Business Law

Business Law

Nigel Savage, BA, LLM, PhD
Professor of Law
Department of Legal Studies
Trent Polytechnic

Robert Bradgate, MA, Solicitor
Lecturer
Department of Legal Studies
Trent Polytechnic

London
Butterworths
1987

United Kingdom	Butterworth & Co (Publishers) Ltd, 88 Kingsway, LONDON WC2B 6AB and 61A North Castle Street, EDINBURGH EH2 3LJ
Australia	Butterworths Pty Ltd, SYDNEY, MELBOURNE, BRISBANE, ADELAIDE, PERTH, CANBERRA and HOBART
Canada	Butterworths. A division of Reed Inc., TORONTO and VANCOUVER
New Zealand	Butterworths of New Zealand Ltd, WELLINGTON and AUCKLAND
Singapore	Butterworth & Co (Asia) Pte Ltd, SINGAPORE
South Africa	Butterworth Publishers (Pty) Ltd, DURBAN and PRETORIA
USA	Butterworths Legal Publishers, ST PAUL, Minnesota, SEATTLE, Washington, BOSTON, Massachusetts, AUSTIN, Texas and D & S Publishers, CLEARWATER, Florida

© Butterworth & Co (Publishers) Ltd 1987

British Library Cataloguing in Publication Data

Savage, Nigel
  Business law.
  1. Commercial law——Great Britain
  I. Title II. Bradgate, Robert
  344.106′7   KD1629

  ISBN 0 406 01843 X

Typeset by Colset Private Ltd, Singapore
Printed and bound in Great Britain
by Thomson Litho Ltd., East Kilbride, Scotland.

Preface

This book has grown out of our experience teaching law to students studying the subject in the context of business studies, accountancy and other similar courses involving some study of general legal principles. We felt that there was a need for a text which would present the law in a way which was both stimulating and relevant to such students, demonstrating its impact on the business community. There are a number of books for law degree students which present the law in a contextual setting, but relatively few which do the same for those studying law, perhaps in less detail, on other courses. Equally there are many books which present a thorough exposition of general principles of black letter law relevant to such courses. We have tried to combine the two approaches, with a view to showing the interaction between the law and business activities, and, where appropriate, to criticise and evaluate the legal 'rules'. To this end we have made extensive use of various materials, including, of course, judgments, but also extracts from the writings of legal academics and commentators working in other related disciplines. After all, the law is not static but must develop in response to social changes and, in this context, to new business practices. Only by understanding the underlying justification for a legal rule can the student evaluate its effectiveness in changing circumstances and form an opinion of how the law is likely to, or should be, developed.

Obviously, in including contextual and evaluative material, we have had to make some sacrifices in the coverage of 'black letter law', if the book was not to become impossibly unwieldly. We have tried to strike a balance between the two approaches, so that the book will present a complete coverage of the law. How far we have been successful in our objectives we leave the reader to judge.

We should make some comment on the content of the book. It may at first seem odd that, contrary to the normal practice, Part II, dealing with the law of torts, is longer than Part III, which deals with the general principles of contract. Part III provides a foundation of general principles upon which much of the remainder of the book builds. Part II on the other hand, stands alone and deals with a subject which is having increasing impact upon business activity. In respect of Part VI our original intention had been to omit the statutory aspects of employment law in their entirety. The subject has continued to grow in recent years and to cover it adequately would have increased the length of the book by half again. In the end, however, we have decided to include an overview of the statutory provisions relating to the termination of employment, because of their special relevance to business and 'managerial discretion', and for the sake of completeness. However, we would stress that it is intended to provide no more than an overview; for a more detailed coverage the student will no doubt turn to one of the several specialist works on the subject.

Part I, 'Business Regulation, the State and the Legal Process,' marks the most radical departure from the model of the traditional general legal principles text. In it, rather than the detailed coverage of the sources of law and the court system, to which, in our experience, students find it difficult to relate, we have tried to place the regulation of business activity within its economic and political context.

The book is essentially intended for students of English business law although inevitably much of the material applies to Scotland and we have made reference occasionally to Scots law. The law is as stated on the 1st January 1987 although we have been able to include some later developments at proof stage.

It is traditional for the preface to a new book to offer thanks to those who have assisted in its production, and we wish to hold with that tradition. The idea for this book was conceived by the first named author almost six years ago; its gestation period since has been long and at times painful. We must therefore extend our thanks to our publishers for their patience and for their help and assistance in the general production of the book. We must also extend our thanks to Stephen Bailey, Senior Lecturer in the Department of Law at Nottingham University, who kindly read Part II, and to our colleagues Stewart Oliver and Erika Kirk who read respectively Parts VII and V. For their comments and advice we are grateful, for any errors which remain we take full responsibility. We also wish to thank Jean Bunn who patiently typed the whole thing, coping in the process with our two illegible scripts. Finally we must thank our respective partners, Linda and Beverley, for their patience (most of the time) in accepting our regular disappearance behind piles of books and papers and the disruption to normal home life.

Nigel Savage
Robert Bradgate
Department of Legal Studies
Trent Polytechnic
Nottingham

Contents

Table of Statutes

References in this Table to *Statutes* are to Halsbury's Laws of England (Fourth Edition) showing the volume and page at which the annotated text of an Act may be found. Page references in **bold** type indicate where the section of an Act is set out in part or in full.

Table of Statutes

List of Cases

Part I
Business regulation, the state and the legal process

Chapter 1
Business Regulation

Growth of regulation

1.0.0 The twentieth century has witnessed a massive growth in the state regulation of business activity. In that period the UK economy has moved from one based on capitalism and free enterprise to a mixed economy which necessarily envisages a prominent role for the state as both owner and regulator.

During the period of the industrial revolution from the late eighteenth century through the nineteenth century the predominant political and economic philosophy was that of laissez-faire. The values of the era were those of free trade and free competition. Such values envisaged only a minimal role for state interference. The laissez-faire philosophy manifested itself in all aspects of life including the attitudes of the judiciary. The legal equivalent of the prevailing economic philosophy was the notion of contract negotiated on the basis of freedom and equality. As Selznick observed:

> 'Contract became a device for entering legally unsupervised relations.'[1]

The parties to a contract were assumed to be bargaining on equal terms and the principle of caveat emptor (let the buyer beware) required each party to act according to his own judgement. In the context of employment, the same notions of freedom and equality were applied resulting in the development of the contract of employment which could be terminated at will. Such a contract brought little in the way of security for the workforce but gave businessmen much flexibility. As Selznick observes:

> 'The free labour market of burgeoning capitalism was real enough, and contractual freedom did much to create it. It does not follow, however, that contract was an adequate foundation for governing the employment relationship. The law could not and did not treat the conditions of employment as the outcome of free bargaining and mutual assent. Rather the concept of contract was adapted to what had to be done to maintain the organisational strength of the business enterprise.'[2]

Once Parliament and the courts had accepted the notion of the limited liability company the legal framework supporting the capitalist philosophy of the era was complete, and in many respects remains intact to this day. The capitalist demanded a framework within which he could maximise the benefit to be derived from his capital without putting it at risk and which gave him complete freedom to withdraw and reinvest in more profitable outlets. The law provided this by a combination of the corporate form

3

entered into by a simple contract. Whereas hitherto corporate status had been granted as a privilege by the sovereign, it became a right:

> 'the charter which had once drawn its force from the grant of the sovereign became a bargain among the enterprises. Who was to limit the terms of the bargain? As in other areas of the law . . . it came to be assumed that the bargainer knew best his own interest and how to secure it, and that the sum of the interests of the bargainers equalled the interests of the whole society.'[3]

Despite the prevailing political and economic philosophy during the period of the industrial revolution, it would be wrong to suggest that there was no government regulation of industry. In fact many of the regulatory statutes which form the basis of modern business law originate from statutes and reforms initiated in that period. The initial impetus for the industrial revolution was supported by the removal of dated restrictions on trade and industry, but as the machinery of government came to terms with the economic and social consequences of the industrial revolution, a new legal and administrative framework regulating economic activity was erected. For example, the framework of company law based on registration and disclosure was in place by the second half of the nineteenth century[4] and there was a succession of statutes dealing with hours of work and conditions in factories. Although the notion of consumer protection is regarded as a twentieth century phenomenon, many of the statutes covering weights and measures and the Merchandise Marks Act dealing with the marking and description of goods are examples of early attempts at consumer protection. As Atiyah points out:

> 'Consumer protection was a major legislative preoccupation throughout the nineteenth century, and it was not by any means confined purely to prevention of fraud . . . Since fraud was often difficult to prove, it was very common for Parliament to legislate on the principle of preventing modes of commercial behaviour which facilitated fraud . . .'[5]

Indeed the modern method of affording protection to consumers by requiring persons who provide certain services to be registered was used in respect of doctors in the Medical Act 1858.

1   Selznick, *Law, Society and Industrial Justice* (1969) p 131. See also Pt III.
2   Op cit pp 135–136.
3   Chayes, *The Modern Corporation and the Rule of Law in The Corporation in Modern Society* (Mason (Ed), 1970,) p 36.
4   See Pt VII.
5   Atiyah, *The Rise and Fall of Freedom of Contract* (1979) p 545.

Factors influencing growth of business regulations

1.1.0   In the period since the end of the nineteenth century a number of factors have influenced the legal environment of business. These include institutional growth, the consumer movement and the increasing role of the state.

Institutional growth

1.1.1   Perhaps the most significant factor has been the rise of the modern business enterprise. Along with trade unions, the corporate body has emerged as a centre of power in society. Drucker observed in 1946 that limited companies had become 'the dominant institution of the western industrial system.'[1] The largest comprise an enormous concentration of wealth and power; international companies such as BP with over 450 subsidiaries operating in over 50 countries have become supranational organisations whose internal policy decisions may have as much impact on a community's economic life as government decisions. The controllers of such organisations exercise considerable influence over a nation in terms of decisions on employment, investment production and pricing.

The famous American academics Berle and Means demonstrated the structural changes in the modern business enterprise brought about by the increasing concentration of industry. In their book, *The Modern Corporation and Private Property*, published in 1932, they illustrated the increasing divorce of control from ownership. Unlike the early business enterprises which were both owned and run by the same persons, modern enterprises are effectively controlled by the management who may have a relatively small ownership interest in the company. Berle and Means concluded that the company 'had ceased to be a private business device and had become an institution.' With the increasing size of companies and the unwillingness or inability of shareholders to exercise effective ownership restraints on management, the shareholders—

> 'have surrendered the right that the corporation should be operated in their sole interest'

and the community is in a position—

> 'to demand that the modern corporation serve not only the owners or controllers but all society.'[2]

Berle observed in 1955 that the

> 'birth of private collective ownership has created problems of legitimacy, it is not possible to justify it in terms of individual private rights which have a limited scope and personal significance. The modern institution of the corporate enterprise has hidden behind accidents of legal form which have shielded the massive growth of power from legal control.'[3]

Hence the need for greater state regulation of business activity particularly in the area of competition law.

A further feature of institutional growth has been the massive increase in ownership of shares by institutional investors such as insurance companies, unit trusts and pension funds. Such institutional holdings have in recent years increased at the expense of direct holdings. The number of individual UK shareholders fell from 2.5m in the 1950s to 1.75m in 1981, and the proportion of shares held directly in UK companies from 54% in 1963 to 22% in 1984. The proportion of shares held by institutions in the same period has increased from 27.8% to 60%.[4] Clearly, the managers of such institutions are in a position to exercise considerable influence, often discreetly, over a company's management. A notable example of institutional influence in the UK was the decision of the Prudential Assurance Co Ltd to support a minority shareholders' action against the management of Newman Industries in 1980.[5]

In recent years the government has made strenuous efforts to promote private share ownership through the privatisation programme and the growth of employee share ownership schemes.

1 *Concept of the Corporation* (1946) p 9.
2 *The Modern Corporation and Private Property* (revised edn, 1967) p 311.
3 Berle, *Capitalist Revolution* (1955) p 27.
4 See 'Financial Times' 11 January 1986.
5 *Prudential Assurance Co Ltd v Newman Industries Ltd (No 2)* [1982] Ch 204, [1982] 1 All ER 354, CA reversing Vinelott J in [1981] Ch 257, [1980] 2 All ER 841. See also Farrar and Russell, (1984) 5 Co Law 107.

The consumer society
1.1.2 The industrial revolution brought profound changes in the economic and political life of the UK. In the period between 1860 and 1900 it has been estimated that the real wages of urban workers increased by 60%.[1] Coupled with the extension of the franchise, the growing economic and political power of the mass of consumers inevitably had a fundamental impact on business activity and regulation. The increasing spending power of the public and the mass production of consumer durables such as bicycles, sewing machines and furniture brought novel problems for the law and business regulators. There was a need for a more rational legal framework regulating the use and abuse of credit selling.[2] The mass manufacture and marketing of prepackaged goods required the judiciary to extend the boundaries of negligence law[3] and Parliament to recognise the legitimate expectations of the consumer in respect of the quality of goods supplied. For most of the nineteenth century the major innovations had been in the methods of production: goods had been manufactured more efficiently. In the twentieth century the innovations have come in the actual goods manufactured, from sewing machines to motor vehicles, electrical goods and more recently micro-computers. Advertising has been used to fuel consumer wants rather than to educate and inform the consumer.[4]

As goods became technologically more complex and the techniques of persuasion more sophisticated, the contractual model which envisages equality and freedom of contract between consumer and business became increasingly transparent. Hence the need to redress the imbalance by reinforcing the legal framework regulating business in favour of consumers.

1 See Mathias, *The First Industrial Nation* (1878).
2 See Part 5.
3 See Part 2.
4 Expenditure on advertising in 1985 amounted to £4.5 bn: *Advertising Associations Statistical Yearbook 1986.*

Increasing role of the state
1.1.3 By the 1920s it was apparent that the era of laissez-faire was coming to an end in favour of state intervention in economic affairs. The influential economist J M Keynes observed in 1927 that—

'progress lies in the growth and recognition of semi-autonomous bodies within the state—bodies whose criterion of action within their own field is solely the public good as they understand it, and from whose deliberations motives of private advantage are excluded, though some place it may still be necessary to leave, until the ambit of men's altruism grows wider, to the separate advantages of particular groups, classes or faculties—bodies which in the ordinary course of affairs are mainly autonomous within their prescribed limitations, but are subject in the last resort to the sovereignty of the democracy through Parliament.'[1]

As we shall see, such bodies exist today across a broad spectrum of business activity.[2]

The two World Wars accelerated substantially the growth in government control and management of the economy. Government itself became a purchaser on a massive scale. In 1945 the Labour Party assumed power on a programme influenced by Keynes' economic theories. There followed a period in which government intervention in the economy became the norm. Coal mines, electricity and gas suppliers and iron and steel were all taken into public ownership. Government agencies with massive budgets assumed a central role in the economic life of the country. The mixed economy became an acceptable fact of political and economic life.

1   *The End of Laissez-Faire* (1927).
2   See 2.5.7.

Chapter 2

The State, the Law and the Legal System

The role of the state

2.0.0 Friedmann considered the state in contemporary society represents—

> 'a focus of centralised power which results from the balance between various contending social and economic interests, and as the embodiment of certain ideas of justice and public interest encompassing the community as a whole. Millions of individuals are in fact at the same time organised in one or the other of the thousands of economic and social groupings that make up the fabric of contemporary society and unorganised individuals who face the power of officialdom, or a large corporation, a labour union, or a professional association. As such they look to the state for protection and implementation of some basic principles of justice. In a pluralistic society, of which the "mixed economy" is an important aspect, the help of the state may be invoked either against private power (eg price controls) or against public power (eg through judicial restraint on administrative arbitrariness). In the latter case one arm of the state is used to control another.'[1]

Friedman identifies four basic functions of the state in the modern economy.[2] First, it provides a cushion of social services to guarantee a minimum standard of living for everyone. Second, it operates as an entrepreneur on an increasing scale. Third, it acts as a regulator to protect the wider public interest or particular groups or individuals in society. Fourth, it is responsible for the judicial process. In the following paragraphs we shall examine each of these functions in the context of the UK.

1   Friedmann, *The State and the Role of Law in a Mixed Economy* (1971), p 10.
2   Op cit p 3.

The Welfare State

2.1.0   As the British economy became more and more dependent on a large and efficient workforce, it came to be recognised in the nineteenth century that welfare support would benefit the economy by improving the productivity of the workforce. Thus the Victorians laid the foundations of a welfare state by legislating to improve environmental conditions. Such improvements did not, however, provide any direct financial assistance for the poor. The extension of the franchise and the rise of the trade union movement, however, saw considerable improvements. Welfare provisions were enacted to mitigate the worst excesses of the free market economy. Thus, in 1897 the Workmen's Compensation Act was passed imposing strict liability on employers for accidents to employees arising out of their work. There followed a system of national insurance against unemployment and sickness[1] and, some years later, the system was extended to cover old age and death.[2]

In the period after the Second World War the framework of the modern welfare state was laid which sought:

'to abolish want by ensuring that every citizen willing to serve according to his powers has at all times an income sufficient to meet his responsibilities'.[3]

The modern welfare state therefore ensures that there are minimum standards of income, health, nutrition, housing and education available to every individual. In addition the state provides benefits and allowances through the system of taxation and occupational welfare rights such as sick pay, additional pension provision, holiday pay and health and safety provisions.[4]

In terms of the law and legal process regulating business activity, many of the welfare rights that exist today represent an acceptance by the state that the growth in the number and variety of risks to which individuals are exposed necessitates that responsibility be shifted to the state, rather than rely on any process of adjustment between the parties.[5]

1   See National Insurance Act 1911.
2   See Widows', Orphans and Old Age Contributory Pensions Act 1925.
3   The Beveridge Report, para 444.
4   For a full account of such welfare provisions see Ogus and Barendt, *The Law of Social Security* (1982).
5   See generally 11.0.5.

State enterprise

2.2.0   In a mixed economy the state plays an increasingly significant role as entrepreneur. Even in the latter part of the nineteenth century in the UK, central and local government bodies were playing an increasing role in terms of the ownership and management of commercial operations in areas such as telegraph services, public transport, electricity undertakings and gasworks. The twentieth century saw a massive increase in such quasi-commercial operations as successive governments accepted the economic and strategic advantages flowing from the ownership and control of sectors of the economy.

In general, three types of state enterprise have emerged in western economies. First, enterprises operating through a central or local government department. Such enterprises operate with varying degrees of managerial and financial independence. Second, autonomous public corporations established by statute or royal charter. In the UK this has, until recently, been by far the most favoured form of state enterprise. Third, state ownership of shares in private enterprise undertakings varying from majority control, to right of veto or minority holding.

Nationalised industries in the UK

2.2.1   Since the Labour Government's programme of nationalisation following the Second World War, the public corporation has been the favoured vehicle for the ownership and management of industries such as steel, coal, gas, electricity, postal and telephone services. Some industries have been denationalised since the war but there remains a broad consensus on the desirability of retaining some industries in the public sector.[1]

British public corporations are usually created by statute and enjoy a separate and independent legal status. They are administered by a governing body appointed by the government and are required to balance revenue and expenditure: any profits are required to be invested in the enterprise. In terms of day to day operations a public corporation enjoys no special privileges or immunities and is fully liable in law. As Friedmann asserts:

> 'In their commercial and managerial aspects they resemble commercial companies and they have an essentially private law status. But in so far as they fulfil public tasks on behalf of the Government and Parliament they are public authorities, as such subject to control by the Government within the limits defined by statute and developed by convention.'[2]

The motives behind the growth in state enterprise are a combination of the ideological and the economic. Public ownership has been seen as a means of enhancing public accountability over the use of the country's resources. It was considered that if the state had control over the 'commanding heights' of the economy it would facilitate the planning and management of the economy. In some respects the nationalised industries have been used as a tool for implementing economic policy. A further argument in support of nationalisation is that the industries can use social costs and benefits as criteria for their operations in addition to commercial criteria.

The opponents of nationalisation argue that the industries tend to be inefficient. In most cases the enterprise will have a monopoly or at least dominant market position. It is argued therefore that this reduces the competitive pressure under which private sector organisations operate, to minimise costs. Nationalised industries are not subject to the ultimate pressure of commercial insolvency; political pressure will always ensure that further public funds are available.

The most difficult problem for state enterprises has been the relationship with the Government Minister responsible for their activity and the overall political pressure from central government. The pressures, both direct and indirect, to draw back from unpopular plant closures, or to make investment decisions on grounds other than commercial criteria, have often been intense and fundamentally compromise any notion of management autonomy.[3]

Invariably the statute regulating the corporation will provide for some form of consumer representation on a Consumer or Consultative Council. Such councils have, however, often been criticised for their low public profile, lack of finance, inadequate staffing, and too cosy a relationship with the corporation over which they are supposed to act as a consumer watchdog.[4]

1   But see 2.2.4.
2   *A Theory of Public Industrial Enterprise in Hanson* (ed) (1955) p 20.
3   See generally, R E Thomas, *The Government of Business* (1976).
4   See NCC Report, *Consumers and the Nationalised Industries* (1976).

State ownership of shares in limited companies

2.2.2   This form of state enterprise has not been favoured in the UK. In those industries where it exists or has existed, it has often arisen as a result of a crisis in a prestigious company that has forced the government to act, rather than the product of any economic philosophy.[1] The British Government holds shares in British Leyland and British Petroleum.

The Labour Government in 1967 established the Industrial Reorganisation Corporation (IRC) whose function was to promote and assist the reorganisation and development of any industry. The IRC was, however, abolished by the Conservative Government in 1971, some of its functions being transferred to the Department of Industry.[2]

In 1975 the Labour Government resurrected the idea when they created the National Enterprise Board (NEB) under the Industry Act 1975. One of the functions of the NEB was to extend public ownership into profitable areas of manufacturing industry.[3] In essence the NEB served largely as an investment bank, development agency and holding company, rather than as an instrument of nationalisation[4] and was firmly tethered to the Department of Industry.

The ownership and possible control of private sector enterprises by government or government agencies poses difficult problems of accountability, not least in the tension between the mechanisms of public accountability through Ministers, Parliament and the public at large and the mechanisms of accountability built into company law.[5] As Ganz observes, government investment in industry—

> 'raises the basic problem of using private bodies for public purposes. The company or the contract state is the result. It represents the reverse side of the corporate state, in that it shows the difficulty of making private bodies publicly accountable for the public money they receive and of using private law mechanisms for public ends . . . Because government directors cannot represent the public interest where it conflicts with the interests of the shareholders, the government has to rely on indirect pressures or other means, such as conditions of contract, and grants of assistance, or planning agreements, to ensure that companies use public money for public purposes.'[6]

1   Eg the government resale of Rolls Royce in 1971.
2   See Industry Act 1972.
3   Industry Act 1975, s 2(2)(c).
4   See generally, Ganz, *Government and Industry* (1977) Ch 4.
5   See Part 7.
6   Ganz, op cit, pp 106–107.

Finance for business

2.2.3   In recent years both the range and volume of finance for business provided by state agencies has substantially increased. The provision of government aid has become an important tool in economic planning in terms of encouraging investment and innovation, particularly in the field of information technology. In addition an important part of government policy towards reducing unemployment is creating a favourable environment in which small firms can start up and flourish.

The massive scope and range of state assistance available to business has become so significant that it represents an important aspect of corporate planning. The decision to locate a factory in one area of the country as opposed to another can have a significant impact on the amount of state aid provided.

In general, assistance comes from three sources. First, assistance from the Department of Trade and Industry. Such assistance may be divided into that which is available nationwide and that which is available to promote development in the regions. The assistance available may be to support innovation and scientific research, assist with export finance, promote energy conservation or simply be of a general nature to be awarded by the Department at their discretion but according to clearly expressed guidelines of eligibility.

The second source of finance is that which is provided by a number of statutory agencies. Such agencies may operate in a particular region, or in respect of particular activities. They include such bodies as the Scottish and Welsh Development Agencies which may provide finance or premises for business, the Highlands and Islands Development Board which may offer discretionary assistance to business carrying out development in its area; the Council for Small Industries in Rural Areas which may provide loans for business in areas of declining population and the British Technology Group which co-ordinates the provision of assistance in the area of technical innovation by providing for investment and aid for small business, particularly start-ups.

The third major source of assistance is from the European Economic Community (EEC) principally in the form of Community Regional Grants. Assistance from the EEC comprises 'quota aid', which is provided to each member state as a fixed amount of 'quota' and 'non-quota aid' which may be earmarked for particular projects in any member state.

In addition to the above areas of assistance, local authorities operate schemes to assist investment in business by way of loans, grants or guarantees. The Conservative Government since 1979 has embraced a policy of deregulation.[1] Consistent with this policy under the Local Government, Planning and Land Act 1980 the establishment of enterprise zones was authorised. Such zones seek to encourage business activity by the removal of certain tax burdens and the relaxation or modification of various statutory or administrative controls within a specific area. Along similar lines to enterprise zones are 'free zones'[2] which assist businesses within a specific area by allowing concessions on the payment of customs duties or value added tax in respect of goods or materials entering the designated area.[3]

1   See 2.5.9
2   See Finance Act 1984.
3   For a full account of all the various sources of finance to industry see Burgess, *Corporate Finance Law* (1985) Ch 8.

Privatising state enterprises
2.2.4   One of the central planks of the Conservative Government in the period 1979 to date has been one of returning state owned enterprises to the private sector, and thereby subjecting them to the discipline of market forces. This policy has been termed privatisation.

In its broadest sense, privatisation involves four activities.[1] First, the introduction of charges for goods and services produced by the public sector which were formerly provided at no charge. Second, the contracting out to the private sector of work formerly undertaken in the public sector. Third, selling off to private individuals and organisations publicly owned enterprises. Fourth, relaxing statutory monopolies and licensing arrangements which exclude firms in the private sector from competing in certain markets. In the context of state enterprise, the third and fourth aspects are the most relevant.

The third aspect involves converting the whole or part of a public corporation into a public limited company[2] by means of offering its shares to the public. Thus in 1981 British Aerospace was privatised and in 1982 the National Freight Corporation[3] and the oil and gas exploration and production activities of the British National Oil Corporation were privatised. In addition, British Rail has sold off its hotel interests to the private sector and its Sealink subsidiary in 1984. The most ambitious projects have been the privatisation of British Telecom under the Telecommunications Act 1984 and British Gas in 1986. In addition to such sales the government has also reduced its holdings in private sector companies such as BP and Cable and Wireless.

In the case of some privatisations the government has retained a strategic shareholding in the company, with a power to appoint directors. Such holdings are not intended to be used as a means of interfering with management or in support of a wider economic policy. For example, in the prospectus inviting the public to subscribe for shares in Britoil, written on behalf of the government, it stated:

> 'HM Government does not intend to use its rights as Ordinary Shareholders to intervene in the commercial decisions of the company.'[4]

In order to deter unwelcome corporate predators from taking over a privatised company the government may retain a 'Special Share' which can be invoked to outvote the other shareholders. In general, the government's role in privatised companies is passive, as Steel asserts:

> 'The Government therefore sees its role as an absentee, at most, as a largely inactive institutional shareholder.'[5]

Under the fourth type of privatisation a number of public corporations which hitherto have had monopolies have had to face competition from the private sector. Thus, the Post Office's letter monopoly was relaxed under the British Telecommunications Act 1981 and British Airways has faced increasing competition from private sector independent airlines.

The privatisation of public utilities such as British Telecom and British Gas poses special problems, since their services are natural monopolies. In the case of nationalised monopolies, Ministerial intervention, the Consumer Councils and public opinion may serve to mitigate any abuse of monopoly power. Thus there is an obvious need to build into a privatisation scheme some form of regulation to ensure that the company does not exploit its market power. The model for such regulation is provided by the British Telecom (BT) privatisation programme where the legislation set up an Office of Telecommunications (OFTEL) under a Director General of Telecommunications to provide independent supervision of BT as opposed to direct government regulation. The functions of the OFTEL relate to the licensing of telecommunications operators and the general supervision of the industry. Under the system any person who runs a telecommunications system requires a licence. In the case of public systems only BT and Mercury

Communications Ltd have full national licences; private systems are licensed separately. The licences lay down the regulatory and competitive framework within which the services must be provided.

OFTEL must also investigate consumer complaints and is given the powers of the Director General of Fair Trading in respect of monopoly reference in the telecommunications industry.[6] The Director may establish advisory bodies and has power to give advice and assistance to litigants in cases involving the telecommunications code.[7]

Given the political impetus it is likely that OFTEL will provide the statutory model for future regulatory agencies in privatised sectors of the economy. In essence the rationale of such agencies is to provide some motivation for the enterprise towards operating efficiently, ensure that consumers are effectively represented and support the public service aspects of the enterprise's operations.

1   See Heald, *Privatisation: Analysing its Appeal and Limitations Fiscal Studies* (1984) 5(1), pp 36–46.
2   See Part 7.
3   This was sold off to its employees.
4   Britoil (1982) p 17.
5   Steel and Heald (eds), *Privatising Public Enterprises* (1985) p 104.
6   See 2.7.1.
7   A code conferring power on operators in respect of plant on other persons' land.

State regulation

2.3.0   We have already identified three specific factors that have influenced the growth of business regulation in the UK.[1] The variety and scope of judicial, legislative and administrative controls that exist today in order to alleviate the perils and inequalities of unfettered business activity are immense. Such controls may be classified along the following lines: first, judicial and legislative controls in respect of the regulation of relations between private individuals, that is the law of contract and tort.[2] Second, legislative and administrative controls regulating a particular trade, profession, or other business activity with a view to imposing standards of behaviour in the conduct of business and protecting the public against unfair trading practices. Third, controls designed to protect the public interest against the concentration of private economic power, that is, monopolies, mergers and restrictive practices regulations. Fourth, controls designed to safeguard the environment, such as planning regulations.[3] It is proposed to examine these four classifications in some detail.

1   See 2.0.0.
2   Termed 'private law'. See Parts 2 and 3.
3   See Friedman, *The State and the Role of Law in a Mixed Economy* (1971).

Restraints on private law[1]

2.4.0   The essence of much of the law of contract is that the parties to a bargain themselves define and regulate its content. As Chayes observed:

> 'what the law of contract has provided is a device by which private persons are enabled to some extent to stabilize and make predictable—to control—the future. That is, they are enabled to make their own law

to govern their own affairs. The state lends its judicial machinery to enforce this personal law, if necessary. The law appears to exhaust itself in defining the conditions on which the public force will be enlisted to effectuate the private end. And it is true that these conditions, in our system at least, are elastic enough to permit a wide range of autonomously directed private activity.'[2]

Thus the courts and Parliament laid down the basic conditions for contracting in terms of competence and capacity. Certain factors were identified as grounds for affecting contractual relations, such as fraud and misrepresentation, but the general attitude was one of non-interference in private contractual relations. As Lord Devlin observed in 1956:

'The courts could not relieve in cases of hardship and oppression because the basic principle of freedom of contract included freedom to oppress.'[3]

The use of standard form contracts by business to impose all or nothing terms on a contracting party exposed the notions of freedom and equality as fictional. The attitude of the courts to such contracts has been ambiguous. On the one hand they have regarded standard contracts as an entirely legitimate form of business dealing. On the other hand, they have sought to impose some standards of fair dealing in terms of the treatment of the contracting party not relying on the standard terms of contract.

The state has, however, intervened to impose compulsory terms of contract on the parties in certain circumstances such as minimum non-excludable standards of quality and fitness for purpose and has subjected certain terms excluding or limiting a person's liability to a standard of reasonableness.[4] In the case of the employment contract, state intervention from 1963 gradually built into the employment relationship minimum statutory rights in respect of dismissal.[5]

1   See Part 3.
2   Chayes, 'The Modern Corporation and the Rule of Law' in Mason (ed), *The Corporation in Modern Society* (1960) p 32.
3   Devlin, *The Common Law, Public Policy and the Executive* (1956) 'Current Legal Problems' p 10.
4   See Unfair Contract Terms Act 1977; Sale of Goods Act 1979; Supply of Goods and Services Act 1982.
5   See Employment Protection (Consolidation) Act 1978. See Selwyn's *Law of Employment* (1985, 5th edn).

Direct regulation

2.5.0   The state has adopted a variety of techniques in order to regulate and influence business activity. In general the motivation for such regulation has been on the basis of a combination of economic and moral grounds. It may be considered necessary to regulate a sector of the economy in order to promote competition and restore confidence in the market for goods or services, or promote greater efficiency. Regulation may also be considered necessary in order to deter fraudulent or unfair practices, or redress the inequalities between trader and consumer.

In a recent White Paper on streamlining the regulatory framework, the government recognised that:

'Every industrialised society needs regulations, covering most aspects of social and economic activity. These regulations are designed to ensure the

15

safety of the public, set a framework for employee/employer relations, protect individuals from health and safety hazards at work, protect the environment and are even required to bring in government revenue.'[1]

1   *Building Businesses . . . Not Barriers* Cmnd 9794 (1986), p 1.

Self-regulation

2.5.1   A popular technique of business regulation in the UK has been that of allowing individuals or institutions to regulate themselves as an alternative to regulation by a government agency. Self-regulation has played a key role in regulating those involved in the control of corporate activities and the securities market and it has also been adopted in the case of professional services. More recently, self-regulation has been used as a means of supporting the rights and expectations of consumers through the development of codes of practice by trading associations.

A useful definition of self-regulation was given by the Bank of England in their evidence to the Wilson Committee, 'Reviewing the Functioning of Financial Institutions'. They considered that self-regulation originated:

'in the realisation by a group of individuals or institutions that regulation of their activities is desirable in the common interest, and their acceptance that rules for the performance of functions and of duties should be established and enforced. Typical of such arrangements are those to which members of professional bodies subscribe in order to establish appropriate standards of professional conduct and competence. In some cases the enforcement of such standards is entrusted to a committee of a profession or of practitioners in a market. Frequently, however, the enforcement of the regulations may be entrusted to an authority outside the group, which is or becomes customarily recognised and obeyed and which may also become the initiator of new regulations. In both cases the system can be described as self-regulation, the first intrinsically so, the second by common consent.'[1]

Notable examples of self-regulation have been the City Code on Takeovers and Mergers policed by the Panel on Takeovers and Mergers[2] and also the Stock Exchange which regulates the conduct of its members and controls security dealings in respect of listed companies.

1   *Second Stage Evidence* Vol 4 (1977) p 89, para 5.
2   See 37.0.2.

Advantages of self-regulation[1]

2.5.2   The advantages of self-regulation have been identified along the following lines:
(a)   In general the costs of regulation are borne by the profession concerned and ultimately the market, not the taxpayer. It is considered appropriate that those who use the market should contribute to the burden of maintaining it.
(b)   The regulators are experts in their own field.
(c)   The system has the virtue of speed and flexibility in the absence of rigid legal procedures and detailed technical rules.
(d)   The rules can be updated and amended to accommodate developments

much quicker than changes in the law can be achieved.

(e) Business is perhaps more likely to comply with the spirit of self-regulatory standards as well as the letter.

(f) The system encourages stronger professional integrity and discipline within a profession or trade.

(g) In general, the law operates at the margin, it imposes minimum standards. Self-regulatory standards may operate from a higher threshold.

(h) The system may operate with more informality and the regulators may be more inclined to offer advice, assistance and a preliminary ruling.

(i) The sanction of disapproval, public censure and damaged reputation may be more powerful than legal sanctions. A business may be more inclined to comply with informal peer group pressure than a full frontal attack from a regulatory agency.

1   See Rider and Hew, 'The Regulation of Corporation and Securities Law in Britain—the Beginning of the Real Debate' 1977 19 Mal LR 144, 168. See also *Review of Investor Protection Report* Cmnd 9125, 1984.

The disadvantages of self-regulation

2.5.3   The alleged disadvantages of self-regulation are:

(a) Despite the use of lay or independent representation, self-regulators give the appearance of being judge and jury in their own cause.

(b) In most instances the only effective remedy is expulsion which invariably is only a threat since it is either too draconian or simply ineffective.

(c) Regulation only extends to those who are members of the association. Unless membership is compulsory by law, complete coverage of the market is impossible and therefore undermines the credibility of the system.

(d) Because of the absence of legal basis, the self-regulatory body has limited powers, particularly in respect of investigation.

(e) There appears to be some doubt about whether self-regulatory agencies possess qualified privilege from liability in defamation.[1]

(f) The agencies can be expensive and wasteful due to unnecessary duplication and conflicting approaches.

(g) There is a lack of public accountability and control over the appointment of the regulators. Appointments may be made on the basis of social pre-eminence rather than administrative competence.

(h) In view of the often vague jurisdictional basis of some self-regulatory agencies, difficulties can arise if they are challenged in the courts.

(i) Self-regulatory agencies are much less certain and predictable than the law.

(j) In an environment of intense competition and rivalry and vast potential rewards, such as exists in the newly liberated securities market, the sanctions of the law rather than the cultural bonds of membership, may be more effective.

Self-regulation and legal regulation are not mutually exclusive. Indeed the new legal framework regulating the securities market under the Financial Services Act 1986, is based on self-regulation supported by a statutory legal framework.[2] As Page asserts, however, in practice self-regulation is only practicable if three conditions exist: there must be an association, it must be sufficiently motivated to regulate the behaviour of its members, and it must maintain sufficient powers of control for this purpose.[3] In the absence of any of these conditions, the very threat of external legal regulation may be sufficient to promote self-regulatory activity. This occurred in 1968 when threatened statutory intervention resulted in a strengthened City Code and Takeover Panel. Those self-regulatory bodies performing a public duty are, however, subject to scrutiny by the courts under the judicial review procedure.[4]

1   See 5.0.4.
2   See Part 7.
3   'Self-Regulation: The Constitutional Dimension' MLR 1986 Vol 49, 149.
4   See *R v The Panel on Takeovers and Mergers, ex p Datafin and Prudential–Bache Securities Inc* FT Commercial Law Reports 6 December 1986. See also 37.0.2.

Codes of practice
2.5.4   One aspect of self-regulation that has proved increasingly popular across a wide range of business activities is the use of codes of practice. As well as the City Code on Takeovers there are codes of practice covering consumer rights in their dealings with certain trades and industries and codes dealing with advertising policed by the Advertising Standards Authority.

Under 124(3) of the Fair Trading Act 1973 the Director General of Fair Trading is under a duty to encourage trade associations to prepare codes of practice for guidance in safeguarding and promoting the interests of consumers. The Director General has always considered that encouraging the creation of codes is one of his most important functions[1] and there are now some twenty codes covering areas such as travel, electrical appliances, the motor industry, cleaning and laundering.

In 1984 the Director General observed that—

> 'codes have several advantages over legal regulations; they are more flexible, can be readily revised and responsibility for enforcement rests with those who have close knowledge of the trade. Many practices can be dealt with, for instance, lack of clarity in documentation, delays in servicing, or periods of time for which spare parts for appliances will be available which it may not be feasible to cover by the precise wording appropriate to legislation.'[2]

He did, however, recognise that codes have the weaknesses inherent in any self-regulatory system: difficulty of enforcement and non-applicability to those traders who are not members of the relevant association.

> 'Enforcement depends on discipline by the trade association itself and the role of enforcement does not always sit well with the trade association's quite different role as representative and advocate for its members in its dealings with government and the public. It is especially difficult if exclusion from membership is not perceived by members as either a likely occurrence or as a deterrent. The other weakness of codes, their non-applicability to non-members, is self-evident. It is a weakness which is serious for the consumer who happens to deal with a non-member and it is a matter of resentment for trade association members that other traders appear to be competing unfairly because they are free from the restraints of the code.'[3]

It has been suggested that a way round these disadvantages would be to create a statutory duty on business to trade fairly in consumer transactions. Such a duty would be enforceable only through codes of practice prepared by the Office of Fair Trading (OFT) for each sector of trade, after appropriate consultation. A failure to observe the codes could then be enforceable under existing OFT powers to seek assurances and apply for court orders.[4]

1 See *Second Report of the Director General of Fair Trading* (1975) p 9.
2 Borrie, *The Development of Consumer Law and Policy—Bold Spirits and Timorous Souls* Hamlyn Lecture (1984) p 75.
3 Ibid.
4 See 2.6.0.

Disclosure
2.5.5 The disclosure philosophy represents a central thread running through many aspects of business regulation. In company law, the requirement to disclose financial and other corporate information and lodge such information with the Registrar of Companies dates from 1900.[1] Disclosure is also used to protect consumers by compulsorily requiring manufacturers to provide information in respect of the origin, content and safety of goods. There are also requirements on traders to provide specific information in respect of contract terms.

In general, disclosure of information may be justified on one or more of the following grounds:
(a) It facilitates competition by ensuring that customers/consumers/ investors are better informed, thus allowing them to make a more rational choice between different goods, facilities or services.
(b) It minimises the risk of fraud or similar impropriety. For example, many of the rules being put forward by the newly created Securities and Investments Board and the Marketing of Investments Board Organising Committee as part of the new legal framework regulating financial markets are designed to raise levels of integrity and prevent conflicts of interest arising by requiring the disclosure of specific details on such things as a firm's material interest in a transaction and the commission received by a representative.
(c) It may also alert persons to specific risks and hazards in using a product, thus reducing the risk of accidents.
(d) It is arguable that it is a basic right of the public in a democratic society to be fully informed. Indeed, disclosure may be said to facilitate equality of opportunity in the market place.

A regulatory policy based on disclosure is only effective however if supported by an adequately resourced policing body and effective remedies in the event of non-disclosure for those for whom the information was intended. Much also depends on how the information is presented and, in the case of financial information, the conventions and the principles adopted in arriving at a final figure.

1 See 31.2.0.

Licensing
2.5.6 A more direct form of regulation is the requirement that persons in certain trades or professions be licensed with a central government department, the local authority or a self-regulatory agency.[1] In some instances a

licence may be required for certain specific activities such as granting credit, or processing personal information on a computer.[2]

The essence of licensing a business activity is that the applicant for a licence is required to satisfy certain statutory conditions and qualifications. Such conditions usually seek to ensure that the applicant is financially solvent and is a fit person to carry on the activity, fitness being assessed according to previous business activities, involvement in crimes, fraud or dishonest or unfair business activities. The legislation may give to the administering body a broad discretion to refuse an application; on the other hand, possession of a qualification may be sufficient to admit an applicant.

The great benefit of licensing is the threat of withdrawal of the licence. Grant of a licence is in effect granting the right to trade or engage in a particular activity. If a person contravenes the rules of conduct or criminal or civil law, they run the risk of their licence being withdrawn and, hence, their livelihood put at stake.

The problem with a system of licensing is that it is only effective if supported by adequate administrative and enforcement resources to ensure thorough vetting of applicants and maintenance of standards. It was for this reason that the Director General of Fair Trading recently recommended that persons engaged in the car servicing and repairing trade should not be subjected to a licensing system.[3] A response to the cost argument is that licensing systems can in part at least, be self-financing if a realistic fee is set for the issue of a licence.

In general licensing schemes can be used to cover entire occupations or specific activities or products sold. Schemes are often administered by the local authority. In some instances the requirements are adoptive in the sense that local authorities may elect to licence or not. The following are occupations that require some form of licence: pet shops, riding establishments, killing and dealing in game, betting, bingo operators, radio communication, selling petroleum, selling milk, pubs and off-licences, taxi-operators and street traders.

In addition all businesses must register or at least notify the Inland Revenue of their activities, Customs and Excise where their turnover exceeds the VAT threshold, the DHSS where they employ staff for national insurance and sick pay and the Factory Inspectorate where they use industrial premises.

Consistent with the preference for self-regulation in the UK, invariably an occupational licensing scheme will be administered by a professional association. For example, under the new legal framework regulating financial markets, persons engaged in investment business are required to be registered with recognised self-regulatory agencies that are, in turn, subject to the supervision of the Securities and Investment Board and ultimately the Secretary of State for Trade and Industry. Persons engaged in such business will be subjected to a formidable array of rules dealing with such matters as disclosure of information to clients, soliciting business and protecting clients' business.[4]

In some instances the state simply lays down a minimum qualification in order to engage in a trade or profession rather than formally require a licence. For example the company secretary of a public limited company must be qualified in accordance with the provisions of the Companies Act 1985;[5] company auditors must be similarly qualified.[6]

Perhaps the best example of licensing covering a particular business activity is in respect of the licensing of credit in the UK. This is covered in more detail in Part 5. At this stage it is sufficient to point out that despite the immense administrative and financial burden, the system gives the Director General of Fair Trading considerable discretion to influence general commercial morality and business practice. Licences can be refused or withdrawn not only on the basis of activities in the credit business but also on the basis of the general behaviour of the person. Thus a car salesman who consistently flouts the law on falsification of mileage readings may have his licence to grant credit withdrawn.

A more recent example of statutory control of a particular activity was the Data Protection Act 1984. Under this legislation anyone engaged in processing personal information on a computer is required to register the nature and scope of their activities with the Data Protection Registrar. A failure to register, or engaging in processing activities not covered by a particular registration entry, or breach of the principles of the legislation can result in criminal penalties and a prohibition on processing any personal data.[7]

A much less bureaucratic form of licensing is what is termed negative licensing. This system allows all persons to engage in the business or activity but permits an agency to withdraw a licence or prohibit an individual from trading if evidence comes to their notice that they are unfit to trade, according to specified criteria. Such a system imposes less of a burden on traders but still has to be adequately financed and tends to be limited to influencing the very worst fringe element in a trade. This system was adopted in 1979 to regulate the activities of estate agents.[8]

A powerful argument against a system of occupational licensing is that it may tend to encourage monopoly practices. In 1971 the Monopolies Commission considered that certain aspects of occupational licensing, whilst beneficial in areas such as health and safety, could have an adverse effect on the public,[9] particularly in the area of pricing. Indeed, in recent years certain professions have come under growing scrutiny in respect of certain of their activities which arguably inhibit price competition.

1 See 2.5.1.
2 See Data Protection Act 1984.
3 *Car Servicing and Repairs* A Report by the Director General of Fair Trading, July 1985, p 27.
4 See 38.0.6.
5 S 286(1).
6 CA 1985, s 389.
7 See Savage and Edwards, *A Guide to the Data Protection Act* (1985, 2nd edn).
8 Estate Agents Act 1979.
9 Monopolies Commission *A Report on the Public Interest and Restrictive Practices* Cmnd 4463, 1970.

The institutional framework of state regulation

2.5.7 In addition to controlling the regulation of business activity by placing legislation before Parliament, creating the right environment for self-regulatory agencies, and operating disclosure and licensing schemes, state agencies are involved in the administration of a wide variety of laws regulating business activity.

A number of central government departments play a major role in enforcing and administering the regulatory framework. The principal ones are as follows:

2.5.7 The State, the Law and the Legal System

a) The Department of Trade and Industry (DTI)
The DTI plays the most important role in regulating business activity. Indeed out of 12,500 staff employed in the DTI over 5,080 work in the regulatory field.[1] The Department is responsible for the regulatory framework covering companies, including insolvency, and the new framework based on the Financial Services Act 1986 regulating the investment business, including insurance. It is responsible for competition, merger law and policy and consumer law. The Secretary of State is therefore responsible for the work of the Office of Fair Trading, the Monopolies and Mergers Commission and numerous other consumer-orientated committees and councils. Telecommunications regulation and the work of OFTEL also comes within the DTI's responsibilities.

In addition to regulatory functions the DTI also has responsibilities in the area of research and development, regional policy including financial aid and overseas trade.

b) The Home Office (HO)
The HO is responsible for the regulatory framework covering such activities as firearms, dangerous drugs, explosives, poisons and licensing laws. It is also responsible for trading laws covering shops. The new legal framework regulating the processing of personal data and the activities of the Office of the Data Protection Registrar also comes within the HO's responsibilities.

c) The Department of Employment (DE)
The DE has overall responsibility for employment and industrial relations law and policy. This includes administering the redundancy payments scheme and an increasingly significant role in manpower policy. In the latter respect the DE works closely with the Manpower Services Commission, a body that has a wide range of powers to assist persons in selecting, training for, and obtaining employment.

The DE is also responsible for the work of the Health and Safety Commission which supervises the promotion of health and safety at work.

d) The Department of the Environment
In the context of business regulation, the most significant activity in this Department is that of overseeing the law regulating the use of land, including planning, pollution and other environmental issues.

The local authorities also play a significant role in the regulation of business. In many instances the local authorities have responsibility for the grass roots enforcement and implementation of regulatory laws emanating from central government departments and the OFT. In terms of business activity they are responsible for the enforcement of a wide range of statutes covering trading standards, in particular the Weights and Measures Act 1985, Food Act 1984, Consumer Credit Act 1974 and the Trade Descriptions Act 1968. The latter has, in particular, had a significant impact in dealing with misleading descriptions applied to goods, misleading prices and statements in respect of services.[2] In addition local authorities are responsible for the direct enforcement of planning and environmental laws.

1 See 'Financial Times', 24 July 1986.
2 See Harvey, *The Law of Consumer Protection and Fair Trading* (1982), 2nd edn), Ch 12.

2.5.8   In respect of other institutions of the state that are involved in the regulation of business, the Office of Fair Trading (OFT) is arguably the most significant. The OFT was established in 1973 under the Fair Trading Act and the Director General has the following major statutory responsibilities:
(a) A number of functions in respect of monopolies, mergers, restrictive practices and uncompetitive practices.
(b) Take action against persons carrying on business who persist in conduct detrimental to the consumer.
(c) Keep under review the carrying on of commercial activities in the UK relating to the supply to consumers in the UK of goods and services and collect information with a view to the ascertainment of practices which may adversely affect the economic interests of consumers.
(d) Receive and collate evidence that becomes available to him in respect of activities in (c) above, which appears to be evidence of practices which may adversely affect the economic, health and safety or other interests of consumers. The Director can then refer such practices to the Consumer Protection Advisory Committee and changes in the law may then ensue.
(e) Supervise the enforcement and administration of the Consumer Credit Act, publish information for consumers and encourage associations to draw up codes of practice.
(f) Supervise the working and enforcement of the Estate Agents Act 1979.

Two other institutions that have a significant impact on business regulation in the area of financial services are the Bank of England and the Chief Registrar of Friendly Societies. The Bank of England exercises a supervisory role over banks and similar deposit-taking institutions under the Banking Act 1979. The Chief Registrar of Friendly Societies is responsible for supervising the activities of building societies. Under the terms of the Building Societies Act 1986 the Registrar's powers have been transferred to a Building Society Commission, which has wider powers to oversee the activities of building societies operating within a legal framework which enables them to offer a much wider range of services than hitherto.

In addition to central and local government agencies that are involved in the regulation of business activity, the institutions of the European Economic Community (EEC) play a significant role in business regulation. When the UK joined the Community in 1973 under the terms of the European Communities Act 1972, it became subject to all the rights, powers, liabilities and restrictions contained or arising under the Treaties of the Community, the principal one being the Treaty of Rome. In essence the central objectives and activities of the EEC are:
(a) the elimination of customs duties and restrictions;
(b) the establishment of a common customs tariff and common commercial policy;
(c) the abolition of obstacles to freedom of movement for persons, services and capital;
(d) the adoption of a common agriculture and transport policy;
(e) the institution of a policy ensuring that competition is not distorted;
(f) the 'approximation of the laws of member states to the extent required for the functioning of the Community.'

In general the impact of membership of the community has been in the area of competition and company law, [1] employment and social security law and the rights of individuals and firms to establish themselves in other member states.

The centre of power and authority in the Community lies with the Council of Ministers and the Commission. The Council represents the governments of the individual member states. The basic function of the Council is to ensure some co-ordination of the general economic policies in the Community and to take appropriate decisions, usually on the basis of proposals from the Commission. The Commission's functions and powers fall into three groups. First, the initiation and co-ordination of policies. This includes making a study of the particular problems of the Community and making proposals for legislation. Second, certain executive actions in terms of formulating regulations and directives, either on its own account or under the direction of the Council. Third, the Commission acts as guardian of the Treaties of the Community. This function involves considering alleged infringements by individuals, undertakings or member states and taking appropriate enforcement measures. Areas of particular significance over which the Commission exercises influence are in relation to the free movement of goods, persons, services and capital, the Common Agricultural Policy and Competition Policy. In addition, the Commission has important budgetary functions and administers a number of special funds including a Regional Development Fund.[2]

1   See 31.2.0.
2   For a more detailed exposition of these matters see Lasok, *The Law of the Economy in the European Communities* (1980). See also the European Communities (Amendment) Act 1986 whch implements changes to the constitutional framework of the Community by allowing certain measures in the Council to be implemented on a qualified majority vote, replacing the requirement of unamity. The powers of the Commission are also increased.

Deregulation
2.5.9   A key feature of the Conservative Government's policy in the period 1983–1987 has been that of reviewing the regulatory framework surrounding business activity. It is considered that in order to promote enterprise, assist the expansion of businesses and hence reduce unemployment there is a need to reduce significantly the level of government regulation of the business community, particularly in the case of small businesses.

The targets for action are as follows:
(a)   regulations which served their purpose in the past but which are now no longer in keeping with current circumstances;
(b)   regulations which were introduced with the best of motives but which have worked out differently from the way Parliament intended;
(c)   where there is some duplication of coverage, with different regulatory systems dealing with the same or similar activities;
(d)   regulations which impose burdens out of proportion to their benefits.[1]

An Enterprise and Deregulation Unit (EDU) has been set up to pursue deregulation throughout all departments of government. The EDU is in a sense a proxy for the voice of business, but the main responsibility for ensuring that burdens are reduced is on the individual Departments. The EDU can however initiate consideration of particular areas, especially where a number of departments may be concerned, and make proposals for change.

The model for the EDU is the US experience with the Office of Management and Budget which looks at the costs and benefits of all new regulations promulgated by the US government and requires them to be explained and justified by each department of state.

A key feature of the review of UK regulations is the compliance cost. All proposals by Departments for regulations will be subjected to an assessment of the costs and benefits to business, government and the economy.

1   *Building Businesses . . . Not Barriers* Cmnd 9794 (1986) p 1.

Control of unfair trading practices

2.6.0   Under the terms of Part Two of the Fair Trading Act 1973 (FTA) the Director General of Fair Trading may refer a consumer trade practice to the Consumer Protection Advisory Committee on the basis that it adversely affects the economic interests of consumers. A consumer trade practice is a practice which relates to the terms and conditions on which goods and services are marketed, the manner in which such terms and conditions are communicated to consumers and the methods of promotion, selling and paying for the sale of goods and services.[1] The practice must specifically affect consumers' 'economic interests'[2] and additionally either mislead or pressurise consumers or involve them in contracts which include inequitable terms.[3]

Where the Director General makes a reference to the Committee he is required to publicise the reference and specify the precise effect that the practice has in terms of the statutory definition. The Committee will then systematically investigate the proposals, inviting representations from interested bodies. Within three months of the reference the Committee must then report to the Secretary of State for Trade and Industry stating that they agree with the Director's proposals or require some modifications to them. If the Secretary of State 'thinks fit' he may then make an order under the authority of the FTA[4] which must be laid before Parliament and approved by both Houses. If the proposals are duly approved they become law and contravention of them constitutes a criminal offence. The orders made by this process are enforceable by the local authorities who liaise closely with the Office of the Director General.

The procedure for considering proposals and the somewhat narrow definition of consumer interests has resulted in very few references. An additional problem has been delay on the part of the government after receiving reports from the Committee.

The first successful reference under these provisions resulted in the Consumer Transactions (Restrictions on Statements) Order 1976 which prohibits certain statements which would be void under the terms of the Unfair Contract Terms Act 1977.[5] The second reference covering mail order advertisers was substantially modified by the Committee and resulted in the Mail Order Transactions Information Order 1976. The order requires that mail order advertisements directed at consumers which suggest that prepayment has to be made should state the name and address of the business. A third order in 1977, the Business Advertisements (Disclosure) Order 1977, prohibits advertisements that create the impression that a proposed sale is a private sale, as opposed to a sale in the course of business.[6]

The procedure for making a reference has at least had a beneficial effect in terms of highlighting suspect practices. The relatively low number of references is perhaps understandable when one considers that the procedure involves designating as a criminal offence something that is essentially a breach of the spirit of the civil law.

A more effective weapon that the Director may use against delinquent traders is the power to seek undertakings from them to refrain from engaging in a persistent course of conduct detrimental to consumers which is in breach of civil or criminal law. The conduct can be detrimental to consumers in economic terms, or in respect of health and safety or otherwise and must be unfair according to specific statutory criteria. Broadly, the criteria involve contraventions of duties, prohibitions or restrictions under criminal law whether or not there has been a conviction, and breaches of civil law obligations, whether or not proceedings have been brought.[7] Thus the Director can initiate action against traders where he has received complaints from consumers or a local authority, that a trader is persistently supplying goods that are not fit for their purpose under the terms of the Sale of Goods Act 1979,[8] even though the individual consumers have not raised specific actions through the courts.

Initially in an investigation the Director General has a duty to use his best endeavours to obtain a satisfactory written assurance from the trader to refrain from breaking the law. If the trader refuses to give such an assurance or, having given one, fails to observe it, the Director may bring proceedings in the courts. A failure to comply with a court order amounts to a contempt of court with consequent threat of an unlimited fine or imprisonment. Company directors, managers and other senior officers who are shown to have consented to or connived at the detrimental course of conduct may also be subject to the requirement to give undertakings.[9]

The Director General has adopted a policy of releasing the text of all assurances with background details: this policy has clearly enhanced the effectiveness of the statutory procedure. It has been suggested, however, that the provisions could be strengthened by widening their scope beyond breaches of the law to include breaches of accepted standards of commercial behaviour as defined in codes of practice.[10]

1   FTA 1973, s 13.
2   FTA 1973, s 14.
3   S 17.
4   S 22.
5   See 18.0.12.
6   See 21.2.1.
7   FTA 1973, s 34.
8   See 21.3.0
9   S 38.
10 See *A General Duty to Trade Fairly*, A Discussion Paper, OFT (1986).

Economic law

2.7.0   In modern mixed economies it is now generally recognised that the unrestrained forces of the market may result in consequences that are contrary to the public interest. For many years governments have used legislative and administrative machinery in order to outlaw excessive concentrations of economic power and undue restrictions on freedom to trade.

The courts through the development of the common law have asserted some influence over restrictive agreements.[1] However, modern UK competition law originated in the Monopolies and Restrictive Practices (Inquiry and Control) Act 1948. Under the Act the Board of Trade could require the

Monopolies and Restrictive Practices Commission to investigate situations in which at least one third of goods were being supplied by or to the same person, or two or more persons were acting to prevent or restrict competition in relation to particular goods.

In general it is possible to identify two basic approaches to competition law in mixed economies. First, there is what may be termed the per se or prohibitory rule and second, there is the case by case or rule of reason approach. There are elements of both approaches in UK competition law. In the first approach, the law absolutely prohibits certain types of market behaviour or structure. There is no question of considering the merits of a particular case. An example of this approach is to be found in the prohibition on resale price maintenance under the Resale Prices Act 1976. The dominant policy in respect of UK competition law is, however, the case by case approach. Such an approach accepts that there is some merit in attempting to draw a distinction between favourable and adverse market behaviour and structures. Obviously it necessitates some form of guidance or criteria against which the particular activities can be evaluated, in the UK the central factor being the 'public interest'. In some areas the statute may assist the judicial or administrative body charged with the task of considering a case, by means of an express or implied presumption against certain activities or agreements.

There are seven basic areas of competition law in the UK. These are described briefly below.

1   See 16.0.5.

Dominant market power

2.7.1   Where a firm exercises monopoly market power or a dominant role in the market the authorities may take action. It is considered that if a firm is able to dominate the market there is less pressure on it to be efficient and minimise costs and thus it is detrimental to the economy. The firm can restrict supplies, artificially inflate prices and thereby damage consumer interests.

Under the terms of the Fair Trading Act 1973 (FTA 1973), where a business or group of inter-connected businesses supply at least 25% or more of a particular product or service in the UK, they can be referred to the Director General of Fair Trading or the Secretary of State, for review by the Monopolies and Mergers Commission (MMC). A reference to the MMC may also be made where a group of firms supplying at least 25% of the market act in such a way as 'to prevent, restrict or distort competition.'[1] There does not have to be a formal agreement between the firms so long as their conduct is seen to impair competition.

There is no legal obligation placed upon firms to notify the authorities if they consider that they are caught by the provisions of the Act. The Director General of Fair Trading, however, plays an important role in monitoring commercial activity and has a specific duty to collect information about monopoly situations and uncompetitive practices, and give advice and assistance to the Secretary of State.[2] Statistical information is collected, press reports noted and if the Director General's suspicions are aroused that a monopoly situation may exist, he can require the supply of all the necessary information.[3]

If a matter is referred to the MMC it will normally have to deliberate on two issues. First, whether a monopoly situation exists as defined under the statutory provisions, and second, whether it operates or may be expected to operate, against the public interest. The FTA lays down a number of guidelines on the precise nature of the public interest. There is, however, no guidance on the weight to be attached to a particular factor and the list is not exhaustive. The Act requires the MMC to take account of 'all matters which appear in the particular circumstances to be relevant.'[4] The factors identified are the desirability of maintaining and promoting effective competition; promoting the interests of consumers; reducing costs and developing of new products; maintaining and promoting the balanced distribution of industry and employment in the UK and encouraging overseas competitiveness.

The very broad definition of public interest gives considerable discretion to the MMC in deciding, on a case by case approach, whether a monopoly or dominant market position exists.

When the MMC makes its report and recommendations the Secretary of State has a wide range of powers. He can prohibit or modify a particular practice, transfer or vest property in other bodies or simply keep a practice under surveillance.[5] Once again the Director General has a key role in monitoring compliance. Indeed, as an alternative to making a formal order the Director General may be requested to consult with the parties concerned and obtain undertakings from them to take remedial action.[6]

In general the approach of the MMC has been pragmatic. There is evidence to suggest that it has contributed to the reduction of a number of serious abuses arising from a dominant market position. Action following reports has led to reduced prices (colour films, the drugs Librium and Valium), the relaxation in exclusive dealing and similar monopoly type arrangements (petrol, wallpaper, colour films) and the ending of certain discriminatory pricing policies (clutch mechanisms).[7]

1   FTA 1973, s 6(1)(c).
2   FTA 1973, ss 2(2), 2(3).
3   FTA 1973, s 44.
4   FTA 1973, s 84.
5   FTA 1973, Sch 8.
6   FTA 1973, s 88.
7   See Pass and Sparkes, 'Dominant Firms and the Public Interest: A Survey of the Reports of the British Monopolies and Mergers Commission,' Anti-Trust Bulletin 25(2), 437–84.

Mergers
2.7.2   The FTA 1973 provides that all proposed mergers which would lead to at least 25% of a market being supplied by one firm or which would involve assets taken over of £30m or more must be considered for referral to the MMC by the Director General. The same public interest guidelines must be considered as those that apply in the case of dominant market powers. In essence the MMC have to form a judgement on how a proposed alteration in market structure is likely to prejudice the public interest.

Only a small proportion of all mergers are ever referred and in practice most mergers are brought to the attention of the Director General before they are formalised in order to obtain a view as to the likelihood of a referral. If this tactic is not adopted the affected parties run the risk of an investigation taking place after a deal has been struck with all the attendant inconvenience and cost that such investigation would bring. Indeed a recent tactic adopted by predatory firms has been to agree to dispose of a part of a target company that is likely to give rise to a referral. Thus in a recent bid for Distillers the Guinness organisation agreed to sell some of their famous drink brands after the takeover to reduce its share of the drinks market to an acceptable level.[1]

The policy adopted in the UK towards mergers has been subjected to some criticism in recent years.[2] In particular it is argued that the authorities take into account too many extraneous considerations rather than relying solely on the overall impact of a merger on competition. However, given the wide statutory terms of reference which necessitates a pragmatic approach such a criticism is inevitable. In general, as Whish asserts, 'the system of control adopted is a benign one and is essentially predisposed in favour of mergers.'[3] Undoubtedly political considerations are a significant factor in the decision to refer and the final outcome.

Following a report of the MMC the Secretary of State may use his wide array of powers. Normally, the Director General will be invited to obtain undertakings from the parties concerned.

Newspaper mergers are subject to tighter control since such mergers may raise issues which cannot be judged solely according to economic criteria.[4]

1   See *Sunday Times* 20 July 1986.
2   See *Financial Times* 6 June 1986, 'How to spur competition'.
3   Whish, *Competition Law* (1985) p 589.
4   FTA 1973, ss 57–62.

Restrictive practices
2.7.3   By contrast to the legislation dealing with monopolies and mergers, the legislation dealing with the public interest aspects of restrictive agreements between firms takes a less neutral stance. Under the Restrictive Trade Practices Act 1976 (RTPA 1976) agreements relating to goods or services are presumed to be against the public interest unless it can be shown that they provide one or more benefits which outweigh any detriment to the public interest.

Under the RTPA 1976 four categories of agreement are registrable with the Director General: restrictive agreements as to goods; information agreements as to goods;[1] restrictive agreements as to services; and information agreements as to services. The agreements caught by the provisions are those which involve at least two or more persons and it extends to all 'agreements or arrangements' irrespective of whether or not they are intended to be legally binding.[2] As Cross J observed:

'all that is required to constitute an arrangement not enforceable in law is that the parties to it shall have communicated with one another in some way, and that as a result of the communication each has intentionally aroused in the other an expectation that he will act in a certain way.'[3]

The Director General is required to place all registrable agreements on a public Register of Restrictive Agreements and he must refer all registered agreements to the Restrictive Practices Court (RPC) unless he is satisfied that the restrictions do not warrant proceedings and the Secretary of State concurs in that view. The Director General has wide powers to obtain information if he has reason to suspect that a registrable agreement exists; indeed such agreements are often revealed in the course of research by the MMC.

A further point of contrast with the monopolies and mergers provisions is that the public interest considerations are determined by judicial process before the RPC and not the MMC. The RTPA 1976 provides that any restriction accepted or information provision made in an agreement to which the Act applies is deemed to be contrary to the public interest unless the RPC is satisfied that one or more of the following circumstances apply:

(a) the restrictions are reasonably necessary to protect the public against injury;
(b) removal of the restrictions would deny to the public specific and substantial benefits or advantages;
(c) the restrictions are reasonably necessary to counteract measures taken by a person not party to the agreement with a view to preventing or restricting competition;
(d) the restrictions are necessary to enable the parties to negotiate fair terms of supply from persons not parties to the agreement who control a preponderant part of the trade or business;
(e) the removal of the restrictions would be likely to have a serious and persistent effect on the level of unemployment;
(f) the removal would be likely to cause a reduction in the volume or earnings of export business;
(g) the restrictions are reasonably required for the maintenance of other restrictions not found by the court to be against the public interest;
(h) the restrictions do not restrict or discourage competition to any material degree.[4]

The court must additionally be satisfied that the restrictions are not unreasonable having regard to the balance between the above circumstances and any detriment to the public resulting from the operation of the restriction.

In terms of enforcement of these provisions, if a registrable agreement is not registered it is void and unlawful to give effect to it. Any person adversely affected by the agreement may bring a civil action for damages. Unlike the decisions of the MMC which are advisory, the final decision of the RPC is binding on the parties in the same way as decisions of the ordinary courts. If the court decides that an agreement is contrary to the public interest it may make a declaration to that effect. Orders may also be made against the parties to the agreement preventing them from giving effect to the agreement and against trade associations who assist their members to break an order. Undertakings may be sought from the parties concerned which can then be incorporated in the court's final order.

In recent years the legislation regulating restrictive practices has come under increasing criticism. It has, for example, been argued that the use of a judicial body is inappropriate to determine whether agreements are contrary to the public interest, especially given the absence of a clearly articulated policy basis for the legislation and somewhat vague criteria.[5] It has also been suggested that the enforcement provisions are insufficient to deter and detect secret cartels and that the Director General should be given greater discretion not to refer certain minor agreements to the RPC. The government announced in June 1986 a review of UK competition law and policy, including the operation of the FTA 1973 and RTPA 1976. A Green Paper is expected in the summer of 1987.

1 Agreements to exchange information on specified matters.
2 RTPA 1976, s 43.
3 *Re British Basic Slag Ltd's Agreements* (1962) LR 3 RP 178 at 195–196.
4 RTPA 1976, s 14 and s 19.
5 See Stevens and Yarney, *The Restrictive Practices Court* (1965); *A Review of Restrictive Trade Practices Policy*, Cmnd 7512, 1979.

Anti-competitive practices

2.7.4 In a review of the RTPA 1976 and anti-competitive practices of individual firms published in 1979[1] a proposal was advocated which envisaged giving the Director General powers to selectively investigate practices which restricted, distorted or prevented competition. Such an investigation would not be dependent on the existence of a monopoly and would not be as extensive and time-consuming as those for monopolies and mergers. These proposals were later adopted by the newly elected Conservative Government in the Competition Act 1980 (CA 1980). The Act gives the Director General power to carry out an investigation in order to establish whether a person has been or is pursuing a course of conduct amounting to 'an anti-competitive practice.' The Director General must then report on the matter, specifying the persons concerned, the goods and services in question and whether he considers it necessary to refer the matter to the MMC. In order to avoid a reference the persons concerned may give binding undertakings to the Director General but in the absence of such undertakings a 'competition reference' may be made to the MMC. The MMC investigates whether the conduct has taken place and whether it operates against the public interest, according to the same criteria that applies in the case of monopolies and mergers. In the case of an adverse report the Secretary of State may request the Director General to seek appropriate undertakings from the persons concerned and in the event of refusal to enter into, or failure to comply with, an undertaking, the Secretary of State has power to make an order prohibiting the persons from engaging in the practice.

An anti-competitive practice is one which has the effect of restricting, distorting or preventing competition in connection with the production, supply or acquisition of goods in the UK or any part of it or for the supply or securing of services in the UK or part of it.[2] Such a practice may, for example, involve some form of price discrimination between different groups of customers, or predatory pricing whereby goods are sold for a time at below cost in order to push competition out of the market and later raise the prices. Alternatively the practice may relate to distribution matters such as provisions restricting customers to rent only terms or exclusive supply whereby supplies are only provided to one outlet in an area, thus restricting competition between the buyer and any competitors in the area.

To date there has been little in the way of research as to the impact of the 1980 Act. There have been fewer investigations than was initially anticipated but this may be partly attributable to the fact that the Director General has been able to effect informal settlements of disputes without the need for a formal investigation. The operation of the CA 1980 is not included in the review of competition law and policy announced by the government in June 1986.

1 See 2.7.3, note 5.
2 CA 1980, s 2.

Nationalised industries

2.7.5 The CA 1980 also provides that nationalised industries may be referred by the Secretary of State for investigation by the MMC. A reference may be made in order to consider any question relating to the efficiency of an industry, the services they provide or a possible abuse of a monopoly position. The MMC may be required to consider whether the industry is, in respect of the above matters, acting according to the public interest. They cannot, however, consider any matters relating to financial obligations or guidance in respect of those matters given to the industry by government. Given such restrictions and the fact that references can only be made by a government minister, the potential effectiveness of the provisions is limited.

Resale price maintenance

2.7.6 Resale price maintenance is the practice where a manufacturer fixes the price at which his goods may be resold. It is considered that to deprive traders of the opportunity to compete with one another by lowering their prices is an impediment to competition and efficiency. On the other hand, it could be argued that if permitted it would provide some protection for small traders against the massive strength of large scale supermarket chains.

Under Part I of the Resale Prices Act 1976, there is a prohibition on collective resale price maintenance and under Part II a similar prohibition on individual resale price maintenance. Part I covers agreements or arrangements entered into collectively between suppliers to boycott or discriminate against traders who are in breach of a resale price condition. The provisions can be enforced by proceedings brought by the Director General and any person harmed by the collective action would have a right to take action for breach of statutory duty.

Under Part II any term or condition of a contract of sale by a supplier to a dealer, or of any agreement between a supplier and a dealer relating to such a sale, is void in so far as it purports to establish or provide for the establishment of minimum prices to be charged on the resale of goods.

However, under the Act it is possible for classes of goods to be referred to the RPC for exemption from Part II on the grounds of the public interest. An exemption will be granted under s 14 if it can be established that the maintenance of minimum resale prices is necessary on the grounds of maintaining quality and variety, maintaining retail outlets, keeping prices low, preventing danger to health in consequence of misuse by the public, or the provision of necessary services. Even where one or more of these conditions is satisfied, no exemption will be granted if the maintenance of resale pricing would be detrimental to the overall public interest.[1]

In the event of an exemption being granted, the condition as to resale price is enforceable against any person who is not a party to the sale and who acquires the goods with notice of the condition. The Act does not preclude the common practice of producers recommending a resale price to traders.

1 Only two exception orders have been made covering books and medicaments.

The EEC dimension

2.7.7 Since the UK became a member of the European Economic Community (EEC) UK firms operating in other member states are subject to the competition rules of the Treaty of Rome, which established the EEC. The relevant articles of the Treaty are contained in Articles 85 to 89 and are heavily influenced by the political and economic objectives of the Community. Unlike the RTPA 1976, EEC competition law applies to agreements according to their economic effects not their legal form, the emphasis being exclusively on competition and not the wider questions of public interest that form such an influential part of UK domestic law.

A further point of contrast between the two systems is that there are fewer institutional lawyers forming part of EEC competition law. The European Commission based in Brussels plays the central role in competition in terms of policy, negotiation, investigation, enforcement including imposing penalties and the granting of limited exemptions. Unlike the UK institutions, which are for the most part reactive, the Commission does not need to wait for complaints in order to take action, they can mount unannounced dawn raids on firms in order to obtain incriminating documentation.

The European Court of Justice hears appeals from the decisions of the Commission and, in addition, deals with points of law referred to it by national courts. Indeed national courts are increasingly being utilised by individuals, in the direct enforcement of EEC competition law.

The pillars of EEC competition law are Articles 85(1) and 86 of the Treaty. Article 85 prohibits the following agreements on the grounds that they are incompatible with the common market:

'all agreements between undertakings, decisions by associations of undertakings and concerted practices which may affect trade between member states and which have as their object or effect the prevention, restriction or distortion of competition within the common market.'

The article then lists the type of agreements likely to restrict competition, including those that directly or indirectly fix purchase or selling prices or other trading conditions, those that limit or control production, markets, development or investment, those that share markets or sources of supply, those that apply dissimilar conditions to equivalent transactions with other trading parties, thereby putting them at a competitive disadvantage, and those that make the conclusion of contracts subject to acceptance by the other party of additional obligations which, by their nature, have no connection with the subject of such contracts.

Paragraph 2 of the Article declares that any agreement or decision prohibited under the Article is automatically void.

With the emphasis on 'object or effect', and the general nature of the prohibitions, it is clear that the Commission has immense potential power to influence competition policy within the EEC.

Although Article 85 has a wide coverage there are sectors to which it does not apply, including coal and steel, nuclear energy, agricultural transport and the public sector. Some of these areas are subject to special rules and special political considerations between member states. In addition, under Article 85(3) the Commission may declare Article 85(1) to be inapplicable to agreements, decisions or concerted practices which contribute to improving the production or distribution of goods or promote technical or economic progress. The exemption cannot however be granted unless consumers receive a fair share of the resulting benefit and the agreement does not impose restrictions which are not indispensable to the attainment of these objectives nor substantially eliminate competition in respect of the products in question.

An exemption may be granted on the basis of an individual application to the Commission or under one of a number of block exemptions issued by the Commission under powers given by the Council of Ministers. Such block exemptions have been granted under the terms of Article 85(3) covering exclusive distribution agreements, exclusive purchasing agreements, motor vehicle distribution schemes, and research and development agreements.[1]

Article 86 of the Treaty provides that any abuse by one or more undertakings of a dominant position within the common market or in a substantial part of it shall be prohibited as incompatible with the common market in so far as it may affect trade between member states. There follows a list of types of abuse similar to those listed under Article 85 such as unfair pricing, the imposition of unfair trading conditions and limiting production markets or technical developments, to the prejudice of consumers. The list is not, however, intended to be exhaustive.

In some respects the provisions of Article 86 are similar to those that exist in the UK to deal with anti-competitive practices under the CA 80 and the provisions of the FTA 1973. The fundamental difference between the two systems, however, is that general public interest factors are not taken into account: under Article 86 the central issue is market dominance. In addition, unlike the decisions of the MMC which are subject to a political veto, the Commission's view is final, subject of course to a limited right of appeal to the European Court.

Indeed a major point of contrast between UK domestic competition law and Articles 85 and 86 is in terms of enforcement. The Commission has wide powers to order infringements of the Articles to be terminated, to enter into formal or informal settlements, and impose fines and penalties. In addition, the competition provisions of the Treaty are directly applicable in the domestic courts of the individual member states and UK courts cannot enforce contracts that contravene them. Furthermore, a third party harmed by an infringement of either Article can apply for an injunction or damages.[2] This represents a very significant advantage over UK domestic law in that a firm affected by an infringement can itself initiate action in the courts. Under both the FTA and the CA 80 an aggrieved third party can only urge the appropriate authority to exercise its discretion and mount an investigation. It should be emphasised of course that the EEC competition rules can only be invoked when trade with another member state is affected.

In the event of any conflict arising between domestic competition law and EEC law, the latter takes precedence.[3]

1   See Whish, *Competition Law* (1985) pp 195–205.
2   See eg *Garden Cottage Foods Ltd v Milk Marketing Board* [1984] AC 130, [1983] 2 All ER 770, HL.
3   See Whish, op cit pp 21–22.

Environmental regulation

2.7.8   One of the consequences of industrialisation and the heavy concentration of industry has been an increasing threat to the condition of the environment. The very decision to locate a business in a particular area poses difficult problems in terms of land usage and compatibility with the surrounding area. It also creates problems in respect of the infrastructure such as the adequacy of communication systems and the proximity of resources, including the workforce. The manufacturing and production process may expose the workforce to dangers in respect of health and safety and emissions from a factory may cause damage to the environment and the economy by polluting the land, air or waterways.

In all of the above areas the state has imposed a legal framework enforced by specialist agencies in order to protect the environment. Thus most land development, including building operations or change of use of land, requires permission from the local authority under the terms of the town and country planning legislation. The Health and Safety Commission and the Health and Safety Executive are responsible for health and safety conditions inside and immediately outside places of work. The Industrial Air Pollution Inspectorate enforces a variety of statutes and the Radiochemical Inspectorate carry out statutory duties through the local authorities. Water pollution is controlled by the various water authorities.

A particular problem in the past has been the lack of a unified approach to pollution of the environment. However, as from April 1987 the Government created a unified pollution inspectorate with the Department of the Environment. The new Inspectorate of Pollution brought together the four agencies with responsibilities for air pollution, radiochemicals, hazardous waste and water pollution.

The state, the law and the legal system

2.8.0   The state represents the very source of the legal rules governing all members of society, including those engaged in business activity. The state is also responsible for administering the legal framework and for the provision of a system for the judicial resolution of disputes between members of society. Given the direct participation of the state in economic activity, it might be assumed that there is a fundamental conflict between the functions of the state as entrepreneur and regulator, and the function as law maker and arbiter. However, the concept of the separation of powers within the state serves to provide a check to such conflicts.

The institutional structure of the state in the UK consists of three elements. These are the Executive, the legislature and the judiciary. Constitutional laws and conventions seek to provide checks and balances between the three elements and ensure that no one element takes too much power. Given the inherent flexibility of the UK constitution there are, however, areas of overlap and inevitably tensions may arise between the three elements of government.[1]

The Executive consists of the Cabinet and Her Majesty's Ministers and Civil Service. It represents a massive organ of the state which is essentially required to carry out the will of Parliament. The Monarch is the nominal head of state but the real power lies with the Prime Minister who is chosen by the Monarch on the basis of being able to command majority support in the House of Commons. Supreme legal power lies with Parliament and as such, Parliament may pass or repeal any law it wants. In reality the Executive is able to control Parliament and the vast majority of legislation enacted by Parliament is initiated by the Executive.

The judiciary represents the arbiter role of the state. At the head of the judiciary is the Lord Chancellor who presides over the House of Lords, the Lord Chief Justice who is the senior criminal law judge and the Master of the Rolls, who is the senior civil law judge. The Lord Chancellor straddles the executive and judicial organs of government in as much as his appointment is political, he sits in the Cabinet, presides over the House of Lords in its legislative and judicial functions, acts as a judge and is also involved in the appointment of other judges.

The main function of the judiciary is to adjudicate dispassionately upon disputes. The essence of the work of a judge is to find the facts upon the evidence presented to him, apply the law to the facts as found and give judgement.

A fundamental feature of the judicial system in the UK is that of the independence of the judiciary. In order to ensure the integrity and impartiality of judges they are not directly under the control of the legislature or the Executive.[2]

1   See generally Hartley and Griffiths, *Government and the Law* (1981, 2nd edn).
2   Judges can only be removed on an address by both Houses of Parliament.

Classification of law

2.8.1   In order to understand the legal framework regulating business activity it is important to appreciate at the outset two fundamental classifications of the law. First, there is the distinction between public and private law. Public law is concerned with the law involving the state, whereas private law is concerned with matters arising between persons within the community. Much of the discussion in the following chapters is concerned primarily with private law such as contract, tort, and commercial transactions. A second important classification is between criminal law and civil law. Criminal law is concerned with the prosecution of crimes, such prosecutions usually being initiated by the state. In the event of a prosecution being successful, the person found guilty will be liable to punishment. Civil law is concerned with actions by one individual (the plaintiff) against another person (the defendant) to establish legal rights or seek compensation for loss suffered. Much of the discussion in this book is concerned with the various categories of civil law including contract, tort, commercial law and company law.

Sources of law

2.8.2   The principal sources of law regulating business activity in the UK are judicial precedent, legislation and regulations, directives and decisions of the EEC.

Judicial precedent

2.8.3   One of the most fundamental aspects of the English legal system is the doctrine of binding precedent. The essence of it is that a decision made by a court, particularly a senior court, is binding on other courts in subsequent cases where the facts are similar. It is argued that the process of deciding cases on the basis of precedent brings uniformity and consistency which are considered to be important features of any judicial system. The law that emerges through the system of judicial precedent is often termed 'the common law'.

In earlier centuries a practice developed whereby a litigant could petition the Lord Chancellor where the application of the common law resulted in injustice or an inequitable situation. The Lord Chancellor could exercise his discretion to remedy such injustice and over the years in the Court of Chancery, where petitions were heard, rules and principles known as equity were developed which supplemented the common law. Two examples of equitable relief are the remedies of specific performance whereby a defendant may be compelled to perform his contractual obligations and the injunction which may be used to prevent a defendant from carrying out specified activities or to compel him to act in a specified way. Since the Judicature Acts 1873–75 the rules of equity have been applied in the same courts as the common law and whilst the discretionary nature of the rules has been maintained, the influence of the system of judicial precedent has somewhat eroded the flexibility of equity and its ability to dispense justice in individual cases.

The system of judicial precedent is based on the hierarchical structure of the courts in England. The decisions of the higher courts are more than mere authoritative statements of the law but are binding in all subsequent cases where the facts are similar irrespective of whether or not the later court considers the decision to be correct. The most authoritative decisions are those of the appellate courts, the Court of Appeal and the ultimate appeal court, the House of Lords. The decisions of these two courts form the precedents that comprise the common law. Decisions of lower courts of first instance, such as the High Court, are persuasive in the absence of any authoritative precedent from an appeal court.

The essence of the doctrine of precedent is that all courts are bound to follow the previous decisions of courts which are higher in the system. Thus a decision of the House of Lords is binding on all other courts, including the House of Lords in subsequent cases. However, since 1966 the House of Lords no longer regards itself as rigidly bound by its previous decisions, where it appears right to depart from a precedent. A decision of the Court of Appeal is binding on all courts below it and on future decisions of the Court, but not binding on the House of Lords. Lower courts, such as the High Court, are therefore bound to follow the decisions of the two appeal courts, and normally follow the previous decisions of the High Court. The decisions of lower courts such as the High Court, or the courts of other jurisdictions may be considered to have persuasive rather than binding value.

It is important to appreciate exactly which aspect of a judgement represents the binding precedent. In practice a case may be broken down into three elements. First, a statement of the facts, with an indication by the judge which of them are material. Second, a statement by the judge of the legal principles which may be raised by the material facts and are the reason for the decision. Such statements are normally made after a review of the existing precedents and legal principles. Third, the actual judgement after the application of the law to the facts as found.

The second element, the legal principle, is often termed the ratio decidendi of the case and it is that element that makes the binding precedent, and it is at that stage that the legal issues will be debated and previous precedents cited to the judge. For example, in a case involving injuries sustained by a consumer as a result of consuming a soft drink that contains a poison it is sufficient that a precedent be found which supports the general proposition that a manufacturer of such goods owes a duty of care to consumers in specified circumstances.[1] It is not necessary to find a case with exactly the same facts.

On occasions the judge will comment on the law relating to the type of case before him in general terms, perhaps discussing hypothetical situations. Such comments are termed obiter dicta and, though not binding, they may have some persuasive authority.[2] In practice it is often very difficult to identify the ratio of a case and to distinguish it from the obiter comments and a judge may exercise considerable influence over the development of the law by his selection of precedents. As two distinguished academics have pointed out:

> 'talk of finding the ratio decidendi of a case obscures the fact that the process of interpreting cases is not like a hunt for buried treasure, but typically involves an element of choice from a range of possibilities.'[3]

Indeed, the judges can have a profound impact on the development of the law, particularly in an area where there is no previous precedent or legislative guidance. In such a situation the judge is required to decide the case before him in accordance with general principles and his decision becomes the original source of a new precedent. To that extent judges can be said to be law makers as well as simply discovering and expounding existing law. Indeed, since the House of Lords considered itself not bound by its previous decisions it has been in a position to exercise a significant creative influence in respect of the law. For example, in recent years the House of Lords have completely reformulated the legal principles in the area of tax avoidance schemes to the extent that where a series of transactions takes place, some of which have no commercial purpose other than tax avoidance, tax liability will arise.[4] Hitherto, it was considered entirely legitimate for a person to arrange his affairs in order to minimise tax liability. Under the new principles any scheme which has no 'business purpose' could be challenged.

The advantages of the system of precedent are said to be its certainty, uniformity and flexibility. It has also the capacity to permit the law to develop in that new rules can be established or old ones adapted to meet new circumstances and the changing social and economic environment.

A criticism of the system is its rigidity in that once a precedent is created it is binding even if in application it results in injustice to an individual litigant. This rigidity may be mitigated by a number of factors. First, a judge may seek to avoid the application of a precedent by arguing that the material facts of the earlier precedent case differ from the facts of the case before him. In such circumstances the precedent may be distinguished and the judge permitted to deviate from it. Second, given the hierarchical structure of the courts, a precedent may be overruled either by a higher court or, in the case of a House of Lords precedent, by their Lordships in a later decision. Some judges are, however, reluctant to overrule precedents apart from very exceptional circumstances. They are particularly sensitive to criticism that they are usurping the supreme law-making function of Parliament.

It has been suggested that:

> 'It would be in the interests of the development of the common law if . . . the decisions in the higher courts were accorded only persuasive, and not binding authority . . . if in an exceptional case, the Court of Appeal or even a High Court judge comes to the conclusion that a principle is unworkable or no longer in keeping with the general view of

society, the judge in the lower court should be entitled to say so and to decide according to his conscience or conviction.'[5]

1 See generally Part II.
2 See eg *Hedley Byrne & Co Ltd v Heller & Partners Ltd* [1964] AC 465, [1963] 2 All ER 575, HL.
3 Twining and Miers, *How to do Things with Rules* (1982 2nd edn) p 286.
4 See WT *Ramsey Ltd v IRC* [1982] AC 300, [1981] 1 All ER 865, HL; *Furniss v Dawson* [1984] AC 474, [1984] 1 All ER 530.
5 Schmitthoff, *Journal of Business Law* (1982), p 290.

Legislation

2.8.4 Although the judiciary has the ability to influence the development of the law, Parliament is the supreme law maker in the UK and the judiciary cannot override legislation or indeed, challenge its validity. The judiciary can, however, significantly influence the impact of legislation when called upon to interpret the meaning of a particular section.[1]

Legislation is the body of rules enacted by Parliament in the form of statutes or Acts of Parliament which proceed through a number of stages in the form of bills. Most legislation is initiated by the government and is introduced in the form of a government bill. It may be in the form of a consolidating statute which gathers together several Acts on one topic and then re-enacts them for the sake of simplicity, such as the Companies Act 1985; a codifying statute which seeks to enact some or all of the common law rules in a particular area such as the Partnership Act 1890; a statute to implement government policy in the area of business, competition and the economy such as the Telecommunications Act 1984; a statute to implement an obligation entered into by the government under an international convention or treaty, such as the Data Protection Act 1984; or a statute introduced to regulate a particular activity identified by the government or an agency such as the Law Commission or Office of Fair Trading, as requiring legislative action such as the Unfair Contract Terms Act 1977. Private members of Parliament have a right to introduce a Private Members Bill but few succeed unless they have the support of the government.

With the increased pace of social and economic change over the years and the massive extension in the functions of government, Parliament has increasingly resorted to delegated legislation. Many modern statutes regulating business are complex and both the government and industry need time to formulate detailed rules and adjust to the demands of a statute. Parliament may therefore pass a statute which enables the Secretary of State concerned to draw up regulations as and when required to complete the scheme of the legislation.[2] Such regulations are, however, subject to Parliamentary scrutiny and in some cases must be approved by both Houses.

Delegated legislation has considerable advantages in the saving of Parliamentary time, including greater flexibility in responding to changes in circumstances by redrafting regulations and dealing with complex issues which Members of Parliament may not be competent to discuss sufficiently. On the other hand, the use of delegated legislation on an increasing scale means that the law-making process is moved out of the control of the elected representatives. However, as stated above, safeguards have been introduced in order to allow Parliament to exercise greater scrutiny over delegated legislation.

1 See 2.8.5
2 See eg the Consumer Credit Act 1984.

The interpretation of statutes

2.8.5   In the event of a dispute arising over the interpretation of a statute it falls on the judiciary to make a decision as to the precise meaning of the words used in the statute. It may be of course that the particular words have already been subjected to judicial scrutiny and in such event the judge may be bound by the doctrine of precedent to accept the meaning attributed to the words by a previous decision.

In essence the function of the judge is to ascertain the intention of Parliament according to the words used in the statute. In the vast majority of cases the intention of Parliament will be perfectly clear from the words used. In a minority of cases, however, there may be some ambiguity or doubt as to the precise scope of a section. In such a case the judge is called upon to interpret the relevant section in accordance with accepted rules of interpretation. An obvious approach for the courts might be to consult the official Parliamentary Debates or the Government White Paper or official report that may have preceded the legislation. The courts have however rejected such an approach, preferring to discover Parliament's intention from the words stated in the actual legislation.

There are at least three recognised rules of interpretation. First, the 'literal rule' whereby the judge will give effect to the literal meaning of the words used however unjust or undesirable such as interpretation proves to be. Second, the 'golden rule' which applies where a literal interpretation gives rise to an absurd result. In such a situation the judge is permitted to modify the literal meaning so as to avoid such a result. Third, the 'mischief rule' which permits the judge to interpret the words in the context of the mischief that the statute was seeking to remedy.

In the same way that the judiciary can have a creative impact on the law through the doctrine of precedent, statutory interpretation allows the judiciary some room for creativity. Some judges—

'regard the interpretation of a statute as essentially an exercise in grammar, based on a strict distinction between the legislative and the interpretative function.'[1]

They are sensitive to the criticisms that a more creative approach might be seen as representing a challenge to the law-making function of Parliament. Other judges, however, regard interpretation as a 'process of purposeful collaboration based on an understanding of the legislative process.'[2] Lord Denning once observed that:

'We sit here to find out the intention of Parliament and of Ministers and carry it out, and we do this better by filling in the gaps and making sense of the enactment than by opening it up to destructive analysis.'[3]

On appeal, however, his attitude was described as a

'naked usurpation of the legislative function under the thin disguise of interpretation.'[4]

1 Friedmann, *Law in a Changing Society* (1972 2nd edn) p 56.
2 Ibid.
3 *Magor and St Mellons RDC v Newport Corpn* [1950] 2 All ER 1226, at 1236, CA.
4 [1952] AC 189 at 191 per Lord Simonds.

The European Economic Community

2.8.6   Since the UK joined the EEC under the terms of European Communities Act 1972, community law has become incorporated into UK law. To a certain extent therefore the position of the UK Parliament as the supreme law-making body has been eroded. The 1972 Act provides that all rights, powers, liabilities, obligations, restrictions, remedies and procedures under the various treaties of the Community are effective under UK law, and the judiciary is required to accept the authority of community law.

The sources of EEC law are the treaties of the Community which automatically form part of the law of the member states, and the regulations and directives of the Council and Commission. Regulations and directives are a form of secondary legislation issued in order to enable the objectives of the treaties to be achieved. The former are of general application, binding and directly applicable in all the member states; the latter are addressed to the member states to specifically implement by changing their own laws to conform with the requirements of the Directive. In the UK Directives are implemented either by statute or by delegated legislation.

A further source of law in the Community is the decisions of the European Court of Justice. The court has no inherent law-making authority and there is no doctrine of binding precedent; its work is concerned with matters of interpretation under the laws of the Community and ensuring the institutions of the Community act validly. Although there is no doctrine of precedent, inevitably, a body of rules constituting the decisions of the Court is emerging which represents a powerful persuasive influence on Community law.

The machinery for dispute resolution

2.8.7   Given the nature and complexity of business activity it is inevitable that disputes arise. Disputes may be between two parties to a contract, or between persons engaged jointly in a business enterprise or between a person engaged in business and an organ of the state; whatever the context of the dispute, it is essential in the interests of justice and the efficient use of economic resources, that machinery be available for its resolution. Disputes can use up valuable resources in terms of finance, managerial time and loss of trade, particularly where there is a continuing relationship between the parties as in the case of partners or those involved in the management or financing of companies, or between an employer and employee.

Although disputes cannot always be prevented, the prudent businessman will, at the appropriate time, take certain measures to minimise the likelihood of conflict and consider ways of facilitating the resolution of any dispute that may arise. Such measures may include consultation with the 'in house' or outside solicitor on the likely legal implications of a new venture; the development of clear lines of responsibility within the organisation and effective communication between the different departments or groups involved; a thorough investigation of all potential suppliers, clients and customers; careful scrutiny of contract terms and awareness of the importance of clauses such as exclusion terms, liquidated damages clauses, reservation of title clauses, and arbitration provisions; in the case of long term contracts, the need to monitor continually performance and provide machinery for adjusting the terms of the contract in the event of changed circumstances.[1]

In the event of a dispute arising in the course of business there are a variety of methods available for resolving it. The simplest method is by direct negotiation between the parties resulting in a compromise solution; indeed predictably this is much the most favoured and successful form of dispute resolution. In some areas the state provides machinery to facilitate the negotiation of an amicable settlement between the parties; one example is the role of the Advisory Conciliation and Arbitration Service in assisting the settlement of industrial relations disputes.

Failing a negotiated settlement, the parties may resort to litigation, arbitration or one of a number of developing alternative forms of dispute resolution.

1   See generally Parts 3 and 4.

The courts
2.8.8   The costs involved in litigation are notoriously high and even though a successful litigant may be awarded costs against his losing opponent he is unlikely to recover all of his costs. Decisions to resort to the courts therefore require careful consideration. Much depends upon the nature of the dispute and amount at stake. Once a court has given judgement in favour of one side, the conflict may not be at an end since the other side may decide to lodge an appeal to a higher court which may mean that the dispute will drag on for a number of years: even if there is no appeal, it may be necessary to take further steps through the courts to enforce payment of any award which is made.

Initially a solicitor will be instructed to take the first steps towards litigation and if a settlement is not forthcoming, the solicitor may instruct a barrister to conduct the case. If the litigation is on a large scale or involves complex points of law, the solicitor will undoubtedly recommend seeking the services of a Queen's Counsel, that is, a senior barrister with special knowledge and expertise in the particular area. At each stage the costs of the exercise are substantially increased.

Under English law the courts are structured according to whether the matter is one of criminal law or civil law. Obviously in the case of business disputes litigation will proceed through the civil courts. That does not, however, mean that persons engaged in business are not subject to penalties imposed through the criminal courts; many of the regulatory statutes enforced by state agencies are underpinned by criminal sanctions.

The most important feature of the court structure in England is its hierarchical nature. Each court has its own specified jurisdiction based on the nature of the case and, often, the amount claimed. Some courts deal exclusively with original disputes, others deal exclusively with appeals from lower courts.

In terms of the volume of business the county court is the most important. Its jurisdiction includes actions in contract and tort, but only if the amount claimed does not exceed £5,000, and bankruptcy proceedings without financial limit. There is also a small claims procedure whereby claims not exceeding £500 are referred to arbitration by the county court registrar. The system enables smaller claims to be dealt with swiftly and with the minimum of formality and procedure. The small claims arbitration procedure was introduced in 1973 in response to research by the Consumer Council[1] which showed that the county court was mainly being used as a debt collection agency by public utilities, mail order houses and large businesses, who would employ either their own 'in house' or regular outside legal staff, familiar with the court system and able to bring regular claims. The procedure allows cases to be decided without a full hearing, for instance on the basis of written submissions, and provides that in most cases when the sum involved does not exceed £500, no costs will be awarded to the winner. The aim of this last rule is to encourage litigants in person to bring small claims which would not merit the cost of employing a solicitor. They may do so without fear that they will be made responsible for the legal costs of their opponent if the claim fails. However, the rule may have a damaging effect by discouraging people with strong but small claims from seeking legal advice: they will not recover the cost of such advice even if the claim succeeds. In a recent study on behalf of the Lord Chancellor's Department it was suggested that the small claims procedure is largely fulfilling its aim of providing a forum where small claims can be litigated without a lawyer's help. In 1985 nearly 45,000 disputes were dealt with through the procedure. However, the survey revealed that small claims are not always dealt with quickly and take between 16 and 36 weeks to resolve. A consultation document proposes that the procedure be extended to claims up to £1,000 and county court registrars take a more active approach to the handling of claims. The document also proposes the idea of introducing a new system of 'judicial arbitration' in the county court for claims between £1,000 and £5,000.[2]

Where a dispute is one which the county court is not competent to handle the case will be heard in one of the divisions of the High Court. These are the Chancery Division, the Family Division and the Queen's Bench Division. The first deals with disputes in company and partnership law, bankruptcy and mortgages and the specific performance of contracts; the second with family law, issues such as divorce and adoption, and the third with a wide variety of disputes including actions in contract and tort and the judicial review of administrative action by government bodies. The jurisdiction of the Queen's Bench Division in contract and tort has no financial limit—upper or lower. It therefore overlaps that of the county court and when a claim is for £5,000 or less a litigant may be able to choose the forum in which to bring his case. The choice of forum may be affected by a number of factors. County court actions may be dealt with more quickly and cheaply: a solicitor may appear as advocate in the county court whereas in the High Court a barrister must be retained. On the other hand it is felt that High Court proceedings can more easily be controlled by the parties, that High Court proceedings are more imposing and threatening, and that procedures for enforcement of judgments may be better in the High Court than in the county court. In order to discourage the use of the High Court for small claims, rules of court provide that if a claim is brought in the High Court and less than £3,000 is recovered, costs will only be awarded on a scale appropriate to a county court claim. This may result in the successful litigant being seriously out of pocket; moreover, if less than £600 is recovered in the High Court, the winner will normally recover no costs at all.

Most High Court actions are begun by the issue and service of a writ. The parties must then exchange pleadings in which each sets out, broadly, the nature of his case. In a case where there is no real defence—for instance a simple debt claim or a claim on a dishonoured cheque—the plaintiff may be able to get judgment very early in the proceedings. If that is not the case, the court will give directions to enable the case to be prepared for trial: problems of evidence may be dealt with at this stage. When all is ready the case will go to trial. However, even when the successful party has judgment that may not be the end of the matter. It may be necessary to take steps to enforce it—particularly if the defendant is not insured against the particular type of liability. Enforcement procedures may include instructing an officer of the court to seize and sell goods, obtaining security over property such as a house or shares, or obtaining payment to the judgment creditor of a debt due to the judgment debtor. The threat of insolvency proceedings may be useful to persuade a debtor to pay.

In the county court, procedure is similar but the action is commenced by summons; the directions stage is reached much earlier and a case is likely to come to trial much more quickly than in the High Court.

Each division of the High Court has specialist courts operating to deal with clearly defined categories of business. The Chancery Division has the Companies Court which deals with matters arising under company legislation and the Queen's Bench Division has the Commercial Court. The latter court deals with commercial actions including:

> 'any cause arising out of the ordinary transactions of merchants and traders and, without prejudice to the generality of the foregoing words, any cause relating to the construction of a mercantile document, the export or import of merchandise, affreightment, insurance, banking, mercantile agency and mercantile usage.'[3]

The basic features of the Commercial Court's operations are its relative speed, and simplicity and flexibility in terms of procedure. The strict rules of evidence may be relaxed and the judges are available at short notice at any stage of the action on the initiative of either party; disputes can thus be dealt with quickly. Unfortunately in recent years the case-load has increased to such an extent that delays have caused some concern. In April 1986 the government appointed a firm of accountants to try and identify the main causes of delay, cost and complexity in the handling of commercial cases.

Other important courts are the Restrictive Practices Court[4] which deals with trading agreements under restrictive practices legislation and the Employment Appeal Tribunal which hears appeals on points of law from industrial tribunals hearing applications under employment and trade union legislation.

Appeals from these courts go to the Court of Appeal (Civil Division) and finally to the House of Lords. In exceptional circumstances appeals may be made directly to the House of Lords from the High Court.

In recent years a number of tribunals have been created to deal with disputes arising out of claims under welfare and employment legislation. Such tribunals usually comprise a legally qualified chairperson and two other non-legal persons. The objective of such tribunals is to dispense justice in an environment with the minimum of formality and delay. In the context of business, the industrial tribunals dealing with claims for redundancy payment, unfair dismissal and discrimination at work have played an important role in providing employees with accessible machinery for enforcing rights against employers.

In the case of disputes involving the law of the European Economic Community, recourse may be had to the European Court.

1 *Justice Out of Reach* (1970.)
2 See Civil Justice Review, 'Small Claims in the County Court' (Lord Chancellor's Department) 1986. See also Civil Justice Review Paper No 6: General Issues (1987).
3 Rules of the Supreme Court, Order 72, r 1(2).
4 See 2.7.3.

Arbitration
2.8.9 Arbitration has long been a popular method of settling business disputes arising out of a contractual relationship. It is used extensively in the settlement of international trading and maritime disputes and in the construction industry. The terms of a contract invariably require that disputes be referred for settlement to one of a number of institutions, such as the Court of Arbitration of the International Chamber of Commerce or the London International Arbitration Centre. On the other hand, the contract may simply provide for the appointment of a single arbitrator or arbitration panel, to be agreed by the parties. In order to avoid disputes over the procedure it has become common practice for arbitration clauses to refer to the United Nations Commission on International Trade Law Arbitration Rules (1976). These rules provide a framework of procedure which, if adopted, can avoid lengthy disputes on the operation of the arbitration.

It is argued that the great advantage of arbitration over litigation is cost and speed. Such advantages are not always readily apparent. In trading disputes the issues may involve shipments dating back a number of years and may raise complex technical points which require considerable time to be set aside for discussion and argument.

Arbitration is favoured in business disputes for three basic reasons.[1] First, the proceedings are held in private thus avoiding the exposure of sensitive disputes to the glare of publicity. Second, the parties can actually agree on the identity of the individual or organisation to settle the dispute. As Schmitthoff points out—

> 'In international disputes the parties are sometimes disinclined to go to the national courts. They prefer their dispute to be settled by persons with an international outlook.'[2]

Third, arbitration is intended as a once and for all mechanism for resolving a dispute, as opposed to litigation which may involve appeals to higher courts, thus creating further uncertainty and greater cost. Arbitrations in the UK have not always carried a guarantee of such certainty and have been exposed to judicial scrutiny. In recent years, encouraged by reforms instituted by the Arbitration Act 1979, arbitration awards have carried a much greater degree of finality. The judiciary have treated arbitration with much less suspicion than hitherto. In the words of Sir John Donaldson:

> 'Courts and arbitrators are in the same business, namely the administration of justice. The only difference is that the courts are in the public and the arbitrators in the private sector of the industry.'[3]

Under the Arbitration Act 1979 the parties may refer preliminary points of law to the courts but an appeal against an award requires the consent of all the parties, or permission of the court which is only granted if the legal issue substantially affects the rights of one or more of the parties to the arbitration agreement.[4] In certain circumstances the parties may even agree to exclude any possibility of judicial review at the outset.

1   See Schmitthoff, 'Why arbitration is the favoured method of dispute settlement' *Financial Times* 4 October 1985.
2   Ibid.
3   *Bremer Vulkan Schiffbau und Maschinenfabrik v South India Shipping Corpn Ltd* [1979] 3 WLR 471 at 479.
4   See *Pioneer Shipping Ltd v BTP Tioxide Ltd* [1982] AC 724, [1981] 2 All ER 1030, HL.

Alternative dispute resolution
2.8.10   In recent years a number of alternative dispute resolution schemes (ADRs) have emerged. Many of them, however, are simply variants on litigation or arbitration.

The Director General of Fair Trading has encouraged trading associations to introduce codes of practice, some of which include conciliation and arbitration schemes for consumers. A number of professional organisations have introduced an Ombudsman officer to whom persons can take a grievance about the way their business has been handled. Usually the service is provided free of charge, and does not preclude later litigation. However, like any system of self-regulation it only works if all practitioners belong to the ombudsman scheme. The first system was the launch of the Insurance Ombudsman Bureau in 1981 which provides a conciliation service for UK personal policy holders of the member companies. This was followed by the Banking Ombudsman in 1986 which is a scheme run by the five major clearing banks and the Scottish banks, and deals with disputes between individual customers and partnerships and the banks concerned and can make awards of up to £50,000 which are binding on the bank but not the complainant. The Banking Ombudsman will only consider a complaint if it has first been considered by the senior management of the bank concerned. A similar scheme is proposed for building societies under the Building Societies Act 1986 and for the stock market on the initiative of the Council of the Stock Exchange. The Securities and Investment Board also plans to launch an Ombudsman scheme to deal with disputes between an investor and investment firms.[1]

In the USA where the legal costs of business corporations are estimated at $80bn a year[2] a variety of conciliation and 'mini-trial' schemes have been introduced in an attempt to reduce the cost of dispute resolution. The Federal Bar Council introduced a scheme designed to reduce pre-trial procedures whereby a 'special counsel' or 'adjudicator' is appointed to make an award on the merits, under a fixed time schedule and with full control over procedure. The Zurich Chamber of Commerce has also introduced a scheme based on the American idea of a 'mini-trial' and designed for international commercial disputes.[3] A panel comprising two senior officers of the parties concerned and an independent chairman hears the issues and seeks to arrive at a settlement. Submissions are limited to 25 typed pages and an overall time limit of 30 days is fixed. In the event of no agreement emerging at the expiration of 30 days, the panel makes a settlement recommendation, which in the absence of unanimity, is submitted by the chairman.

1   See 38.0.6.
2   See Herman, 'Disputes: the other way' *Financial Times* 9 October 1983.
3   Ibid.

The judiciary and the government

2.8.11   In addition to resolving disputes arising out of commercial claims, the courts also reserve the right to examine the activities of the executive in order to ensure compliance with the law. This process is known as judicial review and involves the judges of the Queen's Bench Division of the High Court in scrutinising the decision-making process of government departments, local authorities and other agencies of the state. The scrutiny is not based on a challenge of the decision itself but on the decison-making process. It might be that the decision was based on an incorrect view of the particular legal provision, or that the body concerned ignored important factors or took into account irrelevant factors or that there was a fundamental procedural irregularity such as a lack of consultation or failure to allow an interested party an opportunity to state their case. If any of the above grounds are found to exist the courts may quash the decision of the body concerned. In 1977 the procedure for judicial review was simplified[1] and in recent years there has been a substantial increase in the number of applications.[2] Amongst the bodies that have been challenged in addition to government departments are the Monopolies and Mergers Commission in respect of takeover references, the Independent Broadcasting Authority over a decision to block a takeover bid by Rank for the Granada Group and British Coal over its decision to close a colliery. A recent landmark decision was *R v The Panel on Takeovers and Mergers, ex p Datafin and Prudential-Bache Securities Inc*[3] in which the Court of Appeal held that the Panel was a body within public law and its decisions can be scrutinised by the courts under judicial review procedure, despite the fact that the Panel is a self-regulatory body with no legal status. This decision has immense potential significance for all self-regulatory schemes. Provided, however, that a body complies with the basic standards of fairness enshrined in the grounds for judicial review, the courts have no power to intervene further.

1   See Supreme Court Act 1981, s 31.
2   In 1981 there were 533 applications, in 1985 this had increased to 1230. See *Financial Times*, 6 May 1986.
3   FT Commercial Law Reports, 6 December 1986.

Part II
The law of torts

Chapter 3

The Law of Torts

3.0.0 In any society individuals and organisations must interact, and in the course of their interaction their interests may come into conflict; the activities of one may—actually or potentially—harm another, in his person, his property or his pocket. One of the functions, indeed a major function, of law in any developed society is to provide a means of resolving such disputes so as to limit the resort of the injured party to self-help. The law may attempt to compensate the party harmed, to punish the party inflicting the harm, or to combine both courses. Later, on a more sophisticated level, the law may seek to deter individuals from inflicting harm, and to set general standards for behaviour. In English law these functions are fulfilled by the criminal law and by the law of obligations,[1] generally seen to be made up of the law of contracts and the law of torts.

1 An increasingly important role is played by regulations which, while not part of the law of obligations, are not truly criminal in character. Such regulations, for instance under the Health and Safety at Work etc. Act, play a vital role in setting and raising standards of behaviour.

Tort and contract
3.1.0 We will see in Part III that the law of contract is primarily concerned with commercial relationships between parties who agree to deal together, and, through the doctrine of freedom of contract, with obligations voluntarily undertaken. The law of torts, on the other hand, regulates the behaviour of individuals, and imposes obligations upon them in relation to their behaviour, even when their interaction with others is not voluntary. Indeed, the largest single part of the law of torts, the law of negligence, is concerned with perhaps the clearest example of non-voluntary interaction, accidents—although as we shall see, in many cases of negligence there is in fact a voluntarily undertaken relationship between the parties and, indeed, liability often depends on the existence of such a relationship.

Traditionally the law of contracts has been viewed entirely separately from the law of torts. Contract law is said to depend on obligations voluntarily undertaken, whereas the law of torts is concerned with obligations imposed on all parties, by the general law, regardless of consent, and there is much in this distinction. However, it must be treated with care, for, as we will see, in many situations contractual obligations are imposed on parties without any real consent, whether through the mechanism of implied terms, particularly those statutory implied terms which cannot be excluded or

51

modified,[1] or through the artificial finding of an agreement. At the same time, consent is relevant in the law of torts. Thus in some cases consent may be a defence to a claim;[2] moreover, when contractual and tortious liabilities overlap, the contract may modify or exclude tortious liabilities. Similarly it is said that liability in contract is strict—that a party may be liable for breach of contract without being at fault—whereas liability in tort is based on fault, but this distinction also embodies an oversimplification. The parties to a contract may be relieved of liability when they are not at fault, both through the general law of frustration[3] and through the use of contractual terms— exclusion clauses[4] and force majeure clauses—modifying their liability; at the same time some forms of tortious liability—trespass,[5] defamation[6] or liability under *Rylands v Fletcher*[7]—may arise regardless of the fault of the tortfeasor. It is true that in the law of negligence, which is by far the most important aspect of the law of torts in modern society, liability is imposed because of some measure of blameworthiness in the defendant's conduct. But we will see that even in negligence liability may be imposed on parties who are not personally at fault—for instance, the vicarious liability imposed on employers[8] for acts of their employees—and that in many instances the standard of care required of a defendant by the law of negligence is fixed so artificially high as to be, effectively, strict.

Further, a distinction has in the past been drawn between contract and tort on the basis of the grounds of compensation available. A party to a contract is liable for not doing what he has promised to do; a defendant in a negligence action is liable for doing what the law prohibits—acting carelessly. As Weir has put it:

'Contract law is productive, tort law is protective. In other words, tortfeasors are typically liable for making things worse, contractors for not making them better.'[9]

Finally, the two have been distinguished in the past by the rule that damages were not available in tort for a plaintiff who suffered loss only to his pocket —purely economic loss. A plaintiff could only recover for such economic loss if he had suffered it as a result of a breach of contract—and then only if he had paid for it and his loss was caused by the other party to the contract. However, recent decisions have cast doubts even on this distinction.[10]

The result is that the line between contractual and tortious liability is no longer so clear as it was, and in recent years the courts have shown an increasing inclination to bring the two sets of rules together. There is much to be said in favour of such an approach since very often a claim could be framed either in tort or in contract, for instance when a contract includes an implied term that one party will take reasonable care.[11] It makes sense that the result of the case should not turn on the chance of how the plaintiff chooses to frame it.

1   For example, the implied terms in the Sale of Goods Act 1979; see 21.0.0.
2   Volenti non fit injuria. See 8.0.3.
3   See 17.0.4.
4   See 18.0.0.
5   See 4.0.0.
6   See 5.0.0.
7   (1866) LR1 Exch 265 (1868) LR 3 HL 300, Ex Ch. See 10.0.9.
8   See 9.0.4.
9   Int Encl Comp L xi Ch 12, p 5.
10   See *Junior Books Ltd v Veitchi Co Ltd* [1983] 1 AC 520, [1982] 3 All ER 201, HL.
11   See eg Supply of Goods and Services Act 1982, s 13. See 25.0.2.

Tort and crime

3.2.0   The distinction between tort and crime is more clear cut than that between tort and contract. At its simplest, tort and crime are dealt with in different courts;[1] moreover, whereas a jury will sit with a judge in the Crown Court to hear the more serious criminal cases, there are few juries in any civil cases (with the exception of defamation).

A more important distinction between the two lies in their purposes. The purpose of the law of crime is primarily to punish the wrongdoer—and thus to raise standards of behaviour and deter others.[2] The principle of tort is to compensate the injured party, rather than to punish.[3] However, even this distinction is not entirely clear cut. Criminal courts now have limited powers to make compensation orders against a criminal in favour of his victim[4] and the Criminal Injuries Compensation Scheme provides financial compensation for victims of violent crime—although paid by the government rather than by the wrongdoer. On the other hand a tort claim may exceptionally lead to an award of punitive damages, for instance when a defendant has sought deliberately to commit a tort with a view to making a profit out of that wrong, at the plaintiff's expense.[5]

At the same time, many incidents may give rise to both civil and criminal liability. For instance, assault is both a crime and a tort; similarly public nuisance is a crime but also leads to tortious liability if any one person is particularly injured. A road accident may well lead to both a prosecution for careless (or reckless) driving and a civil claim for damages. On the other hand many acts are criminal but not tortious, or tortious but not criminal; most notably there is no criminal liability for trespass to land so that, contrary to the well-known warning, trespassers generally won't be prosecuted.[6]

There is, however, one way in which both criminal and tortious liability seek to secure the same purpose: both seek to set—and maintain—standards of behaviour, by prescribing certain acts and prescribing penalties therefor.[7]

1   The Magistrates and Crown Courts for crime; county and High Court for tort. The same judge might well deal with both types of case however. See generally above 2.8.8.
2   This is a simplification: there is, of course, much debate amongst legal philosophers and others as to what is the true position of the criminal law—or of the law of torts, come to that.
3   This too is a simplification; see below.
4   Powers of Criminal Courts Act 1973, s 35 gives the criminal court limited power to make compensation orders against a wrongdoer in favour of the victim of a crime.
5   For instance in the case of defamation; see below 5.0.0.
6   Vividly illustrated by the controversy in 1986 over the so called 'hippy convoy' which led to the creation of a limited form of criminal trespass: s 39 Public Order Act 1986.
7   Whether or not either is effective as a means of setting standards is open to debate; see below.

The function and purpose of tort

3.3.0   As we have already noted the law of tort is one of the mechanisms by which the law seeks to regulate the interraction of members of society. A large part of the function of tort is thus the striking of a balance between the conflicting interests of members of society. This is most easily seen in the tort of nuisance: for instance, if my factory gives off noxious fumes causing an unpleasant smell which deters diners from visiting my neighbour's restaurant, the law of nuisance must balance my right to use—and the public interest in my using—my factory with my neighbour's right to use his property; a similar balancing exercise permeates the whole of the law of torts. Thus a balancing of interests may affect the standard of care in negligence so that, although it would be negligent of me to drive at a high speed a lorry containing a heavy piece of lifting equipment improperly secured and held in place by my colleagues, I may not be negligent if I and my colleagues are firemen rushing to an emergency, even if one of my colleagues is injured.[1] The public interest in our effecting a rescue alters the standard of the duty of care I owe my colleagues. Similarly almost the whole of the law of defamation is concerned with striking a balance between the right of freedom of speech and the right to protect one's reputation.

The law cannot exist in a vacuum: it must respond to and cope with social change. The early forms of tortious liability were concerned with directly inflicted harm in the tort of trespass, and with the protection of property in trespass and nuisance. But with the industrial revolution and increased mobility and industrialisation came increased potential for harm. That change has continued and indeed its pace has increased. In the 19th century the law had to cope with an increasing number of accidents in two situations—on the roads and at work. Moreover, the increased mobility of society meant not only that there were more—and more serious—accidents but that those accidents were more likely to be between strangers. The old forms of tortious liability were not well suited to deal with these developments and the law responded by developing and extending new forms of liability, notably the tort of negligence. At first there was a reluctance to allow recovery in some situations—for instance when carelessness at work led to the injury of one worker by a colleague—for fear of exposing a tortfeasor to too extensive a liability. As we shall see, although that reluctance has gradually been overcome in specific situations—the doctrine of 'common employment' for instance, is long gone—the argument against imposing too extensive liability, against opening the 'floodgates of litigation' still flourishes.

Indeed, the floodgates argument is perhaps even more important today than it was one hundred years ago. Continued developments, particularly in transport and industry, have increased the risk of accidents in terms of both their number and their seriousness.

> 'The toll on life, limb, and property exacted by today's industrial operations, methods of transport, and many another activity benignly associated with the "modern way of life" has reached proportions so staggering that the economic cost of accidents represents a constant and mounting drain on the community's human and material resources.'[1]

The Pearson Committee reporting in 1978 gave average figures for the annual number of accidents in the years 1973–1975. Over that period an average of 7,696 people were killed on the roads each year, with a further 403,000 injured; 1,300 were killed at work with 720,000 injured. Those figures alone, however, do not reflect the whole story. In a modern industrial society one accident may have much more wide-reaching consequences than would have been the case 100 years ago. Thus if an airliner crashes, hundreds of passengers may be killed; if it crashes over a population centre the number of potential victims is hugely increased. To take a further extreme but chilling example, an accident at a chemical or nuclear plant could have effects spreading over a vast area and even crossing national boundaries. Furthermore, the manner of causing harm in a modern society may be more subtle and with wide-ranging consequences which are difficult to anticipate. The driver of the excavator severs an electricity supply cable, cutting off the supply to a factory and the factory is therefore put out of action for several hours losing potential future profits;[2] the local authority inspector fails to supervise properly the construction of a building's foundations: several years later the building has changed hands a number of times and begins to collapse;[3] the accountant is careless in his audit of a company's accounts: an investor invests in the company relying on these accounts but the company is actually worth considerably less than the accounts suggested.[4] These situations are all beginning to pose new problems for the law of torts, as the judges extend the law of negligence into new areas to cope with new developments.

The law must be responsive to other factors than simply technological change. It must also reflect changing moral views and, increasingly, its economic implications are failing to be considered.

In particular as the emphasis of tort was shifting from the rather straightforward problem of directly inflicted damage—dealt with by trespass—to more subtle liability for loss caused indirectly, with the development of negligence, there was a parallel shift so that liability in negligence depended on some degree of fault or blameworthy conduct (carelessness) on the part of the defendant. Thus, although the purpose of tort damages is primarily to compensate the victim, there is here an element of retribution: the tortfeasor's liability depends on him being at fault. Gradually, however, the requirement of fault on the part of the tortfeasor has been eroded so that, increasingly, liability is imposed on parties who are in no way blameworthy. A well-known example is the vicarious liability of the employer for the torts committed by his employees. In this situation there is a person—the employee—at fault, but the person who pays for the damage caused is not blameworthy. There are many other instances of strict, ie without fault, tortious liabilities being imposed by statutes; moreover, even in some cases where liability is imposed on the grounds of negligence, the standard of care required by the courts is now so artificially high that there is legal liability without moral fault. An example is in the field of motor accidents: an American survey conducted in 1970 concluded that in Washington the average 'good' driver committed nine driving errors every five minutes behind the wheel. A good driver was one who had not been involved in a traffic accident during the preceding four years.[5]

The motive for this shift away from fault as the basis of liability has come from a growing consideration of the second factor mentioned above—the economic effectiveness of the law of torts. In fact the motorist who is held liable for an accident does not personally pay damages to his injured victim; no more so does the employer personally compensate his injured employee or third parties injured by his employees. Instead the tortfeasor will—if he has been sufficiently prudent to insure—pass the loss on to his insurer. The insurer will then distribute that loss amongst his insureds by way of increased premiums and the tortfeasor may well bear only a small part of the loss in that way and (possibly) by the loss of any no claims bonus. Increasingly businesses and even private individuals have made use of insurance to protect themselves from the effects of their own loss-causing conduct; indeed, public liability cover is increasingly found in domestic insurance policies. However, in the case of many 'high risk' activities, insurance is compulsory: obvious examples are the compulsory third party cover which every motorist must carry and employer's compulsory insurance to cover injury to employees. This widespread use of insurance has obvious benefits for the victim of an 'accident' who can look forward with near complete certainty to recovering damages from the insurance company regardless of the financial status of the person who injured him; equally, the tortfeasor benefits because he himself does not have to bear the potentially crippling costs of his torts; instead the loss will be spread amongst all insureds engaged in a similar activity by way of increased premiums; and, moreover, if the premium payers are themselves in business they will in turn pass on the increased cost of insurance to their own customers by way of increased prices, so that ultimately the consumer will pay for accidents caused by a defective product, for example. There can be no doubt that the courts have in recent years begun to take account, albeit tacitly, of the availability of insurance both in imposing liability and in fixing the level of damages; modern contract law openly recognises the availability of insurance as a factor in assessing the reasonableness of an exclusion clause.[6]

The availability and use of insurance has arguably had a profound effect on the development of the law. Moreover, it raises interesting and complex questions about the true functions of the law of torts, its effectiveness in fulfilling those functions, and whether those functions might better be fulfilled by some other system. These questions have come in for frequent and continued scrutiny in recent years both from lawyers and economists. However, before we can consider the effectiveness of the law we must consider the law itself.

1   J G Fleming, *'An Introduction to the Law of Torts'* (1985) p 1.
2   *Spartan Steel and Alloys Ltd v Martin & Co (Contractors) Ltd* [1973] QB 27, [1972] 3 All ER 557, CA.
3   See *Dutton v Bognor Regis UDC* [1972] 1 QB 373, [1972] 1 All ER 462, CA.
4   *JEB Fasteners Ltd v Marks, Bloom & Co (a firm)* [1981] 3 All ER 289.
5   'Driver Behaviour and Accident Involvement: Implications for Tort Liability' (1970) pp 177–8.
6   Unfair Contract Terms Act 1973, s 11(4)

'Tort' defined

3.4.0   At its simplest 'tort', as students of French will recognise, means simply 'wrong' or 'wrongful act'. In a legal context, a 'tort' is a civil wrong, as distinct from a criminal wrong—even though, as observed above, the same act may often be both a tort and a crime. However, as is often the case, this simple description gives a less than complete picture. A plaintiff can only bring an action for a tort if he has suffered damage, or loss, due to the wrongful conduct of the defendant: this has led Friedman to speak instead of 'civil harms' rather than 'civil wrongs'.[1] This is a major weakness of the law of negligence as a standard-setting device: the court can only declare that the defendant failed to exercise a proper standard of care after he has so done and after at least one plaintiff has suffered as a result.

We can therefore redefine 'tort' as 'wrong + damage' when ' + ' really means 'causing', because, as we shall see, a plaintiff may only claim against the defendant if his damage was caused by the defendant's wrongful act. However, we must still further refine our definition. For it is not every act of a defendant which might be regarded as morally 'wrong' which will found an action in tort; a plaintiff may sue only if his harm is caused by an act which falls into a recognised category of wrong, or 'tort'. Thus he may complain of trespass to his person, property or goods; he may sue in nuisance if, for example, his property is troubled by noxious fumes from neighbouring premises; in defamation if his reputation is injured by an untrue publication; or in negligence if, for example, his person or property is damaged due to another's carelessness. In contrast, imagine a plaintiff who owns a small retail business. A larger concern opens a shop nearby; it checks on the plaintiff's prices and then deliberately undercuts them to drive him out of business. The 'plaintiff' has no tort action even though he has clearly suffered loss; there is no tort of 'unfair competition', or 'unfair trading'. Moreover he would still have no complaint if his larger neighbour was motivated not by economic considerations but by simple personal malice.

Even if the plaintiff suffers loss or harm due to a legally recognised 'wrong' he will only be able to sue if the type of loss he has suffered is recognised as compensatable. In recent years the law of negligence has had to grapple with two difficult areas, in relation to plaintiffs who suffer nervous shock and economic loss. The latter is of particular relevance to us and we examine it in detail below.[2] However, suffice to say for now that until recently it was clear that a plaintiff who suffered only economic loss due to a defendant's negligence could not sue: although the 'wrong' was recognised, the 'harm' was not.

We are now nearer to producing a more workable—if more lengthy—definition of tort. A plaintiff may successfully bring a tort action if he can show that he has suffered a recognised type of damage because of conduct by the defendant which the law recognises as wrongful. It now becomes apparent that there is much flexibility in such a definition. A court may deny a plaintiff a remedy by deciding that the defendant's act was not wrongful; or that the plaintiff's loss is not of a recognised type, or that the plaintiff's loss was not caused by the defendant's conduct, and all of these devices have, at various times, been used to restrict the number of claims that might be brought. Equally, by recognising a new type of wrong or a new type of harm the court may 'create' a new class of tort action in response to changing social circumstances. This was, effectively, what the courts did in the leading case of *Rylands v Fletcher*,[3] holding that a person who brings onto and keeps on his land anything dangerous and likely to do damage if it 'escapes' is strictly liable for any damage it may cause if it does escape. This case, decided in 1866, at a time of a rapid increase in industrialisation and a shift away from agricultural land use is perhaps the classic example of the law responding to changing circumstances. Similar response can be seen in the watershed decisions of *Donoghue v Stevenson*[4] allowing a consumer, for the first time, to sue a negligent manufacturer of a defective product, and *Hedley Byrne & Co Ltd v Heller & Partners Ltd*[5] which opened the door for negligence actions against professional advisers. Of course, those very same factors which provide the law with the flexibility to respond to new circumstances also impart to it a degree of uncertainty.

---

1   Friedman, *Law in a Changing Society* (1972) Ch 5.
2   See 7.1.5.
3   (1866) LR 1 Exch 265; (1868) LR 3HL 330, HL.
4   [1932] AC 562, HL.
5   [1964] AC 465, [1963] 2 All ER 575, HL.

Torts and business

3.5.0   A brief examination of the contents page of any major tort text book will reveal that there are many different types of legally recognised 'wrong-torts'. Our concern is with the law relating to business and, whilst there is no reason why a business cannot commit—or be victim of—any tort, particularly through its vicarious liability for its employees—we shall concentrate on those forms of tortious liability which seem most apposite, in particular negligence and its various extensions, and, to a lesser degree, nuisance, However, before turning to those, we will look briefly at one or two other heads of liability.

Chapter 4
Trespass

4.0.0 Trespass is the oldest surviving form of tortious liability. We are all familiar with the (inaccurate) warning that 'trespassers will be prosecuted' and hence with the idea of trespass to land. However, a trespass may also be committed 'to the person' and 'to goods'. We will look at all three types of trespass in turn.

Trespass to land
4.0.1 Any direct interference with land in the possession of another is a trespass. The important word in the definition is 'direct' because it is the directness of an incursion which distinguishes trespass from nuisance, which deals with indirect incursions and interference. By way of example, it is clearly a trespass if I deliberately break into a factory at night when I have no right to be there. Equally, it is a trespass if I deliberately dump rubbish into my neighbour's property; but it is only a nuisance if my fence collapses into his garden. However, the case law suggests that the distinction between 'direct' and 'indirect' interferences will often be difficult to draw.[1]

Trespass is concerned with a direct incursion onto or interference with the property of another. It is no defence to a trespass claim that the defendant did not intend to trespass. Provided his entry onto or interference with the property was intentional, ie conscious, he will be liable in trespass even though he believed that he had a perfect right to act as he did. Thus the rambler who strays unintentionally from the footpath is a trespasser even if the footpath is hidden by snow drifts. Moreover, trespass is said to be 'actionable per se' that is, a plaintiff may sue without proving he has suffered any loss, although in a trivial case such as that outlined above, the plaintiff would be ill-advised to sue since his damages would probably be nominal at best.

The practical importance of trespass is largely in its relation to other legal topics. Thus a person who enters premises as a trespasser with intent to commit certain offences commits the crime of burglary;[2] a trespasser may not be entitled to the same degree of protection from dangers on premises as would be a lawful visitor; and a person in possession of property may use reasonable force to evict or prevent entry by a trespasser. However, a note of caution must be sounded. If the trespasser is in possession of property, it is a criminal offence to use force to evict him—even if the person using force is the lawful owner.[3] Here is the real practical importance of 'trespass'. A person entitled to possession of property—often the owner—must go to court to take summary proceedings to evict a trespasser. He may also be able to claim 'mesne profits'—that is, the value of the land (normally its rental value) for the duration of the trespass. Typically such proceedings may be brought against squatters—often travellers who have entered onto vacant land. In fact by the standards of civil court actions generally, such proceedings are very speedy and the procedure straightforward. However, as demonstrated by the furore which surrounded the activities of the so-called 'hippy convoy' there was widespread feeling that they were still too cumbersome. The Public Order Act 1986 has therefore imposed criminal liability in limited circumstances where two or more persons have entered land as trespassers having a common purpose of residing there for any period.[4]

1   See *Southport Corpn v Esso Petroleum Co Ltd* [1954] 2 QB 182, [1954] 2 All ER 561, CA and [1956] AC 218, [1955] 3 All ER 864, HL where there was a difference of judicial opinion.
2   Theft Act 1968, s 9.
3   Criminal Law Act 1977, s 12(3) makes it an offence to use force to gain entry to premises if there is any person on the premises opposed to such entry, subject to certain exceptions.
4   Public Order Act 1986, s 39. See Card (1986) 'Public Order: the New Law'.

Trespass to the person
4.0.2   Trespass may take three forms: an assault which represents an act causing someone reasonable fear of an immediate battery; a battery which is the intentional application of force to another person and false imprisonment which is the infliction of bodily restraint not authorised by law.

Trespass to goods and related torts
4.0.3   There are a number of ways in which one may wrongfully interfere with another's chattels. The law is now largely governed by the Torts (Interference with Goods) Act 1977 which deals generally with all types of 'wrongful interference' with goods belonging to another. As a result of the Act many of the older complexities relating to this class of torts have been removed, but some of the detailed law remains unclear.

a) Trespass to goods
Any direct interference with another person's possessions amounts to a trespass. Like other trespasses, to land and to the person, trespass to goods is actionable per se so that in theory at least mere handling of another's chattels without permission would amount to a tort. However, that is subject to the general caveat that damages would be nominal in such a case. Trespass would mostly only be relevant in cases of deliberate damage to goods. Thus the modern Luddite who deliberately damages machinery could be sued in trespass—if he could be identified and caught.

b) Conversion
Conversion, on the other hand, does have real practical importance. Any person entitled to possession of goods may sue in conversion any person who deals with those goods so as to deny his right to possession, or who asserts rights over them in denial of his right. Normally, of course, the person entitled to possession of goods will be the owner, but it is possible for ownership and possession to be split—for instance when goods are hired or

rented. In that case it might be that both the owner and the hirer could sue a third party who wrongly dealt with the hired goods.[1]

What actions on the part of the defendant will give rise to an action in conversion? Any act which denies the rights of the true owner or possessor will suffice, including taking the goods away, selling them, receiving them, retaining them or destroying them. Moreover, liability is strict: the defendant may be liable in conversion even though he did not know that the property he was handling belonged to the plaintiff, and believed it to be his own. Take as a fairly simple example a case where the plaintiff's property is stolen by a thief, A; he then sells the property to B, who keeps it in good faith. It is sold, in turn, to C, D and E, all of whom buy in good faith, and is discovered by P, the plaintiff, in E's hands. Quite clearly A, the thief, converted P's property, but in the normal way of things the thief will not be available to be sued and, if he is, will probably not be worth suing. However, because of the rule 'nemo dat quod non habet' (a person cannot give what he has not got) the thief who never owned the goods could not pass a good title to B; in turn none of C, D or E ever became owners. In fact by receiving, keeping and selling the goods they have all in turn converted them and P may choose to sue any or all of them in conversion even though they handled the goods in complete ignorance. Any individual defendant would have a defence only if he could show that one of the transactions through which he acquired his title was an exception to the 'nemo dat' rule so that he had in fact become owner of the goods.

If the plaintiff can make out a case in conversion he may claim either the specific return of the goods concerned or payment of their value, in either case together with any consequential loss.[2]

The practical importance of conversion can be illustrated by reference to two relatively recent cases. In *Howard E Perry & Co Ltd v British Railways Board*[3] the defendants held steel belonging to the plaintiffs in depots. There was a strike and the plaintiffs attempted to collect their steel. The defendants, fearing a sympathy strike by their own employees if they allowed the plaintiffs to collect the steel, refused to let them do so. The plaintiffs successfully sued them in conversion.

A second possibility is illustrated by the recent proliferation of reservation of title clauses in suppliers' conditions of sale.[4] Under such a clause a supplier of goods sells goods on credit but provides that they shall not become the property of the buyer until paid for. He may further provide that upon demand, or on the happening of certain events, the seller shall be entitled to repossess the goods. Until recently there have been serious doubts about the effectiveness of such clauses—and indeed those doubts are not yet entirely resolved. Normally the seller only seeks to exercise his rights on the buyer becoming insolvent when he will demand the return of the goods from a receiver or liquidator. He in turn may challenge the validity of the clause and refuse to return the goods. In so doing he lays himself open to an action in conversion. This is what happened in the leading case of *Clough Mill Ltd v Martin*[5] when the Court of Appeal upheld the validity of the reservation of title and held the receiver personally liable in conversion.

One final point should be mentioned. The Torts (Interference With Goods) Act 1977 recognises the difficulties faced by persons who do work on chattels belonging to another—for instance the mechanic who repairs a car. It is not uncommon for such goods to remain uncollected when the owner receives a sizeable repair bill. The repairer would then be faced with a choice between the inconvenience of keeping the goods or of disposing of them and risking an action for conversion. The Act allows the repairer, after serving appropriate notices on the owner, to sell the goods without fear of a claim in conversion.[6]

1   The defendant would not have to pay double damages. The Act (s 7) allows damages to be apportioned between two or more plaintiffs and (s 8) requires a plaintiff to identify in his pleadings any other person who, to his knowledge, has an interest in the goods.
2   The court may order the defendant to deliver up the goods; alternatively it may give the plaintiff a choice between (a) an award of damages (assessed by reference to the value of the goods) or (b) an order that the defendant should either hand over the goods or pay their value: s 3 T(IG) A 1977. The plaintiff may therefore not insist upon delivery up, as of right.
3   [1980] 2 All ER 579, [1980] 1 WLR 1375.
4   Such clauses are discussed more fully below, 24.3.0.
5   [1984] 3 All ER 982, [1985] 1 WLR 111, CA.
6   T(IG) Act 1977, s 12.

Chapter 5
Defamation

5.0.0　The tort of defamation is concerned with the protection of that most ephemeral of interests protected by the law, reputation. It is 'the most difficult of all torts [and] certainly the oddest'.[1] Much of its oddity derives from its history, traced back to the days of Star Chamber, and its piecemeal development and occasional half-hearted attempts at reform. It has often been criticised but survives. Here is a clear example of the balancing of interests with which tort law is so often concerned, interests which raise strong feelings for they are, on the one hand, the plaintiff's interest in his good reputation, and on the other the defendant's right to—and indeed the public interest in—freedom of speech. Critics of the law will say that it does not strike a fair balance between those interests and that it imposes an excessive fetter on the press. It is certainly true that newspapers and magazines will arrange for any article which might be contentious to be vetted, prior to publication, by lawyers for fear of a libel writ. Contrast British journalism, say the critics, with that in the United States where the law of defamation is far more favourable to the press and less protective of the plaintiff's feelings. Is it any wonder that investigative journalism flourishes far more freely in the USA than in England? One wonders whether, had the Watergate affair occurred in this country, it would ever have come to light? Or would the story have been killed by an editor, on the advice of his lawyers, fearful of protracted and expensive legal proceedings?

If defamation is concerned with the protection of reputation, why discuss it in a work on business law? A moment's thought will reveal that, in fact, defamation law can impinge in a real way upon those in business. Care must be taken in advertising products that one does not defame one's competitors—or indeed anyone else. In one case[2] an advert for Fry's chocolate depicted a cartoon of a famous amateur golfer with a bar of chocolate protruding from his pocket. He successfully sued on the grounds that the advertisement implied that he had accepted payment for the advertisement and therefore prostituted his amateur status. References given for employees are another area in which a business must exercise care, although certain defences may apply.[3] On the other hand, a businessman may feel that he has been the victim of defamation; indeed, due partly at least to the high cost of defamation actions, businessmen—some more than others—are frequent plaintiffs. Moreover, even a company can have its reputation damaged and sue in defamation.[4] Indeed, in one case a jury awarded a company a total of £175,000 for its hurt feelings.[5] This rule has been criticised, and with some justification. After all, only a *living* natural person can sue: after my death you may say what you like about me without fear of action by my estate or relatives. No one would deny that a company which suffers financial loss should be entitled to compensation, subject to being able to prove that loss. However, as we shall see below, a plaintiff can, in certain circumstances, obtain damages in defamation without having to prove financial loss: he is compensated because his reputation is lowered in the minds of others, and therefore for his hurt feelings—but a company is an artificial legal person so how can it have feelings?

It should be borne in mind that the law of defamation is not the only restriction the law imposes on unbridled freedom of speech. There are other legal—and non-legal—constraints which may be equally important for business. For instance, in the field of advertising there is considerable self-regulatory control exercised by the Advertising Standards Authority which controls, inter alia, advertisements which are misleading or which disparage a competitor. A similar but more specific control is exercised under new regulations which govern advertisements issued by parties involved in a company takeover battle. These regulations were promulgated in response to several particularly extravagant take-over battles which were fought recently in the pages of the national press. Legal regulation includes the Trade Descriptions Act, governing misleading statements made about products, the Contempt of Court Act and Official Secrets Act. However, the law of defamation is unique in that it alone awards damages for the protection of injured reputation.

1   Weir, *A Casebook on Tort* (5th edn, 1983) p 429.
2   *Tolley v J S Fry & Sons Ltd* [1931] AC 333, HL.
3   A claim of qualified privilege would normally be made: see below 5.0.4.
4   *South Hetton Coal Co v North-Eastern News Association* [1894] 1 QB 133. Even a local authority has been allowed to sue: *Bognor Regis UDC v Campion* [1972] 2 QB 169, [1972] 2 All ER 61.
5   *Rubber Improvements Ltd v Daily Telegraph Ltd* [1963] 1 QB 340, [1962] 2 All ER 698 CA, affd, [1964] AC 234, [1963] 2 All ER 151, HL, hereafter *Lewis v Daily Telegraph Ltd*. £100,000 was awarded against the *Daily Mail*, £75,000 against the *Daily Telegraph*. The House of Lords, on appeal, overturned the decision that the statement in question was defamatory.

Slander and libel

5.0.1   In fact it is misleading to speak of 'the tort of defamation'. Defamation is really two torts—slander and libel. The distinction goes back to the days of Star Chamber when libel was dealt with by that court, slander by the common law courts. 'Libel is a defamation in permanent form—typically, in writing, but extending also to pictures, statues and the like.'[1] Spoken words, on the other hand, are slander. Records, tape recordings and the like create problems. There is no decided case, although it has been held that a cinema film was libellous.[2] Radio, television and theatrical performances are all treated as libel by virtue of statute.[3]

The importance of the distinction between slander and libel lies in the remedies available to the plaintiff. If he complains that he has been slandered he may only recover damages if he can show that, as a result, he has suffered actual financial loss. By contrast, if he is libelled, he is entitled to damages without proof of loss: libel is 'actionable per se'. Obviously, if he has suffered actual loss his damages will include that loss. However, in four special cases slander is also actionable per se. Those are when the slander consists of imputations:

(a) of commission of a criminal offence punishable by imprisonment;
(b) of suffering from an infectious disease;
(c) of unchastity or adultery in a woman or girl (but not in a man or boy!);
(d) calculated to disparage the plaintiff in his lawful office, profession, calling, trade or business.

1 *Monson v Tussaud* [1894] 1 QB 671, CA.
2 *Youssoupoff v Metro-Goldwyn-Mayer-Pictures Ltd* (1934) 50 TLR 581, CA.
3 Defamation Act 1952, s 1; Theatres Act 1968, s 4(1).

Practical problems
5.0.2 We have already adverted to the high cost of defamation proceedings. Before turning to the law itself, one or two points are worth noting. The law of defamation is itself complicated; its problems are compounded because there are special technical procedural rules which relate only to defamation proceedings; these relate particularly to the pleadings in the action and the points a party must raise. For instance a plaintiff may plead that a statement is defamatory because of special facts, not included in the statement, but known to those who hear it. This is an innuendo; the rules require him to plead the innuendo and explain it. Similar rules apply if he alleges words have a special meaning, or to a defendant who wishes to plead justification. As a result, practitioners dealing with defamation, especially at the Bar, tend to be specialists. In fact, defamation proceedings are notoriously expensive. What is more, legal aid is not available for defamation proceedings, with the result that only the wealthy can really afford to sue to assuage their hurt feelings. This is particularly the case when one bears in mind that it is not unknown for a court to make a minimal award of damages—say 1p—coupled with no order for costs. Such a contemptuous award effectively says that the plaintiff has won his case, but really should not have brought it because his complaint was trivial. All this tends to mean that defamation actions are almost exclusively the preserve of the wealthy, well-known media and sports personalities and some especially sensitive businessmen.

Another oddity is that defamation actions are one of the few areas of civil litigation in which juries are still used to make decisions of fact. Indeed, either party has a right to insist on a jury trial if he so wishes.

One final point can be made. Defamation proceedings used to be open to a particular type of abuse when a plaintiff subjected to adverse publicity would issue what became known as a 'gagging writ'. In such a case a plaintiff would issue a writ with the intention of preventing further publication or discussion of the matters of which he complained. This was possible because, as the law stood, it would have been a contempt of court to discuss the matter after issue of a writ. In such cases the plaintiff could then pursue his action no further—indeed, often his sole purpose would be to silence even valid criticism, rather than proceed to trial. The practice was widely criticised, notably by Lord Denning MR.[1] It is no longer possible: the Contempt of Court Act 1981 provides that it is only contempt of court to publish material which creates a substantial risk that justice will be seriously impeded or prejudiced in relation to proceedings which are 'active', and civil proceedings are not 'active' until actually set down for trial.[2] It is thus no longer possible for a plaintiff to issue a gagging writ and thus silence his critics.

1   *In Wallersteiner v Moir (No 2)* [1975] QB 373, 508n, [1975] 1 All ER 849, CA.
2   S 2(3), Sch 1.

The defamation action
5.0.3   In order to succeed in a defamation action the plaintiff must show that the defendant published a statement which related to the plaintiff and was defamatory of him. We have already noted that a 'statement' may be oral or written and may include a pictorial representation, statue, performance and so on. We must now look, briefly, at the meanings of 'defamation' and 'publication'.

a) Defamatory
The classic definition of a defamatory statement is one which 'tends to lower the plaintiff in the opinion of right thinking people generally' or that it will expose him to 'hatred, contempt or ridicule'[1] or tend to make him be shunned or avoided by other persons.[2] Thus a statement that a man is incompetent, or corrupt or immoral would clearly be defamatory. So, it is held, is a statement that a person is insane or a woman has been raped—even though such matters should evoke sympathy rather than ridicule. On the other hand, a statement that a person had passed information to the police leading to a prosecution for unlawful gambling was held not to be defamatory, even though untrue, because right thinking members of the public would not think less of him for being so public-spirited—even if his fellow club members (who had been enjoying the gambling) did.[3] Similarly, mere abuse or insult is not defamatory.

We have already seen how a plaintiff may claim that he has been defamed by 'innuendo' when his case is that words used of him, although not of themselves defamatory are made so by additional information known to the receiver of the statement. Thus in *Tolley v J S Fry & Sons Ltd,*[4] the depiction of the plaintiff in the cartoon was only defamatory if his amateur status was known. In *Lewis v Daily Telegraph Ltd*[5] the *Daily Telegraph* published the headline 'Inquiry on firm by City Police' and the *Daily Mail* published a similar story headlined 'Fraud Squad Probes Firm.' Both the company involved and its chairman sued, alleging that the headline and stories could be understood to mean that they were guilty of fraud. The House of Lords held, however, that the words could only bear that defamatory meaning if there was an innuendo—if some additional information was known to readers.

In *Capital and Counties Bank Ltd v George Henty & Sons*[6] the defendants, after a disagreement with the plaintiffs' branch manager, sent circulars to customers saying they would not accept cheques drawn on the plaintiff bank; the plaintiff claimed that the circular implied it was insolvent and sued for libel. The claim failed, the House of Lords ruling that the alleged innuendo was not one which a reasonable man could draw.

b) Publication
The plaintiff will only succeed if he can show that the defamatory words were published to someone other than himself. However, 'publication' requires no more than that the defamatory words are spoken to any one

other person. Thus there will be publication if an employer dictates a defamatory letter to a secretary, even if the letter is then not sent, or is sent only to the plaintiff.[7] Moreover, the defendant is probably liable for every repetition of the defamatory statement which follows, provided he should reasonably expect it to be repeated. There are dangerous possibilities here: for instance, if a business wrongly addresses a letter which (mistakenly) alleges an account is unpaid and that it believes the debtor to be insolvent, there would clearly be a publication and almost certainly libel. If a potentially defamatory letter is sent to a businessman at his business address, it should be marked 'private' or 'personal', because it can be expected that otherwise it will be opened by his secretary or other staff and there will then be a publication to the opener.[8]

However, it is not only the original author of a libel or slander who 'publishes' it. In addition so does any person who repeats it. In the case of written libel in say, a newspaper, the author of the article, the newspaper editor, printer and publisher are all also liable. Indeed, even distributors of the newspaper may be sued, unless they can show that without negligence they did not know and had no reason to know that the material was libellous.[9]

1 *Byrne v Deane* [1937] 1 KB 818, [1937] 2 All ER 204, CA.
2 *Youssoupoff v Metro-Goldwyn-Mayer Pictures Ltd* (1934) 50 TLR 581.
3 *Byrne v Deane*, supra.
4 [1931] AC 333, HL.
5 [1963] 1 QB 340, [1962] 2 All ER 698; affd [1964] AC 234, HL.
6 (1882) 7 App Cas 741, HL.
7 There may be a defence of qualified privilege, see *5.0.4*.
8 *Pullman v Walter Hill & Co* [1891] 1 QB 524, CA.
9 *Vizetelly v Mudie's Select Library Ltd* [1900] 2 QB 170, CA.

Defences
5.0.4 A defendant may, of course, deny that he made a statement that related to the plaintiff or that was defamatory of him. In addition he may seek to rely on one of a number of special defences which apply only to defamation proceedings. We can do no more than comment briefly on them.

a) Justification
The defendant may plead that his comments were justified—that is, that what he said was true. For instance in *Lewis v Daily Telegraph Ltd*[1] the plaintiffs alleged that the words 'Fraud Squad Probes Firm' were defamatory according to their natural meaning, as well as arguing defamation by innuendo. The *Daily Telegraph* successfully pleaded justification—the Fraud Squad *was* probing the firm!

This may seem ironic. After all, a true accusation may well hurt even more than an untrue one. The obvious justification for the rule is that a plaintiff cannot complain of damage to his good name if he does not deserve a good name. However, there is no right of 'privacy' in English law; thus there is nothing to stop a newspaper (for example) publishing anything about anyone, provided it is true, no matter how little the public interest in such revelation or merit in the story.

5.0.4   Defamation

b) Fair comment on a matter of public interest

As noted above, defamation balances the right to freedom of speech with the right of the individual to his good name. The public interest in free speech requires that fair criticism should be able to be freely expressed and this defence seeks to allow that. In order to rely on it, a defendant must show (a) that he commented on a matter of public interest: this may include politics, public affairs, business and art; (b) that the facts upon which he bases his comments are true; and (c) that his comments were fair—that is, honestly believed.

c) Privilege

In some circumstances it is in the public interest that there should be total freedom of expression. In fact English law divides such circumstances into two categories. In those few cases where freedom of expression is regarded as paramount, 'absolute privilege' is granted: a defendant cannot be sued for statements made in such circumstances. In other cases the interest in free speech is less, and the defendant will lose the protection if it is shown that he acted maliciously. Malice in this context means that the defendant had no honest belief in the truth of his statement, or that he used the privileged occasion for an improper purpose—for instance, solely to damage the plaintiff.

(i) Absolute privilege   Statements made in the following circumstances are absolutely privileged and will not found an action:
1. Statements in Parliament.
2. Statements made by any party, litigant, lawyer, judge or witness in court during proceedings, but only if relevant to the proceedings.
3. Executive privilege—communications between Officers of State.
4. Communication between solicitor and client.
5. Fair and accurate newspaper reports of court proceedings, provided they are published contemporaneously with the proceedings.

(ii) Qualified privilege   The full extent of this defence is uncertain. It applies, generally, when communication is justified by the interests of the maker or recipient of the statement. Thus it will apply when the parties have a common interest in making and receiving the statement, for instance, if a reference is given by an ex-employer to a prospective employer.

Qualified privilege will also protect a defendant who makes a statement to protect his own interests—for instance, a brewer who answers a complaint about his beer with an allegation that the publican is suspected of having watered it.[2] Fair and accurate reports of Parliamentary proceedings attract qualified privilege; and a defendant may be able to raise this defence if he has a legal, moral or social duty to make the statement to the recipient.

It is worth noting, in passing, that American law via the constitutional right to free speech, allows much greater latitude to the press than does English law. There is no public interest or 'right to know' which would allow an English newspaper to claim any form of privilege for publishing statements defamatory of a public figure—even of a holder of high public office.

d) Innocent publication

It has already been noted that a person who repeats a defamatory statement is potentially liable, even though he did not know that the statement was defamatory. Indeed, defamation is a tort of strict liability. A defendant will be liable even though he believed his statement to be true, or even if he did not know of the existence of the plaintiff or of circumstances which made a seemingly innocent statement defamatory. For instance if a newspaper publishes a story about Mr Fred Smith without further description, it may unintentionally libel a different Mr Fred Smith. However, in such cases there is a special defence under the Defamation Act, whereby a potential defendant may make an offer of amends—normally an apology and retraction—provided that without negligence he did not know that the words could refer to the plaintiff or could be defamatory of him. If such an offer is made, a plaintiff rejects it at his peril, because the offer to publish a retraction will provide a defence in any subsequent proceedings.[3]

1   [1963] 1 QB 340, [1962] 2 All ER 698, affd [1964] AC 234, HL.
2   *Osborn v Thomas Boulter & Son* [1930] 2 KB 226, CA.
3   Defamation Act 1952, s 4.

Damages
5.0.5   A plaintiff may be able to suppress or prevent publication of a defamatory statement by obtaining from a court an injunction to restrain publication. However, such is the public interest in free speech that such an order will only rarely be made. Instead the plaintiff will normally be left to his remedy in damages. The problem with awarding damages as a remedy for defamation lies in assessing the value of a man's reputation. Obviously if the plaintiff has suffered economic loss—for instance, loss of his job—he should recover that loss. But when only his reputation is damaged, damages may be difficult to assess. In fact, if there is a jury, it falls on them to assess damages and awards may fluctuate widely. We have already referred to the award in *Lewis v Daily Telegraph Ltd* (£100,000 and £75,000 in 1964!) and at the other end of the scale, to nominal awards. Commenting on the defects of the law in this area, Weir writes:

> 'the action for damages [is used] in order to perform three distinct purposes: (a) to permit people to clear their reputation from unfounded allegations; (b) to allow people to claim compensation for the harm they suffer because others have abused their freedom of speech and (c) to repress gratuitous vituperation, scurrilous disparagement and malignant calumny. Only for (b) is damages the appropriate remedy. For (a) we need a procedure for retraction or correction, and for (c) we need the public stocks.'[1]

1   Weir, *Casebook on Tort* (5th edn, 1983) p 432.

Malicious falsehood
5.0.6   We noted above that a businessman may sue in defamation for damage to his reputation, and that a limited company may do likewise. However, such actions only lie for attacks on the plaintiff personally. If instead it is his goods or business which is improperly disparaged he must rely on one of the separate torts which are grouped under the title 'malicious (or "injurious") falsehood'. For instance, if the defendant falsely claims that property offered for sale by the plaintiff is his (the defendant's) or is encumbered in some way, he commits slander of title. Similarly an adver-

5.0.6 *Defamation*

tisement maliciously impugning the goods of a competitor would constitute a malicious falsehood (slander of goods). However, in protecting what is clearly an economic interest rather than simply reputation, the law is more circumspect and in order to bring a claim under this head a plaintiff must show:

(a) that the defendant's statement was untrue;
(b) that the defendant acted maliciously; and
(c) that he has suffered actual economic loss.[1]

Of course, a certain amount of leeway is expected—and allowed—in advertising and a mere sales puff will not be actionable. In practice the self-regulation of advertising by the Advertising Standards Authority is probably a more important regulatory mechanism than the law in this area.

1 *Royal Baking Powder Co v Wright, Crossley & Co* (1900) 18 RPC 95, HL.

Chapter 6
Economic Torts

6.0.0 We noted above that, as a general rule, the fact that a person has suffered injury due to the conduct of another will not enable him to claim damages. A plaintiff must show he has suffered a loss due to conduct which is legally recognised as wrongful. Moreover, the defendant's bad motive will not, of itself, make him liable: 'if it was a lawful act, however ill the motive might be, he had a right to do it.'[1] As noted above, the principle extends into the field of business activity, so that it is not of itself tortious to trade so as to drive a competitor out of business. This was well established by the turn of the century. In *Mogul SS Co Ltd v McGregor Gow & Co*[2] the plaintiffs complained that the defendants were using unfair methods of competition with a view to driving the plaintiffs out of business. They claimed damages and an injunction. They failed. A man has a —

> 'right to trade . . . But the right . . . to trade is not an absolute but a qualified right—a right conditioned by a like right in . . . all her Majesty's subjects, and a right therefore to trade subject to competition. Now I know no limits to the right of competition in the defendants—I mean no limits in law. I am not speaking of morals or good manners. To draw a line between fair and unfair competition, between what is reasonable and unreasonable, passes the power of the courts. Competition exists, when two or more persons seek to possess or enjoy the same thing. It follows that the success of one must be the failure of the other.'[3]

The justification for such a rule is not simply the inability of the courts to distinguish between fair and unfair competition. It is rooted in the philosophy of a capitalist economy.

> 'A great deal of human activity, especially economic activity, involves conflict with opposing interests of others. The very notion of competition, foundation stone of our capitalist system, countenances, if not actively encourages friction in which one enterpriser advances himself at the cost of another, for the assumed good of society generally. The inefficient, the weaker, are thus eliminated from the economic process. Obviously rules of law which would flatly condemn conduct calculated to cause economic disadvantage or ruin to a competitor would be so flagrantly at odds with the basic tenets of the political economy as to be altogether hors de concours.'[4]

However, the law does not give free rein to competing economic interests: all

71

is not fair or lawful in business whatever the rule in other areas. Indeed we have seen there is considerable statutory control—notably through the Restrictive Trade Practices Act 1976 and related legislation.[5] The common law too has imposed limits, thus within the law of contract there is the doctrine of restraint of trade and a growing recognition of duress as a factor which may invalidate a contract.[6] The law of torts has seen the development of a group of economic torts allowing a party injured by certain forms of economic activity to obtain compensation and/or a court order to bring to an end the offending activity. These economic torts do have relevance for the business world but, not surprisingly perhaps, they have been developed mainly in the area of modern society where competing economic interests collide head on, in the (battle) field of industrial relations and where growth has been particularly rapid in the last twenty years or so. A full discussion of industrial relations law is beyond the scope of this work, but the so-called 'economic torts' merit discussion not only because of the relevance of industrial relations to business, but also because of the implications for commercial activity generally.

Before looking at the individual torts, a note of caution needs to be sounded. This area of law is of relatively recent origin and is still developing; moreover it is notoriously volatile and it must be seen against the backdrop of industrial relations law generally and the changing statutory framework which has extended or restricted the rights and immunities of trade unions according to the political colour of the day. This has no doubt contributed to the difficulties of some of the decisions and, probably, to the development of new forms of liability.

Typically the economic torts involve at least three actors: the defendant tortfeasor, the injured plaintiff and some third party between the two on whom the defendant exerts some influence in order to harm the plaintiff. The leading case of *Allen v Flood*[7] identified two possible bases of liability; in one case the defendant does some unlawful act to the middle man in order to damage the plaintiff. In the other the defendant uses lawful means to make the middleman act unlawfully vis à vis the plaintiff. The rules have developed within the compartments of a number of separate torts, but as the forms of liability develop and grow it is increasingly tempting to see in them the form of a more generalised tort of deliberately causing economic loss by unlawful means.

1   Per Lord Hatherley in *Bradford Corpn v Pickles* [1895] AC 587 at 594, HL.
2   (1889) 23 QBD 598, CA.
3   (1889) 23 QBD 598 at 612, CA.
4   Fleming, *An Introduction to the Law of Torts* (2nd edn, 1985) p 215.
5   See 2.7.0.
6   See 16.0.5.
7   [1898] AC 1, HL.

Conspiracy
6.0.1   Conspiracy has a long history as a crime, but has also existed as an independent tort for over eighty years. In *Allen v Flood*[1] the House of Lords held that there was no liability in tort on an individual who deliberately caused economic harm to another, even if his sole purpose was to cause such loss. He could only be liable if he used unlawful means to inflict harm: this is simply a reflection of the decision in *Bradford Corpn v Pickles*. However, three years later the House of Lords held that when two or more people

combine to inflict economic harm on another they may be held liable in damages for the tort of conspiracy. The case, *Quinn v Leathem*,[2] concerned a dispute between employer and trade unions over the former's employment of non-union members; the union leaders threatened a strike against a customer, to persuade him to withdraw his custom from the plaintiff, as a means of putting pressure on him. The result of the case was therefore that it was tortious for two or more to do together what would not be tortious if done by one alone.

There was no question that it is the tort of conspiracy for two or more persons to conspire together to do an unlawful act to injure another; *Quinn v Leathem* created a second strand of liability in which combination alone was actionable. We should point out here that liability for the tort of conspiracy in either form does not depend on any unlawful act actually being done to the plaintiff: if (for instance) two persons conspire to and do assault or defame the plaintiff he can sue both as joint tortfeasors in the appropriate tort of trespass or defamation. Because the (developing) trade union movement depended on combination by workers, the new liability put a powerful weapon in the hands of employers and Parliament responded to *Quinn v Leathem* by granting immunity to trade unions from that form of conspiracy liability.[3] However, the tort itself survives and subsequent decisions of the courts have done much to neutralise its effect. In particular it seems that a conspiracy will only be tortious if its prime aim is to injure the plaintiff. A defendant may plead that his action was justified, including pursuit of his own interests. In the *Harris Tweed* case of 1942[4] traditional crofters on the Isle of Lewis joined with the Transport and General Workers Union to defeat more modern manufacturing methods. Traditionally Harris tweed had been manufactured from yarn produced on the island; however, the plaintiffs, new manufacturers, proposed to import yarn spun on the mainland, threatening both the traditional crofters and the members of the union who produced yarn on the island. The crofters and union struck a bargain whereby, in return for a closed shop for spinners working on the island, the union arranged for its members at ports on the mainland to black consignments to and from the plaintiffs. The plaintiffs sought an injunction to end the blacking of yarn intended for them, pleading a conspiracy. The claim failed. The House of Lords held that the true purpose of the parties to the agreement was to further their own legitimate interests rather than to harm the plaintiffs. There was therefore no actionable conspiracy.

This of course leaves difficulties, not least, what the outcome should be when the defendants have mixed motives as they often will. The answer seems to be that in such a case the furtherance of his own interests must be the main purpose of his action if he is to escape liability. It used to be thought that the restriction on liability recognised in the *Harris Tweed* case only applied to conspiracies of the *Quinn v Leathem* type, when the agreement is to do an act lawful in itself; in the case of a conspiracy to do an unlawful act, it would be no defence to claim that the real motive was self-interest. However, doubt has been cast on that by the House of Lords decision in *Lonrho Ltd v Shell Petroleum Co Ltd (No 2)*[5] when the plaintiffs, who owned an oil pipeline, claimed damages for conspiracy on the grounds that they had suffered loss caused by the prolongation of sanctions against South Africa caused by the defendants' evasion of the oil embargo imposed by the Government. The claim failed and the defendants were allowed to argue the self-interest defence. However, there are unlawful means and unlawful means: in this case the claim based on breach of embargo seems weaker than one based on a breach of contract and light years from a conspiracy to injure through criminal or tortious acts.

1   [1898] AC 1, HL.
2   [1901] AC 495, HL.
3   Trade Union Act 1906, s 1.
4   *Crofter Hand Woven Harris Tweed Co Ltd v Veitch* [1942] AC 435, [1942] 1 All ER 142, HL.
5   [1982] AC 173, [1981] 2 All ER 456, HL.

Intimidation
6.0.2   The tort of intimidation, like that of conspiracy, deals with two situations. Firstly, D may threaten unlawful acts against P in order to influence his behaviour: for instance, a 'protection scheme' clearly the tort of intimidation by D against P. However, in its more contentious form the tort involves threats made by D against X, with a view to influencing X's behaviour vis à vis P, and injuring P. P is not himself the victim of threats, but he is the intended victim of D's action and he may sue D in the tort of intimidation. The leading example is *Rookes v Barnard.*[1] The plaintiff, who worked for BOAC, left his union. The defendants who were union officials and two of whom worked for BOAC, threatened a strike unless BOAC dismissed the plaintiff. It was conceded that a strike would have been a breach of contract by BOAC employees. In order to keep the peace, BOAC dismissed the plaintiff with full notice, so that there was no breach of his contract of employment. He successfully sued the defendants: they had threatened BOAC with an unlawful act—a breach of contract, with a view to harming the plaintiff. It is worth noting that BOAC had committed no legal wrong vis à vis the plaintiff, and that a threat of breach of contract is now sufficient unlawful act for this purpose.[2] Obviously a threat of criminal or tortious action would also suffice; it is less clear if (for example) a non-criminal breach of statutory duty would do so.

1   [1964] AC 1129, [1964] 1 All ER 367, HL.
2   Previously threats of physical violence were necessary; before *Rookes v Barnard* the tort had been forgotten since 1793!

Inducing a breach of contract
6.0.3   In recent years this has come to be the most important of the 'economic torts'—perhaps not surprisingly in view of the importance of contracts as the basis of business. In the face of various legislative immunities granted to Trades Unions the tort has continued to grow so that it is now of rather uncertain ambit and, indeed, may be in the process of metamorphosing into a more general economic tort.

In its simplest form this tort is relatively straightforward. A has a contract with B; C exerts pressure—or offers inducement to B to force him to break the contract, thereby injuring A. Under the doctrine of privity of contract A has no action against C for breach of contract: he may sue B on the contract, but not C. However, he may sue C in tort for inducing the breach of contract. The action has its roots in claims by employers against competitors who tempted away their employees. The leading case however involves an opera singer. In *Lumley v Gye*[1] the plaintiff had a well-known opera singer,

Miss Johanna Wagner, under contract to sing exclusively for him. A rival persuaded Miss Wagner to break her contract and sing in his hall instead. The plaintiff successfully sued the rival for inducing Miss Wagner to break her contract.

The basis of this liability is fairly clear. The defendant must know of the contract, or at least deliberately turn a blind eye to it,[2] and intend it to be broken. This last point is important. If I urge someone to leave their employment and come to work for me I am not liable if I intend that person to give and serve proper notice under his contract. If this were not the case recruitment consultants (so-called 'head hunters') would forever commit this tort. Of course, if I interview someone for a job and they tell me that they have to give three months' notice to the current employer, I will be liable if I tell them to start on Monday.

Another variant of this tort is even more straightforward. Here D interferes directly in a physical manner. For instance in one case[3] P had a contract with a car manufacturer to use P's tyres on his cars. When a car was on display, D, a rival tyre manufacturer, removed P's tyres and replaced them with his own. Such behaviour obviously goes beyond condonable sharp practice and our law would be in a poor state if it failed to impose liability on D in such a situation.

There is, however, a third type of liability which is altogether more contentious and of a far less certain extent. It is also the most important form of liability for practical purposes. In this situation D's intervention in P's contract is only indirect. Typically there is a chain of parties: for instance P contracts with X. D persuades Y, who is an employee of X, to break his contract of employment and to refuse to deliver goods to P. Here D has induced a breach by Y of the contract between him and X. However, the real target of D's action is P, and the law will allow P to sue. This situation arises in industrial disputes in the context of what is known as 'secondary action': D is a union in dispute with P; to strike at P it persuades its members (Y) who work for customers or suppliers (X) to black P's goods. The only preconditions for liability are firstly that D must know of the contract between P and X and secondly that he must interfere by unlawful means. Normally that will be by committing the tort of *Lumley v Gye* vis à vis Y. If there is no unlawful act, there is no liability. This is illustrated by comparing two cases. In the first[4] a union was in dispute with a printer and approached the company which supplied it with paper saying that its members who worked for the paper company would object to making deliveries. To avoid trouble with its own work force the paper supplier stopped making deliveries and did not ask its workforce to make them. As a result there was no breach of contract by the employees—they had disobeyed no order—and so when the printers sued, the union officers were not liable. In another case,[5] however, a union persuaded its members not to return to the plaintiffs barges belonging to the plaintiffs. The union members worked for customers of the plaintiffs who had hired barges from them. They refused to return the barges, thereby breaking their own contracts of employment and putting their employers in breach of their hire contracts. The plaintiff barge owners successfully sued the union leaders for the tort of inducing a breach of the hire contracts. The required unlawful means were present here for the union had induced breaches of its members' contracts of employment.

The requirement of unlawful means again raises questions on the meaning of the term 'unlawful means'. Obviously a tort including the threat of breach of contract or inducing a breach of contract will suffice. However, in one commercial case it was held that an arrangement which would amount to a potential breach of restrictive trade practices legislation would be sufficient.[6]

Even more contentious is the exact scope of this tort. The typical case involves four parties. However there is no reason why there cannot be a longer chain so that the plaintiff—the real target of the defendant's action—is more remote. In one recent case[7] the plaintiffs were ship owners; they chartered a ship and the charterers let it out on a sub-charter; the sub-charterer entered into a contract with a tug company. The defendant union, to strike at the plaintiff ship owners, blacked the ship at the harbour, thus interfering with the contract between ship owners and charterers.

In some respects it is misleading to speak of 'inducing a breach of contract': the defendant will still be liable even if he interferes in a contract without producing a breach. In *Torquay Hotel Co Ltd v Cousins*,[8] another trade dispute case, the defendants sought to interrupt supplies of fuel oil to a hotel. In fact, as is typical, the supply contracts included a force majeure clause which protected the supplier from liability for breach of contract if deliveries were interrupted by industrial disputes. Lord Denning was prepared to hold that it was sufficient if the defendant had by unlawful means interfered with performance of a contract, even if he had not induced a breach, and other decisions since have followed and supported that line.

Liability is not confined to interference with contracts. It has been held[9] that interference with the equitable duties of insurance agents to account to their principals for monies in their possession was actionable on similar grounds and it now appears that the courts are prepared to recognise a more general tort of 'interference with business by unlawful means'.[10]

1 (1853) 2 E & B 216.
2 *Emerald Construction Co v Lowthian* [1966] 1 All ER 1013, [1966] 1 WLR 691, CA.
3 *GWK Ltd v Dunlop Rubber Co Ltd* (1926) 42 TLR 376; on appeal 42 TLR 593, CA.
4 *D C Thomson & Co Ltd v Deakin* [1952] Ch 646 [1952] 2 All ER 361, CA.
5 *J T Stratford & Son Ltd v Lindley* [1965] AC 307, [1964] 3 All ER 102, HL.
6 *Brekkes Ltd v Cattel* [1972] Ch 105, [1971] 1 All ER 1031.
7 *Merkur Island Shipping Corpn v Laughton* [1983] 2 AC 570, [1983] 2 All ER 189, HL.
8 *Torquay Hotel Co Ltd v Cousins* [1969] 2 Ch 106, [1969] 1 All ER 522, CA.
9 *Prudential Assurance Co Ltd v Lorenz* (1971) 11 KIR 78.
10 See *Merkur Island Shipping Corpn v Laughton*, above.

The employment law background

6.0.4 We have observed that most of the decisions which have expanded the scope of the 'economic torts' have been in the field of industrial disputes; we have observed also that labour law generally is beyond the scope of this book. However, we must briefly mention the framework of industrial legislation within which the law has largely developed. From the decision in *Quinn v Leathem*[1] onwards the story here has been one of ebb and flow, of judicial decisions apparently creating new liabilities, followed by the legislative granting of new immunities, followed by the creation of yet more liabilities. This has led to an unfortunate tendency for the law in this area to be seen as a creation by the judiciary hostile to the interests of organised labour, either because the judges, coming from a strongly individualistic tradition, are incapable of sympathy with the collectivist aims of trade unions, or, at its more extreme, because of alleged class or even political bias. Such issues are, of course, important, but they are not within the scope of this work. However, in recent years the legislative pendulum has swung towards subjecting trade unions to greater regulation and moves have been made to restrict the immunities granted by previous legislation. In a nutshell[2] the present position is that trade union officials are immune from most of the economic torts[3] we have discussed, provided they are committed in the course or furtherance of a trade dispute.[4] However, that immunity only attaches to actions in the course of official industrial action taken after a secret ballot of members.[5] No ballot—no immunity. Furthermore, immunity is removed altogether from secondary action directed at parties other than immediate customers or suppliers of the employer in the dispute.[6] It remains to be seen whether the less amenable legislative climate for industrial action will lead to a reduction in judicial creativity in this area.

1 [1901] AC 495, HL.
2 What follows is a summary in outline of the combined effects of the Trade Union and Labour Relations Act 1974 (as amended), Employment Act 1980 and Trade Union Act 1984. For a full detailed discussion the reader should see one of the specialist works on labour law: eg I T Smith and J C Wood, *Industrial Law* (3rd edn) p 470; B Perrins, *Trade Union Law* C17 to C19.
3 Obviously there would be no immunity for (say) intimidation by threats of physical violence.
4 TULRA 1974, s 13.
5 TUA 1984, s 10.
6 Employment Act 1980, s 17.

The commercial background

6.0.5 The fact that the development of the modern economic torts has largely taken place in the field of industrial conflict should not obscure the fact that they are capable of general application and could be of great importance in the field of commercial relations. On the other hand, the torts only form one strand of the restrictions on business activity. They must be seen alongside restrictions on contract terms imposed by the common law restraint of trade doctrine; by legislation such as the Restrictive Trade Practices Act 1976 and Resale Prices Act 1976; and the restrictions on cartel agreements imposed by Article 85 of the EEC Treaty in the interests of promoting free trade and competition.[1]

Nevertheless, the development of tortious liability could have major implications for British business and competition generally, since it makes available a remedy in damages. Its potential can be illustrated by reference to the litigation in the United States (based on US anti-trust law) arising out of the liquidation of Laker Airways and the allegation of unfair competition by other airline companies.

It takes a relatively sophisticated legal system to protect economic interests. In the now emerging tort of unlawful interference with business, English law has moved a long way from the doctrine of *Bradford Corpn v Pickles* and towards the protection of such interests. Indeed, it is worth contrasting the protection granted to economic interests against deliberate injury with the uncertainty which still surrounds the recognition of economic injury negligently inflicted.[2] The ghost of *Bradford Corpn v Pickles* clings hard, however, and English law has chosen to focus on the (unlawful) means employed rather than the end sought. That has imparted uncertainty and controversy into this area of law.

1   See 2.7.0.
2   See 7.1.5.

Passing off

6.1.0   There is one fringe form of tortious liability concerned with the regulation of unfair competition, and it therefore merits mention here. However, in many ways passing off is more closely connected with actions for the infringement of intellectual property rights such as copyright, patents and trade marks.

In its simplest form the tort is committed when one person presents his goods or services to the public in such a way as to make them appear to be the goods or services of another, so that, in effect, the 'interloper' attempts to trade on the goodwill of another business. The law recognises goodwill as 'the benefit and advantage of the good name, reputation, and connection of a business. It is the attractive force which brings in custom'[1] and 'nobody has any right to represent his goods as the goods of somebody else.'[2] The action may thus, obviously, be used when the defendant mimics the plaintiff's goods or services, for instance by producing counterfeit perfume or Levi jeans. In such cases, of course, the plaintiff would probably also have a claim for infringement of his trade mark: he may choose to rely on that action or sue for passing off instead.[3]

However, passing off is not limited to cases of direct copying. It may be used when the defendant presents his business in such a way as to make it appear to be connected with that of the plaintiff.[4] In an Australian case,[5] a record was released with a sleeve depicting a well-known dancing couple. They successfully sued to restrain distribution and sale of the record: the defendant had wrongly deprived the plaintiffs of their right to choose whether to bestow or withhold their professional recommendation, and therefore of the chance to charge for that recommendation. The court explained the basis of the tort as:

> 'once it is proved that A is falsely representing his goods as the goods of B, or his business to be the same as, or connected with, the business of B, the wrong of passing off has been established.'

However, passing off has even wider application. Thus a successful action was brought by representative producers of champagne to restrain the sale of a drink labelled 'Spanish Champagne'.[6] True champagne must be produced from grapes grown in the Champagne district of France and by the champagnoise method. 'Spanish Champagne' was trading on the goodwill of these producers; similar injunctions were awarded to restrain the sale of 'English Sherry' (sherry is produced from grapes grown in Jerez in Spain)[7] and 'English Advocaat'.[8]

In order to succeed in a claim the plaintiff must show (i) that the defendant has made a misrepresentation, (ii) about goods or services, (iii) in the course of his business, (iv) to prospective customers or consumers of his goods or services, (v) which as a foreseeable consequence, damages, the business or goodwill of the plaintiff. Normally the plaintiff will establish this by showing that it is likely that a substantial number of ordinary customers will be deceived or misled by the defendant's statement. If he can make out his case and has suffered actual damage, the plaintiff may recover damages or seek an account of profits from the defendant: alternatively if damage is likely, he may apply for an injunction to restrain the defendant.

The protection given to the plaintiff by passing off, may seem to be similar to that provided by the tort of malicious falsehood. They differ, however, in two respects. First, in an action for malicious falsehood, the plaintiff must prove malice; passing off focuses, instead, on the impact of the defendant's conduct on the public: it is enough if a substantial number of people are likely to be misled or confused, regardless of the defendant's intention. Second, malicious falsehood concerns untrue statements made by the defendant about the plaintiff and his goods: in passing off the defendant makes misleading statements about his own goods or services so that they appear to be connected with the plaintiff.

1   Per Lord MacNaghten in *IRC v Muller & Co's Margarine Ltd* [1901] AC 217 at 223, HL.
2   Per Lord Halsbury in *Reddaway v Banham* (1896) 13 RPC 218 at 224, HL.
3   The Trade Mark Act 1938 (in respect of goods) and Trade Mark (Amendment) Act 1984 (dealing with services) preserve the right of a plaintiff to sue for passing off instead of for infringement of a registered trade mark.
4   This is similar to the protection afforded by the power of the Registrar of Companies to refuse to register a new company's name if it is too similar to a name already on the register: see 33.2.1.
5   *Radio Corpn Pty Ltd v Henderson* [1960] NSWR 279.
6   *Bollinger v Costa Brava Wine Co Ltd* [1960] Ch 262, [1959] 3 All ER 800.
7   *Vine Products Ltd v Mackenzie & Co Ltd* [1969] RPC 1.
8   *Erven Warnink BV v J Townend and Sons (Hull) Ltd* [1979] AC 731, [1979] 2 All ER 927, HL.

Chapter 7
Negligence

7.0.0 The tort of negligence is concerned with damage inflicted on the plaintiff by the defendant's failure to take reasonable care. Thus, unlike the torts we have so far examined, negligence is concerned not with the protection of one particular interest but with a whole range of interests. Negligence focuses on the manner in which the plaintiff is injured. Negligence may thus provide a basis for a claim for a plaintiff injured in an accident on the road or at work—or possibly for his relatives who witness his injury; for the plaintiff injured by his surgeon's carelessness; for the plaintiff whose property is damaged by a defective product; or for the plaintiff who buys shares on the strength of poor investment advice and thus suffers financial loss. Thus it is true to say today that negligence is the most important of the forms of tortious liability, both in terms of the number of areas with which it deals and, due largely to the sheer volume of accidents, especially on the roads and at work, the number of cases brought to court. It was not always so—indeed, 150 years ago negligence was almost unheard of as an independent tort. It sometimes provided a mental element in other forms of tortious liability—for instance in some types of nuisance—but little more. During that period negligence has grown to such an extent that not only does it now overshadow the other torts in importance, but it threatens to swallow them up. It is surely no coincidence that that period of growth has coincided with a period during which, as we noted earlier, our society has changed more and faster than at any other time in history. The tort of negligence has provided the flexibility with which the law has been able to respond to the changes created by growing industrialisation, mobility and general social change.

Definitions, terminology and policy
7.0.1 A law which imposed liability on a defendant for all the harm, of whatever type and by whomsoever suffered, caused by his failure to take care would impose an intolerable burden on potential defendants. It would, to adopt a much used phrase, 'open the floodgates of litigation' intolerably wide. In fact the law does not do that and there are a number of devices which can be used to set boundaries to liability.

It is common to define negligence along the lines

> 'The defendant is liable for all damage caused by his breach of duty to take reasonable care, provided that that damage is not too remote.'

This allows the tort conveniently to be broken down into a number of elements: there must be a duty to take care; a breach of that duty; damage to the plaintiff; a causal link between that damage and the breach of duty; and the damage must not be too remote. Such a breakdown is convenient and we will use it in our examination of the law which follows. However, a note of caution should be sounded at the outset. The compartments we have just defined are not watertight. Indeed, the law of negligence is bedevilled by a confusion of terminology so that at times the judges seem to be using words like Humpty Dumpty to mean 'just what I choose it to mean'. This is particularly true in relation to 'duty of care' and 'remoteness of damage': different judges and commentators may well analyse the same set of facts under either head, or they may choose to say that the defendant did not cause the plaintiff's loss. Even the apparently straightforward problem of 'was the defendant careless?' is susceptible to similar complication; for carelessness involves a failure to take reasonable care to avoid foreseeable injury, so that a judge might say—

'This result was not foreseeable, so there was no duty of care/the defendant was not careless/the damage is too remote.'

Lord Denning, amongst others, has recognised this tendency in himself.

'The more I think about these cases, the more difficult I find it to put each into its proper pigeon hole. Sometimes, I say "there was no duty". In others I say: "The damage was too remote." '[1]

These problems should not cause too much alarm. In reality the various labels do no more than mask the real issue, which, in any doubtful situation, is whether, as a matter of policy, liability should be imposed or not. Indeed, Lord Denning has recognised this: he went on, in the case just quoted,

'I think the time has come to discard these tests which have proved so elusive. It seems to me better to consider the particular relationship in hand, and see whether or not, as a matter of policy, economic loss should be recoverable or not.'[2]

These words are indicative of a more general and growing trend to recognise that the law of negligence is concerned with policy issues—which party can best, or should, insure against a particular kind of loss? Above all, how far should the defendant be liable for the results of his carelessness? Once this is recognised we can also recognise that the various labels of 'duty', breach', 'causation', and 'remoteness' are used from case to case to impose a limit on the potential liability of a defendant. Which label is used to justify a particular decision is less important than the policy question of whether the line between defendant and plaintiff and their conflicting interests has been drawn in the right place.

Having issued that warning we can now turn to look at the elements of the tort of negligence and, for convenience's sake if for no other, we will adopt a 'traditional' categorisation.

1 *Spartan Steel and Alloys Ltd v Martin & Co (Contractors) Ltd* [1973] QB 27 at 37, CA.
2 Ibid.

The duty of care in negligence

7.1.0   In recent years there has been a growing tendency for cases at the frontiers of the law of negligence to turn on the denial or establishment of a duty of care. This element of the tort has thus become the principal tool by which the judiciary controls the growth of the tort in the interests of policy.

The classic formulation of the test for the existence of a duty of care is now taken to be that of Lord Atkin in the famous case of *Donoghue v Stevenson*,[1] the 'snail in the bottle' case. The plaintiff had gone into a Glasgow café with a friend; the friend had bought a bottle of ginger beer for the plaintiff; the bottle was opaque and sealed. The plaintiff had consumed half of its contents over an ice cream float before the remains of a snail, in an advanced state of decomposition, dropped from the bottle. The plaintiff claimed to have suffered shock and gastroenteritis as a result. However, she had no contract with the café proprietor: she therefore sued the manufacturer of the ginger beer in negligence. The point in issue in the case was therefore whether the manufacturer of a defective product owed a duty of care to the ultimate consumer of it. The House of Lords held that a duty did exist, but in the course of his speech Lord Atkin decided that the time had come to state a general principle as to the existence of a duty of care. The general principle, he explained, is based on a moral notion of wrongdoing for which the defendant must pay—but in a practical world the law must impose limits on the range of complainants entitled to legal relief.

> 'The rule that you are to love your neighbour becomes in law: You must not injure your neighbour, and the lawyer's question Who is my neighbour? receives a restricted reply. You must take reasonable care to avoid acts or omissions which you can reasonably foresee would be likely to injure your neighbour. Who then, in law, is my neighbour? The answer seems to be persons who are so closely and directly affected by my act that I ought reasonably to have them in contemplation as being so affected when I am directing my mind to the acts or omissions which are called in question.'[2]

This marked the first attempt by an eminent judge to elucidate general principles on this subject. Previously the courts had approached the question of whether a duty of care existed on a case by case basis. It was always possible for the courts to recognise a duty situation by analogy with one already recognised ('The categories of negligence are never closed')[3] but this dictum recognised the need for a more general statement of principle.

In fact, however, for some time there was a tendency to take a narrow view of the decision in *Donoghue v Stevenson*, restricted to the consumer/manufacturer situation. This then treated Lord Atkin's statement as strictly obiter, although entitled to respect because of the eminence of its maker. However, in the last twenty years there has been a growing willingness to adopt a more general approach. In 1970 Lord Reid[4] gave his view that Lord Atkin's statement should—

> 'not be treated as if it were a statutory definition. It will require qualification in new circumstances. But I think that the time has come when we can and should say that it ought to apply unless there is some justification or valid explanation for its exclusion.'

In fact the 'Atkin dictum' will not serve as a complete definition of 'duty of care' as it stands. Above all it places too much emphasis on 'foreseeability' and tends therefore to make duty and breach of that duty one and the same issue. However, in 1976 Lord Wilberforce[5] gave further guidance on the correct approach to the duty of care question.

'First one has to ask whether, as between the alleged wrongdoer and the person who has suffered damage, there is a sufficient relationship of proximity or neighbourhood such that, in the reasonable contemplation of the former, carelessness on his part may be likely to cause damage to the latter, in which case a prima facie duty of care arises.

'Second, if the first question is answered affirmatively, it is necessary to consider whether there are any considerations which ought to negate, or to reduce or limit the scope of the duty or the class of person to whom it is owed or the damages to which a breach of it may give rise.'

Although some reservations have been expressed about it recently, this formulation reflects the modern approach. There is a tendency to speak of proximity between the parties, rather than foreseeability. Moreover, it clearly admits that the question whether or not a duty of care should exist is one of policy. Provided there was such proximity between the parties that damage to the plaintiff was a foreseeable result of the defendant's carelessness, a duty of care exists unless there are policy reasons why it should not.

1 [1932] AC 562.
2 [1932] AC 562 at 580.
3 Per Lord MacMillan [1932] AC 562 at 619.
4 *Home Office v Dorset Yacht Co Ltd* [1970] AC 1004 at 1027, HL.
5 *Anns v Merton London Borough Council* [1978] AC 728 at 751, HL.

Duty, remoteness and policy

7.1.1 In certain cases it is well established that a duty of care is owed. Such areas include those which are, in terms only of the number of incidents, the most important dealt with by the tort of negligence. Thus a duty of care is owed by drivers to other motorists and road users; a duty is owed by workers to take care not to cause physical injury to fellow workers; and of course after *Donoghue v Stevenson*, a manufacturer of goods owes a duty to the ultimate consumer to take care in manufacture so that the goods do not cause injury or damage to other property.

On the other hand, in several situations the existence of a duty of care, or the extent of any which does exist, is far less clear. We have already noted the tendency to use the duty question almost interchangeably with the remoteness of damage question to produce the same result. Essentially the question for the court, in deciding whether or not to impose liability on a defendant for a particular act is 'Did this defendant owe a duty to this plaintiff to take care to avoid causing this type of injury inflicted in this particular manner?' The tendency is to deal with broad issues of principle under the heading 'duty of care' leaving factors related to the particular circumstances of a case—the individual characteristics of the parties, the manner of infliction of harm—to be dealt with under 'remoteness'. Although this is by no means an absolute division it is one we shall adopt here.

There are three broad policy factors which may affect the decision whether to recognise a duty of care in a particular situation:

(a) *the nature of the act causing the loss*: for instance, should a defendant be liable for omissions, as well as for positive acts? For harm inflicted by careless words? Should there be liability for negligence in the exercise of statutory powers?

(b) *The nature of the loss suffered*: how far is a defendant liable for nervous shock suffered by persons who witness an accident or its aftermath? How far is he liable to the plaintiff who suffers only financial loss rather than physical injury or property damage?

(c) *The parties involved*: policy consideration may affect the extent of the duty imposed on a local authority,[1] or on an advocate presenting his client's case in court.[2]

Of course, any particular case may raise a combination of these policy issues: thus the liability of a local authority for failing properly to utilise its powers of inspection under the building regulations, and thereby allowing a defective building to be constructed, raises policy issues related to the status of the defendant, the type of loss suffered by the plaintiff (normally purely economic) and the nature of the act in question (an exercise of a statutory power—or even an omission). The identity of the plaintiff was also a factor in one recent case.[3]

1 See *Anns v Merton London Borough Council* [1978] AC 728, [1977] 2 All ER 492, HL below, 7.1.4.
2 *Rondel v Worsley* [1969] 1 AC 191, [1967] 3 All ER 993, HL below, 7.1.9.
3 *Governors of the Peabody Donation Fund v Sir Lindsay Parkinson & Co Ltd* [1985] AC 210, [1984] 3 All ER 529, HL.

Omissions
7.1.2 Although Lord Atkin's formulation of duty of care in *Donoghue v Stevenson* spoke of 'acts or omissions' it is generally true that the common law has been reluctant to impose liability on a defendant for negligent failure to act to the same extent as for negligent acts themselves. As Fleming explains:

> 'the force of organised society which we call law is fully employed by restraining men from committing affirmative acts of harm and shrinks from converting courts into an agency for forcing men to help each other.'[1]

The underlying justification for this attitude is that, whereas the law recognises the right of everyone not to have his condition made worse by the act of another, he should only be entitled to have it improved if he has paid for that improvement. Thus only a contract, voluntarily undertaken with quid pro quo, imposes a duty to act.

However, to take the view that there is no liability in negligence for omissions would be too simplistic. First, there are many 'omissions' which can equally well be classified as negligent acts, for instance, the driver who fails to stop at a red traffic light is driving carelessly. In a line of recent cases occupiers of land have been held liable for negligently allowing hazards— which they had not created—to escape and damage neighbouring property. Possibly there is a modern tendency to impose a duty to act to deal with dangers for which the defendant is in some way responsible. In a Canadian case,[2] for instance, a yacht owner invited friends to go for a cruise on a lake; one fell in and, due to the owner's bungling attempts at rescue, drowned, as did another guest who had gone to the rescue upon seeing the owner's attempt fail. It was held that the owner did owe a positive duty to guests to rescue them from the perils of the voyage, and a duty to other potential rescuers by his action not to put them in danger. An even more intriguing American case[3] held a psychiatrist liable when, knowing of the homicidal intention of a patient, he failed to warn the intended victim. What would be the position in English law of an employer who, having honestly given a glowing reference, then discovered that his ex-employee had been guilty of acts of dishonesty? Would he be liable for failing to warn the new employer?[4]

1 Fleming, *An Introduction to the Law of Torts* (1985 2nd edn) p 39.
2 *The Ogopogo* [1970] 1 Lloyd's Rep 257.
3 *Tarasoff v Regents of the University of California* 17 Cal (3d) 425 (1976)
4 This hypothetical example is posited by Dias and Markesinis, *Tort Law* (1984) p 54.

Third parties
7.1.3   A related question is how far a person is liable for the acts of third parties. Generally the answer is 'not at all'—at least when the act of the third party is deliberate. Often it is said that the deliberate act of the third party breaks the 'chain of causation'.[1] However, it is clear that in certain circumstances the law does impose liabilities for the acts of third parties. An employer, for instance, owes certain duties to his employees to provide a safe work place and a safe system of work. Such duties are said to be 'non-delegable' so that the employer may be held liable to an injured employee even if the immediate cause of the injury was an independent contractor for whom the employer is not vicariously liable.

In other situations the law imposes a duty to control or guard against the actions of third parties, at least when those actions are foreseeable. Thus, for instance, a painter left alone in a house failed to lock it when he went for lunch. He was held liable for the burglary which resulted.[2] He had assumed, vis à vis the owner of the house, responsibility for its security. Similarly there may be a duty to control persons under one's charge: it was held that Borstal officers were under a duty to control trainees under their charge so that their employer (the Home Office) was liable for the damage done when the unsupervised trainees ran amok in a harbour damaging several boats.[3] The point in both these cases is that the acts of the third parties were the foreseeable—indeed the likely—consequence of the defendants' carelessness.

1 See 7.3.2.
2 *Stansbie v Troman* [1948] 2 KB 48, [1948] 1 All ER 599, CA.
3 *Home Office v Dorset Yacht Co Ltd* [1970] AC 1004, [1970] 2 All ER 294, HL. Cf *Smith v Littlewoods Organisation Ltd* [1987] 1 All ER 710; *Hill v Chief Constable of W. Yorkshire* (1987) 137 NLJ 222.

The exercise of statutory power
7.1.4   We have seen that in a mixed economy a number of regulatory functions are entrusted to public bodies empowered to oversee and control the activities of businesses and individuals. Such powers include those exercised by trading standards departments, licensing powers and the power to supervise and control building development. In recent years the courts have had increasingly to consider how far, if at all, such public bodies are liable for negligence in the exercise of their powers. This line of cases raises

many policy issues, including questions of liability for omissions and/or failing to control third parties. It is also illustrative of the general approach of the courts to the 'duty' question.

Most of the recent cases have concerned the exercise by local authorities of their powers under the building regulations to supervise construction work. In the leading case of *Anns v Merton London Borough Council*[1] the plaintiffs were leasehold occupiers of flats in a block. The walls of the flats began to crack and it transpired that the block had been built on inadequate foundations. The plaintiffs sued the council for negligence in either making no inspection of the foundations at all, or in making an inadequate inspection. The council denied that it owed any duty of care to the plaintiffs or other occupiers, arguing that it could not be challenged if it failed to inspect at all[2] and so could not be worse off if it did decide to inspect but inspected badly. The House of Lords rejected that argument and held the council did owe a duty of care. Whilst the council had no absolute duty to inspect, it had a duty at common law to exercise its discretion to inspect property and on proper grounds. A decision not to inspect could therefore be challenged if made without such consideration. If the council did decide to exercise its powers, it then came under a duty of care to carry out a proper careful inspection.

The *Anns* decision raises a number of problems of policy. Local authorities are elected bodies with a number of calls on their limited resources: inspecting construction work is only one such call. Lord Wilberforce recognised this in *Anns* holding that even after it had decided to carry out an inspection the council would still have a legitimate discretion as to how to deploy its resources and carry out the inspection. It also left open the problem of to whom the duty was owed: it seemed that all future owners or occupiers of the property could, foreseeably, be injured by its deterioration and were therefore potential plaintiffs.

In fact in *Anns* the plaintiffs were tenant–occupiers; in the earlier case of *Dutton v Bognor Regis UDC*[3] it was an owner-occupier who bought from the original builder. The courts which decided those cases thought that they would be of limited application but in fact a flurry of litigation followed, gradually expanding the duty of local authorities by extending the class of persons to whom it was owed.[4] The high water mark of this tide of opinion came when the Court of Appeal held[5] that the duty was owed to an original developer of a site, despite a statement to the contrary by Lord Wilberforce in *Anns*.[6] The effect of this decision was, in the words of Weir, to force 'honest citizens who pay rates' to compensate 'a money-grabbing financier lurking behind a corporate facade'[7] for his own carelessness.

Since that decision the same question has come before the courts twice more and the House of Lords and Court of Appeal have retreated by restricting the class of persons to whom the duty of care is owed. In *Governors of Peabody Donation Fund v Sir Lindsay Parkinson & Co Ltd*[8] the plaintiff was a developer; its own employees had deviated from plans approved by the local authority and installed rigid rather than flexible drains which proved unsuitable and had to be replaced at great expense. The developer sued the council for failing to correct the negligence of its own employees. The issue, as Lord Keith saw it, was 'whether (the council) owed a duty to Peabody to warn them that they were heading for financial disaster.'[9] Although the loss suffered by the developer was foreseeable, creating a relationship of proximity between it and the council, it was not reasonable to impose a duty of care on the council in favour of the developer. The court stressed the purpose of the building regulations—to protect public health and safety, rather than developers' pockets—and pointed out that the developer itself was in breach of the regulations. The same line was adopted in *Investors in Industry Commercial Properties Ltd v South Bedfordshire District Council (Ellison & Partners (a firm), Third Parties)*[10] when the Court of Appeal held that no duty was owed to a developer who relied on independent professional advisers[11] to design his building.

From these cases, we can extrapolate some general guidelines as to the extent of the duty of care on a public body exercising statutory powers.

(a) It can be held liable in negligence for failing to exercise its powers, if that decision is not properly made by a proper exercise of discretion.

(b) It can be held liable for a negligent exercise of its powers, although there is a discretion left to it as to how best to exercise them.

(c) A duty of care will be owed to persons who were reasonably foreseeable as likely to be affected by negligence in the exercise of the power; however, the extent of that duty and the range of persons to whom it is owed may be reduced—or even extinguished—by policy issues. These will include the purpose for which the powers were given.

1   [1978] AC 728, [1977] 2 All ER 492, HL.
2   An argument based on *Kent v East Suffolk Rivers Catchment Board* [1940] 1 KB 319, [1939] 4 All ER 174, CA.
3   [1972] 1 QB 373, [1972] 1 All ER 462, CA.
4   See *Dennis v Charnwood Borough Council* [1983] QB 409, [1982] 3 All ER 486, CA; *Acrecrest Ltd v WS Hattrell & Partners* [1983] QB 260 [1983] 1 All ER 17, CA. Apparently local authorities during this period adopted a more stringent approach to enforcement of the building regulation. Per Woolf J in *Worlock v SAWS* (1981) 260 Estates Gazette 920, cited in Weir, *A Casebook on Tort* (1983 5th edn p 63)
5   *Acrecrest Ltd v Hattrell & Partners* [1983] QB 260, [1983] 1 All ER 17, CA.
6   [1978] AC 728 at 758.
7   Weir, *A Casebook on Tort* (5th edn, 1983) p 63.
8   [1985] AC 210, [1984] 3 All ER 529, HL.
9   At 239.
10 [1986] 1 All ER 787, [1986] 2 WLR 937, CA.
11 The structural engineers who had advised on the foundations were uninsured and not worth suing.

Economic loss

7.1.5   Twenty-five years ago it would have been possible to write 'there is no liability for purely economic loss caused by negligence': that is to say, the common law did not recognise any duty of care on a defendant to avoid causing purely economic or financial damage. By 'purely economic' loss we mean damage which grounds only in financial terms and is not consequent on some injury to the plaintiff in his person or property. Obviously, when damages are the main remedy available for negligence all forms of loss are given an economic value: damages for physical loss or damage are recoverable. Similarly, economic loss consequent on damage to person or property are recoverable. For instance, the plaintiff injured in a road accident can claim his lost earnings for the period of his enforced absence from work. Imagine, however, the situation when A has agreed with B that he will take a lease of business premises which are being built for B by C. C is negligent and delays completing the premises; as a result A's business is damaged because he cannot move into the premises and commence business. A has no contract with C and has suffered no injury or damage to property; his only loss is 'purely economic' and 25 years ago he would have had no claim: C owed him no duty of care.

During the last 25 years, however, there have been a number of developments in this area suggesting a greater willingness by the courts to recognise a duty to take care to avoid causing economic loss. This is important because the loss which can be caused by, for instance, negligently interrupting a business may be substantial. However, whilst some of the developments in relation to recognition of economic loss have been remarkable, many of the decisions are difficult to reconcile and it is often difficult to state precisely when economic loss will be recoverable; moreover, recent decisions have suggested a shrinking back from recognition of economic loss. Despite the developments of the last quarter century it is unlikely that A's claim against C, in our example above, would be any more successful today.

In fact the cases on economic loss fall into a number of separate, although related categories. Unfortunately, these are not sufficiently distinguished in English law with the result that decisions from one category are cited as authority for arguments relating to another, further confounding attempts at rationalisation. There are now signs,[1] however, that the tendency to equate different types of economic loss is waning and there is a growing willingness to recognise that different rules may be applicable to different situations.

1   See eg *Candlewood Navigation Corpn Ltd v Mitsui OSK Lines Ltd, The Ibaraki Maru* [1986] AC 1, [1985] 2 All ER 935, PC.

Liability for statements

7.1.6   Despite the imposition of liability for negligent acts and Lord Atkin's broad enunciation of the neighbour principle in 1932, the common law for a long time resisted any temptation to impose similar liability for negligent statements. There were several reasons for this reluctance. One was the fear that it would expose defendants to liability 'in an indeterminate amount for an indeterminate time to an indeterminate class',[1] for, as Lord Reid explained in *Hedley Byrne & Co Ltd v Heller & Partners Ltd*, whereas an act may cause loss—even catastrophic loss—it will normally do so only once. Words can be repeated and relied on repeatedly:[2] to impose liability in negligence would open the dreaded 'floodgates of litigation' exposing defendants to open-ended liability and bringing forth more cases than the courts could handle. There is some justification in such an argument. For a person who is potentially liable may wish to insure against that liability— indeed, it is socially desirable and economically efficient that he should so do—and yet he may find it difficult if not impossible to obtain adequate insurance cover against such open ended liability. A favourite example often cited is the cartographer who negligently fails to chart a dangerous rock; should he be held liable to all the users of his map who may found on the rock? On the other hand, there are many cases when the category of potential plaintiffs is not so limitless, and yet the same rule has been applied in these also.

Second, it was said that a man might be incautious in his words and not give them proper consideration[3] but that argument amounts to saying 'people should not be liable for being careless because people are careless.'

Third, there was no doubt a widely held view that a person who wants advice should pay for it—in which case he would have a claim in contract if it proved defective—and not look the gift horse of gratuitous counsel in the mouth. Finally, it will be apparent that in most cases careless advice is likely to lead to economic loss rather than physical damage, and we have already noted the reluctance to countenance recovery for economic loss. Furthermore, as Bishop[4] observes, information differs from products in that the person who produces it may not, and usually will not, be able to appropriate all the social benefit that flows from its production. As he points out, once produced, even valuable information can be reproduced to others at little cost and it is difficult legally and practically to control the transmission of information. There is thus a certain symmetry in not imposing liability for negligent statements. Thus as late as 1951[5] it was held that when a potential investor in a company consulted accounts prepared for the company which, due to carelessness in their preparation, gave a misleading impression and, relying on those accounts made a poor investment, he had no claim against the company's negligent accountants, even though they knew that the accounts would be shown to potential investors.

This is not to say that there was no liability at all for false statements. In *Derry v Peek*[6] the House of Lords had held that directors of a company who issued a misleading prospectus could be liable to potential investors provided they were fraudulent. Thus to succeed in a claim for misstatement the plaintiff would have to show that the defendant made the statement deliberately, knowing it to be false, or recklessly, not caring if it was true or false. Mere carelessness would not suffice. The burden of proof on a plaintiff alleging fraud—the tort of deceit-is heavy (because of the stigma attached to the allegation) and, not surprisingly, few actions succeeded. Liability was also imposed in negligence when a careless misstatement caused physical injury[7] but such instances would be few and far between and leave unfounded the main mischief of negligent statements.

1 Per Cardozo CJ in *Ultramares Corpn v Touche* 174 NE 441 at 444 (1931).
2 [1964] AC 465 at 483, HL.
3 Per Lord Reid in *Hedley Byrne & Co Ltd v Heller & Partners Ltd* at 482.
4 'Negligent Misrepresentation: An Economic Reformulation' in *The Economic Approach to Law* P Burrows and C Veljanowski (eds) (1981) p 170.
5 *Candler v Crane Christmas & Co* [1951] 2 KB 164, [1951] 1 All ER 426, CA despite a powerful dissent from Denning LJ.
6 (1889) 14 App Cas 337, HL.
7 *Sharp v Avery and Kerwood* [1938] 4 All ER 85, CA.

Hedley Byrne & Co Ltd v Heller & Partners[1]

7.1.7 In 1963 the House of Lords made a radical departure from the earlier law and for the first time it recognised in principle a duty of care in relation to negligent misstatements. The plaintiffs, advertising agents, were asked to place advertisements for a client, Easipower Ltd. Before so doing they sought a credit reference on Easipower from their own bankers. They in turn contacted Easipower's bankers who advised that Easipower Ltd was 'good for its ordinary business engagements.' That was passed on to the plaintiffs, who placed advertisements for Easipower on the strength of it. When Easipower subsequently went into liquidation the plaintiffs lost £17,000. They sued Easipower's bank in negligence.

In fact the House of Lords held that the defendants were not liable, because they had issued the credit reference subject to a disclaimer of liability. However, the House held that the defendants did owe a duty of care and would have been liable if not for the disclaimer. It will be recognised that Cardozo's objection to liability for statements—the fear of 'open-ended loss'—does not apply here when the bank knew the information would be used by one particular potential creditor. Moreover, as Bishop[2] recognises, there are sound economic and business reasons for imposing liability in this situation. The defendant bank provided the reference in the course of business: if it failed so to do it might lose Easipower's business and also be unable to obtain similar references from other banks for its own customers. Easipower would want the reference to be given to get credit. The plaintiffs' bank would want to provide a service to their customer. However, the House of Lords was not prepared to recognise wholesale liability for negligent statements: there would be liability only 'in appropriate cases'. Unfortunately, it is difficult to extract from the speeches a common view as to what would be 'an appropriate case' but at the least there would have to be some special relationship between the parties so that the defendants had assumed, vis à vis the plaintiffs, responsibility for the advice they gave.

It has proved difficult to define the degree of 'special relationship' required to give rise to liability under *Hedley Byrne*. The requirement is obviously intended to draw a line between casual information or advice given on a social occasion and advice given in the course of business when there can be less objection to the imposition of liability. Lord Devlin in *Hedley Byrne* thought that the liability depended on a relationship between the parties which was almost equivalent to contract. In *Mutual Life and Citizens' Assurance Co Ltd v Evatt*,[3] the Privy Council sought to restrict the decision further to cases when the adviser either had a financial stake in the advice given or where he professed to be in business to give such advice or claimed particular competence. The English courts have, however, declined to follow that course and thus a petrol company was held liable under *Hedley Byrne* to a plaintiff who agreed to take a lease of a petrol station on the strength of negligent over-estimates of the anticipated throughput of traffic.[4] It seems that liability will be imposed if it was reasonably foreseeable that the plaintiff, or the class of people to which he belongs, would rely on the advice and if he acted reasonably in relying on it.

1 [1964] AC 465, [1963] 2 All ER 575, HL.
2 'Negligent Misrepresentation; An Economic Reformation' in *The Economic Approach to Law* P Burrows and C G Veljanowski (eds) (1981).
3 [1971] AC 793, [1971] 1 All ER 150, PC.
4 *Esso Petroleum Co Ltd v Mardon* [1976] QB 801, [1976] 2 All ER 5, CA.

Professional negligence

7.1.8 Notwithstanding the apparent extension in *Esso Petroleum Co Ltd v Mardon*[1] of the class of persons upon whom a *Hedley Byrne* duty of care may be imposed, the main impact of the decision has been on those who are in business to give advice—principally the professions. Given the increasing importance which advice and information assume in a post-industrial society and the consequent growth in the numbers and types of professional advisers and service industries, the implications of *Hedley Byrne* liability are immensely important for business.

Of course, the business adviser is in business: he does not normally give advice free of charge, and a person who pays him for advice or information was able to sue in reliance on the contract even before *Hedley Byrne*. It will normally be an implied, if not an express term of that contract that the adviser should exercise reasonable care in giving advice.[2] However, the duty of care in negligence extends liability in at least three ways. First, the adviser may be liable for gratuitous advice, at least if given in such a situation as to give rise to a 'special relationship'. Second, liability in negligence avoids the rule of privity of contract and extends liability beyond the immediate client or customer who pays for the advice. The only restriction on this liability is that imposed by the need for a special relationship. Third, although doubt has recently been cast on this,[3] tort liability may extend the adviser's liability to his contractual client by allowing him to sue for negligence rather than breach of contract, and thus take advantage of the more favourable rules of limitation of actions applicable in tort.

This last point is illustrated by a case[4] when a solicitor negligently failed to register an option granted to his client to purchase certain land. If such an option is registered it binds third parties; if not, it is not binding. The land was later sold to a third party in breach of the option which was therefore defeated. The client sued the solicitor who argued that his failure to register was a breach of contract and that since that breach had occurred more than six years before the commencement of the action it was barred. It was held, however, that the client could also sue in tort, when his action would not be barred until six years after he suffered loss: the loss was suffered when the land was sold and the option became valueless, so that the claim could proceed. This approach was doubted by the Privy Council in the recent case of *Tai Hing Cotton Mill Ltd v Liu Chong Hing Bank Ltd*,[5] when the bank argued that its client owed it a duty of care to examine bank statements, contending that the duty arose either in contract or in tort. The Privy Council rejected the existence of such a duty and observed that if the bank wished to increase the obligations of its clients it should do so by amending its express contractual terms, to bring the change to the notice of clients. Tort would not impose any greater duty on the client than was imposed by contract, and Lord Scarman added that he preferred to deal with the obligations of parties in a commercial contractual relationship as arising from contract. The parties have control over the terms of a contract and could even bring the relationship to an end, and a contractual analysis avoids the problems of the different limitation periods in contract and tort. However *Tai Hing* is a Privy Council decision and therefore not strictly binding on English courts. It remains to be seen if the dicta in that case will be followed in preference to earlier cases especially in a claim by a client against his adviser.

Because businessmen tend not to give gratuitous advice, the evasion of consideration may seem unimportant. However, it has meant, for instance, that a petrol company was liable in tort for negligent statements made during negotiations for a contract[6] which led to the formation of a contract. If a contract does result from such negotiations a false statement may well give rise to liability under the Misrepresentation Act[7] or, if the statement becomes a term of the contract, for breach of contract. In a recent case[8] it was held that a bank owed a duty of care to a customer who was asked to sign a guarantee. The bank incorrectly explained the nature of the guarantee and it was held that, having assumed the responsibility of explaining the document, it had a duty to do so carefully and accurately.

However, important as these points are, perhaps the most significant implication of *Hedley Byrne* liability from the point of view of the professional is that it extends his liability beyond his immediate client to others who rely on his advice. Thus it has been held that a valuer who negligently prepared a valuation of property for a client owed a duty of care to the bank which provided a mortgage on the strength of the over-valuation,[9] and a surveyor who surveyed a property for a building society was liable to the intending buyer to whom the survey was shown—as the surveyor knew it would be.[10]

Despite the importance of the cases already cited, the profession with perhaps most to fear from *Hedley Byrne* liability is accountancy.

'The increasing growth and changing role of corporations in modern society has been attended by a new perception of the societal role of the profession of accounting. The day when the accountant served only the owner-manager of a company and was answerable to him alone has passed. The complexities of modern industry combined with the effects of specialisation, the impact of taxation, urbanization, the separation of ownership from management, the use of professional corporate management and a host of other factors have led to marked changes in the role and responsibilities of the accountant and in the reliance which the public must place on his work. The financial statements of the corporations upon which he reports can affect the economic interests of the general public as well as of shareholders and potential shareholders . . . With the added prestige and value of his services has come . . . a concomitant and commensurately increased responsibility to the public.'[11]

The judicial recognition of this new role came in England in the case of *JEB Fasteners Ltd v Marks, Bloom & Co*[12] *(a firm)* in which a negligence action was brought against accountants who had audited a company's accounts and included a misleading over-valuation of stock. The accountants knew that the firm was in financial difficulties and that a take-over was likely; in fact the plaintiffs took over the company having seen the accounts. When they discovered the true state of affairs they sued the accountants. The action failed because, it was held, the plaintiffs had not actually relied on them; they would have taken over the company even if the accounts had given an accurate picture. However, Woolf J at first instance held that a duty of care was owed to anyone who could be foreseen as likely reasonably to rely on the accounts. The Court of Appeal approved his decision.

Similar developments have taken place in the USA and in other Commonwealth jurisdictions. The implications for the accountancy profession are enormous. *The Observer* in 1985[13] listed seventeen cases then pending against accountants in common law jurisdictions; the largest was for a specified sum of one billion US dollars. In many cases, accountants may be sued for negligence in failing to discover frauds by companies or their directors. Since accountancy firms carry indemnity insurance, they make particularly attractive targets. However, the impact of frequent litigation has led to an enormous increase in insurance premiums and 'in the case of small to medium-size accountancy firms hit by litigation on this side of the Atlantic the consequences could be lethal. Many will be wiped out.'[14] In recent months arguments have been in favour of legislation to set a maximum liability for auditors.

The concern about imposing liability on professionals in this way is that the sums involved in a negligence action may be wholly disproportionate to the price charged for the services which gave rise to a claim. Fleming puts both sides of the argument:

'Deterrence is not served by excusing auditors, seeing that their pay masters would usually be the last to complain about too favourable a picture of their financial affairs . . . [but] auditors, unlike manufacturers, are unable to distribute the cost among a sufficiently large number of clients or indeed among most of those who use their work product. The effect of imposing unrestricted liability might be either to drive accountants out of business or compel them to resort to extensive disclaimers. Neither consequence would help the public.'[15]

1   [1976] QB 801, [1976] 2 All ER 5, CA
2   See Supply of Goods and Services Act 1982. See 25.0.2.
3   By dicta of the Privy Council in *Tai Hing Cotton Mill Ltd v Liu Chong Hing Bank Ltd* [1986] AC 80 [1985] 2 All ER 947.
4   *Midland Bank Trust Co Ltd v Hett, Stubbs & Kemp (a firm)* [1979] Ch 384, [1978] 3 All ER 571.
5   [1985] 2 All ER 947 [1986] AC 80.
6   *Esso Petroleum Co Ltd v Mardon* [1976] QB 801, [1976] 2 All ER 5.
7   An action under the Act has the advantage that it is for the defendant to show he was not negligent: see 15.0.5.
8   *Cornish v Midland Bank plc* [1985] 3 All ER 513, CA.
9   *Singer and Friedlander Ltd v John D Wood & Co* (1977) 243 Estates Gazette 212.
10 *Yianni v Edwin Evans & Sons* [1982] QB 438, [1981] 3 All ER 592.
11 Per Dickson J in *Haig v Bamford* (1972) 32 DLR (3d) 67.
12 [1981] 3 All ER 289; on appeal [1983] 1 All ER 583, CA.
13 'Auditors—Time for Qualification' *The Observer* 28 July 1985. See also Savage, 'Auditors and the Law. A Critical Review' 1983 4 Co 187.
14 *The Observer*, loc cit.
15 Fleming, *An Introduction to the Law of Torts* (1985 2nd edn) p 63.

Special cases

7.1.9   In certain cases no duty of care is imposed on grounds of public policy. These are principally concerned with the liabilities of judges, advocates and those acting in a similar capacity. Thus it has been established that a barrister may not be sued in negligence by a client disgruntled by the presentation of his case.[1] The reasons are threefold: first, that a barrister owes a duty to the court which may conflict with any duty to his client: thus a barrister may be forced to disclose information prejudicial to his client; second, under the so-called cab rank rule, a barrister cannot choose whom he will or will not represent; third, an action against a barrister would effectively amount to a form of appeal or retrial and there must be an end to litigation at some point. The House of Lords has expressed the opinion that a solicitor acting as advocate would enjoy similar immunity.

On the other hand we have seen that a solicitor acting in his professional capacity may be sued for acts done other than as an advocate and a similar rule applies to barristers for work done outside the court; thus he may be sued for negligence in advice or in the drafting of documents—but not for work done in preparation for a trial which is ultimately connected with the conduct of the case in court.[2]

Obviously a disgruntled litigant cannot sue a judge for negligence in the trial of a case, and the same would apply to any other person acting in a judicial or quasi judicial capacity. However, there must be a dispute and there must be some judicial element to the function if it is to abstract immunity; thus it has been held that there is no immunity for an auditor valuing shares in a private company,[3] nor for an architect issuing certificates of completion of building works.[4]

1   *Rondel v Worsley* [1969] 1 AC 191, [1967] 3 All ER 993, HL—there is no contract between a barrister and the person he represents.
2   *Saif Ali v Sidney Mitchell & Co (a firm)* [1980] AC 198, [1978] 3 All ER 1033, HL.
3   *Arenson v Casson Beckman Ruttey & Co* [1977] AC 405, [1975] 3 All ER 901, HL.
4   *Sutcliffe v Thackrah* [1974] AC 727, [1974] 1 All ER 859, HL.

Other cases of economic loss
7.1.10   In addition to liability for statements, economic loss may arise in other situations.

a) The cable cases
The clearest case of 'pure economic loss' is where there is no relationship or contract between plaintiff and defendant but the defendant, by some negligent act, interrupts the plaintiff's business causing him loss of profit. In a typical case the defendant severs a power line whilst carrying out excavation work, thereby interrupting the electricity supply to the plaintiff's factory (amongst others). In a line of cases the courts[1] have refused to allow such plaintiffs to recover for their loss. There are several justifications for such reluctance, some more convincing than others. First, there is the familiar 'floodgates' argument: the one act of the defendant—for instance, severing a power cable—may affect many businesses: to impose liability for all such losses on the negligent contractor would be potentially crippling. Moreover, it is much easier for individual businesses to take precautions against loss caused to their business in such a way than it is for the negligent contractor: he must insure against an unknown number of claims of unknown amount. The business can insure on the basis of its own knowledge of its own profits. Of course, such an objection applies to the imposition of liability for negligent statements but the number of potential claims are reduced by the need under *Hedley Byrne* to show a 'special relationship'. In a cable case, potential plaintiffs may be able to take practical steps to avoid or minimise loss, for instance by using standby generators or by including in costings an element to cover the loss of production due to such occurrences and similar risks, such as power cuts due to natural causes. Lord Denning has expressed another reason:

'If claims for economic loss were permitted for this particular hazard, there would be no end of claims. Some might be genuine, but many might be inflated or even false. A machine might not have been in use anyway, but it would be easy to put it down to the cut in the power supply. It would be well nigh impossible to check the claims.'[2]

There is much weight in these objections and the law has therefore leaned against allowing recovery of pure economic loss in such cases. Instead the loss is allowed to lie where it falls, allowing it to be spread amongst the whole of the community affected by an incident and, by insurance or by pricing, to be passed on and distributed throughout an industry and, ultimately, its customers as a whole. However, such an approach can produce inconsistencies. For, although pure economic loss is not recoverable, economic loss consequent on personal injury or property damage is recoverable. The difficulties created by this distinction can be seen in two cases. In *SCM (UK) Ltd v W J Whittall & Son Ltd*[3] an electricity cable was damaged, interrupting the supply to the plaintiffs' factory. This in turn caused damage to machinery which, as a result, was out of use for a day. The plaintiffs successfully claimed for the damage to the machine and for the lost profit caused by that damage. They could not have made any claim for lost profits if the machine had not been damaged. The distinction appears even more clearly from the case of *Spartan Steel and Alloys Ltd v Martin & Co (Contractors) Ltd.*[4] This was, again, a case involving the severing of a power line. To avoid damage to machinery the plaintiffs were forced to pour molten metal out of their furnaces: as a result that 'batch' deteriorated in value. Moreover, during the power cuts the plaintiffs were unable to carry out any further melts. They claimed damages for (a) lost profits on the melt in progress at the time of the power cut, which was damaged when it was poured off and (b) lost profits on the other four melts which had not been carried out. By a majority the Court of Appeal held that they could recover damages for (a) but not for (b); (a) was consequential on physical damage to property—the damaged molten metal—but (b) was pure economic loss.

An Australian case provides an interesting contrast. In *Caltex Oil (Australia) Pty Ltd v Dredge Willemstad*[5] the plaintiffs claimed damages following damage to a pipeline which carried their oil. They did not own the pipeline but claimed merely for increased transport costs caused by the need to find some other means to deliver the oil. The High Court of Australia nevertheless allowed the plaintiffs to recover; there is no one line of reasoning in the judgments but it is perhaps worth noting that the English cases have expressed concern about potential multiplicity of claims; in this case only the plaintiffs used the pipeline and therefore only they were likely to be affected by damage to it.

b) Negligent performance of a service and product liability
There are two other situations involving the infliction of economic loss which fall between *Hedley Byrne* and *Spartan Steel*. Suppose that a businessman carries out a service for a client but due to negligence does it so badly that a third party suffers financial loss; for instance a sub-contractor by his negligent work damages the main contractor's employer. At first glance this appears to be similar to the *Hedley Byrne* situation, especially when the service performed is a professional one. However, the difference is that in *Hedley Byrne* the plaintiff acts in reliance on advice; in this situation the plaintiff is injured without any act of reliance on his part.

Despite that difference and despite the general reluctance to allow recovery of economic loss, a number of recent cases have imposed liability in such situations. In *Ross v Caunters*,[6] for instance, a solicitor prepared a will for a client and the plaintiff was entitled to a bequest under the will. However, after the client's death it was discovered that the plaintiff was not entitled to the bequest because the solicitor had given negligent advice to the client and allowed the will to be witnessed by the plaintiff's husband. It was held that she was entitled to sue the solicitor in negligence. This decision could not be based on *Hedley Byrne* because there was no reliance by the plaintiff on the solicitor's advice; instead the judge based his decision on the *Donoghue v Stevenson* principle.

Although cases of this type extend the recognition of a duty of care to avoid economic loss, the extension is relatively small because in each case the plaintiff was a recognisable individual or a member of a very small group. Another line of cases, however, has potentially far wider implications. We have noted above that in *Anns v Merton London Borough Council* the House of Lords recognised a duty of care on a local authority in favour of an owner-occupier of a dwelling, in relation to enforcement of the building regulations. In *Anns* the House of Lords said that the damages recoverable by the plaintiff would be the cost of repairing the dwellings to make them safe. The House treated the plaintiff's claim as one for physical damage but in reality, it looks more like one for economic loss. However, since the duty is owed to all persons who acquire an interest in the dwelling, it appears to be far reaching. A similar duty is owed by the builder himself. This suggests the possibility that a manufacturer of a product might be liable to all persons who acquire that product for loss they suffer due to negligence in manufacture. As we have seen *Donoghue v Stevenson* allows a person who is injured or who suffers property damage due to a defective product to sue the manufacturer in negligence, but if his only claim is that the product is not as good as it should be—and therefore not worth what he paid for it—his only claim normally lies in contract, against the vendor.[7] This is important. If the seller is insolvent the buyer of a defective product has no worthwile claim; on the other hand, if a manufacturer is liable for economic loss caused by a defective product he is open to a potentially enormous liability. That liability is even greater if, as in *Anns*, a duty is owed to subsequent purchasers of the product. One can imagine the case of (say) a car manufacturer who produces a car with defective brakes, all owners of that type of car may be able to claim from him the cost of repairs. If the defect manifests itself after, say, two years a claim could be brought by all persons who own a car of this type at the time the defect appears, not just by original purchasers.

How far the law does now recognise a duty of care on a manufacturer in respect of his customers' economic loss is unclear. In *Junior Books Ltd v Veitchi Co Ltd*[8] a dispute arose out of the construction of a warehouse for the plaintiffs. The defendants were nominated sub-contractors to lay a floor in the warehouse. There was, therefore, no contract between the plaintiffs and defendants. In fact the floor was laid badly and began to break up. The plaintiffs were forced to replace it and claimed for the cost of replacement and damages for the interruption of their business. The House of Lords held that the defendants did owe the plaintiffs a duty of care even in respect of the purely economic loss suffered by the plaintiffs. There was a sufficiently proximate relationship between the parties to give rise to a duty of care in view of the fact that the plaintiffs' architect had selected the defendants to construct the floor, the plaintiffs had relied on the defendants' expertise and the defendants knew the plaintiffs' requirements.

However, in *Muirhead v Industrial Tank Specialities Ltd*[9] the Court of Appeal restricted the application of *Junior Books* in product liability cases. The plaintiff had set up a lobster farm with the intention of storing live lobsters for sale out of season at Christmas. The defendants had manufactured pumps which were installed at the farm to recirculate water in the lobster tanks. The pumps failed because the motors fitted by the defendants were unsuitable for use with the British mains electricity system and the plaintiff therefore sued the defendants in negligence claiming, inter alia, the cost of replacing the pumps and other financial losses as well as the value of his lost lobsters. The Court of Appeal rejected the claim for economic loss distinguishing *Junior Books* on the grounds that whereas in that case there was a special relationship between plaintiff and defendant and the plaintiffs had relied on the defendants, here the plaintiff had relied throughout on the contractors who built his tanks and installed the pumps.

It seems then that for a claim for economic loss to succeed in a 'product liability' case there will have to be a special relationship between plaintiff and defendant involving reliance by the former on the latter. Obviously in most cases that will not exist: whilst it is true that a plaintiff may buy goods on the strength of a manufacturer's name—for instance he may buy 'a new Ford Sierra' rather than 'a new car'—he will in most cases rely on his vendor and only on the manufacturer's reputation in general terms. That will not be enough so that, if the product fails, he will have to rely on his contractual claim against the vendor.

1 See *Weller & Co v Foot and Mouth Disease Research Institute* [1966] 1 QB 569, [1965] 3 All ER 560; *SCM (UK) Ltd v W J Whittall & Son Ltd* [1971] 1 QB 337, [1970] 2 All ER 417; *Spartan Steel and Alloys Ltd v Martin & Co (Contractors) Ltd* [1973] QB 27 [1972] 3 All ER 557, CA.
2 [1973] QB 27 at 38.
3 [1971] 1 QB 337, [1970] 2 All ER 417.
4 [1973] QB 27, [1972] 3 All ER 557, CA.
5 (1976) 136 CLR 529.
6 [1980] Ch 297, [1979] 3 All ER 580.
7 See 21.2.0.
8 [1983] 1 AC 520, [1982] 3 All ER 201, HL.
9 [1986] QB 507, [1985] 3 All ER 705, CA.

The status of claims for economic loss after Junior Books

7.1.11   We have seen that the consequences for business of negligence claims for economic loss may be potentially catastrophic. Moreover, it is more difficult for a potential defendant to protect himself against liability in negligence than against liability for breach of contract. If a businessman makes a contract he may seek to protect himself against a claim by the other contracting party by including in the contract a clause excluding, or limiting his liability for breach.[1] However, if a third party is allowed to sue him in tort—as the employer sued the sub-contractor in *Junior Books*—he may 'bypass' any such exclusion clause.[2]

Where will such a negligence claim succeed? Despite attempts by some writers to speak of 'economic loss' in general terms, it appears that there are a number of different situations and that different rules apply to each.

a) Negligent statement
A person who suffers loss by relying on negligent advice will be able to claim against the adviser provided he can show a special relationship; that he relied on the advice, it was reasonable for him to do so and it was foreseeable that he would do so.

b) Negligent performance of a service
A person who suffers loss because of the negligent performance of a service by the defendant for a third party will be able to claim provided it was foreseeable that he would be so affected and there is a sufficiently proximate relationship between him and the defendant.

c) Product liability

The buyer of a defective product will only be able to claim against the manufacturer in rare cases where he has relied on the manufacturer. It may be that *Junior Books* will be restricted to cases of nominated building sub-contractors.

d) Pure economic loss

In *Junior Books*, Lord Roskill doubted the decision in *Spartan Steel*.[3] However, in view of the decisions subsequent to *Junior Books*,[4] it seems likely that a plaintiff will have no claim for purely economic loss outside the above three situations.

1   See 18.0.0.
2   Careful drafting may extend the benefit of an exclusion clause to a third party—see *New Zealand Shipping Co v Satterthwaite* (below 18.0.1). In *Muirhead*, Robert Goff LJ thought, obiter, that the defendant might be able to rely against the plaintiff on an exclusion clause in its contract with its own purchaser, but it is unclear if that is correct.
3   At 547.
4   In *Leigh and Sillivan Ltd v Aliakmon Shipping Co Ltd, The Aliakmon* [1986] 2 All ER 145, [1986] 2 WLR 902 the House of Lords, following established authority, rejected a claim for damages by a buyer of goods under a c.i.f. contract to whom the risk of damage to but not ownership of the goods had passed.

Nervous shock

7.1.12   A person who witnesses an accident to another person, or one who himself has a 'near miss' may suffer shock as a result: can he claim damages for that shock from the person responsible for the accident? In the past the courts have been reluctant to admit claims for nervous shock, on grounds very similar to those advanced against allowing recovery of economic loss. First, it is said, it is difficult to test the genuineness of claims for shock; however, as psychiatry comes to be regarded more highly as a science, this argument loses some of its face. Second, the courts are wary of opening the familiar floodgates of litigation: a person who causes an accident in a busy street could be exposed to a vast number of claims if all those who witnessed it could come forward with a claim for damages for shock. However, recent cases suggest a greater willingness by the courts to allow claims for nervous shock, although awards of damages remain low when compared to those for physical injuries.

It must be understood that damages for shock are just that—the law does not allow damages for grief or upset at the loss of a loved one or relative. Older cases[1] restricted claims for nervous shock to cases in which the plaintiff feared for his own safety and was in the 'area of impact'. However, that rule has gradually been relaxed and the House of Lords[2] has held that the sole test is whether it was reasonably foreseeable that the plaintiff would suffer shock. If so, a duty is owed to him. In deciding if the plaintiff's shock was foreseeable, three factors appear to be relevant:

(a) the relationship between the plaintiff and the person injured. A claim by a relative is likely to succeed (depending on other factors); it is far less clear if the 'ordinary bystander' may claim;

(b) the plaintiff's proximity to the accident: the witness present at the time is more likely to succeed than one who comes on the scene later who sees it from a distance;

(c) how the plaintiff discovers the accident, whether personally or through some third party.[3]

Obviously there must be some limitation. With modern telecommunications a camera team may be on the scene of a particularly gruesome accident almost at once and have television pictures of it in every home in time for tea. It would be harsh on the defendant to expose him to claims by everyone who saw the pictures.[4] However, it is unclear when the line is now drawn. In *McLoughlin v O'Brian*[5] the plaintiff was told by a friend of an accident involving her husband and children. She arrived at the hospital soon after to find one child dead and her husband and other children seriously injured and distressed. Not surprisingly her claim succeeded.

1 See eg *Behrens v Bertram Mills Circus Ltd* [1957] 2 QB 1, [1957] 1 All ER 583.
2 In *McLoughlin v O'Brian* [1983] 1 AC 410, [1982] 2 All ER 298, HL.
3 He must witness the accident—or its aftermath—in person, not merely by a report from a third party.
4 The House of Lords in *McLoughlin v O'Brian* did not rule out claims by persons witnessing an accident by simultaneous broadcast.
5 See note 2 above.

Negligence—breach of duty

7.2.0 The fact that, in a certain situation, the law imposes a duty of care on a defendant does not of itself make him liable in negligence.

A defendant is liable only if the plaintiff can show that he was at fault; 'fault' in this context connoting that the defendant has failed to discharge his duty of care towards the plaintiff. The standard of care required of defendants by the law is that of the reasonable man—

> 'Negligence is the omission to do something which a reasonable man, guided upon those considerations which ordinarily regulate the conduct of human affairs, would do, or doing something which a prudent and reasonable man would not do.'[1]

It is important to appreciate that the standard against which the defendant is measured is an objective one. This is important, for as we shall see below, it releases the court from the need to make any inquiry as to the personal attributes or circumstances of a particular individual. Furthermore, it allows the law to be flexible. In any new set of circumstances the question 'was the defendant negligent?' can be rephrased as 'What would the reasonable man have done in this situation?' and, of course, the reasonable man must change with the times and adapt himself to technological developments. What would have been 'unreasonable' or negligent in 1920 may not be so today, and vice versa. It is worth repeating though, that although liability depends in theory on fault, in certain areas, especially those such as road traffic accidents when third party insurance is compulsory, the courts have raised the standard of 'reasonable care' so artificially high that the 'man on the Clapham omnibus' could have no realistic hope of ever attaining it.

The objective nature of 'the reasonable man' is one half of the test of reasonable care; the other is concerned with the balancing of risk and benefit. The law requires that a defendant take reasonable care, and what is reasonable will depend on the surrounding circumstances. In America, Judge Learned Hand expressed this in terms of an equation: if the burden of avoiding an accident is less than the probability of such accident occurring, multiplied by the seriousness of its consequences, then it is negligent not to avoid it.[2] However, this equation must be treated with great care: it would be wrong to understand it in purely economic terms. The social and other non-financial consequences of a potential accident may well require expenditure to avoid its occurrence even though such expenditure is unjustified on economic grounds alone.

1   Per *Alderson B in Blyth v Birmingham Waterworks Co* (1856) 11 Exch 781 at 784.
2   *United States v Carroll Towing Co* 159 F 2d 169 at 173 (2d Cir 1947).

The reasonable man: the objective standard
7.2.1   The defendant is measured against the standard of 'that excellent but odious character'[1] the 'reasonable man'. It is thus no defence for a defendant to plead that he was doing his best, if his best does not satisfy that standard. This is most clearly illustrated by the case of *Nettleship v Weston*[2] where it was held that a learner driver should be measured by the standard of the ordinary, reasonably competent driver with no allowance being made for his own lack of skill. At its most extreme, this approach means that no allowance will be made for the defendant who is stupid or who suffers from any mental infirmity. Although this may seem harsh on the individual defendant who is subjectively innocent it must be borne in mind that the plaintiff is also innocent of blame; and, in many cases, it will be the defendant's insurers rather than he himself who pay any damages awarded.

On the other hand, the physical characteristics of an individual may be relevant. A one legged man would be judged by the standards of a reasonable one legged man, and thus would be expected to cross a road with the speed of a reasonable one legged man: however, a court might well hold that a reasonable one legged man would not have started to cross in the first place! Similar allowance may be made for age, at least in the cases of the very old or young.

In fact it is often the physical attributes of the plaintiff, rather than of the defendant, which affect the outcome of a case. Most often they arise in relation to the question of contributory negligence[3] on the part of the plaintiff: in that case the issue is just the same as that involved in deciding if the defendant was negligent. However, the physical attributes of the plaintiff may also be relevant to the standard expected of the reasonable defendant. Thus, for example, the number of blind people who use the streets alone is sufficiently large for a reasonable man working on the pavement to foresee their presence and take appropriate precautions to protect them as well as the fully sighted.[4]

1   A P Herbert, *Uncommon Law?*
2   [1971] 2 QB 691, [1971] 3 All ER 581, CA.
3   Below 8.0.2.
4   *Haley v London Electricity Board* [1965] AC 778, [1964] 3 All ER 185, HL.

The reasonable businessman
7.2.2   The standard required of a defendant businessman, tradesman or professional is, similarly, that of the reasonable person pursuing that particular business, trade or profession. Moreover, if a person does work which is outside the scope of his own normal business he will be judged as a reasonable practitioner of that particular type of work. Thus no allowance is made for an individual's personal lack of skill: 'I was doing my best' is no defence. In one case a DIY carpenter was judged by the standards of a

reasonably competent carpenter.[1] On the other hand, a person is only judged by the standards of an ordinary reasonably competent member of his particular trade or profession; he will only be judged as a specialist if he professes to be a specialist.

One final point: although an individual cannot rely upon his own lack of competence as a defence, he may be absolved of liability if he can show that he brought his lack of skill to the plaintiff's knowledge before undertaking the particular task, for then not only does the defendant not claim—expressly or impliedly—any special skill, but also the defendant may argue that the plaintiff has voluntarily assumed the risk of harm due to his lack of skill.[2]

What, then, is the standard of the reasonable businessman, tradesman or professional? He must behave as a reasonably competent practitioner of his particular trade or profession, and it is possible to identify several attributes of the reasonably competent practitioner; many of these have been described in cases involving allegations of negligence by doctors, but they are undoubtedly of general application.

The reasonable man will keep up to date with developments in his field: for instance a doctor may not say 'I do not believe in anaesthetics. I do not believe in antiseptics. I am going to continue to do my surgery in the way it was done in the eighteenth century'.[3] However, in judging the conduct of a defendant the court will compare it with standards and knowledge current at the time of the incident in question and not with the benefit of hindsight. In one case[4] a man was paralysed as a result of an injection given to him in hospital by an anaesthetist. The anaesthetic had been contaminated by a disinfectant which had seeped through an invisible hairline crack in the glass ampoule in which the anaesthetic was stored. At the time of the accident the possibility of such an occurrence was not known, but was known by the time the case came to court. The plaintiff argued that the disinfectant should have been stained with dye to show up any contamination, but the claim failed. As Denning LJ said 'We must not look at the 1947 accident with 1954 spectacles'.[5]

A defendant is liable for failing to take reasonable care. If there is a legitimate division of professional opinion in a particular field a defendant will not be held negligent if he follows one strand of opinion, provided that that is a course a reasonable member of the profession could adopt. The justification for such an approach is obvious: in a case alleging negligence in the course of a trade or profession the court is likely to be faced with conflicting expert evidence. It would be impossible for the court to choose between such experts and thus it will not do so. Similarly, the courts recognise that a professional may make a mistake or an error of judgment without necessarily being negligent. Thus, for instance, it has been held that a show jumper who misjudged the speed of his horse and collided with a photographer in the ring was not liable;[6] and in a case of alleged medical negligence the House of Lords adopted a similar approach.[7] However, it must be stressed that an error of judgment may amount to negligence if it 'show(s) a lapse from the standard of skill and care required to be exercised to avoid a charge of negligence'.[8]

As we have observed, cases alleging negligence in the course of a business or profession will often turn on expert evidence of generally accepted practice, and it will be difficult for a plaintiff to succeed in a claim of negligence against a defendant who can show he has followed the normal practice in his field. However, the question for the court is always 'did the defendant act reasonably?' and the court may therefore find a defendant liable notwithstanding that he has followed normal practice. In *Lloyds Bank Ltd v EB Savory & Co*[9] a woman paid into her bank account cheques drawn by her husband on his employers; the bank was held negligent in that when she had opened the account it had failed to ask the woman for details of her husband's employment—even though evidence showed that it was not the normal practice of banks to seek such information. In this way the court may raise standards of behaviour in particular fields of business. Of course, the court is more likely to adopt such a course in relation to questions of business or commercial practice than in cases involving allegations of medical negligence.

1   *Wells v Cooper* [1958] 2 QB 265, [1958] 2 All ER 527, CA.
2   Volenti non fit injuria: see 8.0.3.
3   Per McNair J in *Bolam v Friern Hospital Management Committee* [1957] 2 All ER 118, [1957] 1 WLR 582 at p 85.
4   *Roe v Minister of Health* [1954] 2 QB 66, [1954] 2 All ER 131, CA.
5   Ibid at 84.
6   *Wooldridge v Sumner* [1963] 2 QB 43, [1962] 2 All ER 978, CA.
7   *Whitehouse v Jordan* [1981] 1 All ER 267 [1981] 1 WLR 246.
8   Ibid per Lord Roskill.
9   [1933] AC 201, HL.

Balancing risks: taking reasonable care
7.2.3   A reasonable man will exercise reasonable care to avoid causing harm to his 'neighbour' but the degree of care which he might regard as reasonable will vary according to circumstances. This is reflected, at least partly, in Learned Hand's formulation of negligence mentioned above. There will come a time when the marginal cost—in both financial and social terms—of achieving further reduction in a particular risk will outweigh the benefit gained by such reduction. For instance, statistics show that the driving of motor vehicles increases the risk to pedestrians of accidental injury and death; however, no-one would say that it is therefore negligent merely to drive. Similarly the number and severity of road accidents could probably be reduced if the speed of vehicles were reduced to (say) ten miles per hour; but the cost to business—and therefore to society—of such a reduction would outweigh any benefit gained and so the courts are unlikely to hold that to drive at more than ten miles per hour is automatically negligent.

In deciding whether a defendant has taken reasonable care, a court will then examine the surrounding circumstances, and we can identify a number of factors which may affect its decision.

a)   The likelihood of harm
'People must guard against reasonable probabilities but they are not bound to guard against fantastic possibilities.'[1] This really amounts to no more than a restatement of the general principle that the law requires a man to take reasonable care: he must guard against those consequences of his actions which are reasonably foreseeable.

b)   The seriousness of harm
Obviously the likelihood of harm cannot be the sole factor which influences a defendant's behaviour: he must also take account of the seriousness of the

likely consequences of his acts. A reasonable man will guard against even a remote possibility of serious harm. This is reflected in Learned Hand's formulation of risk as 'probability of an accident occurring multiplied by the seriousness of its likely consequences'. The approach can be seen in *Paris v Stepney Borough Council*.[2] The plaintiff, as his employers (the defendants) knew, had only one good eye: he was not provided with goggles for his work and was injured at work when a splinter entered his one good eye, blinding him. It was held that, although it would not have been negligent to fail to provide goggles for normally sighted employees, the employer had been negligent in not providing them for the plaintiff because the consequences for him of injury to his eye were more serious than they would be for a fully sighted employee.

c) The value of the defendant's conduct
The likelihood of causing serious injury must be balanced against the social value of the defendant's conduct. We have already observed that the social desirability of increased mobility is generally held to justify the increased risk of accidents generated by faster travel. Similarly a risk which would not ordinarily be justified might be justified by circumstances: for instance an emergency requiring prompt action. In *Watt v Hertfordshire County Council*[3] the plaintiff was a fireman; he was called out with his colleagues to an accident where a woman lay trapped beneath an overturned vehicle. A heavy jack was needed to shift the vehicle, but the fire brigade did not have a suitable vehicle to convey it; the jack was therefore carried in a lorry with the plaintiff and several colleagues holding it. The plaintiff was badly injured when the jack slipped during the journey and he sued in negligence. The Court of Appeal held that the claim failed: although it might ordinarily have been negligent to transport the jack unsecured in this way, the risk here was justified by the need to protect life and limb. Denning LJ explained:

> 'It is well settled that in measuring due care you must balance the risk against the measures necessary to eliminate the risk. To that proposition there ought to be added this: you must balance the risk against the end to be achieved. If this accident had occurred in a commercial enterprise without any emergency there could be no doubt that the servant would succeed. But the commercial end to make profit is very different from the human end to save life and limb.'[4]

d) The cost of eliminating the risk
As Denning L J indicated in the words quoted above, the court must also take into account the extent of the precautions needed to reduce or eliminate the risk in question, and balance the cost of such precautions against the likelihood of harm and its likely seriousness. However, as his words also indicate, the court is likely to be slow to recognise mere financial cost as justifying a failure to take care. In every case the question is would it be reasonable to incur the cost of precautions to avoid the risk of harm? Nevertheless, in *Latimer v AEC Ltd*[5] the floor of the defendants' factory was left slippery after a flood; they used their available supplies of sawdust to try to soak up the oily water on the floor and sent out for more sawdust. In the meantime the factory continued to work and the plaintiff was injured when he fell on the floor. It was held that the employers had not been negligent as they had taken all practicable precautions against such an accident and the

only way to further reduce the risk would have been to close down the factory altogether. A similar approach was adopted in *Withers v Perry Chain Co Ltd.*[6] The plaintiff was known to be susceptible to dermatitis and sued her employer in negligence when she contracted the disease. Her employer had moved her to a job where she would have as little contact with grease as possible and the only further precaution he could have taken would have been to dismiss her. Not surprisingly, therefore, the court held that reasonable care had been taken in all the circumstances.

1 Per Lord Dunedin in *Fardon v Harcourt-Rivington* (1932) 146 LT 391 at 392, HL.
2 [1951] AC 367, [1951] 1 All ER 42, HL.
3 [1954] 2 All ER 368, [1954] 1 WLR 835, CA.
4 Ibid at 838.
5 [1953] AC 643, [1953] 2 All ER 449, HL.
6 [1961] 3 All ER 676, [1961] 1 WLR 1314, CA.

Proof of carelessness
7.2.4 In a civil case the burden of proof lies on the plaintiff to prove each and every element of his case on a balance of probabilities. In a negligence case he must therefore prove that it is more likely than not that the defendant failed to exercise reasonable care. Often, he will call expert evidence to explain what the defendant did and what is the general accepted practice in the particular trade or profession. However, by their very nature accidents tend to come as something of a surprise to their victim: the plaintiff may therefore be hard pressed to show how an accident came about. How then is he to prove that the defendant was negligent? In many cases the plaintiff will be assisted by two rules of evidence.

c) Civil Evidence Act 1968, section 11
An accident may give rise to a criminal prosecution in addition to a civil claim for negligence. This is particularly so in the case of road accidents when there is likely to be a prosecution for careless driving. When the accident does result in a criminal prosecution the plaintiff will wait until after that prosecution has been concluded before bringing his claim because by s 11 of the Civil Evidence Act 1968, the fact that a person has been convicted of an offence in criminal proceedings may be given in evidence in civil proceedings and has the effect of reversing the burden of proof so that it is for the person convicted to show that his conviction was wrong or is irrelevant to the civil case. Thus in many road accident cases the burden falls on the defendant to show that he was not negligent.

b) Res ipsa loquitur
There are situations when common sense indicates that an accident would not have happened without carelessness on the part of someone. For instance, if the plaintiff is injured by a barrel which falls from an upper floor window of the defendant's warehouse,[1] the plaintiff is entitled to take the view that such things are not everyday occurrences and to look to the defendant for an explanation. The rule of 'res ipsa loquitur' is no more than a legal reflection of that rule of common sense but, perhaps because it is expressed in Latin, the rule has acquired a mystique and reputation for difficulty which it does not deserve. 'Res ipsa loquitur' effectively means 'The facts speak for themselves' and if the rule applies, the plaintiff is

released from the burden of proving negligence and can call on the defendant to show that he was not careless.

In order to rely on the rule the plaintiff must show that two conditions are fulfilled. First, he must prove that the accident was caused by something under the defendant's exclusive control. He will not be able to call res ipsa loquitur in his aid if the defendant can show that some third party could have interfered with the cause of the accident. Thus it was held that the maxim did not apply in a case where the plaintiff fell out of a moving train through a door which was not properly locked.[2] A passenger could have tampered with the door between the time of the train leaving the station and the accident. Second, the circumstances of the accident must be such that it would not normally have happened without negligence on the part of the defendant. Thus the maxim is singularly applicable to product liability claims: for instance, a consumer is entitled to say to a manufacturer 'Snails do not ordinarily become sealed in ginger beer bottles. Explain how this happened', but it can also apply to cases against professionals provided the two conditions are fulfilled. Thus the maxim has been applied in cases of alleged medical negligence,[3] where a patient is entitled to say 'While I was in your hands something has been done to me which has wrecked my life. Please explain how it has come to pass'.[4]

The defendant may deny that the maxim applies: he may show that he was not in sole control of the thing which caused the harm, or that the accident could have occurred without negligence. However, if the maxim does apply the onus is then thrown onto the defendant to prove that he was not negligent: he must either show how the accident came to happen and that he took all reasonable care to avoid it; or, if he does not know how it happened, that he had taken all reasonable care: in other words, that he had a foolproof system to guard against mishaps of the kind which occurred.

The burden on a defendant is a heavy one, as is shown by the case of *Henderson v Henry E Jenkins & Sons and Evans*.[5] The brakes failed on a lorry owned and operated by the defendants and it was discovered that the failure was caused by loss of brake fluid from a hole in a corroded brake pipe. The plaintiff relied on res ipsa loquitur; the defendants showed that they had inspected the lorry in accordance with the manufacturer's instructions and advice of the Ministry of Transport, and that the hole could only have been discovered by removing the pipe. However, it was held that they had failed to disprove negligence. They should also have shown that nothing had happened during the life of the vehicle to create suspicion that the pipe might be damaged.

1 As in *Byrne v Boadle* (1863) 2 H & C 722.
2 *Easson v London and North Eastern Rly Co* [1944] KB 421 [1944] 2 All ER 425, CA. Contrast *Gee v Metropolitan Rly Co* (1873) LR 8 QB 161, Ex Ch where the accident occurred shortly after the train left a station, and whilst the doors were under the railway company's control.
3 Eg in *Roe v Minister of Health* [1954] 2 QB 66, [1954] 2 All ER 131, CA and *Cassidy v Minister of Health* [1951] 2 KB 343, [1951] 1 All ER 574, CA.
4 Per Denning LJ in *Roe v Minister of Health* loc cited at 81.
5 [1970] AC 282, [1969] 3 All ER 756, HL.

Negligence—damage, causation and remoteness
7.3.0 It is not enough to make a defendant liable in tort to show that he has been careless; liability depends on someone suffering damage as a result of that carelessness. This may seem obvious—after all, if no one has suffered

damage, who is going to sue?—but it is important for three reasons. First, it distinguishes negligence from certain other torts such as trespass and defamation, which are actionable 'per se'—ie without proof of damage. Second, it means that, for instance, a manufacturer can allow as many snails as he likes into his ginger beer bottles without attracting liability provided that, by good fortune, no one suffers injury as a result. The value of negligence as a device for the protection of the public is therefore, to some degree at least, reduced because negligence cannot come into play until at least one person has been injured. The task of keeping snails out of ginger beer bottles, of making products safe and stopping drivers from driving too fast is better left to some part of the public or criminal law system.[1] Third, since damage must accrue to the plaintiff before he can claim, his cause of action in negligence does not accrue until he has suffered damage, and so time does not begin to run against him for the purposes of limitation of actions until that time. As we have seen above, this can be much to the plaintiff's benefit, especially when compared with the rule for claims arising from breach of contract (where the cause of action accrues at and time begins to run from the time of the breach, even though no damage results until much later).[2]

However, the defendant's carelessness coupled with the plaintiff's damage will still not fix the defendant with liability. There must be a connection between the two: the plaintiff's damage must have been caused by the defendant's negligence.

In fact the requirement of causation is a general one applicable to torts actionable on proof of damage, but because most of the difficulties thrown up by the requirement appear in cases of negligence, we consider it here. No doubt the rule conforms to a general concept of what is right and proper: the defendant is only liable if he was at fault and is only required to pay for the damage which he caused. On the other hand, we should not pursue that argument too far because, as we shall see, the law on 'causation' is often shrouded in technicalities.

The law does not stop there, however, for to fix a man with liability for all the damage which is caused by his actions might create an impossible burden. Imagine, for instance, the case of a man who suffers a minor injury in an accident for which the defendant is responsible. The victim is rushed to hospital and given an injection, but, due to a rare blood condition, suffers an adverse reaction to it and dies. Is the defendant to be liable for the death? The law recognises that there must be a limit to a defendant's liability and seeks to find that limit through rules governing remoteness of damage. This problem is not unique to negligence; it occurs in many other areas, most notably in relation to breach of contract. In tort, however, it is closely connected with the problem of causation and so we consider it below.

1   This is not to say that tort does not fulfil a useful role in compensating an actual victim, although it is debatable whether that role could be better fulfilled by some other system. See 11.0.5.
2   See 17.1.6.

Causation in fact

7.3.1   We have said that, in order for the defendant to be liable to the plaintiff, the plaintiff's damage must have been caused by the defendant's negligence. It is not necessary for it to be the sole cause—all events have numerous different causes at different levels of abstraction. What is required is that the defendant's negligence be *one* cause of the plaintiff's loss and be sufficiently closely connected to it that the law should recognise it as a cause and should therefore hold the defendant liable. This issue is often referred to as 'causation in fact' to distinguish it from problems of remoteness, referred to as 'causation in law.'

In many cases there will be no doubt about causation: for instance in a simple road accident case it will be obvious that the plaintiff was injured when the defendant's car mounted the pavement so that, if the car mounted the pavement because the defendant drove negligently, the injury was caused by the negligence. In others, causation may be a matter of factual dispute: for instance, the plaintiff becomes ill after taking medication manufactured by the defendant; the plaintiff may have to show that the make up of the drug caused his illness in scientific terms. In other cases, however, causation may throw up very difficult problems.

The test normally adopted by a court seeking a causal link between the defendant's negligence and the plaintiff's loss is to ask 'would the loss have been suffered but for the defendant's negligence?' and in many cases this so-called 'but for' test will produce acceptable results. Thus, if it is answered in the affirmative, the plaintiff would have suffered loss even if the defendant had not been negligent and the defendant will not be held liable for that loss. In *JEB Fasteners Ltd v Marks, Bloom & Co (a firm)*[1] the court found that the plaintiffs would have taken over a company even if the defendant accountants had not negligently over-valued its stock. The defendants were therefore not liable for the plaintiffs' loss. On the other hand, the 'but for' test may occasionally lead to the imposition of liability as in a case[2] when a lorry jacknifed due to its driver's negligence, and blocked the road; a second lorry coming on the scene was also driven negligently and skidded in trying to avoid the lorry, killing a pedestrian. The court held both drivers liable because the accident would not have happened but for the negligence of both: the negligence of the first defendant had created a dangerous situation which was still continuing at the time of the accident.

It is for the plaintiff to prove his case on a balance of probabilities. The 'but for' test may create difficulties for him especially in cases involving equivocal scientific or medical evidence. There are signs, however, that the courts will be prepared to relax the burden on plaintiffs. In *McGhee v National Coal Board*[3] the plaintiff worked in dusty conditions; the defendant employers provided no shower or bathing facilities and the plaintiff had to cycle home each night caked in dust and sweat. He contracted dermatitis and sued. He could not categorically show that his dermatitis would not have occurred but for the failure to provide showers, but the House of Lords held that it was enough that he could show that their absence had significantly increased his risk of contracting the disease.

Unfortunately the 'but for' test breaks down in cases when a combination of factors cause the plaintiffs' loss. The example often cited is of two fires which break out at the same time and both invade the plaintiff's property to burn down his house. If the plaintiff sues the person responsible for either fire, the defendant could argue that the house would have burned anyway because of the other fire. Obviously, such a result would be unfair to the plaintiff and the law abandons the 'but for' test to allow him to sue either or both fire starters. They in turn would have rights of contribution inter se.[4] The same rule would not apply when only one of the fires was started tortiously: if the plaintiff were then allowed to sue the negligent fire starter he would—possibly—receive a windfall. He would therefore not be allowed to recover. This may seem unfair to the plaintiff: it can be contended that it avoids unfairness to the defendant. One solution might be to allow the plaintiff to recover part of his loss from the defendant in such a case, making a proportionate reduction in his damages to reflect the possibility that he would have suffered the loss anyway.

Similar problems occur when two causes overlap; the plaintiff is injured by A; B then acts so as to aggravate the injury. To what extent are A and B liable? It is well established that a tortfeasor takes his victim as he finds him. This may often be to his disadvantage as in the case of the so called egg shell skull when the plaintiff is especially susceptible to injury; but it may work to his advantage so that if the plaintiff's car needs a respray because of a collision with A but before it is repaired is hit again by B's car in such a way that that collision would have necessitated a respray, B will not be liable at all: he has caused no additional damage.[5] On the other hand, what of the first tortfeasor? Can he argue that, as events turned out, the plaintiff would have been injured later by someone else, and so reduce his own liability? He cannot. In *Baker v Willoughby*[6] the plaintiff's leg was injured by the defendant; later he was involved in a hold up and shot in the same leg. The defendant argued that he should only be liable for the injury up to the time of the shooting, but the court held him fully liable as if the shooting had not happened. The justification is that the plaintiff would otherwise fall between two tortfeasors: the second injurer (the robbers in *Baker*) would only be liable for damaging an already damaged leg and the plaintiff would never get full compensation even if he sued both. However, a different approach is taken when the second injury is not caused tortiously: in that case the defendant responsible for the first injury is only liable for the period until the second.[7]

The problem is that in applying the 'but for' test the court is asking a hypothetical question; only rarely will it be able to answer it with certainty. Atiyah[8] points out the example of a man on the way to the airport who is killed in a collision caused by the negligence of D; the aeroplane the plaintiff was to catch crashes during the flight, killing all passengers. The real question in such a case is should the defendant be held liable for the plaintiff's death in such a case?

1   [1983] 1 All ER 583, CA. Above 7.1.8.
2   *Rouse v Squires* [1973] QB 889 [1973] 2 All ER 903, CA; cf *Dymond v Pearce* [1972] 1 QB 496, [1972] 1 All ER 1142, CA.
3   [1972] 3 All ER 1008, [1973] 1 WLR 1, HL. See also *Hotson v East Berkshire Area Health Authority* [1987] 1 All ER 210, [1987] 2 WLR 287, CA.
4   See 8.1.1.
5   *Performance Cars Ltd v Abrahams* [1962] 1 QB 33, [1961] 3 All ER 413, CA.
6   [1970] AC 467, [1969] 3 All ER 1528, HL.
7   As in *Jobling v Associated Dairies Ltd* [1982] AC 794, [1981] 2 All ER 752, HL.
8   *Accidents, Compensation and the Law* (1980, 3rd edn) p 117.

The chain of causation
7.3.2   We have examined above the problems of causation in situations where two or more events contribute to the plaintiff's loss. A related question is how far, if at all, is a defendant to be held liable for damage sustained by the plaintiff where there is between his careless conduct and the infliction of harm on the plaintiff, independent action by some other party, or, indeed, by the plaintiff himself. In approaching this question the courts and

text book writers use many descriptive tags. We will use 'chain of causation', but it should be borne in mind that the essential question here is '*should* the defendant be held liable for the plaintiff's loss in the light of the intervening event?'. It is linked closely with the problem of remoteness and, as we have seen in looking at the problems of duty of care, is therefore to a large degree a question of policy.

I Breaking the chain: acts of third parties
7.3.3   A court will be reluctant to hold that even a conscious and deliberate act by a third party will break the chain of causation if that act was a reasonably foreseeable result of the defendant's negligence—even if the intervening act was itself tortious or criminal. Thus, when Borstal officers were negligent in their supervision of Borstal trainees allowing them to escape from custody, the officers' employer was held liable in negligence for the damage the boys did when they stole a yacht and rammed another in Poole harbour.[1] Similarly, a decorator left alone in a house was held liable in negligence when he left the house unattended but failed to lock the door. A burglar thus gained access to the house and stole property from it.[2] The justification for such a rule was explained by Lord Reid in *Home Office v Dorset Yacht Co Ltd*:

> 'Unfortunately tortious or criminal action by a third party is often the very kind of thing which is likely to happen as a result of the wrongful careless act of the defendant.'[3]

Such cases have obvious implications for warehousemen, carriers and others in the business of caring for other people's property. Normally such people will be in a contractual relationship with the owner/bailor of goods and their relationship will depend on the contract (including implied terms) so that a suitable exclusion clause can be inserted to restrict liability. However, as we have seen, liability in tort can arise independently of contract so that, for instance, a sub-bailee who has no contract with the owner of property might still be liable to him for its loss and as we shall see, it is more difficult for him to protect himself by use of an exclusion clause.

   In the *Dorset Yacht* case Lord Reid expressed the view that an intervening act would break the chain of causation unless it were 'something very likely to happen'. This is really only an application of the more general rule that the law of negligence requires a person to take reasonable care to guard against reasonably foreseeable consequences and it will suffice as a general rule. However, in some cases a defendant may be held liable even despite a wholly unreasonable and unlikely act of a third party. For instance in *Philco Radio and Television Corpn of Great Britain Ltd v J Spurling Ltd*[4] the defendants were warehousemen who negligently delivered inflammable waste to the plaintiffs. The waste should have gone elsewhere. The boxes were not marked so as to indicate the inflammable nature of their contents. While they were awaiting collection a typist employed by the plaintiffs touched one of the boxes with a lighted cigarette for a 'lark'. The resulting conflagration seriously damaged the plaintiffs' factory. The defendants were held liable and at least one member of the Court of Appeal would have held them liable even had the typist intended to start a fire. The decision can perhaps be explained by the fact that the conduct of the defendants, in misdelivering highly inflammable material in unmarked boxes, was regarded as extremely negligent. On the other hand, all these cases can be criticised: the plaintiffs in *Stansbie v Troman, Home Office v Dorset Yacht Co Ltd* and *Philco v Spurling* were all better placed than the defendants to insure their property.

By contrast, even a foreseeable action may be held to break the chain of causation. In *Quinn v Burch Bros (Builders) Ltd*[5] the plaintiffs negligently failed to provide their employees with proper equipment; the employees therefore improvised an unsafe system of work, and were injured as a result. The employers admitted that this was exactly what they would expect employees to do, but were held not liable: the employees' acts had broken the chain of causation. In this case too the court does not seem to have addressed the policy issues fully, for surely the point of requiring employers to provide proper equipment is to guard against just such an accident.

Where the third party acts in an emergency created by the negligence of the defendant, his action will rarely, if ever, be held to break the chain, even if unforeseeable.[6] It is to be expected that people will panic and behave in unexpected ways in an emergency. A defendant who has created that panic can hardly expect to rely on it to avoid liability for the consequences of his negligence.

1   *Home Office v Dorset Yacht Co Ltd* [1970] AC 1004, HL.
2   *Stansbie v Troman* [1948] 2 KB 48, [1948] 1 All ER 599, CA.
3   At 1030.
4   [1949] 2 KB 33, [1949] 2 All ER 882, CA.
5   [1966] 2 QB 370, [1966] 2 All ER 283, CA.
6   See eg *Scott v Shepherd* (1773) 2 Wm Bl 892; *The Oropesa* [1943] P 32, [1943] 1 All ER 211, CA.

II Breaking the chain: act of plaintiff
7.3.4   A similar approach is taken where the plaintiff is himself responsible for some action between the defendant's negligence and his own resultant loss. If his conduct is reasonable in the circumstances, if it can be treated as having been foreseeable, it will not be held to break the chain of causation. The picture is, however, complicated because prior to 1945 it was a complete defence to a negligence claim for the defendant to show that the plaintiff had caused his own loss. Faced with an 'all or nothing' situation the courts may, on occasion, have stretched legal principle to avoid exonerating a defendant and depriving a plaintiff of all compensation. However, the court now has power to apportion responsibility for an accident and make a reduction to the plaintiff's damages when his conduct has contributed to his loss[1] so that 'contributory negligence' is now only a partial defence to a claim.

Despite the possibility of a reduction of damages for contributory negligence it may still be that in an appropriate case a plaintiff's conduct could be considered so unreasonable as to make him wholly the author of his own misfortune and break the chain of causation. On the other hand there may be cases when the plaintiff's conduct is totally disregarded and does not even reduce his damages. An example of the latter would be when the plaintiff has acted in an emergency created by the defendant;[2] the plaintiff's case will be even stronger if he acted to protect others rather than himself: the law tends to take a generous view of rescuers. However, the plaintiff must be acting in a genuine emergency, rather than a merely inconvenient situation. In a case where a woman found herself locked in a public lavatory and attempted to climb out over the door by climbing on a toilet-roll holder, her conduct was regarded as unreasonable and so led to a reduction in the damages awarded to her for injuries suffered when the toilet-roll holder rotated and deposited her on the floor.[3]

Even apparently irrational behaviour may not affect a plaintiff's claim. In one case the plaintiff suffered depression as a result of injuries caused by the defendant's negligence and took his own life. The defendant was held liable for his death.[4] The case is best regarded as an application of the 'egg shell skull' principle: the defendant was responsible for the damage to the plaintiff's mental and emotional condition even though it went further than might have been expected. By contrast if the plaintiff acts deliberately and rationally but unreasonably, his act will be taken to break the chain: as, for instance, when an injury caused by the defendant left the plaintiff's leg liable to give way unexpectedly. He knew that but attempted to descend a steep flight of steps unaided; he fell and was injured when his leg gave way. He recovered no damages for the fall from the defendant as his decision to descend the stairs broke the chain of causation.[5]

1 Law Reform (Contributory Negligence) Act 1945. See 8.0.2.
2 Eg *Haynes v Harwood* [1935] 1 KB 146, CA.
3 *Sayers v Harlow UDC* [1958] 2 All ER 342, [1958] 1 WLR 623, CA.
4 *Pigney v Pointers Transport Services Ltd* [1957] 2 All ER 807, [1957] 1 WLR 1121.
5 *McKew v Holland, Hannen and Cubitts (Scotland) Ltd* [1969] 3 All ER 1621, HL.

Remoteness of damage

7.3.5   As we have seen, a single act of negligence can have far reaching consequences. It may be months before the snail in the ginger beer bottle poisons anyone or it may be years before the negligence of the builder and building inspector manifests itself in crumbling foundations and cracked walls. Substantial damage may be caused by a single momentary lapse, as in the case of severed cables resulting in economic loss. Imagine a scaffolding pole negligently dropped on a building site. It strikes a spark which ignites a fire destroying the site. The law has tended to baulk at throwing the full consequences of one negligent act onto the shoulders of a defendant. There are several reasons for this reluctance. One is an almost emotional or instinctive feeling that it would be unfair to impose extensive liability on a defendant responsible for only a trivial error. Another is the fear that unlimited or extensive liability might prove crippling to an individual or a business, and a feeling that society should encourage enterprise. The first instinct raises the point that the object of damages in tort is to compensate the plaintiff rather than punish the defendant: and that to restrict compensation may leave the equally innocent plaintiff out of pocket. The second is answered by the fact that a business may be able to spread loss through the community by increased prices, a result which might be thought socially desirable. Both factors take no account of the increased and increasing availability of insurance cover: in some areas such as driving motor vehicles or an employer's liability to his employees, insurance is compulsory; in others liability insurance is widespread.

Nevertheless, the law has used a number of devices for keeping liability within bounds. We have already seen how 'duty of care' is used as a restrictive test: during the 19th and early 20th centuries, at a time of industrial expansion, many restrictions were placed on a tortfeasor's liability to prevent placing excessive burdens on business, in the interests of society as a whole. Thus, for instance, an employee could not sue his employer for the negligence of his colleague: the doctrine of common employment meant that he was taken to have consented to carelessness.[1] Similarly, until 1932, manufacturers were safe from suit by consumers of their defective products. Today, when the potential consequences of a single incident may be even more far reaching, the law still places limits on recovery in certain situations. An important device for limiting liability in this way is the concept of 'remoteness of damage'. It has a close affinity with 'duty of care': indeed, we have seen that in many cases a question may be phrased either as one of remoteness or as one of duty of care. The important point to recognise is the underlying policy basis for the rules of remoteness. Policy perhaps explains why rules of remoteness seem to be less strictly applied to claims for personal injuries than to those for property damage or economic loss: partly because of sympathy for the physically injured plaintiff, but partly perhaps because of the potentially much more extensive loss which can be caused by damage to property—for instance, in the case of the loss of a ship or a building. This policy background was recognised in a famous American case when a judge explained that remoteness means—

> 'that because of convenience, of public policy, of a rough sense of justice, the law arbitrarily declines to trace a series of events beyond a certain point. That is not logic. It is practical politics.'[2]

1 See 9.0.1.
2 Per Andrews J in *Palsgraf v Long Island RR* 248 NY 339 (1928).

Elements of remoteness
7.3.6 There are several aspects of the relationship between the tortfeasor and his victim which a court may seize upon in order to limit recovery of damage which is 'too remote'. The first is the identity of the plaintiff himself: it may be that no damage to the plaintiff was foreseeable at all, regardless of possible harm to others. In a celebrated American case[1] a railway porter negligently pushed a passenger causing him to drop a parcel. Unknown to the porter the parcel contained fireworks which were detonated: the explosion caused a weighing machine some way off on the platform to fall, injuring the plaintiff. An action by the plaintiff claiming damages failed: it was not foreseeable that *he* would suffer any damage. Similar considerations apply to some cases of nervous shock or economic loss; as we have seen, they can equally be analysed as cases of 'no duty of care' and we have dealt with them in that context.[2]

In general a defendant will be held liable for the plaintiff's injuries if it was foreseeable that harm would be caused to a member of a group or category to which the plaintiff belongs. However, as we have seen, in cases of economic loss where damage may be particularly extensive, the courts tend to apply a more restrictive test and require foreseeability of harm to the individual plaintiff.[3]

The remaining factors all relate to the damage suffered by the plaintiff. The court could limit recovery by reference to the type of damage suffered, the manner in which it was caused or its extent. We will look at each of these in turn. We will see that the general test applied by the courts is that of foreseeability: in general a defendant is not liable for unforeseeable harm. It is important to distinguish 'foreseeability' in this context from 'reasonable foreseeability' in relation to negligence itself. In that context, as we have seen, foreseeability is used as an indicator of carelessness: if some harm is foreseeable then the plaintiff's failure to avoid it may be negligent. Here foreseeability fulfils a different role: if the particular type of damage suffered was not foreseeable the defendant is not liable for it even though he was negligent because some (different) type of damage was foreseeable.

1 *Palsgraf v Long Island RR* 248 NY 339 (1928).
2 See 7.1.0.
3 This is the approach taken in *Junior Books Ltd v Veitchi Co Ltd* and *Muirhead v Industrial Tank Specialities Ltd*. However, a more liberal approach was taken in *JEB Fasteners v Marks Bloom & Co (a firm)*. See 7.1.5.

The kind of damage
7.3.7   There is no doubt that the law does impose restrictions on the kind of damage for which a defendant is liable. What is less clear is just what the terms of that restriction are. In the case of *Re Polemis Furness and Withey & Co*[1] the Court of Appeal held that if some damage to the particular plaintiff was foreseeable, the defendant was liable for all damage which resulted directly from his negligence. A stevedore carelessly dropped a plank into the hold of a ship. It was foreseeable that that would do physical damage to the ship. However, unknown to anyone the hold was full of petrol vapours from a previous cargo. The plank struck a spark, igniting the vapours and destroying the ship. The defendants were held liable. Physical damage was foreseeable; all that was unforeseeable was its extent.

However, doubt was cast on that by the subsequent Privy Council decision in *The Wagon Mound*.[2] The defendants were responsible for a spill of oil which resulted in a slick in a harbour. The slick was carried by tide to the plaintiffs' jetty where welding work was being done on two ships. The plaintiffs stopped welding, fearing a fire, but were advised by experts that there was no fire risk from oil on water. They therefore resumed work and the jetty and the two ships were destroyed by fire when the oil was ignited. They sued the defendants but it was held that the defendants were not liable. The Privy Council held that damage by fire was unforeseeable; damage by oil pollution could have been anticipated but the damage which had been caused was of a different kind.

The Wagon Mound test then holds the defendant liable only for damage of a kind which was foreseeable. In fact, the only difference between that and the *Polemis* test is in the definition of 'kind of damage': *Polemis* categorises damage broadly as 'physical damage'; *The Wagon Mound* differentiates between different types of physical damage, between oil fouling and fire. Moreover, as we shall see, decisions since *The Wagon Mound* whilst purporting to apply that rule, have not done so consistently.

Given that *The Wagon Mound* test is correct, how foreseeable must a type of damage be before the plaintiff can sue for it? In a second case arising from *The Wagon Mound* incident[3] the Privy Council held that the defendant is liable provided that the particular kind of harm was foreseeable as 'a real risk . . . which . . . a reasonable man . . . would not brush aside as far-fetched.' In that case, which was brought by the owners of the two ships damaged by fire in the incident, expert evidence showed that there *was* a slight foreseeable possibility of fire; that was enough, held the Privy Council, to make the defendants liable: fire was foreseeable, fire was what had happened.

113

As we remarked above, whilst *The Wagon Mound* test is easy to put in words it has proved difficult to apply in subsequent cases. Thus some cases have taken a broad view of 'type of loss', drawing no distinction between frostbite through driving an unheated van over a long distance in winter and other personal injury due to driving in such conditions, which was foreseeable;[4] others have drawn fine distinctions between types of injury so that a warehouseman who contracted a rare and unforeseeable disease from contact with rat urine could not obtain damages even though it was foreseeable that he might suffer from rat bites.[5] Similarly, some cases have held that the defendant is only liable if the manner in which the plaintiff suffered his injury was foreseeable; thus where an asbestos lid fell into a vat of molten metal it was foreseeable that it might cause a splash and injure the plaintiff; there was no splash but an unforeseeable chemical reaction followed and produced an eruption a few moments later. It was held the plaintiff could not obtain damages.[6] By contrast, in *Hughes v Lord Advocate*[7] the plaintiff, a small boy, entered a workman's tent and knocked a paraffin lamp into a hole, causing an explosion. The House of Lords held that the plaintiff could recover damages: it was foreseeable that he might suffer burns; the House refused to distinguish between burns and an explosion stressing that the lamp was a known source of danger.[8]

1   [1921] 3 KB 560, CA.
2   *Overseas Tankship (UK) Ltd v Morts Dock and Engineering Co Ltd, The Wagon Mound* [1961] AC 388, [1961] 1 All ER 404, PC.
3   *Overseas Tankship (UK) Ltd v Miller SS Co Pty (The Wagon Mound (No 2))* [1967] 1 AC 617, [1966] 2 All ER 709, PC.
4   *Bradford v Robinson Rentals Ltd* [1967] 1 All ER 267, [1967] 1 WLR 337.
5   *Tremain v Pike* [1969] 3 All ER 1303, [1969] 1 WLR 1556.
6   *Doughty v Turner Manufacturing Co Ltd* [1964] 1 QB 518, [1964] 1 All ER 98, CA.
7   [1963] AC 837, [1963] 1 All ER 705, HL.
8   Indeed, the lamp was a positive attraction to small children.

Extent of damage
7.3.8   It is well established that, provided the type of damage in question was foreseeable, the defendant is liable for all the damage of that type which in fact results, no matter that it may be far more extensive than might have been anticipated. Often the line between 'extensive damage of the same type' (recoverable) and 'damage of a different type' is somewhat fine. Thus in *Vacwell Engineering Ltd v BDH Chemicals Ltd*[1] the defendants delivered a gas to the plaintiffs in glass ampoules; it was known that the gas would react with water in a violent way. The ampoules had labels affixed to them and a visiting Russian scientist put a consignment into a sink of water to remove the labels. One broke and the chemical reacted with water but more violently than expected: the explosion killed the scientist and severely damaged the factory. The court held that a violent explosive reaction was foreseeable, as was some damage to property, and held the defendants liable for the full extent of the damage.

The rule that the defendant is liable for the full unforeseeable extent of damage of a foreseeable type applies even when the damage is more extensive because of some existing condition of the plaintiff. This is the so called 'egg shell skull' rule: if X strikes Y a light blow on the head but, because Y has a thin skull, the blow causes serious injury or death, X is fully liable even though had Y had a normally thick skull he would have received no more than a bump and a headache. We have seen the same rule applied to 'egg shell personalities',[2] and it would apply equally to claims for property damage. However, the courts have refused to apply the same rule to claims for economic loss. In *Liesbosch, Dredger (Owners) v SS Edison (Owners)*[3] the plaintiffs' dredger was sunk due to the defendants' negligence. The plaintiffs were in the middle of a contract which included penalty clauses for delayed completion. They were financially unable, however, to buy a replacement at once and therefore hired one at a high cost. They claimed damages but the Privy Council refused to take account of their lack of funds and rejected the claim for damages to cover the high cost of hire. A clear line was drawn between cases of physical damage and personal injury on the one hand and economic loss on the other, although little justification was given. Perhaps this is just one more example of the reluctance of the courts to countenance recovery of damages in tort for purely economic loss. The law may recognise an egg-shell skull or wall, even an 'egg-shell personality', but not an 'egg-shell wallet':

> 'in the varied web of affairs the law must abstract some consequences as relevant, not, perhaps on grounds of pure logic, but simply for practical reasons.'[4]

1 [1971] 1 QB 88, [1969] 3 All ER 1681.
2 See *Pigney v Pointers Transport Services Ltd* [1957] 2 All ER 807, [1957] 1 WLR 1121.
3 [1933] AC 449, HL.
4 Per *Lord Wright* at p 158. There are signs of a greater willingness to take account of a plaintiff's financial circumstances: see eg *Martindale v Duncan* [1973] 2 All ER 355, [1973] 1 WLR 574, CA. (P waited for insurance company approval before having car repaired and in the meantime incurred hire charges) *Dodd Properties (Kent) Ltd v Canterbury City Council* [1980] 1 All ER 928, [1980] 1 WLR 433, CA.

Remoteness in contract and tort

7.3.9 It remains to say a little by way of comparison between the rules of remoteness of damage which apply in tort cases and those applicable in claims for breach of contract. This is important because of the possibility, as we have seen, that the plaintiff may be able to bring parallel claims for breach of contract or in negligence. In contract cases remoteness is governed by the rule in *Hadley v Baxendale*[1] as explained in subsequent cases.[2] That allows the plaintiff to recover for (a) damage arising naturally—in the ordinary course of events—and (b) damage due to special circumstances but only if the plaintiff knew, or ought to have known, of those circumstances at the time the contract was made. In either case, provided the type of loss was foreseeable, the defendant is liable for all of it, regardless of its extent.[3] However, in *Koufos v Czarnikow*[4] the House of Lords explained that the type of loss must be foreseeable as a 'serious possibility' or 'very substantial possibility' and that this test requires a higher degree of foreseeability than that which applies in tort. In *H Parsons (Livestock) Ltd v Uttley Ingham & Co Ltd*[5] Lord Denning expressed the view that in cases of physical loss the test of remoteness should be the same in contract and tort, and that the less strict tort test from *The Wagon Mound (No 2)* should apply. He pointed out that *Koufos v Czarnikow* and other contract cases on remoteness dealt with financial loss, the most common consequence of a breach of contract (especially a commercial contract).

Whilst there is much to be said for this approach in that it seems illogical that the plaintiff's chances of recovery should vary according to how he words his claim, there is no other judicial support for this view at present. In *Parsons* the other members of the Court of Appeal reached the same result by a different route. Moreover, as we have seen, since *Parsons* was decided the law of tort has come increasingly to recognise claims for financial loss, increasing the possibility of overlap between contract and tort.

1   (1854) 23 L J Ex 179.
2   See 17.1.3.
3   The majority view in *H Parsons (Livestock) Ltd v Uttley Ingham & Co Ltd* [1978] QB 791, [1978] 1 All ER 525, CA.
4   [1969] 1 AC 350, [1967] 3 All ER 686, HL.
5   [1978] QB 791, [1978] 1 All ER 525, CA.

Chapter 8
Defences and Remedies

8.0.0 The defendant in a tort action may always seek to avoid liability by denying an element of the plaintiff's case. For instance, in a negligence case the defendant may deny that he owed a duty of care, or that he was careless at all, or that his negligence caused loss to the plaintiff. In defamation he might deny that he made a statement at all, or that it was defamatory. In addition there are certain specialised defences applicable to individual torts —most significantly to defamation—and we have examined these in their appropriate contexts. However, there are a number of more generalised defences which apply to negligence and to other torts, and it is to these that we now turn.

Inevitable accident, act of God and necessity
8.0.1 In certain situations all three of the above may amount to defences, but they are of limited application in negligence cases. Inevitable accident really amounts to a denial of negligence: it might be pleaded as such in a case when the plaintiff relies on res ipsa loquitur and the defendant cannot show how the accident happened. He is then reduced to showing that he took all reasonable care and the accident must have been truly an 'inevitable accident'.

'Act of God' refers to an accident which results from the operation of natural forces. It is most often encountered as a defence to a claim under the rule in *Rylands v Fletcher*.[1]

Necessity may be a defence to certain torts: for instance it might apply in trespass to justify an operation on an unconscious person: the operation would otherwise be a battery (doctors prefer to have consent from someone). It might also provide a defence to an assault or battery, for instance in a case of self-defence: the force used by the defendant must then be proportionate to the force used against him which he seeks to repel. However, it is difficult to imagine an application of necessity in a negligence case.

1   See 10.0.9.

Contributory negligence
8.0.2 It is a defence, albeit a partial one, to a negligence claim to show that the plaintiff was himself at fault and partly the author of his own misfortunes. We noted above that it used to be the law that, if a person was himself

117

at fault and contributed to his own loss, he could not make a successful negligence claim at all. Since 1945 the court has had power to take account of a plaintiff's negligence which contributes to his injury and to reduce his damages accordingly. The Law Reform (Contributory Negligence) Act 1945 provides in s 1 that:

> 'When any person suffers damage as the result partly of his own fault and partly of the fault of any other person or persons, a claim in respect of that damage shall not be defeated by reason of the fault of the person suffering the damage, but the damages recoverable in respect thereof shall be reduced to such extent as the court thinks just and equitable having regard to the claimants' share in the responsibility for the damage.'

The defence is clearly available in cases of negligence and analogous cases under the Occupier's Liability Acts. It does not apply to conversion or trespass to goods and its application in other torts is open to question, although it probably does apply in nuisance. However, what is clear is that the defence may not be used in a case arising solely in contract: what is unresolved is how this rule applies where the plaintiff may claim in tort or contract, especially in view of the dicta in the *Tai Hing Cotton Mill Case* that the plaintiff should claim in contract only: it seems that a plaintiff may have his own contributory negligence ignored by suing in contract, as the Privy Council preferred in *Tai Hing*.

If the defence does apply, the court must first ask if the plaintiff was at fault, and second, if that fault contributed to his injury or loss. In a negligence case the plaintiff's fault will most often be a failure to take reasonable care for his own safety and the considerations mentioned above in relation to breach of duty generally in negligence, apply equally here, subject to the caveat that the courts seem to accept a lower standard of care from the plaintiff for his own safety than they would expect of a defendant for the safety of others. Second, the court must decide to what degree the plaintiff's lack of care contributed to his loss. It is worth stressing that what is in question is not whether he contributed to the accident, but whether he contributed to his own *loss or injury*. Thus it has been held that a motor-cyclist's failure to wear a crash helmet[1] and a motorist's failure to wear a seat belt[2] both amount to contributory negligence: both tend to exacerbate accident injuries although no one could say that failure to wear a seat belt makes a collision more likely.

If the plaintiff has been at fault and thereby contributed to his own loss the court must reflect that contribution by making a reduction in his damages, by such amount as is just and equitable. For instance, it has been held that a motorcyclist's failure to wear a helmet should generally lead to a 15% reduction in damages;[3] a motorist who fails to wear a seat belt could expect a 15%–25% reduction of damages for injuries suffered in a collision.[4] The court approaches this question by deciding what sum it would otherwise award, the extent of the plaintiff's contribution to his loss expressed as a percentage or fraction, and then reduces the damages by that fraction. Thus, for example, a motorist injured in a collision caused by the negligence of another driver, but who was not wearing a seat belt, could be found to be 25% contributorily negligent. If the court would have awarded £2,000 for his injuries he will actually receive £1,500.

Finally, we should mention the possibility of identification. In certain

118

situations one person is identified with the negligence of another. The most common example is an employer's identification with the contributory negligence of his employee. Thus if an employee is involved in a collision whilst driving his employer's van, and the court finds the employee 25% contributorily negligent, the employer can sue the other driver (who, ex hypothesi, is 75% to blame) but will have his damages reduced by 25%.

1 *O'Connell v Jackson* [1972] 1 QB 270, [1971] 3 All ER 129, CA.
2 *Froom v Butcher* [1976] QB 286, [1975] 3 All ER 520 CA.
3 *O'Connell v Jackson* cited above.
4 *Froom v Butcher*, cited above.

Volenti non fit injuria

8.0.3 It would seem unjust if a person could sue another for damage for which he himself was wholly responsible. The law has many devices to avoid allowing such claims: the chain of causation may be broken, the plaintiff may be said to be 100% contributorily negligent; or he may be taken to have excused the defendant by consenting to what would otherwise be a tort: volenti non fit injuria. If consent does apply, it is a total defence to a claim. Thus a patient who consents to an operation cannot sue his surgeon, even though the operation would otherwise be a technical battery. In this area it has recently been held that English law, unlike US law, has no concept of 'informed consent'; a surgeon's failure fully to inform his patient of the nature and risks of an operation will not vitiate the consent so as to make him liable in trespass but might amount to a negligent breach of duty by the surgeon.[1] Similarly one sportsman cannot sue another for injuries sustained whilst playing the game—at least for injuries sustained whilst obeying the rules of the game. Players do not consent to deliberate foul play.

However, consent no longer has much application in the important area of negligence. During the period of expanding industrialisation, the defence served an important role in limiting the potential liability of employers,[2] in the guise of the doctrine of 'common employment' which held that an employee agreed to run the risk of negligence by his fellow employees and so could not claim against the employer. This fiction was based on the notion that the employee could choose whether or not to work with his colleagues—but, the choice was really a stark one: take it (and work) or leave it (and be out of a job).

The fiction of common employment was abandoned by legislation in 1948.[3] The use of consent as a defence to claims by employees had been restricted since 1891 by the House of Lords in *Smith v Baker & Sons*.[4] The plaintiff worked in a quarry under a crane which regularly swung heavy loads above his head. His protests to his employer had no effect and he was eventually injured by a load falling from the crane. It was held that his decision to carry on working did not amount to consent and he was entitled to claim against his employer. In fact, the 'lessening need for protecting industry from meeting the cost of its accidents'[5] (due in part to the requirement for employers to have compulsory insurance against employees' injury claims) has led to the virtual disappearance of the defence; nevertheless in exceptional cases it may still be invoked even between employer and employee, as in one case[6] where two shot firers chose deliberately to disregard both their employer's instructions and a statutory obligation which was placed on them personally. They were injured as a result of their corner cutting and each sought to sue the employer as liable for the default of his colleague. The court held that each had consented to the breach of duty by the other and so could not claim.[7]

1   *Sidaway v Board of Directors of Bethlaem Royal Hospital and the Maudsley Hospital* [1985] AC 871.
2   Claims by employees were at that time probably the most likely to be brought against employers due to the high risk of accidents in young industries, and were therefore a serious threat to the development of industry.
3   Law Reform (Personal Injuries) Act 1948, s 1.
4   [1891] AC 325, HL.
5   Fleming, *An Introduction to the Law of Torts* (1985, 2nd edn) p 160.
6   *ICI Ltd v Shatwell* [1965] AC 656, [1964] 2 All ER 999, HL.
7   The case is exceptional because the relevant statutory duty was laid on shot firers personally.

Consent and negligence today

8.0.4   If consent is to operate as a defence at all the plaintiff must have actually consented to the risk in question. It is not enough that he merely knows of its existence—although in certain situations a notice warning of a danger may effectively preclude a claim by giving the plaintiff the chance to protect himself.[1] Further, consent must be genuine and freely given. The courts have regularly refused to allow consent to be invoked against rescuers who come to the aid of persons put in danger by a defendant's negligence:[2] after all, it is in the public interest to encourage public spirited attempts at rescue.

It is difficult to apply consent to negligence which consists of carelessness but it may apply where a deliberate course of conduct is held negligent. However, 'consent' may be invoked to prevent a duty of care arising in the first place: thus it is said that sportsmen owe no duty of care to spectators injured by ordinary hazards of the game.[3] On occasion, however, consent may come into play after a defendant has been negligent: in such a case the plaintiff with full knowledge of the negligence and danger voluntarily assumes the risk of that danger. In one case[4] workmen in a scrapyard found an unexploded bomb amongst the scrap. They rolled it to a colleague, the plaintiff, and encouraged him to hit it with a hammer; he did so and attempted to sue his employer. The court held that in any case the employer was not liable for practical jokes committed by employees, but added that this would have been a case of volenti.

Such examples are, however, rare. Contributory negligence is far more flexible and is increasingly preferred. Moreover the Unfair Contract Terms Act has reduced the possibility of relying on notices to reduce liability. The Act provides[5] that as regards liability arising in the course of a business, a person cannot by reference to any notice or contract term exclude or limit his liability for personal injury or death caused by negligence, which is defined to include common law negligence and liability under the Occupiers' Liability Act 1957 as well as liability arising under a contractual obligation to take reasonable care. Liability for other loss, including damage to property, can be excluded if the exclusion is reasonable. A defendant might still seek to argue that an effective exclusion clause brought the risk in question to the notice of the plaintiff and that he therefore consented to it. The Act therefore expressly provides that this is not to be the case.[6] However, a notice may still be effective: under the Occupiers' Liability Acts 1957 and 1984 an occupier of premises owes duties of care to persons coming onto his premises; a notice giving a clear warning of a danger which gives a visitor (or trespasser) chance to protect himself might be sufficient to discharge the occupiers' duty of care.[7]

1 The notice may discharge the duty placed on an occupier of premises under the Occupiers Liability Act 1957: see 9.2.0.
2 Eg *Haynes v Harwood* [1935] 1 KB 146, CA.
3 *Murray v Harringay Arena Ltd* [1951] 2 KB 529, [1951] 2 All ER 320n, CA.
4 *O'Reilly v National Rail and Tramway Appliances Ltd* [1966] 1 All ER 499.
5 Unfair Contract Terms Act 1977, s 2(1). See 18.0.6.
6 Ibid, s 2(3).
7 See 9.2.0.

Limitation of actions

8.0.5 A person who claims that he has been legally wronged by another cannot wait indefinitely to bring his claim to court. The law requires him to commence his action within a certain period and provides that if he does not do so his claim will be statute barred and any action he may bring will fail. There are sound reasons for such a rule: it would be unfair to a potential defendant to force him to live under the perpetual threat of litigation and, more practically, there is a need to get actions into court as quickly as possible, whilst evidence is still fresh. This is particularly important when a case may turn on oral testimony rather than documentary evidence, given the frailty of human memory. The Limitation Act 1980 therefore provides that claims in tort (and contract) must be brought within six years of the plaintiff's cause of action arising,[1] with the exception that personal injury actions (where eye witness testimony tends to play a more important role) must be brought within three years.[2] It is important to note that the limitation period does not commence until the plaintiff's cause of action is complete: in tort that is when the plaintiff suffers damage. The result is that the limitation period for tort claims tends to be more generous than that for contract claims, where the cause of action arises at the date of breach of contract. This distinction can produce anomalies when a plaintiff may choose to sue either in contract or in tort—as is often the case in professional negligence cases.

Nevertheless, the limitation periods are relatively generous: moreover, the plaintiff only has to commence proceedings within the period. If he sues in the High Court he need only issue a writ from the court office; he then has a further year before he must serve the writ; and even thereafter, most civil litigation is notoriously slow.

Because of the importance of oral eye witness testimony in cases which involve a claim for damages for personal injury, the 1980 Act requires any action to be commenced within three years of the cause of action. However, such a short period (and indeed even the full six year period) can work to the serious disadvantage of a plaintiff who has suffered 'latent damage' which does not manifest itself until later. The problem first became apparent in claims by workers who had contracted pneumoconiosis due to working in dusty conditions. By the time their disease was diagnosed and attributed to the default of a former employer, it was too late to sue. However, the 1980 Act now protects plaintiffs in that position by providing that in such cases the three year period will not start to run until the plaintiff either knows or ought to know of his condition, his right to sue and that it is attributable to the particular defendant.[3] In deciding what the plaintiff ought to

121

know the court will take account of what the plaintiff could have discovered had he taken such professional advice as a reasonable man would have taken.[4] Further, the court has an absolute discretion to allow an action to proceed even though commenced outside the limitation period:[5] the discretion might be exercised in favour of a plaintiff whose claim was late because of the negligent default of his advisers—although in such a case the court might prefer to leave him to sue his advisers in negligence instead, to discourage professional incompetence.

Similar problems can arise in the case of negligently constructed buildings; it may be years before inadequate foundations are revealed as cracks in the walls. The Limitation Act 1980 as originally drawn did not deal with this point and in *Pirelli General Cable Works Ltd v Oscar Faber & Partners*[6] the House of Lords held that time begins to run against the owner of a defective building from the time when damage occurs, even though he does not discover it then and could not reasonably do so. In the *Pirelli* case therefore time began to run from the time cracks first appeared in a chimney, which evidence showed, must have been in 1970, even though the cracks were not discovered until 1977. Moreover, in extreme cases a building might be so defective as to be 'doomed from the start' in which case time would run from the date of its completion.

Such a rule could obviously work great hardship to a potential plaintiff, especially if one bears in mind the financial value of buildings—domestic and commercial. The Latent Damage Act 1986[7] therefore provides an alternative to the normal six years rule in all cases other than personal injury claims. When damage cannot be discovered immediately a plaintiff must bring a claim within three years from the time when he discovers the damage or, when with reasonable care he should have discovered it. In any case the action must be brought within fifteen years of completion of the building. There remains the problem of the building which is 'doomed from the start'. However, it seems that examples of such edifices will be rare[8] and, in such a case the damage would probably become apparent within six years of construction.

1   S 2.
2   S 11.
3   S 11(4), s 14.
4   S 14(3).
5   Limitation Act 1980, s 33.
6   [1983] 2 AC 1, [1983] 1 All ER 65, HL.
7   Amending the Limitation Act 1980.
8   See *Ketteman v Hansen Properties Ltd* [1985] 1 All ER 352, [1984] 1 WLR 1274, CA.

Remedies—damages

8.1.0   The principal remedy in most tort claims—and almost the only remedy in negligence cases—is an award of damages. The court orders the defendant—or, in fact in many cases, his insurance company—to pay a sum of money to the plaintiff to compensate him for the injuries he has suffered. The aim of an award of damages is to compensate the plaintiff for his loss and the award should seek to put him in the position he would have been in had the tort not been committed. In contrast, an award in a contract case seeks to put the plaintiff in the position he would have been in had the contract been performed,[1] reflecting the fact that a breach of contract claim is about something that should have been done but wasn't whereas a tort action is about something which should not have been done but was. Thus as a general rule a plaintiff cannot sue in tort if he has suffered no damage, although there are exceptional cases like libel and trespass of torts actionable per se. In exceptional cases, in fact, a court may award the plaintiff damages over and above the amount needed to compensate him. In *Rookes v Barnard*[2] however, the House of Lords held that such awards of exemplary or punitive damages should rarely be given: their most important use is, as we have seen, to prevent a defendant making a calculated profit out of his tort. A court may also award aggravated damages, when the award is increased to reflect the defendant's deliberate affront to the plaintiff's feelings. On the other hand the compensatory nature of damages is reflected by the power to award nominal damages—for instance when the plaintiff has suffered no real loss (as in a simple trespass to land causing no damage to property) or even contemptuous damages of 1 p, generally in cases of defamation when the court disapproves of the plaintiff bringing a 'technical' claim. Normally the plaintiff awarded contemptuous damages will also be left to pay his own costs.

An award of money is of course ideally suited to a claim for economic loss. Thus, for instance, the owner of a factory whose production is tortiously interrupted could claim for the lost profits whilst production was held up. The plaintiff will, of course, have to prove his loss, but subject to that he can recover all his lost profits and also other sums reasonably incurred in trying to minimise his loss.

Claims for damage to property also present relatively few problems. Property can normally be valued fairly accurately and in most cases an award of money will enable a person to replace or repair property damaged or destroyed. Thus if property is destroyed a plaintiff can claim the difference between the value of the property immediately before and its value (normally only scrap) after destruction. It should be stressed, however, that the award is not the cost of a replacement: if the plaintiff's old car is written off he is entitled to the value of an old car, not the cost of buying a new one. This is perhaps more important in the case of industrial machinery: there is, after all, a thriving market in second hand cars, but the business which loses an old but important machine may have to buy a new one to replace it. Nevertheless, damages will only cover the value of the old, destroyed machine. By contrast, if property is only damaged the plaintiff can recover the reasonable costs of repair. Moreover it seems that if he reasonably delays repairing, for instance whilst awaiting an insurance assessment[3] and approval, and the cost of repairs escalates in the meantime, he can claim the cost of repairs at the date they are effected. Furthermore, he is entitled to compensation for loss of use of his property while it is repaired—normally the cost of hiring a replacement. In the event of damage or destruction the plaintiff can also claim the additional costs of transporting a replacement to site, profits lost due to delay and so on.[4]

Claims for damages for personal injuries present altogether different problems. We refer below to the difficulties of fixing a monetary value on damage to life and limb. Given that the courts can only seek to compensate the plaintiff in financial terms, there remains the problem of calculating an award. A person run down in the street or injured at work suffers immediate pain; he may suffer long term effects such as a limp or even a personality change; moreover he will probably be absent from work for a time; he may incur expenses visiting hospital and so on; he may never be fit to return to his former job. The award of damages must seek to compensate him for all these things and, in fact, awards of damages for personal injuries are normally divided into two heads: general and special damages. The award of general damages covers those items which cannot be valued exactly at the time of trial: it thus includes a sum for pain, suffering and loss of amenity (such as the plaintiff's inability to play football after a leg injury) and the judges are guided by awards for similar injuries in other contemporary cases. It also includes a sum for future loss of earnings. In assessing future loss the court must assess how much the plaintiff would have earned had he not been injured, and then deduct the amount he is likely to actually earn—for instance he might be incapable of work at all; or he might have had to take a less senior job with diminished pay and prospects. To calculate future loss, the court will assess what the plaintiff's annual net earnings would have been had he not been injured, deduct any actual earnings, and multiply by an appropriate figure in the light of the plaintiff's age to reflect the remainder of his working life. However, since the plaintiff receives his damages in one lump sum and can invest it to earn interest, and to allow for the ordinary hazards of life, the 'multiplier' will be less than the number of years he can expect to work. On the other hand, if the accident has reduced the plaintiff's life expectancy, he is entitled to be compensated for his prospective lost earnings on the basis of his life expectancy before the accident.[5] Otherwise the defendant would pay less to a plaintiff who suffered serious injury reducing his life expectancy than to one who suffered only minor injuries.

Special damages are awarded for losses which can be valued more or less exactly at the date of trial. As well as damages for property damaged or destroyed in the accident, they will include expenses for travelling to hospital and out patient appointments, the cost of medication[6] and, of course, wages or salary lost to the date of trial. The award for lost wages is based on net wages; moreover, to allow the plaintiff to claim for the whole of his wages would over compensate him because he will normally be entitled to some state benefits during his absence from work. Certain benefits are therefore deducted in full, or in part, from the damages awarded.[7]

We have seen how the Limitation Act requires a plaintiff to bring an action within a fairly short time after an accident. This could cause difficulties since in many cases the full long term effects of an accident may not be known for some time: for instance, will the plaintiff recover? Will he develop complications in later life? Often the medical answer to such questions can only be 'maybe'. The plaintiff in such a case would have to commence his action within three years of his injury and would be left with the option of delaying bringing his case to trial, or accepting a speculative award. To alleviate such problems the court now has power to make an award of provisional damages,[8] when the plaintiff is compensated immediately on the assumption that a named complication does not develop, but the court order allows him to return to court at a later date if such condition does develop.

We have also noted that often civil cases take a considerable time to come to trial: in the meantime the plaintiff is out of pocket, injured but uncompensated. To ameliorate his position the Rules of Court allow him to apply to the court for an interim award of damages in personal injury cases where he is likely to succeed; and in any case, the court has power to award interest on damages awarded at trial to reflect the fact that the plaintiff has been deprived of the use of the money pending trial.

1 *Hadley v Baxendale* (1854) 23 LJ Ex 179. See 17.1.3.
2 [1964] AC 1129, [1964] 1 All ER 367, HL.
3 *Martindale v Duncan* [1973] 2 All ER 355, [1973] 1 WLR 574, CA.
4 Such damages were allowed in the *Liesbosch Dredger (Owners) v SS Edison (Owners)* [1933] AC 449, HL, subject to a deduction for living expenses in the lost years.
5 The so-called 'lost years': *Pickett v British Rail Engineering Ltd* [1980] AC 136, [1979] 1 All ER 774, HL.
6 He is entitled to claim the cost of private health care if he chooses to be treated privately rather than on the NHS.
7 Law Reform (Personal Injuries) Act 1948, s 2(1).
8 Supreme Court Act 1981, s 32A.

Joint tortfeasors

8.1.1 We have already seen how two or more persons may be jointly liable to the plaintiff for one injury. This can occur when the negligence of separate parties combines to cause one injury to the plaintiff as when, for instance, two cars collide and injure a pedestrian: in that case the two drivers are concurrently liable for the plaintiff's injuries. Alternatively, it can occur when two parties are both liable for the same injury as when they act deliberately together to injure the plaintiff, or when an employer is vicariously liable for the torts of his employee; in that case the two are said to be jointly liable. In either case the plaintiff may choose to sue either tortfeasor or both together;[1] in practice he will generally choose to sue both together, because, whilst if he chooses to sue only one he may later commence a new action against the other—perhaps because he has obtained a judgment which remains unpaid: he will normally be penalised by not being awarded costs in the second action.

If two or more joint tortfeasors are found to be jointly liable to the plaintiff, he can choose to enforce any judgment he obtains against any one individual. In practice, of course, he will choose to enforce judgment against the defendant best able to pay: in a case of vicarious liability this will normally be the employer who is more likely to be insured. This rule protects the plaintiff against the possibility that one defendant might be insolvent. However, where two or more persons are jointly or concurrently liable to the plaintiff for the same damage they are entitled to claim contributions inter se;[2] thus if the plaintiff chooses to sue only one of the parties responsible for his loss, the defendant can take third party proceedings against any person who is liable to contribute to the damages. In practice the plaintiff in such a case would join in the third party as a second defendant to his action. The court must then apportion liability for the plaintiff's loss between the joint or concurrent tortfeasors on such basis as seems just and equitable.[3] This apportionment will not affect the plaintiff's right to enforce judgment against whichever defendant he chooses—unless one is found 100% responsible; it only affects the obligations of the co-defendants amongst themselves. However, it will be obvious that if the plaintiff has enforced judgment in full against one defendant because his co-tortfeasors are insolvent, the right of contribution will be worthless for practical purposes.

1 Civil Liability (Contribution) Act 1978, s 3.
2 Ibid, s 1(1).
3 Ibid, s 2(1).

Injunctions

8.1.2 Damages are awarded to compensate a plaintiff who has suffered harm due to a defendant's conduct; of course, in many cases it would be preferable to prevent harm occurring. The civil law may seek to do this by use of an injunction; a court order requiring a named person to do something (mandatory injunction) or to desist from doing something (prohibitory injunction). For obvious reasons injunctions are not suitable to negligence actions: various statutes require motorists to drive carefully, manufacturers to produce safe products and employers to take care for the safety of employees; they do not prevent accidents. On the other hand an injunction is singularly appropriate to certain torts—to bring an end to a nuisance, to prevent a potential 'passing off' or to restrain unlawful industrial action. Since an injunction is a court order, failure to obey it will be a contempt of court and may result in the imprisonment of the defendant in contempt.

However, useful as they are, injunctions are not available 'as of right'. An injunction is an equitable remedy and is therefore only available subject to certain restrictions. It will not be awarded if damages would be an adequate remedy for the plaintiff; and he may lose his right to an injunction if he delays too long before going to court, or if he himself is in some way blameworthy.

Obviously the value of an injunction lies in the ability to make a 'preemptive strike': to restrain a defendant before he causes harm. How can that be done, in the light of the comments we have made about the time it takes to get a civil case to trial in the High Court? The answer lies in the courts' power to award an interlocutory injunction at a very early stage of the proceedings without a full trial. The plaintiff can obtain such an order which effectively preserves the status quo if he can show he has an arguable case and that the balance of convenience favours the granting of an injunction.[1] This is not a strict test and to protect defendants against groundless injunctions the court will normally require a plaintiff who seeks an interlocutory injunction to give an undertaking to the court to pay compensation to the defendant if the plaintiff does not succeed at the eventual trial.[2]

An injunction is a court order; often a party against whom an injunction is sought will voluntarily agree to submit to a restriction, at least where the plaintiff gives a suitable undertaking in damages. In such a case the defendant will give an undertaking to the court in terms similar to those of the injunction sought against him. Such an undertaking has the same effect as an injunction insofar as a breach of it is a contempt of court and punishable as disobedience of an injunction.

1 *American Cynamid Co v Ethicon Ltd* [1975] AC 396, [1975] 1 All ER 504, HL.
2 Because in an industrial dispute one interlocutory injunction may decide the issue once and for all, the courts adopt a more strict approach to a plaintiff's request for an interlocutory order in such a case.

Chapter 9

Special Forms of Liability in Negligence

9.0.0 The general rules of negligence which we have already examined are modified in a number of situations. Some of these are so important that they require separate examination.

Employer's liabilities
9.0.1 Industry has an enormous potential for harming both those who work in it, its customers and consumers and even innocent members of the public. Large, powerful and fast-moving machinery may be inherently dangerous, or become dangerous through poor maintenance or improper use; workers doing boring or repetitive tasks may become inattentive or may simply feel 'under the weather'. Moreover, it is not just industrial work which carries the capacity to injure. Office workers can suffer serious injuries lifting packages or furniture, or simply through using unsafe furniture or spending too much time using a visual display unit, and whilst the capacity of office work or light manufacturing to cause physical injury to those outside the enterprise is less than that of heavy industry, we have already seen that a clerical error or poor advice may result in serious economic loss.

In many cases the person responsible for a tortious act at work which causes injury to another, or to himself, will be an employee of an individual or organisation. Indeed where, as in most cases, the business is carried on by a corporate body, or by a nationalised industry, an individual employee must be responsible for individual acts, since bodies corporate, whilst legal persons, have no hands of their own to pull the levers of industry. Someone must pay for the injuries caused by such persons: we could choose to impose liability on the individual personally responsible for a particular tort, but in general our society has chosen instead to impose liability on the employer, be he individual or corporate. That liability can arise in two ways: the employer may be liable for the torts of his employees, or he may be made liable for his own personal default. We will look at both in turn.

Vicarious liability: introduction
9.0.2 An employer is made vicariously liable for the tortious acts of his employees committed during the course of their employment. Thus, for

instance, if a delivery van driver negligently runs down a pedestrian or if a surveyor negligently values a property the injured victim of negligence may sue the employer in either case. It used to be the case that an employee injured by a colleague could not sue their employer as being vicariously liable for the tort. The courts adopted the fiction of 'common employment' to protect employers, and therefore young and expanding industries, from the extensive liability which such claims would produce, by the pretence that one workman consented to run the risk of the carelessness of colleagues. However, with the statutory abrogation of the rule of common employment[1] and the House of Lords decision in *Smith v Baker & Sons*[2] the way was open for the imposition of vicarious liability on employers for injury to members of their own workforce.

The imposition of vicarious liability on an employer may seem harsh: after all, he is not personally at fault. However, there are several justifications for the rule. First, it protects the equally innocent plaintiff by giving him a choice of defendants, for the individual employee responsible for his injury is jointly liable with the employer—one of whom should be a man of substance and, in all probability, insured. Second, it can be argued that since the employer benefits from the acts of his employees, he should equally bear the burden of them although, as we shall see, an employer may be held vicariously liable for acts which in no way benefit his business. However, by making the employer bear such costs, his products or services may be made more accurately to reflect the social and economic costs of their production. Third, if it is accepted that accidents are an unfortunate fact of life, the cost of which should be borne by society in general, the employer is better placed than his employee to distribute the cost of tort damages, by insuring against loss, and by passing on the increased costs of damages and insurance premiums to all his customers in the form of higher prices.

1   Law Reform (Personal Injuries) Act 1948, s 1.
2   [1891] AC 325, HL.

Vicarious liability: the employee

9.0.3   Whilst it may be desirable that tort damages should be paid by those best able to insure against them and redistribute them, there must be a limit to vicarious liability; our system would not countenance the transfer of liability from a tortfeasor to a third party with whom he has no link simply because the third party is better placed to redistribute the loss. Vicarious liability is therefore limited so that an employer is liable only for the torts of his employees or, in exceptional cases, of his agents.[1] The distinction traditionally drawn is between an employee and an independent contractor: the employer is vicariously liable for the torts of the former but not of the latter. The distinction can be justified because an independent contractor will, in all probability, be in business on his own account and so be able to effect his own insurance and distribute his own costs to customers via pricing.

The problem is to distinguish between the employee and the independent contractor. As we shall see later,[2] this distinction is important for other reasons besides vicarious liability, and over the years the courts have developed a series of tests for distinguishing between the two. It must always be borne in mind that different considerations may affect the decision when the court is considering the imposition of vicarious liability to protect an outsider, than when it is considering the tax status of an alleged contractor or a worker's entitlement to claim employment protection rights such as unfair dismissal or redundancy. The test originally favoured was the control test: a man was the employee of another if the other had the right to control not only what he did but also how he did it. However, whilst such a test worked well enough in an early industrial society when employers were often self-made entrepreneurs, it broke down in the face of the growing special-isation and expertise of modern society. How could an airline director tell a pilot how to fly, or a Health Authority tell a surgeon how to operate? The courts therefore sought an alternative test—partly out of a desire to impose vicarious liability in such cases to protect the victims of torts. At first the 'integration' or 'organisation' test was proposed:[3] a man is an employee if his work is integrated into the organisation rather than merely incidental to it. However, this 'test' really does no more than restate the question and offers little help. Instead the courts now favour a 'multiple' test which takes account of a number of factors, such as how tax and national insurance are paid, who provides equipment, whether the 'employee' must perform a task personally or can provide a substitute.[4] Control is still a factor—often an important one—but the newer test provides a more suitable test for the diffi-cult cases of expert employees.

There may be cases when an individual is clearly an employee, but it is not clear who is his employer. Temporary workers are often 'hired out' by agencies, and it is common for heavy machinery to be hired out with an operator. Who then is to be liable for the 'hired' employee: his general employer, or the one for whom he is working? The courts adopt an approach similar to the 'multiple test' and will look at factors such as which 'employer' is responsible for paying the employee, and deducting tax and national insurance; the length of the hiring; who gives orders to the employee, ie who controls him. If machinery is provided with the employee, that may be a very significant factor: if the machinery is complicated and the employee a specialist it is highly likely that his 'general' employer—who owns the machinery—will be responsible for his torts.[5]

1 See below 29.3.0.
2 See Part VI.
3 Per Denning LJ in *Stevenson Jordan & Harrison Ltd v MacDonald & Evans*. [1952] 1 TLR 101.
4 See *Ready Mixed Concrete (South East) Ltd v Minister of Pensions and National Insurance* [1968] 2 QB 497, [1968] 1 All ER 433; below.
5 See *Mersey Docks and Harbour Board v Coggins and Griffith (Liverpool) Ltd* [1947] AC 1, [1946] 2 All ER 345, HL.

Vicarious liability

9.0.4 The imposition of vicarious liability is justified on the grounds that the employer benefits from the activities of his workforce and should therefore bear the burden of any torts they may commit. Obviously in the light of that argument the employer should only be made liable for torts which benefit him, or for those which are incidental to acts for his benefit, and generally this is the case. The employer is only liable for tortious acts committed in the course of employment. There are, however, exceptional cases when an employer is made liable even for deliberate acts which are in no way of benefit to him.

An employer will clearly be liable for torts which he expressly or impliedly authorises. Such authorisation is rare, however, and the most important aspect of vicarious liability is liability for the negligent acts of employees. It is well established that an employer is vicariously liable for his employees' negligent performance of their duties, such as the van driver's careless driving. Liability extends to peripheral or incidental acts—such as the case of the petrol tanker driver who lit a cigarette while making a delivery,[1] or even, in one case, when an employee working on site away from home was driving into town for lunch.[2] On the other hand liability is not imposed for acts such as travelling to or from work in the morning, nor when the employee does something wholly different from the task for which he is employed during working hours. Thus for instance when a bus conductor attempted to drive a bus, and caused an accident, his employers were not liable: he was not employed to drive buses at all and so his negligence was outside the scope of his employment.[3] (If the bus driver had allowed the conductor to drive, the employer might have been held liable for the negligence of the driver).

By an extension of the above reasoning, an employer is exempted from liability if the employee does something which he has expressly prohibited. However, because of the need to protect the innocent victims of torts and (probably) the widespread use by employers of insurance cover, the courts have drawn a distinction between cases where the very act in question is prohibited and cases where the employer has prohibited a particular way of doing the job. In the latter case the employer is held liable for his employees' negligence. The line between the two situations is often difficult to draw. Thus when drivers of two bus companies were in the habit of racing to pick up passengers, one company forbade its drivers to race. When one driver did race in the face of that prohibition, the employer was nevertheless held liable on the grounds that all it had prohibited was a particular way of doing the job, ie driving the omnibus.[4]

In certain situations the employer's liability is extended even to deliberate acts by his employees. Thus in one case[5] a solicitor's managing clerk defrauded a client of the firm of a substantial sum of money. The solicitor who employed him was held liable even though the tort was deliberate and for the personal benefit of the clerk rather than his employer. The justification for imposing liability on the employer was that he had put the clerk in a position where he could appear to represent the firm and obtain the trust of clients.

One situation which could cause difficulties is that of the practical joker. Every office and factory has at least one practical joker: is the employer to be held liable if a joke goes wrong and a fellow worker or member of the public is injured? The answer is usually 'no'. The employer is not held vicariously liable for deliberate practical jokes, such as the case of the scrap workers who persuaded a colleague to hit an unexploded shell with his hammer.[6] However, as we shall see shortly, the employer may be personally liable for his own negligence if he knew, or should have known, of the employee's propensity for pranks and that he was therefore a danger to colleagues.

1   *Century Insurance Co Ltd v Northern Ireland Road Transport Board* [1942] AC 509, [1942] 1 All ER 491, HL.
2   *Harvey v R G O'Dell Ltd* [1958] 2 QB 78, [1958] 1 All ER 657.
3   *Beard v London General Omnibus Co* [1900] 2 QB 530, CA.
4   *Limpus v London General Omnibus Co Ltd* (1862) 1 H & C 526, £x Ch. cf *Conway v George Wimpey & Co Ltd* [1951] 2 KB 266, [1951] 1 All ER 363, CA with *Rose v Plenty* [1976] 1 All ER 97, [1976] 1 WLR 141, CA.
5   *Lloyd v Grace Smith & Co* [1912] AC 716, HL. See also *Armagas Ltd v Mundogas SA, The Ocean Frost* [1986] AC 717, [1986] 2 All ER 385, [1986] 2 WLR 1063, HL (below, 29.4.1).
6   *O'Reilly v National Rail and Tramway Appliances Ltd* [1966] 1 All ER 499. See also *Smith v Crossley Bros Ltd* (1951) 95 Sol Jo 655, CA. Cf *Harrison v Michelin Tyre Co Ltd* [1985] 1 All ER 918, [1985] ICR 696 where the employer was held liable for a practical joke.

Vicarious liability: defences and indemnity

9.0.5 Where an employer is held vicariously liable for the torts of an employee, he steps into the shoes of the employee for all purposes. Thus he can raise any defence which would have been available to the employee personally. In particular, if the employee could have pleaded contributory negligence or even consent against his victim, the employer can likewise raise that defence.

Where vicarious liability applies the employer and employee are jointly liable to the plaintiff; the employee is not absolved from responsibility for his act. In practice, however, if there is no dispute about vicarious liability the victim will normally choose to sue only the employer who is likely to have greater resources, and probably insurance, to meet the claim. In *Lister v Romford Ice and Cold Storage Co Ltd*[1] the House of Lords held that where an employer is held vicariously liable for the torts of an employee, he is entitled to be indemnified against that liability by the employee. This caused some controversy: if the employer is insured against liability his insurance company could pay any damages awarded but then enforce the indemnity against the employee through their right of subrogation; but the insurance company is paid, by premiums, to assume that very risk. Legislation was threatened and to avert it insurance companies agreed that they would not seek to enforce the employer's indemnity. Thus in practice the indemnity is never enforced although it could be relied on by an uninsured employer.

1 [1957] AC 555, [1957] 1 All ER 125, HL.

Employers' personal liability

9.0.6 The Pearson Committee Report[1] stated that every year some 1,300 people are killed in accidents at work, and over 700,000 are injured. Gradually society has come to recognise the right of the casualties of industry to be compensated, either out of the profits of industry or by society in general. As Fleming puts it:

'the law has veered in less than a century from the extreme position of economic liberalism, which offered little in the way of protection for the working man because it was feared that this would impair the free operation of the market and thereby impede progress, to a point when nowadays it is unquestioned that industry owes the highest social obligation to exert itself towards accident prevention and the care of its casualties.'[2]

In fact compensation for those injured at work is provided by a number of different systems. Much comes from the social security system which, being based on flat rate contributions, does not reflect that certain activities such as mining are additionally hazardous (so that such industries are effectively subsidised by other areas of industry). However, an employer may be held liable in tort for injuries suffered by his employees, and therefore have to pay them compensation. Moreover, he is required by law to carry insurance cover[3] against such liability so that the employee is guaranteed compensation. The imposition of liability on the employer meets the requirement that 'the cost of the product should bear the blood of the working man'[4] as ultimately accident costs are passed on to and distributed amongst all the consumers of the goods or services of the industry in question.

1   Cmnd 7034 1 para 958, 1977.
2   Fleming, *An Introduction to the Law of Torts* (1985) p 91.
3   Employers' Liability (Compulsory Insurance) Act 1969.
4   Lloyd George, quoted by Fleming, op cit p 91.

Employers' liability: the nature of the duty
9.0.7   As we have seen, if an employee is injured by the negligence of a colleague, he may hold his employer vicariously liable; the abolition of 'common employment' and virtual abandonment of volenti non fit injuria as defences in such cases have removed major obstacles in the way of compensating injured employees. Moreover, even contributory negligence is reduced in scope, for the courts are prepared to recognise that an employee doing boring and repetitive work may well be inattentive to his own safety. However, vicarious liability is imposed when another was at fault: the law goes further and imposes certain personal duties on an employer to ensure the safety of his employees. These duties are said to be non-delegable, in that the employer cannot escape liability by saying that he personally delegated performance to a third party, such as an independent contractor, and took reasonable care in selecting that third party.

The duties were articulated in *Wilson and Clyde Coal Co Ltd v English.*[1] An employer is under a duty to see that reasonable care is taken to provide his employees with a safe place of work, a safe system of work, safe fellow employees and safe equipment. It should be noted that in each case the duty is to take reasonable care: liability is personal and non-delegable, but not absolute. The standard of reasonable care is flexible, as we have seen. Thus in *Latimer v AEC Ltd*[2] the employer had done all that was reasonable to protect his workforce when the only further thing he could have done was to close down his factory altogether. On the other hand in *Paris v Stepney Borough Council*[3] the employer was required to supply goggles to the plaintiff who was blind in one eye. It will generally not be enough for an employer to say that he prescribed a system of work; he will have to show, also, that he took care to see that it was put fully into effect.

The obligation to provide a safe place of work will extend beyond the employer's own premises; thus he must take reasonable care to see that they are safe when working on site or at a customer's premises. Of course, the flexibility of 'reasonable care' may mean that less is required of him in such a case than when employees are on his premises.

The obligation to provide safe fellow employees means that an employer may be personally liable for employing a practical joker: for although we have seen that he is not vicariously liable for practical jokes and the like, if he employs someone whom he knows, or ought to know, is a joker and a danger to his fellows, he will be personally liable for his own lack of care.

The obligation in respect of equipment is even more strict. It is no defence for an employer to say that he took care in the selection, purchase, provision and maintenance of equipment: the Employer's Liability (Defective Equipment) Act 1969 provides that if an employee is injured by equipment which is defective because of negligence in its manufacture, he may sue his own employer. The employer may in turn seek an indemnity from the manufacturer in tort, or from his vendor relying on implied terms in the contract of sale, but the employee is protected from the need to identify the manufacturer. The importance of this provision is emphasised by the recent decision that 'equipment' includes a 91,650 tonne bulk tanker.[4]

1 [1938] AC 57, [1937] 3 All ER 628, HL.
2 [1953] AC 643, [1953] 2 All ER 449, HL.
3 [1951] AC 367, [1951] 1 All ER 42, HL.
4 *Coltman v Bibby Ltd, The Derbyshire* [1986] 2 All ER 65, [1986] 1 WLR 751

Statutory protection

9.0.8 The employer's vicarious liability and duties under *Wilsons and Clyde Coal Co Ltd v English* arise at common law. In addition there is an immense amount of statutory provision designed for the protection of employees. Much of this provision is now contained in the Health and Safety at Work etc. Act 1974 and regulations made thereunder. Such legislation may well support the duties on employers by criminal sanctions and enforcement by the Health and Safety Executive. In addition, the legislation may expressly provide, or a court may so interpret it, that a person injured as a result of a breach of the legislation may make a civil claim for damages.[1] Such a possibility is important because often the regulations are expressed in absolute terms, for instance that a certain piece of machinery be fenced. Liability is then strict so that an employer cannot escape even by showing that he took all reasonable care or even that he could not have used a particular machine had it been thoroughly fenced,[2] unless the legislation expressly incorporates a defence that it was 'not practicable' to comply with the requirements.

1 See 9.0.9 below.
2 See eg *Close v Steel Co of Wales Ltd* [1962] AC 367, [1961] 2 All ER 953, HL.

Breach of statutory duty

9.0.9 We have already seen that much of the control of business activity depends on legislation of various types. Such legislation may establish standards, require things to be done or prohibit certain actions; non-compliance may result in the imposition of criminal penalties. Non-compliance may also lead to injury to a particular identifiable individual and in certain situations the individual so injured may be allowed to bring a civil action, for damages or even an injunction, based not on a failure to take reasonable care but on the mere fact of non-compliance with the statute. The action is then one for 'breach of statutory duty'.

The most important application of the civil action for breach of statutory duty is in the field of industrial accidents. We have already noted the large number of injuries suffered at work, and in response to those statistics, successive governments have passed a large amount of safety legislation to protect employees. However, the action for breach of statutory duty may have other important uses: thus, for instance, it provided the basis for the grant of an injunction to record companies and recording artists, to halt the activities of 'bootleggers' which constituted a criminal offence. The majority of the Court of Appeal held that the plaintiffs could obtain an injunction if they could show, as they did, that they had a special private right adversely affected by contravention of the statute.[1] The same legislation more recently provided the basis for a claim for damages by the executors of the late actor

Peter Sellers against a film company using out-takes from his 'Pink Panther' films to produce a new film.[2]

1   *Ex p Island Records Ltd* [1978] Ch 122, [1978] 3 All ER 824, CA.
2   *Rickless v United Artists Corpn* (1985) Times, 17 June.

Statutory duty: the availability of civil remedies
9.0.10   Often a statute may expressly provide that a person injured due to its contravention should be entitled to bring a civil suit. One such is the Consumer Safety Act 1978;[1] alternatively the statute may expressly prohibit a civil suit, as is the case with the Nuclear Installations Act 1965.[2] However, a very large number of statutory provisions do not make any express statement about the availability of a civil remedy and a court must then decide if such a remedy is to be allowed. This results in a mass of expensive and time consuming litigation and it might be better if Parliament could make its intention clearer in the relevant legislation.

The difficulty is that no general rule about the availability of a civil remedy can be laid down. The court must search for the intention of Parliament. Each case therefore depends on the construction of a particular piece of legislation and upon the circumstances of a particular case. Lord Denning has referred to the problem as 'a guess work puzzle' and said 'you might as well toss a coin to decide it.'[3] However, some rules are discernible. First, if a statute imposes a duty or requirement but provides no remedy, civil or criminal, for its breach, the court is more likely to infer that a person injured by breach should be entitled to make a civil claim: otherwise the legislation would have no sanction. Second, the court will look for the policy of the legislation. If it was passed for the protection of a particular class of persons or groups in society, a member of that group who suffers injury due to its contravention will normally be allowed to make a claim. However, in *Ex p Island Records Ltd*[4] the Court of Appeal expanded this rule to hold that even where legislation is not passed for the benefit of a particular group, a person who suffers special loss or interference with his property rights due to contravention may sue.

However, whilst such 'rules' may offer useful guidelines they can be no more than that; each case will depend on the view the court takes of the policy of the particular piece of legislation. In general the plaintiff must show that he is a member of the class for whose protection the legislation was passed; it has been held that legislation requiring adequate electrical wiring was for the protection of persons working in factories and so when a fireman was electrocuted by defective wiring whilst fighting a fire in a factory, he could bring no action.[5] The plaintiff will only succeed if he can show that the injury he suffered was the type the legislation was intended to guard against; thus, for instance, a requirement to keep livestock fenced in pens when carried by ship was held to be for the prevention of the spread of disease. A plaintiff whose unpenned sheep were washed overboard could thus make no claim.[6] Furthermore, a plaintiff will only succeed if he can show that the manner in which he was injured was covered by the legislation. The Factories Act 1961 requires every dangerous part of any machinery to be securely fenced. When pieces of machinery broke off from an unfenced machine and, flying out, injured the plaintiff, he was unable to bring a claim; the Act was intended to keep workers out of the machine, not to keep bits of the machinery in.[7]

1 S 12(1)b.
2 S 6(1).
3 *Ex p Island Records Ltd* [1978] Ch 122 at 134.
4 [1978] Ch 122, [1978] 3 All ER 824, CA.
5 *Hartley v Mayoh & Co* [1954] 1 QB 383, [1954] 1 All ER 375, CA.
6 *Gorris v Scott* (1874) LR 9 Exch 125.
7 *Close v Steel Co of Wales Ltd* [1962] AC 367, [1961] 2 All ER 953, HL.

Strict liability
9.0.11   The action for breach of statutory duty has sometimes been described as 'statutory negligence'. However, this is misleading. Liability for breach of statutory duty is very strict in the sense that if a person is in breach of a statutory provision, he is held liable even though he took all reasonable care to prevent contravention. This is well illustrated by the infamous case of *John Summers & Sons Ltd v Frost*,[1] which arose out of the Factories Act 1961 requirement that 'every dangerous part of any machinery shall be securely fenced'. The plaintiff operated a grinding wheel; it was fitted with a guard, but part of the moving wheel had to be exposed to use it. The plaintiff was injured when his thumb came into contact with the wheel. His employers were held liable to him for breach of the statute even though had the wheel been wholly fenced, it would have been unusable.[2]

This is, however, an extreme case. Many statutory requirements now incorporate an element of reasonableness by requiring compliance 'so far as is reasonably practicable'. If the provision in Frost had been couched in those terms, the employer would probably have had a defence.

In the field of industrial injuries, where breach of statutory duty plays its biggest role, there are strong arguments for not imposing strict liability on employers. After all, an injured employee will normally be entitled to compensation from the state through the social security system[3] without proof of fault, and to impose additional liability on employers regardless of fault imposes an unwarranted burden on industry without raising standards. The courts seem now to be prepared to take that fact into account. In any case, even when liability is 'strict' the standard of care imposed may not be unreasonable. The regulations, at least in the field of industrial accidents, are normally a response to high accident rates and particularly hazardous activities; they will normally merely put in statutory form what steps ought to be taken anyway by a reasonable employer to minimise such accidents. Further, although an employer may not plead 'volenti non fit injuria' against a claim for breach of statutory duty, he may be able to rely on the partial defence of contributory negligence, although, as noted elsewhere, the standard of care required, particularly of the manual workers who are most at risk, may be low.

1 [1955] AC 740, [1955] 1 All ER 870, HL.
2 The particular rule has since been reversed by the Abrasive Wheel Regulations 1970, reg 3.
3 Industrial injuries benefit.

Special forms of liability in negligence: liability for products
9.1.0   We have already remarked that in a modern, complex society our scope for causing damage to each other is greatly enhanced. This is nowhere

more apparent than in the context of product liability: a defective product may cause injury to someone far removed in time and space, and by several transactions, from the original manufacturer. If the defect is the result of faulty design, the injury may be reproduced time and again and affect a large number of victims. The question which the law must answer is who is to bear the cost of losses caused by defective products, whether defective in manufacture or in design. The early answer was to leave liability to fall on the ultimate consumer who suffered injury, unless he could pass it to his vendor via the contract between them. Gradually, however, the law has adopted the view that liability should be passed to the party best able to redistribute the loss as widely as possible. Thus the liability of retailers has gradually been extended and there has been an increasing willingness—both judicial and legislative—to pass liability to the manufacturer.

Retailers and consumers

9.1.1 A consumer who buys goods from a retailer has a contract with him. In the event that the goods prove defective he may sue on the contract and, since 1893, he has been able to rely on statutory implied terms that the goods should be reasonably fit for their purpose and of merchantable quality.[1] The liability of the retailer is contractual and is therefore strict: it is no defence that he was not personally at fault. Moreover, since 1973[2] in the case of consumer contracts it has been impossible for him to exclude liability for breach of those implied terms by reference to any contract term or notice. Contractual liability extends to personal injuries or damage to other property caused by the goods; moreover purely economic loss, such as the cost of repairing or replacing the defective goods themselves is covered.[3]

Generally a consumer-buyer has no contract with the manufacturer of goods. However, where the manufacturer offers a guarantee—as, of course, he commonly does—it is possible for the guarantee, in certain circumstances, to create a second contract between the manufacturer and consumer giving the consumer-buyer express rights to repair or replacement of defective goods. In that case the guarantee may not exclude or restrict the manufacturer's liability for defects due to negligence in manufacture.[4]

However, in most cases the consumer-buyer will have no contract with the manufacturer. He may of course sue his vendor in contract, and leave him to sue his wholesaler, in turn, and so on up a chain of transactions until liability is passed back to the manufacturer—but that is expensive. Moreover, although it is a cliché that a chain is only as strong as its weakest link, it is true. The chain of litigation breaks down if one party in it has become insolvent, or has otherwise gone out of business: if the retailer has disappeared or is insolvent the injured consumer can recover no compensation via the contract route.

1 Sale of Goods Acts 1893, s 14; now Sale of Goods Act 1979, s 14(2), (3).
2 Supply of Goods (Implied Terms) Act 1973; now Unfair Contract Terms Act 1977, s 6.
3 Subject to the rule in *Hadley v Baxendale*, see 17.1.3.
4 Unfair Contract Terms Act 1977, s 5. See 18.0.9.

Liability in tort: Donoghue v Stevenson

9.1.2 There is thus a serious lacuna in the contractual protection of consumers; the position is worse where the buyer is not the eventual consumer as where, for example, goods are bought as a gift. The ultimate consumer-beneficiary then has no contract with the retailer and, by virtue of the doctrine of privity of contract, cannot obtain redress from him for any loss he suffers. The purchaser may, of course, sue on the contract, but he may have suffered no loss, or at most the loss only of the price of the goods. It was just such a situation which led to the landmark decision in *Donoghue v Stevenson*.[1] We have already discussed its importance in the general law of negligence; its importance in this particular field cannot be overstated. Before *Donoghue* it had been the law that the manufacturer of a product who sold it, generally to a distributor or wholesaler, could be liable to that party on the contract of sale but could not owe any other duties over and above those created by the contract. Thus the manufacturer was safe from suit by the consumers of his products. In *Donoghue*, however, the House of Lords rejected that fallacy and held that a manufacturer could be sued by a consumer who suffered injury due to negligence in manufacture. Lord Atkin explained the duty thus:

> 'a manufacturer of products, which he sells in such a form as to show that he intends them to reach the ultimate consumer in the form in which they left him with no reasonable possibility of intermediate examination, and with the knowledge that the absence of reasonable care in the preparation or putting up of the products will result in an injury to the consumer's life or property, owes a duty to that consumer to take reasonable care.'[2]

Gradually the liability recognised in *Donoghue* has been extended to a whole range of products. The liability has also been extended by a later decision that the manufacturer can only escape liability if at the time he parted with the product there was a probability, rather than a possibility, of the product being examined[3] so that he could reasonably rely on that examination to reveal any defects. If an examination was not probable at that time, the manufacturer remains liable even though the goods were examined, but the defect was not discovered;[4] on the other hand, if it was probable that the goods would be examined, the manufacturer may escape liability even though no examination in fact took place.[5]

1   [1932] AC 562, HL.
2   Ibid, p 599.
3   *Paine v Colne Valley Electricity Supply Co Ltd and British Insulated Cables Ltd* [1938] 4 All ER 803.
4   The examiner might also be negligent and therefore concurrently liable.
5   As in *Evans v Triplex Safety Glass Co Ltd* [1936] 1 All ER 283.

Implications of negligence liability

9.1.3   The stress placed on the probability of intermediate inspection only underlines that the manufacturer is liable under *Donoghue* for negligence, for failure to take reasonable care. He may be able to fulfil the duty of reasonable care by issuing with the product a suitable warning to the consumer or someone in the chain of distribution to carry out such an examination, or notifying them of known risks. 'Reasonable care' is a flexible standard, so that it can be adapted to new circumstances: for instance, a lower standard of care might be accepted in the case of goods marketed as seconds.

Since the manufacturer is liable for negligence, it falls to the plaintiff consumer to prove that he was negligent: that may be difficult—and expensive—to establish. However, in many cases he will be able to rely on the fact of an accident and res ipsa loquitur to throw the burden of proof onto the manufacturer; moreover, it will not be enough for the manufacturer to show that he has a 'foolproof system': human error can always creep into such a system, the fact of the accident will suggest that it did and the manufacturer will be vicariously liable for the negligence of his employees.

On the other hand, the manufacturer will have the benefit of defences normally available in tort. In particular he may be able to rely on contributory negligence by the consumer, for instance where he has disregarded instructions or used the product wrongly.[1] Further, since liability is in negligence, there is considerable doubt as to whether the manufacturer would be liable for purely economic loss. He clearly is liable for personal injuries or property damage caused by the defective product. On the other hand, in the light of the decision in *Muirhead v Industrial Tank Specialities*[2] and its interpretation of *Junior Books Ltd v Veitchi Co Ltd*,[3] it seems that the relationship between consumer and manufacturer will rarely be close enough to impose on the latter liability for purely economic loss—such as the cost of repairing or replacing the product. This restriction may be particularly important where the 'consumer' is in fact buying goods for use in a business. On the other hand, if goods are unsafe, and a threat to life and limb, the consumer may be able to claim the cost of making them safe: in *Anns v Merton London Borough Council*[4] such costs were categorised as property damage rather than economic loss.

1   *Farr v Butters Bros & Co* [1932] K QB 606, CA.
2   [1986] QB 507; [1985] 3 All ER 705, CA, above 7.1.10.
3   [1983] 1 AC 520, [1982] 3 All ER 201, HL.
4   [1978] AC 728, [1977] 2 All ER 492, HL.

Policy considerations
9.1.4   As we observed above, and elsewhere, it is regarded as desirable that the law of tort should impose liability on the party who is best able to bear it and redistribute it as widely as possible. That argument favours imposition of liability for defective products on the manufacturer who can obtain insurance and pass on the increased cost of premiums to his customers as an increase in prices. Ultimately, the manufacturer who persists in the manufacture of defective goods will find that his prices become uncompetitive; he will then be forced out of business, but this too can be seen as encouraging efficiency and therefore socially desirable.

It is well known that in most manufacturing processes a certain percentage of goods produced will be defective. Random sample testing allows for, and condones, defects within a certain tolerance both of degree and frequency. The decision as to what tolerance is acceptable is one for management based on a cost-benefit analysis: if a product with a known percentage chance of causing harm does cause harm, it seems right that liability for that harm should be imposed on the person who decided that that risk was justifiable. In this way the imposition of liability on manufacturers reduces the likelihood of cynical decisions to market known defective products: an example often cited is the decision of the Ford Motor Corporation in the United States to market the Ford Pinto with a known design defect (the position of the fuel tank) and to meet ensuing product liability claims, rather than redesign the vehicle. There is, however, one difficulty here. Once product liability is imposed for negligence in design rather than for negligence in manufacture, the courts may find themselves in difficult waters for the very reason that design decisions are executive decisions based on cost-benefit analysis. As Atiyah observes[1] a decision by a court on design-negligence would amount to a legislative act: it would establish a precedent for other manufacturers which they would feel bound to follow. It is by no means clear that the judges are suited or qualified so to 'second guess' designers or managers whose economic decisions may have implications—for instance in relation to employment prospects—for society in general. Nor is it generally thought right that the judges should abrogate to themselves a legislative function: the establishment of acceptable minimum standards is thought to be the job of Parliament. In this country, therefore, the courts have generally been reluctant to impose liability for negligence in design rather than in the manufacturing process. In America, however, the judges have begun to impose liability for design defects on the basis of a cost-benefit analysis.

1   *Accidents, Compensation and the Law* (1980 3rd edn) p 60 ff.

Legislative control
9.1.5   British law has for some time imposed a degree of legislative control on product safety standards. The Consumer Safety Act 1978, replacing earlier legislation,[1] empowered the Secretary of State to make regulations controlling the composition, design, safety and so on of goods. Non-compliance with any such order was a criminal offence, and any person injured as a result of breach of any such regulation would be able to bring a civil claim for breach of statutory duty. However, the 1978 Act is to be repealed and be replaced by wider powers contained in Part II of the Consumer Protection Bill before Parliament. That will give the Secretary of State new powers to make regulations controlling the content, design etc of goods, including orders restricting their availability for sale and requiring prescribed information to be supplied with them. Such regulations could thus control or prohibit the supply of, for example, dangerous toys, lead levels in paint or require information or warnings to be supplied with drugs offered to the public. The Secretary of State will have wide enforcement powers, including to prohibit the supply of goods altogether, or to require warnings to be supplied with them. Further enforcement powers will be delegated to other public bodies including, perhaps, local authority trading standard departments, who will have powers, inter alia, to issue notices suspending the supply of goods for up to six months, and to apply for orders for forfeiture of goods which breach the regulations. It will be a criminal offence to sell, offer for sale or even to possess for supply goods which do not comply with a 'general safety requirement', including where they are defective within Part I of the Bill[2] and where they do not comply with regulations made under the Bill. Although an action for breach of statutory duty may still be available to anyone injured by goods which breach the general requirement, its importance will be greatly diminished as a result of the provisions contained in Part I of the Bill.

1   Consumer Protection Acts 1961, 1971.
2   See below, 9.1.6.

Proposals for reform

9.1.6   We have adverted above to the difficulties posed for the consumer by the fact that product liability is based on negligence; principally the difficulty of proving negligence by the manufacturer—although that is to some degree alleviated by reliance on res ipsa loquitur. In America those difficulties of proof have been largely overcome by shifting the basis of product liability from negligence to strict liability—both for production and design defects, the latter generally on the basis of a cost/benefit analysis, as already mentioned. That shift has been achieved by judicial decision.

In recent years there has been a growing call for a similar shift in this country—such a change would require legislation and there have been various proposals for reform. In 1977 the Pearson Committee[1] proposed the imposition of strict liability on manufacturers of both finished products and components, and on importers and 'branders' of own brand goods for death or personal injury caused by defective products. A product would be 'defective' if it failed 'to provide the safety which a person is entitled to expect having regard to all the circumstances including the presentation of the product.' A warning on packaging might thus be effective to reduce the standard reasonably to be expected. Liability would continue for ten years from production; it would be a defence for a producer to show that the product was not defective when it left him or that he did not put it into circulation. In addition it would be a defence that he did not circulate it in the course of a business; and intermediate distributors of products would not be liable—so long as they identify the supplier or manufacturer on request.[2] Pearson justified the imposition of strict liability arguing that the producer, who profits from the success of a product, should accept its losses; that he was best placed to arrange insurance and redistribute loss; that strict liability would raise safety standards; and that all consumers should have the same protection as a consumer-purchaser.[3]

Pearson's proposals were not implemented but at the end of 1986 the British government introduced into Parliament the Consumer Protection Bill, Part I of which was intended to implement the EEC Directive on product liability. Although criticised in several quarters, it seems likely that the Bill will pass into law without significant amendment. The Bill will impose on the producer of a defective product strict liability for death, personal injury or damage to private property caused by the product. 'Producer' is given an extended definition and includes not only the manufacturer of a finished product or component but also—(i) any person who wins or abstracts a substance, and (ii) any person who carries out any industrial or other process to which an essential characteristic of the product is attributable.[4]

Moreover, strict liability is imposed on any person who, although not himself the producer of a product, imported it into the EEC or who holds himself out as if he were the producer, for instance by applying his own brand name, trade mark or packaging to the product.[5] Thus, for instance, a supermarket which sells goods under its own brand label could be held liable as if he were a 'producer' even though the goods were manufactured by someone else. Finally, any person who supplies a defective product may be held liable to any person who suffers damage due to the product if he is asked by that person to identify the producer, importer or 'brander' of the product and fails to do so within a reasonable time.[6]

The Bill defines a product as defective if its safety 'is not such as persons generally are entitled to expect'. The court is to have regard to any packaging, instructions etc. supplied with the product and to 'what might reasonably be expected to be done with or in relation to the product.'[7] This last is in line with judicial interpretation of the Sale of Goods Act 1979 which has held that goods are not unmerchantable where they could be rendered safe or usable if treated in the manner which might reasonably be expected.[8] In general the definition of defect follows that proposed by the Pearson Committee, both being based on the earlier Strasbourg Convention.[9] The reference to reasonable expectations suggests a similarity with the law of negligence. Moreover, controversially, the English Bill allows a producer to rely on a 'development risks' defence. Such a defence is permitted but not compulsory within the terms of the EEC Directive. Thus it will be a defence for a producer to show that:

> 'the state of scientific and technical knowledge at the time when he put the product into circulation was not such as to enable the existence of the defect to be discovered.[10]

This defence, often referred to as a 'state of the art defence', would be particularly important in fields of 'high tech' developments, such as aircraft and vehicles, and drug developments. It was considered and rejected by Pearson. Although it might be thought unfair to impose on a manufacturer liability for compensating injuries which were impossible to avoid, and despite the fear that the absence of a development risks defence might inhibit the development of new products, contrary to the interests of consumers,

> 'to exclude development risks from a regime of strict liability would be to leave a gap in the compensation cover, through which, for example, the victims of another Thalidomide disaster might easily step.'[11]

However, the British government has no doubt been influenced in favour of a 'development risks defence' by the desire to maintain the competitiveness of British industry and by the fact that several other member states are thought to be in favour of allowing such a defence for their producers. An attempt at the Committee stage in the House of Lords to withdraw the defence from drug manufacturers failed.

Although the Directive allows for the imposition of a financial limit on liability (70 million ECU—about £41,000,000), the British government has decided against fixing a ceiling on the grounds that the limit is so high its absence will have no effect on competitiveness.

A producer may not exclude or limit his liability for damage under the Bill by reference to any contract term, notice or otherwise.[12] However, the producer will be able to rely on a defence of contributory negligence where a person suffers damage partly due to his own default and partly due to the defective product.[13]

Notably, the Bill imposes strict liability only for death, personal injury or property damage. There is no liability under the Bill for purely economic loss, including the diminution in value of, or damage to, the product itself. This may be narrower than the liability which may exist in negligence in rare cases. Further, the producer is only liable under the Bill for damage to property which is ordinarily intended for private use and was intended by the person who suffered the damage for his own private use. Small claims for property damage, where compensation would not exceed £275, are excluded from the Bill's scheme.[14]

The threat of the imposition of strict product liability has caused a measure of disquiet amongst British manufacturers. They point to the experience of the United States where product liability awards have been so high that some companies have been unable to obtain adequate insurance cover. In July 1986, for instance, Ford apparently faced product liability claims for sums in excess of $4 billion.[15] Some manufacturers have responded by withdrawing products from the market altogether. However, comparison with the American experience may be misleading: juries are used in product liability cases there and they decide the level of awards and naturally have a tendency to sympathise with the injured plaintiff; juries are not used in personal injury cases in the UK. Moreover, the American contingency fee system which allows a lawyer to take a case for an agreed proportion of the damages if it succeeds (and nothing if it fails) is thought to encourage litigation. Contingency fees are prohibited in Britain as unethical. Interestingly, the American jurisdictions are currently considering imposing a maximum financial limit on product liability claims; however, they do not allow a development risks defence.

The Bill expressly preserves existing liabilities. The statutory scheme will therefore exist side by side with the manufacturer's common law liability for negligence. The absolute prohibition on recovery for pure economic loss and the limitation on small claims for property damage mean that the statutory scheme is in some respects narrower than liability in negligence.

What is clear is that implementation of the EEC Directive will assist plaintiffs by reversing the burden of proof: the manufacturer of a defective product must show that he made it as safe as could be expected in the light of circumstances at the time he put it into circulation. In view of the availability of the development risks defence, we shall have to wait to see if it does more than that

1 Cmnd 7054, 1977.
2 The injured consumer thus always has an identifiable 'target' to sue.
3 Who can sue in contract where liability in contract is strict.
4 Cl 1(2).
5 Cl 2(2).
6 Cl 2(3).
7 Cl 3.
8 See eg *Heil v Hedges* [1951] 1 TLR 512, below 21.2.2.
9 Convention on Products Liability prepared by the Council of Europe and opened for signature in 1977.
10 Cl 4(1)e.
11 Cmnd 7054, 1977.
12 Cl 7.
13 Cl 6(3).
14 Cl 5(4).
15 NLJ 1986, p 645.

Special forms of liability in negligence: liability of occupiers for premises

9.2.0   Activities can put people at risk of all kinds of loss or injury; few 'things' are inherently dangerous, but premises, because of their size and complexity, are an exception. A building or structure can pose dangers to those who enter it and those dangers may not be traceable to any human activity or even omission; this is particularly true, of course, in the case of premises used for business. We have seen how the law of negligence imposes liability on persons for injuries caused by their activities (and sometimes omissions) but it is only comparatively recently that the law has come to recognise that an occupier of premises should be liable for injuries or losses sustained by visitors to those premises as a result of the state of the premises themselves rather than of any activity he carries on there. Until the 19th century an Englishman's home was so much his castle that he owed his visitors no duty other than not to lead them into danger. Gradually, however, that privileged position has been eroded and the law has come to recognise that occupation of premises carries with it a concurrent responsibility to persons who came onto those premises. At first the law laid down a series of categories of visitors, and the duties owed to them by the occupier varying according to the degree to which their visit benefitted him. In 1957 categorisation was abandoned and the Occupiers' Liability Act imposes one common duty of care, owed to all lawful visitors. Nevertheless, the law has long baulked at imposing upon the occupier of premises liability for injury to trespassers, who come unbidden, for purposes—often dishonest or wrongful—of their own and whose presence might be unforeseeable. On the other hand it has gradually been recognised that not all trespassers are undeserving, and that some, such as children attracted to forbidden and dangerous premises, are all too foreseeable. At first then the common law relaxed its strict attitude to trespassers; now the Occupiers Liability Act 1984 imposes a statutory duty in favour of trespassers. However, the duty so created differs from that owed to lawful visitors under the 1957 Act and so it is still important to distinguish between lawful visitors and trespassers.

Lawful visitors and trespassers
9.2.1   Anyone who enters premises with the permission, express or implied, of the occupier will be a lawful visitor. Obviously, therefore, persons expressly invited, and those such as theatre-goers with a contractual right to enter, will be lawful visitors. Permission to enter may be implied, and an implied permission is normally given to members of the public to come onto premises at least as far as the door for the purposes of transacting lawful business—unless excluded by a sign such as 'No hawkers or circulars'. Permission to enter can be withdrawn, but the visitor must be allowed a reasonable time to leave voluntarily before being ejected. Certain persons— including, but by no means only, the police, and officers of public utility boards—may have statutory powers of entry in certain circumstances: they too are lawful visitors when exercising such powers.

Anyone who comes onto premises other than as a lawful visitor will be a trespasser. It should be noted that a person may have permission to enter premises at certain times or for certain purposes: if he enters at other times or for other purposes[1] he may be a trespasser. In addition, a person may have permission only to enter certain parts of premises: the cinemagoer is not invited into the projection room. If he exceeds his licence by entering a forbidden part of the premises, he makes himself a trespasser.

1   See eg *R v Smith, R v Jones* [1976] 3 All ER 54, [1976] 1 WLR 672, CA.

Occupiers
9.2.2   The duties imposed by both the 1957 and 1984 Acts are thrown on the occupier of premises. It is worth noting that although he may be the owner of premises he is not necessarily their occupier. The crucial test of an occupier is whether he has control of the premises. Thus it is possible for two

persons to have sufficient control to be 'occupiers': for instance, a brewery and the manager of a tied house were both held to be occupiers of the manager's first floor living quarters over the public house: the brewery had retained sufficient control to qualify as an occupier.[1] In another case a company retained architects to supervise the conversion of premises into a bowling alley. The company employed to instal bowling lanes stored a substantial amount of valuable equipment on the premises but it was damaged by rain water penetrating through an incomplete doorway. Both the architects and the owners were held to be occupiers because they had[2] 'control'. Landlords are in a special position. When, as is often the case, a landlord retains the 'common parts' of a divided building, such as lifts, entrance lobbies and stairs in an office block or flats complex, he will be treated as the 'occupier' of them for the purposes of the 1957 Act.[3] Further, as against the tenant he will be liable for breach of covenant if he fails to repair in breach of an obligation placed on him by the lease. This liability is extended by statute[4] so that where the lease places on the landlord an obligation to repair, he owes a duty of care to 'all persons who might reasonably be expected to be affected' by defects resulting from breach of that obligation. Thus if a person other than the tenant suffers personal injury or damage to property due to a defect in the premises arising from or continuing because of the landlord's failure to repair, the landlord is liable to that person. He will not be so liable when he has no obligation to repair. Liability to third parties thus depends on the terms of the lease. Of course, when there is a long lease, especially of business premises, it is common for the tenant, rather than the landlord, to be liable for most repairs.

1   *Wheat v F Lacon & Co Ltd* [1966] AC 552, [1966] 1 All ER 582, HL.
2   *AMF International Ltd v Magnet Bowling Ltd* [1968] 2 All ER 789, [1968] 1 WLR 1028.
3   *Cunard v Antifyre Ltd* [1933] 1 KB 551.
4   Defective Premises Act 1972, s 4.

The common duty of care
9.2.3   The Occupiers' Liability Act 1957 requires an occupier to take—

> 'such care as in all the circumstances is reasonable to see that the visitor will be reasonably safe in using the premises for the purposes for which he is invited or permitted by the occupier to be there.'[1]

It is notable that the standard is like that in negligence generally, one of reasonable care; and so, like the general negligence standard, it is flexible. Thus an occupier must expect children to be less careful for their own safety than adults would be, and take correspondingly more care for them; in contrast he can expect specialists who come onto his premises to carry out some job within their own expertise to exercise more care to protect themselves against hazards of that job. Thus in *Roles v Nathan*[2] when two chimney sweeps came to seal a sweephole and were killed by fumes when they lit a fire in the flue, contrary to instructions, the occupier of the premises was not liable:

> 'If it had been a different danger, as, for instance, if the stairs leading to the cellar gave way, the occupier might no doubt be responsible, but not for these dangers which were special risks ordinarily incidental to their calling.'[3]

Since the duty is to exercise reasonable care 'to see that the visitor will be reasonably safe' the occupier may fulfil his duty if he gives sufficient warning to enable the visitor to take care for his own safety. Notices may

144

also be relevant in other ways. If a notice denies access, any person who enters in defiance of it will be a trespasser and therefore, it seems, entitled to a lower standard of care from the occupier. Moreover, an occupier may by contract or notice restrict or even exclude the common duty of care in respect of premises which are not used for business.[4] However, for our purposes business premises are more important and the Unfair Contract Terms Act 1977[5] now prevents a person who occupies premises for the purposes of a business from excluding or restricting his liability under the Occupiers' Liability Act 1957 for personal injury or death. He may restrict or exclude liability for damages to property, but only insofar as the exclusion or restriction satisfies the test of reasonableness.

The occupier of premises may also be liable for damage or injury suffered by visitors due to the faulty execution of any work of maintenance, repair or construction. Obviously an employer-occupier will be vicariously liable for his employees in the ordinary way; he may also be held liable for the dangerous state of premises created by independent third party contractors. He will not be held liable, however, if he acted reasonably in entrusting the work to an independent contractor, exercise reasonable care in the choice of a competent contractor and took reasonable care to supervise the contract.[6] This last requirement may mean that he should employ a 'properly qualific[1] professional man such as an architect, surveyor or a naval architect or Lloyd's surveyor'; of course, the average occupier does not have sufficient expertise to supervise works himself and, at least in the case of major works, it is normal practice to retain an architect or surveyor to supervise and generally manage the works.

1   S 2.
2   [1963] 2 All ER 908, [1963] 1 WLR 1117, CA.
3   Per Lord Denning MR at 1123.
4   Occupiers Liability Act 1957, s 2.
5   S 1(3); s 2.
6   S 2(4)b.

Trespassers

9.2.4   The duty owed to trespassers differs from that owed to lawful visitors. In fact, under the 1957 Act no common duty of care is owed to trespassers at all. For years the courts held that an occupier's only liability to trespassers was not to injure them deliberately or recklessly.[1] The trespasser, it was argued, forces himself on the occupier. However, the rule was modified in a number of cases—for instance by the doctrine of 'allurement' designed to protect child trespassers who tend to be attracted to the very places which are forbidden and dangerous—and in 1972 the House of Lords[2] held that the occupier of premises did owe a humanitarian duty of care to trespassers provided that a reasonable man would have known that trespassers were likely to be on the premises and the occupier did know of the danger on the premises.

In fact this amounts to an application of the 'reasonable care' duty of negligence to the particular problem of trespassers: the standard of care required is flexible and is lower towards trespassers than to lawful visitors. However, the protection of trespassers has now been put on a statutory footing by the Occupiers' Liability Act 1984 which provides that an occupier owes a duty to non-lawful visitors[3] if:
(a) he knows, or has reasonable grounds to believe, that a danger exists;

(b) he knows or has reasonable grounds to believe that non-lawful visitors may come into its vicinity; and

(c) the risk is one against which he can reasonably be expected to provide protection.

Whilst it remains to be seen what standard of care the courts will require of an occupier under the 1984 Act, it seems likely that the duty will be lower than that owed to lawful visitors. A warning notice may often suffice—although, of course, the standard will vary according to the circumstances; in particular warnings are unlikely to be regarded as sufficient where child trespassers are concerned, at least when the presence of child trespassers is foreseeably likely.

1   *Robert Addie & Sons (Collieries) Ltd v Dumbreck* [1929] AC 358, HL.
2   *British Railways Board v Herrington* [1972] AC 877, [1972] 1 All ER 749, HL.
3   The same standard is applied to visitors to National Parks.

Vendors and lessors of premises

9.2.5   We have so far been concerned with defects which arise during a person's occupation of premises. Until very recently the law took the view that, regardless of liability during occupation, a person's responsibility for premises came completely to an end when he parted with them. We have seen above that the rule has gradually been relaxed in the case of landlords who do now owe a duty to·all persons affected by their failure to repair, in accordance with obligations in the lease. The position of vendors of premises has remained highly favoured until very recently, so that the rule 'caveat emptor' (let the buyer beware) continued to be applied to sales of land long after it had been abrogated for the sale of goods. The view of the law was that 'fraud apart, there is no law against letting a tumble-down house.'[1]

However, where the vendor is also responsible for any works of construction or modification to premises he does now owe a duty. Statute imposes a duty on 'every person who does work of construction or conversion in connection with the provision of a dwelling';[2] the duty is owed to every person who acquires an interest in the dwelling and requires him 'to see that the work is done in a professional manner, with proper materials and so as to be fit for human habitation.' This at first appears to be a very wide ranging liability, particularly since liability is imposed on all persons—builders, architects, surveyors and so on—involved in the construction of the house, and is owed to all persons who acquire an interest in the house (although no action can be brought after six years from the completion of the dwelling). However, the practical application of this provision is very much restricted because it applies only to dwellings, and not to those built under an approved scheme such as the National House Builders Council Scheme (which provides insurance cover for a period of ten years against faulty construction of new houses). In practice, most new houses are built under the NHBC scheme.

The common law too has come to recognise a duty on builders in connection with the construction of dwellings, through cases such as *Anns v Merton London Borough Council*.[3] This duty may well be wider than the statutory one, since it clearly applies even to houses protected by the NHBC scheme; and it seems that it applies to commercial properties as well as to dwellings.[4]

1   Per Erle CJ.
2   Defective Premises Act 1972, s 3.
3   [1978] AC 728, [1977] 2 All ER 492, HL.
4   *Hone v Benson* (1978) 248 Estates Gazette 1013.

Chapter 10
Nuisance

Liability for the use of land: private nuisance

10.0.0 Land is one of the most valuable assets a person may own; not surprisingly the law has developed a number of rules which protect a person's interest in property. We have already seen how the law of trespass gave early protection against invasion of property. Through the tort of private nuisance the law has given protection against less direct interference with property rights, and we may define private nuisance as 'any unreasonable interference with a person's enjoyment of land or with his rights over it.'

In fact, the law of nuisance recognises that rights of land use are not absolute: one man's activities on his land may injure his neighbour, whether the context be that of a domestic householder soiling his neighbour's washing or of fumes from a chemical plant putting off potential customers at a nearby hotel. The law of nuisance is therefore concerned with striking a balance between competing claims to land use and as such it is only one of several systems of regulation; playing only a subsidiary role as a supplement to those other systems. Thus the public control exercised by local authorities through the grant or refusal of planning permission is a very important element in the control of land use; moreover, by 'zoning' areas and designating them for a domestic or industrial user, for example, the local authority can minimise the scope for conflict. A similar, more local and private, control is exercised through the imposition on neighbours of restrictive covenants. Such covenants, typically imposed on the sale of land, restrict its user for the benefit of a neighbouring property. Their value lies in that, as an exception to the normal rule of privity of contract, they bind the land upon which they are imposed and can therefore be enforced against all persons who acquire an interest in it. The role of these last two systems is principally regulatory; private nuisance, on the other hand, fulfils a role which is primarily remedial, for, although a plaintiff may seek an injunction to restrain future continuation of a nuisance which has commenced, he may also seek damages for harm suffered due to a past nuisance. Nuisance can also be seen as an element in the system of environmental protection. However, once again its role is only a subsidiary one, the major role being played by various statutory controls over pollution, noise levels and the like.[1]

We have said that nuisance concerns 'unreasonable interference with enjoyment of property' and that a court considering a nuisance claim must balance the interests of plaintiff and defendant. This may, at first glance, seem like the language of negligence and there are indeed situations when a defendant is only held liable in nuisance if he knew, or ought to have known, of a source of interference. However, unreasonableness here refers to the impact of the defendant's conduct on the plaintiff, rather than with the blameworthy nature of the defendant's conduct; and the balancing exercise here is between the competing interests of the parties, whereas negligence involves an assessment of risk.

1   See 2.7.8.

Interference with land

10.0.1   Use of land may cause physical damage to another's property. If it does so, such damage is actionable in nuisance. However, interference with enjoyment short of physical damage may also ground an action. Thus the annoyance caused by smells from fish and chip shops[1] or stables[2] has been held to be a nuisance, as, in one case, was the fact that the defendants used premises for the purposes of prostitution.[3] It is important to distinguish between cases of physical damage and those of mere interference with enjoyment because, not surprisingly, the courts adopt a different approach to the two types of case and are more likely to look favourably upon a plaintiff whose claim is for physical damage; after all, if an interference does result in physical harm it is difficult to categorise it as anything other than 'unreasonable'. However, the distinction may not always be readily apparent. For instance, fumes and vibrations may result in actual damage to property: if they do so, then they are correctly categorised as physical damage, as when acid fumes from a smelting works caused damage to the plaintiff's trees and shrubs.[4]

Physical damage may be caused, more obviously, by things encroaching onto property. Here a distinction must be drawn, between nuisance and trespass. A direct encroachment by one person onto another's land is trespass; an indirect encroachment is nuisance. Thus if a neighbour builds a wall in the wrong place so that it is actually placed on his neighbour's adjoining property, that is a trespass. But if something originally placed on the defendant's land encroaches onto the plaintiff's property, as when a wall correctly placed collapses, that is a nuisance. Thus overhanging branches or encroaching tree roots, water overflowing from a blocked drain[5] and even a burial mound which slipped after heavy rain, have all been held to constitute a nuisance.[6]

1   *Adams v Ursell* [1913] 1 Ch 269.
2   *Rapier v London Tramway Co* [1893] 2 Ch 588, CA.
3   *Thompson-Schwab v Costaki* [1956] 1 All ER 652, [1956] 1 WLR 335, CA.
4   *St Helens Smelting Co v Tipping* (1865) 11 HL Cas 642.
5   *Sedleigh-Denfield v O'Callaghan* [1940] AC 880.
6   *Leakey v National Trust for Places of Historic Interest or Natural Beauty* [1980] QB 485, [1980] 1 All ER 17, CA.

Unreasonableness

10.0.2   There are a number of identifiable factors which a court may take into account in balancing the interests of plaintiff and defendant and assessing how far the plaintiff can be expected to tolerate the impact upon him of the defendant's conduct. This is important: if any trivial interference with enjoyment of property could result in a claim for nuisance, industry could rapidly be brought to a halt. Everyone must be prepared to put up with a certain amount of inconvenience in order that we can all enjoy the benefits of a modern industrial society; the question is 'how much must one tolerate?'

One factor which may enter the equation is the nature of the locality in which the plaintiff's land is situated.

> 'What would be a nuisance in Berkeley Square would not necessarily be so in Bermondsey, and when a locality is devoted to a particular trade or manufacture carried on by the traders and manufacturers in a particular and established manner not constituting a public nuisance, judges and juries would be justified in finding . . . that the trade or manufacture so carried on in that locality is not a private or actionable wrong.'[1]

This argument is two-edged: a plaintiff who lives in a quiet residential area will more easily be able to complain of industrial noises, smells and vibration than would a plaintiff living in an industrial area. However, the courts are unlikely to allow a defendant to justify causing physical harm by reference to the character of the neighbourhood. Thus in *St Helen Smelting Co v Tipping*[2] when fumes damaged the plaintiff's plants, it was no defence that there were many smelting works in the area.

The frequency of an interference is also a relevant factor. A land owner may be expected to put up with one isolated event or even an occasional annoyance, but not one regularly and frequently repeated. However, one isolated incident which results in physical damage may undoubtedly amount to a nuisance.

On the other hand, it is generally no defence for a defendant to show that his conduct is socially valuable. For instance, opening a factory in the middle of a residential district may well create new jobs, but that would probably not be taken to justify keeping residents awake with the noise of night working, or, annoying them with fumes and smoke. However, there are signs that the courts may refuse an injunction when they feel that a defendant's conduct has social value, especially when the plaintiff's complaint is relatively trivial, leaving the plaintiff to his remedy in damages.[3] However, it may be a defence for a defendant to show that his conduct was expressly, or impliedly, authorised by statute. Thus a nuisance may be held to be authorised if it can be shown to be an inevitable result of some activity authorised by Parliament. In *Allen v Gulf Oil Refining Ltd*[4] the House of Lords held that a statute which expressly authorised the purchase of land and the construction of an oil refinery must also impliedly authorise the operation of the refinery, and therefore the consequent unavoidable interference with neighbouring property.

> 'Parliament can hardly be supposed to have intended the refinery to be nothing more than a visual adornment to the landscape in an area of natural beauty.'[5]

The reluctance to award an injunction in such a case, which would have the effect of closing the refinery, is understandable; however, the Act which authorised the purchase of land gave statutory rights of compensation to those whose land was compulsorily purchased to build the refinery, but nothing to those affected by its operation. The refusal of the courts to award compensation for nuisance in such a case means that a few landowners are required to shoulder the burden of operation of a refinery for the good of society as a whole. If the refinery were ordered to pay compensation it could pass that cost to consumers as higher prices, and society as a whole would pay for the activities from which it benefits.

The defendant's state of mind, while not the principal factor in the balancing of interests, may nevertheless be relevant: the cases clearly illustrate that if he acts maliciously to annoy his neighbour, his malice may result in him being held liable in nuisance. This was the case, for instance, in *Hollywood Silver Fox Farm Ltd v Emmett*[6] when the defendant deliberately fired guns on his own land with the intention of interfering with the breeding of silver foxes on his neighbour's land. In such a case the defendant is clearly not pursuing any legitimate interest of his own so that the balance of interests clearly favours the plaintiff.

What if the plaintiff is only affected by the defendant's conduct because his property, or the use to which he puts it, is especially sensitive and therefore susceptible to harm? It is quite clear that if he only suffers harm because he puts his property to some special use, which renders it exceptionally sensitive he may not complain: he can only expect the same protection as the public generally, and not extra protection for his own extra-sensitive activities. Thus in the case of *Bridlington Relay Ltd v Yorkshire Electricity Board*[7] the plaintiffs were unable to claim in nuisance when the defendant's power lines interfered with the transmission of television signals, since the lines would not have interfered with a normal user of land.

However, this rule only prohibits a claim when the sole reason the plaintiff suffers harm is his own special sensitivity. If the defendant's activities would interfere with an ordinary use of property but the plaintiff suffers additional harm because his use is exceptionally sensitive, he may claim and will recover damages for all the harm he suffers. Thus in a case where a factory emitted noxious sulphur dioxide fumes, the plaintiff was able to claim for damage to orchids grown for his business.[8]

1 *Thesigner J in Sturges v Bridgman* (1879) 11 Ch D 852 at 865, CA.
2 (1865) 11 HL Cas 642.
3 See *Miller v Jackson* [1977] QB 966.
4 [1981] AC 1001, [1981] 1 All ER 353, HL.
5 Per Lord Diplock in *Allen v Gulf Oil Refining Ltd* [1984] AC 1001, [1981] 1 All ER 353, HL at 1014.
6 [1936] 2 KB 468, [1936] 1 All ER 825; see also *Christie v Davey* [1893] 1 Ch 316.
7 [1965] Ch 436, [1965] 1 All ER 264.
8 *McKinnon Industries Ltd v Walker* [1951] 3 DLR 577.

Who is liable?
10.0.3 Obviously a person who creates a nuisance, on his own or another's property, is liable for it and, of course, an employer is vicariously liable for nuisances created by his employees. However, in addition, the occupier of premises may be held liable for a nuisance which emanates from his land even though he did not create it. However, the occupier will only be held liable in this way if he knew, or ought to have known, of the source of the nuisance and failed to take reasonable steps to curtail it. Effectively then he is held liable for negligently allowing the nuisance, a dangerous situation, to continue as, for instance, in *Sedleigh-Denfield v O'Callaghan*[1] when the plaintiff's land was flooded by water escaping from a blocked drain on the

defendant's land. The drain had been blocked by a trespasser, but the defendants ought to have been aware of the risk of flooding and were therefore held liable. In *Leakey v National Trust for Places of Historic Interest or Natural Beauty*,[2] the defendants, the National Trust, owned land upon which there was a burial mound. The mound was known to be prone to subsidence and, after a dry summer and wet autumn, the plantiffs, who owned adjoining land, warned the defendants that the mound was unsafe. The defendants did nothing and part of the mound slipped onto the plaintiff's land. The defendants were held liable in nuisance.

In addition, an occupier may be held liable for acts which he has authorised. Thus an occupier has been held liable for the nuisance created by noise and dust from building work on his premises, even though the work was carried out by an independent contractor.[3]

1   [1940] AC 880.
2   [1980] QB 485, [1980] 1 All ER 17, CA.
3   *Matania v National Provincial Bank Ltd and Elevenist Syndicate Ltd* [1936] 2 All ER 633, CA.

Remedies for a nuisance
a) Injunction
10.0.4   A plaintiff who complains that an activity interferes with his enjoyment of property will normally want that activity brought to an end. In most cases, therefore—at least when he complains of a continuing nuisance such as fumes, noise or vibration rather than a single occurrence—he will seek an injunction to bring to an end the defendant's activities. We have already examined the nature of injunctions generally, and seen that being equitable in nature they are only available at the discretion of the court. When deciding whether or not to award an injunction to restrain future nuisance, the court must decide whether the interests of an individual (often particularly sensitive or litigious) should prevail over the interests of a wider group, or even of society as a whole. For instance, an order which prevents night shift working at a factory may have far-reaching social and economic consequences, causing unemployment and even damage to the national economy. We have already seen that it is no defence to a claim of nuisance that the defendant's activities are socially valuable; should that fact prevent the grant of an injunction? The court has a general discretion in all cases to refuse an injunction and award a plaintiff damages in lieu thereof, and yet in the past the courts have shown themselves remarkably reluctant to exercise this power, on the grounds that to order damages would effectively allow a defendant to 'buy' a right to commit a nuisance.[1]

This approach can be criticised. It is argued that if the courts were more willing to order damages in lieu of injunction, industrial and other 'nuisance-making' but socially desirable activities would be allowed to continue, whilst compensating the persons affected by them, forcing industry and ultimately its consumers, to pay the cost of its activities. Such a result would certainly be regarded as 'economically efficient.' On the other hand, given the importance many people attach to land, and the enjoyment of it, it can be argued that no sum of money could properly pay for disturbance and annoyance especially when the plaintiff complains of interference with his home. In any case, it may be very difficult for a court to put a proper value on a 'nuisance-making' activity. Instead, by awarding (or threatening) an injunction the court can leave the parties to negotiate and fix a fair price at which the plaintiff will release his right to restrain the defendant's activities. Thus, for example, if a factory may be forced by injunction to cease night working to prevent a nuisance to an adjoining householder, the factory may offer him compensation or even purchase his property at a price which allows him to rehouse himself elsewhere. If the parties are prepared to agree compensation, a settlement can be reached; if the householder does not wish to move, however, an award of damages only would amount to the compulsory purchase of his right not to be disturbed. Such extreme measures, it is thought, should only be sanctioned by Parliament. The availability of the injunction allows the householder to put his own value on his right to 'non-disturbance'.

1   See *Shelfer v City of London Electric Lighting Co* [1895] 1 Ch 287, CA; in *Miller v Jackson* [1977] QB 966, [1977] 3 All ER 338, CA the Court of Appeal refused an injunction which would have halted the playing of cricket on a village green; but in *Kennaway v Thompson* [1981] QB 88, [1980] 3 All ER 329, CA an injunction was granted to stop power boat racing which created a noise problem.

b) Abatement

10.0.5   The law does allow a measure of 'self help'. Thus, instead of seeking a court order, a plaintiff may take steps himself to 'abate' a nuisance. However, because of the dangers of friction between neighbours, the courts take a restrictive view of the right of abatement. It should only be exercised in a clear case; if the plaintiff must enter the defendant's property in order to abate a nuisance, he must first give notice, except in an emergency; and, in any case the plaintiff must do no more than is necessary to bring the nuisance to an end. The clearest example of abatement of a nuisance would be the right of a person to lop tree branches which overhang his property; but if he chooses to do so, he must cut them back no further than the boundary and must return the branches to the owner of the tree.

c) Damages

10.0.6   We have noted, above, the courts' power to grant damages in lieu of awarding an injunction. In addition, when the plaintiff claims in respect of a past nuisance, the court may award damages for any loss the plaintiff can show he has suffered. Monetary compensation will obviously be appropriate in cases of property damage or single occurrences; it may also be awarded, however, in cases involving an interference with business, as, for example, when the plaintiff complains that fumes from the defendant's factory have deterred customers from visiting his restaurant. When damages are awarded they may cover personal injury, damage to property and economic loss, as in the case of damages for negligence; moreover, it is now established that the rules of remoteness of damage are the same in nuisance as those applying in negligence.[1] This explains why the plaintiff whose premises are especially susceptible to damage may recover compensation for the full extent of the damage suffered, once he has established a case of nuisance.

1   *Overseas Tankship (UK) Ltd v Miller SS Co Pty* [1967] 1 AC 617, [1966] 2 All ER 709, PC.

Defences

10.0.7 A defendant may escape liability if he can show that a nuisance was created by an 'act of God'; but even then he must show that he did not and could not reasonably know of it, or that he took all reasonable steps to bring it to an end.[1] It may be a defence, as we have seen, that the nuisance was expressly or impliedly authorised by statute.[2]

A defendant may acquire a prescriptive right to continue an activity which he has carried out over a long period of time, and a nuisance will therefore cease to be actionable after twenty years. However, a prescriptive right can only be acquired in respect of an activity which could form the subject of an easement and the period of twenty years will only start to run from the time the activity became a nuisance. In *Sturges v Bridgman*[3] the plaintiff doctor moved into property and began to use part of it as a surgery; he complained that noise from the defendant's adjoining premises was interfering with his business. The defendant's argument that he had been carrying on his business for more than twenty years was to no avail: his activities only became a nuisance when the plaintiff began to use his premises as a surgery.

This case also illustrates one other point; a plaintiff may complain of a nuisance even though he moved to it; in the balancing exercise it is no defence for the defendant to show that his activities began before the plaintiff's arrival.

1 See *Goldman v Hargrave* [1967] 1 AC 645, [1966] 2 All ER 989, PC where the defendant was held liable when he failed to extinguish a fire caused by lightning striking a tree on his land.
2 See 10.0.2.
3 (1879) 11 Ch D 852, CA.

Public nuisance

10.0.8 So far we have discussed only private nuisance. There is a separate, though closely related, tort of public nuisance. This tort encompasses a range of different types of activity; the most important category consists of various interferences with the user of the highway. Public nuisance is primarily a crime, but any person especially affected by a public nuisance may sue for damages.

Rylands v Fletcher

10.0.9 This is really a separate head of liability; we mention it briefly because, whilst it differs in many ways from liability in nuisance the two can be seen as controlling similar activities. Indeed, in many cases the line between *Rylands v Fletcher* and nuisance liability may not be clear and a plaintiff may plead both in the alternative. It takes its name from a case in 1867[1] in which a land owner was held liable when water escaped from a reservoir built on his land, flooding adjoining mine workings. Neither the land owner, nor any person for whom he was liable, was negligent; however, the House of Lords laid down a general principle of strict liability that anyone 'who for his own purposes brings upon his land anything likely to do mischief if it escapes must keep it in at his peril.' The rule has two main applications: to dangerous and unusual things brought onto land—thus it has been applied not only to obvious dangers such as explosives or chemicals but even, in one case, to a fairground chair-o-plane ride[2] which detaching itself from its mounting, injured a sightseer, and in another, to people—[3] and to obviously large collections of natural substances as in

Rylands v Fletchers itself, when the deciding factor in favour of the defendant's liability was the potential for damage created by the sheer volume of water.

Liability under *Rylands v Fletcher* is strict. However, it is hedged about with a number of restrictions which greatly reduce its impact on business activities. First, the defendant is only liable for things he has brought onto his premises for his own purposes; he is not held liable for the escape of things which occur naturally. Second, the dangerous object must actually escape: if (say) explosives in a munitions factory injure a worker then he or she must sue in negligence:[4] a passerby, on the other hand, could, probably, rely on *Rylands v Fletcher*. Third, the defendant's use of his premises must be 'non-natural' or, perhaps more correctly, abnormal. Thus, for instance, domestic gas and water supplies, whilst brought into the house for the purposes of the householder, and not being natural occurrences, are nevertheless regarded as a 'natural user', commercial bulk, accumulations, of the same substances would, probably, be regarded as 'non-natural'—perhaps because of their greater capacity to cause harm.

In addition, a defendant may be able to rely on a number of defences. He will not be liable if the escape is caused by the 'act of a stranger', such as a trespasser, or due to 'act of God'—that is to say, natural forces which exceed human anticipation. In addition he may be able to plead that the escape was due to the plaintiff's own conduct and thus raise a partial (contributory negligence) or even a complete defence ('act of plaintiff') or even claim consent. However, perhaps the most important restriction on *Rylands v Fletcher* liability is the willingness of the courts to hold that statutory authority excludes liability. When statute imposes a duty on a public—or private—body to do some act involving the accumulation of potentially dangerous substances, it may expressly exclude liability; but even if it does not do so the court may hold that the statutory duty impliedly excludes liability.[5] Since many potentially dangerous accumulations are brought together by public bodies—such as water and gas boards—or under statutory authority, this is a serious restriction and it has been widely criticised.

There is much to be said for imposing strict liability on the controllers of especially dangerous things or operations so that persons injured by such operations may obtain redress without the need to prove negligence. This is particularly true when the operations are part of a commercial business or public utility: the users of the service, or the public generally, are then made to bear the costs of the operations from which they benefit. However, there is no good reason why such strict liability should be linked to land use, as it is under *Rylands v Fletcher*. The Pearson Commission[6] proposed a statutory scheme of strict liability to be imposed on persons in control of 'things or operations' requiring close supervision because of their especially hazardous nature, or because they are 'likely, if they go wrong, to cause serious and extensive casualties'. The scheme has not been adopted.

1   (1865) 3 H & C 774; revsd (1866) LR 1 Exch 265; on appeal (1868) LR 3 HL 330.
2   *Hale v Jennings Bros* [1938] 1 All ER 579, CA.
3   *A-G v Corke* [1933] Ch 89.
4   *Read v J Lyons & Co Ltd* [1947] AC 156, [1946] 2 All ER 471, HL.
5   See *Green v Chelsea Waterworks Co* (1894) 70 LT 547, CA when there was a statutory duty to provide a water supply; contrast *Charing Cross Electricity Supply Co v Hydraulic Power Co* [1914] 3 KB 772, CA when the defendants had a statutory power but no duty and were held liable.
6   Cmnd 7054 1978—I para 1643.

Chapter 11

The Effectiveness of the Tort System: Some Alternatives

11.0.0　We observed earlier that in recent years the tort system has come under increasing scrutiny from lawyers and economists (amongst others) who have called into question its effectiveness. Having looked briefly at the law itself we are now in a position to look at some of those arguments.

However, we immediately come up against a problem. Before we can assess the effectiveness of the tort system we must decide what are, or should be, its objectives, and what those objectives are or should be is far from clear. Moreover, insofar as the law of torts, and particularly that part upon which we have focused, the law of negligence, has more than one objective, much of the difficulty in this area springs from the fact that those objectives are often in conflict.

We began by simply stating that the purpose of an award of tort damages is to compensate the victim of a tortious act. There is no doubt that that is indeed a major function of the tort system. However, the system suffers from two defects. First, it is primitive in that its only remedy is an award of financial compensation. There are many forms of loss for which damages are awarded, upon which no sensible financial value can be placed: pain and suffering due to physical injury, distress at the loss of one's sight or the ability to take part in sports and games or at the loss of a loved one—a small child perhaps. However, that deficiency in the tort system is shared by any other system which might replace it and, if we accept that such losses should be compensated then they can only be so in financial terms.

The system is more fundamentally flawed by being based on the fault of an identifiable defendant. If I am run down by a drunken driver or am injured by a product made dangerous by negligence in its manufacture, I can claim compensation from the driver or manufacturer (or, in fact, from their insurers). But if I am injured in a road accident when no one is at fault, or if the manufacturer can show that he took all reasonable care in the manufacturing process, I will receive no compensation through the tort system, even though my injuries and losses are no less severe. The same is true of the individual who suffers loss not caused by any other person; for instance, he who is disabled by illness or whose house falls down through the action of natural forces. It is true that, as we have seen, the burden on a plaintiff who must show fault is lessened by a number of devices—by the doctrine of res ipsa loquitur, which may allow him to rely on a presumption of fault, by vicarious liability which allows him to proceed against a blameless but financially sound defendant, by the (statutory) imposition of strict liability on those carrying out hazardous undertakings or by the judicial raising of the standard of reasonable care, particularly where insurance is available. The fact remains, however, that in many cases the plaintiff will be compensated only if he can show that an identifiable individual caused his loss and was at fault. Why should that be? The answer seems to be, at least in part, in an overlap with other ideas of the purposes of the law and tort; with the idea that its purpose is to shift losses and that it is just for a plaintiff wishing to shift his loss onto another to first show that that other was to blame; and with the idea that the law of tort should fulfil a deterrent function.

Vindication

11.0.1 Before moving on to consider the deterrent and loss shifting functions of tort law it is worth mentioning another role it performs, albeit one which is perhaps a little unfashionable. There can be no doubt that an award of damages does help assuage the feelings of an injured plaintiff, in part at least because he is able to vindicate himself: a court action is public and allows him publicly to show that he is right and that the defendant is in the wrong. This is most clearly seen in relation to the law of defamation where a successful plaintiff awarded only nominal damages and no costs will still feel vindicated by the court's decision; but it can be seen also in less obvious situations: in a nuisance action, for instance, or even in a negligence case. As we move on to consider more fashionable aspects of the function of tort law, and its success in fulfilling those functions, it is important not to lose sight of the value of providing the plaintiff with the satisfaction of his 'day in court'. How many times have lawyers heard their clients announce, 'It's not the money; its a matter of principle'?

Deterrence

11.0.2 So far we have accepted, largely without question, that the law of tort fulfils a deterrent function and may therefore raise or set standards of behaviour. It is by no means clear that the law of tort should act as a deterrent; it is even less clear that it does effectively fulfil that function. There is no doubt that in some cases a decision in a past case may raise standards of behaviour and so exercise a deterrent function. For instance, in *Reffell v Surrey County Council*[1] it was held that a school was negligent in using ordinary, rather than toughened, glass in doors. As a result, many local authorities replaced the glass in the doors in their schools with toughened glass. However, even in a case such as this, as Professor Atiyah observes,[2] it is by no means clear that this is a desirable result, for how is the court to rule that a local education authority should spend its (limited) resources on installing toughened glass rather than, say, on new text books?

We can see the deterrent effect even more clearly in the well-known practice of newspaper publishers submitting all contentious material to the scrutiny of their lawyers for fear of a libel action. However, a court decision may often provoke a less beneficial reaction in potential defendants. They may seek to avoid a ruling, for instance by relying on an appropriate exclusion clause or notice (as happened after *Hedley Byrne & Co Ltd v Heller & Partners Ltd*[3]). Thus in *Yianni v Edwin Evans & Sons*[4] it was held that a valuer who carried out a survey for a building society was liable to the intending purchaser to whom the society showed the survey report. As a result of that decision building societies are now much more cautious about showing such surveys to purchasers; and if they do so at all, they do so under cover of an extensive exclusion of liability. One might question whether this is to the advantage of house purchasers. Alternatively, potential defendants may seek to nullify the effects of a decision by taking out insurance against liability. We will return to this point below.

However, if we accept that the law of tort should have a deterrent function, we must then ask how effective it is in that role. The answer may vary from area to area, for several reasons. Let us first consider the role of negligence in relation to road accidents. If a driver is not deterred from driving negligently out of fear for his own safety, it is hard to see how the fear of an award of damages will improve his driving—even if he were to pay the award. This view is supported by evidence from other areas: for instance, the well-publicised adverse health effects of smoking have not brought an end to cigarette smoking, and nor, for that matter, have financial penalties in the form of regular price increases.

Moreover, the deterrent effect of an award of damages is further diluted when we take insurance into account. For if the potential tortfeasor is insured he need not fear an award of damages because the only financial cost to him will be an increased premium—and possibly the loss of a no claims bonus—which will rarely equal the amount of the award. Moreover, if the defendant is in business, he can pass on the increased insurance costs to his customers, at least up to the point when his prices become uncompetitive. On the other hand, as we have already seen, insurance benefits the plaintiff who is assured of his damages. Thus we see here a conflict between the interests of potential tort victims (the deterrent function) and those of the individual plaintiff (the compensation function).

There is a further related weakness in the effectiveness of tort law as a deterrent. For, as we have seen, partly because of the availability of insurance cover, the courts have increased the standard of behaviour required of defendants, in some cases to levels which are artificially high. If the standards required by law are set so high that they cannot be attained, how can the law set or raise standards? To take the example of road accidents, if a driver can be said to be negligent when he is performing to the standard of the average driver—as he no doubt can[5]—the imposition of legal liability is unlikely to improve his driving.

On the other hand, a tort action may have some valuable deterrent effect. For instance, a threat of legal proceedings coupled with possible adverse publicity may lead to the settlement of—even unmeritorious—cases. However, a threat of publicity in newspapers or on TV may be equally effective. Similarly, the threat of adverse publicity may, in the area of dangerous products, lead to the withdrawal from sale of such items. Generally though, the tort system is weak as a deterrent and ineffective as a raiser of standards; other methods are more effective. A tort action can only be brought after someone has been injured; if there is no injured party there will be no action at all. Much more effective is advance regulation—for instance by Parliamentary regulation setting minimum safety standards. The enforcement of such standards is perhaps better dealt with by the criminal law when a prosecution can be brought without the need for someone first to suffer injury or loss.

1 [1964] 1 All ER 743, [1964] 1 WLR 358.
2 *Accidents, Compensation and The Law* (1980, 3rd edn) p 563.
3 [1964] AC 465, [1963] 2 All ER 575, HL.
4 [1982] QB 438, [1981] 3 All ER 592.
5 See 3.3.0.

'Loss shifting'

11.0.3   In recent years it has been popular in academic legal circles to speak of tort law as 'shifting' loss caused by a defendant's wrongdoing, shifting it from the plaintiff to the defendant. Such a description really amounts to no more than a restatement of the compensation objective coupled with the 'fault principle', insofar as the plaintiff must justify shifting his loss onto the defendant, and he may only do so if he can show the defendant is at fault. However, there are several drawbacks to this approach. First, as we have seen, some losses simply cannot be shifted, except in crudely financial terms. Second, there is the problem of when a loss should be shifted. English law has, as we have seen, adopted the solution of shifting loss when the defendant can be shown to be at fault; however, insistence on fault may leave uncompensated many deserving plaintiffs—or may lead to an artificial finding of fault on the part of a defendant. Finally, and not least, is the danger that a substantial award of damages may financially ruin the defendant.

This last danger is mitigated somewhat by the availability to potential defendants of insurance cover. Moreover, insurance allows an award of damages effectively to be spread over a larger group. Thus writers have begun to speak instead of 'loss distribution', a more sophisticated version of 'loss shifting'. However, this leaves unresolved the question of over which group the particular loss should be distributed. Insurance means that loss is spread over all persons carrying out any particular potentially hazardous activity. For instance, the increased cost of road accidents is spread via motor insurance over all drivers. However, as Professor Atiyah has observed, the distribution of losses via insurance is relatively unsophisticated, in that even though the claims record of a particular driver may, via the no claims discount system, affect his premium, his premium is still largely dependent on the claims of drivers generally and—

> 'there are substantial grounds for believing that the whole premium rating structure of motor insurance is based on a hotchpotch of irrationalities, mythologies and traditional practices rather than on any scientific or statistical basis.'[1]

Even more significantly in the context of business, employers' liability insurance premiums to cover the costs of accidents at work are generally based on the experiences of a whole group of similar businesses rather than on the characteristics of the individual business.[2] Indeed, given the immense number of variable factors which might contribute to or cause an accident it is difficult to see how any premium rating system could be wholly scientific.

A third alternative terminology is to speak of 'risk allocation'. By this it is meant that the law decides which of two parties should bear the risk of loss caused by an accident. Effectively this means who should bear the cost of insuring against a particular loss. One solution is to impose that expense on the person who causes the damage—but that leads to the problem of deciding what factor is the cause of a particular loss. Another solution is to impose loss on the party at fault: but that leads back to a discussion of 'fault' and the problems of compensating those who suffer loss where no one is at fault. A third alternative would be to impose the risk on the party who can most easily insure against it. That might be the person who can most easily assess the risk of occurrence of an accident (the defendant) or the person who can most easily assess the extent of the potential loss (generally the plaintiff). This last factor has often been put forward as an argument against imposing on a defendant liability for purely economic loss.[3] There is, of course, no reason why all these factors—causation, fault and insurance— should not be taken into account in deciding where to allocate risk. However, we can see that to speak of 'risk allocation' is only really restating the problem.

1 Atiyah, *Accidents, Compensation and the Law* (1980, 3rd edn) p 572.
2 Ibid, p 574.
3 Eg in the so-called 'cable cases', see 7.1.0.

General deterrence

11.0.4 In recent years a number of writers, principally in America, have advocated a less legalistic approach which would take account of the economic considerations involved in an award of tort damages. Such commentators have evolved a theory of what the function of tort law should be, known as 'general deterrence'.

The starting point for this theory is the economists' ideal that the price of any commodity in a perfect market economy should fully reflect its production costs:[1] the consumers of goods and services can then make a fully considered decision whether or not to purchase them, with full knowledge of their true cost. Any losses caused by a product or service should be allocated to that product or service as a production cost. Thus, for example, if my factory gives off noxious fumes which damage a nearby garden centre, then the loss suffered should be regarded as a cost of my business. The law should therefore make me liable for that loss. Similarly if I manufacture goods with an inherent defect which makes them dangerous, I should bear the cost of accidents caused by those goods. Those accident costs will have to be passed on to my customers and so, to keep my products attractive, I will have to reduce their accident costs by making my product safer, or reducing pollution from my factory. I will then continue to reduce pollution or to make products safer until it ceases to be economic for me to do so: for instance when the cost of further measures to reduce pollution will exceed any damages I may have to pay; or when the risk of accidents caused by my products is so low that further safety improvements will be uneconomic.

The principle objection to such an approach is that, in giving emphasis to economic considerations, it seems to underplay other factors which might be thought to be socially desirable objectives for the law. For instance, it might be desirable for social reasons to reduce pollution beyond the 'break even point'—although this could be achieved by increasing the damages payable for nuisance in the example given, thus 'moving' the break-even point. Furthermore, it places great faith in the capitalist economic system. The approach has been criticised. Abel argues that 'the capitalist must be as unsafe as he can get away with being';[2] he 'must sacrifice the health and safety of others—workers, consumers, those affected by environmental danger',[3] and he cites examples of Ford in the United States building a car which was known to have a design defect (an unsafe petrol tank) and of American Airlines continuing to fly a DC10 known to be faulty.

Other criticisms can be made. Professor Calabresi, a leading exponent of the theory of general deterrence, has applied the theory particularly to accidents, a major concern of the law of torts. He argues that—

159

'the principal function of accident law is to reduce the sum of the cos[t] of accidents and the cost of avoiding accidents.'[4]

This recognises that the costs of accidents, and many other losses with which the tort system deals, are losses to the whole of society. This is particularly clear in the case of accidents which cause personal injury where not only are damages paid out by insurers spread through the community by increased premiums and increased prices; but also society must bear extra costs such as hospital treatment for the accident victim, the loss of his potentially valuable labour to the economy, losses in tax revenues due to the victim's inability to earn, payments to the victim from the welfare system, the cost of maintaining and operating emergency services, and so on. Calabresi argues that this function of reducing accidents and related costs can best be performed if the tort system first identifies the causes of accidents and then imposes legal and financial liability for those accidents on those responsible for causing them. He cites the example of seat belts in cars and argues that if the manufacturers of cars without seat belts had to pay the accident costs caused by such cars they would in turn have to pass on those costs to the potential buyer; the buyer, in turn, would have a choice between paying extra for a car fitted with seat belts, or buying a car without belts, but paying extra to cover its accident costs.[5]

Professor Atiyah criticises this approach.[6] First, he observes, it is difficult to designate any one factor as the cause of an accident. An 'accident' may be due to a combination of factors. Second, there is the difficulty of defining an activity: for instance, should we speak of accidents caused by driving, or by car driving? Should we distinguish between driving for pleasure and driving for business? Between different categories of drivers? Third, as we have already observed, these theories can only operate in a capitalist economy; moreover, they place great faith in consumer preference: a consumer might, perversely, decide not to buy the cheaper accident-avoiding car, for instance because he preferred the other's colour or style. Finally, Atiyah observes, these theories take no account of social factors, for instance the possibility that it might be desirable to reduce injuries caused by the absence of seat belts in cars even if it is more expensive to fit compulsory seat belts. General deterrence allows activities of all kinds to be carried on, provided the actor is prepared to pay. It cannot alone provide a sufficient social framework.

The proponents of general deterrence have, in the main, been American despite the greater weight given to free market economic theories in Britain in recent years. So far such theories have had little impact on the development of tort law, especially in this country. However, Atiyah argues[7] that the law does, in fact, already reflect general deterrence because the modern common law and free market economies share a common root in the laissez-faire philosophies of the 19th century. He concludes that the insurance system provides a combination of general deterrence with 'loss spreading': varied premiums fulfil a deterrent role, but costs are spread amongst all policyholders carrying on similar activities.[8]

1   See R Coase, 'The Problem of Social Cost' (1960) 3 Jnl of Law and Economics. These and the following theories are discussed more fully in Atiyah, *Accidents, Compensation and the Law* (1980, 3rd edn) Ch 24.
2   R L Abel, 'A critique of American Tort Law' (1981) British Journal of Law and Society Vol 8 no 2.
3   Ibid.

4   Calabresi, *The cost of accidents: A Legal and Economic Analysis* (1970).
5   Calabresi in Keeton, O'Connell & McCord (eds), *Crisis in Car Insurance* (1968).
6   Atiyah, *Accidents, Compensation and the Law*, (1980, 3rd edn) p 582 ff.
7   Ibid, p 594.
8   Ibid, p 604.

Accident compensation: alternatives to tort

11.0.5   In discussing the purposes and functions of tort law we have concentrated on that part which deals with accidents—not surprisingly because negligence constitutes the most important element in the law of torts and, numerically speaking, the law of negligence is mainly concerned with accidents which cause personal injuries. Moreover, the question of how best to compensate accident victims has come under increasing scrutiny in recent years, culminating in the UK in the Report of the Pearson Committee in 1978.[1]

The tort system is not the only means which exists in our society for compensating accident victims. Alongside it exists a plethora of other systems: an accident victim may, additionally, receive compensation from his own personal accident insurance policy; from the state social security system, via sickness benefit (including statutory sick pay); disablement benefit, industrial injury benefit; through the state run Criminal Injuries Compensation Scheme; from his own employer (sick pay); charities and so on. Of these systems, the social security system is responsible for compensating the greatest number of accident victims, so much so that Pearson spoke of it having relegated the tort system to the role of 'junior partner'. On the other hand the tort system is disproportionately generous to those it compensates; Pearson reported that the tort system paid out annually some £202 million to 215,000 accident victims, whereas the social security system paid out £421 million to 1.5 million victims—paying approximately only one third as much to each victim.

Moreover, the overlap of various systems makes for further inequality. The injured party able to make a claim under the tort system may be able to claim substantial sums as compensation for 'pain and suffering' and loss of amenity, for which the state system would pay nothing, and may be able to claim twice, or more, from different sources for the same injury. On the other hand the system as a whole still leaves out many accident victims altogether, for instance, the man who breaks his leg falling in the bath will get nothing from the major schemes and must rely on sick pay from the state, or his employer, unless, which is unlikely, he had the foresight to take out his own accident insurance policy. Many commentators have thus come to regard the system as a whole, and the tort system in particular, as unfair. In addition, the tort system is inefficient in that larger sums may have to be paid in legal costs to get the money where it is needed, in the hands of the victim, and the system is slow to deal with claims especially if contested, because of the need to prove fault in order to establish liability. By contrast, a system based on social security would be fairer, more efficient and has the added benefit that it spreads the cost of accidents over society as a whole.

Thus there have been growing calls for a move away from a tort-based system. In 1974 New Zealand abolished tort damages for personal injuries replacing them with a single state social security fund financed by contributions from employers, the self-employed and motorists.[2] All accident victims are entitled to compensation without proof of fault. In 1978 the

11.0.5 The Effectiveness of the Tort System: Some Alternatives

Pearson Committee reported in England and produced a less radical set o' proposals. Broadly the Committee proposed that the state system for deal ing with accidents at work should remain. However, there should be a new state fund to compensate victims of road accidents who would not have to show any other person to have been at fault. The fund would be financed by a tax on petrol. Pearson felt that its terms of reference did not include con sideration of the abolition of the tort system, but in any case advocated it retention so that anyone who could prove fault in another person should be entitled to seek tort damages.

Many commentators have criticised the Pearson proposals for not going far enough and advocating wholesale abandonment of the tort system fo' personal injury compensation. Of course, even if that were done, the tor' system would remain important for dealing with property damage and, a we have seen, increasingly with economic losses. However, even the timorous proposals which Pearson did make have been largely ignored and the tort system remains at the heart of accident compensation in the UK. A least, however, Pearson and the debate which preceded it have served to transfer attention away from the defendant and proof of his fault to the plaintiff and his need for compensation.

1 *The Report of the Royal Commission on Civil Liability and Compensation for Persona Injury* Cmnd 7054, 1978.
2 Implementing the proposals of the Woodhouse Report, 'Report of the Royal Commissio of Inquiry on Compensation for Personal Injuries in New Zealand' 1967.

Part III
Contract

Chapter 12

Agreement

Influences on contract law

12.0.0   The exchange of goods and services is the central feature of business activity and contract law provides the means of supporting exchange transactions in our society. In essence the law of contract facilitates the process of exchange, supporting the expectations of the parties in respect of performance of the undertakings forming part of an agreement.

Much of the theoretical framework of modern contract law originated in the eighteenth and nineteenth century. It was a period of rapid economic and political change. The traditional mercantile economy was superseded by the economic doctrine of laissez-faire founded on notions of individualism and the capitalist society. The cornerstone of the doctrine was that if individuals were left free to pursue their own economic self-interest they would inevitably maximise profits and thus benefit society as a whole. Contract law played a central role in the new economic order since it was by means of a contract that the individual's self-interest would be finalised. As Selznick observes, 'Contract law was to be liberating and facilitative, a channel for the release of energies.'[1]

The law came to embody the predominant values of the era—freedom, self-government and equality.[2] It was assumed that the parties to a contract freely entered into it in pursuit of self-interest and that its terms were necessarily fair and reasonable if both parties were in agreement. The judiciary for the most part have doggedly continued to support these values, although in many respects they are inappropriate in a modern consumer society. In recent years, however, Parliament has placed some restrictions on contractual freedom.

In the following paragraphs we examine some of the essential aspects of contract law and practice.

1   *Law Society and Industrial Justice* (Russell Sage Foundation, 1969) p 53.
2   See Friedman, *Law in a Changing Society* (2nd edn, 1972).

The agreement

12.1.0   For there to be a legally binding contract there must be an agreement, that is, a reasonably definite understanding between two or more persons. In terms of the law the paramount factor is the intention of the parties to be inferred from their words or conduct. If it is found that the intentions of the parties were not the same, there can be no agreement; there is said to be an absence of 'consensus ad idem' or 'meeting of the minds'.

165

12.1.0–12.1.1 Agreement

In view of the fact that the term 'agreement' covers an enormous number of situations ranging from the simple cash sale over the counter, to protracted negotiations over large building or engineering contracts, the law was required to develop a simple and rational model of the negotiation and agreement process. This was done by reducing all agreements to two parts—the offer and the acceptance. If, from the words or conduct of one of the parties, it is possible to identify an offer, it will be turned into an agreement if and when the other party intimates acceptance. It should be stressed at this point that in any dispute over the existence of a contract the courts seek to give effect to the intentions of the parties as manifested or apparent from their dealings which may not, in exceptional circumstances, necessarily be their actual intentions. For example, if A sets out the terms of a proposal which meets the requirements of an offer and delivers it to B who promptly accepts it, there is a contract even though A may later argue that he did not intend it to be an offer or that he had serious reservations over its terms. Such an approach has been called the objective test of agreement and it has been adopted largely as a matter of convenience. It would be impossible for a court to decide what an individual's actual intent was at a particular moment in time. In addition, it would be unjust to allow a person to indicate by the terms of a transaction a particular intention and then claim before a court that they did not mean what was apparently intended. Thus the expression 'meeting of the minds' refers to the apparent or legal meeting of minds.

The offer

12.1.1 Most agreements can be reduced to an offer by one party (the offeror) and an acceptance by the other (the offeree or acceptor). In those cases where it is difficult to identify an offer and acceptance, the courts may nevertheless conclude that there is an agreement, perhaps at the cost of 'forcing the facts to fit uneasily into the marked slots of offer and acceptance . . .'[1]

For example, in *Clarke v Earl of Dunraven and Mount-Earl, The Satanita*[2] two competitors in a yacht race had written to the secretary of a yacht club agreeing to be bound by the rules of the club. The House of Lords held that a contract was created between the competitors and that the one competitor whose yacht had been damaged could recover damages from the other in accordance with the rules. The facts do not, however, fall easily into the 'marked slots of offer and acceptance' and it is very difficult to state exactly when each competitor made an offer to the other and when such offer was accepted.

Atiyah argues that in some cases—

'it may be very difficult, if not impossible, to find a real offer and acceptance or to decide who is the offeror and who is the offeree. Such cases show that to insist on the presence of a genuine offer and acceptance in every case is likely to land one in sheer fiction.'[3]

To amount to an offer the law requires a clear intention to contract on terms that are reasonably definite. Thus if the language used is tentative and the negotiations are merely at an exploratory stage, it may be concluded that contractual relations are not yet contemplated. If a party states, 'I would like to get £2,500 for my car', or 'I will not sell for less than £10,000', it can be said that the negotiations are still at a preliminary stage. The statements cannot be converted into agreements by the other party saying 'I accept' since they are not intended to be legal offers. Similarly, inquiries and replies are not offers. Thus in *Harvey v Facey*[4] the plaintiffs telegraphed to the defendants, 'Will you sell us Bumper Hall Pen? Telegraph lowest cash price'. The defendants replied, 'Lowest cash price for Bumper Hall Pen, £900.' The plaintiff responded, 'We agree to buy Bumper Hall Pen for £900 asked by you. Please send us your title deeds'. It was held that there was no contract. The second telegram was merely an indication of the lowest price should the defendants decide to sell; it was not an offer which was capable of acceptance in the terms of the third telegram.

1 Lord Wilberforce in *New Zealand Shipping Co Ltd v A M Satterthwaite & Co Ltd* [1975] AC 154 at 167, PC.
2 [1897] AC 59, HL.
3 *An Introduction to the Law of Contract* (1981) p 43.
4 [1893] AC 552, PC.

An offer distinguished from an invitation to treat
12.1.2 The existence of a legal offer indicates a willingness to enter into a legal obligation, as opposed to merely entering into negotiations or inviting other persons to make offers. It is necessary therefore to distinguish an offer from 'an invitation to treat' which is in effect an indication by someone that they are ready and willing to receive offers. A person making an invitation to treat is not bound to accept any offer made in response.

Thus the courts have had to pronounce on a number of familiar business situations and their decisions have been based as much on business convenience as on any expression of intention by the parties. For example, it has long been held that the publication of a catalogue or circular advertising goods for sale is an invitation to treat. The display of goods in a shop window is also an invitation to treat[1] since it is argued to hold otherwise might mean that there would be more customers willing to buy than a shopkeeper is able to supply.

It is argued that—

'it would be wrong if a shopkeeper was obliged to sell goods to a man he hated or a barber to cut the hair of a filthy person merely because his window display or price list was on offer. Secondly, there would be no opportunity to rectify mistakes and where an article had, by mistake, a ridiculously low price tag, then acceptance would create a very uneconomic situation for sellers, and in supermarkets and department stores could lead to wholesale fraud where unscrupulous buyers switched prices.'[2]

Similarly the display of goods on a supermarket shelf is an invitation to treat. The offer is made by the customer and is accepted or rejected at the cash desk.[3] This means that where goods are wrongly priced the customer cannot insist on taking them at the marked price, the cashier may simply refuse to accept the customer's offer. The rule may even apply where the goods are described as a 'special offer'.

Not all advertisements or displays are, however, expressions of a willingness to trade. In one case it was held that a notice displayed at the entrance to an automatic car-park was an offer[4] which was accepted when the customer drove in. In the case of advertisements of rewards for the return of lost property, or information leading to the conviction of a criminal, it is generally accepted that the offer is made in the terms of the advertisement and is accepted when someone performs the necessary act. For example in *Carlill v Carbolic Smoke Ball Co*[5] the defendants advertised that they would pay £100 to anyone contracting influenza after using their product in the prescribed manner. The plaintiff used one of the smoke balls according to the directions but caught influenza. The company refused to pay her the £100 arguing that it was a contract 'with all the world' and such a contract was not recognised by the law. In addition they argued that the advertisement was too vague to amount to an offer. The Court of Appeal, however, held that the advertisement was an offer to the world at large which was converted into a binding contract when someone duly performed the conditions.

1   *Fisher v Bell* [1961] 1 QB 394, [1960] 3 All ER 731.
2   Smith and Street, *The Consumer Adviser* (Institute of Trading Standards, 1978) p 63.
3   *Pharmaceutical Society of Great Britain v Boots Cash Chemists (Southern) Ltd* [1953] 1 QB 401, [1953] 1 All ER 482, CA.
4   *Thornton v Shoe Lane Parking Ltd* [1971] 2 QB 163.
5   [1893] 1 QB 256, CA.

Auction sales
12.1.3   In the case of auction sales the mere advertisement of an intended sale is not an offer or promise to hold the sale, since the seller may accept an offer to sell the goods before the date of sale. To hold otherwise would mean that anyone who advertises a sale may become responsible for the travelling expenses of everybody who attends.[1]

On the other hand, it has been held that if an auction is advertised as 'without reserve', the advertisement has the effect of an offer which is accepted by the person who attends the auction and makes the highest bona fide bid.[2] If a reserve price is then imposed, or the auctioneer fails to 'knock' down to the highest bidder, the auctioneer is liable for breach of that contract.

At the actual sale the auctioneer's demand for bids is merely an invitation to make offers, which he may accept or reject. The Sale of Goods Act 1979 confirms such a view by providing that a sale by auction is complete when the auctioneer announces its completion by the fall of the hammer, or in other customary manner, and until such announcement is made any bid may be retracted.[3]

1   *Harrison v Nickerson* (1873) LR 8 QB 286.
2   *Warlow v Harrison* (1859) 1 E & E 309. The reasoning is supported by the House of Lords in *Harvela Investments Ltd v Royal Trust Co of Canada (CI) Ltd* [1986] AC 207, [1985] 2 All ER 966, HL.
3   S 57(2).

Tenders
12.1.4   Often a local authority will declare that the provision of goods or services is open to tender. Such an announcement is an invitation to treat not an offer. Thus the person who submits a tender makes the offer. The person who invites the tender is not bound to accept the highest or lowest unless he has expressly committed himself to do so in the invitation. There may be

good reasons why, for instance, the cheapest tender to carry out building work may not be the best. Sometimes the invitation to submit tenders will be for the supply of goods as required. In such event any offer is treated as a standing offer which may be accepted from time to time as required and in that case the offeror is always able to revoke his offer before individual orders are placed and the offeree is under no obligation to place orders. Alternatively, the invitation may be for the supply of definite services or a definite quantity of goods over a period of time; in that case the acceptance of a tender concludes a contract which is binding on both parties.

In *Harvela Investments Ltd v Royal Trust Co of Canada (CI) Ltd*[1] the House of Lords had to consider the validity of a tender in the form of a referential bid.[2] The defendants wished to sell a number of shares in a company, the plaintiffs and one other shareholder were keen to acquire their shares as they would give either of them control of the company. The defendants therefore invited both interested parties to submit tenders to buy the shares in the form of sealed bids, to be submitted by a certain date. The other interested party submitted a referential bid and the defendants treated that as the highest bid.

The House of Lords held that by the wording of their invitation the defendants had committed themselves to accept the highest bona fide bid. The referential bid was therefore invalid.

1   [1986] AC 207, [1985] 2 All ER 966, HL.
2   The bid was expressed in the following terms: '. . . $100,000 in excess of any offer which you receive which is expressed as a fixed monetary amount and which is higher.'

Termination of offers

12.1.5   An offer will be terminated either by revocation, rejection, lapse of time or death.

a) Revocation

An offer may always be withdrawn provided it has not been properly accepted, since until acceptance takes place no legal obligation arises. Even where the offeror agrees to keep the offer open for a specified period, he may under English law withdraw it at anytime without liability. The only situation where the offeror will be bound on such a promise is where he enters into a separate contract to keep the offer open. Such a contract must, however, be supported by consideration. For example, an option contract may be used whereby the offeree gives the offeror consideration in the form of cash in return for the offeror's promise to keep the offer open. Once accepted, the offeror cannot withdraw during the specified period. The position under Scots law is preferable to the English position. Scots law does not require consideration and is thus able to protect the offeree's expectations in such a situation by enforcing a promise to keep an offer open. In 1975 The Law Commission argued that English law should be changed so as to make offers open for a definite period binding when made in the course of business.[1]

Where the offeror seeks to withdraw an offer he must communicate his change of mind to the offeree. Such communication must be received by the offeree before it is effective. There is no parallel rule to that which regards a postal acceptance as communicated once it has been posted.[2] In a business context it ought to be sufficient that the revocation arrives on a working day and it should be regarded as having been communicated even if it remains unopened. Similarly, if the offeree deliberately keeps out of the way or closes the office to avoid receipt of the revocation, it will nevertheless be regarded as effective. Communication of revocation may be indirect in the sense that if the offeree is advised of the revocation by a reliable third party it will be regarded as an effective revocation.[3]

b) Rejection

If the offeree rejects an offer either outright or by including a counter-offer, the original offer is cancelled. Like the offer and the revocation, a rejection takes effect only when it has been communicated. Thus if the offeree rejects the offer but later changes his mind, provided that he communicates his acceptance before the rejection is received by the offeror, there will be a contract. It is important to distinguish between an outright rejection or counter-offer[4] and a simple approach for further information. Thus an offer would not necessarily be rejected by an enquiry as to whether the offeror would grant credit.

c) Lapse of time

Where no time limit is placed on the offer it may nevertheless be terminated by the passage of a reasonable length of time. What is reasonable depends on the circumstances of each case. Thus if the language used in the offer denotes a sense of urgency, for example, 'I must hear from you very soon', the time within which the offer must be accepted will be shorter than if no such words were used. Similarly, the use of a telegram to send the offer suggests a degree of urgency. Prevailing market conditions may also be a significant factor. If the price of goods is fluctuating rapidly, a reasonable time might be measured in terms of hours.

d) Death

Where the offeror dies before acceptance the offer will lapse. Notice of the death must, however, reach the offeree before he communicates acceptance. Similarly, death of the offeree will normally terminate an offer, unless the offer was made to the world at large.

1   Working Paper 60.
2   See 12.11.0.
3   See *Dickinson v Dodds* (1876) 2 Ch D 463, CA.
4   See 12.1.7.

Acceptance
12.1.6   An offer is turned into a binding contract by an acceptance of its terms without qualification. To be effective there must be some external manifestation of acceptance evidenced by words or conduct and duly communicated to the offeror. In most cases the offeree will promise to perform his part of the bargain in return for performance by the offeror of his promise. This is said to be a bilateral contract, an exchange of promises. On the other hand the offer may simply call for a single act to be performed, such as using the smoke ball in the *Carlill* case, which when performed constitutes acceptance. This is known as a unilateral contract consisting of a promise by one party, the offer, and an act of acceptance by the other party. By far the most common type of contract, particularly in the business context, is the bilateral contract.

An acceptance is an expression by which the offeree indicates consent to be bound by the terms of the offer. Whilst it is preferable that the offeree expressly accepts the offer, it is not necessary. Any language or conduct showing that the offeree is assenting to the deal is sufficient.[1] Often however business negotiations are complex and protracted and it may be extremely difficult to state precisely when an agreement in terms of offer and acceptance has been reached. Naturally the businessman, particularly in times of uncertainty and inflation, may wish to retain a degree of flexibility which the conceptual straitjacket of offer and acceptance does not allow. In the course of negotiations counter proposals and qualifications may be submitted and even when the parties consider that a broad agreement has been reached they may still wish to retain a degree of room for manoeuvre.

1 See *Brogden v Metropolitan Rly Co* (1877) 2 App Cas 666, HL.

Counter-offers
12.1.7 A party's response to an offer will not constitute an acceptance unless it unequivocally accepts all the terms of the offer. Although the courts will tolerate trivial variations and variations which simply spell out a term which the law would in any event imply, any attempt to introduce new or revised terms amounts to a counter-offer and a rejection rather than an acceptance. The courts have also been prepared to distinguish between an outright counter-offer and a mere request for information, such as whether the offeror would be prepared to allow credit terms[1] which keep the offer alive and capable of acceptance. The difficulties over deciding upon the precise time at which an agreement was reached because of the introduction of new terms are illustrated in the case of *Brinkibon Ltd v Stahag Stahl und Stahlwarenhandelsgesellshaft mbH*.[2] The case concerned an agreement between a Swiss company and an English company for the sale of steel. The negotiations proceeded as follows:
1. On 26 April 1979, the plaintiff company sent from London a telex offering to buy the steel.
2. On 3 May the defendants replied by telex sent from Switzerland stating that they accepted the offer subject to certain amendments including a' stipulation that if freight rates rose the price would be increased accordingly. They also requested the plaintiff to open a letter of credit by which the defendants could be paid (this is a common practice designed to facilitate international trade whereby a buyer instructs his bank to open a credit in the seller's favour at a bank in the seller's country).
3. On 4 May the plaintiffs instructed their bank to open a letter of credit. On the same day they sent a telex from London to the defendants informing them that the arrangements had been made.
4. On 21 May the defendants informed the plaintiffs that they intended to withdraw from the transaction.
The problem facing the House of Lords was to decide when acceptance took place so as to determine whether the English or Swiss courts had jurisdiction to decide the case. The plaintiffs argued that the English courts should hear the case because the contract was made either at stage 2 (on 3 May) when the telex was sent or stage 3 when they opened the letter of credit. The House of Lords stated that the telex of 3 May would have concluded the

contract when it was received in London if it amounted to a proper acceptance. However, it sought to introduce new terms into the agreement and was therefore a counter-offer. The act of the plaintiffs in opening a letter of credit did not amount to acceptance and completion of the contract because they had not yet communicated acceptance to the defendants. The contract was made when the telex of 4 May actually reached the defendants in Switzerland and the Swiss courts therefore had jurisdiction.

1   *Stevenson, Jacques & Co v McLean* (1880) 5 QBD 346.
2   [1983] 2 AC 34, [1982] 1 All ER 293, HL.

Battle of forms
12.1.8   The counter-offer rules are particularly important in cases where each party is using its own standard terms which will, as between a buyer and seller, differ on such topics as price fluctuations, right to cancel and liability for loss or damage. This has been described as the 'battle of forms.'

For example, in *Butler Machine Tool Co Ltd v Ex-Cell-O Corpn (England) Ltd*[1] the plaintiff company made a quotation offering to sell a machine tool to prospective purchasers subject to certain printed terms, it being stated that 'these terms and conditions shall prevail over any terms and conditions in the buyer's order'. The conditions included a price variation clause, the price of the goods to be that ruling at the date of delivery. The buyers made an order on their own standard terms which did not include a price variation clause. At the foot of the buyers' order was a tear-off acknowledgement of receipt which stated 'we accept your order on the terms and conditions stated therein.' This was completed and returned by the seller with an accompanying letter which stated that the buyers' order was being entered in accordance with their revised quotation. The goods were delivered late and prior to delivery the sellers sought to make use of the price variation clause. The buyers refused to pay the additional sum and the sellers therefore brought an action to recover the increase due under the clause contained in their original offer. The sellers argued that they had made it clear from the start of negotiations that they would only contract on their own terms and conditions, including a price variation clause. The buyers argued that their response to the offer, being on different terms, was a counter-offer, which negated the original offer.

It was held by the Court of Appeal that the contract had been concluded on the buyers' terms when their counter-offer had been accepted by the sellers' return of the acknowledgement slip.

Despite the evident problems created by the so-called battle of forms, in practice any conflicts tend to be sorted out by a process of negotiation in the ordinary course of business. Indeed such empirical research as exists suggests that not all business contracts are entered into under the strictly formalistic model that contract law envisages. On simple cost-benefit grounds persons involved in business tend to avoid a legalistic approach to the resolution of contractual disputes. For example, Beale and Dugdale carried out some research in 1974 on contracts between businessmen and observed that:

'there was considerable awareness of the fact that in many cases an exchange of conditions would not necessarily lead to an enforceable contract, and in some that the last set of conditions might prevail . . .

But most firms seemed unconcerned about the failure to make a contract. They usually tried to ensure that they referred to their conditions in any written communication which would prevent the letter "accepting" the other party's terms, but no more, and some were not even concerned with that.

In commercial terms, therefore, the result of an exchange of "back of order" conditions did not offer a complete contrast to a negotiated contract on the one hand or an informal exchange of letters on the other: the number of issues planned would vary enormously, but there would be definite agreement on certain of them. Legal enforceability seemed secondary to reaching a common understanding . . .'[2]

Difficulties may arise where parties have failed to reach agreement on the contract terms, and therefore no contract exists but one party has performed their part of the proposed bargain. This situation arose in the case of *British Steel Corpn v Cleveland Bridge and Engineering Co Ltd.*[3] CBE entered into negotiations with BSC for the manufacture of 137 cast steel nodes to be used in the centre of the steel frame of a bank in Saudi Arabia. After some discussions, CBE sent a letter of intent requesting BSC to 'proceed immediately . . . pending the preparation and issuing to you of the official form of contract.' (Such letters are frequently used in business by developers proposing to tender for a contract and who need to sub-contract certain of the work to other chosen firms. The letter enables the subcontractor to prepare estimates and perhaps commence preliminary work but does not create any binding contractual obligation.) The letter of intent was followed by a telex request that BSC should deliver the goods in a particular sequence.

BSC would not agree to supply the nodes on the basis of any conditions other than its own, but in the expectation of an order, it began to manufacture. They subsequently delivered 136 nodes, but retained the final one pending payment. This final node was trapped in the factory by a steel strike in 1980. On its eventual delivery BSC claimed £229,832 as the price of the nodes and CBE counterclaimed £867,335 for damages for breach of contract in delivering late.

The central issue before the court was to decide whether a contract existed between CBE and BSC because if no contract existed there could be no action for breach. CBE argued that there was a contract based on the letter of intent and a request for delivery in a particular order and BSC's subsequent conduct in manufacturing the goods.

Robert Goff J held that the correct analysis of the situation was that the parties both confidently expected a formal contract to eventuate. To expedite performance under that anticipated contract, one party requested the other to commence the work, and they then complied. As, contrary to expectations, no contract was entered into, the performance of the work done was not referable to any contract whose terms could be ascertained and the law simply imposed an obligation on CBE to pay a reasonable sum for the work carried out pursuant to the request.[4]

1   [1979] 1 All ER 965, [1979] 1 WLR 401, CA.
2   'Contracts between businessmen: Planning and the use of contractual remedies', 2 British Journal of Law and Society (1975) p 59.
3   [1984] 1 All ER 504.
4   See 17.1.5.

Communication of acceptance

12.1.9   As already indicated, there can be no acceptance until the offeror is informed, either by words or conduct, that the offeree assents to the terms of the offer. To rule otherwise would place the offeror in an invidious position, since he would not know whether he had entered into a contract or whether he could make other offers. On the other hand the offeree is unlikely to suffer any serious injustice if there is no contract because of lack of proper communication.

As a matter of law however, there must be actual communication. Thus if an oral acceptance is drowned by an aircraft flying overhead or interference on a telephone line, there will be no valid communication. As the *Brinkibon* case above illustrates, telex messages are regarded as being the same as oral communication so there can be no acceptance until the telex message is received. In that case[1] Lord Wilberforce considered the problem of exactly when a telex acceptance should be treated as received. There are several possibilities, for example, the time it is printed on the recipient's machine; the time it is removed from the machine by the recipient; or the time when it should have been removed in the ordinary course of business. He concluded that there could be no hard and fast rule but in every case the question would depend on the circumstances, ordinary business practice and the expectations of the parties. It has been suggested that should there be a breakdown in communication because of an act or omission on the part of the offeror, there may nevertheless be a valid communication. This might arise where, for example, the offeror replaces the phone at an important stage in the discussion. There is, however, little authority for such a proposition.[2]

The offeror can always dispense with the need for communication, either expressly or impliedly. In contracts involving the performance of an act it is assumed that the very act of performance is sufficient indication of assent to the offer without the need to communicate it to the offeror. Such an assumption is based on the commonsense view that if a person advertises a reward for the return of a lost dog they do not expect the police or members of the public to respond by writing a note of acceptance. Thus in the *Carlill*[3] case the plaintiff accepted the offer when she purchased the smoke ball, and no formal communication of acceptance was therefore envisaged.

Although communication of acceptance may be dispensed with, the offeror cannot couch the offer in such terms that acceptance will be presumed unless the offeror hears to the contrary. In other words, silence cannot amount to acceptance.[4] Thus if goods are left on the doorstep with a note to the effect that unless the offeror is notified within so many days he will assume there is a contract, the offeree is under no obligation. Indeed under the Unsolicited Goods and Services Act 1971 the offeror may be considered as making a gift to the customer. If, however, the customer uses or consumes the goods it may be argued that he has manifested an assent to a contract and he would be bound.

1   See 12.1.7.
2   See Lord Denning in *Entores Ltd v Miles Far East Corpn* [1955] 2 QB 327, [1955] 2 All ER 493, CA.
3   See 12.1.2.
4   *Felthouse v Bindley* (1862) 11 CBNS 869.

Postal acceptance

12.1.10   If an acceptance is sent by post it takes effect as soon as it is posted. By adopting this rule the courts have elected to promote the convenience of the offeree. The rule may be justified on the basis that the offeror, by expressly or impliedly allowing acceptance to be made by post, must accept the risk of failure of the postal system. Thus if the acceptance is lost in the post or is seriously delayed the offeror bears any hardship. If the offeror wishes to protect himself against such hardship he can always insist under the terms of the offer that the postal rules will not apply and that acceptance does not take place until a postal communication is actually received.

Since the postal rule is justified primarily on grounds of common sense, in application it will always be subject to common sense limitations. Thus, if in all the circumstances use of the post is unreasonable, perhaps because of impending industrial action by postal unions, the postal rules may not apply. In addition, if the offeree fails properly to address or stamp the letter of acceptance it is reasonable that he should suffer any loss that results. In *Holwell Securities Ltd v Hughes*[1] Lawton LJ observed that—

> 'In my judgement, the factors of inconvenience and absurdity are but illustrations of a wider principle, namely, that the rule does not apply if, having regard to all the circumstances, including the nature of the subject matter under consideration, the negotiating parties cannot have intended that there should be a binding agreement until the party accepting an offer or exercising an option had in fact communicated the acceptance or exercise to the other.'

1   [1974] 1 All ER 161 at 167, CA.

Revocation of acceptance

12.1.11   Assuming that the postal rules apply to a particular transaction and an acceptance is duly posted thus concluding a contract, may the acceptor withdraw the acceptance after posting it but before it has reached the offeree? A strict application of the general rule should forbid such a practice since once the contract is complete there can be no withdrawal by either party. The Scots case of *Countess Dunmore v Alexander*[1] has often been cited to support the proposition that an offeree may be permitted to withdraw. The case is, however, very old, the facts obscure and the issue before the court was not of direct relevance to the question of recalling a letter of acceptance by a faster means of communication, but involved the simultaneous receipt of two letters. Decisions in other jurisdictions have not permitted such a withdrawal by an acceptor.[2] In any event the offeror can always protect himself against the risks of such a practice by the insertion of an appropriate term in the offer.

1   1830 9 Sh (Ct of Sess) 190.
2   See for example the South African case of *A to Z Bazaars (Pty) Ltd v Minister of Agriculture* 1974 (4) SA 392.

Vague agreements

12.1.12   As indicated earlier the businessman does not share the lawyer's desire for certainty and precision in contractual relations. There may be good reason for seeking to postpone a precise formulation of the price to be paid and in times of recession and inflation the businessman will be understandably reluctant to commit himself to a rigid contractual framework over a long period of time. Indeed, familiarity and mutual trust arising out of a continuing business relationship on reasonably well defined terms may serve to explain any uncertainty in a particular agreement.

The law will tolerate some degree of laxity in contractual relations, but there must always be present the fundamentals of a bargain, with perhaps only the minimum left to further agreement. The courts will certainly not give effect to an agreement that is so vague that they have, in effect, to make a contract for the parties. Thus if terms are used that refer to a previous course of dealing or whose meaning can be explained by reference to a trade custom or external standard, the courts will enforce the contract. Indeed trade custom and practice may even be applied to fill in any gaps in the agreement.

In some cases the parties may prefer to defer the question of pricing. In such a case it would not necessarily be fatal to the conclusion of a contract. Indeed s 8(2) of the Sale of Goods Act 1979 provides that if an agreement for the sale of goods does not specify a price for goods then a reasonable price will be payable. Thus the courts will normally give effect to a contract, even though the price is to be fixed at a future date, if some machinery is laid down for fixing a price either by arbitration, reference to a market price at a particular time, or some other means.[1] If, on the other hand, the contract simply provides that the price will be fixed at some future date by a further agreement, the courts are more likely to consider that no binding contract has been made. For example, in *King's Motors (Oxford) Ltd v Lax*[2] it was held that an option in a lease for a further period of years at such rental as may be agreed upon between the parties was void on grounds of uncertainty even though the option had been exercised. If, however, the parties consider the agreement to be binding and act upon it over some time, the courts may consider it to be valid. This would be particularly so where the party seeking to rely on the invalidity derived benefits from the agreement.

If the agreement is silent or vague as to a fundamental matter and there is no provision for resolution of the matter then there will be no contract. In one case it was held that an agreement to supply a van on 'hire purchase terms' was not a valid contract on the basis that it was vague and—

> 'the parties never in intention nor even in appearance reached an agreement . . . They did, indeed, accept the position that there should be some form of hire purchase agreement but they never went on to complete their agreement . . .'[3]

1   See *Bushwall Properties Ltd v Vortex Properties Ltd* [1976] 2 All ER 283, [1976] 1 WLR 591, CA.
2   [1969] 3 All ER 665, [1970] 1 WLR 426.
3   *G Scammell & Nephew Ltd v Ouston* [1941] AC 251 at 269, HL.

Agreements subject to formal execution

12.1.13   Frequently the parties may agree on the important terms of a contract but express themselves in terms that such agreement is 'subject to contract', or 'subject to a formal contract to be drawn up.' Such terms usually mean that the parties are postponing the conclusion of a contract until a later date, thus giving either party the right to withdraw without obligation. It is common in the case of contracts for the sale of land that the agreement be 'subject to contract'. Such an expression is taken to mean that neither party is bound until a formal written contract is exchanged. The practice enables the buyer to undertake a thorough investigation of the ownership of the property. However, on a buoyant market it may enable the seller to 'gazump' the buyer, that is, delay signing the formal contract unless the buyer agrees to increase his offer. This contrasts with the practice in Scotland where it is common for a written offer and acceptance to be exchanged at an early stage which gives rise to a personal contract between the parties. Title is then investigated and the more formal process of transfer and registration takes place at a later date.

Where the parties use a term similar to 'subject to contract', if it can be construed that their intention was that an agreement should take effect immediately, with perhaps some minor points left to be resolved when a formal document is drawn up, the courts may nevertheless consider there to be a contract. In *Branca v Cobarro*[1] an agreement was stated to be a 'provisional agreement until a fully legalised agreement, drawn up by a solicitor and embodying all the conditions herewith stated, is signed.' The court held that the word 'provisional' indicated that the parties intended that the agreement be binding, although it would be replaced by the formal contract. If the term 'subject to contract' had been used or even 'tentative agreement' it would probably have indicated a contrary intention.

1   [1947] KB 854, [1947] 2 All ER 101, CA.

Conditional agreements

12.1.14   Sometimes a contract is dependant upon the occurrence of an event which neither party is necessarily bound to bring about, for example, buying a car on condition that it satisfies a particular test, or the purchase of a house subject to mortgage facilities being obtained. The effect of such conditions is largely a matter of interpretation of the contract and assessing the precise intention of the parties. It may mean that there is no agreement at all, as in the 'subject to contract' cases and either party can withdraw. Alternatively, it may mean that contractual relations are suspended until the particular event or condition precedent as it is sometimes called, has taken place. In such a case the courts may consider that either party can withdraw until they know whether the condition will be satisfied. It may be that one party will be bound to do his best to fulfil the condition.[1]

A contract may also be subject to a condition subsequent. In other words, the contract comes to an end on the occurrence of a particular condition. Thus in *Head v Tattersall*[2] a contract for the sale of a horse was subject to the condition subsequent that the buyer could return it within a stated time if the horse did not fit the description applied to it. The buyer was held to be entitled to return the horse when he found that it did not meet the description even though it had been injured whilst in his possession.

1   *Marten v Whale* [1917] 2 KB 480, CA.
2   (1871) LR 7 Exch 7.

Chapter 13

Consideration and Intention

13.0.0 Simply because two parties make an agreement does not necessarily mean that the agreement will be enforceable. English contract law requires agreements to be supported by consideration unless they are made under seal. A contract made under seal is one made by deed, that is, a written document signed, sealed (in most cases by attaching a red disc to it) and delivered by the person executing it. The term delivery does not refer to actual delivery but simply some words or conduct showing an intent to be bound by the party in question.

Consideration represents the element of mutual action or quid pro quo that English law requires to be present in a contract. It is recognition of the idea that a contract is nothing more than a bargain between the parties, thus stressing the commercial origins of contract law. A person cannot expect something for nothing; if a party requires the benefit of a promise to do something he must himself respond by promising to do or refrain from doing something. Thus in a contract for the sale of goods the consideration will be the promise to pay in return for actual or promised delivery.

The necessity for consideration means that a gratuitous promise, unless made under seal, is not binding.

Past consideration

13.0.1 Since consideration is the price of a promise, past consideration is insufficient. For example, if someone renders a service and is, at a later date, promised some payment, the promise is not supported by consideration and would not therefore be enforceable. If, however, there is a request to perform a service, the circumstances might suggest that some form of payment was implied, in which case the contract would be supported by consideration. In such a situation if a precise amount was not fixed at a later date, the party would be able to claim reasonable remuneration for the service supplied.[1]

1 See 17.1.5.

Consideration must move from the promisee

13.0.2 If a person wishes to enforce a promise it is necessary for him to show that he provided consideration. Such a rule is expressed in the term, 'consideration must move from the promisee'. It means that only the parties to a contract can acquire rights and obligations under it, and a third party cannot claim under the contract. For example if A promises B and C in a joint agreement to pay £10 to C for services to be rendered to A by B, although C is a party to the contract he cannot enforce it because no consideration moved from him. B may do so because he gave consideration for A's promise.

The adequacy and sufficiency of the consideration

13.0.3   In general the courts will not be concerned with the adequacy of the consideration. It is irrelevant that the parties happen to have concluded a bargain which on the face of it is much more favourable to one party than the other. Indeed, often the consideration may be purely nominal. Thus in *Chappell & Co Ltd v Nestle Co Ltd*[1] it was held that wrappers from chocolate bars could form part of the consideration even though they were thrown away. There are, however, a number of instances where the courts will not accept an act or promise as sufficient to constitute consideration.

a) Existing legal duty
A promise by one party to do what may already be legally demanded of him does not amount to consideration. If, however, the promisor undertakes to do more than is required by law, that may constitute consideration.

b) Existing contractual duty
Similarly, where a person is under a contractual obligation to do something, a promise to perform, it cannot be sufficient consideration in return for a promise by the party to whom the contractual duty is already owed. If the party promises something additional to the existing contractual obligation, however insignificant, the need for consideration is satisfied. Thus if A employs B to perform a particular task and later promises him more to complete the job, such a promise is unenforceable. B is already contractually bound to complete the task. If, however, B undertakes to perform an additional task, it would be good consideration for the promise.

c) Existing contractual duty to a third party
It seems that a promise to perform, or the performance of a pre-existing contractual obligation to a third party can be valid consideration. In *New Zealand Shipping Co Ltd v A M Satterthwaite & Co*[2] it was held that an offer made to one party to unload the offeror's goods from a ship in return for the offeror exempting the offeree from any liability for damage to the goods was good consideration. This was so even though the offeree was contractually bound to unload the goods by virtue of a contract with a third party:

> 'an agreement to do an act which the promisor is under an existing obligation to a third party to do, may quite well amount to valid consideration . . . the promisee obtains the benefit of a direct obligation.'[3]

1   [1960] AC 87, [1959] 2 All ER 701, HL.
2   [1975] AC 154, [1974] 1 All ER 1015, PC.
3   At 166.

Discharge and variation of contract

13.0.4 Clearly the parties to a contract may often seek to discharge or vary the terms of an agreement. In either case the variation or discharge must be supported by consideration. Often there is little difficulty in identifying such consideration, for example, in a contract of sale where delivery and payment are postponed. If, however, a variation is made for the benefit of one party, although it is capable of benefiting both parties, the courts will hold there to be no consideration, as, for example, where payment is made at a place other than that fixed under the contract simply for the convenience of the debtor.

Where two parties agree to bring a contract to an end before performance is complete, such an agreement would be effective to discharge the contract since it would be supported on either side by consideration; both parties agree not to seek further performance in return for being absolved further performance.

If one party completes his performance and then promises to release the other party from his obligation to perform, such a promise would not be binding unless supported by consideration. However, s 62 of the Bills of Exchange Act 1882 provides that if the holder of a bill of exchange or promissory note either unconditionally renounces his rights in writing or delivers the instrument to the person liable, the effect is to discharge the obligation even though no consideration is received. For example, if a seller takes a cheque in payment and duly renounces it there will be an effective discharge.

In respect of variation of a contractual debt the courts have experienced considerable difficulties in evolving a rational policy that accords with general business practice. Strictly speaking, if X owes Y a certain sum and Y subsequently promises to accept a lower amount X has provided no consideration for Y's promise and therefore Y can later recover the rest of the debt.

Such a situation arose in *Foakes v Beer*[1] and the House of Lords, with some regret, did not see fit to challenge the rule. In some respects the rule is clearly contrary to the realities of business since to a creditor in financial difficulties part payment may offer some benefit.

Lord Blackburn observed in the *Foakes* case that:

'All men of business everyday recognise and act on the ground that prompt payment of part of their demand may be more beneficial to them than it would be to insist on their rights and enforce payment of the whole.'[2]

In order to provide some protection for legitimate business practices there are a number of situations where the worst effects of the rule may be mitigated. The following are regarded as sufficient consideration:
1. Where part-payment is made together with some other benefit, irrespective of its value.
2. Where the method of performance is varied, such as payment of a smaller sum on a date earlier than fixed or payment at a different place, where it is more convenient for the creditor.[3] It used to be considered that part-payment by cheque was good consideration for a promise to extinguish a debt payable in cash. Such a view was, however, rejected by the Court of Appeal in 1966 when they held that in modern business there is no practical difference between cash and a cheque which is duly honoured.[4]

3.   When the promise to accept a smaller sum is made under seal.
4.   It is common practice where a debtor is in financial difficulties for him to make an arrangement with his creditors for them to accept only a given proportion of their debt in satisfaction of the full amount. In such circumstances although there is no apparent consideration, the courts are prepared to hold that a creditor may not recover any more than the agreed proportion. Such an approach has been justified on the basis that to allow otherwise would be a fraud upon all the parties involved in the composition agreement.
5.   Similarly, if a third party pays part of a debt in full settlement, it will be recognised as a complete discharge of the debt.[5]
6.   The general doctrine of promissory estoppel may be used to prevent a party from renegeing on a promise not to enforce, or to suspend, strict contractual rights, where it would be inequitable to allow him so to do. The doctrine derives from the body of English law known as equity, which developed over the years to correct the inefficacy or injustice of the ordinary principles of English common law.[6] Thus if a strict application of the common law results in an inequitable situation a litigant may ask the courts to exercise their discretion under the rules of equity in order to make good the defects of the common law in a particular situation.

The doctrine of promissory estoppel was first used in the context of part payment of a debt by Denning J in *Central London Property Trust Ltd v High Trees House Ltd.*[7] The case concerned a landlord who made a promise, not supported by consideration, to accept half rent from his tenant so long as the difficulties caused by the Second World War prevailed in respect of sub-letting. In 1945 the landlord demanded full rent, which he was held entitled to do since the promise was limited to war time conditions.

Denning J considered that had the claim been made for full arrears the doctrine of promissory estoppel would have applied to prevent the landlord from claiming the underpaid rent. He had made a promise which was intended to be acted upon by the tenant and when it was duly acted upon the landlord would have been denied the right to claim the underpaid rent, on grounds of equity.

The doctrine may be therefore used to mitigate the worst effects of *Foakes v Beer*. In general its application is limited to the following circumstances.

1.   There must be an unambiguous promise made by a party to a contract, either expressly or impliedly, that he does not intend to enforce his contractual rights. The promise must have been intended to be acted upon and the promisee must have changed his position on the basis of the promise.
2.   Since the remedy is an equitable remedy the promisor is only barred from reneging on the promise if it would be inequitable for him to do so. This is assessed by reference to the position of the promisee taking account of the extent to which he has changed his position on the faith of the promise. If the promisee has extracted the promise fraudulently or by using improper pressure, he may not be able to seek the assistance of the doctrine. For example, if the creditor is in a weak financial position and the debtor suggests that he accept half the payment due in full satisfaction of the debt, or he gets nothing, the debtor's conduct would prevent him from obtaining the benefit of an equitable remedy.[8]
3.   It is said that the doctrine may only be used 'as a shield and not as a sword'. This means that it cannot create a new cause of action if nothing

existed before. Thus in *Combe v Combe*[9] a husband made an informal promise to pay maintenance to his wife. On his failing to make the payment the wife made a claim on the basis that she had acted on his promise in not seeking a court order for maintenance. She was unable to sue on a contract, since she had provided no consideration for the promise. The Court of Appeal rejected her claim on the basis that the doctrine does not create new rights, it only prevents a party asserting rights that he has under an existing contract.

4.   Where the doctrine of promissory estoppel applies, its effect is to suspend a contractual obligation, not terminate it. Thus, on giving reasonable notice, the promisor may legitimately restore the full contractual rights. This means that where the right is of a periodic nature, such as the payment of rent, full payment may be demanded once the promisor has served notice on the promisee, but unpaid amounts relating to the duration of the promise may not be claimed.

If the promisee cannot resume his position the court may however consider that the promise was final and irrevocable, in which case it will terminate the obligation.[10]

1   (1884) 9 App Cas 605, HL.
2   At 622.
3   *Pinnel's case* (1602) 5 Co Rep 117a.
4   *D & C Builders Ltd v Rees* [1966] 2 QB 617, [1965] 3 All ER 837, CA.
5   *Good v Cheesman* (1831) 2 B & Ad 328.
6   See 2.8.3.
7   [1947] KB 130, [1956] 1 All ER 256.
8   See note 4 above.
9   [1951] 2 KB 215, [1951] 1 All ER 767, CA.
10 See *Ajayi (trading under the name and style of Colony Carrier Co) v R T Briscoe (Nigeria) Ltd* [1964] 3 All ER 556, [1964] 1 WLR 1326, PC.

Intention to create a legal relationship

13.1.0   Contract law requires the parties to an agreement to have intended to create a legal obligation. It is normally presumed that the parties to a social, family or other domestic arrangement do not intend to create legal relations. Thus an agreement to play golf, or an arrangement over household expenses, or even a car pool arrangement between neighbours,[1] would not create a legally binding contract unless there were clear indications to the contrary.

On the other hand, in the absence of any indication to the contrary it is assumed that the parties to a business agreement expect such an agreement to be legally binding. Unless they state quite clearly that it is not intended to have legal effect, no matter how trivial it may be, it will nevertheless be presumed to be legally binding. Thus in *Esso Petroleum Ltd v Customs and Excise Comrs*[2] the petrol company organised a marketing promotion in order to encourage the public to buy their petrol. It involved giving a free World Cup coin to any motorist who bought four gallons of petrol. In the action which arose out of a claim for purchase tax, the House of Lords concluded that even though the scheme stressed that the coins were free and the scheme was purely for advertising purposes, there was a contract to supply coins to any motorist who purchased four gallons of petrol. Thus if the company had failed to supply a coin to a motorist he could technically have sued them.

Agreements between employers and trade unions provide an interesting example. Such agreements often contain considerable detail on such things as rates of pay, hours of work, and grievance procedures. Often the terms of such agreements will be incorporated into the individual contracts of employment of the workers covered by the agreement and thus be enforceable by and against the individual employee. Such agreements are not, however, legally enforceable as between the employer and trade union. In *Ford Motor Co Ltd v Amalgamated Union of Engineering and Foundry Workers*[3] the court considered that in the context of the British system of industrial relations such agreements present:

> 'grave practical problems of enforcement and, reached against a background of opinion adverse to enforceability, are in my judgement not contracts in the legal sense . . . Without clear and express provisions making them amenable to legal action, they remain in the realm of undertakings binding in honour.'[4]

Such a view is now confirmed by statute. Section 18 of the Trade Union and Labour Relations Act 1974 provides that such collective agreements are presumed not to be legally binding unless they are made in writing and expressly state that the agreement is to be legally binding.

1 *Coward v Motor Insurers' Bureau* [1963] 1 QB 259, [1962] 1 All ER 531, CA.
2 [1976] 1 All ER 117, [1976] 1 WLR 1, HL.
3 [1969] 2 QB 303, [1969] 2 All ER 481.
4 At 496.

Chapter 14

Statements Made in a Contractual Setting

14.0.0 In the course of negotiations leading to the conclusion of a contract many statements may be made by the parties either orally or in documents. When an initial inquiry is made by a buyer, the seller may well commend the virtues of his product in terms of quality, durability and perhaps aesthetic merits. The potential buyer may pose specific questions on certain issues, perhaps seeking assurances in order to be certain that the product will meet commercial or domestic requirements. The buyer may even insist that certain of the assurances be committed to writing in order to emphasise their importance.

In the event of a dispute arising at some later date it may be necessary to subject statements made in a contractual context to closer scrutiny in order to determine their status and effect. In general it is possible to identify three categories of statement made in the context of a contract. First, those statements which amount to sales talk such as extravagant advertising claims and honest expressions of opinion. Examples of such statements would be 'this car is the best and smartest of its type' or 'a superb bargain, it will run for ever.' This kind of statement does not have any impact on the contractual relationship between the parties. Such statements are merely value judgments which are not capable of being tested against any objective standard. Invariably the person making the statement is merely asserting his belief, not necessarily guaranteeing that such a belief is well founded.

Second, there are statements of fact which are made to induce a party to enter into the contract but which fall short of forming part of the terms of the contract. For many years the victim of an innocent misstatement of fact had no remedy other than a right to rescind the contract. However, since the Misrepresentation Act 1967 a person can now claim damages for innocent misrepresentation.[1]

The third category of statements are those which are intended to have contractual and binding effect forming part of the terms of the contract. Breach of such terms will entitle the innocent party to claim damages and, in some cases, termination of the contract.[2]

In practice it is often difficult to decide whether a particular statement is a term or a representation. However, in the absence of any clear indication by the parties a statement is more likely to be regarded as forming part of the contract if it is made at a significant stage in the negotiating process, if it is of central importance to the contract, or it is made by the party with the greater degree of expertise or professional skill.[3]

184

At this point it is intended to discuss those statements forming the terms of a contract.

1 See 15.0.5.
2 See 17.1.0.
3 See *Dick Bentley Productions Ltd v Harold Smith (Motors) Ltd* [1965] 2 All ER 65, [1965] 1 WLR 623, CA and *Oscar Chess Ltd v Williams* [1957] 1 All ER 325, [1957] 1 WLR 370, CA.

Express terms and formality

14.0.1   The express terms of a contract are those that are specifically identified and agreed by the parties at the time the contract is made. They may be agreed in writing or orally. Such terms may vary in importance and the consequences of non-observance will depend upon whether a term is classified as a condition or a warranty.[1]

As a general rule the parties to a contract may enter into it in any form they choose. Apart from a number of special circumstances, a contract will be equally binding whether it is made under a formalised procedure, by informal writing or by word of mouth. In general it is always preferable that the terms are expressed in writing in order to avoid uncertainty and dispel any doubts should a dispute arise. Indeed a number of modern statutes expressly require certain contracts to be in writing where it is considered that one party is likely to be bargaining from a weak position, or where the law considers that some formality is required in order to give a party the opportunity to ponder on the onerous obligations they are undertaking. For example, the Consumer Credit Act 1974 requires regulated agreements to be in a form prescribed in accordance with regulations made under the Act.[2] Some statutes simply impose an obligation on one party to provide certain written particulars for the other party within a specified period.[3]

Certain contracts are so special that the law requires them to be entered into by deed, which should be written, sealed and delivered. The person who executes it must also sign it or place their mark on it.[4] Among the contracts that are required to be entered into by deed are leases for more than three years[5] and agreements not supported by consideration, such as a gratuitous promise.

Some contracts are invalid unless they are in writing, although the writing need not be executed under seal. The requirement for writing will be satisfied by the signature of one or both parties. Contracts in this group include:
(a) contracts of marine insurance. These contracts are not admissible in evidence unless embodied in a marine policy signed by the insurer and stating the name of the assured, or of some person who effects the insurance on his behalf;[6]
(b) bills of exchange and promissory notes;[7]
(c) regulated agreements under the Consumer Credit Act 1974. If not in the correct form such agreements are only enforceable against the debtor or hirer by a court order.[8]
The Statute of Frauds Act 1677 required a number of contracts to be evidenced in writing. Although the requirement was repealed in respect of most of the contracts by the Law Reform (Enforcement of Contracts) Act 1954 there remain two important classes of contract where no action may be brought unless they are evidenced by some note or memorandum. These are contracts of guarantee (a promise to answer for the debt or default of another), and contracts for the sale of land or any interest in land.[9]

The absence of written evidence does not make the contract invalid: it simply renders it unenforceable. The written evidence may thus be supplied at any time after the contract has been made provided that it clearly gives recognition to the existence of the contract. In general the courts have been somewhat liberal in their interpretation of the statutory requirement. The note or memorandum must contain details of the contract, the names of the parties, the subject matter, the consideration in the case of a contract for the sale of land, and any special terms in reasonable detail. Although it is required to be signed by the party 'to be charged', an initial or printed signature is quite sufficient.

Even where there is no written evidence the law recognises that where the parties have purported to enter an oral contract for the sale of land and one party has performed his part of the bargain, hardship and injustice may be caused if the mere absence of documentary evidence permitted a party to withdraw. Thus the equitable doctrine of part performance may assist the party who has taken possession of the land as against the other party seeking to rely on the absence of written evidence to render the agreement unenforceable. In general the party relying on the doctrine must have been induced, or allowed to change his position in reliance on the contract to such an extent that it would be fraud to allow the other party to take advantage of the lack of formality. Equivocal acts, such as the payment of money, are not generally treated as sufficient part performance although the payment of money together with other acts may be sufficient.[10] The doctrine of part performance will only operate if the contract is one where the courts are prepared to exercise their discretion to order specific performance.

1 See 17.1.1.
2 See Part V.
3 See Employment Protection (Consolidation) Act 1978, ss 1 and 3.
4 For example, a deed is executed by a company when its seal is affixed in the presence of and attested by its secretary and a director.
5 Law of Property Act 1925, ss 52 and 54.
6 Marine Insurance Act 1906.
7 Bills of Exchange Act 1882.
8 See Part V.
9 Law of Property Act 1925, s 40.
10 See for example *Steadman v Steadman* [1976] AC 536, [1974] 2 All ER 977, HL.

Written contracts and the parol evidence rule

14.0.2 Over the years the courts have developed a basic rule that parol or oral evidence cannot be admitted to add to or vary the terms of a written contract. Indeed, the rule extends to all extrinsic evidence whether it is oral or in writing. In effect the rule represents the common sense approach that when parties to a contract stipulate in writing all the express terms of their agreement, evidence contradictory or altering those terms will be inadmissible largely because it would be irrelevant.[1] The rule does not therefore prevent parties from alleging that the written terms are not a complete record of the transaction. Thus when parties arrive at a definite written contract there is a strong presumption that it is intended to contain all the terms of their bargain, but it is a presumption that can be rebutted.[2]

The courts may consider that a separate oral promise forms the basis for an independent or collateral contract.[3] In any event the courts can order the rectification of a document that does not accurately record the intention of the parties.[4]

1 See Law Commission No 154, 1986.
2 See *Gillespie Bros & Co v Cheney, Eggar & Co* [1896] 2 QB 59 at 62 per Lord Russell.
3 *De Lassalle v Guildford* [1901] 2 KB 215, CA.
4 *Craddock Bros v Hunt* [1923] 2 Ch 136, CA.

Standard form contracts

14.0.3 The growth in economic activity generated at the time of the Industrial Revolution resulted in the creation of a massive market for goods and services. Alongside this growth in mass consumption there developed standard modes of doing business and standard documentation in contractual relations. In effect the standard form contract became the legal equivalent of mass production, and any idea of freedom and equality in contractual relations became something of a fiction. Slawson criticised the use of standard form contracts in the following terms:

'Private law which is made by contract in the traditional sense is democratic because a traditional contract must be the agreement of both parties. Unless a contract is coerced, therefore, the "government" it creates is by its nature "government by and with the consent of governed". But the overwhelming proportion of standard forms are not democratic because they are not, under any reasonable test, the agreement of the consumer or business recipient to whom they are delivered.

Indeed, in the usual case, the consumer never even reads the form, or reads it only after he has become bound by its terms. Even the fastidious few who take the time to read the standard form may be helpless to vary it. The form may be part of an offer which the consumer has no reasonable alternative but to accept . . . The effect of mass production and mass merchandising is to make all consumer forms standard and the combined effects of economics and the present law is to make all standard forms unfair . . . The conclusion to which all this leads is that practically no standard forms, at least as they are customarily used in consumer transactions, are contracts. They cannot reasonably be regarded as the manifested consent of their recipient because an issuer could not reasonably expect that a recipient would read and understand them.'[1]

1 Quoted in 'Judicial Control of Standard Form Contracts', Trebilcock and Dewes in *The Economic Approach to Law* (Burrows and Veljanovski (Eds)) p 94.

Benefits of standard form contracts

14.0.4 The use of standard form contracts brings considerable commercial advantages. For the business user they reduce the time and cost of negotiations and are an efficient means of reducing the administrative costs of selling goods and services. Coupled with the enormous technological advances made in the whole process of handling and storing information in recent years, preprinted standard forms are an important contribution to business efficiency. It would clearly be a waste of time to produce individual contracts each time a new transaction is made, although the rise of the word processor means that standard forms may now be modified to meet the demands of individual contracting parties.

However sophisticated, the law of contract cannot possibly meet the needs of every trade and provide for all contingencies. By the use of standard contracts business concerns are able to calculate and apportion risks and confidently delegate the selling function to employees without yielding the authority to bargain, thus minimising the risk of disputes arising.

Standard contracts may also bring benefits for individual consumers. It should not be assumed that bargaining necessarily ensures a fair deal. Standard form contracts are a useful vehicle for informing consumers of their rights and how to proceed if difficulties arise. Consumers also benefit in that if transaction costs are reduced then, assuming a competitive environment, such reductions may be passed on to the consumer in terms of pricing policies.

Thus provided that the use of standard form contracts is subjected to adequate controls by the courts, Parliament and regulatory agencies, they are defensible. If they are used as a means of imposing wholly unreasonable terms on a contracting party because of their inferior bargaining position, then they clearly are not defensible. In general, contract law regulates the use and abuse of standard form contracts by the imposition of basic standards of fairness in respect of the procedure for incorporating standard terms into contracts and subjecting standard terms excluding liability to a test of reasonableness.[1] In addition, in exceptional circumstances, the courts have been prepared to acknowledge inequality of bargaining as a ground for attacking the validity of a contract.[2] Both of these areas are dealt with in later paragraphs.

1 See 18.0.0 and 18.0.3.
2 See 15.0.8 and 16.0.5.

Implied terms
14.0.5 Although the standard form contract containing express contract terms is a common feature of modern business practice, inevitably the sheer volume and variety of transactions that take place in the economy means that some agreements will be entered into in circumstances where there is an incomplete record of the agreement. Certain details may be omitted from the express terms of the contract because the parties are dealing in an environment that generates standard terms of dealing based on custom or practice; on the other hand, the parties may have genuinely neglected to foresee a particular problem which turns out to be the cause of a dispute. In most such cases any omissions may be dealt with by a process of informal negotiation but, in the event of litigation, the courts may be invited to imply certain terms into a contract. In general such terms may be implied by examining the context in which the contract was made and the authority of the courts to imply terms may vest in trade usage, the previous dealings of the parties, the common law or statute.

a) Previous dealings
When parties have regularly contracted on the same terms, the courts will invariably be prepared to assume that a transaction was intended to be on the same terms as the previous course of dealings.[1]

b) Trade usage or custom
Where the parties make a contract in the context of a particular market or trade, the customs of the market or trade may be imported into the terms of their contract. The custom must however be consistent with the express terms of the contract as Lord Jenkins observed:

> 'An alleged custom can be incorporated into a contract only if there is nothing in the express or necessarily implied terms of the contract to prevent such inclusion and, further that a custom will only be imported . . . where it can be so imported consistently with the tenor of the document as a whole.'[2]

c) Business efficacy
The courts may apply a term into a contract where it is necessary to give business efficacy to the contract.[3] In the words of Lord Pearson:

> 'An unexpressed term can be implied if and only if the courts find that the parties must have intended that term to form part of the contract; it is not enough for the court to find that such a term would have been adopted by the parties as reasonable men if it had been suggested to them: it must have been a term that went without saying, a term necessary to give business efficacy to the contract, a term which although tacit, formed part of the contract which the parties made for themselves.'[4]

d) Common law
In certain classes of transaction the courts have stated that, in the absence of an express exclusion, implied terms will be incorporated as a matter of law into all contracts of that class. Many such implied terms have now been codified in statutes. For example in contracts for the sale of goods the Sale of Goods Act 1979 implies terms in respect of title to sell, description applied to the goods and quality.[5] As the range of transactions increased, the courts modified and extended traditional implied terms covering such matters as quality of goods provided or the standard of care and skill that is expected of a party.

A feature of some terms implied by statute is that they cannot be excluded by the express terms of the contract.[6]

1 *McCutcheon v David Macbrayne Ltd* [1964] 1 All ER 430, [1964] 1 WLR 125.
2 *London Export Corpn Ltd v Jubilee Coffee Roasting Co Ltd* [1958] 2 All ER 411 at 420, CA.
3 *The Moorcock* (1889) 14 PD 64, CA.
4 *Trollope & Colls Ltd v North West Metropolitan Regional Hospital Board* [1973] 2 All ER 260 at 268, HL.
5 See 21.0.0.
6 See 21.8.0.

Chapter 15
Factors Affecting the Validity of Contracts

15.0.0　Some contracts may have the appearance of being based on consent but may nevertheless be challenged because of some defect present at the time the contract was entered into. It may be that the parties misunderstand each other, or one party misleads the other or obtains consent by improper means; such factors may seriously affect the validity of a contract.

Contract law distinguishes between those factors which render a contract void and those which render a contract voidable. A void contract is one which is devoid of any legal effect. Any payments made or property transferred under it are recoverable. In effect no legal relationship exists between the parties.

A voidable contract is one which is, in effect, cancellable by one of the parties because of some factor affecting its validity induced by the other party. It differs from a void contract in that it is valid and binding until the innocent party exercises the option to cancel or rescind it. The effect of rescission is, however, to cancel the contract from the beginning and therefore each party is required to return benefits received; in as much as it is possible the parties are restored to the position they would have been in had the contract not been entered into. If such restoration is not possible then the right to rescind may be lost; similarly the right to rescind may be lost where the innocent party indicates a willingness to proceed with the contract or, in the case of goods, a third party acquires the goods before rescission takes place.

Mistake
15.0.1　Not every mistake affects the validity of a contract. A contract will not automatically be rendered void simply because one or both parties have misunderstood a situation. For example, if X purchases some land from Y believing it to be suitable for a particular purpose and it turns out to be wholly unsuitable, X will not be able to challenge the validity of the contract on the grounds of mistake. If, however, Y had deliberately misled X he may have a remedy on grounds of a misrepresentation, which will be dealt with in the following paragraphs.

A contract can be rendered void for mistake in two situations:
(a) if the parties reach an agreement but both make the same mistake on a fundamental question of fact;
(b) if the parties are fundamentally at cross-purposes.

190

a) Shared mistake

In the absence of express intention to the contrary, if the parties have arrived at an agreement on the basis of a shared fundamental misunderstanding as to the facts, the contract will be void for mistake (if both parties share the misunderstanding). If, however, the contract provides that the risk as to the particular fact in question falls on one or other of the parties, then the courts will give effect to such intention and the contract will be valid. For example in *Clark v Lindsay*[1] one party agreed to rent a room along the route of Edward VII's coronation procession. The terms of the contract provided that in the event of the procession being cancelled, the room would be made available on any later date when the coronation was rearranged. The procession was cancelled because of the King's illness and it was held that the contract was not void for mistake but valid and both parties were bound by the terms of the contract in respect of the rearranged day. In a similar case when the parties did not allocate the risk of a cancellation the court held the contract to be void for mistake when the procession was cancelled.[2]

The mistake must be of a fundamental nature either in relation to the existence of the subject matter or its identity. An obvious example is where the parties make a contract and neither party is aware that the subject matter has perished or been resold before they made their agreement. A more difficult question is the extent to which a mistake as to the quality of the subject will render the contract void. Here again, if a seller undertakes that the subject matter has a particular quality, he will shoulder the risk should the particular quality be lacking. On a number of occasions judges have observed that where the parties make a fundamental mistake as to quality the contract may be rendered void but there has been no actual case to support such a view. In *Bell v Lever Bros Ltd*[3] the company wanted to terminate Bell's contract and agreed to pay him £30,000 compensation. It was subsequently discovered that the company could have dismissed Bell without compensation for certain breaches, which Bell had forgotten about. It was argued that both parties had made a mistake as to the quality of the contract of employment in that they had believed it was only determinable by Bell's agreement when it was in fact determinable at the company's instance without agreement.

The House of Lords did not, however, accept such a view and held that the company had obtained precisely what they had bargained for. Although the judgements support the view that a fundamental mistake as to quality may render a contract void, in terms of their Lordships' decision on the facts of the case it is hard to imagine a factual situation where a mistake as to quality will render a contract void. Indeed Lord Atkin observed that:

> 'A buys a picture from B; both A and B believe it to be the work of an art master and a high price is paid. If it turns out to be a modern copy A has no remedy in the absence of representation or warranty.'[4]

The common law thus takes a very narrow view of the type of mistake which will render a contract void.

In certain circumstances equity intervenes where a contract is made on the basis of a shared mistake. Thus in the interests of justice and equity a contract may be rescinded and the parties restored to their original position, with some allowance made if one party has received a benefit at the expense of the other party.

The nature of the equitable remedy denies a precise formulation of what

191

type of mistake will permit equity to intervene. Nevertheless, it clearly encompasses a much wider definition of mistake than the common law admits. Thus where an insurance company paid out a claim on a policy which they considered was valid but which in fact was a voidable policy, it was held that they could rescind the claim agreement and recover the amount paid, even though it was valid at common law.[5]

In *Grist v Bailey*[6] a flat was sold in the mistaken belief that it was free from rent control. The court held that the contract was not void at law but the mistake as to quality was of a sufficient nature as to permit equitable intervention. The contract was therefore set aside on terms that the party should be given the opportunity to buy the property at its proper market value under a new contract.

However, if a party affirms the contract after the mistake has been discovered or a long time has elapsed since the contract was made, rescission may not be permitted.

b) Mistake not shared

If the parties to a contract are completely at cross purposes over some matter central to the contract it may be rendered void. It is important to stress at the outset, however, that it is only in very exceptional circumstances that the courts will consider that a contract is void at common law. If the parties are apparently agreed on the same terms and the same subject matter there will be a valid contract even though one of them is mistaken. As stated earlier, the basic test of whether an agreement exists is objective, irrespective of what a person might intend in his mind; if he conducts himself in such a way and on such terms that a reasonable person would consider that he is assenting to the particular contract there will be a valid contract based on such conduct and terms. In exceptional cases, however, the contract may be held to be void even though only one party is mistaken, at least where his mistake is known to or induced by the other party for he cannot claim to have been misled by the apparent consent of the mistaken party. On the other hand it may be that the parties are completely at cross purposes or that the circumstances are so ambiguous that a reasonable person could not decide the true intention of the parties. In that case, the contract will be void, for the parties have in fact not reached the objective appearance of agreement.

The cases suggest that a mistake made by one contracting party may affect the contract in three types of situation:

(i)   mistake as to identity of the contracting party;
(ii) mistake as to subject matter of the contract;
(iii) mistake as to the terms of the contract.

i) Mistake as to identity

Where a mistake is made as to the identity of one of the parties it is usually induced by fraud and will in any event make the contract voidable. Where the mistake is such that one party thinks that he is contracting with X when in reality he is contracting with Y, the contract will be void. The question as to whether the contract is void for mistake or voidable for fraud is of paramount importance to a third party who may subsequently have bought the goods which were the subject of the contract. If a contract for the sale of goods between A and B was void for mistake, then B cannot pass title to the goods to a subsequent purchaser, C. Thus A can recover the goods from C at a later date. If, however, the original contract between A and B is voidable for fraud then B can pass a good title to C thus preventing A from rescinding the contract and recovering the goods. In essence, therefore, the courts are presented with the difficulty of deciding which of two innocent parties, A or C, is to suffer as a result of B's fraud, since in such circumstances B will either be impecunious or absent.[7]

In *Cundy v Lindsay*[8] Lindsay was given an order for handkerchiefs from a rogue called Blenkarn, who deliberately signed his name so as to resemble Blenkiron & Co, the name of a reputable firm known to Lindsay. The goods were duly dispatched to Blenkarn who resold them to Cundy. The court held that the contract between Lindsay and Blenkarn was void for mistake as to identity since they had only intended to sell to Blenkiron & Co. Lindsay was therefore able to recover the price of the goods from Cundy. By contrast, in *Kings Norton Metal Co Ltd v Edridge, Merrett & Co Ltd*[9] a rogue named Wallis offered to buy goods in a letter headed 'Hallam & Co' which made reference to a number of depots and a large factory. 'Hallam & Co' was in fact an alias for Wallis. The goods were supplied to and resold by Wallis. The court held that the contract was not void for mistake as to identity, the mistake was simply in relation to the credit worthiness of the other party, not his identity.

The courts approach the problem by distinguishing between a mistake as to identity which will render a contract void and a mistake as to a particular attribute, such as credit worthiness, which will not have that effect. Where the parties deal on a face to face basis it will normally be presumed that a party intended to deal with the person before him. Thus in *Lewis v Averay*[10] a party claimed to be Richard Greene, an actor, when he bought a car. He produced a pass to Pinewood Studios to substantiate his claim and was allowed to take the car, whereupon he resold it. The seller was unable to rebut the presumption that he intended to deal with the person in front of him and he failed to establish that identity was of crucial importance to him. Where a party makes a serious attempt to check on the identity of the other party, for example by checking in a telephone directory, this may be sufficient to establish that identity was of fundamental importance.[11]

ii) Mistake as to subject matter

Here too the general rule applies so that the unilateral mistake of one party will not normally affect the contract. It is clear that a mere mistake as to the quality or value of the subject matter will not avoid the contract. Thus if a purchaser of oats wrongly believes them to be old oats when in fact they are new, his mistake has no impact upon the contract. However, if the mistake is so fundamental that the mistaken party thinks he is dealing with something completely different than is in fact the case, the contract will be vitiated. This is particularly likely if the mistake is known to the other party or has been induced by his conduct.[12] Alternatively the parties may be entirely at cross purposes. In that case the outward appearance of agreement will be entirely superficial and a closer examination of the facts will reveal that there is no genuine agreement. Thus in *Raffles v Wichelhaus*[13] there was a contract to buy cotton which was arriving from Bombay on a ship called 'Peerless'. There were in fact two ships called 'Peerless' both of which sailed from Bombay with cotton, one departing in October and one in December. The buyer thought that he was buying the October shipment and the seller thought the December shipment was the subject matter of the contract. It was held that the contract was void for mistake on the basis that both parties had different consignments in mind.

If, however, the mistake relates to quality but not the essential nature of the subject, it will not avoid the contract.

iii) Mistake as to terms of the contract

By contrast it seems that if one of the parties is mistaken about the terms of the contract that mistake will make the contract void. Thus, although a contract to buy oats will not be void merely because the buyer believes the oats to be old, it will be void if he mistakenly believes that the seller is warranting that they are old.[14] In *Hartog v Colin and Shields*[15] the sellers offered to sell hare skins at a price per pound when in fact they meant, as the buyer well knew, to fix a price per piece, there being several pieces to the pound. It was established by the court that both trade practice and the pre-contract negotiations suggested that the sale should be on a price per piece basis. It was therefore held that the contract was void because of the sellers' fundamental mistake.

At common law the effect of the mistake is to render the contract void if the courts consider the mistake operative. Equity, on the other hand, may offer a greater degree of flexibility in order to do justice to both parties. In general in a claim for specific performance equity will, however, follow the common law. Thus if the contract is valid at common law notwithstanding the mistake, specific performance may be awarded.[16] If, however, the contract is void specific performance will normally be denied.[17] Much depends upon the circumstances of the case and whether it is reasonable to grant the remedy; thus in one case it was suggested that the remedy would be refused: 'where a hardship amounting to injustice would have been inflicted upon the mistaken party by holding him to his bargain and it was unreasonable to hold him to it.'[18]

The court may also set aside the contract in order to do justice to both parties, imposing certain terms on them.[19]

1 (1903) 88 LT 198.
2 See *Griffith v Brymer* (1903) 19 TLR 434.
3 [1932] AC 161, HL.
4 At 224. See also *Leaf v International Galleries* [1950] 2 KB 86, [1950] 1 All ER 693, CA.
5 *Magee v Pennine Insurance Co Ltd* [1969] 2 QB 507, [1969] 2 All ER 891, CA.
6 [1967] Ch 532, [1906] 2 All ER 875.
7 The Law Reform Commission have recommended that the innocent third party should be permitted to retain goods even where the original contract was void. 12th Report (1966) Cmnd 2958.
8 (1878) 3 App Cas 459, HL.
9 (1897) 14 TLR, 98, CA.
10 [1972] 1 QB 198, [1971] 3 All ER 907, CA.
11 See for example the much criticised decision of *Ingram v Little* [1961] 1 QB 31, [1960] 3 All ER 332, CA.
12 *Scriven Bros v Hindley & Co* [1913] 3 KB 564.
13 (1864) 2 H & C 906.
14 *Smith v Hughes* (1871) LR 6 QB 597.
15 [1939] 3 All ER 566.
16 See *Tamplin v James* (1879) 15 Ch D 215, CA.
17 See *Webster v Cecil* (1861) 30 Beav 62.
18 See footnote 16 at 221.
19 *A Roberts & Co Ltd v Leicestershire County Council* [1961] Ch 555, [1961] 2 All ER 545.

Mistake and rectification

15.0.2   Where both parties have made an agreement and proceeded to embody it in a written document which fails to represent their agreement accurately, the equitable remedy of rectification may be available. Under this remedy the court will, after considering the appropriate evidence, rectify the mistake so that the document truly reflects the intention of the parties.

A document will normally only be rectified if both parties have made a mistake as to its contents. However, a party may be granted rectification if he mistakenly believed a term was in the document and the other party knew of such mistake but nevertheless permitted the contract document to be drawn up. In *Joscelyne v Nissen*[1] one party shared a house with his daughter-in-law and proposed that she take over his business. In the preliminary negotiations it was agreed that she would also take over the household expenses but the written contract placed no such liability on the daughter-in-law who some time later refused to pay the household bills. The Court of Appeal permitted the document to be rectified in accordance with the earlier oral arrangement despite the fact that such an arrangement was not, in itself, a binding contract.

1   [1970] 2 QB 86, [1970] 1 All ER 1213, CA.

Mistake in signing a document

15.0.3   The general rule is that where a person signs a contractual document he is bound by it irrespective of the fact that it is not the type of arrangement he intended or that he simply failed to read it. However, if the document is radically different in effect from the document he thinks he is signing and he was not careless, he may plead non est factum (it is not my deed). Such a plea is, however, difficult to establish in the case of a literate adult of sound mind. In *Saunders (Executrix of Will of Gallie) v Anglia Building Society*[1] an elderly widow signed a deed of assignment of a lease without reading it because her spectacles were broken and she had been induced to think the document was a deed of gift to her nephew. The building society advanced £2,000 on the faith of the document. The House of Lords rejected a plea of non est factum and considered that in view of the object. of the exercise, to raise money on security of a house, the two transactions were in effect much the same. The lady was clearly careless in not reading the document or consulting expert advisers. Thus in the case of a person of full contractual capacity the plea will rarely be established unless they are blind or perhaps illiterate. A person cannot rely on a plea of non est factum if they sign a document containing blanks which are later filled in by a third party otherwise than in accordance with instructions.[2]

1   [1971] AC 1004, [1970] 3 All ER 961, HL.
2   *United Dominions Trust Ltd v Western* [1976] QB 513, [1975] 3 All ER 1017, CA.

Misrepresentation

15.0.4   Where a person enters into a contract as a result of an untrue statement made by the other party the validity of the contract may be affected and in addition damages may be awarded to the innocent party. It may be that the misrepresentation induces a fundamental mistake in which case it will render the contract void under the principles discussed in the preceeding paragraphs. If it does not induce such a misunderstanding but is nevertheless a material misrepresentation of the facts to such an extent that it was the deciding factor in inducing the other party to contract, it will render the contract voidable. In addition if it was untrue it may give rise to an action for damages and even where it was made quite innocently English law provides, under the Misrepresentation Act, that damages may be awarded.

In general, for a misrepresentation to be the basis for any kind of contractual relief it must be:
(a) a misrepresentation of fact;
(b) it must be material;
(c) it must have induced the contract;

a) Misrepresentation of fact

A misrepresentation may be either by words or conduct but it must be in respect of an existing fact. A statement of fact must be distinguished from one of opinion, a statement as to the future, or a statement of law.

Some statements are intended purely as vague sales talk and if they are unfounded they will not affect the validity of the contract. Thus in one case[1] land was sold as 'fertile and improvable' and it turned out to be of no use and completely abandoned. The court however considered that the representation was simply a florid opinion not a representation of fact. In general therefore if the statement is incapable of actual verification, for example, a statement as to the possible profits of a business, it will be a matter of opinion and thus if it turns out to be untrue it will not affect the contract.

In *Bisset v Wilkinson*[2] the seller of a farm which had never been used for stock, told a purchaser that it would support 2,000 sheep. The court considered that such a statement on the farm's capacity was a matter of opinion. In such cases the other party has every opportunity to make independent inquiries as to the matters in question.

Where, however, a person makes a representation of opinion or belief which he does not in fact hold, or where he has no reasonable grounds for such a belief, he may make a misrepresentation of fact. For example, if a party states that he believes an article to be a genuine antique, when in fact he actually believes it to be a copy, he misrepresents a fact in respect of his state of mind. In *Smith v Land and House Property Corpn*[3] the seller of property described a tenant as a 'most desirable tenant' when in fact the tenant was in arrears. It was held that such a statement was not simply of opinion but clearly involved a misrepresentation of fact in that the seller impliedly represented that he had reasonable grounds for such a belief.

The statement of fact must also be distinguished from a statement of future intention. If a party makes a promise as to the future and fails to fulfil the promise, the other party must establish that the promise formed part of the contract and thus amounts to a breach of contract. If it does not form part of the contract he will not be entitled to any remedy since it was not a misrepresentation of an existing fact. However, a statement of future intention will constitute a misrepresentation of fact if, when it was made, the maker did not honestly hold that intention. Thus in *Edgington v Fitzmaurice*[4] a company issued a prospectus stating that funds raised would be used in the improvement of buildings. The real intention was, however, to use the money to discharge the company's debts. It was held that the misrepresentation of present intentions was a misrepresentation of fact for when they made the statement as a matter of fact they had no intention of using the money for the promised purpose. Thus, the 'state of a man's mind is as much a fact as the state of his digestion . . . A misrepresentation as to the state of a man's mind is, therefore, a misstatement of fact.'[5]

If a person makes a contract as a result of a misrepresentation of law he will have no remedy. It is assumed that both parties have equal access to the law and are able to take independent legal advice if necessary. However, as in the case of statements of opinion, where a person makes a statement of law which he knows to be untrue, such a statement will affect the validity of the contract because he misrepresents his state of mind.

In general a misrepresentation as to the meaning of legislation or the construction of a document is a question of law whereas a misrepresentation as to the content of a document would be one of fact.

In general concealment will not affect the validity of a contract even if it is clear that the other party has the wrong impression. For example, where one party agrees to take the lease of a mine knowing it to contain valuable deposits, the other party will not be permitted to avoid the consequences of his deal simply on the grounds that he was not aware of the true value of the property. Lord Curriehill remarked in a Scottish case:

> 'Concealment by a contracting party is not held in law to be fraudulent, if he is not under an obligation to disclose what he conceals to the other contracting party. The understood object of parties in entering into bargains in business matters is to make gain, and neither is bound to inform the other of the grounds upon which he makes his prospective estimate of gain.'[6]

Silence may, however, give grounds for relief in the following situations:

1. Where a silence distorts a fact, for example, if the seller of land states that all the farms on the land are let but neglects to say that tenants have given notice to leave. Similarly, where a factual statement is made and events render the statement false before the contract is made, the party making the statement is under an obligation to notify the other party otherwise the contract will be voidable.[7]
2. Where the contract is one of the utmost good faith or 'ubberrimae fidei'. If the contract is one where one party is in possession of all the material facts and the other party is therefore obliged to place confidence in his disclosure of all the facts, a failure to make disclosure will render the contract voidable. The principal example is the contract of insurance where it is said that: 'the underwriter knows nothing and the man who asks him to insure knows everything'.[8] Thus the insured is required to disclose all material facts which would influence the prudent insurer. The failure to disclose material facts by an insured entitles the insurance company to refuse to honour a claim under the policy. The operation of the rule was illustrated in the case of *Lambert v Co-operative Insurance Society Ltd*[9] which concerned a policy of insurance on some jewellery. The plaintiff had not been asked any questions on her husband's previous criminal convictions and had not volunteered any information. The policy had been taken out in 1963 and renewed every year until 1976 when the plaintiff made a claim. In the course of

settling the claim it was revealed that the plaintiff's husband had criminal convictions and the insurance company therefore sought to repudiate the policy. The Court of Appeal held that the plaintiff had failed to disclose a material fact and the policy was therefore avoided.

A contract of insurance can be avoided even where the actual claim on it is unrelated to the undisclosed fact. For example, if a policy covers fire and theft and the insured fails to disclose a criminal conviction the fact that a claim is subsequently made for fire damage would not prevent the company avoiding the claim. The rule has been the subject of much criticism on the basis that many individuals taking out insurance are not aware that such a duty exists. Even if they are aware of the duty, moreover, it is extremely difficult to know precisely what information would be regarded as material to a prudent insurer.[10]

3. In certain cases the nature of the relationship between the parties demands full disclosure of all material facts; in particular relationships of a fiduciary nature based on mutual trust. This category includes those between principal and agent, partners, and a company promoter and the company.

b) Material misrepresentation

For a misrepresentation to affect the validity of a contract it must relate to a material matter. In general if the matter is such that it would have affected the decision of a reasonable man to enter into the contract, it is sufficiently material. It does not therefore extend to trivial aspects of the contract. The contract may, however, provide that all representations irrespective of their importance are to be regarded as material. This often occurs in contracts of insurance and means that the slightest misstatement gives rise to the right to set the contract aside. For example in *Dawsons Ltd v Bonnin*[11] a motor insurance proposal for a lorry asked where it was to be garaged. The proposer wrongly assumed that it was garaged at an address in central Glasgow when in fact it was garaged on the outskirts of the city. There was a clause in the contract to the effect that all representations on the proposal form were regarded as material (such a clause in insurance contracts is often referred to as 'a basis of the contract clause') and the insurance company was, therefore, permitted to repudiate the policy despite the relatively trivial nature of the misrepresentation. Like the rule on non-disclosure of material facts in insurance contracts, this practice has been subjected to criticism.[12]

c) Inducing the contract

The misrepresentation must have been the factor or one of the factors which induced the other party to enter into the contract. Thus if he knew the truth of the matter he cannot complain of the misrepresentation. In general if a misrepresentation has been made of such a kind as is likely to induce a party to contract, the fact of inducement will be presumed. However, it is always possible to rebut the inference where it can be proved that the other party did not allow the misrepresentation to affect his judgement. Thus if the party takes steps to verify the truth of a representation and makes the contract in reliance on their own investigation, the implication of inducement will have been rebutted. Similarly, if the other party was not aware of a misrepresentation when the contract was made he may not, at a later date, rely on it in order to set the contract aside. For example, if a person buys shares in a company he cannot rescind the contract if at a later date he discovers false statements about the company in a prospectus.[13]

1 *Dimmock v Hallett* (1866) 2 Ch App 21.
2 [1927] AC 177, PC.
3 (1884) 28 Ch D 7, CA.
4 (1885) 29 Ch D 459, CA.
5 Ibid at 482.
6 *Gillespie v Russell* (1859) 21D HL 13, 15.
7 See *Dimmock v Hallett* (1866) 2 Ch App 21 and *With v O'Flanagan* [1936] Ch 575, [1936] 1 All ER 727, CA.
8 *Rozanes v Bowen* (1928) 32 Ll Rep 98 at 102.
9 [1975] 2 Lloyd's Rep 485, CA.
10 See MacKenna J's observations in the *Lambert* case at 491 and Law Commission Report No 104, 1980.
11 [1922] 2 AC 413, HL.
12 See Law Commission Report No 104, 1980.
13 *Re Northumberland and Durham District Banking Co Ltd exp Bigge* (1858) 28 LJ Ch 50.

Remedies for misrepresentation

a) Rescission

15.0.5 A misrepresentation normally makes a contract voidable which means that until the innocent party elects to avoid the contract it is valid. Rescission enables the innocent party to recover any property transferred under the contract or any payment made in advance, whilst at the same time he must restore any property he obtained under the contract. Rescission may be carried out by either the commencement of legal proceedings, or by giving notice to the other party. In cases where goods have been obtained by fraud it is often impossible to trace the individual concerned in order to effect rescission. This may present difficulties since where the goods are resold before rescission the third party will obtain a good title as against the original owner. In the case of *Car and Universal Finance Co Ltd v Caldwell*[1] it was held that notification to the police was sufficient to amount to rescission so that if, after such notification, the goods are resold to a third party they may be recovered. Such a situation clearly prejudices the interests of the innocent third party and the Scottish decision in *Macleod v Kerr*[2] to the effect that notification to the police does not constitute rescission, may be preferable.

In order to avoid hardship and injustice to either the person who was responsible for making the innocent misrepresentation or an innocent third party, the law recognises that in certain circumstances the right to rescission may be withdrawn.

Where a third party purchases the subject matter of the contract in good faith and before rescission is effected, he will acquire a good title to the property and thus the original owner is prevented from rescinding the contract and recovering the property.

If a party proposes to rescind a contract he must be able to restore the other party to the position in which he was before he entered into the contract. Obviously if goods have been consumed restitution is impossible. Precise restitution is not, however, necessary. Thus where the goods have diminished in value or otherwise deteriorated or changed, rescission may still be permitted.[3]

If a party recognises the validity of the contract after he has become aware of the misrepresentation he thereby waives his right to rescind it. For example, a person who has purchased shares in reliance on a prospectus in which there appears a material misrepresentation will lose his right to rescind if he accepts a dividend, attends and votes at a meeting or does any other act consistent with continued ownership in the knowledge of all the material facts.[4]

Undue delay in rescinding a contract may preclude a party from exercising his right. This can be viewed as one aspect of recognition of the validity of the contract under the above paragraph. Clearly if a party is aware of any irregularity in the making of the contract but delays in taking action it represents evidence of affirmation. Even where the party is not aware of the defect for some time and acts promptly on discovering the true position, the time factor may negate the right to rescind. In *Leaf v International Galleries*[5] a picture was purchased that had been innocently attributed to Constable. Five years later the purchaser discovered that the picture was not by Constable and sought to rescind the contract. The Court of Appeal held that despite the fact that the purchaser acted promptly, the right to rescind had been lost because of lapse of time.

b) Damages
Damages may be claimed for misrepresentation under five categories in English law.

(i) Fraudulent misrepresentation If a person makes a false statement which he either knows to be false, or which he made without belief in its truth or recklessly not caring whether it was true or false, the statement will amount to fraud and thus be actionable as a civil wrong. Such an action will lie irrespective of its impact on the contract. Negligence in making a false statement is not sufficient to support a claim for fraud; there must be some element of conscious dishonesty. For example, in *Derry v Peek*[6] the directors of a company issued a prospectus containing a statement that the company had obtained authority to operate a tramway by steam power. The statement proved to be false but it was established that the directors honestly believed it to be true, they had misunderstood the negotiations with the Board of Trade. It was held that the directors were not liable because of the absence of dishonesty. They genuinely believed the statement to be true, albeit that they were careless in failing to verify the position.

(ii) Damages for a negligent misrepresentation Since the observations of the House of Lords in *Hedley Byrne & Co Ltd v Heller & Partners Ltd*[7] it has been accepted that damages may be awarded where a person has suffered loss as a result of a negligent statement made by a professional or business person. This matter is dealt with in Part 2.

(iii) Damages for negligent misrepresentation under the Misrepresentation Act 1967 The Misrepresentation Act 1967 provides in section 2(1) that damages are payable 'where a person has entered into a contract after a misrepresentation has been made to him by another party.' The section provides a much more effective remedy in the context of contractual statements than the common law action based on negligence. All the innocent party is required to show is the existence of a contract after the

misrepresentation was made. Unlike an action based on negligence, the burden is thrown onto the person who makes the statement to prove that 'he had reasonable grounds to believe and did believe up to the time that the contract was made that the facts represented were true.' In other words, he is assumed to have been negligent unless he proves the contrary.

(iv) Damages in lieu of rescission   Section 2(2) of the Misrepresentation Act 1967 provides that where a person enters into a contract after an innocent representation has been made to him, and he would be entitled to rescind the contract—

> 'then, if it is claimed in any of the proceedings arising out of the contract that the contract ought to be or has been rescinded, the court or arbitrator may declare the contract subsisting and award damages in lieu of rescission.'

The court must, however, be satisfied that it would be equitable to do so, taking account of the nature of the misrepresentation and the loss that would be caused by it if the contract were upheld, in addition to the loss that would be caused to the other party in the event of rescission.

It must be stressed that damages under this subsection are awarded instead of rescission, not in addition to rescission. Further, the power cannot be exercised in the case of a fraudulent misrepresentation nor where rescission is barred (see (a) above). Section 2(2) does not establish a right to damages, it merely bestows upon the court a discretion to make an award. In the event of damages being awarded under s 2(1) of the Act, the court must take account in that award of any damages under s 2(2).[8]

1   [1965] 1 QB 525, [1964] 1 All ER 290, CA.
2   1965 SC 253.
3   See *Armstrong v Jackson* [1917] 2 KB 822.
4   *Scholey v Central Rly Co of Venezuela* (1868) LR 9 Eq 266n.
5   [1950] 2 KB 86, [1950] 1 All ER 693, CA.
6   (1889) 14 App Cas 337, HL.
7   [1964] AC 465, [1963] 2 All ER 575, HL, and see 7.1.6.
8   S 2(3).

The Misrepresentation Act—exclusion of liability
15.0.6   Section 3 of the 1967 Act, as amended by s 8 of the Unfair Contract Terms Act 1977, makes the exclusion or restriction of any liability or remedy arising out of a misrepresentation subject to a test of reasonableness.[1]

1   See 18.0.11.

Duress
15.0.7   Since consent lies at the heart of all agreements it follows that if consent is obtained by improper pressure there will be no agreement. Thus if consent is obtained by actual or threatened violence calculated to produce fear of loss of life or physical harm, the contract may be avoided. To constitute duress the threat must be unlawful in that it amounts to a crime or a tort. Such a situation rarely arises in practice. Of more immediate relevance is the effect of duress to goods and the wider notion of economic duress. In recent years the English courts have come to accept that a threat to

goods or to break a contract may amount to duress. As Lord Scarman observed in *Pao On v Lau Yiu Long* :[1]

> 'there is nothing contrary to principle in recognising economic duress as a factor which may render a contract voidable, provided always that the basis of such recognition is that it must always amount to a coercion of will, which vitiates consent.'

Mere commercial pressure would clearly be insufficient; the threats must be of an unlawful character. Thus in the *Universe Tankships Inc of Monrovia International Transport Workers Federation*[2] it was held that the threat by a union to black an employer's ship unless the employer made a number of payments, including a contribution to the union welfare fund, amounted to economic duress thus permitting the employer to recover the sums paid to the fund. Lord Diplock observed that:

> 'The rationale of economic duress was that where the apparent consent of a party was induced by illegitimate pressure from the other party, that consent was revocable unless approbated expressly or by implication after pressure had ceased.'[3]

As Lord Diplock implies in the above quotation duress renders a contract voidable.

1   [1979] 3 All ER 65 at 79, PC.
2   [1983] 1 AC 366, [1982] 2 All ER 67, HL.
3   At 384.

Undue influence—extortionate and unconscionable bargains

15.0.8   Undue influence in English law falls into two distinct groups. First, equity may extend to protect an individual who makes a contract under a form of pressure which falls outside the ambit of duress. The coercive act need not be unlawful but there must be present some form of exploitation by one party to their advantage, over a weaker party. Second, where a special relationship exists between persons based on trust and confidence there is a presumption of undue influence. Such a relationship exists between solicitor and client, doctor and patient, parent and child. It may extend to any relationship where one party takes advantage of the other party by virtue of a relationship based on trust and confidence. The person in whom confidence is placed is required to rebut the presumption by, for example, evidence that the other party had access to independent advice before the agreement was made. In order to render a contract voidable it must be established that the contract was manifestly disadvantageous to the weaker party.[1]

As a general rule contract law does not recognise extortion as a ground for challenging the validity of a contract. If the price is excessive or because of unequal bargaining power between the parties, one party is forced to accept a bad bargain, the common law provides no remedy. The general attitude has always prevailed that it is not for the courts but the parties themselves to decide whether the terms of a contract are a good bargain.

Equity may, however, grant relief against unconscionable bargains but such relief has been granted infrequently. In particular it has been granted in order to protect someone who is poor, ignorant and has been disadvantaged by another. In *Cresswell v Potter*[2] a wife in the course of a matrimonial dispute agreed to transfer her share in the matrimonial home to her husband for a grossly inadequate consideration. The Court of Appeal set aside the contract on the grounds that the disposition was at an undervalue, she had no independent advice, was poor and in the context of property transactions, ignorant. Such decisions are essentially based on the absence of independent advice and may often be explained in terms of fraud, duress or undue influence rather than on the basis of any notion of unconscionable bargain.

In *Lloyds Bank Ltd v Bundy*[3] the Court of Appeal set aside a transaction largely on the basis that the person involved had received no independent advice. In reviewing the case law Lord Denning observed:

> 'through all these instances there runs a single thread. They rest on inequality of bargaining power. By virtue of it the English law gives relief to one who without independent advice, enters into a contract on terms which are very unfair or transfers property for a consideration which is grossly inadequate, when his bargaining power is grievously impaired by needs or desires or by his own ignorance or infirmity or pressures brought to bear on him by or for the benefit of the other. When I use the word 'undue' I do not mean to suggest that the principle depends on proof of any wrongdoing. The one who stipulates for an unfair advantage may be moved solely by his own self-interest unconscious of the distress he is bringing to the other.'[4]

The difficulty with such a wide concept as Lord Denning envisages is that it undermines the certainty of contract law and in effect introduces a mechanism for deciding each case on its merits or as one American academic observes it is 'a licence for courts to decide cases by instinct alone.'[5]

In the context of disputes arising out of agreements in restraint of trade, a number of cases have been decided on the basis of protecting a weaker party against a harsh agreement.[6] For example, in *Schroeder Music Publishing Co Ltd v Macauley*[7] it was considered that the music publishing company's standard form contract was void on the basis that it was an unreasonable restraint of trade. Lord Diplock stated:

> 'It is, in my view, salutory to acknowledge that in refusing to enforce provisions of a contract whereby one party agrees for the benefit of the other party to exploit or to refrain from exploiting his own earning-power, the public policy which the court is implementing is not some 19th century economic theory about the benefit to the general public of freedom of trade, but the protection of those whose bargaining power is weak against being forced by those whose bargaining power is stronger to enter into bargains that are unconscionable. Under the influence of Bentham and of laissez-faire the courts in the 19th century abandoned the practice of applying the public policy against unconscionable bargains to contracts generally . . . If one looks at the reasoning of the 19th century judges in cases about contracts in restraint of trade one finds lip service paid to current and economic theories but if one looks at what they said in the light of what they did, one finds they struck down a bargain if they thought it was unconscionable as between the parties to it, and upheld it if they thought that it was not.
> So I would hold that the question to be answered as respects a contract in restraint of trade of the kind with which this appeal is

concerned is: was the bargain fair? The test of fairness is, no doubt, whether the restrictions are both reasonably necessary for the protection of the legitimate interests of the promisee and commensurate with the benefits secured to the promisor under the contract.'[8]

The problem for business is how to distinguish between a hard bargain which is the hall mark of the market economy and a harsh bargain which may be invalidated. Perhaps the line between such bargains is best left for Parliament and public agencies such as the Office of Fair Trading to identify. Such is the case in respect of extortionate credit bargains[9] where detailed statutory guidelines are laid down.

1 *National Westminster Bank plc v Morgan* [1985] AC 686, [1985] 1 All ER 821, HL.
2 [1978] 1 WLR 255n.
3 [1975] QB 326, [1974] 3 All ER 757, CA.
4 At 339.
5 Leff, 'Unconscionability and the Code: The Emperor's New Clause' 115 UPa L Rev 485, 527 (1967).
6 See 16.0.5.
7 [1974] 3 All ER 616, [1974] 1 WLR 1308, HL.
8 At 623.
9 See 28.7.1.

Chapter 16
Contracts and Public Policy

16.0.0 Although the law of contract is centred on the doctrine of freedom of contract, the courts reserve the right to declare that a contract is void on the grounds that its object is illegal or offends against current morality. In some cases Parliament has intervened to declare specific agreements void, unenforceable or subject to the specific scrutiny of a public agency before declaring them valid.

Inevitably what may be regarded as offensive at one time may be regarded as acceptable in another era. Indeed one judge has observed:

> 'The determination of what is contrary to the so-called policy of the law necessarily varies from time to time. Many transactions are upheld now by our courts which a former generation would have avoided as contrary to the supposed policy of the law. The rule remains, but its application varies with the principles which for the time being guide public opinion.'[1]

1 *Evanturel v Evanturel* (1874) LR 6 PC 1 at 29.

Contracts illegal by statute
16.0.1 Certain types of contract are declared to be illegal by statute. The nature and effect of such illegality varies according to the terms of the particular statute. Some statutes expressly render the entire contract illegal, thus for example, the Life Assurance Act 1774 makes illegal contracts on the life of a person in whom the proposer has no insurable interest.

Where a contract is not expressly prohibited by a statute, it may be a matter of interpretation as to whether the contract is impliedly forbidden. Simply because a statute is contravened does not automatically render a contract illegal.[1] If a statute imposes some penalty for entering into a particular type of contract and the purpose of the penalty is merely to raise revenue, the contract will not be illegal.[2] If, on the other hand, the purpose is to protect the public, the contract will be impliedly prohibited.[3]

The effect of illegality very much depends upon whether the creation of the contract is prohibited or whether the manner of its performance renders it illegal. In the former case, neither party will be able to enforce the contract unless the illegal parts of the contract can be separated from other parts of the bargain. If the statutory provision is one which is designed to protect a particular class of person as opposed to simply imposing a general prohibition, a party who is a member of that class can enforce it.[4] Where the

205

contract was lawful in formation but illegally performed, the party responsible for the illegal performance will not acquire any rights or remedies under the contract.[5] The innocent party will, however, be permitted to enforce the contract.

1   *Archbolds (Freightage) Ltd v S Spangleltt Ltd* (Randall, Third Party) [1961] 1 QB 374, [1961] 1 All ER 417, CA.
2   *Smith v Mawhood* (1845) 14 M & W 452.
3   *Cope v Rowlands* (1836) 2 M & W 149.
4   *Nash v Halifax Building Society* [1979] Ch 584, [1979] 2 All ER 19.
5   *Anderson Ltd v Daniel* [1924] 1 KB 138, CA.

Contracts illegal at common law

16.0.2   The courts have held certain types of contract to be illegal on grounds of public policy. It has been said that the notion of public policy is 'a very unruly horse, and once you get astride of it you never know where it will carry you.'[1] This aspect of the role of the judiciary depends essentially upon how wide a discretion should lie with judges to declare certain activities harmful. The predominant view today is that the significant areas of public policy are matters for Parliament rather than the judiciary to regulate. The courts therefore exercise a restrained creative role in this area of the law. As Lord Simon observed:

> 'The overriding rule is the general one that the courts of law must recognise their limitation for decision making—that there are many matters on which the decision is more appropriately made by the collective wisdom of Parliament on the advice of the executive briefed by officials who have investigated over a wide field the repercussions of the decision. Such, for example, are those decisions which affect the . . . public safety or in contradistinction to decisions where the subject matter is lawyer's law.'[2]

The generally accepted categories of cases in which the courts will declare a contract to be illegal are:
(a)   contracts to commit a crime or tort;[3]
(b)   contracts that are sexually immoral;[4]
(c)   contracts liable to corrupt public life;[5]
(d)   a contract to defraud the revenue;[6]
(e)   contracts prejudicial to public safety;[7]
(f)   contracts prejudicial to the administration of justice.[8]
If the formation of a contract is illegal under the common law it is unenforceable. In general therefore neither party can sue on the contract. Despite the illegality, title passes under an illegal contract so that money or goods transferred under it cannot normally be recovered.[9]

1   *Richardson v Mellish* (1824) 2 Bing 229 at 252.
2   *D v National Society for the Prevention of Cruelty to Children* [1978] AC 171 at 235.
3   *Berg v Salder and Moore* [1937] 2 KB 158, [1937] 1 All ER 637, CA.
4   *Pearce v Brooks* (1866) LR 1 Exch 213.
5   *Montefiore v Menday Motor Components Co Ltd* [1918] 2 KB 241.
6   *Miller v Karlinski* (1945) 62 TLR 85, CA.
7   *Sovracht (V/O) v Van Udens Scheepvart en Agentuar Maatschappij (NV Gebr)* [1943] AC 203, [1943] 1 All ER 76, HL.
8   *R v Andrews* [1973] QB 422, [1973] 1 All ER 857, CA.
9   *Kingsley v Stirling Industrial Securities Ltd* [1967] 2 QB 747, [1966] 2 All ER 414, CA.

Contracts void at common law
16.0.3 Certain types of contract are treated as invalid at common law on grounds of public policy. These include contracts prejudicial to the state of marriage, contracts to oust the jurisdiction of the courts and contracts in restraint of trade. It is intended to concentrate on the last two types of contracts.

Contracts to oust the jurisdiction of the courts
16.0.4 A contract the effect of which is to preclude a party from submitting questions to the courts is void.[1] Such contracts must be distinguished from those which provide that a dispute shall be referred first to arbitration for settlement. A great many commercial agreements include such provisions and are perfectly valid[2].

1 *Baker v Jones* [1954] 2 All ER 553, [1954] 1 WLR 1005.
2 See 2.8.9.

Contracts in restraint of trade
16.0.5 A contract in restraint of trade is one which unreasonably restricts a person from carrying out his trade, skill or profession. At one time all restraints of trade were regarded as void because by their nature they tend to create monopolies. However, over the years the courts have allowed certain restrictions to be enforced where they can be justified in the interests of the parties and are not detrimental to the public interest. Thus the general test to be applied to such contracts is that they are presumed void unless it can be proved otherwise. The courts will enforce restraints if the party seeking enforcement can prove that the restraint is reasonable between the parties and the other party fails to establish that the restraint is unreasonable in terms of the public interest. In essence the courts have to balance their natural inclination towards giving effect to a bargain between two parties against the economic interests of society in promoting competition and the social interest in ensuring that a party is not locked into an oppressive arrangement.

Contracts in restraint of trade are frequently used in the context of employment, to restrict an employee's future employment prospects; in agreements for the transfer of business to make sure that the seller does not compete with the buyer of the business; in franchise agreements whereby one party agrees to take all supplies from a particular manufacturer; and agreements between traders and manufacturers to restrict output or maintain the selling price of goods or services. The doctrine is not however limited to these classes: 'the classifications must remain fluid and the categories can never be closed.'[1]

a) Employment
If employees have access to trade secrets or are in a position to influence clients, it is legitimate for an employer to seek to protect his interests by including a clause in the contract of employment limiting the employees' ability to abuse their knowledge or influence. Such clauses normally require the employees not to be employed or conduct a business competing with the employers. The restrictions are normally limited in terms of the geographic area covered and the duration.

Such restrictions are presumed void unless they satisfy the twin tests of reasonableness as between the parties and the wider public interest. In general the courts will only permit the use of such clauses where they seek to protect the legally recognised interests of an employer, trade secrets and business connections. In essence the courts have to balance the protection of such interests against the legitimate rights of workers to sell their expertise and carry out their trade or profession. Restraints which simply seek to impede competition will not be enforced.

In employment cases the courts have to be mindful of the disparate bargaining power between an employer and an employee which in cases of doubt may necessitate erring on the side of the employee.

The term 'trade secrets' encompasses any confidential information, secret formulae or processes imparted in the course of employment.[2] It does not include general skills, aptitude or technical knowledge,[3] which all employees acquire in the course of employment.

As regards business connections the employee must be in a position where he is able to acquire influence over clients. If the employee is not sufficiently associated with clients a restraint will be unenforceable.[4]

The reasonableness is determined by examining the nature of the interest protected against the scope of the restraint. If the restriction is wider than is reasonably necessary in order to protect an employer's legitimate business interests it will not be enforced. This will depend upon such factors as the geographic area of the restraint, its duration, nature of the business, and precise terms of the restraint. For example, in *Fitch v Dewes*[5] the House of Lords enforced a life long restraint against a solicitor's managing clerk practising within seven miles of his principal's office after the end of his employment. It was considered reasonable because of the degree of influence that a managing clerk is able to exert over clients. By contrast in *M and S Drapers (a firm) v Reynolds*[6] it was held that a five year restraint against a collector/salesman was too wide in view of his relatively lowly status in the company.

Even where the restraint is held to be reasonable between the parties it may be held to be unenforceable on the grounds of the wider public interest, if its effect is to deprive the community of services from which it could derive benefit.[7]

b) Transfer of a business
When a person sells a business they sell, in addition to the tangible assets, the goodwill of the business. This has been expressed as the:

> 'whole advantage whatever it may be, of the reputation and connection of the firm, which may have been built up by years of honest work or gained by lavish expenditure of money.'[8]

The law will therefore protect the buyer's legal interest in the goodwill and even in the absence of a specific restraining clause, prevent the seller from canvassing customers of the business.

A buyer may, however, seek further protection by inserting an appropriate clause in the contract preventing the seller competing with the business. Such restraints are subject to similar considerations as those in employment contracts. They are presumed void unless reasonable between the parties and in the wider public interest. A restraint in the sale of a business will not be enforced if it is simply intended to restrict competition.

It must be aimed at protecting the interest (goodwill) in the business acquired. For example in *Vancouver Malt and Sake Brewing Co Ltd v Vancouver Breweries Ltd*[9] a company had a licence to brew beer but the only trade carried on by them was the brewing of sake. They agreed to sell the business, including the goodwill, and covenanted not to brew beer for fifteen years. It was held that since the company did not brew beer there was no goodwill to pass to the purchasers and the covenant was merely a restraint on competition which was therefore void.

In terms of the reasonableness of such clauses since the buyer and seller of a business tend to be on a more equal bargaining footing than employer and employee, the courts are more inclined to enforce the restraint. The restraint however must still be reasonable in scope, duration and area. In one case a world-wide restraint for 25 years was held to be reasonable against the seller of an armament business in view of the world-wide spread of the customers.[10]

c) Franchise agreements
In general the courts have been prepared to endorse sole agency agreements particularly where they have become part of the accepted pattern or structure of a trade. They have, however, always reserved the right to subject such agreements to tests of reasonableness.[11] For example, a contract under which a songwriter agreed to provide exclusive services to a publisher who did not give any assurance that the works would be published was held to be void. It was considered by the House of Lords that the agreement was the result of unequal bargaining power and was capable of enforcement in an oppressive manner.[12]

Agreements between garage proprietors and oil companies under which the garage agrees to sell no other brand in return for financial assistance, have been the subject of some litigation. In *Esso Petroleum Co Ltd v Harper's Garage (Stourport) Ltd*[13] the House of Lords held that such agreements were subject to the restraint of trade doctrine. Their Lordships held that a 21 year agreement was unreasonable because it was longer than necessary to protect Esso's interest. A restraint of four years five months was, however, upheld by their Lordships since it was reasonably required by Esso in order to protect their network of outlets, their systems of distribution and stability of sales. In return the garages obtained a rebate on the price of petrol and financial support. It seems therefore that the courts are prepared to protect commercial interests in this context as opposed to the narrower legal interests that have been stressed in employment cases.[14]

In the Esso case the House of Lords were able to support their observations by reference to a Monopolies Commission Report in 1965 on the Supply of Petrol which recommended a five year limit on all 'tied garage' agreements. However, the public interest consideration tends to be viewed in the context of restrictions on an individual's freedom to work rather than any wider economic considerations to promote competition. Ungoed-Thomas J expressed the orthodox view in the following terms:

'It seems to me right in principle and in accordance with the habitual inclination of the court not to interfere with business decisions made by businessmen authorised and qualified to make them. This seems to me to be a proper recognition of freedom of contract within the doctrine of restraint of trade.'

He declined to consider any wider economic or business matters on the grounds that they were matters for 'policy decisions by business administration, Government or Parliament.'[15]

d) Restrictive trading agreements
Agreements in which manufacturers or traders seek to restrict competition, output or maintain prices are also subject to the restraint of trade doctrine. They are, therefore, void unless proved to be reasonable in terms of the parties and the public. With such agreements the public interest tends to be of central importance since an agreement may be reasonable between the parties but unreasonable in the public interest because it is calculated:

> 'to produce that state of things which is referred to as a pernicious monopoly, that is to say, a monopoly calculated to enhance prices to an unreasonable extent.'[16]

Provided that restrictive trading agreements are not contrary to the wider public interest, the courts have been prepared to enforce them, even where the interests they seek to support are purely commercial such as customer lists.[17] Indeed, with such agreements the parties may rarely be in dispute themselves since they normally derive a mutual benefit from continuing the agreement. The difficulty with such agreements may be that third parties are prejudiced by their existence and the courts were reluctant to allow a third party to challenge an agreement made between two other parties. However in *Eastham v Newcastle United Football Club Ltd*[18] a footballer was granted a declaration that the retain and transfer system operated by the rules of the Football Association and the regulations of the Football League were not binding upon him as they were an unlawful restraint of trade.

In view of the obvious need to protect third parties and the wider public interest, restrictive agreements are now largely regulated by statute and were considered in Part 1.

1   *Esso Petroleum Ltd v Harper's Garage (Stourport) Ltd* [1968] AC 269 at 337.
2   See *Forster & Sons v Suggett* (1918) 35 TLR 87.
3   *Herbert Morris Ltd v Saxelby* [1916] 1 AC 688, HL.
4   *S W Strange Ltd v Mann* [1965] 1 All ER 1069, [1965] 1 WLR 629.
5   [1921] 2 AC 158, HL.
6   [1956] 3 All ER 814, [1957] 1 WLR 9, CA.
7   See *Wyatt v Kreglinger and Fernan* [1933] 1 KB 793, CA.
8   *Trego V Hunt* [1896] AC 7 at 24, HL.
9   [1934] AC 181, PC.
10 *Nordenfelt v Maxim Nordenfelt Guns and Ammunition Co* [1894] AC 535, HL.
11 See *Martin-Baker Aircraft Co Ltd v Canadian Flight Equipment Ltd* [1955] 2 QB 556, [1955] 2 All ER 722.
12 *Schroeder Music Publishing Co Ltd v Macauley* [1974] 3 All ER 616, [1974] 1 WLR 1308, HL. See also 15.0.8.
13 [1968] AC 269, [1967] 1 All ER 699, HL.
14 See also *Alec Lobb (Garages) Ltd v Total Oil GB Ltd* [1985] 1 All ER 303, [1985] 1 WLR 173, CA.
15 *Texaco Ltd v Mulberry Filling Station Ltd* [1972] 1 All ER 513 at 525.
16 *A-G of Commonwealth of Australia v Adelaide SS Co Ltd* [1913] AC 781 at 796, PC.
17 See *McEllistrim v Ballymacelligott Co-operative Agricultural and Dairy Society Ltd* [1919] AC 548, HL.
18 [1964] Ch 413, [1963] 3 All ER 139.

Restraint of trade and severance

16.0.6   If a contract is contrary to public policy it is void and therefore unenforceable. The courts will not substitute a more reasonable term for the offending restraint. However, they may sever the void terms from the valid terms provided that the terms can be severed as they stand without rewriting the agreement or affecting the overall nature of the agreement.[1]

1   *Nordenfelt v Maxim Nordenfelt Guns and Ammunition Co* [1894] AC 535, HL.

Contracts void by statute

16.0.7   Certain statutes render a contract void and therefore unenforceable. Examples of such legislation are the Restrictive Trade Practices Act[1] and legislation rendering wagering and gaming contracts void.[2]

1   See 2.7.3.
2   See Gaming Act 1845; Gaming (Amendment) Act 1982; Betting, Gaming and Lotteries Act 1963.

Contractual capacity

16.1.0   As a general principle the law recognises that all persons have the capacity to enter into contractual relations. However, in order to protect young persons against their own immaturity, the mentally ill or those in a state of intoxication against persons taking advantage of their state of mind, the law restricts their contractual capacity. In addition, where corporate bodies are formed with a particular objective in mind the law restricts their contractual capacity to their stated objects or the terms of the statute under which they were created.[1] The law must also, however, strike the right balance between placing limitations on the contractual capacity of persons and protecting the legitimate rights and expectations of those persons who deal in good faith with individuals or corporate bodies on whom the law has placed such restrictions.

1   See 33.3.0.

Age

16.1.1   Under the Family Reform Act 1969 the age of majority was reduced from 21 to 18. Persons below that age have a limited contractual capacity.

The approach that English law somewhat unsatisfactorily[1] adopts is to divide contracts made by minors (the term used to describe persons under eighteen) into different categories ranging from valid contracts to those which are rendered void.

a) Valid contracts
A minor may validly enter into two types of contract:

(i) Contracts for necessary goods and services   The term 'necessary' is taken to include most goods and services that are reasonably necessary to maintain the minor, taking account of his particular circumstances. It therefore extends to cover food, clothing, transport and education. It must be shown the goods and services supplied were necessary, taking account of the minor's circumstances at the time of the sale and when they were delivered.[2] Section 3 of the Sale of Goods Act 1979 provides that where

goods are sold and delivered to a minor he must pay a reasonable price for them, which may not necessarily be the contract price.

(ii) Contract of employment   A contract of employment is binding on a minor if it is of benefit to him. The minor will not be bound if the terms are harsh or oppressive in any way. The rule also extends to contracts of apprenticeship and any other contract under which the minor makes a living by the exercise of some trade or profession.[3] Curiously, however, the principle does not extend to trading contracts. Thus if a minor carries on a business he will not be liable on any contracts entered into in the course of trade, regardless of whether or not the contract is beneficial.[4]

b) Voidable contracts
There are a number of agreements where both the parties are bound, but the minor is given the option to avoid or repudiate the contract. These are:
1. A contract by a minor to buy or sell land.
2. A purported lease by or to a minor.
3. A contract by a minor to bring property into a marriage settlement.
4. A contract by a minor to purchase shares.
5. A partnership agreement. Although a minor can become a partner and share in the profits, he is not liable for debts of the partnership during his minority. He will, however, be liable for such debts after attaining the age of majority, if he fails to repudiate the contract.

The minor is required to exercise his right to repudiate the contract during minority or within a reasonable time of reaching majority. What is a reasonable time depends on the factual circumstances. The minor's ignorance of his right to repudiate will not necessarily relieve him from the consequences of undue delay in exercising the right.

The effect of repudiation is to relieve the minor of all future liability. There would appear to be some uncertainty as to whether repudiation relieves the individual concerned from liabilities which have built up before repudiation.[5] There is no right however to recover money paid under the contract unless there has been a total failure of consideration, that is the individual received nothing of what he has bargained for.

c) Void contracts
Section 1 of the Infants Relief Act 1874 renders certain contracts 'absolutely void.' It applies to:
1. Contracts for the repayment of money lent or to be lent to a minor.
2. Contracts for goods supplied or to be supplied, other than necessary goods.
3. Accounts stated (admission of a debt). In effect this is no longer necessary since an account stated is regarded as prima facie evidence of a debt; of itself it creates no liability.

Such contracts cannot be enforced by or against the minor. In the case of transactions involving credit or other financial accommodation, if the lender obtains an indemnity against loss from an adult it can be enforced. An indemnity must however be distinguished from a guarantee of a minor's debt by an adult which cannot be enforced: since the loan is void there can be no debt to guarantee. Sometimes the distinction between a guarantee and an indemnity can be fine and in cases of doubt the courts will usually be swayed towards the indemnity interpretation.[6]

Contracts under this group have some legal effect in that the property in the goods (ownership) passes when they are delivered to the minor. Such a rule represents an exception to the general principle that property does not pass under a void contract and it serves to protect the innocent third party who acquires the goods from the minor.[7]

In general money paid, or property transferred, under a void contract cannot be recovered by the minor unless there has been a total failure of consideration.[8]

d) Other contracts
A minor is not bound by other contracts not covered by the above provisions, such as contracts for the supply of goods by the minor, or a loan by a minor. They will however bind the adult party although it seems that the minor cannot obtain specific performance of the contract.[9] Section 2 of the Infants Relief Act 1874 provides that a debt entered into during minority cannot be rendered enforceable against the minor by a promise to pay made after majority. In the case of contracts which do not give rise to a debt on the part of a minor the section goes on to provide that such contracts are not enforceable against the minor by his ratification after minority but a fresh promise to perform will be enforceable. Clearly, it is more likely to be a fresh promise if additional terms are added or the original terms varied in some way.

1 See the Latey Committee's Report Cmnd 3342 Part IV (1967). See the Minors' Contracts Bill 1987.
2 *Nash v Inman* [1908] 2 KB 1, CA.
3 See *Chaplin v Leslie Frewin (Publishers) Ltd* [1966] Ch 71, [1965] 3 All ER 764, CA.
4 *Mercantile Union Guarantee Corpn v Ball* [1937] 2 KB 498, [1937] 3 All ER 1, CA.
5 See *North Western Rly Co v M'Michael* (1850) 5 Exch 114 at 125 and *Blake v Concannon* (1870) IR 4 CL 323 for contrasting views.
6 See *Yeoman Credit Ltd v Latter* [1961] 2 All ER 294, [1961] 1 WLR 828, CA.
7 See Part 4.
8 See *Pearce v Brain* [1929] 2 KB 310.
9 *Flight v Bolland* (1828) 4 Russ 298.

Insanity
16.1.2 Under English law contracts made by someone mentally ill are voidable at their instance if the other party knew of their inability to comprehend the nature of the transaction.[1]

1 *R Leslie Ltd v Sheill* [1914] 3 KB 607, CA.

Drunkenness
16.1.3 The fact that a person was drunk at the time he entered into a contract will not necessarily affect the validity of the contract. However, if a person is so drunk that he is unable to give true consent the contract may be voidable at his option. English cases[1] stress the additional requirement that the other party has knowledge that the person was incapable of understanding what he was doing but clearly in most instances if a person is so drunk as to negative any consent it will be readily apparent to the other party.

A drunken person to whom necessaries are sold and delivered is under the same liability to pay a reasonable price for them, as is an insane person.

Malins v Freeman (1836) 2 Keen 25 at 34.

Corporations

16.1.4   The basic principle in relation to the contractual capacity of corporate bodies is that such capacity depends upon the terms of their constitution. In general there are three ways in which a company may be formed. First, by registration under the Companies Act 1985. Second, Private Act of Parliament (statutory companies). Third, by Royal Charter (chartered companies).

A body incorporated by royal charter has power to enter into any contract unless expressly forbidden by the charter. Companies incorporated by statute cannot enter into any contracts unless they are expressly or impliedly authorised to do so under the terms of the statute. Any purported contract outside the statutory powers is described as ultra vires (beyond the powers) and is void.

The most common form of corporate body is the company registered under the Companies Act. This is an area to which we shall return in later paragraphs.[1] In the context of the present discussion however, it is sufficient to say that companies registered under the Companies Act are required to state the broad objects of the enterprise in a memorandum of association which is placed on public display. A company cannot enter into any contract which is not reasonably incidental to the achievement of its stated objects. If it does so, the contract will be void and unenforceable, even if it was approved by all the shareholders. However, the rights of innocent third parties may be protected in certain circumstances where they have entered into an ultra vires contract with a company. The Companies Act 1985 (s 35)[2] provides that if a party in good faith enters into a contract decided upon by the directors of the company then the contract is enforceable against the company irrespective of any provisions in the company's memorandum.

1   See 33.3.0.
2   See 33.3.2.

Trade unions

16.1.5   A trade union is not a corporate body but statute has given such organisations the capacity to enter into contracts and to sue and be sued in their own name in proceedings founded on contract.[1]

1   Trade Union and Labour Relations Act 1974, s 2(1).

Chapter 17

Discharge, Breach and Remedies

Discharge

17.0.0 Contracts entered into in the course of business impose obligations on both parties. Once such obligations have been performed by the parties as envisaged under their agreement, the contract will be discharged.

A party who fails to perform his obligations may be in breach of contract. In that event the innocent party may be entitled to treat the contract as discharged. Alternatively the failure to perform may be due to a radical change in the circumstances which will excuse non-performance and discharge the contract.

Discharge by payment

17.0.1 Where performance of a contract is by payment of a specific sum of money, the contract will be discharged when the sum has been paid. Such payment should be in legal tender which consists of those notes and coins which by law must be accepted in payment of a debt.

Discharge by performance

17.0.2 For performance to discharge a contract it must be in accordance with the terms of the contract. It is important therefore to determine the precise nature of the contractual obligations and compare them with the contractual performance. The general rule is that each party must perform what they have bargained to do and it is no defence to claim that the performance effected is as commercially acceptable as that promised if it does not correspond.[1] The law will however tolerate microscopic deviations.[2] If some flexibility is required it is important that it is built into the terms of the contract by the use of appropriate words signifying that some latitude is allowed.

1 See *Arcos Ltd v EA Ronaasen & Son* [1933] AC 470, HL.
2 *Shipton, Anderson & Co v Weil Bros & Co* [1912] 1 KB 574.

Time for performance

17.0.3 If a contract does not stipulate a time within which a performance must be completed, then the contractual obligations must be performed within a reasonable time. If performance is not so carried out damages may be recovered for breach of contract.

Where a time for performance is specified the key consideration is whether time is of the essence. If it is, the provision in the contract is classified as a condition and a failure to perform in time will amount to a breach of contract entitling the other party to sue for damages and treat the contract as terminated.[1]

1   See 17.1.1.

Discharge by frustration

17.0.4   Even the most sophisticated and well planned contract cannot foresee all eventualities. In the context of a business contract, particularly one where performance is over a period of time, unforeseen events may take place which render performance impossible, or more difficult or more expensive and thus unprofitable. It may be a substantial increase in the price of materials, wage increases at a national level increasing the costs of a project, fire damage in a factory or changes in government policy rendering performance illegal or more expensive because of increased import or export duties. Certain foreseeable problems can be covered by appropriate general clauses in a contract such as a price variation clause or a force majeure clause where the parties can provide for foreseeable difficulties such as price increases on raw materials or suspension of the contract in the event of industrial action. If, however, the parties fail to provide for the adjustment of contractual rights and duties in certain eventualities, the courts are reluctant to interfere and order such adjustment and will expect the parties to perform their respective obligations. Thus in one case[1] where goods were shipped from Port Sudan to Hamburg the House of Lords considered that the closure of the Suez Canal did not frustrate the commercial objective of the contract, even though such closure made performance a great deal more onerous. The position would however have been different had the contract specified that the route would be via the Suez Canal.

Where an event takes place which strikes at the very objective or purpose of a contract, then the courts may be prepared to regard such event as frustrating the contract thus terminating it without attributing fault to either party. Such would be the case where the subject matter of the contract becomes unavailable or is destroyed;[2] where death or personal incapacity supervenes to prevent performance in contracts involving personal service;[3] where there is a change in the law or circumstances which makes performance of the contract illegal[4] or where there is a fundamental change in the circumstances rendering performance radically different from that which was envisaged when the contract was made.[5]

The courts will not however interfere in those cases where performance has simply become more difficult or expensive,[6] or where the frustrating event was induced by one party's failure to follow an appropriate course of action, or they were otherwise at fault. Much may depend upon the terms of the contract in that it may impose a strict responsibility on one party in respect of a particular matter, in which case, the responsibility for failure to produce the desired result will be borne by that party.

Thus the court will only hold that a contract is frustrated by some event which was unforeseen by the parties and for which their contract makes no provision.

If a court holds that a contract has been frustrated, the contract is terminated from that time onwards and the parties are relieved from performance of all future obligations, although they remain liable for performance already rendered or which had already become due. At common law the rule was that all loss lay where it fell at the time of frustration: money paid before the frustrating event was unrecoverable but no further sums were payable, even though one party might have received a benefit from the other. The position is now governed, however, by the Law Reform (Frustrated Contracts) Act 1943 which is intended to mitigate the harshness of the common law rule. However, its drafting is far from clear and it is a measure of the extent to which the Act is distrusted by businessmen and lawyers alike that there is, to date, only one reported decision on the application of the Act.[7] It seems that in general, when contracts are frustrated, contracting parties prefer to deal with the problem by negotiation.

The Act applies to all contracts except (a) a charterparty other than a time charter or charter by demise; (b) contracts of insurance and (c) contracts to which s 7 of the Sale of Goods Act 1979 apply.[8]

The Act provides that:

(a) all monies paid before the date of frustration are repayable; sums which had already fallen due but had not been paid cease to be payable;

(b) if, however, the party to whom such sums were paid or payable has incurred expenses in performing his side of the contract before the date of frustration, the court may allow him to keep a sum, not exceeding the amount of the prepayment, towards those expenses (s 1(2));

(c) if before the date of frustration one party has received a 'valuable benefit' (other than the payment of money) under the contract from the other, then the court may order him to pay such sum not exceeding the value of the benefit, as the court considers just (s 1(3)). In the only reported case[9] on the Act it was held that the court should assess the value of the benefit after the frustrating event. In the particular case this allowed the court to take into account a potential claim for compensation against the Libyan government after nationalisation of an oil concession, which increased the value of the benefit. However, such an approach could cause problems: in *Appleby v Myers*[10] a contract to instal machinery in a factory was frustrated when, shortly before completion, fire destroyed the factory and machinery. Valuing the benefit after the fire would mean that the installer would still get nothing for his work even under the Act. In addition it seems that the party who has provided the benefit may only claim the lesser of the cost to him of providing the benefit and the value of the benefit to the other party.[11]

1 *Tsakiroglou & Co Ltd v Noblee Thorl GmbH* [1962] AC 93, [1961] 2 All ER 179, HL.
2 *Taylor v Caldwell* (1863) 3 B & S 826.
3 *Poussard v Spiers and Pond* [1876] 1 QBD 410.
4 *White and Carter Ltd v Carbis Bay Garage Ltd* [1941] 2 All ER 633, CA.
5 See *Metropolitan Water Board v Dick Kerr & Co Ltd* [1918] AC 119, HL and *Krell v Henry* [1903] 2 KB 740, CA.
6 *Davis Contractors Ltd v Fareham UDC* [1956] AC 696, [1956] 2 All ER 145, HL.
7 *BP Exploration Co (Libya) Ltd v Hunt (No 2)* [1982] 1 All ER 925, [1979] 1 WLR 783.
8 See 22.1.3.
9 See note 7.
10 (1867) LR 2 CP 651, Ex Ch.
11 See note 7.

Breach and remedies

17.1.0 In the event of a party failing without lawful reason to perform his contractual obligations he will be in breach of contract. Such breach may be a total refusal to perform any of the obligations under the contract at the time fixed, or an announcement in advance of an intention not to perform; the latter event is known as anticipatory breach. On the other hand, the breach may be incomplete or defective performance causing loss or injury to the other party.

Where one party is in breach the innocent party may seek redress by taking certain action himself in response to the other party's breach, by initiating litigation in order to compel performance or claim monetary compensation or by activating an arbitration clause in the contract and allowing an independent third party to resolve the dispute.[1]

1　Arbitration was discussed at 2.8.9.

Self-help remedies[1]

17.1.1 An innocent party may quite legitimately refuse to perform his contractual obligations until the other party has performed, or is ready to perform, his obligations. Indeed, the innocent party may refuse to perform his obligations at all and decline any further performance by the other party because of the initial breach. The remedies of withholding performance and termination for breach are indeed closely related. In essence they are both dependent on the breach being a serious breach going to the root of the contract.

Obviously if one party fails to perform at all, or manifests an intention not to perform a fundamental part of the contract, the law will consider that such repudiatory behaviour will entitle the innocent party to take the appropriate action. In less clear cut cases, the law makes the distinction between major breaches which strike at the root of the bargain and minor ones which do not have that effect. The issue is determined by considering what the intention of the parties was at the time the contract was made. The breach of a major part of the contact is often termed a breach of condition and a minor breach, a breach of warranty. In essence, it is not necessarily the seriousness of the breach that designates a term a condition but the importance attached to it by the parties as manifesting itself in the wording of the contract or surrounding circumstances. Indeed if a term of a contract is designated a condition then breach of it, however insignificant, will allow the other party to terminate the contract. Where the parties considered that a term is less important, then breach of that term will enable the innocent party to claim damages only.[2]

A further approach to the question of deciding whether a party is entitled to terminate a contract for breach is based on an examination of the consequences of the breach. As Diplock J said:

> 'There are, however, many contractual undertakings of a more complex character which cannot be characterised as being 'conditions' or warranties . . . Of such undertakings all that can be predicted is that some breaches will and others will not give rise to such an event . . .; and the legal consequences of the breach . . ., unless provided for expressly in the contract, depend upon the nature of the event to which the breach gives rise and do not follow automatically from

a prior classification of the undertaking as a 'condition' or 'a warranty'.[3]

In effect, instead of classifying a term, the courts may simply examine the extent of the breach as against the value of the performance of the contract as a whole.

The two approaches each have their advantages. An approach based simply on classifying the term has the advantage of predictability and certainty. As Megaw LJ observed:

> 'One of the essential elements of law is some measure of uniformity. One of the important elements of the law is predictability. At any rate in commercial law, there are obvious and substantial advantages in having, where possible, a firm and definite rule for a particular class of legal relationship, eg as here, the legal categorisation of a particular definable contractual clause. . .'[4]

On the other hand, an approach based on the seriousness of the breach introduces a measure of flexibility allowing the courts to manufacture a 'common sense' solution.

Where a party signifies an intention not to perform a major part of the contract in advance such anticipatory breach enables the innocent party to treat the contract as discharged, without waiting for the date fixed for performance. A party is not however bound to accept such a breach as discharging the contract. He may ignore the breach and continue to insist on performance, in which case the contract continues in existence until the due date.

1 See also Part IV.
2 See 17.1.3.
3 *Hong Kong Fir Shipping Co Ltd v Kawasaki Kisen Kaisha Ltd* [1962] 2 QB 26 at 70, CA.
4 *Maredelantia Cia Nariera SA v Bergbau-Handel GmbH, The Mihalis Angelos* [1970] 3 All ER 125 at 138–129.

Judicial intervention
17.1.2 If an innocent party cannot obtain satisfaction by self-help remedies he may have to resort to judicial proceedings.[1] Judicial remedies include the following.

a) Specific performance
The courts have the equitable remedy of compelling a party to perform his contractual obligations. Specific performance is not, however, considered appropriate where damages would be an adequate remedy and is rarely resorted to in the context of business contracts except in the case of agreements for the sale of land.

b) An injunction
An injunction is an order of the court directing a person not to break a contract. It is particularly appropriate in enforcing negative stipulations in contracts, for example, lawful restraints on trade.[2]

c) A claim in debt
Where a contract provides for payment in return for goods or services, delivery of the goods or carrying out the service entitles the party to the

amount provided for in the contract. In such circumstances the party completing performance can bring a debt action to recover the contract price.

d) Damages³

The innocent party may make a claim for monetary compensation. The objective of such compensation is to put the innocent party in the position he would have been in had the contract been performed. The intention is not to punish the offending party but to compensate the innocent party. Whilst damages in tort usually seek to restore the position that existed before the tort, damages in contract aim to reflect the position after the contract.

1   See also Parts I and IV.
2   See 16.1.5.
3   See also 17.1.3. and Ch 24.

Damages

17.1.3   In general damages are awarded to compensate the innocent party to the extent of his contractual expectations or his loss of bargain. Thus if A has paid £200 to B for goods which have not been delivered and the open market price has increased to £400 by the delivery date, A can claim his £200 back from B plus £200 for his loss of bargain.[1]

An alternative way of looking at damages is on the basis of reliance loss. A party may incur expenditure in reliance on the contract which will be wasted if the other party fails to perform. This includes all expenditure wasted in attempting to carry out the contract and, in certain circumstances, expenditure incurred prior to the contract in anticipation of it.[2] If the innocent party made a bad bargain in that their reliance loss exceeds the value of the contract, then, only a proportion of the loss can be recovered.

Damages in contract are not restricted to pure economic loss but may be awarded for personal injury, pain and suffering, inconvenience and discomfort.[3] Whether a party may be awarded damages for emotional distress arising out of a breach is probably dependant on whether the contract is one which involves the provision of enjoyment or peace of mind as is the case with contracts involving travel and leisure.[4]

Clearly the practicalities of economic activity demand that some limit be placed on the nature and scope of the loss that can be claimed as a result of a breach of contract. As one learned judge observed:

> 'The law cannot take account of everything that follows a wrongful act; it regards some subsequent matters as outside the scope of its election, because it were infinite for the law to judge the cause of causes or consequences of consequences. In the varied web of affairs the law must abstract some consequences as relevant, not perhaps on grounds of pure logic but simply for practical reasons.'[5]

The law of contract will only allow a person to recover damages where the loss suffered was caused by the other party's breach of contract. Thus if the loss would have occurred irrespective of the breach, no damages would be payable. Similarly, if the loss was the result of an intervening act by a third party which was not foreseeable as the consequence of the breach, it will be regarded as too remote. The rules on remoteness of damage were formulated in the famous case of *Hadley v Baxendale*[6] and provide that damage is not too remote if:

(a) the loss arises naturally, ie according to the usual course of things, from the breach of contract as the probable result of it. In other words, any person in that position would have been likely to suffer that loss; or

(b) the loss could reasonably be supposed to have been in the contemplation of the parties, when they made the contract, as the probable result of it.

In practice, a person will only be able to recover damages for such loss as was within the reasonable contemplation of the parties as the probable result of its breach had they had their attention drawn to the possibility of the breach which did in fact occur. What was within the reasonable contemplation of the parties depends on their knowledge and such knowledge can be either imputed or actual.[7] Everyone is taken to know the ordinary course of things under the terms of rule (a) of *Hadley v Baxendale* and hence the loss that is the probable result of a breach of it. If a party has actual knowledge of special circumstances (over and above the ordinary course of things) of such a kind that the breach in these special circumstances would be liable to cause more loss, rule (b) in *Hadley v Baxendale* makes that additional loss recoverable. In effect as Posner asserts:

> 'the general principle . . . is that where a risk of loss is known to only one party to the contract, the other party is not liable for the loss if it occurs. This principle induces the party with knowledge of the risk either to take any appropriate precautions himself or, if he believes that the other party might be the more efficient loss avoider, to disclose the risk to that party and pay him to assume it. In this way incentives are generated to deal with the risk in the most efficient fashion.'[8]

Provided that the type of loss is within the reasonable contemplation of the parties, damages can be recovered, even if the actual extent of the loss is not within the contemplation of the parties. For example in *Parsons (Livestock) Ltd v Uttley Ingham & Co Ltd*[9] a hopper was supplied for the storage of pig food nuts. The hopper was improperly ventilated and the pig nuts became mouldy with the result that the pigs contracted a rare disease causing the death of 254. Clearly the supply of a defective hopper was a breach of contract, but the question to be decided was whether the farmer could claim for the loss he sustained as a result of the death and sickness of his pigs. In awarding such damages the Court of Appeal considered that if the breach had been brought to the attention of the parties and they had asked themselves what was likely to happen they would have contemplated the serious possibility that the pigs would have become ill, hence damages were awarded for the death and sickness of the pigs since the type of loss was within the contemplation of the parties. The fact that the extent of the loss may not have been in contemplation of the parties was not relevant.

Once a contracting party becomes aware of a breach of contract, he must take reasonable steps to mitigate the loss, since the law will not allow a party to recover damages for loss which could reasonably have been avoided. Thus if a buyer is not supplied with goods on the due date he may purchase substitute goods on the open market and claim any difference in price from the original seller; the duty to mitigate, however, encourages the buyer to make a repurchase with reasonable haste and on reasonable terms. If there is undue delay or the substitute goods are purchased at an exorbitant price, the amount awarded will reflect the loss he would have suffered if the damage had been mitigated.

The duty to mitigate only requires the innocent party to act reasonably, he is not expected to go to excessive lengths such as embarking on hazardous litigation or risking his business reputation.[10]

In the case of an anticipatory breach of contract the innocent party has an option to either accept the breach, terminate the contract immediately and sue for damages, or affirm the contract and await the date fixed for performance and then bring an action for damages. If the termination option is selected the party is under a duty to mitigate his loss immediately; if, on the other hand, he waits until the date fixed for performance, he is under no obligation to mitigate his loss before performance is actually due.[11]

1 See also 24.0.3.
2 *Anglia Television Ltd v Reed* [1972] 1 QB 60, [1971] 3 All ER 690, CA.
3 *Jarvis v Swans Tours Ltd* [1973] QB 233, [1973] 1 All ER 71, CA.
4 *Bliss v South East Thames Regional Health Authority* [1985] IRLR 308, CA.
5 *Lord Wright in Liesbosch, Dredger (Owners) v Edison SS (Owners)* [1933] AC 449 at 460.
6 (1854) 23 LJ Ex 179.
7 See *Victoria Laundry (Windsor) Ltd v Newman Industries Ltd* [1949] 2 KB 528, [1949] 1 All ER 997, CA.
8 Posner, *Economic Analysis of Law* (2nd edn) pp 94–95.
9 [1978] QB 791, [1978] 1 All ER 525, CA.
10 See *Pilkington v Wood* [1953] Ch 770, [1953] 2 All ER 810.
11 *Gebruder Metelmann GmbH & Co KG v NBR (London) Ltd* [1984] 1 Lloyd's Rep 614, CA.

Agreed damages

17.1.4 The parties to a contract may provide in the terms of the contract that a specified amount will be payable in the event of breach. Such clauses in the contract are referred to as liquidated damages clauses and are a sensible precaution against the cost and difficulties inherent in the judicial process of proving damages. As Sweet comments:

'Both contracting parties often wish to control their risk exposure, and permitting them to do so encourages risk-taking. The performing party may also wish to avoid the feared irrationality of the judicial process in determining actual damages. He may also be fearful that the court will give insufficient consideration to legitimate excuses for non-performance, that the court may be unduly sympathetic to the plaintiff's claim, that any loss he incurred should be paid for by the party whose non-performance caused the loss, or that the court may consider contract breach an immoral act. There are also reasons why the non-performing party as well may wish to use a liquidated damages clause. Sometimes a breach will cause damage, but the amount of damages cannot be proven under damage rules.'[1]

Where a contract contains a liquidated damages clause, in the event of a breach, the innocent party may recover the specified amount irrespective of whether the amount is greater or less than the actual loss sustained. However a clause will only be enforceable if it represents a genuine and reasonable pre-estimate of the loss likely to flow from the breach. If a clause is inserted in the contract simply in order to operate as a threat to hold over a potential defaulter, in the event of it being challenged, it will be disregarded by the courts as a penalty and damages will be awarded on the basis of the actual loss sustained. The important question that must be asked in every case is, did the parties intend the sum to be a genuine pre-estimate of the damage likely to be caused by the breach or to operate as a fine for breach? Whether the clause is described as a 'penalty' or as 'liquidated damages' is a relevant consideration but not decisive.

In *Dunlop Pneumatic Tyre Co Ltd v New Garage and Motor Co Ltd*[2] Lord Dunedin set out a number of rebuttable presumptions of intention.

1. A clause will be regarded as a penalty if the amount stipulated is extravagantly greater than the damage which could conceivably flow from the breach.
2. It will be held to be a penalty if the breach consists only in not paying a sum of money, and the sum stipulated is greater than the sum which ought to have been paid.
3. When a single lump sum is made payable by way of compensation, on the occurrence of one or more or all of several events, some of which may occasion serious and others trifling damage, there is a presumption that it is a penalty.
4. It is no obstacle to the sum stipulated being a genuine pre-estimate of damage, that the consequences of the breach are such as to make precise pre-estimation almost an impossibility. On the contrary, that is just the situation when it is probable that pre-estimated damage was the true bargain between the parties.

1 'Liquidated Damages in California' 60 Calif LR 84 at p 86 (1972).
2 [1915] AC 79 at 86, HL.

Quasi-contract

17.1.5 Circumstances may arise in the context of business relations where a person becomes unjustly rewarded at the expense of some other person. In such circumstances, there is a need for the law to provide some mechanism for adjusting the financial relationship between the parties. Since there may be no valid contractual relationship between the parties, the law imposes a general obligation to return money where a party has been unjustifiably enriched at the expense of another. Such claims are often somewhat misleadingly referred to as quasi-contractual claims. Examples of such claims are:

1. Quantum meruit (as much as he has deserved). This represents a claim for reasonable remuneration for goods supplied or services performed. It may arise under a contract where the parties have not made express provision for payment.[1] It may also arise where services have been provided under the terms of a contract which is void[2] or where work has been commenced at a person's request in anticipation of a contract which does not materialise.[3]
2. Money paid under a void contract. Where money is paid in pursuance of a contract that is rendered void such funds can normally be recovered.[4] Money paid under an illegal contract cannot however normally be recovered.[5]
3. Money paid under a contract where there is a total failure of consideration. For example, if under a contract of sale the seller fails to pass a good title to the goods to the buyer there will be a total failure of consideration and the buyer will accordingly be able to claim what he has paid for the goods, even where he has received a benefit, before surrendering the goods to the true owner.[6]

1 See 12.1.12.
2 See *Craven-Ellis v Canons Ltd* [1936] 2 KB 403, [1936] 2 All ER 1066, CA.

3   *British Steel Corpn v Cleveland Bridge and Engineering Co Ltd* [1984] 1 All ER 504. See 12.1.8.
4   See *Strickland v Turner (Executrix of Lane)* (1852) 7 Exch 208.
5   See 16.0.1.
6   See *Rowland v Divall* [1923] 2 KB 500, CA; see 23.1.0.

Time limit on remedies
17.1.6   A right to raise an action for breach of contract may be extinguished by lapse of time. Under the terms of the Limitation Act 1980 an action based on a contract (other than a contract under seal) or an action for an account, cannot be brought once six years has expired from the date on which the cause of action accrued, ie when the breach of contract occurred. However if before expiry of the six-year period the person liable makes a written acknowledgement of the debt or makes any payment in respect of it, the time begins to run again. Similarly, where there is a fraud or mistake, the limitation period does not commence until the innocent party has discovered the fraud or mistake or could have discovered it with reasonable diligence.

The Limitation Act rules do not directly extend to equitable remedies such as specific performance or injunction but the courts apply the rules by analogy.

Chapter 18
Exemption of Liability

18.0.0   It is commonplace for a contracting party to seek to limit or exclude liability for breach of contract. In addition, contract terms may be used to limit or exclude other forms of liability, such as liability in tort. Such exclusions or limitations may be contained in notices displayed at or before the point where a contract is made or may be contained in a standard form contract. As a general rule the use of such notices and clauses is regarded as entirely legitimate. However, because of the potential unfairness of such limitations and exclusions the courts have made some attempt to impose standards of procedural fairness in respect of the use of exclusion clauses.

Judicial control
18.0.1   The general rule is that if a contract has been signed the signature establishes agreement to the terms irrespective of whether the terms were read or understood.[1]

In the event that a contract is not signed then the standard terms excluding or limiting liability may be in a notice displayed prominently where the contract was made or on a ticket or other contract document. The general rule in such cases is that the notice or terms will form part of the contract if the party relying on the clause took reasonable steps to draw it to the other party's attention. In addition, such notice must be given before or at the time of the contract, if it is to be effective.

a) Incorporation
The first question in such cases is to decide whether the clause or notice is contained in a contractual document. Is the document one which a reasonable person would assume contains contractual terms? Was it intended to form an integral part of the contract or was it merely an acknowledgement or receipt for payment? For example, left luggage and railway tickets are usually regarded as contractual documents. Some documents used in the course of business transactions may quite reasonably be considered to contain no conditions. They may simply represent acknowledgement of payment, or be intended as a means of access to the next stage in the contractual relationship, such as allowing admission to a seating area after entering into a contract at a theatre booking office. In *Chapleton v Barry UDC*[2] it was held that a ticket given to a holiday maker who hired a deck chair and on which was printed an exclusion of liability was nothing more than a receipt for payment; it had no contractual effect.

Second, the other party must be notified at or before the time of the contract. Thus an exclusion of liability sent with goods sold is not effective.[3] Similarly, when a guest books in at the reception desk of a hotel the contract is made at that point and a printed notice on the bedroom wall will have no contractual effect.[4]

Third, has reasonable notice of the clause been given? This relates to the manner in which the clause is displayed or otherwise drawn to the attention of the other party and the precise scope of the exemption. The notice must be in a clear and legible form, reasonably prominently displayed on a notice-board or ticket. If the conditions are set out in a second set of documents to which reference is made in a ticket, such notice must be made on the face of the document handed over at the time of the contract. For example the words: 'For conditions see back . . .' or 'Sold subject to the conditions of contract currently in force and obtainable on request' are often used.

As a general rule the wider the exemption the greater the degree of notice required. Thus in *Thornton v Shoe Lane Parking Ltd*[5] the plaintiff entered an automatic car park by taking a ticket from a machine. The words on the ticket stated that the ticket was issued subject to conditions displayed on the premises. One of the conditions sought to exempt the defendants from liability not only for damage to the cars parked but also injury to customers however caused. The plaintiff was injured on return to his car and claimed damages. The defendants, however, claimed the protection of the clause. It was held, first, that the plaintiff was not bound by the terms of the ticket since the contract had been concluded before its issue. Stretching the rules of offer and acceptance somewhat, Lord Denning considered that the offer was made when the proprietors held out the machine as being ready to receive money. The acceptance took place when the customer put his money into the slot. The terms of the contract were those displayed on or near the machine, so long as they were sufficiently prominently displayed. Thus, the customer was not bound by the terms on the ticket since they come after the contract has been concluded. Second, it was held that since the exemption covered liability for personal injury, it required a much more explicit warning and therefore the clause would not, in any event, be allowed to exempt the defendants from so wide a liability.[6]

The test in respect of reasonable notice is based on an objective standard. Thus if reasonable notice has been given to one party, it is immaterial that they did not read or understand the terms either because of blindness, illiteracy or inadvertance.[7]

The situation may be different if the party seeking to enforce the clause knew that the other party could not read or understand the terms.[8] In such a case it might be argued that greater efforts to give reasonable notice are justified.

A further consideration in relation to notice is that where two parties have a record of dealings over a period of time, the courts may infer notice in a particular transaction. Thus if the parties have had a regular course of dealings on the same terms whereby one party excludes or limits liability and on one occasion, the notice is given too late or by accident is not given at all, the courts may imply the exemption clause into the particular contract. In such cases there must, however, be a well established and consistent course of conduct, that is to say, a number of transactions on the same terms. It has, for example, been held that three or four transactions over a period of five years does not constitute a course of dealing.[9] Because of the nature of business contracts it is clearly easier to establish that the terms are included in a business contract by a course of conduct than in a contract with an individual consumer. Indeed, a term may be incorporated into a contract by reference to a course of dealing which is customary in a particular trade, even in respect of parties who have had no previous dealings.[10]

b) Interpretation
Assuming that a particular exemption clause is incorporated into a contract, a further problem for the party seeking to enforce it is the determination of whether the clause applies to the damage or loss that forms the basis of a claim.

An exemption clause will always be construed against the person putting it forward (contra proferentem) that is, against the person seeking to rely on it. Thus if there are ambiguities, the other party will be entitled to take advantage of them.

Often a party will not only seek to restrict or exclude his contractual liability but may also draft the term so as to exclude other forms of liability, in particular, negligence. If such a clause unambiguously purports to exclude such liability it will be enforced, unless a statute declares it invalid or unreasonable. In *Ailsa Craig Fishing Co Ltd v Malvern Fishing Co Ltd*[11] the House of Lords considered that the following clause was wide enough to cover negligence:

> 'If . . . any liability on the part of the company shall arise (whether under the express or implied terms of this contract or at common law, or in any other way) to the customer for any loss or damage of whatever nature arising out of or connected with the provision of the services covered by this contract, such liability shall be limited to the payment by the company of the sum . . .'

Normally, where a party can be held liable in negligence and for breach of a contractual provision, a clause will be construed as only applying to the stricter contractual liabiliy and not negligence. Thus in *White v John Warwick & Co Ltd*[12] the plaintiff hired a cycle under a contract which stated that 'nothing in this agreement shall render the owners liable for any personal injury'. It was held that the clause would not protect the hirers from liability in negligence since it was expressed in general terms; it would be construed as referring only to the stricter contractual liability.

On the other hand where liability can only be for negligence a general clause will protect a party from negligence because clearly it is the only meaning that can be given to it. For example, in *Alderslade v Hendon Laundry Ltd*[13] a contract to launder handkerchiefs was entered into on the basis that liability 'for lost or damaged articles' was limited to twenty times the contract charge. The handkerchiefs were lost due to negligence. It was held that since the only way the laundry could be liable for loss would be for negligence, the clause must be applied to limit liability for negligence. On the other hand, a clause may be interpreted as simply giving notice that the party is not liable except for negligence. For example, in *Hollier v Rambler Motors (AMC) Ltd*[14] a car was badly damaged by fire due to a repairer's negligence. The terms of the purported contract were that 'the company is not responsible for damage caused by fire to customers' cars on the premises.' It was held by the court that such a clause would not protect the repairer since it could be read as simply amounting to a warning to

227

customers that the garage would not be responsible for a fire caused in the absence of negligence. The clause did not protect the garage in respect of damage caused by fire due to their own negligence.

c) Fundamental breach

The most blatant judicial attack on exemption clauses came through the development of the doctrine of fundamental breach. The doctrine emerged from cases such as *Karsales (Harrow) Ltd v Wallis*[15] which involved the purchase of a car on hire purchase terms. The contract contained a term that 'no condition or warranty that the vehicle is road-worthy or as to its condition or fitness for any purposes is given by the owner or implied therein.' The car delivered was a wreck, with the cylinder head broken, all valves burnt out and incapable of self-propulsion. The consumer refused to accept or pay for the car on the basis of its condition. The supplier relied on the exclusion clause. The Court of Appeal held that the car delivered was not the car contracted for. The fundamental breach disentitled the party in breach from relying on the clause.

For many years the doctrine of fundamental breach was regarded as a rule of law and thus no term could operate to protect a party guilty of such a breach. This view was, however, rejected in *Suisse Atlantique Société d'Armement Maritime SA v Rotterdamsche Kolen Centrale NV.*[16] The House of Lords considered that to regard the doctrine as a rule of law would be a restriction on freedom of contract. The doctrine was nothing more than a rule of construction. The question of whether an exemption clause can be relied upon in cases of fundamental breach depends upon the intention of the parties as embodied in the terms of the agreement.

The development of the doctrine of fundamental breach illustrates both the strength and weakness of law reform by judicial ingenuity rather than legislation. The judiciary did at least offer the weaker party some protection when, having entered into a standard form contract with a widely drawn exemption clause, he received in return something totally different from that which he could reasonably have expected. This was before the age of consumerism and the growth of legislation specifically designed to redress the inequality of bargaining power between consumer and supplier. However, the doctrine also illustrates the unsatisfactory aspects of consumer protection by judicial ingenuity in the sense that the rationale behind the doctrine became so confused by successive interpretations that its development become 'aimless and incoherent'.[17] For example, despite the observations of the House of Lords in the *Suisse Atlantique* case the Court of Appeal continued to regard fundamental breach as a rule of law. Even in cases where the parties appear to have entered into a contract well aware of limitations on liability agreed upon, in part, for the purposes of apportioning risk and making insurance arrangements, the Court of Appeal have nevertheless applied the doctrine and struck down exemption clauses.[18]

The matter was, however, clarified by the House of Lords in *Photo Production Ltd v Securicor Transport Ltd.*[19] The case concerned a contract whereby the defendants would make periodic checks of the plaintiff's premises against burglaries and fires. The defendant's patrolman deliberately started a fire in the factory causing loss and damage to the value of £615,000.

The plaintiffs raised an action and the defendant company relied on exemption clauses in the contract. In particular one such clause stated that under no circumstances were the defendant company 'to be responsible for any injurious act or default by any employee . . . unless such act or default could have been foreseen and avoided by the exercise of due diligence.' The Court of Appeal held that there had been a fundamental breach of the contract which precluded the defendants from relying on the clause. The House of Lords however reversed the decision and held that on its true construction the clause clearly and unambiguously applied to what had taken place and thus protected the defendants from liability.

Lord Diplock summed up the views of the House of Lords when he observed:

> 'In commercial contracts negotiated between businessmen capable of looking after their own interests and deciding how risks inherent in the performance of various kinds of contract can be most economically borne (generally by insurance) it is in my view, wrong to place a strained construction on words in an exclusion clause which are clear and fairly susceptible of one meaning only . . .'[20]

The arrangements adopted by the parties were made on the basis of commercial considerations. Clearly the plaintiff company would in any event have to insure their factory against fire. The cost of such insurance would not be any the less if the defendants had assumed responsibility for damage by fire under the patrol service contract. If, however, they had undertaken to accept a greater responsibility they would have been forced to take out liability insurance and increase their charges accordingly. It made sense on economic grounds for the parties to allocate risks on the basis of commercial convenience under the terms of the contract.

The matter has now been put beyond doubt by Parliament. Section 9 of the Unfair Contract Terms Act 1977 now states that if an exemption clause, as a matter of construction, covers the breach and the clause satisfies the general test of reasonableness laid down in the Act, it may be relied upon notwithstanding that there has been a fundamental breach.

e) Oral undertakings

An exemption clause may also be rendered ineffective by an oral under-taking made at or before the time the contract was made which is inconsis-tent with the exemption clause. Thus in *J Evans & Son (Portsmouth) Ltd v Andrea Merzario Ltd*[21] an oral undertaking was given that goods would be loaded under deck. In fact, some of the goods were loaded on deck and were lost overboard during the voyage. It was held that an exemption clause in the written contract excluding liability for loss and giving the carrier complete discretion as to the loading was overridden by the oral assurance.

f) Third parties and exemption clauses

In accordance with the doctrine of privity of contract,[22] if a person is not a party to a contract he cannot claim the protection of an exemption clause, even if the clause purports to confer such protection on the third party.[23] However a third party may be protected by a clause if the original contract was entered into by a party as agent for the third party. For such a situation to arise it must be clear from the terms of the contract that a third party was to be protected, and that the original contracting party is acting as agent for the third party with the appropriate authority. In addition the third party must have provided consideration for the promise conferred upon him.[24]

Similarly a third party cannot lose his right to sue under the terms of an exemption clause in a contract to which he is not a party,[25] unless the contract was entered into by one of the parties as agent for the third party.

1 *L'Estrange v F Graucob Ltd* [1934] 2 KB 394.
2 [1940] 1 KB 532, [1940] 1 All ER 356, CA.
3 *Rutherford & Co v Miln & Son* 1941 SC 125.
4 *Olley v Marlborough Court Ltd* [1949] 1 KB 532, [1949] 1 All ER 127, CA.
5 [1971] 2 QB 163, [1971] 1 All ER 686, CA.
6 See Lord Denning at 169.
7 See for example *Thompson v London, Midland and Scottish Rly Co* [1930] 1 KB 41, CA.
8 See, for example, *Geier (formerly Braun) v Kujawa Weston and Warne Bros (Transport) Ltd* [1970] 1 Lloyd's Rep 364.
9 *Hollier v Rambler Motors (AMC) Ltd* [1972] 2 QB 71, [1972] 1 All ER 399, CA.
10 See *British Crane Hire Corpn Ltd v Ipswich Plant Hire Ltd* [1975] QB 303, [1974] 1 All ER 1059, CA.
11 [1983] 1 All ER 101, [1983] 1 WLR 964, HL.
12 [1953] 2 All ER 1021, [1953] 1 WLR 1285, CA.
13 [1945] KB 189, [1945] 1 All ER 244, CA.
14 [1972] 2 QB 71, [1972] 1 All ER 399, CA.
15 [1956] 2 All ER 866, [1956] 1 WLR 936, CA.
16 [1967] 1 AC 361, [1966] 2 All ER 61, HL.
17 See Trebilcock and Dewees, *Judicial Control of Standard Form Contracts* in *The Economic Approach to Law* (Burrows and Veljanovski (Eds)) (1981) pp 97–98.
18 See *Harbutt's Plasticine Ltd v Wayne Tank and Pump Co Ltd* [1970] 1 QB 447, [1970] 1 All ER 225, CA.
19 [1980] AC 827, [1980] 1 All ER 556, HL.
20 At 568.
21 [1976] 2 All ER 930, [1976] 1 WLR 1078, CA.
22 See 19.0.0.
23 *Cosgrave v Horsfall* (1945) 175 LT 334.
24 *New Zealand Shipping Co Ltd v A M Satterthwaite & Co Ltd* [1975] AC 154, [1974] 1 All ER 1015, PC. See also 19.0.3.
25 *Haseldine v C A Daw & Son Ltd* [1941] 2 KB 343, [1941] 3 All ER 156, CA.

Judicial control—policy issues
18.0.2 The use and abuse of exclusion clauses has been attacked by the courts largely by the covert tools of incorporation and construction. Although standard form contracts may be invalidated where one party takes advantage of a stronger bargaining position,[1] the courts have largely preferred to impose standards of procedural fairness on contracting parties rather than examine the fairness of clauses in substantive terms. The difficulties with such an approach were summed up by Llewellyn in the following terms:

'First, since they all rest on the admission that the clauses in question are permissible in purpose and content, they invite the draftsman to recur to the attack . . . Second, since they do not face the issue, they fail to accumulate either experience or authority in the needed direction, that of making out for any type of transaction what the minimum decencies are which a court will insist upon as essential to an enforceable bargain of a given type. Third, since they purport to construe, and do not really construe, nor are intended to, but are instead a tool of intentional and creative misconstruction, they seriously embarrass later efforts of true construction, later efforts to get at the truth of those wholly legitimate contracts and clauses which call for their meaning to be got at instead of avoided. The net effect is unnecessary confusion and unpredictability, together with inadequate remedy, . . . covert tools are never reliable tools.'[2]

In other words, manipulating the rules of contract and construction in order to protect one party to an unfair contract only serves to distort the basic rules.[3]

1 See 15.0.8.
2 *Llewellyn, The Common Law Tradition* (1960) pp 364–65.
3 See eg Lord Denning's analysis of offer and acceptance in *Thornton v Shoe Lane Parking Ltd* [1971] 2 QB 163 at 169.

Statutory control of exemption clauses

18.0.3   Because of the need to provide more protection against the misuse of exemption clauses, in more recent years Parliament has sought to impose greater control over their application. Justification for legislative action was provided by the Law Commission in their 'Second Report on Exemption Clauses'.

'We are in no doubt that in many cases they operate against the public interest and that the prevailing judicial attitude of suspicion, or indeed of hostility, to such clauses is well founded. All too often they are introduced in ways which result in the party affected by them remaining ignorant of their presence or input until it is too late. That party, even if he knows of the exemption clause, will often be unable to appreciate what he may lose by accepting it. The result is that the risk of carelessness or of failure to achieve satisfactory standards of performance is thrown on to the party who is not responsible for it or who is unable to guard against it. Moreover, by excluding liability for such carelessness or failure the economic pressures to maintain high standards of performance are reduced.'[1]

It follows from such observations that where exemption clauses are used against ordinary consumers they are indefensible unless clearly explained and the consumer is perhaps given some choice as to the terms of their application. Where, however, such clauses are used by two persons acting in the course of trade, on broadly equal terms, with an awareness of the risks and the opportunity to insure, the application of the clause may be justified. In general, legislation regulating exemption clauses has adopted such an approach.

There are a number of examples of statutes that render void exemption clauses within a particular sector of activity. For example clauses which purport to exclude or limit the liability of the operator of a public service road vehicle for causing death or personal injury to a passenger are void.[2] The most significant control of exemption clauses came with the passing of the Supply of Goods (Implied Terms) Act 1973 and the Unfair Contract Terms Act 1977. The former dealt specifically with attempts to exclude terms implied under the Sale of Goods Act and is dealt with in Part 4; it is proposed to concentrate at this stage on the Unfair Contract Terms Act 1977 (UCTA).

1 Law Commission No 69, para 11.
2 Public Passenger Vehicles Act 1981, s 29.

231

UCTA 1977

18.0.4   The Act primarily deals with unfair exemption clauses by placing limitations on their use in the course of business. Some clauses are declared void whilst others are subject to a test of reasonableness. The Act deals with unfair contract terms only in so far as they are exemption clauses; it does not give the courts any general power to re-open a contract on the basis that its terms are unfair. Part One of the Act covers England, Wales and Northern Ireland and Part Two covers Scotland.

UCTA 1977 only applies to business liability, that is, breach of an obligation or duty arising (a) from anything done or to be done in the course of business or (b) from the occupation of business premises.[1] The term business extends to the activities of professions, government departments, local authorities and public authorities.[2]

Certain types of contract are specifically excluded from the scope of the Act. The most important of these is the contract of insurance; other excluded categories include contracts relating to the creation, transfer, or termination of any interest in land, to the creation, transfer or termination of intellectual property rights and interests, to the formation, dissolution or constitution of a company and to the creation or transfer of securities or any right or interest in securities.[3]

1   S 1(3).
2   S 14.
3   Sch 1 para 2.

What is an exemption clause under UCTA 1977?

18.0.5   The Act not only seeks to regulate those clauses which completely deny a party to the contract a remedy but also clauses which have a similar effect.[1] These include the following clauses:

(a)   those making a liability or its enforcement subject to restrictive or onerous conditions. Thus a term requiring the giving of notice of loss within a specified time or in a specified manner would be subject to the reasonableness test;

(b)   those excluding or restricting any right or remedy in respect of the liability, or subjecting a person to any prejudice in consequence of his pursuing any such right or remedy. This embraces the situation where rescission of a contract may be disallowed permitting only damages as a remedy. It also covers a term limiting liability to a specified amount. It was not intended that a liquidated damages clause, that is, a clause agreeing a figure of damages and requiring no proof of loss, would be caught by the Act.[2] Such clauses normally fix the sum payable for breach whether the actual loss is greater or less. An exemption clause simply fixes the maximum amount recoverable; if actual loss is lower, then that amount only can be claimed;

(c)   excluding or restricting rules of evidence or procedure. Thus a term that failure to complain within fourteen days is deemed to be conclusive evidence of proper performance of the contract would be caught.

In addition, a clause which purports to exclude the creation of a legal duty or obligation would be classed as an exemption clause. Thus for the purposes of avoidance of negligence liability,[3] avoidance of liability by a manufacturer's guarantee[4] and avoidance of liability arising in contracts of sale or supply of goods,[5] any term or notice which prevents an obligation or duty from arising will also be treated as an exemption clause. For example a term such as 'the seller does not give any warranty or undertaking that the goods are fit for any purpose'[6] is as much caught by the Act as is one which states that 'all conditions and warranties are hereby excluded.' Similarly, a term which states that no duty of care is owed by one party is caught by the Act to the same extent as one which states that liability for loss or damage is excluded.[7]

Arbitration clauses in contracts are not regarded as exemption clauses. Such clauses do not normally restrict or limit liability but provide a procedure for settling disputes.[8]

1 See s 13.
2 See 17.1.4.
3 S 2.
4 S 5.
5 s 5 and 7.
6 See Ch 21.
7 It should be noted that this part of s 13 does not extend to s 3 (contract liability). Thus, if a contract term does not come within s 2 or s 5-7, it does not operate as an exemption clause if it simply defines the obligations of the parties under the contract.
8 S 13(2).

UCTA 1977—Avoidance of negligence liability[1]

18.0.6 An exemption clause or notice that seeks to exclude or restrict a person's liability for death or personal injury caused by negligence is of no effect.[2] In the case of other loss, such as financial loss or damage to property, such exclusions or restrictions are only valid in so far as the term or notice satisfies 'the requirement of reasonableness'.[3]

The term 'negligence' means:
(a) the breach of any obligation arising from the express or implied terms of a contract to take reasonable care or exercise reasonable skill in the performance of the contract; or
(b) the breach of any common law duty to take reasonable care or exercise reasonable skill; or
(c) the breach of the common law duty of care imposed by the Occupiers' Liability Act 1957.

Thus, in addition to regulating small print exemption clauses in contracts, it extends to regulate the use of a notice seeking to exclude or restrict liability in respect of negligence to visitors who are allowed on to premises and who may have no contractual relationship with the occupier.

1 See also Part II.
2 S 2(1).
3 S 2(2).

UCTA 1977—Avoidance of contract liability

18.0.7 In general s 3 of the UCTA 1977 seeks to subject certain terms in contracts excluding contractual liability to a general test of reasonableness. The section, however, only extends to those contracts where one party deals as a consumer or where one party deals on the other's written standard terms of business. In such contracts, the other party cannot rely on a contract term which:

(a) excludes or restricts any liability in respect of breach of contract; or
(b) purports to entitle him to render a contractual performance substantially different from that which was reasonably expected of him, or to render no performance at all, except in so far as the term satisfies the requirement of reasonableness.

a) Dealing as a consumer

A party deals as a consumer where three conditions are satisfied. First, the alleged consumer neither makes the contract in the course of business nor holds himself out as doing so. Second, the party dealing with the alleged consumer must have acted in the course of business. Third, if the contract involves goods, the goods must be of a type ordinarily supplied for private use, or consumption.[1]

A buyer in a sale by auction or competitive tender is deemed not to deal as a consumer.[2] In terms of the burden of proof it is up to the party dealing in the course of business to establish that the other is not dealing as a consumer.

Key elements of the definition of dealing as a consumer are that the 'consumer' is not acting in the course of business and the goods, if any, are consumer type goods. What happens therefore when someone buys goods for both private use and business use? In *Peter Symmons & Co Ltd v Cook*[3] it was held that a surveyor did not buy a Rolls Royce in the course of business because the car did not form an integral part of the buyer's business, nor was it necessarily incidental to the business. Such a finding may however present difficulties where a business sells a vehicle to an individual and seeks to exclude liability. In such circumstances the individual would not be dealing as a consumer if the business seller was not selling in the course of business.

Problems may also be encountered where a consumer buys goods of a type which may be used in business and privately. For example, if someone buys an industrial vacuum for use at home, is it goods ordinarily bought for private use? Here the courts must take account of changing values and standards of living. At one time a computer would not be regarded as consumer goods, whereas today many consumers are buying microcomputers.

b) Written standard terms

The expression 'written standard terms of business' is not defined. If a definition had been attempted it would doubtless have produced complex problems for the Parliamentary draftsman. The Law Commission in their Report on Exemption Clauses observed that:

> 'We think that the courts are well able to recognise standard terms used by persons in the course of business and that any attempt to lay down a precise definition of a standard form of contract would leave open the possibility that terms that were clearly in a standard form might fall outside the definition.'[4]

The term therefore covers the situation where a business has its own prepared terms or when trade is carried on under terms prepared by a trade association or similar body. A debatable question is the extent to which variation of standard terms takes the contract outside the ambit of the section. There will always be some variation in terms of pricing, quantity and delivery but what of the situation where a standard term is replaced by a term excluding liability because of a special risk? Are the parties still making the contract on 'written standard terms'? It must be presumed that given the opportunity the courts will construe the expression widely and in any event any special factors may always be resolved in the context of the courts' deliberations on the reasonableness issue.

The corresponding section in Part Two amending Scots Law uses the expression 'standard form contract'.[5] It has been held that such an expression includes contracts which contained a number of fixed terms or conditions in contracts of the kind in question by the party in breach.[6] Lord Dunpark also considered that the expression was wide enough to embrace—

> 'any contract whether wholly written or partly oral which includes a set of fixed terms or conditions which the proposer applies, without material alteration, to contracts of the kind in question.'[7]

c) Contract terms

Section 3 only extends to (a) clauses excluding or restricting liability and (b) clauses seeking to substitute a substantially different performance or to totally excuse performance. In respect of the former type of clause it should be emphasised that there may be some overlap with other sections of the Act. For example, if the clause seeks to exclude a contractual duty to take reasonable care it will be void under s 2 in so far as it seeks to exclude liability for death or personal injury. Similarly, if the contract is a consumer contract involving goods, any term seeking to exclude or limit implied terms relating to description or quality of the goods will be void under s 6 or 7 of the Act. Terms which seek to define the extent of the contractual obligation are not caught by s 3.[8]

An example of a contract term in the context of entertainment which claims entitlement to offer a substantially different performance from that which was reasonably expected would be:

> 'management reserve the right to alter the performance of any member of the cast of this production.'

Similar clauses are common in the travel industry where a company may claim the right to change the time, date of departure, or even destination in respect of a holiday.

Contract terms which totally excuse performance are also caught by section 3. For example, a travel timetable often reserves the right of the operator to withdraw a service.

1   S 12(1).
2   S 12(2).
3   (1981) 131 NLJ 758.
4   Law Commission Report No 69, para 157.
5   S 17.
6   *McCrone v Boots Farm Sales Ltd* 1981 SLT 103.
7   At 105.
8   See Law Commission No 69, para 119.

Indemnities

18.0.8 Also subject to the test of reasonableness are indemnity clauses imposed on persons dealing as consumers by another person in respect of liability incurred by that person for negligence or breach of contract.[1] Such clauses are frequently used by car ferry operators in order to shift responsibility to the owners of vehicles for damage caused to other vehicles by employees of the carrier when moving vehicles around.

1   S 4(1).

Exemption clauses in guarantees

18.0.9   Manufacturers' guarantees are a common feature in the marketing of consumer goods. They are usually intended as an expression of the manufacturer's confidence in the product and to reassure consumers when they are deciding which brand to buy. The guarantee will normally involve the manufacturer in a promise to repair, or replace goods or refund the purchase price. Such promises are of course additional to the consumer's contractual rights against the person from whom they bought the goods.

The difficulty with guarantees in terms of general contract law is whether the consumer provides consideration for the manufacturer's promise. Often, however, the guarantee involves returning a card to the manufacturer and such an act might be sufficient consideration.[1] Alternatively, entering into a contract with the retailer might be regarded as sufficient consideration.

Section 5 of UCTA 1977 seeks to prevent a manufacturer using guarantees on the other hand, to give consumers limited additional rights, whilst at the same limiting their own liability for negligence. The section applies in the case of goods of a type ordinarily supplied for private use and consumption where loss or damage (a) arises from the goods proving defective while in consumer use and (b) results from the negligence of a person concerned in the manufacture or distribution of the goods. The effect of the section is to render void any exemption in a guarantee which seeks to exclude the above liability.

A guarantee is anything in writing which contains or purports to contain some promise or assurance (however worded or presented) that defects will be made good by complete or partial replacement, or by repair, monetary compensation or otherwise.[2] Goods are regarded as in consumer use when a person is using them, or has them in his possession for use, otherwise than exclusively for the purposes of a business.

1   See 13.0.0.
2   S 5(2).

Avoidance of liability on sale and supply of goods contracts

18.0.10   UCTA 1977 also places restrictions on the extent to which a contracting party may exclude or restrict the statutory implied undertakings in contracts involving the sale or supply of goods. These undertakings normally relate to title to the goods, description, quality and fitness of purpose. They are examined at 21.8.0.

The reasonableness test

18.0.11   The question of whether an exemption clause satisfies the test of reasonableness is decided by reference to whether the clause was fair and reasonable having regard to the circumstances which were, or ought reasonably to have been, known to or in the contemplation of the parties when the contract was made.[1] In the case of notices which have no contractual effect, the time for deciding whether the clause was reasonable or not is when the liability arose or, but for the notice, would have arisen.[2]

Where a party seeks to restrict liability to a specified sum in reliance on an exemption clause and the question arises whether the restriction is reasonable, regard shall be had in particular to two factors: first, the resources available to that party for the purpose of meeting a potential liability; and, second, how far it was open to him to cover himself by insurance.[3] Thus, where no insurance is available or where only limited cover is available and the additional cover is excessive in relation to the resources of the party relying on the clause, the court may regard a limitation of liability as reasonable. Indeed, as a general rule the courts may be inclined to subject clauses limiting liability to less rigorous scrutiny than clauses which seek to exclude liability.[4]

UCTA 1977 only provides more specific guidance as to the reasonableness issue where contract terms seek to exclude the statutory implied terms in sale and supply of goods transaction.[5] These are laid down in Schedule 2 to the Act and although they are intended as guidance in respect of contracts involving goods supplied under a contract, they may be used as a valuable yardstick for the courts in other types of contract.

The guiding factors are:

(a) the strength of the bargaining positions of the parties relative to each other, taking into account alternative means by which the customer's requirements could have been met;

(b) whether the customer received an inducement to agree to the term, or in accepting it had an opportunity of entering into a similar contract with other persons, but without having to accept a similar term;

(c) whether the customer knew or ought reasonably to have known of the existence and extent of the term (having regard, amongst other things, to any custom of the trade and any previous course of dealing between the parties);

(d) where the term excludes or restricts any relevant liability if some condition is not complied with, whether it was reasonable at the time of the contract to expect that compliance with that condition would be practicable;

(e) whether the goods were manufactured, processed, or adapted to the special order of the customer.

In contracts between two persons who are both acting in the course of business it is likely that the courts will continue to allow risks to be allocated by the use of exemption and limitation clauses and they will not therefore disturb standard commercial practice. Where an exclusion clause is being used against a consumer the courts are, however, likely to be more rigorous in imposing the reasonableness test. Whatever the circumstances, however, it is for the party claiming that a contractual term or notice satisfies the requirement of reasonableness to show that it does.[6]

The difficulty in satisfying the burden of proof, particularly in consumer contracts, is well-illustrated by the few cases which have received some publicity. For example in *Woodman v Photo Trade Processing Ltd*[7] a roll of film taken at a wedding was accepted for developing and printing, subject to a term which limited liability in the event of loss to the replacement cost of the film. When the company attempted to rely on the clause the county court judge held that the clause was unreasonable. The court were particularly influenced by the fact that the consumer had no real alternative since few photographic firms accepted liability for consequential loss. The industry did operate a code of practice which recognised that firms could adopt a two tier pricing system whereby customers could pay a lower price on the basis that the firm excluded liability. The consumer in this case was offered no such choice.

In *Lally v Bird*[8] a county court found clauses in a removal contract limiting liability to a specified amount per article, and requiring all claims to be made within a certain period to be unreasonable.

In a case concerning liability under the Sale of Goods Act the House of Lords held that because the seller in a commercial contract could have insured against the risk of liability to the buyer without having to raise the price of the goods, an exclusion clause was unreasonable.[9]

1 S 11(1).
2 S 11(3).
3 S 11(4).
4 See observations of Lord Fraser in *Ailsa Craig Fishing Co Ltd v Malvern Fishing Co Ltd* [1983] 1 All ER 101 at 105, HL.
5 See 21.8.0.
6 S 11(5).
7 (17 May 1981, unreported). See Lawson, *Exclusion Clauses* (2nd edn 1983) pp 161, 167.
8 (23 May 1980, unreported). See n. 7, p 112.
9 *George Mitchell (Chesterhall) Ltd v Finney Lock Seeds Ltd* [1983] 2 AC 803, [1983] 2 All ER 737, HL.

Unlawful exemption clauses

18.0.12 Under the Consumer Transactions (Restrictions on Statements) Order 1976[1] it is a criminal offence for persons in the course of a business to display at any place where consumer transactions are effected a notice containing a statement purporting to apply, in relation to consumer transactions effected there, terms rendered void by s 6 of UCTA 1977. The prohibition extends to advertisements, statements on goods and any documentation which seeks to exclude liability for the implied terms as to title, description, quality and fitness for purpose in a consumer contract.[2]

The prohibition does not however extend to terms rendered void by s 2(1) (negligence causing death or personal injury) or s 7 (contracts involving the supply of goods) of UCTA 1977. Indeed, there is evidence to suggest that terms excluding liability for death or personal injury are still widely used. Although such terms may be rendered void under the Act, they may deter a person from bringing a claim against a business or be used as a bargaining weapon by a company in a dispute with an individual.[3] By contrast to other jurisdictions, there is no formal administrative control of exemption clauses in the UK.

In Australia, for example, under the Contracts Review Act 1980 of New South Wales there are provisions allowing government officials to apply to the court where a person has embarked, or is likely to embark, on a course of conduct leading to the creation of unjust contracts. The courts may then prescribe or restrict the terms on which that person may enter into contracts of a particular class.[4] The Law Commission specifically rejected any prior validation of standard form contracts.[5]

The Office of Fair Trading is however able to exert some influence over trade associations in the detail of standard contracts that are used in certain industries. In particular, a number of codes of practice drawn up in consultation with the OFT have made recommendations in respect of contract terms.

1   SI 1976 1813.
2   See 21.8.0.
3   See *Financial Times* 24 April 1983.
4   See Borrie, 'The Development of Consumer Law and Policy. Bold Spirits and Timorous Souls' Hamlyn Lectures 1984, 115.
5   Law Commission report 1975 No 69 para 290–314.

Chapter 19

Privity of Contract

19.0.0 It is a fundamental principle of contract law that no one can sue or be sued on a contract unless he is a party to it even if it is made expressly for the benefit of a named third party. For instance, if X and Y make a contract whereby X agrees to pay £500 to Z, Z cannot sue to enforce that promise if X fails to make the payment.[1] The doctrine may have serious implications for a number of familiar business transactions. For instance if A buys goods from B and gives them as a present to C who suffers injury because the goods prove defective, C can bring no claim against B because he was not party to a contract with him. In that situation C's only remedy would be an action in tort against the manufacturer, in which it would be necessary for him to prove negligence, as we have already seen.[2] Moreover, if C's only complaint is that the goods themselves are useless or defective and they cause no injury to him or to his other property, it seems that he will have no remedy. The rule can thus cause considerable inconvenience to the consumer of defective goods and it has been subjected to a considerable degree of criticism.[3] Similar problems can arise where under a contract to do work part of the work is sub-contracted, as regularly happens in the case of construction work. Once again, as we have seen, the tort of negligence has expanded to fill the gap in the protection offered by contract.[4]

1 See *Tweddle v Atkinson* (1861) 1 B & S 393.
2 See 9.1.1.
3 Per Lord Scarman in *Woodar Investment Development Ltd v Wimpey Construction UK Ltd* [1980] 1 All ER 571 at 591, HL.
4 See 7.1.11.

Enforcement by the promisee
19.0.1 Of course, when X makes a contract with Y for the benefit of Z, the doctrine of privity only prevents an action to enforce the contract by Z. If X fails to perform the contract there is nothing to prevent Y suing, as a party to the contract. There is, however, another difficulty for, generally, Y will have suffered no loss and he will not normally be able to recover damages for the loss suffered by Z, unless he is suing as agent or trustee for him.[1] Here there is a problem; Z has suffered loss but cannot sue, Y may sue but has suffered no loss and will therefore recover nothing. In exceptional cases this difficulty may be overcome if Y can obtain an order of specific performance, as is illustrated by the case of *Beswick v Beswick*.[2] An uncle agreed to transfer his coal merchants' business to his nephew in return for the nephew's

240

promise to pay him a pension for life and, after his death, an annuity to his widow. However, shortly after the uncle's death, the nephew ceased payments and refused to make any further payments to the widow. She sued to enforce the contract, both in her own right as beneficiary and as administratrix of her late husband's estate. The action in her own name was defeated by the doctrine of privity but the House of Lords awarded her a decree of specific performance in her capacity as administratrix,[3] in which role she represented her late husband. Exceptionally such an order may mitigate the harshest effects of the privity rule. However, unlike an award of damages, an order of specific performance is equitable and therefore discretionary and so will not provide a remedy in every case.

1   Y may recover damages for losses suffered by Z in special cases when the contract was to provide enjoyment for Z—for instance, a family holiday or a meal in a restaurant: see *Jackson v Horizon Holidays Ltd* [1975] 3 All ER 92, [1975] 1 WLR 1468, CA.
2   [1968] AC 58, [1967] 2 All ER 1197, HL.
3   The House held that damages would not be an adequate remedy: as administratrix the plaintiff had suffered no loss.

Limits of the doctrine
19.0.2   It is always possible for a party to a contract to assign his rights under the contract to a third party. If such an assignment is effected in accordance with the correct procedures the assignee steps into the shoes of the original contracting party and can enforce the contract in his stead. Assignment is the basis of the well known business practice of factoring debts, whereby a creditor assigns to a debt collection agency the right to collect debts due to him. In general the factor pays for the assignment but the sum paid is less than the debt assigned; the assignor benefits by having cash in hand at once and being relieved of the expense and inconvenience of enforcing payment. If such an assignment is made the assignee can be in no better position than the assignor, so that the debtor may raise against the assignee any defence he could have raised against the assignor. All that is required for a valid assignment of legal rights under a contract is that the assignment must be absolute, in writing and written notice of the assignment must be given to the other contracting party (the debtor).[1]

Another exception to the doctrine of privity is created by the law of agency when one person (the agent) makes a contract on behalf of another (the principal). The effect of agency is that the agent, having negotiated and concluded a contract on behalf of his principal, drops out of the picture and there is privity of contract between the principal and third party. Such arrangements are very important in business and we examine the rules of agency in more detail below.[2] For now we should note that there may be an agency even though the agent fails to identify his principal, or even that he is acting as agent and, on occasion, when he in fact has no authority from his 'principal'.

It was thought at one time that the problems created by the doctrine of privity could be avoided by finding that when X made a contract with Y for the benefit of Z, X acted as trustee for Z and held the benefit of Y's promise on trust for him. However, a clear intention to create an irrevocable trust of the promise is required and whilst the notion is supported by older cases,[3] more recent authorities[4] show a marked reluctance to find a trust in such situations, for such a finding would bind X and Y and make it impossible for them to vary or discharge their contract. It seems unlikely that a

241

modern court would find a 'trust of a promise' in any but an exceptional case.

1   Law of Property Act 1925, s 136.
2   Below, Part VI.
3   See eg *In Re Flavell, Murray v Flavell* (1883) 25 Ch D 89, CA.
4   *In Re Schebsman, ex p Official Receiver, Trustee v Cargo Superintendents (London) Ltd and Schebsman* [1944] Ch 83, [1943] 2 All ER 768, CA.

Privity and exclusion clauses
19.0.3   The doctrine of privity has caused particular problems when the parties to a contract have allocated between themselves risks associated with performance of the contract by the use of exclusion clauses. Often actual performance of the contract may be delegated to some third party—an independent sub-contractor, or an employee of one of the contracting parties. We have already seen that, notwithstanding the lack of privity between them, if the other contracting party is injured by the third party's poor performance of the contract, he may be able to maintain an action against the third party in negligence.[1] However, privity remains important, for the lack of privity between plaintiff and defendant third party in such a situation means that the latter cannot rely against the plaintiff on any exclusion clause which may be included either in the main contract between the plaintiff and the main contractor or in the contract between the main contractor and the defendant. Moreover, it has been held that this is so even where all the parties are businessmen and where an exclusion clause in the main contract purports to protect employees, sub-contractors and the like.[2] The rule may thus allow the plaintiff to circumvent what may be, as between two businessmen, a perfectly reasonable allocation of risk, and it has therefore been subjected to much criticism.

However, a way was found to avoid the difficulty in the case of *New Zealand Shipping Co Ltd v A M Satterthwaite & Co Ltd*.[3] The case arose out of the consignment of goods for shipping and the contract between the consignor and the carrier included a clause which limited the liability of the carrier for damage to the goods; the clause went on to extend that protection to any servant, agent and independent contractor employed by the carrier and provided that for the purpose of the limitation the carrier should be deemed to be acting 'as Agent or Trustee on behalf of and for the benefit of' all such employees, agents and sub-contractors. The goods were damaged during unloading by the negligence of stevedores to whom the work of unloading was sub-contracted. Knowing that any claim against the carriers would be subject to the limitation of liability, the consignors brought a claim against the stevedores arguing that they could not rely on the limitation as they were not party to the original contract. The Privy Council held that on the wording of the clause the stevedores were entitled to its protection: not only did it purport to protect them but it was also made expressly on their behalf. In effect the carriers had acted as agents for the stevedores and so created a contract between them and the consignors. The stevedores had provided consideration for the consignor's agreement to let them have the benefit of the limitation clause by carrying out their own contract with the carriers and unloading the cargo. It seems then that a third party will be able to benefit from an exclusion clause provided:
(a)   it is worded so as to protect him;
(b)   the contract is expressed to be made on his behalf, the contracting party

being authorised to act as his agent; and
(c) he provides consideration for the promise to exclude or limit his liability.

1 Above, Part II.
2 See *Adler v Dickson* [1955] 1 QB 158, [1954] 3 All ER 397, CA; *Scruttons Ltd v Midland Silicones Ltd* [1962] AC 446, [1962] 1 All ER 1, HL.
3 [1975] AC 154, [1974] 1 All ER 1015, PC.

The burden of contracts
19.0.4 Just as a third party cannot enforce a contract to which he is not a party, so he cannot be held liable under such a contract. Here too the doctrine of privity is subject to some limitations; it is worth noting, however, that the burden of a contract, unlike its benefits, cannot be held on trust for another, nor can it be assigned. On the other hand, agency does allow the 'transfer' of contractual duties: if X contracts with A who acts as agent for P, as we have seen, the result is to create a contract between X and P as if they had made a contract direct, inter se. P may take benefits and be subject to burdens under that contract.[1]

Special rules apply to covenants affecting land. The rule there is that a covenant restricting the user of a piece of land may be imposed for the benefit of a nearby or neighbouring plot and, provided certain requirements are fulfilled, the covenant will bind the land and restrict its use, no matter that it may change hands. Such covenants are particularly important devices for protecting the value of land, for instance by prohibiting an adjoining owner from carrying on a potential nuisance or offensive business, or restricting development on his land. The rule only applies, however, to covenants which are negative in nature; and, in order to bind future owners, details of the covenant must be registered on registers open to the public.

Although a person may not normally be subject to obligations by a contract to which he is not party, that is not to say that he may not indirectly be restricted by it or incur liabilities as a result of it. As we have already seen,[2] a person who knowingly interferes with another person's contract—for instance by inducing a contracting party to break the contract—may be held liable in tort. Liability may also be imposed under a collateral contract. In *Shanklin Pier Ltd v Detel Products Ltd*[3] the plaintiff pier owners engaged a firm of contractors to paint the pier; they directed the contractors to buy and use paint manufactured by the defendants, relying on the defendants' assurance that the paint would last seven to ten years. In fact it lasted only a few months. The plaintiffs were able to bring an action direct against the defendants; there was a collateral contract between them consisting of the defendants' assurance in return for which the plaintiffs had directed the contractors to buy the defendants' paint. This device has been used to protect the buyer of goods on hire purchase; normally in such a situation the dealer sells the goods to a finance company who in turn resell them to the buyer on hire purchase terms. It has been held, however, that when the consumer is induced to take the goods by statements made by the dealer which turn out to be false, he may sue the dealer for damages for breach of warranty contained in a collateral contract between them.[4]

1 See Part VI.
2 Above 6.0.3.
3 [1951] 2 KB 854, [1951] 2 All ER 471.
4 *Andrews v Hopkinson* [1957] 1 QB 229, [1956] 3 All ER 422.

Part IV
The classification and regulation of business transactions—goods and services

Chapter 20

The Classification of Transactions

Goods and services

20.0.0 In terms of business activity generated through commercial transactions, contracts involving the supply of goods and contracts for the provision of services represent the bulk of commercial activity. Within these two categories, however, there are a number of different classifications of contract each of which may have distinct characteristics and advantages for the parties. Such advantages may vary in their attractiveness over the years with changes in commercial activity, consumer preferences, government fiscal policy and developments in judicial and public attitudes. Some transactions may give rise to statutory duties, the breach of which may involve criminal or civil sanctions. The contract for the sale of goods has inevitably received the most attention from the courts and Parliament largely because contracts of sale are the very essence of commercial activity.

Sale of goods

20.1.0 Section 2(1) of the Sale of Goods Act 1979 (SGA 1979) provides that:

'A contract of sale of goods is a contract by which the seller transfers or agrees to transfer the property in the goods to the buyer for a money consideration, called the price.'

This definition raises three questions. First, what are goods? Second, what is meant by transferring property? Third, what are the consequences of confining sale contracts to a monetary consideration?

20.1.1 Goods are defined in the SGA 1979 as including:

'all personal chattels other than things in action and money . . . and in particular "goods" includes emblements, industrial growing crops and things attached to or forming part of the land which are agreed to be severed before sale or under the contract of sale.'

Thus the Act does not cover the sale of land or intangible assets,[1] such as rights of property which can only be claimed or enforced by action rather than taking physical possession. This means that debts, shares, trademarks and other similar intangible assets are not included in the definition of goods. Money when transferred as currency is also excluded from the definition but is included when it is transferred as an antique or commodity in the foreign exchange market. 'Emblements' are annual crops produced by agricultural labour, such as vegetables and corn, as opposed to things which grow naturally on the land. 'Industrial growing crops' are assumed to include crops produced by labour but which may not mature within a year. Where the sale is of things growing naturally on the land, or fixtures attached to the land, the question of whether it is a sale of goods depends upon severance. If the subject matter of the contract has been severed from the land or is to be severed under the contract, it will be a sale of goods. If, on the other hand, a forest is sold or a right is granted to extract minerals, without an obligation to sever, there would be no sale of goods.

1   That is things or choses in action.

Transferring property
20.1.2   Under a contract of sale, the seller transfers or agrees to transfer the property in the goods. Section 61(1) of the SGA 1979 declares that property means the general property in the goods and not merely a special property. In essence, general property refers to the ownership in the goods. The objective of a contract of sale is to transfer the ownership of the goods from the seller to the buyer. Special property refers to rights other than ownership, such as the right to use goods. For example, in a rental agreement the rental company has the general property in the goods, and the hirer the right of possession, or special property.

A contract may provide for the property to pass immediately to the buyer, in which case it is called a sale, or it may provide that the property will pass at a future time or subject to a condition to be fulfilled called an agreement to sell.[1] An agreement to sell becomes a sale on the date fixed or fulfilment of the condition. A common condition imposed in an agreement to sell is that property will not pass until the buyer has paid the total price. Such an agreement is known as a conditional sale agreement and in effect it is a form of credit, allowing the buyer to pay for goods by a number of instalments, ownership passing to the buyer when the last instalment is paid. Because of the element of credit, conditional sale agreements are regulated by the Consumer Credit Act 1974 in addition to being subject to the SGA 1979.[2]

In the absence of an indication, express or implied, when the property in the goods is to pass to the buyer, the SGA 1979 lays down certain rules.[3] A conditional sale agreement must be distinguished from a credit sale which is a sale of goods under which the price is payable by instalments but there is no reservation of property in favour of the seller. Credit sale therefore differs from conditional sale in that property passes immediately to the buyer, even before the instalments have been paid. Credit sale agreements are regulated under the Sale of Goods Act and also come within certain of the provisions of the Consumer Credit Act 1974.[4]

1   S 2(4) (5) and (6).
2   See Part 5.
3   See 22.0.3.
4   See 26.0.3.

Money consideration
20.1.3 The SGA 1979 restricts contracts of sale to those contracts where the consideration for the transfer of ownership in the goods is a money payment. This distinguishes a contract of sale from a contract of exchange or barter where goods are exchanged for other goods. A part exchange transaction whereby an agreed price is payable partly in money and partly in goods is a sale. In such a transaction the money consideration is fixed under the agreement but the buyer agrees to purchase the goods offered in part-exchange at a price fixed against the price payable by the buyer.[1]

The central question where other goods, or coupons or tokens, are offered as part of the consideration, is whether there is an agreed money price. As far as fixing the price is concerned the SGA 1979 provides that it may be fixed by the contract, or left to be fixed in a manner agreed by the parties or by the course of dealing.[2] Alternatively, if no provision is made for determining the price, the buyer must pay a reasonable price, determined according to the circumstances of the case.[3] The absence of agreement as to the price may suggest that the parties have not yet concluded a contract.

1 See *Aldridge v Johnson* (1857) 7 E & B 885; *G J Dawson (Clapham) Ltd v Dutfield* [1936] 2 All ER 232.
2 S 8(1).
3 S 8(2).

Hire purchase
20.2.0 The ultimate objective of a hire purchase agreement is usually the transfer of ownership in goods to the hirer. To that extent the term hire purchase is purely a colloquialism[1] and such agreements have more in common with conditional sale agreements than hire agreements. In form a hire purchase contract is an agreement to bail[2] or hire goods by the owner (bailor) to the hirer (bailee) with an option to purchase the goods when all the instalments have been paid. The hirer has the right to buy the goods but is not obliged to do so. In reality the hiring is fictional, indeed, the fact that the payments required of the hirer are normally greatly in excess of the payments that would be required in an ordinary hire or rental agreement illustrates the artificial nature of the transaction. In a conditional sale agreement it is intended from the outset that the property in the goods will be transferred ultimately to the buyer because he has 'agreed to buy.'

In common with the conditional sale agreement, the property in the goods in a hire purchase agreement remains with the bailor/owner until the option to purchase is exercised by the bailee/hirer. Since the property in the goods is retained in the owner, if the buyer defaults, the owner has a remedy over the goods in addition to an action for the arrears. Indeed the agreement may provide that the owner has a right to repossess the goods.[3] Modern consumer protection legislation makes little distinction between the two types of transaction in terms of rights and formalities, even to the extent of giving the buyer in a conditional sale agreement the right to terminate the agreement.[4]

Historically, the hire purchase agreement was favoured by business because it offered greater protection against a wrongful sale to an innocent third party by a customer in possession of goods under the agreement. Under the Factors Act 1889 a person who has bought or agreed to buy goods may, in certain circumstances, pass title to the goods to an innocent purchaser. In a landmark decision in 1895 the House of Lords[5] held that a hirer under a hire purchase agreement, who merely had an option to buy, was not one who had agreed to buy within the meaning of the Factors Act 1889 and so could not, by a wrongful sale, pass on title even to a purchaser in good faith. Thus the hire purchase agreement offered greater security for the owner of the goods.

In more recent years hire purchase agreements have proved less popular with business because of increased legislative regulation in order to protect consumers and the imposition of controls by way of minimum deposit, as a means of regulating demand in the economy.

The legal regulation of hire purchase agreements is further complicated by the role of finance companies. Most hire purchase agreements are initiated by a retail trader who sells the goods to a finance company which then enters into either a hire purchase agreement or conditional agreement with the customer.

1   See Report of the Committee on Consumer Credit, Vol 1 Ch 2, Cmnd 4596, 1971.
2   See 20.7.0.
3   See 28.6.5.
4   See 28.6.0.
5   *Helby v Matthews* [1895] AC 471, HL.

Mortgage
20.3.0   Goods may be used as a security for a loan of money. Thus the owner of goods may borrow money in return for a charge or mortgage over the goods in favour of the lender. In such circumstances the owner would retain possession of the goods but the lender would have a right to take the goods in the event of default in repaying the loan or interest. In substance such transactions are similar to hire purchase agreements in that the person in possession of the goods is not the owner. Such mortgages were subjected to legislative control under the Bills of Sale Acts 1878 and 1882 which requires them to be made by written instrument and registered. The rationale of the legislation was that without a system of registration third parties could be induced to advance money to the grantor of a bill of sale under the impression that he was the true owner of the goods in his possession. In practice, however, the Bills of Sale Acts became excessively technical and a trap for the unwary. In the words of the Crowther Committee on Consumer Credit:

'It is difficult to imagine any legislation possessing more technical pitfalls . . .'[1]

One of the factors which contributed to the popularity of hire purchase transactions amongst the business community was that the House of Lords in 1895 held that the Bills of Sale Acts did not apply to such transactions, largely because the Bills of Sale Acts applied where an owner granted a charge; in a hire purchase contract the hirer is not the owner at the time that a right to repossess the goods is granted.

Under the SGA 1979 s 62(4) it is provided that the provisions of the Act do not apply to a transaction in the form of a contract of sale which is intended to operate by way of mortgage, pledge, charge, or other security.

In certain commercial, as opposed to consumer, transactions it is often difficult to categorise a transaction. Indeed, certain refinancing transactions may be deliberately disguised as sales in order to evade the provisions of the Bills of Sale Acts. For example, a sale and lease-back transaction may be entered into whereby goods are sold to a finance company by the owner who promptly takes the goods back under a hire purchase agreement. In substance such an arrangement is broadly akin to a mortgage of goods as security for a loan in so far as a cash amount is advanced to the original seller, who then pays instalments under the hire purchase agreement which cover the original purchase price advanced plus a charge for finance. In the event of a dispute, it would be for the courts to decide whether the sale was a genuine transfer of ownership or merely a loan on security of goods, in which case it will invariably be invalidated by the Bills of Sale Acts. The role of the courts was expressed by Winn LJ in the following terms:

> 'In my definite view the sole or entirely dominant question upon that part of the appeal to which I have so far adverted is whether in reality and upon a true analysis of the transactions and each of them, and having regard in particular to the intention of the parties, they constituted loans or sales. It is clear upon the authorities that if a transaction is in reality a loan of money intended to be secured by, for example, a sale and hiring agreement, the document or documents embodying the arrangement will be within the Bills of Sale Acts; it is equally clear that each case must be determined according to the proper inference to be drawn from the facts and whatever the form the transaction may take the court will decide according to its real substance.'[3]

Another example of a transaction which provides difficulties in terms of sale or security interest is the reservation of title clause.[4]

1 Para 4.212.
2 *McEntire v Crossley Bros Ltd* [1895] AC 457, HL.
3 *Kingsley v Sterling Industrial Securities Ltd* [1967] 2 QB 747 at 780, CA.
4 See 24.3.0.

Contract of exchange or barter

20.4.0 Although contracts of sale are by far the most common form of commercial transaction, contracts where the consideration is not money but other goods or services are not uncommon. Indeed in times of high inflation and unpredictable fluctuations in foreign currency markets, goods provide a reliable form of payment. In the words of an eminent Scots lawyer:

> 'Even if the currency may suffer unwelcome and involuntary dilution in value at the present time, a Scotsman may hope that whisky will not suffer likewise.'[1]

There are, however, a number of transactions which have developed as a result of modern marketing techniques designed to induce consumers to buy a particular brand of goods and which are difficult to categorise. These may involve a consumer collecting coupons and trading them in as part of the consideration for goods, entitling him to a reduction in the price of the goods,[2] or the supply of additional goods as a bonus to which the consumer becomes entitled on purchasing the product being promoted.

Such transactions could be classified as a sale, a barter or even a free gift. In *Esso Petroleum Ltd v Customs and Excise Comrs*[3] the House of Lords had to categorise a transaction which involved giving away a free coin with every four gallons of petrol. Each coin was stamped with the likeness of one of the thirty footballers selected for the English squad in the 1970 World Cup competition; they were of little intrinsic value. The question had to be decided whether the coins were being 'sold' for the purposes of purchase tax. The House of Lords were divided as to which category the transaction fell into. Lord Fraser considered that it was a sale of both articles in one transaction; Viscount Dilhorne and Lord Russell were of the view that the coins were distributed as gifts and Lords Simon and Wilberforce considered that the coins were supplied under a contract but not one of sale because the consideration was not a money payment but an undertaking to enter into a collateral contract to purchase petrol.

A popular trading device in the 1960s was the issue of trading stamps with a purchase of goods. The stamps were intended to be collected by consumers and later redeemed in exchange for goods.[4]

1   T B Smith (1974) 47 Tulane Law Rev 1029, 1042.
2   See *Chappell & Co Ltd v Nestle Co Ltd* [1960] AC 87, [1959] 2 All ER 701, HL.
3   [1976] 1 All ER 117, [1976] 1 WLR 1, HL.
4   See Trading Stamps Act 1964, s 4(1) and (2) and the Supply of Goods (Implied Terms) Act 1973, s 16.

Contracts of work and materials

20.5.0   The distinction between a contract of sale and a contract which involves the supply of some goods and the rendering of a service has always presented the courts with problems. Until 1954 the distinction was of considerable practical importance because contracts for the sale of goods to the value of £10 or more were required to be evidenced in writing as a condition of enforceability, whereas no such requirement was necessary for contracts to provide work and materials.[1]

As stated earlier the objective of a contract of sale is to transfer property in the goods to the seller. The object of a contract for work and materials is the carrying out of a service which involves, in varying degree, the transfer of property in some goods. Greer LJ observed:

> 'If you find . . . that the substance of the contract was the production of something to be sold . . . then it is a sale of goods. But if the substance of the contract, on the other hand, is that skill and labour have to be exercised for the production of the article and that it is only ancillary to that there will pass . . . some materials, the substance of the contract is the skill and experience.'[2]

Thus a contract for the supply of a meal in a restaurant[3] and a contract to make and fit false teeth[4] have been held to be sales, whereas a contract to paint a portrait,[5] repair a car[6] and apply a hair-dye[7] have been held to be contracts for work and materials.

In general however where goods are supplied under a contract for work and material the courts[8] and now Parliament[9] imply terms similar to those implied in sales contracts.

1   This requirement was contained in s 4 of the SGA 1893 which was repealed by the Law Reform (Enforcement of Contracts) Act 1954.
2   *Robinson v Graves* [1935] 1 KB 579, CA.
3   *Lockett v A & M Charles Ltd* [1938] 4 All ER 170.
4   *Lee v Griffin* (1861) 1 B & S 272.
5   *Robinson v Graves* [1935] 1 KB 579, CA.

6   *G H Myers & Co v Brent Cross Service Co* [1934] 1 KB 46.
7   *Watson v Buckley, Osborne, Garrett & Co Ltd and Wyrovoys Products Ltd*[1940] 1 All ER 174.
8   *Samuels v Davis* [1943] KB 526, [1943] 2 All ER 3, CA.
9   See 20.6.0 below.

Contracts for the supply of goods

20.6.0   The ownership of goods can be transferred from one party to another under a variety of different transactions. The most common forms are sale of goods, the conditional sale agreement, credit sale and hire purchase agreements. Parliament has therefore tended to concentrate its attention on these more common transactions when considering regulating commercial activity. The result was that, until recently, a person who acquired goods under a sale or hire purchase contract would have the benefit of certain statutory, and in the case of consumers, non-excludable implied terms; whereas a person who acquired goods under a contract of exchange or work and materials would have to rely either on inserting express terms or terms implied by the common law.

The Supply of Goods and Services Act 1982 (SGSA 1982) remedied that situation by extending statutory implied terms to cover all contracts under which one person transfers or agrees to transfer to another the property in goods[1] other than excepted contracts. Excepted contracts are those contracts already covered by legislation, such as sale, hire purchase, trading stamps, transfer by deed for which there is no consideration and contracts intended to operate by way of mortgage, pledge, charge or other security.

It is noteworthy that the transfer must be under a contract. If therefore the transaction is not supported by consideration (either in kind or cash) it will fall outside the scope of the Act. The section extends to protect a buyer who acquires goods under a contract of sale which gives rise to the acquisition of further goods under a promotional campaign. Such additional goods are transferred under a contract and therefore by the terms of SGSA 1982 attract the same implied terms as goods sold under a contract.[2]

Transactions within s 1 of the SGSA 1982 include exchange contracts; contracts of work and materials;[3] transfers of property in goods by the award of prizes in competitions; the use by a guest in a hotel of consumable goods supplied on the premises.

1   S 1(1).
2   See the discussion in 20.4.0.
3   The materials element of the contract is subject to Part I of SGSA 1982 and work element Part II of the Act. See Ch 25.

Hire

20.7.0   A contract for the hire of goods is classified as a type of bailment and is subject to the rules of common law regulating such transactions. The essence of bailment is the transfer of possession from the owner of goods (the bailor) to the bailee who will deal with the goods bailed in accordance with the instructions of the bailor.[1] In fact 'a contract of hire' embraces a variety of different transactions, including the rental agreement, contract hire, operating lease and finance lease. The common feature of such transactions, however, is that the hirer has the right to possession and with it the right to use and enjoy the goods. By contrast to the other contracts for the supply of goods, the transfer of ownership or financing the transfer of ownership is not contemplated.

It will be recalled that the hire purchase contract is a bailment entitling the hirer to possession but because of the option to purchase the law regulates it in much the same manner as a contract of sale.

The idea of hiring equipment is by no means a modern one. In 1798 it was observed that there were advantages for commerce in extending leasing to all:

> 'interests and possessions whatsoever, being led thereto by that known rule that whatsoever may be granted or parted with for ever, may be granted or parted with for a time, and therefore not only lands and houses have been let for years but also goods and chattels.'[2]

Hiring has proved particularly popular at times of rapid technological change when there may be uncertainty about the reliability or economic life of equipment. For example, in the early days of television sets and more recently, with the growth of video recorders, it proved convenient for consumers to rent the equipment until technology became more reliable and standardised. Under such rental agreements responsibility for maintenance and repair normally rests with the rental company, thus the consumer is freed from the responsibilities and risks of ownership.

A further reason for the popularity of hiring was that such agreements escaped statutory control. The first legislation designed to protect consumers entering into hire purchase contracts was passed in 1938 and in the following years substantial initial deposits and other credit controls were introduced. Such measures only served to encourage the use of hiring agreements.

As the Crowther Committee observed, the—

> 'wide extent of television rental is a phenomenon unique to this country, in other countries people buy their television sets by one means of finance or another. It is difficult not to connect this with the fact that, in the early days of statutory control of the terms of hire purchase lending in this country, rental was exempt, and it was therefore possible to obtain a television set on weekly or monthly payments without the necessity of putting down a substantial initial deposit.'[3]

More recently the terms and conditions of hiring contracts have been subjected to the same degree of control and regulation as sale and credit transactions.

The Consumer Credit Act 1974 recognises that some rental agreements when entered into by individuals are indistinguishable from credit transactions and, therefore, subjects them to similar controls and requirements.[4] The SGSA 1982 implies similar terms into hiring contracts to those that apply in respect of other contracts involving the supply of goods.[5] The Act has a broader coverage than the Consumer Credit Act since it extends to 'contracts under which one person bails or agrees to bail goods to another by way of hire'.[6]

Although the SGSA 1982 makes no distinction between different types of hiring in practice however there are a variety of different categories of hiring each of which has particular characteristics. As stated earlier, the common feature in all of them is possession. It is for that reason that contracts under which services are rendered involving the use of goods which remain under the control of the person rendering the service are not generally regarded as contracts of hire. For example, where a builder hires a crane and driver for a particular job, that would be a contract for services rather than hire, since the supplier of the crane and driver would not be regarded as having surrendered possession of the goods.

Similarly, where ships or aircraft are chartered the contract may provide that the ship or aircraft together with the crew be chartered for a particular voyage or period of time, in which case it would not be a contract of hire but services.[7]

Alternatively, the contract may provide for the ship or aircraft to be leased to the charterer, with or without crew; in such a situation possession is given to the charterer and the crew would be under his control, thus it would be a hiring.[8]

In terms of commercial practice, hiring contracts fall into three categories: leases, contract hire and rental.

1   See *Coggs v Bernard* (1703) 2 Ld Rayns 909.
2   Bacon, *A Treatise on Leases and Terms for Years* (1798) p 7.
3   P 92.
4   See generally Part 5.
5   See 21.0.0.
6   S 6(1). Hire purchase agreements and contracts under which goods are bailed in exchange for trading stamps are excepted contracts because they were regulated under previous legislation.
7   In the case of a ship this type of agreement is known as a charterparty.
8   In the case of a ship this type of charter is known as a charterparty by demise.

Leases

20.7.1   A lease may be described as a contract between a lessor and lessee for the hire of a specific asset selected from a manufacturer or vendor of such assets by the lessee. The lessor retains ownership of the asset. The lessee has possession and use of the asset on payment of specific rentals over a period.[1]

Leasing has become increasingly popular and more sophisticated in the last twenty years. In the early 1960s financial institutions, having concentrated their attention on consumer transactions, began to extend their influence into industrial financing. The use of more sophisticated technology with both a high purchase cost and an inclination to become obsolete much sooner than more traditional plant and machinery, facilitated the growth of leasing. In the 1970s the high rates of inflation and government policy in relation to investment incentives only served to increase the popularity of leasing. The result is that leasing is seen as an attractive alternative to ownership in respect of a wide range of assets from small typewriters and word processors to so called 'big ticket' items like aircraft or drilling rigs. As Goode argues:

'the huge growth in finance leasing illustrates how little importance is attached by the businessman to the legal concept of ownership. To him what matters is the substance, not the form.'[2]

In general leases fall into two divisions: the finance lease and the operating lease.

A finance lease is generally taken to refer to the lease of an asset to a commercial customer for the major part[3] of the asset's economic life under an agreement which is non-cancellable or cancellable with a major penalty. The rentals are fixed so that the lessor recovers the whole, or a major part, of the capital cost together with his outgoings and a profit margin. Common characteristics of a finance lease are: the lessee is usually responsible for repairs, maintenance and insurance; since the equipment is purchased by the lessor, often at the request of the lessee, the responsibility for its condition and suitability rests with the lessee; the risk of obsolescence lies with the lessee; the residual value at the end of the primary rental period is not important to the lessor, indeed, the lessee will have an option to continue the lease at a reduced rent and share in the proceeds of sale.[4] In essence, therefore, a finance lease is a mechanism for financing the use rather than the ownership of an asset.

An operating lease is generally a lease of plant or equipment in which the lessor contemplates that the asset will be let to successive lessees under an agreement which is cancellable at short notice without penalty. The lessor is normally responsible for repairs, maintenance and insurance. The asset will eventually be sold by the lessor and so the residual value of the asset will be important to the lessor. An operating lease is particularly attractive when equipment is required for a short period because of rapidly changing technology. The lessor assumes the risk of obsolescence and such risk is built into the rentals charged. It is a particularly attractive arrangement for a business requiring computing equipment, indeed in the computer industry the manufacturer will often be the lessor, thus placing him in a good position to judge the degree of obsolescence.

1   See Clarke, *Leasing* (1978) p 57.
2   Goode, *Commercial Law* (1982) p 835.
3   For tax purposes not less than 75% of the useful life of the asset. Finance Act 1980, Schedule 12 para 5(1).
4   But the lessee will not have an option to purchase.

Contract hire

20.7.2   The term contract hire is usually employed to denote the letting on hire of motor vehicles for a period usually between 12 and 36 months. Finance houses also use the term to describe arrangements with motor dealers to provide vehicles on a fleet basis to firms. At the end of the agreement the vehicles still possess a reasonable market value and may be repurchased by the dealer. Maintenance costs may be built into the rental charge or be the subject of a separate agreement between the hirer and a garage.

Rental

20.7.3   The term rental agreement is used in the context of consumer transactions to describe short term agreements in respect of motor vehicles or indefinite period agreements covering television or video recorder equipment. Such agreements derive their popularity from the fact of their convenience to consumers, in particular the consumer obtains the benefit of use without the responsibility of repair and maintenance that goes with ownership. Goods may be let on rental by retailers or by specialist rental firms.

Hire or acquire?

20.7.4   There are a wide variety of methods available for the acquisition or financing the acquisition of use of goods. The decision whether to enter into a transaction which ultimately results in the ownership of goods, as opposed to a transaction which permits use with no ownership, is a complex one. For the consumer the decision is fashioned by social and economic considerations, for a business organisation there are complex considerations which are dependent on the individual requirements of the business. Central questions will be the nature of the business, the speed of technological change, and the overall financial state of the business, including existing liabilities.

In a business context leasing can offer greater flexibility than alternative transactions. Much, however, depends upon prevailing conditions at the time a decision is made and in most businesses a range of transactions will be used. A lease can often be arranged at relatively short notice, as an alternative to credit which may be either expensive or unavailable; by contrast to conditional sale or hire purchase where a substantial deposit may be required, in a lease the lessor normally provides all the finance thus assisting the lessee in terms of cash flow requirements and budgeting. Whilst a lease is relatively easy to obtain and the asset quickly available, over the period of the agreement the rental payments may represent an onerous burden on a business. One reason why leasing became so popular was that firms entering into leasing liabilities were not required to disclose such transactions in their balance sheet. Thus when a firm's credit worthiness was being assessed by a financial institution, they could underestimate the financial liabilities of the business, if they relied solely on the balance sheet. This was illustrated in the collapse of Court Line in 1974 and the subsequent investigation by Department of Trade Inspectors.[1] The company had produced annual accounts which made no mention of leasing obligations of £38 million in respect of aircraft since there was no requirement under the law or accounting standards to make such disclosure. In recent years, however, institutions have become much more aware of leasing obligations and more vigilant in identifying them.

The advantages of leasing should be assessed against the possible benefits to be derived from ownership. Where machinery and plant are purchased a business may take advantage of 100% first year capital allowance for the purposes of taxation calculations. In the case of a lease such allowances are not available to the lessee but may be claimed by the lessor and to that extent that benefit may be reflected in the rental. In addition ownership of an asset allows a company to use it as security to underpin its general borrowing requirements; funds may also be generated by the sale of the asset where a company no longer requires it, whereas under a lease the lessor usually takes the benefit of any residual value of the equipment, although in a finance lease such value would only be nominal.

1   Department of Trade Inspectors' Report into the affairs of Court Line Ltd (1978) HMSO.

Chapter 21

Statutory Implied Terms in Contracts for the Sale and Supply of Goods

21.0.0 In response to industrialisation the courts in the nineteenth century developed a number of implied terms in contracts of sale. The industrial revolution resulted in a considerable expansion in the number and complexity of goods on sale. Coupled with the growth in overseas trade and changes in the nature of commerce, inevitably the law came to reassess the obligations of a seller of goods. Llewellyn observed:

> 'Markets widen with improved transportation—internal waterways railroads. This means reliance on distant sellers. Middlemen's dealings mean, sometimes, the postponement of inspection, always they mean some ignorance in the seller of the history of the goods. Industrialisation grows out of and produces standardisation . . . a certain predictability and reliability of goods. Contracts made by description or by sample, which is a form of description, or by specification, which is an elaborate description, become the order of the day. Contracts come increasingly to precede production. Sellers begin to build for good will, in wide markets, to feel their standing behind goods to be no hardship, no outrage, no threat to their solvency from a thousand lurking claims, but the mark of business respectability and the road to future profit. The law of seller's obligation must change, to suit.'[1]

Hitherto the predominant philosophy had been 'caveat emptor' requiring the buyer to make sure that goods obtained were of reasonable quality by properly examining them. The idea that the state should seek to lay down minimum standards in respect of quality and suitability was unacceptable McCulloch notes:

> 'the free competition of the producers is the only principle on which reliance can ordinarily be placed for securing superiority of fabric as well as cheapness. Wherever industry is emancipated from all sorts of restraints, those who carry it on endeavour, by lessening the cost, or improving the fabric of their goods or both, to extend their business and the intercourse that subsists among the different classes of society is so very intimate that an individual who should attempt to undersell his neighbours by substituting a showy and flimsy for a substantial article, would be very soon exposed.'[2]

Industrialisation demanded a move away from caveat emptor, particularly

258

in respect of contracts of sale by description where the buyer placed reliance on the seller to select goods for him.

The original Sale of Goods Act 1893 contained three implied conditions in respect of quality and description. Various amendments were made to these implied terms in the Supply of Goods (Implied Terms) Act 1973, but the current Sale of Goods Act 1979 (SGA) contains the same three implied conditions. In effect they lay down a series of graduated duties upon the seller.[3] First there is an implied condition under s 13 that the goods supplied must correspond with their description. Thus if the buyer orders a green 1984 model of a car, he is entitled to receive a car that fits that description. The more detailed the description, the greater the protection afforded to the buyer. However, goods may correspond with their description but nevertheless be defective. The second implied condition under s 14(2) thus extends the buyer's protection further by providing that goods supplied must be merchantable. Such a condition does not however guarantee that the goods are entirely suitable for the buyer's particular purpose. Hence, the third condition under s 14(3) which covers the more narrow circumstance that goods must be suitable for the purpose for which they are sold.

The SGA 1979 distinguishes between conditions and warranties. A condition is a fundamental stipulation, the breach of which gives rise to a right to treat the contract as repudiated. A warranty is a less material stipulation collateral to the main purpose of the contract, the breach of which gives rise to a claim for damages only.[4]

The terms in ss 13 and 14 are conditions thereby entitling a buyer to reject the goods and recover the price paid. In addition, if the buyer has suffered damage through the breach of condition, he could sue for damages for non-delivery.[5]

As an alternative to rejection of the goods the Act gives the buyer the option of electing to treat breach of the condition as a breach of warranty. In such circumstances the goods would be retained and a claim for damages made.[6]

Even where the buyer does not elect to treat the breach as a breach of warranty, the Act withdraws the right to reject where the buyer has accepted the goods or part of them within the meaning of ss 34 and 35 of the Act.[7] If however the contract is severable, that is, split into smaller contracts and delivered by instalments which are separately paid for, acceptance of one or more instalments would not prevent the buyer from rejecting future instalments for breach of the condition.

The classification of the implied terms as conditions or warranties is somewhat inappropriate today, and apt to produce unreasonable distortions in the law. In particular where a minor or cosmetic defect occurs the courts seem reluctant to recognise that such a defect is a breach of the implied term in s 14(2), because to do so they would classify the breach as a breach of condition, thus giving the buyer the right to reject the goods. To prevent that situation arising the courts tend to hold that a minor defect does not render the goods unmerchantable at all under s 14(2).[8] The remedy for this situation would seem to be to remove the designation condition from the implied terms and set out the consequences of a breach of the implied terms more precisely, giving a discretion to the courts in identifying the appropriate remedy.[9]

The implied conditions in respect of contracts for the sale of goods have now been extended to other contracts for the supply of goods. Thus in terms of the statutory protection provided for a person being supplied with goods under a contract there is little difference between the various types of transaction.

The first class of transaction to which the implied conditions were extended was hire purchase contracts.[10] The Supply of Goods and Services Act 1982 (SGSA 1982) extended the implied terms to all contracts 'where one person transfers or agrees to transfer to another the property in goods'.[11] Thus under a contract for work and materials, the materials supplied must comply with the statutory implied conditions.[12] The 1982 Act also extended the implied conditions to contracts of hire.[13]

The following discussion of the implied terms focuses attention on sale of goods transactions but obviously because of the extension of the implied terms to cover hire purchase, other contracts involving the supply of goods and hire contracts, unless otherwise stated, the discussion applies equally to such contracts.

1 Llewellyn, *Cases and Materials on the Law of Sales* (1930) p 204.
2 McCulloch, *Principles of Political Economy* (1864) p 215.
3 Atiyah, *The Sale of Goods* (7th edn 1985) p 55.
4 See SGA 1979, s 11.
5 SGA 1979, s 51.
6 S 11(2).
7 S 11(4). See 24.1.1.
8 See 22.2.0.
9 See Law Commission Working Paper 85, pp 68–84.
10 The Supply of Goods (Implied Terms) Act 1973, ss 8–11 as amended by the Consumer Credit Act 1974.
11 S 1(1). See 20.6.0.
12 S 3–4.
13 S 8–10.

Implied terms as to description

21.1.0 Section 13 of the SGA 1979 implies a condition in contracts of sale by description that the goods comply with the description. Furthermore, if the sale is by sample as well as description, it is not sufficient that the bulk of the goods corresponds with the sample if the goods do not also correspond with the description.[1]

For s 13 to apply, the descriptive statement must be a term of the contract. Thus the common law distinction between statements that are merely representations inducing the contract and statements that became terms of the contract is relevant in this context.[2] The courts have however largely removed the difficulties inherent in that distinction by their generous interpretation of the scope of s 13.[3]

1 See also SG(IT)A 1973, s 9 and SGSA 1982, ss 3, 8.
2 See 14.0.0.
3 See eg *Beale v Taylor* [1967] 3 All ER 253, [1967] 1 WLR 1193, CA.

Meaning of sale by description

21.1.1 Clearly if the buyer has not seen the goods and is relying on the description it must be a sale by description. Section 13 also extends to the sale of specific goods where the buyer has seen the goods. In *Grant v Australian Knitting Mills Ltd* Lord Wright observed that:

'there is a sale by description even though the buyer is buying something displayed before him on the counter; a thing is sold by description, though it is specific, so long as it is sold not merely as the specific thing, but as a thing corresponding to a description eg woollen undergarments, a hot water bottle, a second-hand reaping machine.'[1]

A sale may be by description even where the buyer selects goods exposed for sale from a supermarket shelf.[2] In *Beale v Taylor*[3] a car was advertised as a 1961 Herald convertible. The car had a 1200 disc at the back which the buyer saw. After purchasing the car it was found that it was a combination of two cars welded together, only one of which was from a 1961 model. The Court of Appeal held that the words '1961 Herald' were part of the contractual description. The buyer had relied in part on a newspaper advertisement and the description of the car. The consequences of this case seemed to be that a sale will be by description in every case where the buyer relies on descriptive words. More recently however the House of Lords appear to have moved away from such a broad interpretation of s 13. In *Ashington Piggeries Ltd v Christopher Hill Ltd*[4] the House of Lords considered that a statement made about goods will only form part of the description if it has been used to identify the goods. Lord Diplock considered that:

'The description by which unascertained goods are sold is, in my view, confined to those words in the contract which were intended by the parties to identify the kind of goods which were to be supplied. It is open to the parties to use a description as broad or narrow as they choose. But ultimately the test is whether the buyer could fairly and reasonably refuse to accept the physical goods proferred to him on the ground that their failure to correspond with that part of what was said about them in the contract makes them goods of a different kind from those he had agreed to buy. The key to section 13 is identification.'[5]

Although his Lordship's observations relate specifically to unascertained goods,[6] they could be applied generally. The matter would seem to be one of degree. Thus in *Reardon Smith Line Ltd v Yngvar Hansen-Tangen*[7] a ship was described as built at Yard No 354 by Osaka Shipbuilding Co Ltd. The House of Lords held that the words Yard 354 were not part of the contractual description of the vessel. The vessel tendered was the vessel contracted for. Lord Wilberforce distinguished between words which identify in that their 'purpose is to state (identify) an essential part of the description of the goods' and words 'which provide one party with a specific indication (identification) of the goods so that he can find them and if he wishes sub-dispose of them.' Words used in this second sense do not necessarily describe the goods: 'Such words can be construed much more liberally than they would have to be construed if they were providing essential elements of the description.'[8]

The following have been held to be a breach of s 13: a contract for common English sainfoin seed is not performed by supplying giant sainfoin;[9] a contract for the supply of foreign refined rape oil not carried out where a mixture of hemp and rape oil was offered;[10] oxalic acid containing 10% of sulphate of magnesium was not oxalic acid within the commercial context of the contract;[11] meat and bone meal containing 5% of cocoa husks was similarly not regarded as complying with the description meat and bone meal.[12] The courts have also held that such matters as method of packing,[13] thickness[14] and date of shipment[15] may be treated as part of the contract description.

1 [1936] AC 85 at 108, PC.
2 S 13(3).
3 [1967] 3 All ER 253, [1967] 1 WLR 1193.
4 [1972] AC 441, [1971] 1 All ER 847, HL.
5 [1972] AC 441 at 503–504.
6 See 22.0.2.
7 [1976] 3 All ER 570, [1976] 1 WLR 989, HL.
8 [1976] 1 WLR 989 at 999.
9 *Wallis Son & Welds v Pratt and Haynes* [1911] AC 394, HL.
10 *Nichol v Godts* (1854) 10 Exch 191.
11 *Pinnock Bros v Lewis & Peat Ltd* [1923] 1 KB 690.
12 *Robert A Munro & Co Ltd v Meyer* [1930] 2 KB 312.
13 *Re Moore & Co and Landauer & Co* [1921] 2 KB 519, CA.
14 *Arcos Ltd v E A Ronaasen & Son* [1933] AC 470, HL.
15 *Macpherson Train & Co Ltd v Howard Ross & Co Ltd* [1955] 2 All ER 445, [1955] 1 WLR 640.

Degree of compliance

21.1.2 The duty of the seller to supply goods complying with the contract description has been interpreted very strictly by the courts. Thus in *Arcos v Ronaasen*[1] half inch thick staves were ordered by the buyers. The staves supplied were between half an inch and nine-sixteenths of an inch but nevertheless fit for the buyer's purpose. The House of Lords held that the buyer could reject the goods.

'A ton does not mean about a ton, or a yard about a yard. Still less when you descend to minute measurements does half an inch mean about half an inch. If a seller wants a margin he must, and in my experience does, stipulate for it . . . No doubt there may be microscopic deviations which business men and therefore lawyers will ignore . . . But apart from this consideration the right view is that the condition of the contract must be strictly performed . . .'[2]

Similarly in *Re Moore & Co Ltd and Landauer & Co Ltd*[3] the buyers agreed to buy 3,000 tins of fruit packed in cases containing 30 tins. On delivery some of the boxes contained only 24 tins, although the overall quantity of tins delivered was correct. Despite the finding by an arbitrator that there was no difference in value between tins packed 30 to a case and packed 24 to a case, the Court of Appeal held that the buyers were entitled to reject the total consignment because of a breach of s 13; the packing formed part of the contract description. Such an inflexible approach has been the subject of considerable criticism, in particular, Lord Wilberforce has described it as 'excessively technical and due for re-examination.'[4]

1 [1933] AC 470, HL.
2 Lord Atkin [1933] AC 470 at 479.
3 [1921] 2 KB 519, CA.
4 *Reardon Smith Line Ltd v Yngvar Hansen-Tangen* [1976] 1 WLR 989 at 998, HL. See also The Law Commission Working Paper 85 (1983) pp 30–31.

Description and quality

21.1.3 The *Arcos* case illustrates that goods delivered may be fit for their intended purpose but nevertheless not correspond with the contract description. By the same token, goods may comply with the description even though they are unfit for the purpose for which they were bought. The point may be considered academic since in such a case the buyer may have a remedy under s 14(2) or (3). However, as we shall see, the provisions in s 14 are more limited in scope than s 13; the point may therefore be of practical significance.

In *Ashington Piggeries Ltd v Christopher Hill Ltd*[1] herring meal containing an ingredient which produced a toxin rendering it unsuitable for feeding to mink, was held to have been properly described as 'herring meal'. Thus if the goods remain in substance the goods contracted for, a defect in quality will not be considered to render the seller in breach of s 13. In a New Zealand case[2] a bull was purchased for breeding purposes. It was described as a 'pure bred polled Angus bull', but unfortunately turned out to have a physical abnormality which prevented it from breeding. In holding that the sale was by description with the implicit assumption that the bull was capable of breeding it was stated:

> 'The respondent could have no use for the animal save for the purpose of serving his cows, and, it is to be observed that it was sold not as a bull merely, but as a pure-bred polled Angus bull. The descriptive words appear to me to be meaningless unless intended to convey the impression that the animal might be used to get this class of stock.'[3]

Thus goods described as 'baby food', or 'cold cure' could not be said to conform to their description if they prove completely unsuitable.

1 [1972] AC 441, [1971] 1 All ER 847, HL.
2 *Cotter v Luckie* [1918] NZLR 811.
3 At 813.

Caveat emptor and the implied term as to quality

21.2.0 Section 14(1) of the SGA 1979 reveals its nineteenth century origins by stating:

> '(1) except as provided by this section and section 15 and subject to any other enactment, there is no implied condition or warranty about the quality or fitness for any particular purpose of goods supplied under a contract of sale.'[1]

Thus caveat emptor remains the guiding light, although it only shines in respect of private sales. In the majority of sales the seller is under a duty to supply goods of merchantable quality and fit for their known purpose.

Section 14(2) provides that where the seller sells goods in the course of business, there is an implied condition that the goods supplied under the contract are of merchantable quality. No such condition applies, however, in respect of defects drawn to the buyer's attention before the contract is made or, if the buyer has examined the goods, defects which the examination ought to have revealed.

1 See also SG(IT)A 1973, s 10 and SGSA 1982, s 4.

In the course of business

21.2.1 Unlike s 13, s 14(2) does not apply to private sales. The seller must be selling in the course of business. 'Business' includes a profession and the activities of any government department or public authority.[1] The provision is expressed in wide terms to insure that the conditions implied by s 14 are imposed on every trade seller no matter whether he is or is not habitually dealing in goods of the type sold.[2] As a consequence it would cover the sale by a firm of business equipment or the vehicles used in the business, even though the goods were not of a type ordinarily sold in that business. In order to protect the public against the unscrupulous trader, regulations make it an offence for a business seller to pose as a private seller in any advertisement.[3]

Where private sellers engage a business agent to sell goods on their behalf, the sale would be regarded as a sale in the course of business unless it is apparent to the buyer that it is not a sale in the course of business. Thus a sale by an auctioneer would be a sale in the course of business unless the buyer knew it was a private sale or reasonable steps were taken to bring it to the notice of the buyer before the contract was made.[4]

1 S 61(1).
2 See First Report on Exemption Clauses 1969 (Law Comm no 24) para 31.
3 Business Advertisements (Disclosure) Order 1977, SI 1977/1918.
4 *Geddling v Marsh* [1920] 1 KB 668; *Wilson v Rickett, Cockerell & Co Ltd* [1954] 1 QB 598, [1954] 1 All ER 868, CA.

Merchantable quality

21.2.2   Until the Supply of Goods (Implied Terms) Act[1] there was no statutory definition of the term merchantable quality. Section 14(6) of the SGA 1979 now provides:

'Goods of any kind are of merchantable quality . . . if they are as fit for the purpose or purposes for which goods of that kind are commonly bought as it is reasonable to expect having regard to any description applied to them, the price (if relevant) and all the other relevant circumstances.'

This definition drew heavily on the earlier case law, emphasising fitness for purpose and reasonableness.

It has been argued that the notion of merchantable quality is an outmoded and inappropriate concept,[2] in an age of sophisticated consumer products. It is in essence an expression of commerce, 'more appropriate . . . to material products such as grain, wool or flour than to a complicated machine.'[3] As Ormrod LJ observed in *Cehave NV v Bremer Handelsgesellschaft mbH, The Hansa Nord*[4]—

'the word has fallen out of general use and largely lost its meaning except to merchants and traders in some branches of commerce. Hence the difficulty today of finding a satisfactory formulation for a test of merchantability. No doubt people who are experienced in a particular trade can still look at a parcel of goods and say "those are merchantable but only at a lower price" distinguishing them from "job lots" or "seconds". But in the absence of expert evidence of this kind it will often be very difficult for a judge or jury to make the decision except in obvious cases.'

If goods are manifestly defective such as a catapult breaking on use[5] or lemonade containing acid,[6] they are clearly unmerchantable. But what of goods that contain imperfections or minor defects? In the *Cehave* case the Court of Appeal held that a consignment of citrus pulp pellets were merchantable despite the fact that they were damaged and 'far from perfect'. The finding of the Court was, however, influenced by the fact that there was an express term allowing the buyer a reduction if the pellets were impaired. In addition, having rejected the goods the buyer had repurchased them at a lower price and used them for the original purpose.

In *Millars of Falkirk Ltd v Turpie*[7] a new car was found to have an oil leak in the power steering system. After some adjustment by the dealer the oil was still leaking and the buyer refused to pay the balance of the price and sought to reject the car on the grounds that it was unmerchantable. It was held that the car was of merchantable quality. Relevant factors were that: the defect was a minor one which could be readily cured at a small cost; the dealers were willing to cure it; the defect was obvious and the risk slight, many new cars had some defects on delivery, and it was not exceptional for a new car to be delivered in such a condition.

In respect of this last factor it has been suggested that the statutory definition has reduced the standard of merchantable quality. If a seller can establish that a particular category of car has a reputation for possessing minor defects, it could be argued that goods delivered with such defects are as fit for the purpose 'as it is reasonable to expect.' Thus a general deterioration in the standards of a manufacturer would mean that a buyer could only reasonably expect goods of a lower standard of quality.[8]

It has been suggested, however, that the statutory definition is wide enough to cover minor defects. For example, when a person buys a new car he does not make the purchase purely for a functional purpose but also for the purpose of enjoying the comfort and aesthetic pleasure to be found in a car of that type and even the admiration of his friends.[9] In the recent case of *Rogers v Parish (Scarborough) Ltd*[10] a Range Rover sold as new had defects in the engine, bodywork, gearbox and oil seals, none of which rendered it undrivable or unroadworthy but which required repairs. The Court of Appeal held that the car was not of merchantable quality. It was considered that the fact that a defect was repairable did not prevent it from making the thing sold unmerchantable; the matter was one of degree. Simply because the vehicle was capable of being driven did not necessarily preclude a court finding that it was unmerchantable. In respect of passenger vehicles 'the purpose for which goods of that kind' were commonly bought includes not simply driving it from one place to another but of doing so with the appropriate degree of comfort, ease of handling, reliability and pride in the vehicle's outward and interior appearance. Much would depend upon the market at which the vehicle was aimed and therefore the price. The vehicle in question had been sold as new and the performance and finish to be expected was therefore that of a model of average standard with no mileage. The expectations raised by the description Range Rover and the price of £16 000 were 'relevant factors'.

In *Bernstein v Pamsons Motors (Golders Green)*[11] the judge observed that the merest cosmetic defect on a Rolls Royce might render it unmerchantable whereas it might not on a humbler car. He commented that no system of mass production could ever be perfect; a buyer of a new car had to put up with teething troubles and have them rectified.

Clearly therefore merchantable quality is a relative expression. Much will depend upon the description of the goods and the price at which they are sold. Thus if goods are sold as second-hand, the buyer cannot expect the same standard of quality as new goods. In *Bartlett v Sidney Marcus Ltd*[12] a second-hand car was on sale for £950. The dealers informed the buyer that the

21.2.2   Statutory Implied Terms in Contracts

clutch was defective and the car would be sold at either £975 with the clutch repaired or £950, leaving the repair to be effected by the buyer. The latter option was chosen by the buyer with the result that the clutch cost £84 to be repaired. The Court of Appeal held that the car was not unmerchantable simply because the repairs cost more than anticipated. Lord Denning observed that:

'on the sale of a second-hand car it is merchantable if it is in usable condition, even though it is not perfect. . . . A buyer should realise that when he buys a second-hand car, defects may appear sooner or later, and in the absence of express warranty, he has no redress.'[13]

Since the car was described as a second hand car with a defective clutch it was not unmerchantable merely because the defect proved more serious.

Obviously if goods are sold at a very low price it may be assumed that they are not of the same quality as goods sold at the normal price. On the other hand if the goods are sold at a reduced price in a clearance sale, the buyer is surely entitled to assume that the goods will be of the same standard of quality as goods sold at the original price. The situation may be different, however, if the goods were described as 'shop soiled' or 'seconds'. In *B S Brown & Son Ltd v Craiks Ltd*[14] in response to an order from the buyers a quantity of cloth was supplied. The cloth was required for making into dresses but the sellers were not aware of this, they thought the cloth was required for industrial purposes. The price paid was higher than the normal price for industrial fabric but less than the normal price for dress fabric. The House of Lords rejected the buyers' claim that the goods were unmerchantable on the basis that the cloth was commercially saleable for industrial purposes albeit at a slightly lower price than the contract price.

It should be stressed however that the *Brown* case was decided before the enactment of a statutory definition of merchantable quality. It is consistent with earlier cases which suggest that where goods have several normal purposes, they need only be fit for one of those purposes in order to satisfy the merchantable quality requirement. Arguably, the statutory definition of merchantable quality requires goods to be fit for all the purposes for which they 'are commonly bought'.[15]

1   S 7(2).
2   See The Law Commission Working Paper 1983 No 85, p 14.
3   Farwell LJ in *Bristol Tramways etc Carriage Co Ltd v Fiat Motors Ltd* [1910] 2 KB 831 at 840, CA.
4   [1976] QB 44 at 80, CA.
5   *Godley v Perry* [1960] 1 All ER 36, [1960] 1 WLR 9.
6   *Daniels and Daniels v R White & Sons Ltd and Tarbard* [1938] 4 All ER 258.
7   1976 SLT (Notes) 66.
8   See 'Merchantable Quality—what does it mean?' Consumers' Association 1979, p 32.
9   Goode, *Commercial Law* (1982) 262. See also *Jackson v Rotax Motors and Cycle Co* [1910] 2 KB 937, CA and *Winsley Bros v Woodfield Importing Co* [1929] NZLR 480.
10 (1986) Times, 8 November.
11 (1986) Times, 25 October.
12 [1965] 2 All ER 753, [1965] 1 WLR 1013, CA.
13 At 755.
14 [1970] 1 All ER 823, [1970] 1 WLR 752, HL.
15 But see *Aswan Engineering Establishment Co v Lupdine Ltd* [1987] 1 All ER 135, [1987] 1 WLR 1 when it was held that goods are of merchantable quality if they are suitable for one or more purposes for which they might, without a price reduction, be used, but they are not required to be suitable for every purpose within such a range of purposes.

Examination of goods and obvious defects

21.2.3 The condition of merchantable quality does not apply in two specific situations. First, 'as regards defects specifically drawn to the buyer's attention before the contract is made'. Thus if the buyer is made aware in specific terms of a particular defect he cannot complain. The defect must however have been drawn to the buyer's attention by some other person, not necessarily the seller.

Second, if the buyer examines the goods before the contract is made, no condition will be implied in respect of defects which that examination ought to have revealed. Thus if a buyer does not examine goods he cannot lose the right to complain of any defects which there may be in the goods. If, however, the buyer specifically waives the right of examination, he may be regarded as voluntarily accepting the risk of defects that would have been revealed by an examination. On the other hand, a clause in a contract which purports to waive the right to examine may be struck down as an exemption clause.

Where the buyer examines the goods the question of whether he loses the right to complain about particular defects depends upon the nature and thoroughness of the examination. If a buyer merely examines the bodywork of a car, he could still complain about defects in the engine. Once the buyer commits himself to an examination he will be prevented from complaining about any defects which his examination should have revealed.

Goods acquired for a particular purpose

21.3.0 Section 14(3)[1] of the SGA 1979 is intended to protect buyers where they inform a seller that goods are required for a particular purpose and the goods are found to be unsuitable for that purpose.

The subsection provides:

> 'where the seller sells goods in the course of business and the buyer, expressly or by implication, makes known—
> (a) to the seller, or
> (b) where the purchase price or part of it is payable by instalments and the goods were previously sold by a credit broker to the seller, to that credit broker,
> any particular purpose for which the goods are being bought, there is an implied condition that the goods supplied under the contract are reasonably fit for that purpose, whether or not that is a purpose for which such goods are commonly supplied, except where the circumstances show that the buyer does not rely, or that it is unreasonable for him to rely on the skill or judgement of the seller or credit broker.'

Thus, in common with s 14(2) the implied term does not extend to private sales but it does cover all goods supplied under the contract.

1 See SG(IT)A 1973, s 10 and SGSA 1982, ss 3 and 8.

Particular purpose

21.3.1 The words 'particular purpose' refer to the specified purpose rather than a special or unusual purpose. Thus where goods only have one purpose and they are unsuitable for that purpose a claim will arise under s 14(3) as well as s 14(2). As Lord Wright observed:

'There is no need to specify in terms the particular purpose for which the buyer requires the goods which is nonetheless the particular purpose within the meaning of the section because it is the only purpose for which everyone would ordinarily want the goods.'[1]

The difficulty arises where the goods may be used for a wide range of purposes, but prove unsuitable for a particular purpose. In such circumstances the seller may be liable under s 14(2) on the grounds that the goods are unmerchantable in that they are unsuitable for one of their normal purposes; the seller's liability under s 14(3) is dependent upon whether the purpose for which the goods prove unsuitable is within the range of particular purposes indicated.

Where the buyer does indicate the purpose for which the goods are required he will be entitled to assume that the goods are suitable for all foreseeable applications within the stated purpose. For example, in *Ashington Piggeries Ltd v Christopher Hill Ltd*[2] the subject matter of the contract was herring meal which can be used for feeding to animals or as a fertilizer. In this instance the sellers were aware that the meal was required for feeding the animals but did not know specifically that it was required for mink. The meal proved unsuitable for mink and the House of Lords considered that once the seller was aware that the meal would be used for animal feed it was reasonably foreseeable that it might be used for feeding to mink and the suppliers were therefore liable under what is now s 14(3). The requirements of the subsection were satisfied by showing that herring meal was often used as a feed for mink.

The particular purpose must be communicated to the seller by the buyer. If the seller is aware of the purpose for which the goods are required either by past transactions or impliedly from the circumstances surrounding the contract negotiations, no further express intimation is necessary.[3]

Communication may be made to the seller in person, his agent, or a credit broker who sold to the seller. The latter case covers the typical situation where consumer goods are sold on credit terms. Normally a consumer will negotiate with a dealer thus communicating purpose to the dealer; the dealer then sells the goods to a finance company, who in turn enters into a transaction with the consumer. In such a situation the finance house, not the dealer, are sellers to whom purpose must be communicated and on whom reliance must be placed. In order to avoid problems for buyers in these circumstances the Act makes it clear that communication of purpose to the credit broker/dealer, and reliance on his skill and judgement is sufficient.[4]

1   *Grant v Australian Knitting Mills Ltd* [1936] AC 85 at 99, PC.
2   [1972] AC 441, [1971] 1 All ER 847, HL.
3   *Manchester Liners Ltd v Rea Ltd* [1922] 2 AC 74, HL.
4   See also Consumer Credit Act 1974, s 56(2) and Part 5, post.

Reasonably fit for indicated purpose
21.3.2   Like the notion of merchantable quality, reasonable fitness is a relative notion. In the case of secondhand cars, for example, reasonable fitness depends upon the age, the price paid and the description applied to the goods. As Lord Pearce observed in *Henry Kendall & Sons (a firm) v William Lillico & Sons Ltd:*[1]

'I would expect a tribunal of fact to decide that a car sold in this country was reasonably fit for touring even though it was not well adapted for conditions in a heat wave but not, if it could not cope adequately with rain. If, however, it developed some lethal or dangerous trick in very hot weather, I would expect it to be found unfit. In deciding the question of fact the rarity of the unsuitability would be weighed against the gravity of its consequences. Again, if food was merely unpalatable or useless on rare occasions, it might well be reasonably suitable as food. But I should certainly not expect it to be held reasonably suitable if even on very rare occasions it killed the consumer. The question . . . is simply "were the goods reasonably fit for the specified purpose." '

Thus if the buyer is unusually sensitive to a particular product and the seller is unaware of this, the goods may still be reasonably fit for the purpose.[2] Where the product is one in which there is a high degree of sensitivity, there may, however, be a duty on the seller to make inquiries with the buyer or accompany the goods with a warning.[3] Once the goods are found not to be reasonably fit for the indicated purpose, the seller will be liable even though the defect could not have been detected by reasonable skill.[4]

1 [1969] 2 AC 31 at 115, HL.
2 See *Griffiths v Peter Conway Ltd* [1939] 1 All ER 685, CA.
3 See *Vacwell Engineering Co Ltd v BDH Chemicals Ltd* [1971] 1 QB 88, [1969] 3 All ER 1681, *Willis v FMC Machinery and Chemicals Ltd* (1976) 68 DLR (3d) 127.
4 See *Frost v Aylesbury Dairy Co* [1905] 1 KB 608, CA; *Henry Kendall & Sons (a firm) v William Lillico & Sons Ltd* [1969] 2 AC 31, HL.

Reliance on the seller's skill and judgement
21.3.3 Section 14(3) will not apply if the buyer does not rely on the seller's skill and judgement, or, if he does so rely, it was unreasonable for him to do so. Reliance will normally be presumed unless the circumstances indicate otherwise. Certainly in a consumer transaction reliance will be inferred, as Lord Wright stated in *Grant v Australian Knitting Mills Ltd:*[1]

'The reliance will seldom be express: it will usually arise by implication from the circumstances; thus to take a case like that in question, of a purchase from a retailer the reliance will be in general inferred from the fact that a buyer goes to the shop in the confidence that the tradesman has selected his stock with skill and judgment.'

Similarly where the seller also happens to be the manufacturer it would be difficult to deny reliance. Simply because the buyer elects to test or subject the goods to analysis will not necessarily negate the inference of reliance on the seller.
    In a great many commercial transactions a buyer may rely partly on their own expertise and partly on the skill of the seller. In such circumstances if the goods are found to be unsuitable, it will be a question of deciding on whom does responsibility rest. To succeed in a claim the buyer must be able to show that the basis of his claim relates to matters in respect of which he placed reliance on the seller.[2]
    If the seller can establish that it was unreasonable for the buyer to rely on his skill and judgement, the implied term will not apply. Such might be the case where goods are being made according to the special instructions of the buyer and the seller indicates that he has no expertise in manufacturing

goods under the required conditions. It is important, however, to distinguish between the situation where a seller seeks to contract out of the implied term and the situation where a seller merely indicates that his skill and judgement cannot be relied upon in the prevailing circumstances. It is unlikely that the courts would allow a seller to evade the implied term simply by inserting a clause in the contract to the effect that the buyer relies on his own skill and judgment.

1 [1936] AC 85 at 94, PC.
2 See *Ashington Piggeries Ltd v Christopher Hill Ltd* [1972] AC 441, [1971] 1 All ER 847, HL and *Cammell Laird & Co Ltd v Manganese Bronze and Brass Co Ltd* [1934] AC 402 at 414, HL.

Relationship with section 14(2)
21.3.4 There is clearly some overlap between s 14(2) and s 14(3). In particular, to satisfy the requirements of merchantable quality goods must be fit for their normal purpose; in terms of s 14(3), goods must be fit for their normal purpose and any other communicated purpose. An important factor will be whether the buyer has examined the goods because if a defect ought to have been revealed by the examination, s 14(2) will not apply. Examination does not however preclude a claim under s 14(3) although it may suggest that the buyer has not relied on the seller's skill and judgement.

Clearly s 14(3) is wider than s 14(2) in that goods may satisfy the requirement of merchantable quality although they may be unsuitable for the precise purpose for which they were acquired.

Contracts of sale by sample
21.4.0 Section 15 regulates contracts of sale by sample. It provides that:

'A contract of sale is a contract for sale by sample where there is an express or implied term to that effect in the contract.'

Merely because the seller provides a sample does not make the transaction a sale by sample. There must be evidence of an intention that the sample is provided in order to allow the buyer to ensure that the bulk of the goods broadly corresponds to the sample.

Lord Macnaghten observed:

'The office of the sample is to present to the eye the real meaning and intention of the parties with regard to the subject matter of the contract which, owing to the imperfection of language, it may be difficult or impossible to express in words. The sample speaks for itself. But it cannot be treated as saying more than such a sample would tell a merchant of the class to which the buyer belongs, using due care and diligence, and appealing to it in the ordinary way and with the knowledge possessed by merchants of that class at the time. No doubt the sample might be made to say a great deal more. Pulled to pieces and examined by unusual tests which curiosity or suspicion might suggest, it would doubtless reveal every secret of its construction. But that is not the way in which business is done in this country.'[1]

Thus, the use of a sample does not preclude the seller being liable for failure to provide goods of merchantable quality. As s 15(2)(b) provides there is an implied condition that:

'the goods will be free from any defect, rendering them unmerchantable, which would not be apparent on reasonable examination of the sample.'

The section also provides that there is an implied condition:

'(a) that the bulk will correspond with the sample in quality,
(b) that the buyer will have a reasonable opportunity of comparing the bulk with the sample.'

In the first implied term, it is not sufficient that the bulk could be made to correspond with the sample by 'some simple process.'[2] The second implied term reflects a general principle enshrined in s 34(1) of the SGA 1979 that a buyer must always have an opportunity to examine goods in order to determine whether they are in conformity with the contract. Unless there is evidence pointing to a contrary intention, the place of delivery is where the bulk must be compared with the sample.[3]

1   (1887) 12 App Cas 284 at 297.
2   *E & S Ruben Ltd v Faire Bros & Co Ltd* [1949] 1 KB 254 at 260.
3   *Perkins v Bell* [1893] 1 QB 193, CA.

How long must goods remain of merchantable quality and fit for their purpose?

21.5.0   In general goods must satisfy the requirements of s 14(2) and (3) at the time of delivery. If a defect manifests itself some time after delivery, it may suggest that the goods were not up to the required standard at the time of delivery. The longer the defect takes to manifest itself the more difficult the buyer's task becomes to establish that the goods do not meet the statutory requirements. The courts would have to consider such factors as the nature of the goods, the price paid, the reasonable expectations of the buyer and any other relevant circumstances. If the goods are under a manufacturer's guarantee and a defect occurs within the guarantee period, that would suggest that the goods may not have been of the requisite quality. As time elapses the likelihood increases of a defect arising out of misuse or some other cause not attributable to the condition of the goods when delivered. When a defect is discovered or even suspected, the buyer is required to act swiftly; a failure to take action may preclude a latter action for damages. For example in *Lambert v Lewis*[1] it was held that the implied condition that the coupling fitted to a Land Rover would be reasonably fit for towing ceased once the farmer became aware that the locking device was defective.

It has been suggested that the absence of an express reference to the durability of goods in s 14 represents a justifiable criticism, particularly in the case of consumer sales. The advantage of such a reference would be that it imposes:

'. . . on the seller the onus of establishing that goods which failed within the durability period appropriate for the class of goods in question were in fact delivered to the buyer in such condition that with normal use and care they would have continued in good order and condition for the durability period in question . . . Since all the expertise in relation to a product lies with the maker, there is much to be said for putting the onus on him . . . and passing the benefit and burden of such an onus down the distributive chain . . .'[2]

Some Codes of Practice issued by trade associations include durability in the statement of the general standard of consumer articles.[3]

1   [1982] AC 225, at 268, [1981] 1 All ER 1185, HL. But see 24.1.1.
2   Goode, *Commercial Law* (1982) p 290.
3   See also The Law Commission Working Paper 85, para 22, pp 19–20.

Implied terms are absolute

21.6.0   The conditions implied by s 14 are absolute and the seller cannot raise as a defence that he took all reasonable care. As Blackburn J stated:

'If there was a defect in fact, even though that defect was one which no reasonable skill or care could discover, the person supplying the article should nevertheless be responsible, the policy of the law being that in a case in which neither were to blame, he, and not the person to whom they were supplied, should be liable for the defect.'[1]

There is no state of the art defence available to a seller by which he could argue that the properties of the product which render it unmerchantable were not recognised as defects by scientific or medical knowledge at the time of the transaction.[2]

This may appear unjust from the point of view of the retail seller who quite blamelessly sells defective goods acquired through the distributive system and for which he may have to pay considerable damages to a buyer. The idea however is that the retailer will pursue his remedies as a buyer against the wholesaler, and eventually the real culprit, the manufacturer will bear the cost when the distributive system yields the buyer to whom the manufacturer first sold. It should be pointed out, however, that whilst a retailer cannot exclude or restrict his liability to the consumer in respect of the implied terms, a wholesaler or manufacturer who sells to a retailer may attempt to limit or exclude their liability to a retail buyer.[3]

1   *Randall v Newsom* (1876) 45 LJQB 364.
2   *Henry Kendall & Sons (a firm) v William Lillico & Sons Ltd* [1969] 2 AC 31 at 84, HL.
3   See 21.8.0.

Implied conditions by trade usage

21.7.0   Consistent with the general principles of contract law, an implied condition or warranty about quality or fitness for a particular purpose may be added to a contract by custom or usage of a trade.[1]

1   S 14(4). See *Hutton v Warren* (1826) 1 M & W 466 at 475.

Excluding the implied terms

21.8.0   The SG(IT)A 1973 radically altered the extent to which the implied terms as to description, merchantable quality and fitness for purpose could be modified or excluded by agreement.[1] Many of the issues were touched upon in the general discussion of exclusion of liability in contracts in 18.0.3. The position may be summarised as follows:

1. Where a buyer deals as a consumer[2] the implied terms in ss 13, 14 and 15 can never be excluded. Indeed, any attempt to exclude the implied terms may result in criminal penalties against a trader.[3]

2. In the case of a buyer who does not deal as a consumer any attempt to exclude the implied terms in ss 13, 14 and 15 will only be valid if it satisfies a test of reasonableness.[4]

These above rules apply equally to hire purchase contracts, and other contracts involving the supply of goods caught by the SGSA 1982.

1   See now Unfair Contract Terms Act 1977 ss 6–7.
2   See 18.0.3.
3   Consumer Transactions (Restrictions on Statement) Order 1976, and see 18.0.12.
4   See 18.0.11.

Chapter 22
Passing of Property and Risk in Contracts of Sale

22.0.0 The SGA 1979 contains detailed rules dealing with the passing of property—by which we mean ownership— and with the time and place of delivery. In many ways these are the heart of the Act: it has been said that: 'the whole object of a sale is to transfer property from one person to another'[1] and whilst it can be argued that the buyer is not concerned with ownership if he receives the use and enjoyment of the goods it is the transfer of ownership which marks out the contract of sale from other contracts, such as bailment, hire and rental, where only possession is transferred. We have already seen that the definition of a 'sale of goods' in s 1 of the Act refers to the transfer of the 'property' in goods.[2]

In reality a buyer is concerned that he should get full possession, use and enjoyment of the goods, without which for many practical purposes his ownership alone would be worthless, and the Act accordingly deals also with those matters.

Two points must then be borne in mind. First, although it is widely said that 'possession is nine-tenths of the law' the rules about title/ownership and delivery/possession are separate and distinct. Thus we will see that the person in possession of the goods is not necessarily the owner and that physical delivery of the goods does not necessarily pass title. The buyer can become owner of the goods before he takes possession of them and, conversely, the seller can remain owner even though he has delivered them to the buyer. As we will see, these rules have caused some difficulties and been the subject of much controversy.

Second, it is important to bear in mind the history of the Act, first passed in response to the needs of businessmen almost 100 years ago. The provisions in this part of the Act have been criticised as being 'highly technical, prejudicial to consumers and out of touch with what happens in practice',[3] and, as we shall see, many of the rules, particularly those about the passing of ownership and risk, are unsuited to the bulk of consumer transactions. Equally, however, some of the rules have been outpaced by developments in commercial and business practice.

1 Atkin LJ in *Rowland v Divall* [1923] 2 KB 500 at 505.
2 20.1.2.
3 Cranston, *Consumers and the Law* (2nd edn, 1986) p 166.

Consequences of the passing of property in sale

22.0.1   Transferring the ownership in and hence the title to the goods from the seller to the buyer has three important consequences. First, unless otherwise agreed, the risk of accidental loss or damage passes to the buyer.[1] If the buyer has had the foresight to arrange insurance cover such risk will cause no hardship. However, the ownership in goods can pass to a buyer even before he takes possession of the goods and in such circumstances insurance cover may not have been arranged.

A second consequence is that until title has passed to the buyer, the seller cannot sue for the price of the goods. As we shall see, the seller cannot sue for the price until he has also at least tendered delivery of the goods; but if title has not passed and the buyer refuses delivery, the seller's only claim is for damages for breach of contract for the buyer's non-acceptance and, as with any claim for damages, he will be under a duty to mitigate his loss[2] (for instance by selling the goods elsewhere). On the other hand, if title has passed to the buyer, even if the buyer refuses to take delivery, the seller is under no duty to mitigate and can simply claim the price. The third consequence is that until ownership passes to the buyer he cannot resell the goods to a third party. Only the owner of goods may dispose of them to another so as to pass a good title to that other. Thus if the buyer attempts to dispose of the goods before he has become owner then, prima facie, the person who acquires them from him will not become owner and will not be able to claim them from the seller. Similarly if the seller attempts to dispose of the goods to a third party after the buyer has become owner, the third party will have no title to the goods. However, as we shall see below, there are important exceptions to this rule contained in the SGA 1979 which mitigate the impact of the rule on third parties. Given these consequences, it is important to be able to identify the time at which the transfer of ownership takes place.

1   S 20.
2   See 24.2.0.

Classification of goods for the purposes of the passing of property

22.0.2   In considering the rules governing the time when ownership passes it is necessary to make two distinctions between different types of goods. The first is that contained in s 5 of the SGA 1979 which makes a distinction between existing goods and future goods; the latter may either be in existence but not yet owned by the seller, or not yet manufactured. Thus a manufacturer might agree to build a specific piece of equipment for sale to his customer: as the machinery is yet to be built the contract is for the sale of future goods. Alternatively an antique dealer might mention to a customer that he intends to acquire a particular piece and the customer agree that he will in turn purchase it from the dealer (no doubt at a profit for the dealer); the goods are in existence but since they are yet to be acquired by the dealer, they are future goods.

Obviously, when goods are not yet in existence, or have not yet been acquired by the seller, property cannot pass to the buyer immediately on the making of the contract. Such contracts must therefore be agreements to sell rather than sales.

Of rather more practical importance is the distinction drawn between specific and unascertained goods, a distinction which cuts across that between existing and future goods. Specific goods are defined in s 61(1) of the Act as 'goods identified and agreed upon at the time the contract of sale is made.' It is possible for future goods to be specific goods—for instance in both the above examples the contract would be for the sale of specific future goods. 'Unascertained goods' are not defined in the Act, but by a process of elimination must be all goods which are not specific. Thus, when at the time the contract is made the parties can identify a particular item as the subject of the contract, the goods are specific: for instance if a customer calls at a garage and picks out a particular second hand car—'That MGB'.

Unascertained goods, on the other hand, are not specifically identified at the time the contract is made but generally fall into two categories. First, those that are wholly unidentified other than by description, for example '100 tons of potatoes', 'a new Ford Escort'. In such a case no source is identified and the seller can fulfil his contract by supplying goods from any source, provided they meet the contract description.[1] Even if he has a particular source—or even a particular item—in mind, he can change his mind and use another for the particular contract. Second, the goods will be unascertained if a particular source is specified, for instance 100 tons of potatoes from a particular field. In such a case the seller may choose which particular goods he will use for the particular contract, but he must supply from the particular designated area.

Such contracts are particularly common in international commodities dealing, when parties might contract for the sale of a quantity of material supplied (existing goods) or to be shipped (future goods) on a particular vessel, for example:

> '1,000 tons of Weston White wheat ex motor vessel Challenger expected to load between 16 and 31 December from Oregon or Washington.'[2]

Obviously many commercial contracts involve sales of unascertained goods, and the sale of commodities from bulk raises special problems.

One other point should be noted in relation to unascertained goods. Although not identified at the time of the contract they will be identified later in some way; they must be, because otherwise no title can pass.[3] The goods are then described as ascertained.

The distinction between specific and unascertained goods is vital in relation to the passing of property and therefore, in relation to the passing of risk. In addition it affects the question whether or not the seller may be excused performance on the grounds of frustration.

1   Sale of unascertained goods will always be sales by description and/or by sample.
2   See *Re Wait* [1927] 1 Ch 606, CA.
3   See SGA 1979, s 16.

The passing of property rules
22.0.3   The SGA 1979 lays down two general overriding rules in respect of the passing of property. First, no property in unascertained goods can pass until the goods have become ascertained; until a particular item or parcel of goods is marked out as the one to be transferred under the contract no one knows which goods are to be transferred, and no property can pass. Second, under s 17 of the SGA 1979 where there is a contract for the sale of specific or ascertained goods the property in them is transferred to the buyer at such

time as the parties intend it to be transferred. In order to determine the intention of the parties the terms of the contract, conduct of parties and surrounding circumstances must be considered. The rule is expressed to apply to 'specific' and 'ascertained' goods: since even goods which were initially wholly unascertained must at some stage become ascertained if title is ultimately to pass. It is always, therefore, open to the parties, expressly or impliedly, to state when property shall pass to the buyer subject to the overriding rule in s 16 that property cannot pass until the goods are identified and ascertained. In practice, even though the passing of ownership is so fundamental to the contract, the parties rarely even consider the point. Certainly in most consumer sales, at least when cash is paid at once, the matter receives little attention: the consumer buyer—and perhaps even the seller—simply assume that the goods will become the buyer's property, probably with no idea as to exactly when that should happen. The only exception to this tendency in consumer sales is when goods are sold on credit terms when the sale will almost always be a conditional sale[1] and the seller will provide, for his own protection, that property shall not pass to the buyer until he has paid the whole price or all the agreed instalments.

Even in the context of commercial transactions, most businessmen probably have little awareness of the importance of the exact time when property passes. However, in recent years following the case of *Aluminium Industrie Vaassen BV v Romalpa Aluminium Ltd*,[2] greater awareness has been generated as to the advantage of the device of the conditional sale, and so the insertion of reservation of title clauses into contracts, stating that notwithstanding delivery of the goods to the buyer, the seller retains the property in them until the price is paid in full, has become widespread.[3] Such clauses are merely an example of a statement of intention under s 17.

Should the seller wish only to postpone the passing of property, his right to do so is bolstered by s 19 of the Act, which underlines the general rule of party intention and gives a specific example of the separation of possession and ownership. It provides that the seller can deliver goods reserving title and a right of disposal, since goods will therefore be in the possession of the buyer but owned by the seller. By far the most common condition imposed by sellers for the passing of title is that the purchase price should be paid. Such a clause gives protection to the seller against the buyer becoming insolvent without having paid. In that event the operation of the clause means that the property in the goods has not passed, the goods are still owned by the seller and he can recover them if payment is not forthcoming. In the absence of the clause the property would have passed to the buyer and the seller's only remedy would be to join all the other creditors of the buyer and prove for the price in the insolvency.

On the assumption that the parties have made no stipulation as to when title is to pass, s 18 of the Act contains five 'rules' which deal with the passing of property. It must always be remembered, though, that the 'rules' only apply if there is no express or implied declaration of intention by the parties: the provisions of s 17 override those of s 18.

See 20.1.2 and Part V.
[1976] 2 All ER 552, [1976] 1 WLR 676.
See 24.3.0.

Passing property—rules one to three
22.0.4 Rule 1 provides that where there is an unconditional contract for the sale of specific goods in a deliverable state, the property will pass when the contract is made, and it is immaterial whether time for payment or delivery is postponed. Thus even where payment is delayed, unless the contract stipulates a contrary intention, the property in specific goods passes immediately the contract is made. Invariably a contrary intention will be apparent, as Diplock LJ observed:

> 'In modern times very little is needed to give rise to the inference that the property in specific goods is to pass only on delivery or payment.'[1]

Rule 1 refers to the goods being in a 'deliverable state'; this means that they are in such a state as the buyer would under the contract be bound to take delivery of them.[2] If the seller agrees to carry out repairs to the goods or modify them in some way, the goods would not be in a deliverable state until the work was completed.

Applying rule 1 then, let us look at a typical situation. P wishes to buy second hand car. He goes to V's garage, and selects a particular car on show (specific goods) agreeing there and then to buy it. He pays for it and agrees to collect it later when he has arranged insurance. Even though the car remains on V's premises title has passed to P, and with it the risk of loss.

Thus we have the unfortunate situation that the person in possession, and therefore in the best position to safeguard the goods, does not bear the risk. In practice, the burden would not be unduly onerous since the risk would undoubtedly be covered by V's business insurance, at little extra cost. The consumer would not have such extensive insurance cover and would, in any events, not take out cover until the vehicle was in his possession.

The position would be otherwise if P ordered a new car not yet in stock (unascertained or future goods), or if V insisted that title does not pass until the cheque is cleared (not an unconditional contract) or if modifications had to be made to the car. The latter event is in fact covered by rule 2 which provides that if the seller is bound to do something to the goods, for the purpose of putting them in a deliverable state, the property does not pass until such thing is done, and the buyer has notice that it has been done.

Rule 2 is the converse of rule 1: it applies when the goods are not in deliverable state at the time of the contract and the seller is required under the contract to do something to them so that the buyer can be required to take delivery. Thus in one case[3] there was a contract for the sale of condensing engine weighing over 30 tons and which was connected to the floor of the premises in which it stood. The contract required the sellers to dismantle the machine and load it for delivery by rail. The engine was badly damaged during loading and the buyers refused to take delivery. The seller contended that title—and therefore the risk of loss—had passed to the buyers at the time the contract was made, but the court rejected the argument: the machine was not in a deliverable state at the time of the contract, because something remained to be done by the sellers: they had to dismantle and load it and title could not pass until that had been done.

A second point should be noted. It is not enough under rule 2 for the seller simply to perform the acts required of him. Title will not pass to the buyer until he has notice that the goods are in a deliverable state. This requirement will protect the buyer who will thus be able to insure his goods.

Applying rule 2 to an example, suppose again that P visits a garage and decides to buy a specific second hand vehicle on the forecourt. He agrees to buy it, but notices that the exhaust is 'blowing' and insists that a new exhaust is fitted before he will take the car. Even if he pays the price then and there, title to the car will not pass to him until a new exhaust is fitted and he has notice of that fact: similarly risk will not pass and if, before he has notice that the work has been done, the car is stolen, he can recover the price.

Rule 3 provides that where the seller is bound to weigh, measure, test or do some other act with reference to the goods for the purpose of ascertaining the price, the property does not pass until such actions have taken place, and the buyer has notice that they have taken place.

1   *R V Ward Ltd v Bignall* [1967] 1 QB 534 at 545, CA.
2   S 61(5).
3   *Underwood Ltd v Burgh Castle Brick and Cement Syndicate* [1922] 1 KB 343, CA.

Passing of property—rule four
22.0.5   Rule 4 deals with goods on sale or return and provides that the property in such goods passes to the buyer:
(a) when he signifies his approval or acceptance or does any other act adopting the transaction; or
(b) where he retains the goods without giving notice of rejection, after the expiration of the time fixed for their return, or the expiration of a reasonable time. What is a reasonable time is a question of fact to be decided by examining all the circumstances.

Rule 4 is something of an oddity. Strictly it does not apply to sales at all because the situations it describes are not sale contracts. When goods are delivered on sale or return or on approval there is some prior agreement between the parties leading to delivery, and the seller is committed to sell. However, the buyer is not at this stage committed to buy: he will do so only if he is satisfied with the goods (delivery on approval) or if he can resell them (sale or return). The transaction is not converted into a sale contract until the buyer notifies his acceptance of the goods by words or conduct.

The rule stipulates four ways title can pass:
(a) when the buyer signals acceptance of the goods;
(b) when the buyer does any act adopting the transaction;
(c) when a time limit for return of the goods is fixed and the buyer returns them beyond that time without giving notice of rejection;
(d) when no time limit is fixed but the 'buyer' keeps the goods beyond a reasonable time for their rejection.

In each case the same act serves as acceptance of the offer to sell and to pass title to the 'buyer'.

Situations (a) and (c) give rise to no difficulties: in those cases the buyer either accepts expressly or else title passes in accordance with the expressed intentions of the parties. For the purposes of situation (d), what is a reasonable time will be a question of fact depending on the circumstances of each case: obviously the time will be shorter if goods are perishable, or the market is subject to fluctuations.

Situation (b) is slightly more difficult. The buyer is treated as adopting the transaction if he does any act inconsistent with the seller's ownership or which prevents the free return of the goods. Thus if he uses or consumes the goods in his business, or resells or pledges or changes them, he adopts the transaction and title passes: the 'buyer' is treating the goods as his own. It is possible for the seller to exclude the automatic operation of rule 4 by including a reservation of ownership until the price is paid; if such a clause is included title will not pass to the buyer under rule 4 if he re-sells, because rule 4 will not apply: the parties have expressed their own intention. Further, if such a clause prohibits re-sale by the 'buyer' then the sub-buyer will not get good title and the seller can recover the goods. However, even such a reservation of ownership will not protect the seller if the goods are used by the buyer in his manufacturing process, especially if the goods are consumed.

Rule 4 deals with the situation when goods are delivered by agreement—ie at the buyer's request. Distinguish the situation when goods are delivered without such a request: unsolicited goods. The rule has no application to such deliveries, which used to be common. Sellers would rely on 'inertia' selling, delivering goods to consumers without prior order and with a statement that, if not wanted, they should be returned within a fixed time, and relying on natural inertia to do their selling for them; the consumer would forget, or not be bothered to return the goods in time and would end up paying the price. In fact the buyer was never legally obliged to pay—the seller was making an offer and the rule, of course, is that silence[1] is not an acceptance—but many did out of ignorance of the law. The practice of inertia selling in this way is now outlawed by the Unsolicited Goods and Services Act 1971. Where unsolicited goods are delivered the recipient must keep them available for collection for six months (or, if he gives notice to the seller, for 30 days). If they are not collected within that time, they become the property of the recipient. Furthermore, he is under no duty to take care of the goods—his only obligation is not to destroy or dispose of them. Finally, it is a criminal offence to demand payment for unsolicited goods.

1   *Felthouse v Bindley* (1862) 11 CB NS 869.

Passing of property—rule five

22.0.6   The final rule in s 18 is concerned, primarily, with unascertained goods. It is probably the most complex of the rules and almost certainly the most important in practice—at least in commercial transactions.

Let us first remind ourselves of the significance of the passing of property and the situations in which it becomes important. Imagine that A sells to B 50 sacks of potatoes from his warehouse, containing several thousand such sacks. Before B has paid for the potatoes the warehouse is burned down: can A claim the price? Or imagine that C is the owner of a bulk cargo of 6,000 tonnes of tapioca being shipped by sea by bulk transporter. He sells 2,000 tonnes each to D, E and F. On discharge at the port of delivery it is found that 1,000 tonnes are mouldy: can D, E or F insist on delivery of any amount? Or can C insist that any of them take any amount? Or, in the same situation, imagine that C had become insolvent before discharge of the cargo, but after D, E and F had paid the sums due from them. C's trustee in bankruptcy now claims the tapioca: can D, E or F claim any part of it?

It should be appreciated that in each of the above cases, involving sales from bulk, the contract was for the sale of unascertained goods. In such a case, the starting point in the search for 'property' is SGA 1979, s 16 which states that in a contract for the sale of unascertained goods no property can pass unless and until the goods are ascertained. This provision is overriding: it cannot be varied or excluded by any agreement of the parties. Thus in the above situation, B would not be bound to pay the price; D, E and F could not insist on any part of the tapioca, even if they had paid for all of it between them. No title to goods can pass under a contract of sale until the goods are ascertained, because until then no one could know which parcel of goods belongs to which buyer. Which 2,000 tonnes of tapioca should go to D, which to E, which to F—or, to put it another way, who should get the mouldy 1,000 tonnes? No doubt the problem—at least in the case of the mouldy tapioca—could be solved by a rule of apportionment; but the law requires certainty.

We will return to this point shortly. Having seen the negative rule in s 16 which prevents the passing, when does title to unascertained goods pass? The answer is provided by s 18 rule 5 which states that where there is a contract for the sale of unascertained or future goods by description, and goods of that description and in a deliverable state are unconditionally appropriated to the contract, either by the seller with the assent of the buyer, or by the buyer with the assent of the seller, the property in the goods thereupon passes to the buyer; and the assent may be express or implied, and may be given either before or after the appropriation is made.

In theory there seems no reason why the parties should not state their own intention as to when title should pass—subject of course to s 16. In practice, however, they are unlikely to do so, except when a reservation of title clause is included to postpone the passing of title. The parties can always vary rule 5 by defining its terms—for example, by requiring the seller to give notice of appropriation, and so on.

The first thing to note about rule 5 is that it applies not only to sales of unascertained goods but also to sales of future goods by description. It could thus apply to sales of specific future goods if sold by description. The reason is simple. Just as a seller of bulk potatoes can decide which sacks to send to which customer, so the engineer building specialist machinery to order for customers could decide to use the machine built for customer P to fulfil an urgent order from very important customer Q, so that title cannot pass until the goods are appropriated to the contract.

For example in one case[1] a carpet was ordered from a supplier who was also contracted to lay it. The carpet was delivered to the buyer and left overnight in his garage, still wrapped in bales. Before it could be laid it was stolen and the court had, therefore, to decide on whom did the loss fall. It was held that property had not passed because the carpet would not be in a deliverable state until it had been laid.

For the property to pass under rule 5 the goods must be unconditionally appropriated to the contract. This requires that they be 'irrevocably earmarked' for the performance of the contract so that the seller can use those goods and only those goods for that particular contract and no other. There will be an unconditional appropriation if the seller delivers the goods to the buyer or gives them to a carrier so that they can be delivered to the buyer, or if he does some other act in pursuance of the contract—for instance seals goods in sacks provided by the buyer, or marks the goods in some way to identify them and gives notice of appropriation to the buyer. On the other hand there is not an unconditional appropriation if the buyer simply sets the goods aside in his own warehouse: he could change his mind and use other goods for the contract.

'To constitute an appropriation of the goods to the contract the parties must have had, or be reasonably supposed to have had, an intention to attach the contract irrevocably to those goods so that those goods and no others are the subject of the sale and become the property of the buyer.'[2]

In fact rule 5(2) gives a specific example of an unconditional appropriation: delivery to the buyer or to a carrier, provided that the seller does not reserve the right of disposal. In such an event the seller effectively puts the goods out of his control.

In *Healy v Howlett & Sons*[3] P contracted to sell 20 cases of mackerel to D in London. He despatched 190 cases by rail from his premises in Valentia, Ireland, to meet D's order and those of other customers, but consigned them to his own order. The rail company at Holyhead was instructed to divide the cases between the various customers. In fact, on arrival at Holyhead the mackerel had already deteriorated due to delay in transit and would be unfit for consumption on arrival in London. D rejected the mackerel and P sued for the price, arguing that property had passed to D at Valentia when loaded on the first train. P failed. He had consigned the goods to his own order and there was therefore no unconditional appropriation until the particular cases were set aside for D at Holyhead. Therefore the goods had been P's property and, therefore, at his risk at the time of deterioration.

On the other hand, in *Wardar's (Import and Export) Co Ltd v W Norwood & Sons Ltd*[4] V contracted to sell P 600 cartons of frozen kidneys out of 1,500 in his cold store. P sent his carrier to collect them and on arrival the carrier found the 600 cartons stacked on the pavement. Loading took four hours and towards the end the carrier noticed some of the cartons dripping: nevertheless he completed the loading and signed a receipt (noting 'in soft condition'!). The kidneys were delivered to P who found them to be unfit for human consumption. The court held that V could claim the price: title had passed when the carrier arrived and presented his delivery order. From then on the cartons on the pavement were under his control and the loss had occurred after that time.

As a general rule, in the case of wholly unascertained goods, the court will not find that there has been an unconditional appropriation until the seller had done the last act he is required to do under the contract.[5] In the case of unascertained goods sold from a specified source, for instance when part of a bulk consignment already at sea is sold, appropriation may come about in a different way: by exhaustion. Suppose V has bought a consignment of 10,000 tonnes of tapioca at sea on board the bulk transporter 'Palamino'. He contracts to sell 2,000 tonnes to A in Rotterdam, 5,000 tonnes to B in Hamburg and 3,000 tonnes to C in London. The Palamino calls at Hamburg and discharges 5,000 tonnes and then at Rotterdam where it discharges 2,000 tonnes; there are now only 3,000 tonnes left, consigned to C: the remaining tapioca thus becomes his property.[6] The same result is reached wherever goods are to be supplied from a specified source and the bulk is reduced in any way so as to leave only enough to fulfil the particular contract—for example because the remainder is stolen, or evaporates.

There is one final requirement before title can pass under rule 5: the appropriation must be assented to by the buyer (or by the seller if the buyer makes the appropriation, for example when P agrees to buy ten cases of wine from V's cellar and V allows P to go and select ten cases.) In practice the need for assent is of little significance because assent can be express or implied and may be given before or after the appropriation. Thus, if the seller gives notice to the buyer that goods have been set aside for him and are ready for collection and the buyer fails to do anything in response he will be taken to assent, impliedly to the appropriation.[7] In most business contracts the buyer will be taken to impliedly assent in advance to an appropriation to be made by the seller: for example where the contract calls for the seller to arrange for physical delivery. Thus in international contracts where the seller has to ship goods, shipment will be an unconditional appropriation to which the buyer assents in advance. Similarly when goods are ordered to be despatched by post, the act of posting will amount to an unconditional appropriation to which the buyer has assented.[8] The goods thus become the buyer's property as soon as they are posted—and he therefore bears the risk of loss in the post.

The rules as to passing of property in unascertained goods can thus be seen to be complex; their results particularly when coupled with the rule that risk passes with ownership,[9] can be unjust and anomalous—particularly in consumer sales. Thus the rule that when goods are sent through the post title passes on posting may severely prejudice the consumer-buyer: it is doubtful if he will even contemplate the possibility that the goods are his before they arrive, yet they are, and he bears the risk of loss in the post. It is most unlikely that he will think to insure against such loss.

In the context of commercial sales the most serious difficulty is for the buyer who pays before delivery: if title has passed before the goods arrive, he is protected against the seller's insolvency. But if he buys an unascertained part of a larger bulk, no title can pass. If the seller becomes insolvent, the buyer cannot claim the goods and is restricted to claiming as an unsecured creditor. In practice he will get nothing. It is well established that no equitable title to goods can pass before the legal title[10]: the rules in SGA 1979, ss 16–19 are exclusive and so the buyer is unprotected until title passes to him—ie until the goods are ascertained and unconditionally appropriated. Furthermore, this is true even when there are several buyers who between them own the whole of the bulk: in *Re London Wine Co (Shippers) Ltd*[11] a company imported stocks of wine which it sold to customers from its cellars. The customers were given 'certificates of title' and paid in full for 'their' wine, but no bottles were separated out for individual customers. The company passed into receivership and the buyers claimed the wine from the receiver. It was held that they failed—even though they owned all the wine between them there had been no appropriation to individual contracts: no one buyer could point to a bottle or a case and say, 'that is mine'.

In such a situation it would appear to be more just to allow the buyer to recover. The American Uniform Commercial Code[12] would do so, by allowing the buyer and the seller to own proportionate shares in the bulk as tenants in common. Similarly, where the bulk which is to be sold to several buyers contains some defective goods it would seem appropriate to apportion the satisfactory and defective goods amongst the buyers proportionately according to their purchases and allow each to recover a reduction in price, or damages, for the defective part—and indeed, when the defect can be discovered in time and the problem be dealt with by negotiation or arbitration, such a solution may be reached. But if the courts are called upon to decide the dispute, s 16 and rule 5 will apply with full rigour.

283

The problem is that the rule, given statutory form almost 100 years ago, is out of step with modern practice and particularly inappropriate to modern commerce when goods are transported and stored in bulk in ever larger amounts and when so much trading in commodities and futures depends merely on the transfer of documents without ever separating out a particular parcel of goods. Bulk transportation and/or warehousing of commodities causes other problems. The bulk may have been supplied by more than one seller, and in that case, should part prove defective, it will prove impossible to identify the buyer or seller of the defective part. The law offers no solution, although commercial practice, at least in the context of futures dealings in commodities, is to allocate buyers to sellers, and allow them to arbitrate their difficulties, regardless of the true situation. Presumably the parties agree in the hope that, at the end of the day, gains and losses will even themselves out.

1   *Philip Head & Sons Ltd v Showfront Ltd* [1970] 1 Lloyd's Rep 140.
2   *Carlos Federspiel & Co SA v Charles Twigg & Co Ltd* [1957] 1 Lloyds Rep 240 at 255, per Pearson J: bicycles packed in cases bearing buyer's name and address: held–title had not passed; seller still had to ship goods.
3   [1917] 1 KB 337.
4   [1968] 2 QB 663, [1968] 2 All ER 602, CA.
5   See Pearson J in *Carlos Federspiel & Co SA v Charles Twigg & Co Ltd* [1957] 1 Lloyd's Rep 240.
6   *Karlshamus Oljefabriker v Eastport Navigation Corpn, The Elafi* [1982] 1 All ER 208.
7   *Pignatoro v Gilroy* [1919] 1 KB 459, PC.
8   This appears to be the case, on the House of Lords authority of *Badische Anilin und Soda Fabrik v Basle Chemical Works, Bindschedler* [1898] AC 200, HL.
9   SGA 1979, s 20; see 22.1.0.
10   *Re Wait* [1927] 1 Ch 606, CA.
11   (1975) 126 NLJ 977.
12   Ss 2–105(4).

Risk, frustration and loss in contracts of sale

22.1.0   A separate issue which must be dealt with in a contract of sale—or indeed in any transfer of property—is who bears the risk of loss? When speaking of risk we are asking 'Who bears the economic risk of loss or destruction of or damage to the goods?' In short, at least in a business context, we are asking, 'Who should insure against loss?'

The problem in a contract of sale is to decide when risk should be transferred. It is self-evident that, in respect of property which I own, possess and control in a static situation, I bear the risk of loss or damage and should insure against it. But problems arise in a dynamic situation, as in sale, where ownership, possession and control are in motion between transferor and transferee—possibly all moving at different times. Who then is to bear the economic risk at any moment? The answer to the question is particularly important in the context of sale, where ownership itself is transferred, because the question of 'who bears the risk' masks other questions, such as 'Is the buyer liable to pay the price, even though the goods are destroyed?' or 'Is the seller liable to find a replacement to fulfil his contract'. (or, if he cannot do so, is he liable to the buyer for damages for non-delivery, for example when the market has moved and the buyer could have re-sold at a profit?)

The concept of risk and the moment of its passing is thus of vital economic importance to buyer and seller. One might think that they would therefore make provision, then, in their contract to deal with the question: this is certainly done in most (if not all) properly drafted hire or leasing agreements, for instance. However, in a sale, all too often no express provision is made. Many sales are made, after all, on a consumer basis; and whether the buyer is a consumer or businessman, the last thing on his mind at the time he is agreeing to buy is the possibility of the destruction of the object bought. In the absence, then, of express provision, it must be left to the law to provide a general solution.

Before proceeding to examine the actual rules, there is one further point which we should make. The allocation of risk answers the question 'Who pays for loss?' (or 'Who insures against loss?') Thus, if V contracts to sell goods to P, and, the goods are destroyed before the transaction is complete, the rules as to the passing of risk tell us who must bear the economic loss. If risk has passed to P, he must pay the price despite the loss of the goods; if risk was still with V, he cannot sue P for the price.[1] However, other liabilities arise from a contract of sale. If V cannot deliver, he may be liable for damages for non-delivery[2] (for example if the market has risen); if P refuses to take delivery, he may be liable for damages[3] for non-acceptance (if the market has fallen). Risk does not tell us whether the parties are excused those liabilities. The answers to those questions depend on the rules as to frustration of the contract, for frustration will bring the contract to an end and excuse further performance. Thus we will also examine below the rules relating to frustration of the contract, and the related rules covering loss of the goods at an even earlier stage—before the contract is even made.

1   P can recover the price if he has paid in advance.
2   Alternatively, if the goods were unascertained, he can tender replacements; the question then is 'Must he pay for a replacement, or can he simply refuse to deliver?' In practice, of course, even if the goods were specific, P may accept replacements.
3   Under s 27 of the SGA 1979 'It is the duty of the seller to deliver the goods and of the buyer to accept and pay for them, in accordance with the terms of the contract of sale'—see below, Ch 24.

The passing of risk
22.1.1   Section 20 of the SGA 1979 sets out the primary rule that risk of loss passes to the buyer at the same time as property passes, irrespective of whether delivery has been made. It is thus quite clear that risk can pass to the buyer, or remain with the seller, regardless of who has possession of or control over the goods. Risk passes to the buyer when property passes, even if the seller still has possession. In order to decide when risk passes it is necessary to examine again the rules about passing of property, and whether the goods are specific or unascertained. Applying the rules together we may see some surprising results. Thus if the seller delivers goods subject to a reservation of title then, prima facie, he retains also the risk of loss even though the goods are in the buyer's possession. On the other hand, if P buys specific goods from V but asks V to keep them until P can collect later, then the risk passes to P at the time the contract is made; if V's premises are burned down in the interim, P is nevertheless liable for the price; the property lost was his property and he therefore must bear the loss. Such a rule may be particularly prejudicial to a consumer buyer, and has been subjected to criticism. If the goods are unascertained at the time of the contract, no title can pass until they are ascertained, by virtue of SGA 1979, s 16 and therefore risk will not pass until then.

The general rule in s 20 is subject to certain exceptions and to a contrary intention expressed by the parties. It is thus always open to the parties to make express provision for the passing of risk. As we have already observed, very often the parties do not do so; however, the practice of making express provision is growing, as is that of making express provision for the passing of title, and for the same reason, the protection of the seller. Thus, where a seller sells goods subject to a reservation of title, whether in a consumer conditional sale or in a business transaction, it is now common to include a provision that, although property is retained by the seller, risk shall pass to the buyer on delivery; it is also common, and good business practice expressly to require the buyer to insure the goods from the time of delivery, to safeguard the seller's position; in the event that the goods are lost, he will be entitled to claim the proceeds of the insurance.

Just as the court may find an implied intention as to when title shall pass, so the court may find an implied intention as to the passing of risk. In *Sterns Ltd v Vickers Ltd*[1] P agreed to buy 120,000 gallons of spirit which was part of a quantity of 200,000 gallons held in a storage tank by T, a third party, on behalf of V. V gave P a delivery order for 120,000 gallons which would authorise T to deliver 120,000 gallons to P, but P did not collect immediately. Since the spirit thus remained as part of the larger bulk, no title could pass at this stage. When P presented the delivery order to draw off the 120,000 gallons, it was found that the spirit had deteriorated. P argued that risk remained with V and claimed that he was therefore entitled to reject the goods. The Court of Appeal however held that even though no title could pass until the contract goods were ascertained from bulk, risk had passed to P when the delivery order was issued, enabling P to collect the goods, and T accepted that order. From that time T held the spirit in proportionate parts for V and P. Since P decided to leave the spirit in the tank it seems proper that he should therefore take the risk; V had done everything necessary to enable P to take possession. However, the case is probably exceptional, and raises interesting problems. For instance, as Atiyah postulates,[2] suppose V owns 200,000 gallons held in two tanks, and only the contents of one tank deteriorate. Can P then claim the whole of the good spirit, or must he take all of the bad or a proportionate share of both?

Section 20 creates two express exceptions to the general rule. First, if delivery is delayed through the fault of either party, then that party bears the risk of any loss caused by the delay: for instance, on Monday, P agrees to buy a desk and V agrees to deliver on Wednesday; however V's van breaks down on Wednesday and he cannot deliver; he bears the risk of any loss from then until he delivers. The position would be different if P called V and asked him not to deliver until Friday; he would then be at fault.

Secondly, when either buyer or seller is in possession of the goods as bailee, he is liable to the other as a bailee. He must take reasonable care of the goods, and he must abide strictly by any agreed terms. He is liable for loss caused by his negligence, but not for purely accidental loss—unless he departs from the agreed terms. For instance, V sells to P; title passes at once, and with it, risk. They agree that V shall deliver in two days. In the interim he is to keep the goods in his warehouse. V is a bailee. If due to his carelessness the goods are stolen, he is liable for the loss. He is not liable if the warehouse is burned down by a purely accidental fire. However, if the parties had agreed that V should store the goods in his shop pending delivery but V stored them in his warehouse, V would be strictly liable for any loss, because of his deviation from the terms of the bailment.[3]

1 [1923] 1 KB 78, CA.
2 *The Sale of Goods* (7th edn, 1985) p 246.
3 Similarly where a buyer receives goods subject to a reservation of title the buyer will owe the duties of a bailee to the seller; when goods are delivered on a sale or return/approval basis, the buyer is a bailee; it is possible that an act by him which causes damage to the goods will operate to pass title to him and, with it, risk.

Risk of loss during delivery

22.1.2 Obviously where goods are to be physically delivered to the buyer there is a real risk of loss or damage to the goods during transit: a lorry may be involved in an accident; or delay may cause deterioration, especially if the goods are perishable. Obviously, the rules about passing of ownership and risk which we have already examined may deal with the situation, but two sections of the act dealing with physical delivery may also impinge upon the issue. First, when the seller is required to send the goods to the buyer and delivers them to a carrier for that purpose, then that is treated as delivery to the buyer,[1] provided the carrier is independent of the seller.[2] Thus, as between seller and buyer, the buyer is regarded as in possession.[3] However, if pursuant to the contract the seller is required to deliver to some specified place, for instance the buyer's premises, then he has not delivered until the goods arrive there and the carrier will be treated as the seller's agent, and the seller will be in possession during transit.[4]

When the seller does deliver by handing goods to a carrier who holds on behalf of the buyer, then the seller must make 'such contract with the carrier . . . as may be reasonable having regard to the nature of the goods and the other circumstances of the case . . .' and if he fails so to do, the seller may be liable for any loss during transit.[5] The seller must therefore make a contract which will allow the buyer to claim against the carrier in the event of loss during transit, and not accept (for instance) an excessively wide exclusion clause.

A further specific provision deals with carriage by sea. Again, for the protection of the buyer, the seller is required to give the buyer such information as will allow the buyer to arrange insurance during transit; if he fails so to do, the seller remains at risk in the event of loss during transit.[6]

We have seen that when the seller contracts to deliver the goods at the buyer's premises, he does not fulfil his contract until the goods arrive. However, in the event of loss during transit, s 33 provides that the buyer must, nevertheless, (unless otherwise agreed) take any risk of deterioration in the goods necessarily incident to the course of transit. This provision is of little practical importance in modern circumstances. First, modern methods of delivery, when goods can be delivered speedily by road or rail and when there are sophisticated packing and refrigeration methods available to protect the goods in transit, should minimise the risk of loss. Second, the section only protects the seller against liability due to ordinary risk of transit: it will not protect him if loss is caused by his own failure to take care. Third, it will not apply in the case of perishable goods when, as we have seen, the implied term of merchantable quality requires that goods should be merchantable when delivered and for a reasonable time afterwards.[7] Professor Goode suggests an example of when s 33 would apply: if V contracts to sell and deliver explosives to P whose premises can only be reached by a bumpy and uneven cart truck; P must bear the risk of loss on that journey.[8]

1   SGA 1979, s 32(1).
2   If the carrier is the seller's employee, the seller is still in possession. If the carrier is the seller's agent, the seller is treated as being in possession.
3   The buyer is therefore liable as a bailee. The basic rule is still, of course, that risk only passes with ownership.
4   The carrier is then the seller's agent: see above. The seller is liable as bailee, even if risk and ownership have passed; but the seller's liability may be modified as SGA 1979, s 33: see below.
5   SGA 1979, s 32(2).
6   SGA 1979, s 32(3).
7   *Mash & Murrell Ltd v Joseph I Emanuel Ltd* [1961] 1 All ER 485, [1961] 1 WLR 862, applying SGA 1979, s 14. See 21.2.0.
8   Goode, *Commercial Law* (1982) p 212.

Mistake and frustration
22.1.3   We have seen that the rules as to passing of risk answer the question of who must pay for the loss of goods; if they are destroyed when at the buyer's risk he must still pay the price. If the goods are lost whilst at the seller's risk, he will not be able to claim the price. But can he be required to deliver, that is, to find alternative goods, as a replacement, or to pay damages for non-delivery? The answer may be vital if the market has moved, so that the cost of replacement goods or the damages payable to the buyer may be substantial, and that answer is to be found in the separate, but related, provisions dealing with mistake and frustration.[1]

We have already discussed the general rules of mistake and frustration in contract. The SGA 1979 contains special rules governing similar situations in sale of goods contracts. These rules are contained in ss 6 and 7 of the Act which provide respectively:

Where there is a contract for the sale of specific goods, and the goods without the knowledge of the seller have perished at the time when the contract is made, the contract is void (s 6). Where there is an agreement to sell specific goods, and subsequently the goods, without any fault on the part of the seller or buyer, perish before the risk passes to the buyer, the agreement is thereby avoided (s 7).

The sections are dealing with loss of the goods at different times. Section 6 deals with the possible perishing of the goods before the contract is made, and mirrors the common law rules of mistake. Section 7 deals with them perishing after the contract is made but before risk has passed to the buyer, mirroring the rules of frustration. Once risk has passed, of course, the buyer bears the risk of loss and the loss of the goods can have no effect on the contract.

Although dealing with loss at different times, ss 6 and 7 both have similar effects since under them the effect of the loss of the goods will be to release the parties from the obligation to perform the contract—ie if they apply, the seller will not be liable for non-delivery. Second, both sections refer to the goods having 'perished' and we must first ask what is meant by 'perishing'. There are very few decisions on the meaning of 'perish' in the context of the SGA 1979. However, there are decisions on the meaning of the word in other contexts, particularly in relation to insurance claims, where the word is used. Clearly goods have perished if they have been totally and irretrievably destroyed. However, deterioration of the goods less than total destruction will also be interpreted as perishing. The leading case is *Asfar & Co v Blundell*[2] where the cargo of dates was on board a ship which sank. Insurance underwriters argued that the dates had not perished; they were a pulpy mass, soaked in sea water and impregnated by sewage, but still existed. Not surprisingly, the court did not accept that argument which 'might commend itself to a body of chemists, but not to businessmen. We are dealing with dates as a subject matter of commerce . . . [The] test is whether, as a matter of business, the nature of the thing has been altered.'[3]

The generally accepted view is that goods have 'perished' within the meaning of the Act when they cease to be merchantable in accordance with the contract. However, that interpretation does create problems: for if goods have perished when they cease to be merchantable, ss 6 and 7 overlap the implied condition of merchantable quality in s 14 of the Act. The difficulty is that under s 14, if the seller delivers goods which are not merchantable, the buyer can treat the contract as repudiated: he can reject the goods and reclaim the price, if paid; but he can also claim damages for consequential loss, for instance, damages for non-delivery, if the market price of similar goods has risen, or damages for other injury or damage caused by the goods. But if the contract is void or avoided by virtue of the goods having perished under ss 6 or s 7, then the seller has no liability under the contract and he is excused liability for damages for non-delivery. It is suggested that, to avoid such difficulties, ss 6 and 7 will never apply when the goods are actually delivered, or where the seller ought to have known of their condition, they will only apply when the goods have deteriorated; they must once have been merchantable and have ceased to be so.

However, 'perishing' also covers situations other than the physical deterioration of the goods. Thus it has been held that goods have perished where they have been stolen. In *Barrow, Lane & Ballard Ltd v Phillip Phillips & Co Ltd*[4] there was a contract for the sale of 700 bags of nuts; at the time of the contract, in fact, there were only 591 bags in the warehouse; the others, presumably, had been stolen. It was held that the goods had perished. However, it is not clear if goods will always be treated as perished when stolen; for instance, a car may be stolen but later be recovered: will it be treated as 'perished' immediately? If not, when will hope of recovering the car be abandoned?

What is clear is that the vendor cannot break his contract with P to sell to another purchaser, (as he might wish to do when the market price has risen dramatically since he made the contract with P) and then try to meet P's claim for non-delivery by relying on s 7: the goods have not then perished.[5]

Having seen when goods will be said to have 'perished', we can look at the detailed rules in ss 6 and 7. Section 6 parallels the common law of mistake, and, indeed, it is thought that it is based on the case of *Couturier v Hastie*,[6] which is generally treated as a case of mistake. The first thing to note is that the section only applies to contracts to sell specific goods; if the contract is for unascertained goods, then it is clearly impossible for them to perish before the contract is made: until the goods became ascertained, there are no contract goods capable of perishing. Even if the seller has a particular source of supply in mind and that source of supply is destroyed, for instance he contracts to supply a new Vauxhall Astra intending to obtain it from a particular supplier and, unknown to him, his supplier's premises and entire stock of cars has been destroyed by fire, then he will not be protected by s 6. However, if the contract requires him to use a particular source—ie the

289

contract is for unascertained goods from a specific bulk—although s 6 will not apply, the ordinary common law rules of mistake may well vitiate the contract.

Second, s 6 only applies when the goods have perished without the knowledge of the seller; obviously, because common sense dictates that if the seller contracts to sell goods knowing that they have already been destroyed he should not be able to escape liability for what amounts to fraud.

Problems are caused by the decision in *McRae v Commonwealth Disposals Commission*,[7] when the defendants contracted to sell to the plaintiffs a named wreck on a named reef. In fact, as neither party realised, neither the reef nor the wreck had ever existed. The plaintiffs claimed the cost of equipping an expedition to recover the wreck as damages for breach of contract; the defendants argued that the contract was void for mistake. The court held that the contract was not void: the defendants had impliedly warranted that the goods existed: ie, they had agreed to bear the risk of there being no wreck. It is argued[8] that s 6 can similarly be excluded by the parties' intention, expressly or impliedly; alternatively *McRae* may be explained on the basis that s 6 cannot apply when the goods have never existed at all.

If s 6 does apply, then the contract is void, just as for mistake. Thus neither party need perform the contract; the seller cannot demand the price, but he will not be liable for non-delivery. There never was a contract.

Section 7 is likewise limited to contracts for specific goods. It is concerned with the perishing of the goods, without the fault of either party, between the making of the contract and the passing of risk to the buyer. It will be apparent then that s 7 will only apply where either of the parties expressly or impliedly includes a reservation of title in favour of the seller, or where s 18 rule 2 or 3 apply. It can never apply to contracts covered by s 18 rule 1, where specific goods are in a deliverable state at the time of the contract and there is no contrary intention, because their ownership, and, with it, risk of loss, will pass when the contract is made. Section 7 will not apply to contracts for unascertained goods, but such contracts could, of course, be frustrated, in which case the common law rules relating to frustration apply; this will be so particularly when the goods are, under the contract, to be from a specified source: if the whole of the goods available at that source are destroyed, the contract will be frustrated.

When s 7 does apply, the effect is to avoid the contract and is therefore as if the contract had been frustrated. However, the rules of the Law Reform (Frustrated Contracts) Act 1943 do not apply.[9] Instead, the parties are released from any obligation further to perform the contract; the seller is absolved from the need to deliver and the buyer can recover the price if he has already paid it. If the contract is frustrated by any other reason than the perishing of the goods, for instance in an international sale, economic sanctions are imposed by the government against the buyer's country, preventing the export of the goods, then the more sophisticated rules in the Law Reform (Frustrated Contracts) Act 1943 will apply: thus, if the seller has incurred expense in preparing to perform the contract (for instance: he has spent money to put the goods into a deliverable state) then he can retain part of any advance payment made by the buyer to offset these costs.

It is far from clear what will happen if only part of the contract goods perish. In *Barrow, Lane and Ballard Ltd v Phillip Phillips & Co Ltd*[10] mentioned above, s 7 was held to apply when 109 out of 700 sacks of nuts had disappeared. However, in that case the sellers were claiming the price of the 109 sacks, and the court merely held that they could not: it is not clear what would have happened had the buyers refused to take the 591 bags which remained. In *H R & S Sainsbury Ltd v Street*[11] V contracted to sell P 275 tons of barley to be grown on his farm. Due to crop failures the crop produced was only 140 tons. Taking advantage of the price rise caused by the shortage, V sold the 140 tons to another buyer, and when P sued him for damages for non-delivery, sought to escape liability on the grounds that the contract was frustrated. Not surprisingly, the court held that he could not do so: the contract was valid and V was bound to offer the 140 tons to P; however, it is still not clear whether, had he done so, P would have been bound to accept.

It is thus apparent that ss 6 and 7 are not without difficulties. However, the difficulties are mostly theoretical, because in practice, despite the apparent importance of the rules as a protection against a claim for non-delivery in a rising market, the sections are rarely invoked: as we have seen there are few decisions on the meaning of 'perishing' and the problems raised by cases like *H R & S Sainsbury v Street* are not worked out; and, to date, there is only one reported decision on the Law Reform (Frustrated Contracts) Act 1943. This may well reflect a distrust in businessmen of the legal rules of frustration and mistake. Alternatively, it may merely indicate that in practice businessmen are willing and able to reach practical and naturally beneficial solutions, perhaps negotiated out of the need to preserve goodwill for the benefit of a future trading relationship without invoking technical and often arbitrary legal rules. Thus, no doubt, even when a contract is for the sale of specific goods and those goods perish, the practical solution may be that, regardless of the legal niceties, both parties will prefer to try to find replacement goods to fulfil the contract, rather than make a claim for non-delivery. Alternatively, the parties may in fact deal with the possibility in advance by including appropriate clauses in their contract— for instance, the contract may deal with the possibility of price fluctuations and require the buyer to pay a higher price in the event of price variation; alternatively a force majeure clause may excuse non-performance caused by events outside the parties' control, such as weather conditions, strikes shortages and the like. In the past when such clauses have come before them the courts have interpreted such clauses very restrictively, and perhaps unrealistically, in the 1983 case *Andre et Cie SA v Tradax Export SA*[12] the Court of Appeal recognised this and suggested that in future the courts should have regard to the wider commercial context, and perhaps in future such clauses may be allowed to be more effective.

1 See 15.0.1 and 17.0.4.
2 [1896] 1 QB 123, CA.
3 Lord Esher, 127.
4 [1929] 1 KB 574.
5 *Goodey and Southwold Trawlers Ltd v Garriock, Mason and Millgate* [1972] 2 Lloyd's Rep 369.
6 (1856) 5 HL Cas 673.
7 (1950) 84 CLR 377.
8 See Atiyah *The Sale of Goods* p 64; Treitel, *The Law of Contract* (1984) pp 219–20.
9 See 17.0.3.
10 [1929] 1 KB 574.
11 [1972] 3 All ER 1127, [1972] 1 WLR 834.
12 [1983] 1 Lloyd's Rep 254, CA.

22.1.4 Passing of Property and Risk in Contracts of Sale

Consumers—passing of property and risk

22.1.4 In the context of the consumer transaction, the rules on the passing of risk have been described as 'grotesque'.[1] Imagine the following transaction. On Saturday P, a consumer, visits a furniture store; he chooses an 'ex-display' wardrobe included in a sale and agrees to buy it and it is agreed that the store will deliver on the following Monday. The goods are specific, and therefore title, and with it, risk, passes when the contract is made. On Sunday, without any fault or lack of care on the part of the store,[2] its premises are burned down. The wardrobe is destroyed. P remains liable for the price.

Even more anomalous is the situation where P buys, for example, a new refrigerator, to be delivered by V in his van the following day. The refrigerator is to be taken by V from his stock of such refrigerators in store. It is therefore unascertained goods, and no title, or risk, can pass until the goods are ascertained. If the refrigerator is taken from store, it becomes ascertained, but whilst in the hands of V's employee is not unconditionally appropriated to P's contract;[3] it is therefore at V's risk until actually delivered at P's premises. On the other hand, if V is to employ an independent carrier, then the carrier will be P's agent.[4] V has to deliver 3 such refrigerators and hands them, together with details of the deliveries, to the carrier. If the delivery van is involved in an accident whilst at least two refrigerators are on board, then the goods remain unascertained, title has not passed and V must bear the risk. On the other hand, if the carrier has delivered two refrigerators before the accident, the goods became ascertained by exhaustion and title and risk pass to P who must therefore pay the price.

The results are clearly complex, and even the straightforward example given first above is probably contrary to the natural expectation of most consumers. Furthermore, the rule linking risk with ownership rather than possession is capable of causing real financial hardship to consumers, since it is unlikely that their general household contracts insurance would cover the loss. However, in practice it is unlikely that retailers would require consumers to bear the risk in such a case. In surveys cited by Cranston[5] the majority of suppliers, either through ignorance of the strict rule or concern to maintain customer goodwill, indicated that they would expect to bear the loss in such situations; furthermore, their insurance would probably be sufficient to cover the loss in such situations.

Why, it may be asked, if the legal rules cause little hardship in practice, bother to complain about them? The answer is that the function of the law is to provide a solution in the case where the parties cannot reach an agreed solution; furthermore, it should provide a clear and certain framework within which agreed solutions can be worked out. The law which regulates business transactions must be responsive to and reflect current business practice, and if it fails to do so it will be ignored in most cases and cause hardship in the few in which it is not. As Gilmour has pointed out,[6] the current rules favour sellers because they were worked out in the last century at a time when the policy of the law was preoccupied with promoting commercial activity at all costs. As has already been observed there is no conceptual need for risk to be linked with ownership, and there is much to be said for abandoning that rule and replacing it with one linking risk to possession in accordance with the expectation of the public and commercial community.

1 Atiyah *The Sale of Goods* (7th ed. 1985) p 249.
2 The store is of course a bailee and will be liable for loss caused by its failure to take care.
3 Delivery to the store's employee does not constitute delivery to a carrier for the purpose of s 18, rule 5(2).
4 Section 18, rule 5(2); s 32(1).
5 Cranston, *Consumers and the Law* (2nd edn. 1984) p 169.
6 Grant Gilmour, 'Products Liability: A Commentary' (1970) 38 U Chi, Law Rev 103; 112–114.

Chapter 23

Who Can Pass Title in Contracts of Sale?

23.0.0 In addition to the rules dealing with the time when title passes, the law has also developed a series of rules as to who can pass title to goods Indeed, the two sets of rules are interrelated because a party who has agreed to buy and has obtained possession of goods may purport to resell them: if he then fails to pay, the rules as to the time when ownership passes tell us that no title had passed to the first buyer, while the rules as to who can pass title deal with the question of whether any title is obtained by the sub-buyer.

In a society which allows private ownership of property, many disputes will arise between competing claimants to property. In the case of land such disputes, at least in so far as they relate to the actual land itself rather than to some linked right in or over it, are more easily avoided, because interests in land tend to greater permanence than those in goods and title to land is recorded in documentary form and all dealings with land are preceded by a thorough investigation of the documentary title. Interests in goods, on the other hand, tend to be less permanent in their duration, and, indeed, the essence of commerce in a capitalist society is that property, and particularly personal property such as goods should be freely alienable and should move and circulate from hand to hand within the economy. At the same time documentary recording of title to personal property and dealings with it is clearly inappropriate for those very same reasons. There is thus greater scope for title conflicts to arise, and with the growth of commerce and the need for goods to circulate, the scope for such conflicts has increased.

Title conflicts can arise in a number of ways. As we have seen, the seller may let his buyer have possession, retaining title to secure payment of the price. If the buyer fails to pay, he will want to recover the goods, but if the buyer has sold on to a sub-buyer, then a conflict arises between seller and sub-buyer. Alternatively, the owner may entrust the goods to a bailee to store, or to an agent to sell; the bailee or agent sells the goods and disappears; the owner will wish to reclaim the goods from the buyer. Or in the most obvious case of all, the goods are stolen from O, their owner. The thief then (perhaps after a series of 'fencing' transactions) sells the goods to an innocent buyer, in whose hands they are found. O, the dispossessed owner, now reclaims the goods. We have in fact already seen examples of this type of situation: the cases involving the effect upon a contract of 'mistaken identity' illustrate the point. Thus in *Ingram v Little* the plaintiffs alleged that they made their contract with 'Hutchinson' whilst labouring under a mistake, because the effect of a mistake is to make the contract void; a void contract has no effect so that 'Hutchinson' never acquired title to the car and therefore no title could have passed to the defendant.

We should stress that although the conflicting claims we have outlined above involved competing claims to the outright ownership of an asset, such disputes may arise between a dispossessed owner and someone who has acquired only a limited interest, for instance a pledgee to whom the thief has pledged goods, or a bank to whom they have been charged.

We have spoken of a dispute between the dispossessed owner and the third party. Obviously, each of them has, in theory, a claim against the real villain of the piece, the thief, defaulting bailee or fraudulent agent. Thus the dispossessed owner can sue anyone who has dealt with his property in such a way as to deny his title in the tort of conversion. Furthermore where there is some contractual relationship between the two, for instance when the owner has bailed the goods, or has entered into a contract of agency, the owner will have a claim for breach of contract. The third party, on the other hand, will have a claim against his vendor for the return of the price he paid for the goods and for damages, under SGA 1979, s 12, which implies into the sale contract a condition that the vendor is the owner of them, a condition which cannot be excluded. However, such claims are, in practice, generally illusory. The middleman, or 'rogue' as he is often called, will either have vanished altogether, or, even if he can be traced, have no money and will not be worth suing. At best, when for instance a buyer in possession of goods subject to a reservation of title sells them on to a sub-buyer, he will have become insolvent. The dispute then boils down to a claim by the original owner for the return of the goods, or their value, against the new possessor. Such a claim will be framed in the tort of conversion, where any person who deals with another's goods in such a way as to deny his title to them, for instance by refusing to hand them over on request, can be made to hand over the goods or pay their value and, in addition, pay damages. Such liability is strict; the third party will be liable even though he is perfectly honest and reasonably believes that he is the owner.

It will be readily apparent that in such proceedings the dispute is really between two innocent parties. As Lord Denning has observed:

'In the development of our law, two principles have striven for mastery. The first is for protection of property; no one can give a better title than he himself possesses. The second is for the protection of commercial transactions; the person who takes in good faith and for value without notice should get a good title.'[2]

In deciding which of these two principles should prevail, the law must decide which of the two innocent parties should bear the loss occasioned by the fraud of the 'rogue'. 'Whatever the solution, an innocent party suffers: the original owner of the property; the innocent purchaser; or a merchant who has bona fide dealt with it'.[3] This is because the law tends to adopt an 'all or nothing' solution to such problems; one party must win, the other lose; and yet much can be said for a middle way, for allowing the court to apportion the loss between the parties. This has been recognised even by eminent judges:

'. . . The relevant question in this sort of case . . . is . . . which of two innocent parties shall suffer for the fraud of a third. The plain answer is

295

that the loss should be divided between them in such proportion as is just in all the circumstances. If it be pure misfortune, the loss should be borne equally; if the fault or imprudence of either party has caused or contributed to the loss, it should be borne by that party in the whole or in the greater part.'⁴

Such calls have, however, gone unheeded. The solution of the law is 'all or nothing' and, as Lord Denning indicated, the law has developed in this regard. The earliest solution was that the original owner should always prevail and could recover his property in all cases; the common law rule was expressed in the maxim 'nemo dat quod non habet' (no one can have a better title than he himself has) and that rule is restated in s 21 of the Act. However, the growth of commerce and the need for goods and finance to circulate, and with it the need for certainty in such transactions, produced a need for greater protection for purchasers and so a number of exceptions to the rule grew up at common law. Those are also retained by the SGA 1979 and are restated by the Act, along with some other purely statutory exceptions.

As we indicated above, s 21 of the SGA 1979 preserves the common law and states that where goods are sold by a person who is not their owner, and who does not sell them under the authority or with the consent of the owner, the buyer acquires no better title to the goods than the seller, unless the owner of the goods is by his conduct precluded from denying the seller's authority to sell.

It will be seen that s 21 itself contains several exceptions to the general rule. The subsequent sections then set out certain other statutory exceptions. There is no discernible policy underlying or linking the exceptions; they are merely specific situations where the general rule is abrogated. However, in several cases the fact that a non-owner was in possession⁵ of goods may enable him to pass a good title to a buyer, illustrating the recognition in English law of the importance of possession of goods. It is also true that many of the exceptions do overlap, so that the law is not always as clear as it might be. We will now look at the exceptions in detail.

1   [1961] 1 QB 31, [1960] 3 All ER 332, CA. See 15.0.1.
2   Denning LJ in *Bishopsgate Motor Finance Corpn Ltd v Transport Brakes Ltd* [1949] 1 KB 322, [1949] 1 All ER 37, CA.
3   Hahlo, *Sale of Another Person's Property* (Quebec Civil Code Revision Commission).
4   Devlin LJ (dissenting) in *Ingram v Little* [1961] 1 QB 31 at 38, CA.
5   Although in none of the cases is possession alone sufficient.

Agency and estoppel
23.0.1   Section 21 itself preserves at least four classes of exception to the general rule; we deal here with three which overlap. Thus s 21 provides that a non-owner can pass title if he sells with the owner's consent, in other words, if he is an agent. The section goes on to refer (indirectly) to a particular type of agency, mercantile agency, to which special rules apply. Finally, a buyer from a non-owner will acquire title if the true owner is 'precluded by his contract from denying the seller's title to sell', covering the situations where the seller is held out by the true owner as his agent, or as the owner of the goods.

A great amount of business is conducted through agents, and in order to protect commercial transactions it is obvious that the buyer from an agent should get good title. When an agent does conclude a contract on behalf of his principal, the principal is bound by the contract and there is a direct contractual relationship between principal and third party so that title to goods passes directly. When the contract concluded by the agent is within his actual authority—ie in accordance with the express instructions given to him—the principal will have no complaint, or at least cannot be heard to make any complaint. However, in certain circumstances an agent may have authority, in law, beyond that actually given to him. Thus the agent may have implied authority; he may have the usual authority given to agents in his particular profession or business; or the third party may be able to rely on the agent's apparent authority. This arises when the third party is allowed to rely on a representation by the principal—ie the owner of the goods—by words or by conduct, that the agent has greater authority than he appears to have. In all these cases, the third party can rely on the agency and will take a good title; the principal will be able to sue the agent for breach of contract and/or his duties as an agent, if he departs from the actual authority given. We will examine these situations again in more detail below in the context of the law of agency. However, we should make clear at this stage, in relation to apparent authority, first that the representation relied on by the third party must be made by the owner; the third party cannot rely on the agent's own assertion of authority, otherwise every thief could claim to be an agent and bind the true owner to his disposition of property. If an agent claims authority which he does not have, the third party may sue him for breach of his warranty of authority. Second, the mere delivery of property by its owner to another will not create an apparent authority.

What happens if the owner gives property to his agent to sell, together with specific instructions, and the agent sells outside the scope of those instructions—ie he exceeds his authority? For instance, O gives his car to A and asks him to sell it 'for not less than £800;' A sells the car to T for £500. Is O bound by the sale, or can he reclaim the car? The answer may, of course, depend on whether A's actual authority was extended by any implied, usual or apparent authority. But in the absence of any such extension the answer is, that it depends on whether A is a professional or an amateur. If he is an amateur—for instance selling the car for a friend, then O is not bound and can reclaim the car. But if it is A's business to sell cars or goods on behalf of their owners, he will be a mercantile agent and his disposition will bind O; T will then get a good title to the car.

Mercantile agency was recognised at common law; the concept was vital for the conduct of commerce, for such is the volume of business done through agents that business relations would be hopelessly uncertain if purchasers from known professional agents could not rely on their authority to sell and take the goods with certainty. However, at common law only a purchaser from a mercantile agent was protected and, as it became apparent that commercial agents might deal with goods other than by outright sale, it became necessary to protect these transactions also. That was done by the Factors Acts. S 2(1) of the Factors Act 1889 provides as follows:

> 'When a mercantile agent is, with the consent of the owner, in posses-
> sion of goods or of the documents of title to goods, any sale, pledge or
> other disposition of the goods made by him when acting in the ordinary
> course of business as a mercantile agent, shall, subject to the provisions
> of this Act, be as valid as if he were expressly authorised by the owner

297

of the goods to make the same; provided that the person taking under the disposition acts in good faith, and has not, at the time of the disposition, notice that the person making the disposition has not authority to make the same.'

Section 21 of the SGA 1979 expressly preserves the provisions of the Factors Act as an exception to the nemo dat rule, and we must now examine the various requirements of s 2(1) of the Factors Act which must be fulfilled before a mercantile agency is created and a buyer or other disposee from an agent can claim a good title.

a)   The agent must be a mercantile agent
We have already said that this means that he must be a professional agent; it must be his business to sell as an agent. Thus when a car was delivered on, hire purchase terms to a company whose business was the hire of cars and which occasionally sold cars from its own fleet, the company was not a mercantile agent and could not sell the car so as to pass good title to the buyer: it never, as part of its business sold vehicles on behalf of others.[1] The phrase is defined in s 1 of the Factors Act: 'a mercantile agent having in the customary course of his business as such agent authority either to sell goods or to consign goods for the purpose of sale, or to buy goods, or to raise money on the security of goods.' However, although the mercantile agent must be a professional, acting in the course of a business, he will qualify even if he acts for only one principal[2] and if the transaction in question is his first as a mercantile agent: as Atiyah comments, 'every business must have a beginning.'[3]

b)   The agent must be in possession of the goods, or of the documents of title to the goods
It should be noted that documents of title include both recognised title documents, such as a bill of lading, and other documents, such as warehouse documents and the like which are used in the course of business as 'proof of possession or control of goods' or which 'authorise or purport to authorise' the transfer of the goods represented. However, a car registration document has been held not to be a document of title.[4]

c)   The agent must have obtained possession of the goods with the consent of the owner
This requirement is rather more important and has generated a certain amount of case law. The starting point is that the owner's consent to the agent's possession is presumed in the absence of evidence.[5] It is therefore up to the owner to show that he did not give his consent. The authority of a line of cases involving fraudulent sales of motor cars is that it makes no difference that the agent obtains consent by a trick.[6]

Once consent has been given, its withdrawal or termination has no effect on a subsequent sale by the agent unless the buyer knows that consent has been withdrawn.[7]

d)   Possession must have been given to the agent for some purpose connected with sale[8]
The law draws a distinction between the situation when the agent has possession of the goods to sell them, or for some related purpose, for

instance to display them and receive offers, and that where he has the goods for some purpose wholly unconnected with sale. In the first case the buyer gets good title; in the second he does not. Thus if I give my car to the garage proprietor to display on his forecourt and receive offers for it, he is a mercantile agent and, if he sells the car, I will be bound. On the other hand, if I leave my car with him to repair and he sells it instead, I can reclaim the vehicle. The distinction may seem odd: presumably in either case it is part of the garage's business to sell cars and, in either case the third party buyer is equally taken in. It can perhaps only be explained in the historical context of the rule, which was designed for the protection of regular commercial trading when it was perhaps less likely that the mercantile agents in question would combine the businesses of repair or storage, with sale. Were the rule otherwise, the owner would always lose his goods if they were sold by his bailee, for instance a warehouseman, and English law has always declined to hold that a voluntary parting with possession is enough to allow the owner of goods to be divested of his title.

A related point is that the agent must have been in business as a mercantile agent at the time he received possession for sale; it is not enough if he becomes a professional agent after he receives possession of the goods.[9]

e) The sale must be in the ordinary course of business of a mercantile agent
This requirement goes further than the requirement that the agent should be a professional. It requires that the sale must be in the form of a normal business transaction: for instance, the sale must be conducted in ordinary business hours, from business premises; in fact it tends to overlap with the requirement that the buyer should act in good faith because, effectively, it means that there must be nothing suspicious about the circumstances of the sale: for instance a sale of a car in a lay-by at midnight would not be a sale in the ordinary course of business—(in the absence of extenuating circumstances). Of course, different trades or businesses will have different, special requirements: thus, for instance, it has been held that a sale of a car without its logbook[10] (registration document) or ignition key[11] would not be a sale in the course of business.

f) The purchaser must act in good faith and take the goods without notice that the agent has no authority to sell
Mercantile agency operates as an exception to the nemo dat rule to pass title to the purchaser. The law has always been reluctant to divest an owner of his title to property except in the most extreme of cases. As we have seen, the mercantile agency exception was created to protect commercial transactions; however, the exception is needed only because a choice must be made between two innocent victims of the agent's wrongdoing. If the buyer is not an innocent victim, the law reverts to the protection of the original owner. It is for the buyer to prove that he acted in good faith and without notice of a lack of authority.[12]

We have seen the historical need for the mercantile agency exception, on the grounds of certainty in commercial transactions. The justice of the rule seems clear; the owner picks his agent, and he is clearly better placed than the buyer to vet his honesty. He, after all, acts through an agent for some benefit to himself, and therefore should bear the risk of any loss caused by the dishonesty of the agent. Indeed, it can be said that, hedged about with restrictions as it is, the rule does not give sufficient protection to the buyer.

However, it should be noted that the original commercial purpose of the rule is now of less importance than it was, and most of the recent cases on the rule have involved the dishonest sale of motor vehicles being leased under hire purchase agreements.

The third exception, based on estoppel, is obviously similar in many ways to that when an agent has apparent authority, sometimes called 'agency by estoppel'. It is noteworthy that in many cases a buyer of goods will alternatively claim he has acquired title on this basis or by purchasing from a mercantile agent.[13] However, this estoppel differs from that which raises an apparent agency, in that although each is based on a representation by the owner of the goods, in the case of apparent agency the representation is that the third party is an agent with authority to sell; in this case the representation is that the third party is the owner of the goods.

The basis of the exception, then, is a representation by the owner of the goods. That representation may be made in words or by conduct: for instance if I stand by and allow someone else to negotiate for and sell my property as if it were his, I will not be able to claim back the property: I will be estopped. It has been held that when the owner of a van completed hire purchase forms in blank to allow a car dealer to pretend to be the owner of the van as part of an elaborate fraud on a hire purchase company, he was by his conduct precluded from denying the dealer's title to sell the van, even though the dealer sold for his own purposes rather than for the jointly planned fraud.[14]

However, it is well established that the owner will not be estopped in this way merely because he parts with possession of his property.[15] Further, it seems that mere carelessness in relation to one's own property will not be enough to estop the owner.

> 'If I lose a valuable dog and find it afterwards in the possession of a gentleman who bought it from somebody whom he believed to be the owner, it is no answer to me to say that he would never have been cheated into buying the dog if I had chained it up, or put a collar on it, or kept it under proper control. If a person leaves a watch or a ring on a seat in the park or on a table at a cafe and it ultimately gets into the hands of a bona fide purchaser it is no answer to the true owner to say that it was his carelessness and nothing else that enabled the finder to pass it off as his own.'[16]

Thus when a car dealer handed over possession of a car and its unsigned registration document to a plausible 'purchaser' before he had received approval of the necessary hire purchase proposal, the Court of Appeal by a majority, and despite a strong dissent from Denning LJ, held that the owner was not estopped by his conduct from recovering the car.[17] More recent cases have tended to approach the issue of 'estoppel by negligence' as part of the general law of negligence. It is not enough to create liability in negligence that a person should be careless; he must have owed a duty of care to the person who has suffered loss. In *Mercantile Credit Co Ltd v Hamblin*[18] a woman signed blank forms believing them to be forms to enable her to obtain a loan on the security of her Jaguar car. In fact they allowed the dealer involved to appear as owner of the car and submit a hire purchase proposal to the plaintiff finance company. The Court of Appeal held that the woman did owe a duty of care to the finance company in signing the form, but, on the facts, she had not been careless because it was reasonable for her to trust the dealer whom she knew socially and who appeared respectable.

The decision of the House of Lords in *Moorgate Mercantile Co Ltd v Twitchings*[19] makes establishing an estoppel by negligence more difficult than hitherto. The case involved the registration of hire purchase agreements with Hire Purchase Information, a body set up by finance companies to register hire purchase agreements in respect of motor vehicles and to give such information to members (and to bodies like the AA and the police) to try and avoid frauds by persons attempting to sell cars which they held under hire purchase contracts. Both plaintiffs and defendants were members of HPI; the defendants received a proposal in respect of a car and made the usual search with HPI. There was, apparently, no agreement registered and the defendants therefore accepted the proposal and bought the car. In fact the car was owned by the plaintiff company and let out on a hire purchase agreement. It appeared that the plaintiffs had failed to register the agreement. However, despite the general practice of hire purchase companies (98% of which were members of HPI), a bare majority of the House of Lords held that the plaintiffs owed no duty of care to other companies, including the defendants, and so could not be estopped by negligence. They recovered the car.

Lord Denning has said that 'the courts, in favouring the original owner at the expense of the innocent purchaser, have run counter to the needs of a commercial country.'[20] Certainly, in allowing the owner of goods to be as careless as he likes with his property they do appear to allow him to have an almost flagrant disregard for the likely effects of his conduct on others, and to take an unjustifiably optimistic view of human nature. After all, the reasonable man locks his door when he goes out; he knows of the risk of theft and it is not too hard to foresee that if his video is stolen someone may be persuaded to buy it, in all honesty and good faith. No doubt the policy of the law is to encourage care in buyers and make it more difficult for the thief to 'fence' property. On the other hand the law is very hard on the innocent purchaser, particularly when the owner has voluntarily parted with his property: he is, after all, at least as well placed as the ultimate buyer to judge the honesty of the rogue who deceives them both.

Most would advocate drawing a distinction between a person deprived of his property by theft and one who loses it in other circumstances. Such distinctions are widely drawn.[21]

> 'Theft, and to some extent loss, have the unpredictability of lightning, and there is relatively little the owner can do to protect himself against them. It is of his own free will, on the other hand, that the owner parts with possession of goods of his own to another by way of loan, lease, deposit, pledge etc and he has every opportunity of investigating the integrity of that person before doing so. It is only fair and equitable, therefore, that the risk should fall on him rather than on the innocent purchaser. The fact that he has, in the first instance, voluntarily parted with possession swings the delicate balance of equity in (the purchaser's) favour.'[22]

However, in the criminal law there is a close link between the thief and the con-man, and it would be difficult to show that an owner deceived by a plausible con-man had been negligent. However, that is to deny negligence not the existence of a duty to take care. In recent years the courts have

301

appeared more willing to impose liability in negligence for causing purely financial loss[23] and perhaps the law represented by *Moorgate Mercantile Co Ltd v Twitchings* is due for a reappraisal.

1   *Belvoir Finance Co Ltd v Harold G Cole & Co Ltd* [1969] 2 All ER 904, [1969] 1 WLR 1877.
2   *Lowther v Harris* [1927] 1 KB 393.
3   Atiyah, *The Sale of Goods* (1985, 7th edn) p 281.
4   *Folkes v King* [1923] 1 KB 282. But the registration document is necessary if the sale is to be 'in the course of business'; *Pearson v Rose & Young Ltd* [1951] 1 KB 275, [1950] 2 All ER 1027, CA.
5   Factors Act 1889, s 2(4).
6   *Folkes v King* [1923] 1 KB 282.
7   Factors Act 1889, s 2(2).
8   *Pearson v Rose & Young Ltd* [1951] 1 KB 275.
9   *Heap v Motorists' Advisory Agency Ltd* [1923] 1 KB 577.
10 *Pearson v Rose & Young Ltd* [1951] 1 KB 275, [1950] 2 All ER 1027, CA.
11 *Stadium Finance Ltd v Robbins* [1962] 2 QB 664, [1962] 2 All ER 633, CA.
12 *Heap v Motorists' Advisory Agency Ltd* [1923] 1 KB 577.
13 See eg, *Heap v Motorists' Advisory Agency Ltd* [1923] 1 KB 577.
14 *Eastern Distributors Ltd v Goldring* [1957] 2 QB 600, [1957] 2 All ER 525, CA.
15 See eg, per Denning LJ in *Central Newbury Car Auctions Ltd v Unity Finance Ltd* [1957] 1 QB 371, [1956] 3 All ER 905, CA.
16 *Farquharson Bros & Co v C King & Co* [1902] AC 325, HL per Lord MacNaghten, at 335.
17 *Central Newbury Car Auctions Ltd v Unity Finance Ltd* [1957] 1 QB 371, [1956] 3 All ER 905, CA.
18 [1965] 2 QB 242, [1964] 3 All ER 592, CA.
19 [1977] AC 890, [1976] 2 All ER 641, HL.
20 *Central Newbury Car Auctions v Unity Finance Ltd* [1957] 1 QB 371 at 381.
21 Eg French and German law allow more extensive rights of recovery to owners who lose their property due to theft.
22 Hahlo, *Sale of Another Person's Property*.
23 See Part 2.

Sellers and buyers in possession
23.0.2   We have seen already that possession and ownership are two separate items; and in particular that title may pass before or after physical delivery. The separation of ownership and possession can create difficulties for a third party purchaser dealing with an apparent owner and the legislation therefore contains a series of rules dealing with the powers of sellers and buyers in possession of goods which they no longer or do not yet own, as exceptions to the nemo dat rule.

a) Sellers in possession
We shall see later that, as a form of statutory security for payment of the purchase price when title has passed, an unpaid seller has a lien over goods in his possession and a right of resale.[1] Where he relies on his lien and statutory right of sale the third party to whom he sells gets good title[2] and the original buyer has no recourse against the seller.[3]

However, the seller may remain in possession even after he has been paid, and he may purport to resell the goods to a second purchaser. It may be that the seller (S) has contracted to sell, but that title has not yet passed to the buyer (P1). The seller can then, of course, continue to deal with the goods as his own and if he sells the goods to a second purchaser (P2) so as to pass title, the first purchaser's only remedy is to claim damages for breach of the contract of sale. More problematical is the case when title has passed to the first purchaser but the seller remains in possession of the goods and purports to resell them to a second purchaser. P1 can still sue S for breach of contract (non-delivery). However, in practice he will often wish to claim the goods from P2—perhaps because S is insolvent.

Section 24 provides that where a person having sold goods, continues, or is, in possession of the goods, the delivery or transfer by that person, or by a mercantile agent acting for him, of the goods or documents of title under any sale, pledge or other disposition thereof, to any person receiving the same in good faith and without notice of the previous sale, shall have the same effect as if the person making the delivery or transfer was expressly authorised by the owner of the goods to make the same.

This repeats, almost verbatim, an exception contained in the Factors Act 1889, s 8 except that that provision is slightly wider, covering also 'any agreement for any sale, pledge or other disposition.' The effect of this exception is that, provided its requirements are fulfilled, the second purchaser (P2) from the seller gets a good title to the goods and can resist a claim by P1. P1's title is extinguished and he is left with only a claim against S for breach of contract. The rule only applies when S remains in possession of the goods; however, there is no need for him to be in possession with the consent of the buyer;[4] furthermore, there is no need for him to remain in possession as seller, the rule was applied in a case where S sold goods to P1 who immediately bailed them back to S under a hire purchase agreement, S never relinquishing possession even though S was now in possession as hire purchase bailee, rather than as seller.[5] The rule would thus cover the common business arrangement of sale and leaseback.

In order for P2 to take good title he must take actual delivery of the goods or of the documents of title. It is that which gives him priority over P1 who did not take physical possession. In addition if he is to rely on the exception P2 must have taken the goods in good faith and without actual notice of the previous sale, and his good faith must exist both at the time the contract is made and at the time he takes delivery if that is later.

It must be noted that, although we have spoken of P2 as a second purchaser, he will be protected if he takes the goods under any sale, pledge or other disposition—and it has been held that 'disposition' has a particularly wide meaning so that it applied where S, who had purchased by means of a worthless cheque, allowed his vendor to repossess the goods, thus defeating the claims of P1 to whom he had sold the goods.[6]

b) Buyers in possession
It very commonly happens that a person buys goods for the purpose of resale. When goods are supplied on credit terms there is thus scope for conflict between the unpaid seller and the sub-buyer. Not surprisingly, therefore, there are several statutory provisions dealing with sales by buyers who have no, or an imperfect, title.

(i) Sale under voidable title The first exception is contained in s 23 of the SGA 1979, which provides that when the seller of goods has a voidable title to them, but his title has not been avoided at the time of the sale, the buyer acquires a good title to the goods, provided he buys them in good faith and without notice of the seller's defect of title.

We have already seen the distinction drawn between contracts which are wholly void, for example for mistake, and those which are merely voidable, for example for misrepresentation.[7] The buyer under a voidable contract is capable of reselling at any time before the contract by which he acquired the goods is rescinded; the effect of s 23 is that, provided the sub-buyer takes the goods in good faith and without notice of the defect in his seller's title (ie of the first seller's right to set the contract aside), he gets a title which is free of that defect and can therefore resist the claim by the first seller.

This exception will, of course, come into play where the original seller has been defrauded, typically by a misrepresentation, for instance where he has been induced into parting with his goods by a representation of creditworthiness and in return for a cheque which is subsequently dishonoured. It is because the buyer with a voidable title can pass a good title to his sub-buyer that sellers in cases such as *Ingram v Little*[8] attempt to establish a mistake, which wholly avoids the contract ab initio: if there is a mistake, the contract is void and the sub-buyer gets no title. However, from the point of view of the sub-buyer the position is the same. It seems harsh that his entitlement to the goods should depend on the highly technical distinction between a mistake and a misrepresentation, void and voidable. Devlin LJ, dissenting in *Ingram v Little*, said:

> 'the dividing line between voidness and voidability is a very fine one . . . Need the rights of the parties in a case like this depend on such a distinction? The great virtue of the common law is that it sets out to solve legal problems by the application to them of principles which the ordinary man is expected to recognise as sensible and just. (H)ere the common law, instead of looking for a principle that is simple and just depends on the theoretical distinctions.
>
> The relevant question in this sort of case is not whether the contract was void or voidable, but which of two innocent parties shall suffer for the fraud of a third.'[9]

However, even if the contract is held to be voidable rather than void, the sub-purchaser is still not wholly safe. His position depends on whether, as between seller and fraudulent buyer, the contract has been avoided. Furthermore, it has been held that, when a seller was defrauded into parting with a car in return for a worthless cheque and could not contact his buyer to rescind, the contract was effectively avoided by him notifying the police and AA and asking them to recover the car.[10]

(ii) Section 25   Section 25 is the converse of s 24 and deals with the sale by a buyer in possession. Like s 24, SGA 1979, s 25 repeats an exception from the Factors Act 1889, s 9. Again, the Factors Act exception is slightly wider than that in s 25, extending also to protect those who acquire the goods under any 'agreement for any sale, pledge or other disposition.'

This exception is of the utmost importance in business practice and, indeed, its importance has increased in recent years. It applies when a buyer gets possession of the goods with the consent of the seller but does not yet have title: if he resells in accordance with s 25/s 9 his sub-buyer will nevertheless get title to the goods. The importance of the rule lies in the increasingly common practice of suppliers supplying goods on credit terms coupled with a reservation of title until the price is paid; the practice has become widespread in the last ten years, since the *Romalpa*[11] case, and reservation of title clauses are now used even when goods are, to the knowledge of both parties, supplied for immediate resale. When the seller has inserted a reservation of title the goods remains his property until payment, notwithstanding delivery. It is common for purchasers to resell before they pay for the goods: indeed, the commercial purpose of allowing credit is to improve the buyer's cashflow and allow him to raise the price by reselling. The purpose of the reservation of title is to give the seller security in the event of the buyer's insolvency; if the buyer is insolvent the seller may recover the goods, and, of course, the nemo dat rule would allow him to recover them from the sub-buyer, even though he may in all probability have paid for them. It would be impossible to conduct business if buyers were forever at risk of goods being repossessed by creditors of their vendors and the exception to the nemo dat rule in s 25 protects the sub-buyer in such a situation and allows business to be conducted and goods to circulate freely with some measure of certainty. The buyer of goods in possession may always pass a good title to them regardless of any reservation of title, if the conditions in s 25 are fulfilled.

Section 25 applies when a buyer who has bought, or agreed to buy, goods gets possession of them with the consent of the seller. It therefore only applies to sale contracts; a bailee in possession of goods subject to a hire purchase contract cannot pass good title under s 25,[12] and s 25(2) assimilates conditional sale agreements to hire purchase agreements, when the contract is one regulated by the Consumer Credit Act and the price is payable by instalments.[13] Section 25 will however cover a sale by a business purchaser who bought goods subject to a reservation of title.[14] Furthermore, it will cover the situation when a buyer has a voidable title. We have seen that by virtue of s 23 he can pass a good title to the goods before his own title is avoided; however, even after his vendor has rescinded the sale contract the buyer will be able to sell under s 25. Finally it should be noted that the sub-buyer will only need to rely on s 25 when the buyer has possession but no title. If title had already passed he could of course pass that title at common law.

If s 25 is to apply the buyer must obtain possession of the goods with the consent of the seller: wrongful possession will not suffice. However, once consent has been given, its withdrawal is ineffective unless the sub-buyer knows it has been withdrawn. This is important since many reservation of title clauses purport to forbid the buyer from dealing with the goods and may require him to deliver them up to the vendor on his insolvency, or perhaps even on request. The effect is that the sub-buyer who complies with s 25 gets a good title even though the original buyer has made default and his vendor has demanded the return of the goods, unless the sub-buyer knows of that. However, as with s 24 of the SGA the sub-buyer is only protected if he actually takes delivery of the goods (or documents of title to them). In addition he must take the goods in good faith and without notice of any rights of the original vendor.

Section 25 has been interpreted by the courts in a way which is potentially restrictive. The difficulty is that the section says that the effect of the sale by the buyer in possession is as if he was a mercantile agent in possession with the consent of the owner. A sale by a mercantile agent must be in the ordinary course of business; a buyer in possession may not be in business but the courts have held that he must sell in circumstances which would be considered to be in the course of business if the sale were by a mercantile agent, eg during business hours.[15]

(iii) Vehicles under hire purchase   Section 25 has no application to a sale by a bailee under a hire purchase agreement: normally a person who buys from a hire purchase bailee gets no title. However, there is a special statutory

305

exception which applies only to sales of motor vehicles held under hire purchase agreements.[16] The effect is to protect a first private purchaser from the bailee provided he takes in good faith; it does not protect a buyer who is either a dealer in motor vehicles or in the business of financing vehicle purchases,[17] even if he purchases for his own use.[18] This should cause no hardship in practice since most dealers are members of HP Information Ltd and can thus obtain information as to whether or not the vehicle is subject to any subsisting hire purchase agreement. However, although a dealer cannot take good title, the first private purchaser can take a good title even if the vehicle has passed through the hands of one or more dealers. On the other hand if the first private purchaser is not bona fide, neither he nor any subsequent private purchaser can take advantage of the exception.

A purchaser of a vehicle is thus protected if he purchases directly from the defaulting hire purchaser; however, very often he will not be the immediate purchaser and may not be able to trace all the links in the chain between the hire purchaser and himself. He may, however, rely on a series of presumptions;[19] the effect is that provided he can show that he was a purchaser in good faith, he will keep the vehicle unless the hire purchase company can show that the first person to acquire the vehicle from the hire purchaser was not a good faith purchaser.

1   Ss 41–43, see 24.2.1.
2   SGA 1979, s 48(2).
3   SGA 1979, s 48(4).
4   *Worcester Works Finance Ltd v Cooden Engineering Co Ltd* [1972] 1 QB 210, [1971] 3 All ER 708, CA.
5   Ibid.
6   Ibid.
7   See Ch 15.
8   [1961] 1 QB 73, [1960] 3 All ER 332, CA. See 15.0.1.
9   At 42.
10 *Car and Universal Finance Ltd v Caldwell* [1965] 1 QB 525, [1964] 1 All ER 290, CA.
11 *Aluminium Industrie Vaassen BV v Romalpa Aluminium Ltd* [1976] 2 All ER 552, [1976] 1 WLR 676.
12 *Helby v Matthews* [1895] AC 471, HL.
13 See 26.0.3.
14 *Lee v Butler* [1893] 2 QB 318, CA.
15 *Newtons of Wembley Ltd v Williams* [1965] 1 QB 560, [1964] 3 All ER 532, CA.
16 Hire Purchase Act 1964, Pt III.
17 HPA 1964, s 29(2).
18 *Stevenson v Beverley Bentinck Ltd* [1976] 2 All ER 606, [1976] 1 WLR 483, CA.
19 HPA 1964, s 28.

Sale in market overt
23.0.3   This exception, contained in SGA 1979, s 22, is an oddity, with little in common with those we have already looked at. The effect is that a buyer of goods will obtain a good title to them provided he buys them in an open, public and properly constituted market, in accordance with the usages of the market and acts in good faith without notice of any defect in title of the seller.

The exception has a very long history: SGA 1979, s 22 merely gives statutory form to an old common law rule.[1] Historically the purpose of the rule is clear: in the Middle Ages it encouraged trade because most sales took place in open public markets and fairs. The dispossessed owner was expected to visit his local market and look for his goods. If he did not, or if he failed to claim them, then he could have no complaint if the goods were sold there: he had, after all, had his chance, and the rule thus encouraged trade.

If the rule is to apply, several requirements must be fulfilled. First, the sale must take place in an open, publicly constituted market: the market must be established by Royal Charter, statute[2] or long established custom. The rule does not apply to sales in ordinary shops, except, by a curious exception, to shops in the City of London: there, because of the historical importance of the City in trade, every shop is treated as market overt,[3] provided the sale takes place on the ground floor, in part of the premises open to the street and is a sale by the shop owner (not to him) of goods ordinarily sold there.

Second, the sale must be in accordance with the usages or customs of the market. However, a sale may be in market overt even though made by a private individual, rather than a trader, provided private sales are allowed by the custom of the market.[4] The sale must take place between sunrise and sunset.[5] Third, as is generally required for an exception to the nemo dat rule to apply, the buyer must buy in good faith without notice of his seller's defect in title.

If a sale is in market overt, complying with s 22, the buyer gets a good title and can resist a claim by a dispossessed owner. The old rule that he would have to return the goods if the thief was prosecuted to conviction has been repealed.[6] There is a power for a criminal court to make a restitution order in respect of stolen goods,[7] but the court will not normally make such an order when there has been a sale in market overt to a bona fide purchaser, or indeed when there is a genuine dispute about ownership.[8]

The market overt rule had a historical justification. In modern conditions it quite clearly shows itself as an anachronism. Its main application will be to cases of stolen goods; indeed it is the only exception to the nemo dat rule which can assist a purchaser of stolen goods, and is probably more important to consumers, or private buyers, than to business purchasers. Even in that context, however, the rule is outdated. It is no longer true that most transactions take place in markets, and with the ease and speed of modern transport the argument that the thief's victim can watch for his property at the local market is rendered nugatory; his goods can be at the opposite end of the country in a day and be sold before he knows they are gone. Similarly although the City of London may once have held a prominent position in relation to trade, it is no longer the site of any significant amount of retail trade, certainly no more so than many other areas, and yet a difference of a few yards in the location of a transaction can place it inside or outside the City, inside or outside the market overt rule.

In 1966 the Law Reform Committee recommended its abolition,[9] but nothing has been done and the rule was reenacted in 1979. An alternative reform, which has much to commend it, would be to extend the market overt rule to cover all retail transactions, in order to bring it up to date and perform the function in the modern context, for which it was originally created. Interestingly, though, the only important recent judicial decision on market overt has restricted the rule still further and added to its curiosity.[10]

1 Cases are known at least as early as 1291.
2 *Bishopsgate Motor Finance Corpn Ltd v Transport Brakes Ltd* [1949] 1 KB 322, [1949] 1 All ER 37, CA.
3 *The Case of Market-Overt* (1596) 5 Co Rep 836.
4 *Bishopsgate Motor Finance Corpn Ltd v Transport Brakes Ltd* [1949] 1 KB 322, [1949] 1 All ER 37, CA.

5   *Reid v Metropolitan Police Comr* [1973] QB 551, [1973] 2 All ER 97, CA.
6   By the Theft Act 1968, s 33.
7   Theft Act 1968, s 28.
8   *R v Church* (1970) 55 Cr App Rep 65, CA.
9   In its 12th Report *Transfer of Title to Chattels*, Cmnd 2958, 1966.
10   *Reid v Metropolitan Police Comr* [1973] QB 551, [1973] 2 All ER 97, CA.

Special powers of sale
23.0.4   There is one final group of exceptions, preserved by s 21(2)b of the SGA 1979, which provide that nothing in it is to affect 'the validity of any contract of sale under any special common law or statutory power of sale or under the order of a court of competent jurisdiction.' The Act thus allows sales, effective to pass good title, by various persons, including court sheriffs and bailiffs selling goods of debtors seized under writs or warrants of execution, sales by pledgees of goods pledged with them, and sales by bailees of goods. It should be noted, however, that under the Torts (Interference With Goods) Act 1977 a bailee of goods, for instance the garage which repairs a car, is required to give notice to the owner, before selling the goods, requiring him to collect them.[1] Finally, a sale may be made by an Officer of the Court acting under a Court Order. Such orders could be made in a wide variety of circumstances, for instance where parties are in dispute about perishable goods, the court might order a sale to prevent deterioration, allowing the parties to fight over the proceeds of sale.

1   Torts (Interference With Goods) Act 1977, s 12.

Implied terms as to title, possession and enjoyment in contracts for the sale and supply of goods

23.1.0   In the event that a buyer does not acquire a satisfactory title to goods and is forced to return them to their original owner, he will seek redress from the vendor. Such redress is based on s 12(1) of the SGA 1979 which implies into contracts for the sale of goods a condition that the seller has a right to sell the goods, or will have at the time property is to pass. The section additionally implies a warranty that the goods are free from undisclosed encumbrances and that the buyer will enjoy quiet possession of them. Under the terms of s 6(1) of UCTA 1977 any contract term purporting or attempting to exclude these implied terms is void.

The effect is that if the vendor of goods has no right to sell, the buyer can reject them and reclaim the price. In the majority of cases, in practice, of course s 12 will only be invoked by the purchaser who has been forced to return goods to a successful dispossessed owner; in fact O, the owner, will sue P, the most recent purchaser in conversion and P will then claim against V1, his vendor, relying on s 12; V1 will claim against his vendor, V2, and so on. In this way liability will be passed back up the chain until a vendor (often the true rogue) cannot be located.

It should be noted that the implied condition is that the seller has a right to sell, not that he is the owner of goods. There is thus no breach if goods are sold by a duly authorised agent.

There may be a breach of s 12 even when the seller is the owner of the goods, if for some reason he has no right to sell them. In *Niblett Ltd v Confectioners' Materials Co Ltd*[1] V supplied tins of condensed milk bearing the brand name 'Nissly'; the Nestle company successfully sought an injunction to prevent P selling the cans, on the grounds of a breach of their trademark copyright. P could not dispose of the cans until they removed the labels. The majority of the Court of Appeal held that there was therefore a breach of s 12: because Nestle could obtain an injunction to prevent V dealing with the tins, V had no right to sell. There was also a breach of the warranty for quiet enjoyment.[2]

The principal requirement is that the seller should have a right to sell at the time property is to pass under the contract. There is no breach if the seller contracts to sell goods which he does not yet own, intending to buy them for his contract before property is to pass. Further, it seems that even if the seller does not have title at the time he sells, but later acquires title, then that title will be fed through to his buyer.[3]

Since the principal term implied by s 12 is a condition, breach of it allows the buyer to reject the goods and, reflecting the importance the law attaches to ownership, to reclaim the price he paid for them, even though he may have had the use of the goods for some time. In *Rowland v Divall*[4] P bought a car in May, and resold it in July. In September it transpired that the car had been stolen and it was repossessed by its original owner. P refunded the price paid by his customer and then claimed a refund of the whole price he had paid to his vendor. The Court of Appeal held he should succeed, even though he and his customer had had four months' use of the car. The court stressed that the buyer did not get what he paid for, namely a car to which he would have title[5] and 'the whole object of a sale is to transfer property from one person to another.'[6] The effect is that the right to reject for breach of s 12, unlike that for breach of the implied conditions in ss 13 and 14, cannot be lost by accepting the goods.

Furthermore, the buyer who claims for breach of s 12 may, in addition to reclaiming the price, claim damages for additional expenses incurred.[7]

The rule in *Rowland v Divall* has been criticised as unduly harsh to vendors. In principle there is no reason why a purchaser could not reclaim the price paid even after substantial undisturbed use and enjoyment of the goods—perhaps even after consuming them. The harshness is particularly clear if one recalls that the vendor will often be blameless. Of course, in reality a purchaser is mostly concerned to get the use and enjoyment of the goods he buys, and if he does get that, he should have no complaint. On the other hand the purchaser is exposed to claims in common law from the true owner, and, if the defect in his title is discovered, he cannot safely sell the goods. In 1966 the Law Reform Committee proposed that the buyer should be required to give credit for any use and enjoyment of the goods[8] and in 1983 the Law Commission proposed similar reforms, although recognising the difficulty of putting a value on use and enjoyment.[9]

Although the implied condition in s 12 cannot be excluded, in certain situations the protection given to the buyer is reduced: when the contract, expressly or impliedly is to sell only such title as the vendor has, there is only a warranty of freedom from undisclosed encumbrances, and of enjoyment free from disturbance by the seller, or a person claiming through him.[10] This exception is narrowly construed. It would cover, for instance, sales by sheriffs' officers or bailiffs, who cannot know that the goods they seize are the property of the debtor.[11]

By virtue of section 8 of the Supply of Goods (Implied Terms) Act 1973, the implied terms in respect of title and quiet possession under s 12 of the

SGA 1979 are extended to hire purchase contracts, with appropriate modifications; similarly s 2 of the Supply of Goods and Services Act 1982 extended the implied terms to all contracts caught by that Act involving the supply of goods.[12] In the case of hire or rental agreements, where the customer is only entitled to possession and use of the goods, the implied term is modified to the effect that the owner or bailor has a right to transfer possession for the period of the agreement, and the customer or bailee will enjoy quiet possession.[13]

1   [1921] 3 KB 387.
2   There was also held to be a breach of the condition of merchantable quality.
3   *Butterworth v Kingsway Motors Ltd* [1954] 2 All ER 694, [1954] 1 WLR 1286.
4   [1923] 2 KB 500, CA.
5   Per Bankes LJ, p 504.
6   Per Atkin LJ, p 506.
7   The buyer will be able to claim an indemnity for his costs of fighting the owner's conversion claim: *Butterworth v Kingsway Motors Ltd* [1954] 2 All ER 694, [1954] 1 WLR 1286. In *Warman v Southern Counties Car Finance Corpn Ltd, W J Amen's Car Sales (Third Party)* [1949] 2 KB 576, [1949] 1 All ER 711, a car buyer rejected the car for breach of s 12 and recovered the price paid plus damages to cover the cost of insurance, repairs and the legal costs of the conversion claim.
8   Law Reform Committee 12th Report: *Transfer of Title to Chattels* Cmnd 2958, 1966.
9   Law Commission Working Paper 'Sale and Supply of Goods', 1983.
10 S 12(3)–(5).
11 In *Niblett Ltd v Confectioners' Materials Co Ltd* [1921] 3 KB 387, Atkin LJ thought that the proviso should be limited to such sales.
12 See 20.6.0.
13 SGSA 1982, s 7.

Chapter 24
Delivery and Payment in Contracts of Sale

24.0.0   We have seen the importance which the law attaches to the passing of ownership, and the separation of possession and ownership which is not only possible but increasingly the norm in commercial transactions. In practice, however, the parties are often less concerned with ownership than with the more immediate issues of the physical availability of the goods for use or resale, and the payment of the price. Indeed very often ownership is irrelevant as between the original contract parties and only assumes importance when third parties become involved. Possession and delivery are however key factors since the buyer's duty to pay the price is linked to the seller's duty to deliver the goods.

Given the practical and legal importance of possession, we should not be surprised that the law supplies detailed rules about delivery. We must make clear from the outset, however, that in law 'delivery' has a meaning different from its colloquial meaning: whereas 'delivery' ordinarily means the physical transport of goods from A to B, normally by the seller or a carrier, in law 'delivery' means no more than the 'voluntary transfer of possession from one person to another',[1] and delivery will normally take place at the seller's place of business, unless the contract makes some other provision.

The basic obligations of buyer and seller under a sale of goods contract are set out in SGA 1979, s 27: 'It is the duty of the seller to deliver the goods, and of the buyer to accept and pay for them, in accordance with the terms of the contract of sale.' This is important for the seller, for until he has tendered delivery he cannot sue for the price; if he tenders delivery, the buyer must accept the delivery, failing which the seller may sue him for damages for non-acceptance. On the other hand, should the seller fail to tender delivery, the buyer can sue him for damages for non-delivery.

How, then, is delivery to be made? We have seen that delivery constitutes merely a voluntary transfer of possession. The rule is that, unless the contract makes express provision to the contrary, delivery is to take place at the seller's place of business or, if he has none, at his home, or, if the contract is for the sale of specific goods in some other place, at the location of the goods.[2] Invariably the contract will make express contrary provision: in most business contracts the seller will undertake physically to deliver the goods at the buyer's place of business, and he will then be obliged to transport them there; if he is merely required to despatch the goods, he fulfils his obligation when he hands them to a carrier, who will be the buyer's agent.[3] Even when the seller is required physically to deliver the goods to the buyer's premises, he fulfils his obligation by handing the goods to a person there who appears to be authorised to receive

311

them.[4] A prudent buyer will protect himself by requiring the seller to get a signature of receipt from some senior employee.

In many business transactions it will be impractical for the buyer to take physical possession of the goods, for instance when commodities are sold in bulk. In such circumstances delivery may be 'constructive', that is, the seller may hand over a document of title to the goods, such as a bill of lading or warehouse delivery warrant.[5] Alternatively the parties may contract to sell the whole of a quantity of goods held in a warehouse, and the seller could symbolically make delivery by handing to the buyer the keys to the warehouse. If the goods are held by a bailee on behalf of the seller, for instance when he sells a quantity of frozen carcasses held in a cold store owned by a third party, there will be a delivery when the third party bailee attorns to the buyer for the goods—that is to say, he acknowledges that he holds the goods on behalf of the buyer. As we have already seen, the seller can also deliver goods by handing them to a carrier who is the buyer's agent.

These instances of non-physical delivery are important, not only because of the link between delivery and payment but also because, once the seller has delivered goods he loses his right of lien over them,[6] which can be a useful lever to obtain payment, or a better remedy than payment if the buyer becomes insolvent.

1   Defined in SGA 1979, s 61. However, a court may find it relatively easy to imply a duty on the seller to make physical delivery to the buyer's premises, especially where the goods are bulky and the buyer is a consumer. Certainly shops selling to consumers tend to deliver to the consumers' home in such circumstances, and may think they are obliged to do so: see Cranston, *Consumers and the Law* (1984 2nd edn) p 171.
2   SGA 1979, s 29.
3   SGA 1979, s 32.
4   *Galbraith & Grant Ltd v Block* [1922] 2 KB 155, where the seller contracted to deliver a crate of champagne to the buyer's premises and left it in the custody of someone at the premises who appeared to be in charge. The buyer never saw the champagne but the court held that the seller had delivered and could sue for the price.
5   Technically most warehouse warrants are not documents of title. Some, however, are given that status by special statutes and some are treated in practice as if they were title documents.
6   A right to regain possession of goods as security for payment. See 24.2.1.

When should delivery take place?
24.0.1   Having considered how the seller should deliver, the next question we must ask is 'When must he deliver?' The answer, of course, is that the parties will make provision in their contract. If no time is fixed, the seller must deliver within a reasonable time and must tender delivery at a reasonable hour.[1] Invariably the parties will expressly provide a fixed delivery date and the important question then is what happens if the buyer does not deliver at the fixed time: can the buyer treat the contract as at an end, or must he accept the goods? The Act itself does not give the answer,[2] but the general rule is that if the contract is silent on the effect of delay, the courts will treat the time for delivery as being of the essence,[3] so that if the seller is late in delivering, the buyer can treat the contract as ended and claim damages. This is in line with the general approach of the courts to stipulations as to time in commercial contracts. Lord Wilberforce gave the reason for this in the case of *Bunge Corpn v Tradax SA*:[4]

> 'It is clearly essential that both buyer and seller (who may change roles in the next series of contracts or even in the same series of contracts)

should know precisely what their obligations are, most especially because the ability of the seller to fulfil his obligation may well be totally dependant on punctual performance by the buyer.'[5]

On the other hand, the time for payment is normally not of the essence,[6] so that the seller cannot treat the contract as ended merely because the buyer is slow in paying. The reason for the difference in approach is recognised in the statement of Lord Wilberforce quoted above: the consequences for the buyer of late delivery may well be catastrophic. One particular sale transaction will often only be one link in a chain of such transactions; the buyer may make a contract to resell the goods, or he may use them to manufacture other goods which he has already contracted to sell. If the seller fails to deliver on time, he will have to find alternative goods to fulfil his contract or find himself in breach, with consequent damage to his commercial reputation. Even if the goods he buys are not for resale, he may intend to use them in his business, so that delayed delivery could cause him lost production and the expense of plant standing idle. On the other hand the seller kept out of his money can be adequately compensated by an award of interest.[7]

Nevertheless, the rule is harsh. Very often, the parties may accept late delivery, but the rule that time is of the essence could be used by an unscrupulous buyer who, having made a bad buy, finds that the market has fallen and can use late delivery as an excuse to end the contract. For this reason most contracts will actually vary the general rules, particularly if the contract is on the seller's standard terms of trading. Thus, for instance, contracts may fix delivery dates by phrases such as 'on or about' a certain date, or provide for deviation from date. Similarly the seller may vary the normal rule and provide that the time for payment shall be of the essence: this may be particularly attractive where he wishes to rely on a reservation of title clause. Alternatively, even when the contract does not vary the general rule, the buyer may prefer to accept late delivery, perhaps in the interests of a good trading relationship, or because the contract terms are better than he could obtain in the open market, or perhaps in return for a negotiated variation—for example an allowance against the price. If the buyer does clearly indicate that he will not insist on delivery strictly in accordance with the contract, he will be held to have waived his right to delivery on the contract date.[8] However, even if he does not immediately fix a new delivery date, he can make time of the essence again by giving reasonable notice that he requires delivery by a certain date.[9]

---

1   SGA 1979, s 29(3), (5).
2   S 10(2) provides that 'Whether any other stipulation [than for payment] as to time is or is not of the essence of the contract depends on the terms of the contract.'
3   *Hartley v Hymans* [1920] 3 KB 475.
4   [1981] 2 All ER 513, [1981] 1 WLR 711, HL.
5   At p 521.
6   SGA 1979, s 10(1).
7   By the rules of court he will be entitled to claim interest on the price if he brings a claim for it. Furthermore, the contract itself will often require interest to be paid if payment is late, or, alternatively, give a discount for early payment.
8   Whether this is interpreted as a waiver or as an example of promissory estoppel is not clear; the effects appear to be very similar. Alternatively the parties may negotiate a full variation of the contract.
9   *Charles Rickards Ltd v Oppenheim* [1950] 1 KB 616, [1950] 1 All ER 420, CA.

What must the seller deliver?

24.0.2 The final question relating to delivery is 'What must the seller deliver?' The quality of the goods he must deliver is defined by the implied terms in s 13–15 of the Act which we have already examined. The seller is required to 'deliver the goods . . . in accordance with the terms of the contract',[1] and, if the goods delivered are defective, the buyer may reject them, and the seller will be treated as not having delivered, thus the buyer may be able to claim the cost of replacements as damages for non-delivery. However, we are concerned here, primarily with the question of quantity: how much must the seller deliver? The Act contains some technicalities, which we shall note before considering normal business practice.

(a) The buyer is not obliged to accept delivery by instalments unless the contract expressly provides for delivery by instalments.[2]

(b) If the seller delivers less than the contract quantity, the buyer may reject the whole consignment, and treat the case as one of non-delivery, or he may elect to accept short delivery and pay only for the goods actually delivered.[3] The seller cannot unilaterally deliver the balance later, because that would be delivery by instalments.

(c) If the seller delivers more than the contract quantity, the buyer has three choices:

   (i) he may accept the contract quantity and reject the excess;

   (ii) he may treat the breach as repudiating the contract and reject the whole consignment;[4]

   (iii) he may accept the whole consignment, paying for the excess ratably at the contract rate.[5]

(d) If the seller delivers goods of the contract description mixed with goods of a different description, the buyer may choose to keep the contract goods and reject the rest, or he may reject the whole of the consignment.[6]

These rules are all, in theory, subject to the restriction that a 'de minimis' variation from the contract quantity will not allow the buyer to reject; however, in the light of decisions such as that in *Re Moore & Co Ltd and Landauer & Co's Arbitration*[7] it will be clear that even a very small deviation from the contract quantity will allow the buyer to reject.

These rules appear harsh, and clearly favour the buyer. In reality, buyers do not reject deliveries for small deviations in quantity. Furthermore, it is common for sellers to protect themselves so that their standard terms of trading will allow them to deliver 'more or less' than the contract quantity: for instance, the contract may allow a limited 'percentage' deviation from the strict contract quantity.[8] Interestingly, in clauses dealt with by arbitration arising from international sales the normal practice is to allow a buyer a reduction in the price for variations in quality or quantity, but not to allow rejection of the goods. This protects the seller against the possibility that a minor deviation may leave him with the goods on his hands accruing freight, storage and interest charges, and prevents the buyer using a minute deviation as an excuse to escape from a bad bargain.

1 SGA 1979, s 27.
2 SGA 1979, s 31(1).
3 SGA 1979, s 30(1).
4 SGA 1979, s 30(2).
5 SGA 1979, s 30(3).

6 SGA 1979, s 30(4). This would apply even if the seller delivers all the proper contract goods plus some others; the buyer cannot be forced to sort out the contract goods from the others, which might be expensive and time consuming.
7 [1921] 2 KB 519, CA, see 21.1.2.
8 Similarly, 'tolerances' may be implied by previous dealings between the parties or by the custom of the particular trade. The rules in s 30 are subject to such provisions: SGA 1979, s 30(5).

Remedies for non-delivery

24.0.3 It is the seller's duty to deliver and, unless the buyer has already indicated that he will not abide by the contract, for instance by saying that he will not accept or pay for the goods, a failure by the seller to deliver will be a breach of contract. The buyer will then be entitled to claim damages for non-delivery. The measure of such damages is similar to the normal measure for breach of contract laid down in *Hadley v Baxendale*,[1] but is slightly modified: damages are 'the estimated loss directly and naturally resulting in the ordinary course of events, from the seller's breach'.[2]

However, when there is an 'available market' for the contract goods, such loss 'is prima facie to be ascertained by the difference between the contract price and the market or current price of the goods at the time or times when they ought to have been delivered or (if no time was fixed) at the time of the refusal to deliver.'[3] The buyer's damages thus depend not on the price he actually pays but on the current market price at the date of breach. He must immediately mitigate his damages by buying in the market: if he fails to do so he must take the risk that if the market price rises, he will have to bear that increase. He may speculate on the market, but entirely at his own risk. Similarly it is irrelevant that the buyer was buying to resell, he can buy replacement goods for his resale in the market, unless he had contracted to resell the exact goods he was buying and the seller knew, or ought reasonably to have known, of that.[4] In addition to 'market price damages' the buyer is also entitled to damages for any special loss—for instance lost profits because he cannot use equipment in his factory, provided such damages would be recoverable under the ordinary rule in *Hadley v Baxendale*, as 'reasonably in the contemplation of the parties'.[5]

The 'market place' rule differs from the normal rule of mitigation of loss in that if the buyer manages to make a particularly good bargain and buy replacement goods at a favourable price, either by prudent negotiation or by delaying and 'playing the market' he keeps the benefit of that bargain; on the other hand, he must bear the risk of his speculation backfiring so that he must pay more. The rule does however avoid the law in the need to speculate: if damages were assessed by reference to the price actually paid by the buyer, there would be difficulties in linking the breach with a particular purchase especially when there was a delay or when the buyer was regularly buying goods.[6] For example, if P regularly buys raw materials for use in his business, which purchase would the court say was made to replace the consignment if the seller failed to deliver? Further, although the rule could trip the unwary, the buyer will be allowed a reasonable time to ascertain the seller's intention not to deliver, and in most cases the buyer's need, whether for raw materials, goods for resale or equipment, will be urgent and he will immediately seek replacements. A prudent buyer who intends to resell will protect himself either by notifying his seller of the fact, or by allowing a delay between the purchase date and resale date, although, of course, he may be reluctant so to do for sensible business reasons: he will wish to make his turnover as quick as possible to assist cashflow and minimise handling and storage costs.

There is an available market where there is a market in which goods of the contract type are freely and interchangeably traded, for instance one ton of coal is as good as a different ton of coal of equivalent quality. Supply and demand must be roughly equal (when the buyer claims for non-delivery, demand must not exceed supply).[7] It has been held that although there is an available market for the sale of new cars,[8] there is no available market for second hand cars,[9] because each is unique and different (although this ignores the fact that there are fairly standard values for second hand cars depending on year, condition and so on, and clearly indicated in publications such as 'Glass Guide'). The market must also be physically geographically accessible to the buyer.

If there is no available market, the damages for non-delivery will then depend on ordinary *Hadley v Baxendale* principles: if the purchase was for resale, the loss of profit on the resale can be claimed; if the purchase was for raw materials or equipment for a business the loss of profits due to loss manufacture can be claimed but, in both cases, subject to the losses having been within the contemplation of the parties.

1   (1854) 9 Exch 341, see 17.1.3.
2   SGA 1979, s 51(2).
3   SGA 1979, s 51(3).
4   *R & H Hall Ltd v W H Pim Jr & Co Ltd* (1928) 30 Ll L Rep 159, HL.
5   See 17.1.3.
6   See Goode, *Commercial Law* (1982) p 345.
7   See *Charter v Sullivan* [1957] 2 QB 117, [1957] 1 All ER 809, CA; *W L Thompson Ltd v Robinson (Gunmakers) Ltd* [1955] Ch 177, [1955] 1 All ER 154.
8   *Charter v Sullivan* [1957] 2 QB 117, [1957] 1 All ER 809, CA.
9   *Lazenby Garages Ltd v Wright* [1976] 2 All ER 770, [1976] 1 WLR 459, CA.

Late delivery
24.0.4   Where the seller indicates that he intends to deliver, but that such delivery will be late, the buyer cannot mitigate by buying replacement goods, unless time was of the essence in which case he can treat late delivery as a repudiation and end the contract. If late delivery is accepted, damages may still be claimed for breach of contract. If the goods were for use in his business he may be able to hire a replacement to cover the delay, and claim the cost of hire. If the goods are for resale his damages are the difference between the market price at the date they should have been delivered and the market price at the date when they were delivered: ie the amount (if any) by which the market has fallen and which he has lost by having to delay reselling. Again the buyer may be in difficulty if he was buying for a specific resale: he will either have to buy replacement goods for that contract, or he will have to risk breaking that contract by at least delaying delivery, and of course that will at least damage his goodwill. He can only protect himself at the negotiation stage, either by allowing a delay, as suggested above, or by making time of the essence of his contract with his supplier.

The buyer's duty to pay and accept
24.1.0   The duty of the seller under a contract of sale is to deliver the goods; the principal duty of the buyer is to 'accept and pay for them in accordance

with the terms of the contract.'[1] Unless the contract stipulates otherwise, payment and delivery are concurrent obligations, in other words the basic rule is 'cash on delivery.' In commercial transactions it is fairly common to allow delivery before payment since trade credit is the lifeblood of much commercial activity.

Where a time is fixed for payment and the buyer fails to meet that date, the seller cannot normally refuse to deliver since time of payment is not of the essence unless the contract expressly provides.[2] Where, however, the goods are perishable the seller may resell them if the buyer does not tender the price within a reasonable time.[3] Similarly, even if the goods are not perishable the seller can serve notice on the buyer requiring payment within a reasonable time—effectively on completion, and if the buyer then fails to pay, re-sell.[4] If the seller does re-sell, he brings the contract to an end by accepting the buyer's repudiation, so he is not liable for non-delivery. However, these rights will be of use only to the seller who has not already delivered the goods on credit terms.[5]

1   SGA 1979, s 27.
2   SGA 1979, s 27.
3   SGA 1979, s 48(3).
4   SGA 1979, s 48(3).
5   Unless the seller relies on a reservation of title clause including a right to repossess and resell: see below.

Acceptance and rejection

24.1.1   The buyer is required to accept the goods unless they do not conform with the contract.[1] If the buyer rejects goods when the seller is not in breach, then such rejection itself amounts to a breach allowing the seller to claim damages. Thus disputes about the quality of goods involve mutual allegations of breach of contract: if the goods were defective, the seller was in breach and the buyer was entitled to reject; on the other hand, if the goods were not defective, then the buyer's rejection was a breach of contract entitling the seller to damages. Such a situation is fraught with uncertainty, hence the commercial world's preference for informal negotiated settlements.

The buyer has a basic right to reject goods for breach of any condition, including the implied statutory condition in respect of title, quality and description. If the buyer does legitimately reject the goods, the effect of rejection is to revest title to the goods in the seller (if it had already passed). The buyer must keep the goods available for collection by the seller,[2] and he will be able to claim either the return of the price, or damages according to the market price rule, plus any consequential loss he may have suffered.

In reality the seller may attempt to repair the goods or replace them with others. Arguably he has a right to do so at law,[3] unless time was of the essence, but often the buyer will be happy for him to do that anyway, either because he wishes to preserve a good trading relationship or because the market price has risen and he wishes to avoid the expense of a re-purchase coupled with the uncertainty and acrimony of a claim for damages.

There is some authority that, subject to the time of delivery being essential, the seller does indeed have a legal right to tender replacement goods,[4] at least when the original contract was for unascertained goods.[5] It has been proposed, however, that the law should be reformed to give sellers an express right to repair or replace—or indeed to give consumers an express right to demand repair or replacement.[6] The seller already has a clear right to 'cure' a defect in the USA.[7] A legal right to cure would bring the law more closely into line with commercial and consumer expectations. Indeed, commercial arbitration claims of defective quality are dealt with by a price allowance and rejection is not allowed because the goods, even if defective, normally have some value and it will generally be easier for the buyer who has access to the local market, to resell than for the seller to recollect and resell. Furthermore, the right to reject is often restricted by contract terms, for instance limitation or exclusion clauses may limit the right to reject or may require defects to be reported within strict time limits.[8]

By s 11(4) of the SGA 1979 the right to reject goods for breach of condition is lost when the buyer has accepted the goods; he may then only treat the breach as a breach of warranty and claim damages. A key question therefore is, what amounts to acceptance?

Section 35 envisages three ways in which a buyer may accept goods. These are as follows:

a) Express intimation of an acceptance
A buyer may expressly signify acceptance of the goods, possibly by signing a delivery note couched in the appropriate language. An acknowledgement of the receipt of goods would not, however, be regarded as an acceptance. There are obvious dangers in intimating acceptance as soon as goods are delivered. One factor is that many goods arrive in sealed units or sophisticated packaging, thus making immediate examination of the contents impossible. Indeed in many cases a defect may not manifest itself until the goods have been put into service. In effect, therefore, by immediately intimating acceptance, the buyer is foregoing his right to examine the goods and thereby considerably restricting his remedies in the event of the goods proving defective.

b) Some act inconsistent with the seller's ownership
Where the buyer accepts by doing some act inconsistent with the seller's ownership, such as reselling the goods, he is not treated as having accepted the goods 'until he has had a reasonable opportunity of examining them for the purpose of ascertaining whether they are in conformity with the contract.'[9] Thus, unlike express intimation, the buyer will not lose his right to reject merely by doing an act inconsistent with the seller's ownership: his right will depend on whether or not he has had an opportunity to inspect. Thus if the goods are delivered direct to a sub-buyer, with no chance for the buyer to inspect, he will not lose his right to reject, at least when the seller knows that there will be an immediate resale.[10] On the other hand if the goods are delivered first to the buyer and then resold and delivered by him to his sub-buyer he should take his chance to inspect the goods, because if he does not he may be taken to have had an opportunity to inspect; his resale is an act inconsistent with the seller's ownership and therefore he will be unable to reject. He may therefore find himself with a consignment of defective goods on his hands if the sub-buyer does inspect and rejects them, as of course he will be entitled to do, and left with no alternative but an action in damages.

In fact any dealing with the goods, including selling them, pledging or mortgaging them, is an act inconsistent with the seller's ownership and so capable of amounting to an acceptance if done after a reasonable opportunity of examining the goods. Of course, the buyer's acceptance is even clearer when he deals with the goods with knowledge of the defect. Similarly, the buyer will be unable to reject if he cannot return the goods in the original form, perhaps because he has consumed them in his manufacturing process. The only exception to this is that the buyer does not lose his right to reject if goods are lost or damaged because of the defect: for example, if V supplies a car with defective brakes and because of the defect the car is written off in a crash, P can reject the car and reclaim the price (as well as claiming damages): V cannot complain that he has not received back the car because it was V's own breach of contract which prevented P returning it.

Where the seller makes constructive delivery by handing over the documents, for example, a bill of lading, representing the goods before physically delivering the goods themselves, it seems the buyer will not lose his right to reject until after physical delivery of the goods, when he has a reasonable opportunity to examine them, unless he complains of a breach which would be evident from the documents, for example late loading.

The law in this area is somewhat unsatisfactory and does not accord with the expectations of the public. The Law Commission has advocated abolishing the concept of acceptance by an inconsistent act, at least in consumer sales, when the uncertainty of the law may make it easier for a dealer to 'fob off' a consumer, denying his right to a refund.[11] Even in commercial sales there seems to be little good reason for the rule: if a buyer is in a position physically to return the goods, because his sub-buyer has rejected and returned the goods to him, why should he be forced to keep defective goods? The only justification would be the possibility that to allow a refund in such a case would prejudice the seller who believed he had made a sale and acted accordingly.

c) Lapse of time

The buyer will lose his right to reject 'when after the lapse of a reasonable time he retains the goods without intimating to the seller that he has rejected them.' Again, however, the right is only lost if the buyer has had a reasonable opportunity to examine the goods. There must, of course, come a time when the seller can safely regard the contract as closed and assume that he is safe from a claim for a refund. If it were not so the position of sellers would be hopelessly uncertain, particularly in commercial transactions when goods and money might change hands several times leaving a long chain of transactions to be disentangled. Further, if the law were to allow long term rejection rights, business costs of sellers would rise and those costs would be passed on to buyers (and ultimately consumers) in the form of increased prices. The obvious difficulty here is to know what is a 'reasonable time': and the parties may choose to avoid any uncertainty by stipulating a time for notification of defects; such a contractual provision will be valid provided it is reasonable.[12] Thus if the buyer does not notify defects within that time he will lose the right to reject. Few such clauses have been tested by the courts, but many provide for very short periods, often as little as 24 hours, especially where goods are perishable.

If the contract makes no provision for notification of defects, what is reasonable will depend on the circumstances of the case: are the goods perishable? Is the market subject to rapid fluctuation? The seller's conduct may also be relevant. If the buyer notifies a defect, the seller may offer to put it right; if he does so, the buyer should not lose the right to reject if he later discovers other defects, or the repair proves ineffective. Such case law as there is, at least in consumer cases (often involving vehicles) suggests that the buyer who reasonably allows the seller to attempt to remedy one, or a series of defects, will not automatically be held to have lost his right to reject by delay.[13] Similarly, if the seller refuses to acknowledge his liability the buyer should not be penalised, at least for reasonable attempts at negotiation.[14] Litigation is expensive and uncertain, and if the buyer is wrong in alleging a defect, his rejection itself is wrongful and lays him open to a claim for damages for non acceptance. However, the safe course is to reject, demand a refund and refuse repairs at once, at least when the goods are clearly defective.

The lapse of time rule is probably more likely to prejudice consumer buyers than commercial buyers, at least where the commercial buyer buys goods for resale or raw materials for consumption. The rule, particularly due to the uncertainty that surrounds it, can work against the consumer; for example in *Bernstein v Pamsons Motors (Golders Green)*[15] the buyer took delivery of a new car and having travelled 140 miles in three weeks the engine seized up. The cause of the trouble was traced to drops of sealant which had got into the car's lubrication system during the assembly process. Repairs had been carried out but the buyer wished to reject the car and recover the price. The court held that the car was unmerchantable but the buyer had lost his right to reject by lapse of time. The judge observed that section 35(1) allowed a reasonable time to inspect the goods and try them out generally, however, the fact that the defect was not discovered until after delivery was irrelevant in assessing what was a reasonable time. He commented that the length of time required would vary according to the nature of the goods: what was a reasonable time for a bicycle would scarcely be adequate for a nuclear submarine.

1   Either for breach of the implied conditions in ss 13, 14 or s 30 or for breach of an express condition.
2   SGA 1979, s 36 provides that the buyer does not have to return the goods.
3   *Borrowman, Phillips & Co v Free and Hollis* (1878) 4 QBD 500, CA, the seller of unascertained goods allowed to re-tender replacement goods after rejection. See Goode *Commercial Law* (1982) p 298.
4   *Borrowman, Phillips & Co v Free and Hollis*, supra.
5   If the contract was for specific goods only they can be tendered under the contract.
6   The Law Commission (WP 85) recommend that a consumer should have a clear right to reject except when the breach is slight and the seller can show that in the circumstances it is reasonable to require the buyer to accept them.
7   Uniform Commercial Code s 2–508.
8   Such clause would be subject to the Unfair Contract Terms Act and must be reasonable. See 18.0.5.
9   SGA 1979, s 34.
10 *Molling & Co v Dean & Son Ltd* (1901) 18 TLR 217.
11 Law Commission (WP 85) para 4.85.
12 Such a clause would be subject to the test of reasonableness under the Unfair Contract Terms Act 1977. See 18.0.5 and 18.0.11.
13 See *Porter v General Guarantee Corpn* [1982] RTR 384.
14 *Manifatture Tessile Laniera Wooltex v J B Ashley Ltd* [1979] 2 Lloyd's Rep 28.
15 (1986) Times, 25 October.

Acceptance of part

24.1.2   What happens if the seller delivers a consignment of goods only part of which is defective? Can the buyer accept the good and reject the bad? The answer is 'no', at least when the contract is not severable, because by virtue of SGA 1979, s 11(4) the right to reject is lost if the buyer accepts the goods 'or part of them'. There is one exception: s 30(4) covers the situation when the seller delivers goods which fit the contract description together with others which do not. The buyer may then accept those goods which conform to the contract description, and reject the others. However, this idea only applies to goods which fail to fit the contract description; it will not allow partial rejection when goods are of the right description but are defective in quality. So, if P is a clothing manufacturer and buys 1,000 yards of red fabric, and V delivers 500 yards of red fabric and 500 yards of blue, P can keep the red and reject the blue; but if V delivers 1,000 yards but 500 yards are soiled, P must keep or reject the whole: if he keeps the good cloth he must keep the bad and can only claim damages.

Once again the strict law appears to be out of step with commercial practice and common sense; why should the buyer not be able to reject the bad part of the consignment? Obviously, in most cases when part of the consignment is defective the parties will attempt to negotiate a settlement and will probably agree to allow partial rejection. The Law Commission[1] has tentatively proposed reform which would allow the buyer to reject part of a consignment which forms a distinct 'commercial unit': presumably the buyer above could reject any individual soiled roll of the fabric.

1   See Working Paper 85.

Instalment deliveries

24.1.3   The strict rule under s 11(4) prohibiting partial rejection only applies if the contract is not severable. However, what happens if there is a contract for instalment deliveries and one or more instalments is defective? Is the whole contract affected, or can the buyer reject the one instalment? The situation may also raise problems for the seller if the buyer rejects one instalment, or refuses payment for one instalment: he needs to know whether or not he must deliver the remaining instalments.

The first question to ask is whether there is one contract or several. This will depend on the documents and language used: if there are separate contracts, then breach of one has no effect on any other. However, the distinction may be difficult to draw. The seller may send one set of terms and conditions to his customers at the commencement of trading, and the buyer place several orders: each will be governed by the standard terms and conditions but each order will create a separate contract. On the other hand the arrangement may be that the buyer buys a bulk consignment and then calls off stock by a series of orders: then there will probably be one contract for the sale of the whole consignment, with separate deliveries. Again, when parties have dealt together regularly they may have highly streamlined (and often rather informal) methods of doing business allowing the buyer to place orders on mutually agreed and understood terms: there will still be a new contract created by each order. In contrast when a number of items are ordered in one order form, or included in one document, they are likely to be treated as part of one contract, even if they are different in nature. Finally it should be noted that if there is in law one contract, a term that each delivery should be treated as a separate contract will not affect the fact of the contract being one contract, but may be treated as creating a divisible contract.[1]

We are primarily concerned with the case in which there are several deliveries made under one contract. Then we must decide whether the contract is severable (or divisible) or 'entire' (or indivisible): if the contract is not severable the buyer cannot accept part and reject part of the contract goods. The Act does contain a definition: a contract will be severable if there are separate deliveries which are to be separately paid for.[2] However, the definition is not exhaustive and in appropriate cases the court may construe a contract as severable even though it does not meet the definition. For instance in *Regent OHG Aisenstadt und Barig v Francesco of Jermyn St Ltd*,[3] the contract was for the delivery of 62 suits by instalments to be determined by the seller. The court held that the contract was severable.

If the contract is not severable, then s 11(4) applies: if the buyer accepts any one instalment he is then precluded from rejecting any other. He cannot accept part and reject the rest unless he can show that his acceptance of part was conditional on the remaining deliveries being to standard.[4] On the other hand a breach in respect of any one instalment is a breach of the whole contract so that if the buyer wrongfully rejects one instalment the seller can treat the whole contract as ended. Further, if the buyer fails to pay for a particular instalment the seller can exercise his lien over later instalments and withhold delivery to enforce payment.

If, however, the contract is severable, each instalment is treated separately. The first consequence of this is that the buyer can accept one instalment and reject another: s 11(4) has no application. Whether or not a breach in relation to one instalment affects the rest of the contract is less clear. For instance, if one instalment is defective, can the buyer refuse future instalments? Or, if the buyer refuses to pay for an instalment, can the seller refuse to deliver future instalments? The answer depends on the seriousness of the breach and the likelihood of it being repeated: what is the ratio of breach to performance? In *Maple Flock Co Ltd v Universal Furniture Products (Wembley) Ltd*[5] there was a severable contract for the delivery of 100 tons of rag flock by three instalments of one and a half tons each per week. Fifteen deliveries were made; the sixteenth was contaminated and unuseable. Two more deliveries, which were acceptable, were made and the buyers then reported the contaminated delivery and refused to accept any more. The sellers sued: a further four deliveries had been made, all acceptable. The court held that the buyer was in breach: he was bound to accept the other deliveries. There was little likelihood of a repetition, and the ratio of good consignments to bad was 21:1. We can contrast the case with *Robert A Munro & Co Ltd v Meyer*[6] when the contract was for the sale of 1,500 tons of meal and bone meal by weekly deliveries of 125 tons. After half the goods had been delivered it was found that each consignment was adulterated with cocoa husks. The court held that the breach was so serious that the buyer could treat the whole contract as repudiated and refuse future deliveries.

> 'If the breach is of such a kind or in such circumstances as reasonably to lead to the inference that similar breaches will be committed in relation to subsequent deliveries, the whole contract may then and there be regarded as rescinded.'[7]

If the contract is divisible the buyer cannot reject an instalment and then claim an overall short delivery under s 30(1) (which would allow him to reject the whole): the court will prefer the more flexible rules of s 31.[8]

The difficulty here for the businessman is in knowing what to do faced with a breach in relation to one instalment. For instance if the buyer rejects and refuses to pay for one instalment, is the whole contract ended? The seller needs to know whether or not he must deliver the next instalment, or if he should immediately try to mitigate his loss by selling elsewhere. Applying the *Maple Flock* test, he must be advised that there is no clear answer: it will depend on the view the court takes of the seriousness of the breach.

1 See for instance *Robert A Munro & Co Ltd v Meyer* [1930] 2 KB 312.
2 SGA 1979, s 31(2).
3 [1981] 3 All ER 327.
4 *London Plywood and Timber Co Ltd v Nasic Oak Extract Factory and Steam Sawmills Co Ltd* [1939] 2 KB 343.
5 *Maple Flock Co Ltd v Universal Furniture Products (Wembley) Ltd* [1934] 1 KB 148, CA.
6 [1930] 2 KB 312.
7 *Millars' Karri and Jarrah Co (1902) v Weddel, Turner & Co* (1908) 14 Com Cas 25 at 29, per Bigham J.
8 See note 3 above.

The seller's remedies

24.2.0   The buyer's duty is to accept the goods and pay the price. If property has passed, or the seller has delivered the goods and the buyer accepted them, the seller can sue for the price,[1] provided that any credit period has expired. However, what can he do if the buyer refuses to accept the goods? He must then sue for non-acceptance and claim damages for breach of contract.

The first point to note is that mere delay in accepting the goods is not itself a repudiation of the contract.[2] However, the seller may be able to claim any extra costs of storage, and insurance as damages. Further, if delivery is delayed due to the buyer's default, the goods will be at the buyer's risk as regards any loss or damage caused by the delay.[3]

However, if the buyer flatly refuses to accept the goods, ie if he rejects them without good reason, the seller can treat the contract as ended. He will then claim damages for non-acceptance, and as with damages for non-delivery, the amount will depend on the existence of an available market. If there is an available market the seller's damages will be the difference between the contract price and the market value at the date when the buyer should have accepted.[4] Thus if the market has risen the seller gets no damages as he has suffered no loss. However, there is one exception: an available market here depends on supply not exceeding demand. If supply does exceed demand the seller will argue that he has lost a sale even if the market' has remained static or moved in favour of sellers. The authorities then allow the seller to claim the lost profits on the transaction. Thus in *Charter v Sullivan*[5] when a car dealer could sell every new Hillman he could get, there was an available market; the market price rule applied. However, in *W L Thompson v Robinson (Gunmakers) Ltd*[6] there was no market for new Vanguard cars when supply exceeded demand and the seller was able to claim lost profit on a lost sale. As we have seen there is held to be no available market in second hand goods.

SGA 1979, s 49.
SGA 1979, s 10(1).
SGA 1979, s 20(2).
SGA 1979, s 50(3).
[1957] 2 QB 117, [1957] 1 All ER 809, CA.
[1955] Ch 177, [1955] 1 All ER 154.

Remedies against the goods

24.2.1 A right to sue the buyer will often not be enough for the seller. Litigation is precarious as well as expensive. The Act therefore gives the seller certain remedies against the goods themselves by way of protection. However, in practice, the remedies are relatively unimportant, because they depend on the goods not having reached the buyer's hands. The self-help remedy of a reservation of title clause gives the seller a far more potent weapon against the goods.[1]

a) Statutory remedies
All the remedies are given to an unpaid seller, and a seller is treated as unpaid if he has been 'paid' with a cheque which has been dishonoured— although he then has additional rights to sue on the cheque.

(i) Lien Provided he has possession and provided either he has not allowed credit or, if he has, the credit period has expired, the seller has a lien over the goods for the price, which allows him to withhold delivery.[2] However, it will be of limited value: if title has not passed to the buyer, then the seller can withhold delivery as owner. On the other hand it will be very rare in business transactions for the seller to keep possession after property has passed: it will be far more common for him to retain title after giving possession to the buyer. The lien might be useful, however, when there is one entire contract for the sale of specific goods, deliverable by instalments: the seller could then withhold delivery of one instalment against payment of the price for a previous one.

(ii) Stoppage in transit The seller loses his lien if he delivers the goods to the buyer, or if he delivers them to a carrier (other than his own agent) to transmit to the buyer.[3] However, if he has passed the goods to a carrier and the buyer becomes insolvent, the seller can stop the goods in transit and recover possession, and his lien.[4] Again, the right will rarely be useful in practice, particularly in view of the speed of modern transport.

(iii) Resale We have already seen that the vendor may resell the goods if the buyer fails to accept them and either they are perishable or the seller has served a notice requiring the buyer to accept the goods.[5] In addition the seller may resell after exercising his lien or right of stoppage in transit. If he does so, even though title may have passed to the buyer, the new buyer gets good title to the goods, but the seller himself remains open to an action for damages for non-delivery.[6]

Additionally, the seller may include an express right of resale in the contract, which will have the effect of preventing property passing.[7]

1   See 24.3.0.
2   SGA 1979, s 41–43.
3   SGA 1979, s 43.
4   SGA 1979, s 44–46.
5   SGA 1979, s 48(3).
6   SGA 1979, s 48(2).
7   SGA 1979, s 19.

Reservation of title in contracts of sale

24.3.0   Business depends heavily on credit—to finance the start-up of wholly new activities, or to improve cash flow—which may be obtained from a range of sources. Institutional lenders such as banks or finance houses may make loans to finance individual large transactions or, more generally, make rolling credit available in the form of an overdraft facility. However, the ordinary trader who supplies goods (or services) to his customers on terms which allow payment to be postponed is equally a supplier of credit. However, whereas the institutional creditor can protect himself against his debtor's default by taking security for his loan, such as a fixed or floating charge,[1] the ordinary trade supplier–creditor will generally not be able to do that so that if the debtor defaults on payment for goods or services supplied, his only remedy will be to sue for the price. That may be a long-winded or expensive process; if the debtor should be insolvent the position is far worse, for the plight of the unsecured creditor in insolvency proceedings is notorious.

This may seem unfair, especially where a supplier sees goods for which he has not been paid sold for the benefit of other, preferred or secured creditors. The trade supplier of goods could, of course, protect himself by delivering the goods under some arrangement which would prevent title passing to the buyer. Hire purchase would be inappropriate in many cases because such contracts normally prevent the resale of the goods supplied under them;[2] since in many business transactions goods are supplied for resale or use in manufacture on credit terms to improve the buyer's cashflow, a prohibition on resale would stultify the transaction. In Europe and the USA a solution was found in the widespread use of the conditional sale agreement[3] under which goods are supplied subject to a reservation of title to the seller pending payment of the price. In 1975 such a clause fell to be considered by the English courts.[4] A Dutch company supplied aluminium foil to an English company under terms which provided that title to the foil would not pass until the buyer had paid the price. The buyer had gone into receivership after taking delivery of the foil for which it had not paid. However, the foil itself had been resold, and the receiver held the proceeds of sale. The supplier claimed those proceeds and the Court of Appeal held that, since the supplier had retained title to the foil, the buyer had sold the foil on the supplier's behalf, so that it could claim the proceeds. We should note that the case did not uphold the reservation of title clause itself: that was conceded by counsel for the receiver so that the Court of Appeal did not have to consider it. However, the decision was seized on by suppliers of goods as a way of providing protection against a buyer's insolvency, and reservation clauses suddenly proliferated in the terms of trading of English suppliers of goods. The clauses even took a common name from the case and became known as 'Romalpa clauses'. 'It is doubtful whether any case decided this century has created a greater impact on the commercial law.'[5]

Since that original decision there has been much litigation about 'Romalpa clauses', and in a recent case, *Clough Mill Ltd v Martin*,[6] the Court of Appeal has finally held that when a seller supplied yarn knowing that it would be used to make fabric before he was paid, a reservation of title to the yarn pending payment was valid. The court added that each case will depend on its own facts, but it seems unlikely that a simple reservation of title clause can now be effectively challenged.

Unfortunately, the law in this area has developed in piecemeal fashion as individual cases have come before the courts, so that the exact effect of reservation of title clauses and their legality is difficult to discern. In a memorable phrase one judge has described the area as 'a maze, if not a minefield.'[7] Part of the difficulty arises from the many different forms which reservation clauses may take. A seller may simply reserve title to the original goods—but if they are re-sold or consumed he will lose his protection; he may therefore seek to add a claim to the proceeds of sale. If the goods are to be used in a manufacturing process he may seek to claim a share in, or all of, the manufactured product, or the proceeds of its sale. In the most extended form of reservation the seller may attempt to keep title to each consignment until he is paid not only for those goods, but any other sums due to him. As we have said, conclusions are difficult to draw, but the following can probably be said with some certainty:

(a) A basic reservation of title, effectively incorporated into the contract of sale, will probably be effective where the goods remain unsold, identifiable and in their original form.[8] However, the seller must reserve 'ownership', or 'legal title' or some such: a reservation of 'equitable and beneficial ownership' allows legal title to pass and is therefore ineffective.[9]

(b) if the goods are used in a manufacturing process:
   (i) if they are detachable—eg motors incorporated in generator sets—the seller may reclaim them;[10]
   (ii) if they are consumed or irreversibly mixed—for example, resin used to manufacture chipboard, the seller will not be able to claim them.[11] If he makes an express claim to the manufactured product, the court may regard that as a charge and, if the buyer is a company, the charge must be registered to be enforceable against another creditor or liquidator.[12] Difficult problems could arise if two or more suppliers have provided raw materials under reservation of title and all claim a share of the product.

(c) If the goods or manufactured product are re-sold:
   (i) the seller will lose his original goods;[13]
   (ii) he may be able to claim the proceeds of sale but the courts are reluctant to imply such a right;[14]
   (iii) if he expressly claims the proceeds the court may treat that claim as a charge—which will need to be registered;
   (iv) in practice a claim to proceeds of sale will often be worthless: if the buyer is insolvent, his bank account will almost certainly be overdrawn.

(d) If title is reserved until payment of other debts besides the price of the particular goods, the position is unclear. There are dicta in *Clough Mill* which suggest such clauses may be valid, but they seem closely akin to a charge.[15]

1 See 34.3.1.
2 See 20.2.0.
3 Such agreements are generally more common in other jurisdictions than in the UK. See 20.1.2.
4 *Aluminium Industrie Vaassen BV v Romalpa Aluminium Ltd* [1976] 2 All ER 552, [1976] 1 WLR 676.
5 Prof R Goode writing in (1977) Times, 11 May.
6 [1984] 3 All ER 982, [1985] 1 WLR 111, CA.
7 Per Slaughton J, *Hendy Lennox (Industrial Engines) Ltd v Grahame Puttick Engines Ltd* [1984] 2 All ER 152 at 159.

8   *Clough Mill Ltd v Martin* [1984] 3 All ER 982, [1985] 1 WLR 111, CA.
9   *Re Bond Worth Ltd* [1980] Ch 228, [1979] 3 All ER 919. See 20.3.0.
10 *Hendy Lennox (Industrial Engines) Ltd v Grahame Puttick Engines Ltd* [1984] 2 All ER 152, [1984] 1 WLR 485.
11 *Borden (UK) Ltd v Scottish Timber Products Ltd* [1981] Ch 25, [1979] 3 All ER 961, CA.
12 Companies Act 1985, s 395, below 34.3.2.
13 By virtue of Sale of Goods Act 1925, s 25, above 23.0.2.
14 A right to proceeds of sale was implied in *Romalpa* but not in *Hendy Lennox* (supra) nor in *Re Andrabell Ltd (in liquidation), Airborne Accessories Ltd v Goodman* [1984] 3 All ER 407.
15 Such a clause was upheld in *Snow (John) & Co Ltd v DBG Woodcroft & Co Ltd* [1985] BCLC 54 but the point was not taken in argument.

Policy considerations

24.3.1   Since the decision in *Romalpa*, reservation of title clauses have become widely used; they have also been subject to frequent challenge by receivers and liquidators of insolvent companies who, charged with maximising assets available for their appointing creditor, or for creditors generally, have resisted retention of title claims which, if successful, would reduce the pot of assets available for distribution. In many cases they have sought to argue that the clause creates a charge which, in the case of a company, will be ineffective unless registered at the Companies Registry.[1] No case so far has considered the effectiveness of retention of title against an unincorporated buyer.

There is no doubt that the purpose of a reservation of title is to provide the seller with security but 'it is possible to achieve security for an unpaid purchase price in different ways with different legal results'[2] and in *Clough Mill* the Court of Appeal held that the sellers had 'chosen not to use the charging method in relation to unused yarn.'[3] The result may appear strange. The seller allows the buyer extensive rights over the goods sold, akin to those of an owner: he may mix the goods with his own, use them, consume them or sell them and indeed the granting of such rights is essential to the transaction, making credit available to the buyer. The goods nevertheless remain the property of the seller. It has been argued that the buyer acts as agent for the seller when he uses or sells the goods, but that too is unrealistic. The buyer's objective is to make a profit for himself and to discharge a debt to the seller.

An effective reservation of title may do much to improve the position of an unsecured supplier-creditor should his customer prove insolvent. However, a number of objections have been raised to such provisions and they raise difficult policy issues which the courts cannot address. First, reservation of title allows the supplier-creditor to gain priority over other creditors in an insolvency, effectively 'leap frogging' the queue and the order of distribution prescribed by statute.[4] Second, it is only one particular group of creditors, the suppliers of goods or materials, who may benefit; similar protection is not available to the supplier of services and to the extent that the position of the supplier of goods is improved, that of other creditors is prejudiced. Third, it is possible that if the widespread use of reservation of title led to a serious depletion in the pot of assets available to institutional credit suppliers, they would reduce the amount of credit made available to business, with possibly wide ranging deleterious effects.[5] Fourth, it is said that suppliers may protect themselves in other ways; by assessing the credit worthiness of customers and negotiating appropriate contract terms, which might improve business efficiency; or by taking out bad debt insurance, premiums for such insurance reflecting the risk of business failure and enabling the cost of premiums to be passed on to customers or clients. The cost of business failure would then be spread more widely over all its ultimate customers. Fifth, it is said that the reservation of title clause gives security without publicity. Whereas (for instance) the bank must register its floating charge in a register open to the public, there is no outward sign that goods supplied subject to reservation of title are not the property of the debtor, who may therefore present a misleading appearance of credit worthiness to the world.[6] However, the same objection can be made to many other arrangements including the ordinary conditional sale, hire purchase and even equipment leases; in many foreign jurisdictions all such security arrangements are alike subject to a registration requirement.[7] In 1971 the Crowther Committee on Consumer Credit[8] recommended a similar scheme for Great Britain and proposed a Lending and Security Act; the Cork Committee on Insolvency Law and Practice[9] approved such a course but also made specific recommendations to deal with problems posed by reservation of title, including that such clauses should be registered to be effective. Neither set of proposals has been taken up, although the Insolvency Act 1986 does provide a moratorium on creditors enforcing rights under a reservation of title clause when an administration order is made with a view to facilitating the recovery of a company in financial difficulties.[10] The law in this area thus remains unclear; an authoritative House of Lords decision might be welcome but would probably not deal with all the points of uncertainty and could not adequately consider the policy issues. Moreover, in the light of the *Clough Mill* decision it is unlikely that such a case would reach the House. However, the government has recently appointed Professor Aubrey Diamond to review the law relating to security interests over moveable property. A consultative paper published by the Department of Trade and Industry[11] suggests that the government is considering the questions of whether security interests should be subject to a general requirement of registration and whether reservation of title clauses should be regarded as creating security interests.

1   Companies Act 1985, s 395. See 34.3.2.
2   *Clough Mill Ltd v Martin* [1984] 3 All ER 982, [1985] 1 WLR 111, CA, per Lord Donaldson at 994.
3   Ibid.
4   See 36.0.15.
5   The possibility was considered in 1982 by the Cork Committee but no evidence of such action was found.
6   The goods will normally appear in the buyer's accounts as his property. But see 20.7.4 above.
7   For example the United States Uniform Commercial Code Article 9; registration is also required in France and Italy.
8   Cmnd 4596, 1971, para 1640.
9   Cmnd 8558, 1982.
10   Insolvency Act 1986, ss 10–11; see 36.0.7.
11   'Security Interests in Property other than Land,-A Consultative Paper' (Department of Trade and Industry, 1986).

Chapter 25

Contracts Involving Services

25.0.0 In contrast to contracts involving the sale and supply of goods Parliament has not subjected contracts involving services to much attention.[1] The Supply of Goods and Services Act 1982 (SGSA 1982) provides that in a contract of work and materials, the material or goods element of the contract are subjected to the three standard implied conditions regulating all contracts for the supply of goods; the service element of the contract falls to be regulated by the provisions of Part Two of the Act. Under such provisions three terms are implied into all contracts under which a person agrees to carry out a service. These are: an implied term that the service will be carried out with reasonable care and skill; that where no time is fixed the service will be carried out in a reasonable time; and where the consideration is not fixed a reasonable charge will be paid. These terms were intended to codify the existing common law not change the law.

It could be argued that the absence of statutory implied terms did not have a wholly detrimental effect on the recipient of a service, since the courts developed common law standards in respect of services, akin to those under the Sale of Goods Act.[2] However, the lack of attention paid to services has meant that exclusion clauses in such contracts have not been regulated as closely as those in sale of goods transactions, particularly in the context of a consumer contract. For example, a consumer entering into a contract for the supply of a service could fall foul of an exclusion clause unless such a clause is held to be reasonable under UCTA 1977,[3] however, where the contract was for the sale of goods an exclusion clause in respect of any of the implied terms is void.[4]

Defining contractual obligations in a statute has the additional advantage over piecemeal common law development, in that it focuses attention on the suppliers' obligations, reminding them of their responsibilities to clients and customers. Statutory provisions offer greater clarity and certainty to the businessman and his adviser should they become involved in disputes and serve as a readily accessible reference point.[5]

Where the public interest is identified as being at risk, Parliament has subjected certain business activities involving services to additional scrutiny. For example, solicitors are closely regulated by statute,[6] the activities of estate agents are controlled under the Estate Agents Act 1979 and persons involved in the credit industry are required to obtain a licence and are regulated by the Consumer Credit Act 1974.[7] In addition many professional associations, with varying degrees of enthusiasm, subject their members to close scrutiny.[8]

1   See Unfair Contract Terms Act 1977.
2   See for example *Greaves & Co (Contractors) Ltd v Baynham, Meikle & Partners* [1975] 3 All ER 99, [1975] 1 WLR 1095, CA.
3   See 18.0.7.
4   See 21.8.0.
5   See 'Service Please. Services and the Law: a Consumer View' 1981 NCC p 23.
6   The Solicitors Act 1974.
7   See 26.3.1 and 2.5.6.
8   See 2.5.1 and 2.5.4.

Service contracts caught by the Act
25.0.1   Unless specifically excluded, the implied terms in the 1982 Act apply to all contracts for the supply of services whether or not goods are also transferred or bailed by way of hire.[1] Thus the provisions regulate the service element of such contracts as the installation of domestic or industrial equipment and plant, vehicle repair and servicing, plumbing and electrical work. Other contracts caught are professional accounting, legal, financial, and similar services, as well as a wide range of domestic and leisure services.

The provisions only apply to services supplied under a contract. Where a person relies on services supplied gratuitously or supplied to some other party, as in the case of an investor relying on the audited accounts of a company they can only sue in negligence.[2] For the purpose of the Act a contract of employment or apprenticeship is not a contract for the supply of a service.

The Secretary of State has the power to make exclusion orders providing that one or more of the implied terms shall not apply to services of a particular description.[3] Two such exclusion orders have been made covering s 13, first in relation to advocates, arbitrators and company directors,[4] and the second in relation to the directors of building societies and members of the committee of management of a society registered under the Industrial and Provident Societies Act 1985.[5]

a) Advocates
This exemption extends to cover the services of an advocate in court or before any tribunal, inquiry or arbitrator and in carrying out preliminary work directly affecting the conduct of the hearing. The reasoning behind the exemption is that to permit someone to sue as a solicitor or barrister for not exercising proper care and skill in court would, of necessity, mean re-opening the judicial proceedings which would be clearly undesirable.

b) Directors
The duties and responsibilities of company directors are laid down in the Companies Act 1985 and in a great deal of case law. It was felt better to exempt directors rather than confuse the existing company law. Some directors also have contracts of employment with their company to cover executive duties that they perform. Since contracts of employment are exempt, the imposition of section 13 on directors would have required the courts to undertake a somewhat artificial and over-complex analysis of the precise capacity in which a particular director was acting. The same reasoning applies to the exemption covering building society directors and members of

the management committee of societies registered under the Industrial and Provident Societies Act 1985.

1 S 12.
2 See 7.1.8.
3 S 12(4).
4 The Supply of Services (Exclusion of Implied Terms) Order 1982 SI 1982/1771.
5 Supply of Services (Exclusion of Implied Terms) Order 1983 SI 1982/902.

Care and skill
25.0.2 Section 13 provides that where the supplier of a service under a contract is acting in the course of business, there is an implied term that the supplier will carry out the service with reasonable care and skill. Like the implied term in respect of quality and fitness for purpose under the Sale of Goods Act, this implied term only applies to services provided in the course of business.

The standard adopted is that of the common law and there are countless authorities laying down general propositions on the requisite degree of care and skill for a particular profession or skill. In general the law is not looking for perfection, the supplier must simply 'exercise the ordinary skill of an ordinary competent man exercising that particular art.'[1]

Lord Denning has said that:

> 'The law does not usually imply a warranty that he will achieve the desired result, but only a term that he will use reasonable care and skill. The surgeon does not warrant that he will cure the patient. Nor does the solicitor warrant that he will win the case. . . . It seems to me that . . . his duty is to use reasonable care and skill in the course of his employment (contract).'[2]

Much depends upon the circumstances of the case and the nature of the trade or profession.[3] Thus carpet-layers were in breach of an implied term when they left the carpet in such a condition that it represented a danger to anyone using the premises.[4] On the other hand, carpet-layers were not in breach of duty when they failed to lay a carpet so that the medallion pattern was central in relation to the width of the carpet.[5]

The implied term does not extend to a requirement that the services provided will be fit for a particular purpose or achieve a desired result. However, in *Greaves & Co (Contractors) Ltd v Baynham, Meikle & Partners*[6] contractors engaged by an oil company to build a warehouse for the storage of barrels of oil had sub-contracted to a firm of structural engineers the work of designing the building, including the floors. It was pointed out to them that stacker trucks carrying drums of oil would be running over the floors. Soon after the warehouse had become operational cracks appeared in the floor, caused by vibration produced by the stacker trucks. It was held that since the engineers had been informed of the purpose of the warehouse, they were in breach of an implied term that if the work was completed in accordance with the design, it would be reasonably fit for the use of loaded stacker trucks.

It has been suggested that a standard of care based on reasonableness is not high enough and that strict liability should be adopted as in the case of goods.[7] Such a change was rejected by the Royal Commission on Civil Liability[8] on the basis that it would present problems in defining the range of

331

services to be covered. It was considered that designers and architects who supply technical information services might be discouraged from supplying advice and information if they were strictly liable. In addition it was suggested that many providers of services in the course of a business have small businesses with few fixed assets, and are thus not as able to bear or insure against the cost of their liabilities as the producers of goods are.

A consultative document on consumer safety supported the reasonableness test on the following lines:

> 'The person performing the service is not therefore in the same position as a seller in that he is controlled by the customer's instructions. He cannot require a customer to order a complete overhaul or even an adequate repair. Rules for servicing must therefore differ from rules governing the sale of goods and it would seem impracticable to require more than that the repair or service ordered by the customers should be competently performed and that it should not be defective or hazardous in itself, and that if it would in itself render the article in use more hazardous it should not be carried out.'[9]

1   McNair J *Bolam v Friern Hospital Management in Committee* [1957] 2 All ER 118, [1957] 1 WLR 582. See 2.12.2.
2   *Greaves & Co (Contractors) Ltd v Baynham, Meikle & Partners* [1975] 3 All ER 99 at 103–5.
3   See 7.2.2.
4   *Kimler v William Willett Ltd* [1947] KB 570, [1947] 1 All ER 361, CA.
5   *CRC Flooring v Heaton* (8 October 1980, unreported). See Lawson, 'The Quality of Services Supplied: Guidance from the Court of Appeal', NLJ 39 1984.
6   [1975] 3 All ER 99, [1975] 1 WLR 1095, CA.
7   See 21.6.0.
8   *Royal Committee on Civil Liability and Compensation for Personal Injury* Cmnd 7054, 1978, p 278.
9   Department of Prices and Consumer Protection: 'Consumer Safety. A Consultative Document' Cmnd 6398, 1976, p 22.

Time for performance

25.0.3   Section 14 provides that where the parties have not agreed a particular time for the performance of a contract, and a time cannot be ascertained from previous dealings or calculated under the terms of the contract, there is an implied term that the service will be carried out within a reasonable time.

This section simply reiterates a well established common law rule.[1] What is a reasonable time is a question of fact and may require expert evidence on the time that a competent supplier would take to complete the work. In *Charnock v Liverpool Corpn*[2] a garage took eight weeks to complete a car repair which should have been completed within five weeks at most. The explanation for the delay was that the garage was short staffed and was giving priority to manufacturers' warranty work. The Court of Appeal held the garage liable for the delay, awarding damages to cover the cost of hiring a vehicle for the additional three weeks beyond the time when the work ought to have been completed.

1   See SGA, s 29 for the equivalent provision in respect of goods.
2   [1968] 3 All ER 473, [1968] 1 WLR 1498, CA.

A reasonable price

25.0.4   If the consideration for a service is not fixed by the contract and there is no provision for determining it in the contract and no previous course of dealings, s 15 provides that a reasonable charge will be payable. Although it is unwise to enter into a contract before knowing the likely charge, a great many transactions are concluded on that basis. For example, accountants and solicitors invariably do not agree a fee before undertaking work on behalf of a client.

What is a reasonable charge is a question of fact. Where however the customer considers that the charge is excessive, it should be disputed immediately. If the charge is agreed to without complaint and later disputed, the earlier agreement will be conclusive evidence that the charge was reasonable.

In order to avoid disputes over the consideration the customer can set an upper limit on the charge. This has the effect that the supplier requires to obtain authority from the customer where the limit is likely to be exceeded. Alternatively an estimate of the cost may be requested which then acts as a target figure and a yardstick if a reasonable charge is required to be assessed. In general an estimate is regarded as a considered approximation of the likely cost involved, the actual contract price may be slightly more or less than the estimate. A quotation price is however generally binding,[1] even where labour costs and materials might have increased. If additional work is requested then the quotation may be exceeded.

1 See *Croshaw v Pritchard and Renwick* (1899) 16 TLR 45.

Part V
Financing the supply of goods and services

Chapter 26

The Development and Regulation of Credit

26.0.0 Credit represents an ever increasing aspect of business activity. In both consumer and commercial transactions credit facilities play a key role in financing the acquisition of goods and services or supporting general business activity. As Galbraith points out: 'The process of persuading people to incur debt and the arrangements for them to do so, are as much a part of modern production as the making of the goods and the nurturing of wants.'[1]

In a business context the word 'credit' is often used to signify a person's financial status: they might be described as a 'good credit risk'. In legal terms, however, the word is used to describe a variety of related financial accommodations. Indeed the Consumer Credit Act 1974 (CCA 1974) states that 'credit includes a cash loan, and any other form of financial accommodation.'[2]

Such accommodations generally fall into two broad categories: lender or loan credit and vendor credit. Lender credit refers to a straightforward loan of funds to a debtor either in the form of a fixed amount or a fluctuating amount as in the case of a bank overdraft, where the funds are not tied to a specific transaction. Vendor credit relates to accommodations where all or part of the purchase price for goods and services is deferred such as in a hire purchase, conditional sale or credit sale. Before the passing of the Consumer Credit Act 1974 the law had treated lender and vendor credit entirely separately, with the result that credit law had become confused and irrational. As the Crowther Committee observed in 1971:

'it is to us of the highest importance to recognise that they are, in fact, two aspects of the same thing—the transfer of purchasing power from one set of persons to another set of persons, against a promise to repay the principal with interest.'[3]

The development of the various forms of credit transaction invariably coincided with parallel developments in government policy, economic activity and consumer behaviour. For example, when the hire purchase transaction became popular it was subjected to increasing regulation in terms of both consumer protection and as a manipulator of economic activity in the economy. Governments could increase or reduce demand in the economy by making changes to the amount required by way of minimum deposit.

337

The following paragraphs describe the principal forms of credit transaction.

1   J K Galbraith, *The Affluent Society* (1970) p 167.
2   S 9(1).
3   *Report of the Committee on Consumer Credit* Cmnd 4596, 1971, para 1.1.2.

The provision of loans/lender credit
26.0.1   A loan is simply an arrangement whereby a debtor is advanced a sum of money which is repaid over a period of time. The debtor agrees to repay fixed amounts over the period of the loan inclusive of interest. The rate of interest will be fixed according to the prevailing market rate at which lending institutions are advancing funds and such factors as the degree of risk for the creditor. Normally the creditor will be aware of why the loan is required but in practice, where funds are transferred directly to the debtor, little control can be exercised over how the loan is used.

The banks are one of the main sources for loans both to individuals and business organisations. In the case of individual personal advances funds may be transferred by way of personal loan or overdraft. A personal loan merely involves the transfer of a fixed sum loan to the account of the debtor and the opening of a loan account which is debited initially with the amount advanced plus interest charges. The loan account operates until the debt has been extinguished over the fixed period.

Overdrafts are a means of allowing customers to overdraw on their current accounts up to a maximum debit balance. Such loans are therefore of fluctuating amount, depending upon how much is paid into and withdrawn from the account at any one time. Overdrafts are intended as a facility for customers whose cash flow varies from time to time; they are not used to finance specific transactions.

Personal loans have become increasingly popular because unlike hire purchase and credit sale, they can be used to finance the purchase of services, for example holidays, as well as goods. The banks offer an attractive source of funds for both individual and corporate clients, since in addition to protection afforded to customers by the contract based consumer protection legislation, banks are subjected to considerable institutional regulation.[1] Other institutions involved in lending are finance houses. These institutions expanded considerably with the growth of hire purchase and a great part of their business is still the provision of instalment credit finance. Finance houses tend to be subsidiaries of banks, large retailers and manufacturers, and other financial institutions. Such institutions have however diversified considerably into such activities as credit card operation, personal loans, and leasing.

In addition to banks and finance houses there are moneylending firms. These are businesses that specialise in advancing cash loans to individuals at rates of interest, usually, in excess of the current market rate. The activities of moneylenders caused considerable concern in the late nineteenth century. A House of Commons Select Committee on Moneylending in 1898 considered that:

> 'the system of moneylending by professional moneylenders at high rates of interest is productive of crime, bankruptcy, unfair advantages over other creditors of the borrower, extortion from the borrower's family and friends, and other serious injuries to the community.'[2]

Moneylenders were subjected to increasing regulation by a series of Money-lenders Acts. Under this legislation they had to have an annual licence, moneylending contracts were required to be evidenced in writing, the true rate of interest had to be stated, restrictions were placed on advertising and canvassing for business, and the courts were given the power to reopen unconscionable bargains.[3] Many of the provisions in the Moneylenders Acts formed the model upon which the Consumer Credit Act was based and which now regulates moneylending, along with other credit transactions.

1   Banking Act 1979.
2   Brit Parl Papers 1898 260, X, 106, p v.
3   See Moneylenders Act 1927.

Secured loans

26.0.2   The lending institutions may often require some form of security before advancing funds. For example, on a long term loan for the purchase of a house the institution will require that a charge (mortgage) over the house be enacted in its favour. Similarly, in the case of a corporate client requiring funds to expand the business the lending institution will require the assets of the company to be charged as security for the loan.[1] Under either of these security arrangements the creditor is given an interest in the property or asset and thus should the debtor default or become insolvent, the creditor can seize the land or assets and sell them to recoup the amount outstanding on the loan.

As an alternative or in addition to a charge over property, the security may take the form of a personal security whereby a third party agrees to guarantee to repay a loan advanced to a debtor in the event of default.

In addition to the sources of finance identified above, building societies play a major role in financing house purchase. However, under the terms of the Building Societies Act 1986 they are now permitted to offer wider credit facilities.

1   See 34.3.0.

Vendor credit

26.0.3   One factor which distinguishes loans or lender credit from vendor credit is that although a loan may be advanced for the purchase of identifiable goods, there is a clear distinction between the person providing the loan and the person providing the goods. In the case of vendor credit, the person who supplies the goods may also supply the credit. For example, in a typical hire purchase transaction[1] a customer identifies the goods he requires and negotiates with the retailer. The retailer will sell the goods to an associated finance company and the finance company will enter into a hire purchase contract with the customer: thus both the goods and the credit are supplied by the finance company although the goods originate from and are despatched by the retailer. The following are the principal forms of vendor credit.

a) Hire purchase

As we have seen the hire purchase transaction became popular in the late nineteenth century to the extent that by 1891 there were probably one million agreements in existence and in that year the Hire Trades Protection Association was formed.[2] Once the House of Lords[3] accepted the theoretical basis of the hire purchase contract as a bailment or hire, with an option to purchase, it flourished as a means of instalment credit. With the mass production of cars, radios, radiograms, vacuum cleaners and other household appliances, the hire purchase contract provided the means by which consumers could enjoy the use of such goods immediately, paying for them over two or three years. From the 1920s the finance houses became a significant element in instalment selling. Retailers could not provide the extensive credit facilities necessary to satisfy demand for the more expensive consumer goods.

The modern finance house owes its origins to three basic sources. First, the companies which were formed in the 1860s to finance the purchase of specialised coal wagons for the railway and colliery companies. Second, the extension to the UK of American companies that had financed a consumer credit boom in the USA. Third, the establishment by UK manufacturing companies of finance houses to support the market in their own goods.

It was in the 1920s that the hire purchase contract assumed its present three-cornered appearance; apart from cash transactions a seller did not sell directly to customers, but to the finance company which then hired to the customer with an option to purchase. Since such transactions were not regarded as loans on security of the goods the restrictive provisions of the Moneylenders Acts and Bills of Sale Act were not permitted to inhibit the growth in hire purchase.

Thus, apart from the general law of contract the hire purchase transaction was free from control, which undoubtedly contributed to its popularity amongst the finance houses. Consumers also derived benefit, as the Crowther Committee observed:

> 'There can be little doubt that this by-passing of the Moneylenders Acts has been in the interests of consumers as a class, since otherwise the great extension of credit to ordinary households, and the higher material standards of living based upon it, would not have been possible.'[4]

However, the Committee proceeded to identify the inevitable corollary of that proposition, that consumers were subjected to abuses and deprived of comprehensive protections that such Acts were intended to afford. A particular abuse was the 'snatch back' of goods by a company for a trivial default by the customer, when nearly all the instalments had been paid. The goods would be disposed of without any compensation to the hirer for the amount paid, and thus a considerable profit would be made for the hiring company.

Because of pressure from public opinion and social reformers, the Hire Purchase Act 1938 was passed with the object of attacking some of the worst abuses in the hire purchase business. Basic formalities were introduced for hire purchase contracts within a financial limit and restrictions were placed on the remedies for default by a customer. There followed a series of statutes gradually extending protection, culminating in the Hire-Purchase Act 1965, many of the provisions of which are now contained in CCA 1974.

(b) Conditional sale agreements

A conditional sale agreement is a contract for the sale of goods in which the property (ownership) remains in the seller until payment of the price or performance of other specified conditions. For reasons already outlined its use has been largely confined to commercial as opposed to consumer contracts, because of the attractiveness of hire purchase. The CCA 1974 largely ignores the conceptual distinction between the two transactions and equates one with the other.

(c) Credit sale

What distinguishes credit sale from conditional sale and hire purchase is that the seller does not reserve the property in the goods. Such agreements have become increasingly popular with large department stores and mail order firms in respect of goods that either do not have a high value or that depreciate rapidly. There is no point in reserving the property in goods if such goods have a limited resale value.

(d) Rental agreements [5]

Although not strictly a form of instalment credit, the Crowther Committee considered that rental agreements should be treated as a form of vendor credit. In much the same way that hire purchase benefited by being relatively free from statutory control until 1938, rental agreements emerged as an alternative to hire purchase when such contracts became subject to greater control. Indeed such agreements remained relatively free from legislative control until the CCA 1974.

1   See 20.2.0.
2   See Crowther Committee (1971) p 43.
3   *Helby v Matthews* [1895] AC 471, HL.
4   P 44.
5   See 20.7.0 to 20.7.4.

Hybrid transactions

26.0.4   By the 1960s a trend was developing towards transactions which did not easily fall into the category of lender or vendor credit. The Crowther Committee termed such agreements 'hybrid transactions' since they were closely tied to the supply of goods or services but retained the flexibility of pure loans. Indeed one reason for the development of such transactions was the growth of a market for the provision of finance tied to the supply of services, for which clearly hire purchase and conditional sale were inappropriate. Finance houses started to provide personal loans to the customers of retailers with whom they had pre-existing arrangements. Thus in legal terms the customer entered into two separate transactions, a loan from the finance house and a sale or supply of services from the retailer. This contrasts with hire purchase, where the finance house supplies both goods and credit. The attraction for finance houses of providing loans through a retailer was that until the CCA 1974 they could not be held responsible for the quality of goods and services supplied.

An increasingly popular form of credit facility is the plastic credit card[1] which in many respects offers more than the opportunity to be supplied with goods or services and is viewed as a convenience by consumers. Credit cards are a form of revolving or 'running account credit' whereby the card holder can use the card during a monthly accounting period to enter into numerous transactions for goods and services up to a credit limit, interest being payable on the amount outstanding at the end of the monthly accounting period. Such credit cards are issued by large scale retailers for use at their own outlets or by banks and finance houses for use at any business designated to accept their particular card, for example Access or Barclaycard/Visa.

The business pays a commission to the credit card company for the privilege of being able to offer the facilities and thereby attract additional customers. Indeed for this reason it could be argued that credit cards, by adding to costs of business in terms of paying the commission and extra administrative arrangements, increase the price of goods and services.

A credit card must be distinguished from a cheque card issued by banks guaranteeing that the cheque in respect of which the card was used will be paid irrespective of whether there are sufficient funds in the customer's account.

Other examples of hybrid transactions are shop budget and credit accounts whereby a customer makes a regular periodic payment into an account and is given credit for a specified multiple of the monthly payment. The customer must then pay for the purchases within a specified period. Check trading is another hybrid transaction. The credit is extended in the form of vouchers or trading checks each carrying a specific value, which can be used at retailer outlets that have arrangements with the check trading company. The retailer is paid by the check company less a commission and the customer pays the check company by instalments.[2]

1   When the Access card was launched 3,800,000 cards were issued in 64 days.
2   In essence such forms of credit are moneylending.

Trade credit

26.0.5   It is important to distinguish the above examples of credit facility which are deliberate and formalised as between the parties, from ordinary trade credit whereby there is often a time lapse between delivery of goods or performance of a service, and payment. Such arrangements whether they be in respect of domestic agreements such as milk and newspaper accounts or between one business and another, are part and parcel of commercial activity. Whilst there is no denying that they are credit transactions, the Crowther Committee considered that it was undesirable to subject such informal arrangements to general credit legislation.[1]

1   Page 3.

The Crowther Committee report

26.1.0   The Crowther Committee considered that credit law as it had developed was deficient in the following respects:[1]
(a) It lacked any functional basis, distinctions between one type of transaction and another being drawn on the basis of legal abstractions rather than on the basis of commercial reality.
(b) The law did not distinguish consumer from commercial transactions.
(c) There was an artificial separation between the law relating to lending and the law relating to security for loans.
(d) There was no rational policy relating to the rights of third parties.
(e) Many statutes were excessively technical.
(f) There was no consistent policy in relation to sanctions for infringement
(g) 'The fact is that the present law relating to credit, based largely on legislation enacted in the last century, is unsuited to modern commercial requirements and fails to tackle everyday problems in a realistic manner.'[2]

The solution was a massive rationalisation of the law regulating all credit transactions. The Committee proposed two statutes: a Lending and Security Act to rationalise the regulation of security interests and conflicts between secured parties and a Consumer Sale and Loan Act which would regulate consumer credit transactions, including a requirement for those involved in the credit industry to be licensed. The first proposal was rejected by the government, the second subsequently became the CCA 1974.

1   See Crowther, Ch 4.
2   P 181.

The Consumer Credit Act 1974

26.2.0   The Consumer Credit Act received the Royal Assent on 31 July 1974, but because of its complexity and comprehensive scope it was not fully implemented until 1985. It repealed much of the existing legislation regulating credit and replaced it with a framework of law based upon common rules and principles applicable to most credit and hire transactions. In essence the CCA 1974 seeks to control trading malpractices, redress bargaining inequality between consumers and traders and regulate the remedies for default.[1]

The controls provided by the Act are:

(a)   the control of the credit industry generally by the issue of licences, restrictions on advertising and canvassing and wide supervisory powers of the Director General of Fair Trading.

(b)   the control of individual agreements on such matters as formalities, termination, cancellation and default.

1   See Crowther, Ch 6.

The Director General

26.3.0   The Crowther Committee favoured the creation of a Consumer Credit Commissioner to oversee the legislation and act as an Ombudsman in the field of consumer credit. It was decided however to extend the scope of the activities of the Director General of Fair Trading to cover credit and thus avoid unnecessary duplication of resources. The principal role of the Director General is in granting, renewing, varying, suspending and revoking licences. In addition he is required to supervise the legislation, disseminate information and advice, and periodically review the operation of the Act.

Licensing

26.3.1   In justifying the need for a system of licensing under the auspices of a regulatory body the Crowther Committee observed that the efficacy of the protective measures concerned with individual transactions is in practice limited:

> 'by the fact that a single individual may be unaware of his legal rights or unable or unwilling to exercise them; and the more unscrupulous type of credit grantor may well take the view that the occasional check on his malpractices by a determined consumer in an isolated transaction is not a serious deterrent, and is outweighed by the financial advantages he may derive from evading the law. There is thus a need for an agency

343

entrusted with the continuing supervision of consumer credit grantors, with power to investigate trading practices, require production of accounts and records and, in the case of serious malpractice, suspend or revoke the offender's licence.'[1]

As noted earlier, a licensing system operated under the Moneylenders Act 1927 but the system was decentralised, with no duty of enforcement placed on any particular agency. Thus in practice enforcement was practically non-existent.

Consistent with the comprehensive nature of the CCA 1974, a licence is not only required by those that provide credit or hire (rental) facilities, but also those involved in ancillary credit businesses. Thus a licence is required to carry on a consumer credit business and a consumer hire business.[2] Local authorities and bodies empowered by a public general Act to carry on such a business are however exempt. In effect all businesses, in so far as their activities comprise or relate to the provision of credit or hire agreements caught by the Act, (such agreements are termed regulated agreements under the Act) are required to be licensed. It is important to realise that the provision of credit or hire agreements need not be the principal business; if credit or hire agreements are made in the course of any business a licence will be required.[3]

The Act identifies five categories of activity as ancillary credit businesses. Thus any business in so far as it comprises or relates to one or more of the following activities requires a licence:

(i)   credit brokerage;
(ii)   debt-adjusting;
(iii) debt-counselling;
(iv)   debt-collecting;
(v)   the operation of a credit reference agency.

(a) *Credit brokerage* relates to the business of introducing individuals to persons that provide either consumer credit or goods under consumer hire agreement. The definition under the Act is wide enough to include the activities of insurance agencies and mortgage brokers, solicitors and accountants arranging loans for clients, estate agents introducing prospective buyers to building societies as well as retail outlets that introduce their own customers to a finance house in order to finance the supply of goods or services.[4]

(b) *Debt-adjusting* relates to renegotiating, on behalf of a debtor/hirer, a debt incurred under a consumer credit or hire agreement. It also covers the situation where a debt is taken over, or otherwise liquidated, in return for payments by the consumer.[5]

(c) *Debt-counselling* is simply giving advice to debtors/hirers in respect of the liquidation of debts due under a consumer credit or hire agreement.[6]

(d) *Debt-collecting* is the taking of steps to procure payment of debts due under consumer credit or hire agreement.[7]

(e) A *credit reference agency* is a person carrying on a business comprising the furnishing of persons with information relevant to the financial standing of individuals, being information collected by the agency for that purpose.[8]

1   P 255.
2   S 21(1).
3   However, a person may not be treated as carrying on a credit or hire business simply because he occasionally enters into such transactions, s 189(2).

4   There is an exemption in s 146(5) for individuals acting as free-lance collectors for check
    traders or agents for mail order.
5   S 145.
6   S 145.
7   S 146.
8   S 145.

Licence applications

26.3.2   There are two types of licence: standard licences and group licences.
A standard licence is issued to a single person (including a company), or to a
partnership or unincorporated body in the name of the partnership or body.
It lasts for ten years and authorises the licensee to carry on the activities
described by the licence.[1]

Group licences are of indefinite duration and are issued by the Director
General to cover persons operating in a particular business, if the public
interest is better served by doing so, rather than by obliging the persons
concerned to apply separately for standard licences. A person covered by a
group licence may also apply for a standard licence, indeed, they must if
their precise credit business activities are not covered by the group licence.
Group licences have, for example, been issued to the Law Society in respect
of solicitors holding practising certificates, to the Institute of Chartered
Accountants in respect of their practising members and to the National Association of Citizens Advice Bureaux covering bureaux registered with them.

Since licensing commenced in 1976 the number of applications for
licences has been over 150,000. A person must be granted a licence if he
satisfies the DGFT that he is a fit person to engage in activities covered by
the licence, and the name or names under which he applies is or are not
misleading or otherwise undesirable. Factors taken into account are whether
the applicant or persons associated with the applicant, have committed any
offence involving fraud, dishonesty, violence or a breach of consumer law;
practised discrimination on sex, colour, racial, ethnic or national grounds;
or engaged in deceitful, oppressive, unfair or improper business practices
(whether lawful or not).[2] Specific factors in the former category include
breaches of the CCA 1974 provisions, convictions under the Trade Descriptions Act 1968, or supplying goods that are not of merchantable quality.
Unfair or improper business practices include variation of the interest rate
stated in an agreement, pressuring consumers into purchases by causing
anxiety about their state of health, and failure to settle outstanding debts on
cars taken in part-exchange.[3]

The decision of the DGFT whether to grant a licence is based on information provided by the applicant on the application form and information
supplied from such sources as local authority consumer protection departments. If the DGFT decides not to issue a licence he must inform the
applicant that he is 'minded to refuse',[4] giving his reasons and inviting
representations. Where the only evidence against granting a licence consists
of complaints, the DGFT has outlined the problems involved in issuing a
'minded to refuse' notice:

> 'Counter statements designed to show that the complaint is
> misconceived may raise sufficient questions about the validity of the
> complaint that we are unable to make a finding of fact on the issues
> raised. In short, it is very difficult for me to arrive at a decision which is

not favourable to the applicant in those cases which are comprised solely of complaints. Such cases are, however, very rare indeed, for we would try to obtain other supportive evidence to lend weight to the proposed case.'[5]

If the DGFT remains unconvinced after considering representation from the applicant, an appeal may be made to the Secretary of State or the High Court on a point of law.[6] Alternatively, the DGFT can seek undertakings from the applicant in respect of future conduct and proceed to issue the licence.

Once the licence has been granted the DGFT has the right to suspend or revoke it should he consider that if it had expired, he would be 'minded to refuse' it.[7] The same procedure would then be followed as in an original application.

1   Fees are payable for a licence; £150 for a company or partnership and £80 for a sole trader, plus £10 for each additional category of business applied for.
2   S 25(2).
3   See eg Annual Report of the Director General of Fair Trading 1981, p 21.
4   S 27(1)(a).
5   Borrie, 'Licensing Practice under the Consumer Credit Act' 1982 J Bus L 91, 95–6.
6   S 34.
7   S 32.

Enforcement of licensing

26.3.3   A person who engages in any activity for which a licence is required without holding a licence in respect of those activities commits an offence.[1] A more potent sanction, however, is that any agreement caught by the Act which is made by an unlicensed business cannot be enforced against the consumer without an order from the DGFT.[2] Where a customer is introduced to a creditor by an unlicensed credit broker the agreement will also be unenforceable even where the actual creditor is licensed.[3] This latter provision, in effect, introduced an element of self-policing into the licensing system. As Sir Gordon Borrie observed:

'Creditors who at one time may have used credit brokers with little thought as to whether they had sufficient integrity or knowledge or were sufficiently reputable intermediaries will now in their own interests ensure that their brokers do not engage in conduct that may make them likely candidates for revocation action.'[4]

In deciding whether to make an order to allow enforcement of an unlicensed agreement the DGFT may consider how far customers were prejudiced by the trader's conduct; whether he would have been likely to grant a licence if an application had been made; and the degree of culpability for the failure to obtain a licence.

1   S 39(1).
2   S 40(1).
3   S 149.
4   Borrie, *The Development of Consumer Law and Policy—Bold Spirits and Timorous Souls* (Hamlyn Lectures, 1984) p 87.

Chapter 27
Regulated Agreements

27.0.0 Although the CCA 1974 introduces a comprehensive framework of law regulating credit and hire agreements, not all such agreements are caught by this Act. As its title suggests the CCA 1974 concentrates on agreements with consumers, thus many credit and hire agreements between corporate bodies in the course of business will fall to be regulated under the common law. The CCA 1974 talks in terms of 'regulated agreements'; only regulated agreements are subject to the requirement of the Act and are defined as consumer credit agreements or consumer hire agreements, other than an exempt agreement.[1]

1 S 189.

Consumer credit agreements
27.0.1 A consumer credit agreement is a personal credit agreement by which the creditor provides the debtor with credit not exceeding £15,000.[1] A 'personal credit agreement' consists of an agreement between an individual (the debtor) and any other person (the creditor) by which the creditor provides the debtor with credit of any amount.[2] An individual includes not only the ordinary consumer but also a partnership or other unincorporated body of persons not consisting entirely of bodies corporate.[3] This means that the Act extends beyond credit agreements where a consumer is the customer and regulates certain business credit transactions provided the customer/debtor is not a corporate body. The Act makes no clear cut distinction between consumer transactions and business transactions such as exists under other statutes regulating transactions.[4]

Credit is defined in very broad terms as including a cash loan and any other form of financial accommodation.[5] Thus the Act applies to many different categories of credit transaction identified earlier. The three common forms of instalment credit: hire purchase, conditional sale agreements and credit sale are specifically defined in terms which, in principle, accord with the observations made in 26.0.3. A hire purchase agreement is one where goods are bailed in return for periodical payments and the property in the goods will not pass until one or more of the following occurs—(a) the exercise of an option to purchase; (b) the doing of any other specified act by any party to the agreement or (c) the happening of any other specified event.[6] A conditional sale agreement is an agreement for the sale of goods or land under which the price is payable by instalments and the

347

property is to remain in the seller until the required conditions are fulfilled. A credit sale is defined on the same terms as a conditional sale except that property passes to the buyer immediately.[7]

As stated above the Act only extends to the provision of credit not exceeding £15,000. It is important to distinguish between the amount of credit provided and the total charge for credit[8] which relates to interest and other charges. The latter is not treated as credit and must therefore be excluded when considering the £15,000 limit. For example goods may have a total price of £22,000; this may include a deposit of £4,000 and interest of £3,000. When the deposit and interest are subtracted from the total price one is left with £15,000 of credit and an agreement within the CCA 1974.

1   S 8.
2   S 8(1).
3   S 189(1).
4   See eg the Unfair Contract Terms Act 1977, s 6.
5   S 9(1).
6   S 189.
7   S 189.
8   S 20.

Classification of credit agreement under the Consumer Credit Act 1974

(a) Fixed sum
27.0.2   Agreements that provide credit of a fixed amount are termed fixed sum credit.[1] Under such agreements it is relatively easy to calculate the amount of credit.[2] In the case of overdraft facilities and credit card transactions it is not so easy to calculate the credit since the amount varies from day to day. Such agreements are termed running account credit under the CCA 1974.

(b) Running account credit
Running account credit is a credit facility which fluctuates from time to time and allows the debtor to obtain cash, goods or services from the creditor or a third party (as in the case of a bank credit card) usually up to an agreed credit limit.[3] The credit limit is the maximum debit balance which is allowed to stand on the account during any agreed period, disregarding permissible temporary advances under the agreement which may exceed the maximum.[4]

Where the credit limit is fixed at £15,000 or below the agreement will be regulated. Indeed, Access and Barclaycard normally set a monthly credit limit below £1,000, depending upon the credit rating of the individual debtor.

The astute credit company may consider that one method of avoiding their agreements being classified as regulated would be either to set no credit limit or a credit limit in excess of £15,000. The Act however covers such methods of avoidance by providing[5] that running account credit will qualify as a regulated agreement if:

(a) the debtor cannot draw more than £15,000 at any one time; or

(b) the agreement provides that if the debit balance rises above a given amount (£15,000 or less), the rate of interest increases or some other condition favouring the creditor . . . comes into operation; or

(c) at the time that the agreement is made it is probable, having regard to the terms of the agreement and any other relevant circumstances, that the debit balance will not at any time rise above £15,000.

Thus, if the accounting period for the credit agreement is set over a year with a credit limit of £20,000 it would still be a regulated agreement under (a) above if the debtor can only draw at any one time an amount up to £15,000. Alternatively, if the credit limit is set at £20,000 but there is a provision whereby interest will be charged at 3% above the usual rate should the debit balance exceed £15,000, such an agreement would be regulated.

(c) Restricted and unrestricted use credit

Consistent with the functional approach to regulation of credit as outlined in the Crowther Report[6] the CCA 1974 distinguishes between restricted use credit and unrestricted-use credit which may give rise either to a debtor-creditor-supplier agreement or a debtor-creditor agreement.

Restricted-use credit is a regulated consumer credit agreement whereby the credit supplied is to finance a specific transaction between the debtor and a person (the supplier) other than the creditor.[7] The essence of such agreements is that the credit funds are transferred directly to the supplier as in the case of hire purchase and credit card transactions. Unrestricted-use credit is credit supplied under any other regulated agreement and the main feature of such credit is that the debtor can use it for any purpose. Even where the creditor makes it a term of the credit agreement that it be used only for a specific transaction, the agreement will still be for unrestricted-use credit if the funds are provided in such a way as to leave the debtor free to use it as he chooses.[8]

The distinction between restricted and unrestricted-use credit is particularly important in relation to canvassing of loan applications,[9] the provisions relating to repayment of credit when an agreement is cancellable[10] and in deciding the classification between debtor-creditor-supplier and debtor-creditor agreements.

(d) Debtor-creditor-supplier agreements/debtor-creditor agreements

By distinguishing between these two types of agreement the CCA 1974 is effectively distinguishing between those agreements where the creditor also supplies the goods, or has a business arrangement with someone to supply the goods (debtor–creditor–supplier agreements, (dcs)) and agreements where there is no connection between the creditor and the supplier of the goods or services[11] (debtor–creditor agreement (dc)).

A dcs agreement can relate to two parties, the debtor/consumer and the creditor/supplier or it can involve three parties: the debtor/consumer, the creditor and the supplier of the goods and services. An example of the former would be the typical hire purchase and conditional sale agreement where the retailer sells the goods to the finance company and they enter into a credit transaction with the customer under which they supply the goods as well as the credit. An example of a three party agreement classified as a dcs agreement would be either:

(i) a restricted-use credit agreement financing a transaction between a debtor/consumer and a third party supplier, made by the creditor under pre-existing arrangements, or in contemplation of future arrangements between himself and the supplier.[12] This covers the situation where a finance house provides loans for the customers of a retailer to purchase goods or services, the customer being introduced to the finance house under a formal arrangement. It also covers credit-card transactions such as Access or Barclaycard, where the credit company enters into a formal contract with the supplier whereby goods or services can be supplied to credit card holders; or

(ii) a second example of a three party agreement is an unrestricted-use credit agreement which is made by the creditor under pre-existing arrangements between himself and a person (the supplier) other than the debtor, in the knowledge that the credit is to be used to finance a transaction between the debtor and the supplier. Thus if consumer/debtor A is buying a car from supplier B and requires finance, B might advise A to approach moneylender C, a credit company with whom B has an arrangement. C knows that the loan is for a particular transaction and advances the funds directly to A (thus rendering it unrestricted-use credit) who then pays for the car.

A dc agreement is obviously any agreement that is not a dcs agreement. Such agreements are not tied to any specific transaction but constitute a simple loan or overdraft facility, the creditor having no business arrangement with a supplier of goods or services.[13] Thus if a bank advances funds to a customer for the purchase of a vehicle, they may be aware of who is supplying the vehicle but provided there is no business arrangement between bank and supplier, the loan will be a dc agreement.

The Crowther Committee explained the rationale behind the distinction between dc and dcs agreements in the following terms.

'Where goods are bought for cash provided by an independent lender there is no reason to regard the sale as any different from a normal cash sale, or to treat the loan as other than a normal loan. Where, however, the price is advanced by the seller or a connected lender the sale and loan aspects of the transactions are closely entwined. The connected lender and the seller, where not the same person, are in effect engaged in a joint venture to their mutual advantage and their respective roles cannot be treated in isolation.'[14]

1   S 10(1)(b).
2   In order to avoid doubt the Act provides that 'the credit provided under a hire purchase agreement is fixed-sum credit . . . of an amount equal to the total price of the goods less the aggregate of the deposit and the total charge for credit' (s 9(3)).
3   S 10(1)(9).
4   S 10(3)(a).
5   S 10(3)(b).
6   See p 184.
7   S 11(1).
8   S 11(3).
9   See 28.0.3.
10 See 28.1.0.
11 Ss 12 and 13.
12 S 12(b).
13 S 13.
14 Para 6.2.24.

Exempt agreements

27.0.3   Certain types of credit agreement are removed from the scope of the legislation. These include mortgages given on land by certain specified bodies.[1] Also exempt are fixed sum debtor-creditor-supplier agreements (other than hire purchase or conditional sale agreements) where the number of payments to be made by the debtor does not exceed four.[2] The intention behind this provision is to exempt trade and domestic credit agreements where the supplier and the creditor may be the same person and the debt is extinguished quickly. As the Crowther Committee observed:

> 'We have not been aware of any special problems that arise in this area . . . Moreover we have been keenly conscious of the undesirability of trying to impose any form of regulation upon such an enormous number of largely informal transactions, unless it is strictly necessary to do so.'[3]

Debtor-creditor-supplier agreements for running-account credit where all indebtedness is extinguished at the end of a specific accounting period are also exempt. This provision relates to one particular form of credit card agreement where the debtor is required to clear the account at the end of each period, as opposed to those agreements where the debtor is merely required to pay a minimum amount at the end of a period thus extending the credit period. Examples of credit cards within this exemption would be American Express or Diners Club.

There is also an exemption relating to low cost debtor-creditor agreements, that is, an agreement where the rate of interest does not exceed the higher of 13%, or 1% above the base rate of the London Clearing Banks in operation on a date 28 days before the date on which the agreement was made. Certain non-commercial and small agreements are also given partial exemption from the Act.[4]

1 Namely, local authorities, building societies, insurance companies, friendly societies, employers and workers organisations, charities, a land improvement company or a body corporate specifically referred to in any public general Act. See s 16(1) and Consumer Credit (Exempt Agreements) (No 2) Order 1985 SI 1985/757.
2 See note (1).
3 Para 1.1.8.
4 See 27.1.2.

Consumer hire agreements

27.1.0   A consumer hire agreement is an agreement made by a person with an individual (the hirer) for the bailment of goods whereby the agreement:
(a) is not a hire purchase agreement
(b) is capable of lasting for more than three months, and
(c) does not require the hirer to make payments exceeding £15,000.[1]
All consumer hire agreements are regulated agreements unless within the category of exempt agreement.

Where the agreement is of indefinite duration terminable on notice by either party, it will be within the Act because clearly it is capable of lasting for more than three months.

In formulating how much the hirer is required to pay, it is simply a matter of assessing the minimum contractual liability. For example, if an individual hires equipment which sets a minimum rental period of two years and a monthly rental of £50, the total he is required to pay under the contract is £1,200 thus bringing the agreement within the Act.

1 S 15.

Exempt hire agreements

27.1.1   The Secretary of State has the power to provide by order that the CCA 1974 should not regulate consumer hire agreements where the owner is a body corporate authorised by or under any enactment to supply gas, electricity, water or a public telecommunication operator and the subject of the agreement is a meter or metering equipment.[1]

1   See Consumer Credit (Exempt Agreements) (No 2) Order 1985 (SI 1985/757).

Non-commercial and small agreements

27.1.2   The basic distinction in the CCA 1974 is between regulated and exempt agreements. The above two classes of agreement fall between the basic distinction in that they are partly regulated by the Act.

A non-commercial agreement is a consumer credit agreement or a consumer hire agreement not made in the course of a business carried on by the creditor or owner.[1] For example, a purely private transaction whereby an individual advances funds to another as a gesture of goodwill or friendship and not in the course of a business, would be classed as a non-commercial agreement. The nature of the exemption afforded to such agreements is in respect of the formalities and cancellation provisions.

A small agreement is a regulated consumer credit or consumer hire agreement for credit or hire payments not exceeding £50. The agreement must be unsecured or secured only by a guarantee or indemnity.[2] Hire purchase and conditional sale agreements can never be small agreements but a credit-sale agreement where the credit does not exceed £50 would be. Small agreements are exempt from most of the provisions of the Act regulating formalities and cancellation rights.

1   S 189(1).
2   S 17.

Linked agreements

27.2.0   Where goods are obtained on credit is common for ancillary contracts such as guarantees, insurance, or maintenance, to be entered into at the same time. Any protection afforded in respect of the main transaction may be substantially undermined if it is not extended to such ancillary or linked agreements, especially since such transactions are invariably used as a vehicle for imposing additional and sometimes excessive charges on a customer. Hence the CCA 1974 introduced the notion of a linked transaction which is entered into by a debtor, hirer or a relative of the debtor or hirer, and another party who will often be the creditor.

A transaction is linked to a regulated agreement (the principal agreement), actual or prospective, if:

(a)   It is entered into in compliance with a term of the principal agreement. For example, a finance house may insist that the debtor under a hire purchase contract for electrical equipment enters into a maintenance agreement with a specified firm.

(b)   It is financed by a debtor-creditor-supplier agreement. Thus when goods are paid for by Barclaycard, the sale will be a linked transaction. Not all debtor-creditor-supplier agreements will involve linked agreements, since the credit and the supply may be contained in one

single agreement regulated under the Act.[1]
(c) It is entered into at the suggestion of the creditor, owner, or a negotiator in respect of the principal agreement, in order to induce the other party to enter into the principal agreement, or for another purpose related to the principal agreement, or, where the principal agreement is a restricted use credit agreement, for a purpose related to a transaction financed, or to be financed, by the principal agreement. This would cover the situation where it is suggested (rather than required as in (a) above) by a dealer or broker arranging a loan that an insurance policy be entered into with a particular company to whom the dealer introduces his client. Such an insurance policy would be a linked transaction.

An agreement for the provision of security cannot be a linked transaction.[2]

In general a linked transaction that is entered into before the making of the principal agreement has no effect until that agreement is made.[3] However, in the case of insurance, contracts (in so far as they contain a guarantee of goods), any agreement for the opening of a deposit or current account, such linked transactions will have effect before the principal agreement is made.[4]

As indicated above, the significance of a transaction being linked is that any rights attached to the principal agreement in respect of withdrawal, cancellation or early settlement extend to the linked transaction.

1   Eg hire purchase.
2   S 19(1).
3   S 19(3).
4   Consumer Credit (Linked Transactions) (Exemptions) Regulations 1983 (SI 1983/1560).

Chapter 28

Control of Credit Agreements

Truth in lending

28.0.0   As indicated in 2.5.5, disclosure as a means of regulation is a popular device for regulating business activity in the UK. The CCA 1974 embraces the disclosure philosophy by the concept of 'truth in lending' and the requirement of business to comply with regulations on advertising, canvassing, quotations and rules on the form and content of agreements. The objective of such regulations is to reduce the inequality of bargaining between the consumer and those offering credit or hire facilities by allowing the consumer to obtain an accurate picture of the nature and scope of facilities on offer.

Advertising

28.0.1   The advertising provisions of the CCA 1974 apply to any advertisement published for the purposes of a business carried on by the advertiser indicating that he is willing to provide credit or to enter into an agreement for the bailment of goods by him.[1]

The potentially wide coverage of those provisions is, however, reduced by exemptions. In practice the controls are restricted to consumer credit and consumer hire businesses that advertise a willingness to enter into regulated agreements and, in addition, businesses which provide to individuals credit secured on land.[2]

The Secretary of State may also provide by regulations that certain advertisements are exempt from the general requirements.[3] The Consumer Credit (Advertisement) Regulations 1980 (SI 1980/54) exempts certain advertisements including those published by building societies, local authorities and other bodies identified in the Consumer Credit (Exempt Agreements) (No 2) Order 1985 (SI 1985/757) as being exempt agreements under s 16.[4]

The provisions extend to every form of advertising, whether in a publication, by television or radio, by display of notices, signs, labels, showcards or goods, by distribution of samples, circulars, catalogues, price lists or other material, by exhibition of pictures, models, films, or in any other way.[5]

Section 44(1) of the CCA 1974 enables the Secretary of State to make regulations covering the form and content of advertisements. The overriding requirement is that such advertisements convey a fair and reasonably comprehensive indication of the nature of the credit or hire facilities offered and their true cost.

The regulations are detailed and complex, laying down what may be included in an advertisement, and how it should be presented and set out. In respect of the charge for credit, regulations require that it be expressed as an annual percentage rate (APR). The regulations divide controlled advertisements into three types: simple, intermediate and full. Where the advertiser merely states his name and his occupation or its general nature, it will be a simple advertisement. If more information is included, such as the price, it will be an intermediate or a full advertisement thus requiring the disclosure of specific details and the omission of certain expressions.[6] These provisions are supported by criminal penalties. It is an offence to contravene the advertising regulations,[7] and to make a false or misleading statement in an advertisement to which the provisions apply.[8]

It is also an offence if an advertisement indicates a willingness to provide restricted-use credit for the supply of goods or services, when the supplier is not selling or providing the goods or services for cash. Thus for example, a business engaged in mail order trading cannot disguise the financial disadvantage of credit by omitting the cash price of goods. If the advertiser commits an offence, the publisher, deviser of the advertisement and any person who procured publication, may also commit an offence.[9]

1 S 43(1).
2 S 43(2), (4).
3 S 43(5).
4 See 27.0.3.
5 S 189(1).
6 Consumer Credit (Advertisement) Regulations, SI 1980/54.
7 S 167(2).
8 S 46.
9 S 47(1), (2).

Quotations
28.0.2 Similar regulations to those covering advertisements have been made in respect of the form and content of quotations.[1] The regulations apply to both consumer credit and hire agreements and also all agreements for the provision of credit to individuals secured on land. The regulations make no distinction between business and private customer. They deal with the situation where a trader receives a request from an individual asking for written information about the terms on which the trader will do business in respect of a particular transaction.

The information provided must include specific information including the APR, the amount of credit and credit limit, details of the payments which may be payable and the difference in treatment of cash and credit transactions.

1 S 52(1) and Consumer Credit (Quotation) Regulations 1980 (SI 1980/55).

Canvassing
28.0.3 The CCA 1974 also prohibits the canvassing of a debtor-creditor agreement off trade premises. Canvassing means soliciting the entry of a consumer into a regulated agreement by making oral representations during a visit not previously arranged. Even where a visit is made in response to a previous request, the offence is still committed if the request was not in writing and signed by, or on behalf, of the person making it.[1] In essence,

355

canvassing is off trade premises if the place the canvasser visits is not the place of business of the creditor/owner, a supplier, the canvasser or the consumer. A further offence in relation to seeking business exists where circulars are sent to minors inviting them to borrow money, obtain goods on credit or hire, obtain services on credit or apply for information or advice on borrowing money or otherwise obtaining credit or hiring goods.[2]

1   S 49.
2   S 50.

Formalities

28.0.4   Parts V–IX of the CCA 1974 regulate the form and content of individual credit or hire agreements. In general the underlying principles behind these provisions are that:[1]

(a) they should be simple to understand and comply with;

(b) there should be sufficient flexibility to allow for those cases where information cannot be provided immediately;

(c) the required information should be kept within reasonable limits and made prominent by, for example, inclusion in an outlined area;

(d) the courts have a general power to dispense with any requirements the breach of which was inadvertent and did not mislead;

(e) sanctions for breach are tailored to the gravity of the offence.

In respect of the last two factors, the sanctions for breach of these provisions are potentially harsh. If the creditor or owner does not comply with the formalities the agreement is 'not properly executed' and cannot therefore be enforced against the debtor or hirer unless either the court makes an enforcement order,[2] or the debtor or hirer consents to enforcement.[3] Theoretically therefore the customer can retain the goods without payment; the courts would, however, be sympathetic to a creditor or owner seeking enforcement of an improperly executed agreement provided the customer had not been prejudiced, especially where the breach was inadvertent or had been remedied.

The provisions do not apply to:

(a) non-commercial agreements;[4]

(b) a debtor-creditor agreement enabling the debtor to overdraw on a current account;

(c) a debtor-creditor agreement to finance the making of payments arising on, or connected with, the death of a person;[5]

(d) small debtor-creditor-supplier agreements for restricted use credit.[6]

1   See Crowther, pp 265–6.
2   S 127(1). See 28.6.0.
3   S 173(3).
4   See 27.1.2.
5   For example payments of capital transfer tax or court fees relating to a grant of representation.
6   See 27.1.2.

Pre-contract information

28.0.5   Section 55 of the CCA 1974 enables regulations to be made requiring specified information to be disclosed to a prospective debtor or hirer before a regulated agreement is made. No regulations have been made under this section, however, most debtors and hirers will receive some information under the advertising and quotation regulations.

Form and content

28.0.6 Regulations[1] also require that a debtor or hirer is made aware in the agreement of his obligations and rights under the CCA 1974, the amount and rate of the charge for credit and any remedies available. In particular the debtor under a hire purchase agreement must be informed of his right of termination, and the limitation on the creditor's right of repossession where the goods are protected.

Such information as is required must, where appropriate, be given prominence and be easily legible and distinguishable. Any financial information must be presented as a whole in the agreement.

The agreement, in a form complying with the regulations, must be signed personally by the debtor or hirer and by or on behalf of the creditor or owner. Signature on a blank form with details provided at a later date is not sufficient.

1 Ss 60–61.

Copies of the agreement

28.0.7 A person entering into a regulated agreement is entitled to receive one, and in some cases, two copies of the agreement. The most common situation is for a customer to sign an agreement at business premises and then pending checks on creditworthiness, the other party will sign at a later date. In such a situation the customer must be given a copy of the unexecuted agreement[1] when first he signs it and also be supplied with a copy of the agreement once it has been signed by the other party and thereby become executed. The second copy must be given to the customer within seven days of the agreement being made.

Where the creditor or hirer has already signed, the customer's signature will convert the agreement into an executed agreement, of which the customer is entitled to one copy. No further copy would then be required.

The debtor or hirer is also entitled to request a copy of the agreement or particulars of the sums paid or payable, during the currency of the agreement.[2]

1 S 62(1).
2 Ss 77–79.

Cancellation

28.1.0 In order to curb the activities of door step salesmen the Hire-Purchase Act 1965 conferred on a hirer or buyer a right to cancel the agreement where it was signed other than at appropriate trade premises. Such 'cooling off' provisions were extended under the CCA 1974 to any regulated agreement in which the antecedent negotiations included oral representations made in the presence of the customer by an individual acting as, or on behalf of the negotiator. The unexecuted agreement must have been signed elsewhere than the business premises of the creditor or owner, any party to a linked transaction or the negotiator.

The provisions do not therefore apply to the situation where high pressure canvassing takes place at the customer's home but the agreement is then signed at business premises some time later.

The cancellation provisions do not apply to non-commercial agreements and small debtor-creditor-supplier agreements for restricted-use credit. In addition they do not apply to agreements secured on land,[1] restricted-use agreements to finance the purchase of land, or bridging loans in connection with the purchase of land.

In the case of a cancellable agreement the Act provides that each copy must contain a notice in the prescribed form indicating the right of cancellation, how and when it may be exercised and the name and address of a person to whom notice of cancellation may be given. If the circumstances are such that a second copy of the agreement is required to be given to the customer, if that agreement is one to which these provisions apply, the second copy must be sent by post. Where a second copy is not required a notice containing the cancellation information must be posted to the customer within seven days of the agreement being made.

The period during which cancellation can be effected begins when the customer signs the unexecuted agreement and expires on the end of the fifth day following the day on which the consumer receives the second copy of the executed agreement or the cancellation notice if no second copy is required.[2]

The cancellation is considered to be effective at the time of posting, even if it is never received. The notice can be served on the creditor or owner, or their agent, a person specified in the agreement, a credit broker or supplier who was a negotiator, and any person who in the course of business acted on behalf of the consumer in any negotiations for the agreement.

Cancellation renders the agreement void together with any linked transaction.[3] Thus payments made are recoverable and the customer must return any goods supplied. Where, however, such goods have become incorporated into land or other goods or supplied to meet an emergency, the cash price must be paid.

In the case of perishable goods, or those consumed by use before cancellation, the customer is under no obligation to return the goods or pay the cash price.[4] It is, however, unlikely that such goods would be delivered to the customer before the cancellation period expires. The rationale of this provision is that the customer should not be deterred from exercising cancellation rights whilst in possession of perishable goods such as might be the case where a freezer is supplied together with frozen food.

Where the customer contributed goods in part-exchange, such goods must be returned within ten days of cancellation; if not, a sum equivalent to the part-exchange becomes recoverable.

It may seem somewhat anomalous that customers subjected to pressure on their own doorstep have a right to cancel regulated agreements but have no such right where goods or services are supplied for cash.[5]

1   There is, however, a pre-contractual period of reflection for the debtor or hirer built into the CCA 1974, see s 58.
2   S 68.
3   See 27.2.0.
4   S 79(2).
5   See 15.0.8.

Withdrawal

28.2.0 It may be that a debtor or hirer has made an offer to enter into a regulated agreement which has yet to be accepted by the other party. In such circumstances the general law of contract permits the offeror to withdraw the offer at any time prior to acceptance.

The CCA 1974 confirms the common law position[1] treating withdrawal in the same manner as cancellation. The provisions are however wider than the general law in that they permit a notice of withdrawal to be served on the creditor, owner, a credit broker or supplier who is the negotiator and any person who, in the course of business carried on by him, 'acts on behalf of the debtor or hirer in any negotiations for the agreement.'[2]

In practice, therefore, a debtor can effect a withdrawal by informing his own solicitor or agent who negotiated the agreement.

1 S 57.
2 S 57(3)(b).

Duty to provide information during the agreement

28.3.0 The debtor or hirer under a regulated agreement has a statutory right to require the creditor or owner to provide information as to the amounts paid under the agreement and amounts outstanding.[1]

1 Ss 77–79.

Dealer/creditor liability

28.4.0 It is relatively commonplace for a supplier of goods to negotiate with a debtor and then for the debtor to enter into a credit agreement with a finance company/creditor. In such circumstances there may be no direct contractual relationship between the debtor and the dealer and thus statements by the dealer could not be incorporated into the contract as terms, or amount to misrepresentation,[1] unless he was acting as agent for the creditor.

Under the CCA 1974[2] antecedent negotiations with the debtor conducted by the supplier in relation to a transaction financed by a debtor-creditor-supplier agreement:

> 'shall be deemed to be conducted by the negotiator in the capacity of agent of the creditor as well as in his actual capacity.'

Thus if the dealer makes a misrepresentation as to the subject matter or terms of the contract he is deemed to have made them as an agent of the finance company. An agreement is void in so far as it purports to exclude the deemed agency arising under the Act.[3]

1 See *Andrews v Hopkinson* [1957] 1 QB 229, [1956] 3 All ER 422 where it was held that statements by a dealer amounted to a collateral warranty, the breach of which entitled the customer to damages.
2 S 56(2).
3 S 56(3).

Joint and several liability

28.4.1 Under the old law in a typical three-party transaction whereby a customer purchased goods from a seller with funds supplied by a connected creditor, the credit company would not incur any liability in respect of defects in the goods, or other breach of contract as between buyer and seller.

The Crowther Committee considered that the buyer supplied with defective goods may:

'find that to secure redress from such a seller he has to incur the worry and expense of litigation, in which the burden of taking the initiative lies on him; and that in some cases the seller's financial position is so poor that it is doubtful whether he will be able to meet the judgment even if the buyer is successful. The buyer's difficulties of pursuing a claim against the seller are enhanced if, whilst wrestling with the financial problems of litigation, he has to go on paying the lender under the loan agreement . . .'[1]

They therefore recommended that where the price payable under a sale agreement is advanced wholly or partly by a connected lender, that lender should be liable for misrepresentations relating to the goods made by the seller and for any breach of the implied terms under the Sale of Goods Act 1979.[2] It was considered that such a change in the law might encourage creditors to exercise some control over the activities of retail organisations in terms of trading malpractices. The withdrawal of credit facilities from a retailer could be a powerful encouragement to comply with basic standards of fair trading.

The Crowther recommendations were enshrined in s 75 of the CCA 1974. The section provides that if the debtor under a three-party debtor-creditor-supplier agreement has, in relation to a transaction financed by the agreement, any claim against the supplier in respect of a misrepresentation or breach of contract, he shall have a like claim against the creditor, who, with the supplier, shall accordingly be jointly and severally liable to the debtor.

The provision does not extend to non-commercial agreements[3] or disputes where the claim relates to any single item to which the supplier has attached a cash price not exceeding £100 or more than £30,000.

There is obviously some overlap between ss 56 and 75 where the negotiator makes a misrepresentation, since the customer will have a claim against the creditor under either provision. Section 56 is however of wider scope than s 75 since it is not confined to three party debtor-creditor-supplier agreements and not subject to financial limits. For example hire purchase agreements, although debtor-creditor-supplier agreements, are not within s 75 because the supplier of the goods and of the credit are the same person.

The real significance of s 75 is that where the debtor is supplied with the goods or services which fall short of his contractual entitlement, he may have a claim against the creditor. Such a claim is a considerable protection against the unwillingness or inability of a supplier to meet a claim. It is particularly useful where the supplier has become insolvent. The extent of such claims may, of course, far exceed the amount of the credit advanced. A claim against the creditor may be made even where the debtor exceeds the credit limit or otherwise contravenes a term of the agreement.[4]

The section refers to the debtor having 'a like claim' against the creditor. There seems to be some doubt about whether this restricts a claim under s 75 against a creditor to a monetary claim or whether it extends to other remedies such as termination for breach of contract. A Scots law case[5] has held that a breach of contract in respect of the supply of a car meant that the debtor had a right to rescind both the contract for the car and the credit agreement. The decision has however been criticised on the grounds that the word 'claim' must be limited to monetary claims for compensation. Further, the creditor is liable for breach of the supply contract on the basis of a like claim against both creditor and supplier; it therefore, cannot be said that the debtor has a right to terminate the credit agreement because there exists no like claim against the supplier for termination of the credit agreement.

Where a debtor does proceed against a creditor, the creditor is entitled to join the supplier as a party to the action and claim an indemnity from him.[6]

1   Para 6.6.25.
2   See Part IV.
3   See 27.1.2.
4   S 75(4).
5   *United Dominions Trust v Taylor* 1980 SLT 28.
6   S 75(2), (5).

Joint liability and credit cards

28.4.2   Where goods or services are wholly or partly paid for by a credit card, the effect of s 75 is that the credit card company may be held liable in damages for breach of contract,[1] in the event of a claim arising against the supplier. Two problems have emerged in this area. First, what is the extent of a credit card company's liability where goods or services are partly paid for by their card? This question arose in the context of claims by customers of Laker Airways when the company went into liquidation. The customers claimed the full return of their money from the credit card organisations. Although the credit card organisations have resisted such claims the consensus of opinion seems to be that since s 75(1) talks of having 'a like claim' against the creditor, the credit card organisations should be liable for the full amount of the debtor's loss.

The second problem in this area relates to the transitional provisions covering s 75. Such provisions make it clear that the section only applies to agreements made after the 1 July 1977. It has therefore been argued that transactions under credit cards issued before that date but effected after the date are outside s 75. The consensus view seems to be that renewal of a credit card is a completely new regulated agreement; thus, if a card has been renewed since 1 July 1977 (normally cards are renewed every two years) transactions under it will be caught by s 75.[2]

1   It must be regulated agreement. It will be recalled that certain single repayment credit agreements such as Diners Club and American Express are exempt. See 27.0.3.
2   Credit card organisations have agreed with the OFT to accept liability up to the amount of the credit where the card was renewed on or after 1 July 1977.

Credit cards and their misuse

28.5.0   The credit card is perhaps the most common form of financial accommodation used today. Where a card is used to acquire goods or services at approved outlets the transactions will be regulated as debtor-creditor-supplier agreements.

The CCA 1974 classifies credit cards along with other similar transactions as credit token agreements, which are 'regulated agreements for the provision of credit in connection with the use of a credit token.'[1] A credit token is defined as a card, check, voucher, coupon, stamp, form, booklet or other document or thing given to an individual by a person carrying on a consumer credit business who undertakes that on production of it the debtor is entitled to receive cash, goods or services from the creditor. Thus credit cards issued by retailing organisations, banks, building societies and other similar organisations are caught by these provisions, as too are checks and vouchers issued by institutions and used by the consumer to acquire goods up to the face value of the voucher. Also caught are cards enabling customers of financial institutions to draw money from a cash dispenser. Cheque cards guaranteeing cheques up to a fixed sum are not credit tokens because although they are issued under a consumer credit agreement the institution is not paying for goods or services but simply honouring the guarantee of payment on the cheque. Consistent with the objectives of the CCA 1974 in terms of consumer protection, it is an offence to supply an unsolicited credit token.[2]

With regard to the misuse of credit facilities, the CCA 1974 lays down the general rule that a debtor under a regulated agreement is not liable to the creditor for any loss arising from the use of the credit facility by another person not acting, or to be treated as acting, as the debtor's agent.[3]

The misuse of credit tokens poses special problems, in the words of the Crowther Committee:

> 'If a card is lost or stolen through what may be a purely momentary carelessness on the part of the cardholder, some time may elapse before he discovers the loss. During that time, a fraudulent third party could easily run up accounts to the full amount of credit provided by the card; and if the card is valid for services such as air travel, entertainment and so on the unfortunate cardholder might well be presented with a crippling bill.'[4]

A debtor cannot be liable for an unauthorised use of a credit token unless he has first accepted the token either by signing it, signing a receipt for it or using it.[5]

Once having formally accepted a credit token, a debtor's liability for its misuse depends, in the first place, on whether the person who misused it acquired possession of the token with the debtor's consent. If such is the case, then the debtor is liable 'to any extent for the loss to the creditor.'[6]

In the case of accidental loss of a credit token the liability of the debtor is limited to £50, during the period beginning when the token ceased to be in the possession of an authorised person and ending when the token is returned to the possession of such a person.[7] The debtor is not, however, liable for any loss arising after the creditor has been given oral or written notice that the token has been lost, stolen or 'is otherwise liable to misuse.'[8]

Particular problems have been identified in respect of the use of cash cards at automated teller machines.[9]

1   S 14.
2   S 51 and see *Elliott v Director General of Fair Trading* [1980] 1 WLR 977, [1980] ICR 629.
3   S 83(1) The rule does not apply to non-commercial agreements and in respect of loss arising from misuse of an instrument regulated by s 4 of the Cheques Act 1957.
4   Para 6.12.5.
5   S 66.
6   S 84(2).
7   S 84(1).
8   S 84(3).
9   See 'Losing at cards. An investigation into consumers' problems with bank cash machines.' (NCC, 1985).

Termination

28.6.0   The Crowther Committee considered that one of the three primary tasks of consumer protection legislation should be regulating the rights which a creditor would ordinarily be able to enforce under the general law. Such regulation may be by imposing restrictions on the exercise of certain types of remedy, such as, the right to repossess goods, or by simply giving greater flexibility to the courts in cases concerning default by debtors.

Building on reforms made by the Hire-Purchase Act 1965, the CCA 1974 provides certain basic rights and protections in the context of termination of regulated agreements. Such provisions seek to strike a balance between consumers and creditors/owners. On the one hand, it is relatively easy for the business creditor to bear most of the risk in default cases by a combination of prudent insurance and pricing policy, thus spreading the burden over all his customers. On the other hand:

'the concept of risk spreading must not be taken too far. Every restriction on a creditor's remedy has to be paid for to the extent to which the creditor is not himself willing or able to absorb the loss or expense in which he is involved by the restrictions on him, this must be passed on to his customers. Hence the good customer is made to subsidise the bad. Moreover, the burden of bad debts bears particularly harshly on the small trader . . .'[1]

1   See Crowther, para 6.1.16.

Termination of consumer credit agreements—early discharge by debtor

28.6.1   In respect of termination of a regulated consumer credit agreement, the CCA 1974 allows a debtor to complete his obligations in advance of the date fixed for termination by making full payment.[1] Such a situation might arise where the debtor has acquired funds from elsewhere and wishes to extinguish his existing credit obligations.

Section 94 gives the debtor a non-excludable right to discharge his indebtedness by serving a notice on the creditor and paying any sums due under the agreement. If a debtor takes advantage of this provision he may claim a rebate in respect of charges for credit.[2]

Early settlement of a debt will also operate to terminate future liability of the debtor or his relative, under a linked transaction.[3] The statutory right to pay off a debt early is supplemented by a right to require a creditor to inform the debtor of the precise amount required to discharge the debt.[4] A failure to comply with a request means that the agreement cannot be enforced while the default continues, and the creditor commits an offence if the default continues for one month.[5]

1   S 94.
2   S 95 Consumer Credit (Rebate on Early Settlement) Regulations 1983 (SI 1983/1562).
3   S 96.
4   S 97.
5   S 97(3) A statement referring to the right to discharge a debt early must be included in the agreement. Agreements Regulations SI 1983/1553.

Termination of consumer hire agreement by hirer

28.6.2   In terms of the hirer's financial commitments, many hire or rental agreements are indistinguishable from credit agreements. A fixed term hiring agreement could commit the hirer to total rental payments equivalent to the hire purchase price of the goods, without any of the advantages of ownership that hire purchase gives a debtor. In 1964 Sachs J observed:

> 'It is becoming increasingly apparent from cases which come before the courts that there is a tendency on the part of some finance companies, at any rate, to try to use contracts of which I have referred to as simple hire in order to ensure that the hirer does not have the protection of the Hire Purchase Act. These contracts of hire to which finance companies are inclined, are simple only in the sense that technically they are not contracts of hire purchase. One has but to look at the contract in this particular case to see in its small print how far from simple it is, either from the layman's or indeed the lawyer's point of view. The sooner the legislature is apprised of this tendency and the sooner it takes in hand the problem, the fewer will be the occasions when financial companies are able to inflict on any unwary hirer hardships of the type that have become manifest in the present case.'[1]

The problems identified by Sachs J have, for the most part, been attacked by the CCA 1974. In particular, s 101 gives the hirer, under a regulated consumer hire agreement, the right to terminate the agreement after at least eighteen months have expired. This right exists even where the agreement may provide for a fixed term longer than eighteen months. The hirer is required to give notice to the owner equivalent to the shortest period between two payments, or of three months, whichever is less.

In general the statutory right to terminate is intended for consumer, as opposed to commercial, hirers. Thus the right does not apply to three categories of agreement. First those which require the hirer to make payments which in total exceed £900 in any year. Second, where the hirer is hiring the goods for business purposes and he selects goods which are later acquired by the owner from another person at the hirer's request.[2] Third, agreements where the hirer requires the goods to hire them out to other persons in the course of business.[3] It is worth pointing out that in the case of the second and third categories, the hirer will generally be a corporate body in which case the agreements would not in any event be regulated hire agreements.

1   *Galbraith v Mitchenall Estates Ltd* [1965] 2 QB 473, [1964] 2 All ER 653.
2   See 20.7.1.
3   S 101(7).

Termination of hire purchase and conditional sale agreements by returning goods
28.6.3   The CCA 1974, s 99, continues a provision originally contained in the Hire Purchase Act allowing the debtor under a regulated hire purchase or conditional sale agreement to terminate it and return the goods. The debtor can exercise the right any time before his final payment is due, by giving notice to the person entitled or authorised to receive the sums payable under the agreement.

The debtor must of course discharge any liability that accrued before the date of termination. In addition, the debtor must normally bring his total payments up to one-half of the total price immediately before termination. The agreement may however provide for a smaller sum to be paid or no sum at all.

The court has a general discretion to order payment of a lesser part of the total price if it considers that such a sum would be sufficient to compensate the debtor.[1] The courts do not however have any discretion to extinguish obligations to pay arrears on the part of the debtor. The debtor must of course return the goods and, if he has failed to take reasonable care of them, the amount payable to discharge the agreement may be increased, in order to recompense the creditor.

As a general rule the longer the agreement has been operational and thus the more payments that have fallen due, the more inappropriate termination under this provision becomes. In such circumstances debtors may consider refinancing by borrowing an amount sufficient to make early repayment under section 94 and thus assuming ownership of the goods. In some circumstances it may even be preferable for a debtor to wait for the creditor to initiate default procedures rather than terminate under s 99.

A decision to terminate may have to be made fairly swiftly if the agreement contains an acceleration clause. Such a clause is a contractual provision requiring immediate payment of all or part of the unpaid balance of the debt on the occurrence of a specific event. Thus if the debtor is in default, all payments fall due under the acceleration clause and the debtor loses the right to terminate since s 99(1) specifically states that the debtor is entitled to terminate the agreement 'at any time before the final payment by the debtor . . . falls due.'

The use of acceleration clauses is justified on the basis that in their absence creditors would be required to bring a series of actions as an instalment falls due, or allow the agreement to expire by which time the possibility of recovery would be remote.[2] Such clauses are liable to be attacked as penalty clauses if they are penal in nature, that is, not a genuine pre-estimate of the creditor's loss.[3]

1 S 100(3).
2 See R M Goode and J S Ziegel, *Hire Purchase and Conditional Sale* (British Institute of International and Comparative Law, 1965) p 110.
3 See *United Dominions Trust v Thomas* [1976] CLY 1618; *Wadham Stringer Finance Ltd v Meaney* [1980] 3 All ER 789, [1981] 1 WLR 39. See 17.1.4.

Termination by the creditor on the debtor's default

28.6.4   Whilst the vast majority of consumer credit agreements are terminated by the consumers making full payment to extinguish their debts, it is not uncommon for some consumers to experience difficulties in meeting payments. In such a situation the consumer is said to be in default.

In general, lower-income consumers are more likely to default than other income groups,[1] simply because they have fewer resources with which to meet unforeseen changes in their financial position. In earlier times it used to be considered that debtors in default had only themselves to blame and must take the consequences for their own recklessness or improvidence. Indeed the Crowther Committee observed that:

'There are many, particularly in the low income group, who are not reckless so much as improvident. They lack the ability to budget or to manage their income. They have little or no sense of values and are not motivated by rational considerations in selecting their purchases. Such people will, for example, spend a slice of their income not on articles they really need but on other less importance items, and they will spend regardless of whether they are getting value for money. Here again, legal protection tends to be largely ineffective . . .'[2]

Modern techniques of persuasion in marketing and advertising goods, services and credit facilities only serve to make matters worse for such 'improvident' consumers. Indeed it has been suggested that some consumers are seduced into a cycle of poverty by the attractions that credit offers, which only serves to exacerbate their financial plight.[3]

The most frequently identified causes of default are illness and unemployment.[4] With increasing levels of unemployment, across all income groups, it may be expected that the level of default will increase. In the final analysis, the most that the law can do in respect of such default cases is to mitigate the hardship by compassionate judicial control over the enforcement of debt and the repossession of goods held by the debtor. As the Crowther Committee observed:

> 'Given the characteristics of the typical honest defaulter, it is extremely difficult to devise administrative and legal measures for protecting him without depriving the much larger number of consumers, who use credit wisely, of its considerable benefits. The best policy beyond much question, is not to restrict or control the granting of credit, but to be more careful in assessing the ability of borrowers to carry the burden of repayment, and to be ready with policies of rescue and remedy for the minority for whom it brings difficulties.'[5]

To that extent the business of credit reference agencies that give information on credit worthiness provides a useful means of preventing reckless or dishonest persons from gaining access to credit facilities.

A regulated agreement may give the creditor or owner certain contractual rights in the event of the debtor or hirer's default. Such rights may include the right to terminate the agreement; demand earlier payment of any sum; recover possession of any goods or land; treat any of the debtor's or hirer's rights as terminated, restricted or deferred, or to enforce any security.

The CCA 1974[6] provides that before a creditor or owner can become entitled to any of the above rights he must serve a notice of default on the other party. The notice must specify the breach, the action needed to remedy the breach if capable of being remedied, or the amount of compensation if the breach is incapable of remedy.

The debtor or hirer is allowed seven days from the date the notice is served, to take the appropriate action, and the notice must state the consequences of a failure to comply with it.

A notice is not required in an action purely for the recovery of arrears or for breach of contract. Similarly, a notice is not required when a creditor treats the right to draw upon any credit as restricted or deferred, and takes the necessary steps to make the restriction or deferment effective.[7] Such would be the case where a bank withdraws a credit-token from a debtor to prevent them from using it.

The Act also protects the interests of debtors in default by providing that a provision increasing the rate of interest in the event of default is of no effect.

1   See Crowther, p 143.
2   Para 6.1.7.
3   See Caplovitz, *Consumer in Trouble* (1974).
4   See Crowther, Ch 3.9 and National Consumer Council, *Consumer Credit* (1980).
5   See 3.7.17.
6   S 87.
7   S 87(2).
8   S 93.

Repossession of goods under hire purchase or conditional sale agreements
28.6.5 The Crowther Committee considered that 'the importance of security in a transaction tends to be exaggerated, and repossession whilst causing hardship to the debtor, is often of little value to the secured party.'[1] The Finance Houses Association pointed out in evidence to the Committee that only one car in forty taken on hire purchase was repossessed, despite the fact that repossession was sought only where the owner found he had no other remedy.[2] In the case of some goods such as household appliances, repossession may be uneconomic in view of the low resale value of such goods. However, repossession is considered valuable not so much because of the actual ability to repossess, as the psychological inducement it gives the consumer to maintain regular payment of the instalments. Furthermore, it may be argued that effectively giving the creditor security in the goods enables credit to be extended to those who otherwise would be unable to obtain it on their rating alone, because of their income.

In order to protect debtors from the risk of repossession of goods by the creditor for breach of the agreement, where the debtor has paid a considerable part of the total price the notion of 'protected goods' was introduced under hire purchase legislation. These provisions are now contained in s 90 of the CCA 1974 which provides that under a regulated hire purchase or conditional sale agreement where the property in the goods remains in the seller, a creditor must obtain a court order to repossess goods when the debtor is in breach of contract and has paid one third of the total purchase price.[3] Any installation charge included in the total purchase price must not be included as part of the total price for the purpose of calculating the one third payment.[4]

A failure to comply with these provisions means that the regulated agreement, if not already terminated, terminates, and the debtor is released from all further liability and is entitled to recover from the creditor all sums paid by him under the agreement.[5]

The CCA 1974 also provides that even where goods are not protected, the creditor under a regulated hire purchase or conditional sale agreement is not entitled to enter any premises to take possession of goods unless a court order[6] is obtained.

These provisions do not apply where the debtor gives his consent at the time of repossession.[7] Similarly, s 90 only refers to recovery of possession from the debtor, thus, there may be no infringement where the creditor repossesses goods which the debtor has abandoned.[8]

Section 90 also makes it clear that its provisions do not apply where the debtor has terminated, or terminates, the agreement. It must be apparent, however, that the decision to terminate was taken consciously knowing of the consequences.[9]

1 See 6.6.45.
2 See 6.6.47.
3 S 90(1).
4 S 90(2).
5 S 91.
6 S 92.
7 S 173(3).
8 See *Bentinck Ltd v Cromwell Engineering Co* [1971] 1 QB 324, [1971] 1 All ER 33, CA.
9 See *United Dominions Trust (Commercial) Ltd v Ennis* [1968] 1 QB 54, [1967] 2 All ER 345, CA.

Repossession of goods on hire

28.6.6 The provisions of s 92 prohibiting entry of premises to recover possession of goods also apply to regulated hire agreements. A further protection for hirers is that where the owner of goods does recover possession of the goods, the courts have a discretion to give relief to the consumer. Such relief may take the form of an order that the whole or part of any sum paid by the hirer to the owner shall be repaid and the obligation to pay the whole or part of any sum owed to the owner in respect of the goods shall cease.[1]

1 S 132.

Judicial control

28.7.0 The CCA 1974 gives the courts extremely wide powers in respect of the control and enforcement of regulated agreements. The following orders may be made.

(a) Enforcement and time orders

An enforcement order is essentially an order to enforce an improperly executed agreement. If an agreement is not properly signed the court cannot make an enforcement order unless some other document containing all the prescribed terms was signed by the debtor.[1] Where an application for an enforcement order is made the court can dismiss it if it considers it just to do so, having regard to the prejudice caused to any person by the contravention and the powers conferred on the court under ss 135 and 136.

The court may also reduce or discharge any sum payable by the debtor or hirer in an enforcement to take account of any prejudice caused by the contravention.[2]

A time order allows the court to require a debtor or hirer to pay sums owed by such instalments and payable at such times as the court considers reasonable having regard to the means of the debtor or hirer. The court may also use a time order to require a debtor or hirer to remedy any breach (other than non payment) within such period as they specify.

(b) Protection orders

The CCA 1974 gives the court power to make orders protecting any property of the creditor or owner, or property subject to any security, from damage or depreciation pending the outcome of proceedings under the Act.[3] This includes orders restricting or prohibiting the use of the property or giving directions in respect of its custody.

(c) Special powers in the case of hire purchase and conditional sale

The Act provides that on an application in respect of a regulated hire purchase or conditional sale agreement for an enforcement order, time order or action by the creditor for recovery of possession of the goods, the court may, if it appears just, make a return order or a transfer order.[4]

A return order is an order for the return of the goods to the creditor; and a transfer order is an order requiring the debtor to return some of the goods to the creditor and vesting the remaining goods in the debtor.[5] A transfer order may only be made where the amount already paid to the creditor by the debtor exceeds the part of the total price in respect of the transferred goods by at least one third of the unpaid balance of the total price. The objective here is to compensate the creditor for the return of used goods.

The debtor may, at any time before the goods enter the possession of the creditor, pay the balance of the total price and, subject to fulfilling any other necessary conditions, claim the goods notwithstanding any return or transfer order.[6]

In the event of a debtor's failure to comply with either a return or transfer order, the creditor may invite the court to cancel the order and substitute an order for so much of the total price as is referable to the goods.

(d) Conditional and suspended orders

Under s 135 the court, if it considers it just to do so, may in an order made by it in relation to any regulated agreement include provisions:

(a) making the operation of any term of the order conditional on the doing of specified acts by any party to the proceedings;

(b) suspending the operation of any terms of the order until such time as the court subsequently directs or until the occurrence of a specified act or omission.

These provisions give considerable flexibility to the courts in their handling of disputes and claims. The powers cannot, however, be used to suspend an order requiring a person to deliver up goods unless the court is satisfied that they are in that person's possession or control.[7] In the case of a consumer hire agreement the provisions cannot be used to extend the period for which the hirer is entitled to possession of the goods.

Section 136 gives a wide general power to the courts in the context of an order made under the Act, to include such provision as it considers just for amending any agreement or security in consequences of a term of the order.

1 S 127(3).
2 S 127(2).
3 S 131.
4 S 133.
5 S 133.
6 S 133(4).
7 S 135(2).

Extortionate credit bargains

28.7.1 We have already seen that under the general law of contract the courts are reluctant to interfere in contractual relations on the grounds that the bargain struck between the parties was extortionate.[1]

Under the Money-lenders Act 1900 the courts had the power to reopen any transaction within the Act that was harsh and unconscionable. They could re-open accounts; relieve the debtor from payment of any sum in excess of what was judged to be fairly due for principal, interest and charges; order repayment of any excess; and set aside any security given. The Moneylenders Act 1927 laid down that there was a rebuttable presumption that an interest rate in excess of 48% per annum was excessive and the transaction was harsh and unconscionable.

The CCA 1974[2] considerably expands on the principles originally laid down in the Moneylenders Act. The provisions allow the courts to reopen a credit agreement where they find the bargain extortionate. The scope of the sections is much wider than regulated agreements since a credit bargain is defined as an agreement where credit of any amount is provided to an individual together with any other transactions which must be taken into account in computing the total charge for credit.

Rather than operating by reference to a fixed rate of interest that is presumed extortionate, the courts are simply directed to consider a number of criteria. Thus a bargain is extortionate if it requires the debtor or a relative of his to make payments which are grossly exorbitant or otherwise grossly contravenes ordinary principles of fair dealing.[3] In deciding whether a bargain is extortionate the following matters shall be considered:

(a) interest rates prevailing at the time the agreement was made;
(b) the debtor's age, experience, business capacity and state of health;
(c) the degree to which the debtor was under financial pressure at the time he made the bargain, and the nature of such pressure;
(d) the degree of risk accepted by the creditor, having regard to the value of any security provided;
(e) the creditor's relationship with the debtor;
(f) whether or not a colourable cash price was quoted for any goods or services included in the credit bargain;
(g) in relation to a linked transaction, factors applicable include how far the transaction was reasonably required for the protection of the debtor or creditor or was in the interest of the creditor;
(h) any other relevant consideration.

In reopening a bargain the courts can effectively rewrite it. They may extinguish liabilities, order repayment of sums paid and order accounts to be taken.[4]

An order can be made under these provisions notwithstanding that its effect is to place a burden on the creditor in respect of an advantage unfairly enjoyed by another person who is a party to a linked transaction.

Proceedings under these provisions to have the bargain reopened may be taken by the debtor or a surety. Alternatively, they may raise the matter in any proceedings to which they are parties, being proceedings to enforce the agreement or any security of any linked transaction or other proceedings where the amount paid or payable under the credit agreement is relevant.

Such judicial guidance as there is suggests that the courts are adopting a fairly even handed approach in dealing with cases under the provisions, deciding each according to its own special facts. Thus in *Ketley Ltd v Scott*[5] a lender advanced £20,500 to a prospective house purchaser at only a few hours' notice at a nominal annual rate of interest of 48%. The court rejected the borrower's argument that the bargain was extortionate largely on the grounds of the borrower's conduct. Similarly in *Wills v Woods*[6] Sir John Donaldson stated that the word was 'extortionate', not unwise, and that the jurisdiction seemed to contemplate at least a substantial imbalance in bargaining power, of which one party had taken advantage.

Such an attitude is consistent with observations made by the draftsman of the CCA 1974 that:

> 'it is likely that the courts will be sparing with relief. The bargain must after all be grossly exorbitant or unfair.'[7]

1 See 15.0.8.
2 S 137–140.
3 S 138(1).
4 S 139(2).
5 [1981] ICR 241.
6 (1984) 128 Sol Jo 222, CA.
7 Bennion 121 Sol Jo 485.

Part VI
Business relations

Chapter 29
Agency

29.0.0 We have seen that, in general, the doctrine of privity of contract prevents a person acquiring rights under or being subjected to obligations by a contract to which he is not party.[1] However, there are clearly many occasions on which a person may wish to use the services of another to negotiate and even conclude a contract on his behalf; he may lack expertise, knowledge of a particular market, area or commodity, or simply be too busy or in the wrong place to make the contract for himself. The problem is particularly acute for business, for any but the smallest operation would rapidly grind to a halt if its principal had to make every contract in person, from ordering stationery and buying tea upwards. Obviously a company cannot contract for itself: it is a person at law,[2] but an artificial person and relies on humans to be its hands and mind and to make its contracts. The law meets this need of business by the concept of agency which modifies the general law of contract and allows one person, a principal, to acquire rights and obligations under contracts made on his behalf by another, the agent. The importance of the concept of agency is explained by Markesinis and Munday:[3]

> 'Commerce would literally come to a standstill if businessmen and merchants would not employ the services of factors, brokers, forwarding agents, estate agents, auctioneers and the like and were expected to do everything themselves. These specialised "middle men", whose main purpose is to make contracts on behalf of their principals, are to be found in all advanced societies and, whether one accepts or deplores some of the economic consequences of this phenomenon, the fact is that the agent's activities are an inevitable feature of a developed economy.'

As that quotation indicates, agents may appear in a number of guises and be known by a variety of names—agent, factor, broker. The business world recognises a number of specialised agents: we have already met the mercantile agent whose business it is to sell or buy goods or raise money on the security of goods belonging to another. There is also the del credere agent who acts as an agent but also guarantees to his principal that third parties will pay their debts under contracts negotiated by him. However, the businessman is not the only one who may use the services of an agent; the services provided by travel agents and estate agents are familiar although the latter is in a special position because, whilst he has authority to find a buyer for a property and to negotiate, he does not ordinarily have any authority to make a binding contract on the vendor's behalf.[4] Professional men may be the agents of their clients, but generally their agency will be restricted to a particular transaction; thus, for instance, a solicitor may be the agent of his client to conduct litigation on his behalf and to negotiate a settlement of proceedings;[5] an accountant may act as his client's agent in relation to (say) negotiations with the Inland Revenue; and a stockbroker buying or selling shares may act as the agent of his client.

However, a note of caution must be sounded; not all those who are called agents are in fact agents in law. Thus, for instance, an 'advertising agency' does not act as agent for its clients when it places advertisements. The importance of this lies in the result that the agency is solely liable for the cost of the advertising space it books; it will in turn look to the client for reimbursement when it charges him for its services.[6] Similarly dealers in goods, particularly motor cars, are often described as 'agents' or 'sole agents' for a particular manufacturer, for example, 'sole Ford agents'. Generally such dealers are not agents at all. They buy goods from the manufacturer and resell them on their own behalf to the customer. There is no contract between customer and manufacturer, as there would be if this were a true 'agency' in the legal sense. Thus if he has a contractual complaint the customer may look only to the retailer for redress. On the other hand, if the dealer is a 'sole agent' he may be able to prevent the manufacturer selling his own goods direct to the public which he would not be able to do if he were a true agent.[7]

Similar difficulties occur in the common situation where a consumer buys goods, such as a car, on hire purchase terms from a finance company. Typically in such a situation the consumer's only contact is with a dealer who arranges the transfer of the goods to the finance company and prepares all necessary forms for completion and signature by the consumer. Parliament has provided that for certain purposes connected with the credit arrangements the dealer is to be treated as the agent of the finance company.[8] As Lord Wilberforce has explained:

> 'the mercantile reality . . . has become well known and widely understood by the public, as well as by the commercial interests involved . . . So far from thinking first of a purchase from a dealer, and then separately, of obtaining finance from an outside source, the identity or even existence of the finance company is a matter (to customers) of indifference; they look to the dealer, or his representative, as the person who fixes the payment terms and makes all the necessary arrangements.'[9]

In the light of that, Lord Wilberforce favoured the view that the dealer is the agent of the finance company for general purposes connected with the transaction, as have other eminent judges. However, the views expressed have been obiter and the matter remains uncertain as there are other eminent judicial pronouncements taking a contrary view.

There are other commonly encountered examples of agency, sometimes in special forms. Thus the powers of directors and other officers of a company to bind the company depend on agency principles;[10] and similarly a partner is regarded as the agent of his partners for the purposes of the firm and its business.[11]

As the above comments illustrate, an agent may be an independent contractor, in business on his own account, who makes his profit by charging fees or commission to his principal. However, that is not always the case, and agents may be employees of their principals, although their powers may, in practice, be limited. Directors of a company are often also employees of the company. We will now examine the general rules applicable to all agents and then turn to some of the special rules which govern the relationship between employer and employee.[12]

1 Above 19.0.0.
2 Below 33.0.0.
3 *An Outline of the Law of Agency* (2nd edn 1986), p 3.
4 *Hamer v Sharp* (1874) LR 19 Eq 108.
5 See (eg) *Waugh v H B Clifford & Sons Ltd* [1982] Ch 374, [1982] 1 All ER 1095, CA.
6 This was the reason for the plaintiff's enquiry in *Hedley Byrne & Co Ltd v Heller & Partners Ltd* [1964] AC 465, [1963] 2 All ER 575, HL; above 7.1.7.
7 *Lamb (WT) & Sons v Goring Brick Co Ltd* [1932] 1 KB 710, CA.
8 Under the Consumer Credit Act 1974, see eg, s 56. See 28.4.0.
9 *Branwhite v Worcester Works Finance Ltd* [1969] 1 AC 552 at 586–7, HL.
10 Below 35.0.3.
11 Below 32.3.0.
12 Below 30.0.0.

The legal basis of agency

29.1.0. An agent is a person who is recognised by the law as having power to enter transactions creating legally binding rights and obligations for his principal. Typically his role is to negotiate and enter into a contract on behalf of his principal although certain special forms of agency may involve the creation of more limited, or wider, obligations. We have already seen how, in the law of torts, the notion of vicarious liability may subject one person to legal liability for the acts of another.[1] Vicarious liability and agency are however separate concepts. Vicarious liability creates only liabilities in tort; agency may create rights or liabilities in contract; vicarious liability is imposed only where there is a relationship of employer and employee; agents, on the other hand, may be self-employed or independent contractors or employees of their principal. In certain situations, however, the two concepts are similar. This is particularly true where an employer is made liable for the deliberate deceptions of his employee.[2] As we remarked above, in such a situation the employee is in no sense furthering his employer's interests—quite the contrary. However, liability is imposed on the employer because he has, by words or conduct, induced the victim of the fraud to believe that the employee was acting in the course of the employer's business, and the victim suffers loss as a result of reliance on that representation.[3] The employer's liability in such a situation is thus closely connected to the concept of ostensible authority, or agency by estoppel, in the law of agency.[4]

An agent is recognised as having power to affect the legal position of his principal only where he has authority so to do. Such authority will often derive from agreement between agent and principal but it may exist even in the absence of such agreement. Generally, once the agent has concluded a contract on behalf of his principal, he drops out of the picture, leaving principal and the third party in a contractual relationship with each other. There are thus potentially, two contracts in an agency situation: one between agent and principal by which the former is authorised and under which certain mutual rights and duties arise; and that between principal and third party created by the agent. However, in certain situations the normal rule breaks down and the agent may not drop out of the picture. There are thus three relationships to be considered: between principal and agent, principal and third party, and agent and third party.

1 Above 9.0.2.
2 As in *Lloyd v Grace Smith & Co* [1912] AC 716, HL; above 9.0.4.
3 Explained in *Armagas Ltd v Mundogas Ltd* [1986] 2 All ER 385 [1986] AC 717, HL.
4 Below 29.2.4.

Principal and third party: the authority of the agent

29.2.0 The power of the agent (A) to bind his principal (P) in a contract with a third party (T) depends on authority given to A by P. In many cases there will be an agreement between P and A by which the former confers authority on the latter; A is then said to have 'actual authority'. It may then be necessary to determine the scope of that authority, which may be extended by implication; or, indeed, the agreement between P and A may be wholly implied. However, an agent may be treated by the law as having authority to bind his principal even when there is no express or implied agreement: a person may be held out by another so that he appears to have authority which he does not actually possess. He is then said to have ostensible, or apparent authority. Further, in addition a person may, in certain limited circumstances, be treated as an 'agent of necessity'.

Unfortunately the courts and writers have not been wholly consistent in their use of terminology when classifying particular situations.[1] There is, moreover, a certain legitimate overlap between implied and apparent authority, and 'usual' or 'customary' authority which may be a variety of either.

Finally, even where a person has acted on behalf of another wholly without authority, the other may in certain circumstances adopt the acts purportedly done in his name and create an agency 'ex post facto' by the doctrine of ratification.

1 Much of the confusion was alleviated by the analysis of Diplock LJ in *Freeman & Lockyer (a firm) v Buckhurst Park Properties (Mangal) Ltd* [1964] 2 QB 480, [1964] 1 All ER 630, CA.

Actual authority

29.2.1 In many cases the agent, A, will have been given actual authority by his principal, P, to contract on his behalf. The basis of such actual authority is some agreement between the parties, which may be express or implied, where the parties act on a tacit mutual understanding that A should act on P's behalf. In addition, where A has express actual authority, its scope may be extended by the implication into the agreement of extra, incidental authority. As between P and A, actual authority is paramount; only while acting within the scope of his actual authority is A entitled to remuneration for his services or an indemnity for expenses;[1] and if he exceeds his actual authority, he may be liable to P for breach of his duties as agent.[2] However, as between P and the third party, T, with whom A contracts, the actual authority may be extended by the apparent or ostensible authority which the agent is allowed to appear to have, so that P may be bound by contracts made by A outside the scope of his actual authority, or even by contracts made after the termination of his actual authority.

1 Below 29.5.0.
2 Below 29.5.5.

Express actual authority

29.2.2 Actual authority is that authority actually given by P to A. It is express if it derives from an express agreement. It is important to note that its basis is agreement and not necessarily contract. Of course, often the agreement between P and A will be contractual: in that case A is entitled to be paid for his services.[1] However, he may have express actual authority even if he agrees to act totally gratuitously. It seems that if he has agreed to act gratuitously, A is not liable if he fails to carry out his appointed task.[2]

In general anyone may act as an agent. An adult, P may appoint a minor to act on his behalf, and any contracts made by A will be fully binding because they are P's contracts. However, the agency agreement between P and A may not be binding on A due to his minority.[3]

Generally, no formalities are required for the express appointment of an agent. The agreement may be oral or written. However, when A is appointed to execute a deed on P's behalf, he must be appointed by a deed, known as a power of attorney.

Where there is an express agreement between P and A, the scope of the latter's authority is purely a question of the construction of the agency agreement; however, the express authority may be extended by any implied power, or by A's apparent authority.

1 Below 29.5.1.
2 Below 29.5.5.
3 Above 16.1.1.

Implied actual authority

29.2.3 A may have authority from P to act on his behalf even though there is no express agreement between them. If from their words and conduct an implicit agreement can be discerned, A will have implied authority to act on P's behalf. It is important to recognise that this is, nevertheless, a species of actual authority for that affects the rights and liabilities of P and A inter se. Obviously in business transactions it is rare to find agents acting on the strength of wholly implicit authority; however examples may arise. In *Hely-Hutchinson v Brayhead Ltd*[1] the Court of Appeal held that on the facts of the particular case, the Board of Directors of the defendant company had impliedly authorised the company's chairman to act on its behalf as if he were its managing director, and to enter into a contract on behalf of the company to indemnify the plaintiff. In a domestic context a wife has implied authority to pledge her husband's credit for household necessaries as a result of their sharing a household,[2] although this rule now appears increasingly archaic.

An agent who has been given express authority may have additional, implied authority. Such authority may be implied under the usual rules by which the courts are prepared to imply terms into contracts. Such implied authority is sometimes categorised as incidental, customary or usual authority.

Incidental authority gives the agent power to do those acts which are reasonably necessary for or incidental to the execution of his express authority. The scope of any incidental authority in any particular case will depend on all the particular circumstances.

In addition, the authority of the agent may be expanded by customary authority: that is, the authority which agents operating in a particular area or business customarily have. However, the court will only recognise a custom in this way if it is certain, notorious (ie sufficiently well known) and reasonable. In *Dingle v Hare*[3] the defendant's agent had contracted to sell a quantity of manure and had warranted it; it was found that it was customary for agents in the particular trade to warrant manure and so the defendant was bound even though he had not authorised the warranty. On the other hand the court would not recognise a custom which purported to allow an agent to buy goods in his own name and then resell to his principal;[4] such a custom would lead to a conflict of interest between agent and principal and would therefore be unreasonable.

Similarly an agent may be held to have usual authority which exceeds his actual authority. Usual authority is that authority which a particular type of agent usually has. Thus, for instance, a solicitor usually has implied authority to compromise an action on behalf of a client.[5] In *Panorama Developments (Guildford) Ltd v Fidelis Furnishing Fabrics Ltd*[6] it was held that a company secretary had implied usual authority to hire cars on behalf of the company, so that the company was liable for the hire charges even though the hirings were unauthorised and, in fact, for the secretary's own benefit. Indeed, the secretary would have usual authority to sign contracts 'dealing with the administrative side of [the] company's affairs', including the hiring of staff and so on. A managing director or chief executive would have wider usual authority to make commercial arrangements binding on the company;[7] by contrast such contracts would not be within the usual authority of the company chairman.[8]

A particular problem which has exercised the courts is the scope of the authority of an estate agent. He has authority to make statements about the property, so that his principal may be liable for misrepresentation if such statements prove false. However, he has no authority to make statements about the permitted user of premises;[9] nor does he have usual authority to sign a binding contract of sale;[10] he may only do that if expressly authorised so to do. In *Sorrell v Finch*[11] the House of Lords had to consider whether or not estate agents have usual authority to take pre-contract 'deposits' from interested purchasers. The practice of taking such payments has become common, although they are taken before a binding contract is concluded and are returnable to the would-be purchaser on demand. The question arises as to who, as between vendor and purchaser, should bear the loss in the event of default by the agent. Here again the law must decide between two innocent parties. If the estate agent has usual authority to take such deposits, the purchaser may look to the vendor to repay any deposit so paid. In *Sorrell v Finch* it was held that the estate agent does not have such usual authority.

A principal may seek to limit his agent's authority; for instance, by excluding the customary authority of a particular market, or by limiting his usual authority as where a company imposes a financial limit on transactions which may be concluded by its managing director. As between principal and agent, such a limit is effective so that if the agent exceeds it he is liable to his principal for breach of duty. However, the principal can only rely on such a limit as against a third party who deals with the agent if the third party knows of the limit; if not he can rely on the agent's usual or customary authority. 'Usual authority' here resembles ostensible or apparent authority and this has no doubt helped to create confusion. A particularly difficult case is *Watteau v Fenwick*.[12] The defendant had appointed one Humble to run an hotel on his behalf; however, the business was carried on in Humble's name. The defendants expressly forbade Humble to buy cigars for the hotel on credit; in defiance of that prohibition he did purchase cigars from the plaintiff. The defendant was held liable for the price; ordering cigars was within the usual authority of an hotel manager and the plaintiff was unaware of the prohibition. The most striking feature of the case is that the plaintiff at all times thought he was dealing only with Humble, and not with him as agent for the defendant. For that reason this could not be a case of apparent authority. However, the result is closely analogous to a case of apparent authority and can perhaps be justified on the grounds that the defendant had put Humble in a position when he could appear to be in charge of the hotel, and stood to benefit from contracts made by him.

1 [1968] 1 QB 549, [1967] 3 All ER 98, CA.
2 *Debenham v Mellon* (1880) 6 App Cas 24, HL.
3 (1859) 7 CBNS 145.
4 *Robinson v Mollett* (1875) LR 7 HL 802. The principal would be bound if he knew of the custom.
5 *Waugh v H B Clifford & Sons* [1982] Ch 374, [1982] 1 All ER 1095, CA.
6 [1971] 2 QB 711, [1971] 3 All ER 16, CA.
7 *Freeman and Lockyer (a firm) v Buckhurst Park Properties (Mangal) Ltd* [1964] 2 QB 480, [1964] 1 All ER 630, CA.
8 As in *Hely-Hutchinson v Brayhead Ltd* [1968] 1 QB 549, [1967] 3 All ER 98, CA.
9 *Hill v Harris* [1965] 2 QB 601, [1965] 2 All ER 358, CA.
10 *Pickering v Busk* (1812) 5 East 38 at 43.
11 [1977] AC 728, [1976] 2 All ER 371, HL. The power of estate agents to take such deposits is now governed by the Estate Agents Act 1979. S 13 makes it clear that the money is held for and is returnable on demand to the purchaser.
12 [1893] 1 QB 346.

Apparent authority

29.2.4   Apparent or ostensible authority is that authority which the agent appears to have. As Diplock LJ explained,

> 'it is upon the apparent authority of the agent that the contractor normally relies in the ordinary course of business when entering into contracts.'[1]

Its basis is a representation by the principal to the other contracting party that the agent has some authority. The other party is entitled to rely on that representation unless he knows it to be false; otherwise his position would be intolerable for he would always have to verify the agent's authority before dealing with him. Since in most cases the agent does actually have the authority he appears to have, that would be an unwarranted burden on both principal and the other contracting party.

The possible coincidence of apparent authority with actual authority can be seen in *Hely-Hutchinson v Brayhead Ltd*[2] where Roskill J at first instance held the defendants liable on the grounds that their chairman had apparent authority as if he was managing director; Lord Denning MR in the Court of

Appeal expressly endorsed that view, but held that the company had given actual implied authority. However, apparent authority can exist even when there is no actual authority: for instance if the agent has not been appointed at all, or where his appointment has been terminated but that fact has not been communicated to the other party.[3] In addition it may operate to expand the authority of an agent who is actually authorised: for instance when his actual authority is subject to an express limit. As we have seen, there is then some overlap between 'apparent authority' and 'usual authority'. The special rules relating to sales by mercantile agents are really an example of apparent authority expanding the agent's powers.[4]

In *Freeman and Lockyer v Buckhurst Park Properties (Mangal) Ltd*[5] Diplock LJ explained the basis of apparent authority and its relationship with actual authority. The latter depends on the agreement, express or implied, between principal and agent and is really of no interest to the outsider. Apparent authority, on the other hand, depends on a representation made by the principal to the other contracting party and does not concern the agent. It is thus a form of estoppel. In order to rely on the agent's apparent authority, a contractor must show:

(a) A representation made to him by the principal. He cannot rely (against the alleged principal) on the agent's own assertions of authority although if the agent purports to have authority he does not have, the contractor may sue the agent for breach of warranty of authority.[6] Problems may arise in the case of companies, which must act through agents. The representation must then be made by someone with actual authority to act on behalf of the company.[7] Typically this will be the Board of Directors and in *Freeman & Lockyer* the outsider was able to rely on the representation by the Board that one of their number had been authorised to act as if he were a managing director and make a contract for the plaintiff's services. The representation may be by words or conduct. In *Freeman & Lockyer* it was enough that the Board sat by and, knowing of his activities, allowed the agent to continue to act on behalf of the company.

(b) The representation must be of fact, not law. Thus an incorrect representation as to the effect of a power of attorney will not lead to apparent authority. The representation ordinarily is that the 'agent' has authority to act on behalf of the principal.

(c) The contractor must rely on that representation and change his position as a result. He cannot rely on a representation made to another party, and he will not be able to claim he relied on a representation if he knew it to be false. It is unclear if a third party is under a duty to enquire as to the agent's authority. It may be that he is, at least when the agent purports to act beyond the scope of the usual authority of an agent of that kind. However, an outsider who deals with a company is protected against having to enquire into the company's internal procedures[8] and is allowed to assume that the powers of the directors to act on behalf of the company are unfettered by its Articles of Association.[9]

If these conditions are fulfilled a contractor who deals with the agent relying on his apparent authority may enforce the contract against the principal even though the agent was not actually authorised to make it. The scope of the authority of an apparent agent will depend on the usual authority of an agent of that particular kind. Thus in *Freeman & Lockyer* the agent was apparently managing director; he had the authority usually possessed by a managing director. However, as between principal and agent, the agent will be liable for breach of duty.[10]

The result may seem harsh on the principal who is bound to a contract he did not authorise; but the law must choose between two innocent parties and favours the third party who would otherwise be misled by the principal's conduct. Moreover, by allowing him to rely on appearances, the rule facilitates commerce.

1 *Freeman and Lockyer (a firm) v Buckhurst Park Properties (Mangal) Ltd* [1964] 2 QB 480 at 504, CA.
2 [1968] 1 QB 549, [1967] 3 All ER 98, CA.
3 As in *Drew v Nunn* (1879) 4 QBD 661, CA; below 29.6.2. Retired partners may, similarly, continue to be liable for debts contracted by the firm after their retirement, by virtue of Partnership Act 1890, s 14(2).
4 Above, 23.0.1.
5 See note 1, above.
6 Below, 29.4.2.
7 See below, 35.0.3.
8 By the rule in *Royal British Bank Ltd v Turquand*, below 35.0.3.
9 By Companies Act 1985, s 35; below 33.3.2.
10 Below, 29.5.5.

Estoppel arising after the event

29.2.5 In the cases discussed above, the principal makes a representation that the agent has authority upon which the third party then relies in entering into a contract. However, an estoppel may also arise as a result of the principal's behaviour after a contract has been made. In *Spiro v Lintern*[1] the defendant instructed his wife to put his house in the hands of estate agents. She had no authority to enter a binding contract for sale but the estate agents acting on her instructions purported to sign one with the plaintiffs as purchasers. The defendant made no objection and allowed the plaintiffs to proceed with the transaction, to instruct architects and builders to make alterations to the property and even to visit it to measure up for those alterations. He then sought to deny the authority of his wife and therefore of the estate agents. He was held to be bound: his failure to disabuse the plaintiff of his mistaken belief that the contract was authorised amounted to a representation that his wife had authority and estopped him from now denying it.

1 [1973] 3 All ER 319, [1973] 1 WLR 1002, CA.

Agency of necessity

29.2.6 Agency of necessity arises, like apparent authority, due to the operation of law rather than any consent of the parties. However, it is in some ways closer to actual authority because, when agency of necessity is established the 'agent' may not only be able to create for his principal rights and obligations vis à vis third parties, but may also himself be entitled to rights against his principal, for instance to claim an indemnity against expenses incurred or to rely on the agency as a defence to a claim by the principal for interference with his property. Indeed, often the only question in issue will be the rights and liabilities of principal and agent inter se.

An agency of necessity arises—

> 'when a person is faced with an emergency in which the property or interests of another person are in imminent jeopardy and it becomes

necessary, in order to preserve the property or interests, to act for that person without his authority.'[1]

The rule is best established in mercantile contracts for the carriage of goods by sea, perhaps because emergencies giving rise to 'imminent jeopardy' are most likely to arise in that situation. Thus a master of a ship may deal with his vessel and its cargo in an emergency to preserve either; he may use the cargo to raise capital for repairs, incur expenses on behalf of cargo owners to preserve the cargo, or even jettison cargo to preserve his ship.[2] An agency of necessity may arise even when the agent had no prior authority, but it may also operate to extend the authority of an appointed agent. In order to claim the benefit of the rule, a party must show:

(a) there was an emergency;
(b) that it was practically impossible to obtain instructions from the principal;
(c) that the agent acted bona fide in the principal's interests;[3]
(d) that the agent acted reasonably in all the circumstances.

The doctrine does not only apply to contracts for carriage of goods by sea; it may apply in other situations and has been applied, for instance, to a contract for carriage by rail.[4] However, in light of modern methods of communication it is unlikely that an agency of necessity will often arise in such circumstances today.[5]

If there is an agency of necessity, the agent may make contracts, for instance for the warehousing of the endangered property, binding on the principal. He may also claim reimbursement for his expenditure, contrary to the general rule that a person who expends money on the property of another is entitled to no payment.[6]

1 *Bowstead on Agency* (1985, 5th edn) p 84.
2 *Notara v Henderson* (1872) LR 7 QB 225, Ex Ch.
3 *Sachs v Miklos* [1948] 2 KB 23, [1948] 1 All ER 67, CA.
4 *Great Northern Rly Co v Swaffield* (1874) LR 9 Ex Ch 132.
5 *Springer v Great Western Rly Co* [1921] 1 KB 257, CA.
6 The general rule is also modified by the Torts (Interference with Goods) Act, which may allow him to claim for improvements to goods if sued by the owner.

Ratification

29.2.7   So far we have been concerned with situations where an agent has, or appears to have, authority from his principal at the time he enters into a transaction. However, a person may purport to act on behalf of a principal when he in fact has no authority. The agent's own representation of authority is not enough to create an apparent authority.[1] In such a case the 'agent' may be liable to the other contracting party for breach of his warranty of authority.[2] However, the law allows the 'principal' to adopt the acts purportedly done on his behalf, by ratifying the agent's contract. If he does choose to ratify the result is as if the agent had always been authorised and there is a contract between the principal and the other contracting party.

A person may only ratify a contract if a number of conditions are fulfilled.

(a) The agent must have purported to act on behalf of the principal who seeks to ratify; an undisclosed principal cannot ratify. If the agent purported to act on his own behalf, or on behalf of someone entirely different, the principal may not ratify. In *Keighley, Maxstead & Co v*

Durant[3] the agent, having no authority, contracted in his own name. His intended principal later purported to ratify the contract and was then sued under the contract by the third party. The action failed because the purported ratification was ineffective. In such a case the third party must settle for his personal action against the agent. In contrast, the named principal can ratify acts done in his name even where the agent acted fraudulently and intended to take the benefit of the contract for himself.[4]

(b) The principal must have been in existence at the time when the agent made the contract. This rule causes difficulty for the promoters of new companies; any contract, even if made on behalf of the company, cannot bind or benefit the company; and the company cannot, after formation, ratify a contract purportedly made on its behalf before incorporation.[5] In such a case the promoters who make the contract are personally liable on it.[6]

(c) The principal can only ratify a contract which he had capacity to make when the agent made it for him. Thus, for instance, if a contract is made by a supposed agent on behalf of a minor, the minor cannot ratify it even after attaining his majority.[7] Similarly a company cannot ratify a contract made on its behalf which would be ultra vires the company.[8]

(d) Similarly the principal cannot ratify a nullity. This is sometimes said to explain why a principal cannot ratify a forgery—for instance when the agent forges the principal's signature.[9] However, this rule can also be explained on the basis that the forger does not purport to act for the principal, but pretends that he is the principal.[10]

(e) If he wishes to ratify, the principal must do so within a reasonable time. This rule is necessary to protect the third party because, as we shall see, ratification has retroactive effect. What is a reasonable time will depend on the facts of each case; obviously the time will be shorter, for example, in relation to a contract to purchase perishable goods or when dealing on a fluctuating market. It has been said that a contract cannot be ratified after the time for its performance, or the commencement of performance, has arrived.[11] Similarly, a principal may not ratify a policy of insurance made on his behalf after the destruction of the insured property.[12]

(f) The principal will only be bound by his ratification if he made it with full knowledge of all relevant facts. Thus he would not be bound to a contract to buy goods if the agent led him to believe that the purchase price was lower than in fact it was.

1 Above 29.2.4.
2 Below 29.4.2.
3 [1901] AC 240, HL.
4 *Re Tiedemann and Lederman Frères* [1899] 2 QB 66.
5 *Kelner v Baxter* (1866) LR 2 CP 174.
6 Companies Act 1985, s 36(4); below 33.3.2.
7 Above, 16.1.1.
8 Below, 33.3.0.
9 *Brook v Hook* (1871) LR 6 Exch 89.
10 Similarly the principal cannot effectively ratify a contract which the law prohibits him making: see *Bedford Insurance Co Ltd v Instituto des Resseguros do Brasil* [1985] QB 966, [1984] 3 All ER 766.
11 *Metropolitan Asylums Board (Managers) v Kingham* (1890) 6 TLR 217. This was doubted in the *Bedford Insurance* case, supra, when the court said, obiter, that the principal could ratify a contract after the time for performance when ratification benefitted the other.
12 *Grover & Grover Ltd v Matthews* [1910] 2 KB 401, CA. There is a special exception for contracts of marine insurance: Marine Insurance Act 1906, s 86.

The effect of ratification

29.2.8 If the principal does choose to ratify the contract made in his name the effect is as if the agent had always had authority to act on the principal's behalf. Thus, the agent is not liable to the principal for exceeding his authority, nor to the other party for breach of warranty of authority. On the other hand there is a valid contract between the principal and third party; and, by the doctrine of relation back, that contract is validated from the time the agent purported to make it. This may seem hard on the third party: it seems to allow the principal to choose whether or not to ratify and, possibly, to play fast and loose in a fluctuating market. However, the harshness is mitigated by the rule that ratification must be in a reasonable time.[1] Further, if the principal does ratify the third party is in the position he always believed himself to be in; whereas if he does not do so, the third party may sue the alleged agent for breach of warranty of authority.[2] It must be remembered that the principal has not authorised the acts of his agent. The difficulty may also be mitigated by the decision in *Watteau v Fenwick*.[3]

If the third party makes an offer to the agent who accepts it, he will be bound to the contract if the principal later chooses to ratify. Moreover, if he purports to revoke his offer after the agent's acceptance but before ratification, his revocation will be ineffective.[4] This is because the ratification has retroactive effect to the time of the agent's acceptance. However, this apparently unfair result can be avoided:

(a) if agent and third party expressly make their agreement conditional upon ratification; the principal must then ratify within a reasonable time;[5]

(b) if the third party knowing of the lack of authority can stipulate a time within which the principal must ratify. Ratification outside that time will be ineffective;

(c) if the third party agrees with the agent to terminate the agreement before it is ratified, any subsequent ratification will be ineffective.[6]

1 Above 29.2.7.
2 Below 29.4.2.
3 Above 29.2.4.
4 *Teheran-Europe Co Ltd v S T Belton (Traders) Ltd,* supra.
5 *Heald v Kenwrothy* (1855) 10 Exch 739—contra *Armstrong v Stokes* (1872) LR 7 QB 598.
6 *Walter v James* (1871) LR 6 Exch 124.

Principal and third party: rights and liabilities

29.3.0 The general rule is that if a duly authorised agent makes a contract on behalf of his principal 'the contract is that of the principal, not that of the agent, and prima facie at common law the only person who can sue is the principal and the only person who can be sued is the principal.'[1] The agent, having performed his allotted task, drops out of the picture; he has no liability under the contract he has negotiated. Were it otherwise, few would willingly act as agents. As we have seen, the same result is reached even when the agent is not authorised provided his purported principal later ratifies his acts. However, although this is the general rule, it is subject to exceptions, particularly in the case of the undisclosed principal. A principal is disclosed if his agent has revealed that he is acting for a principal, whether the principal is named or unnamed. The principal is undisclosed when the agent does not reveal that he is acting for a principal at all and purports to act in his own name.

1 Per Wright J in *Montgomerie v United Kingdom Mutual SS Association Ltd* [1891] 1 QB 370 at 371.

Where the principal is disclosed

29.3.1   In general, when the agent discloses that he is acting for a principal, the contract which results from his efforts is between the principal (P) and other contracting party (X); the agent (A) has no rights or liabilities under that contract. Exceptionally, however, he may be liable on the contract despite the general rule.[1] If A had only apparent authority, it seems that P may be sued but may not sue on the contract.

There used to be a general exception to this rule, that where A acted on behalf of a foreign principal, A alone acquired rights and liabilities under the contract and P could neither sue nor be sued because—

'the foreign constituent has not authorised the merchant to pledge his credit to the contract, to establish privity between him and the home supplier, . . . [and] the home supplier, knowing that to be the usage . . . does not trust the foreigner and so does not make the foreigner responsible to him, and does not make himself responsible to the foreigner.'[2]

However, 'commercial usages are far from immutable'[3] and today, when international trade is commonplace, and there are developed rules of conflict of laws and treaties providing for reciprocal enforcement of judgments, the foreign nationality of the principal will only be one factor, and generally a weak one, for the court to evaluate in deciding whether there is privity between P and X.[4]

If the contract requires the payment of money the general rule is that neither P nor X is discharged from liability by payment to A. This will be important if payment is made to A who then absconds or becomes insolvent. A payment by X to A will only discharge X from liability if A had authority, actual, usual or apparent, to receive payment on behalf of P; otherwise X must make a second payment, if necessary, to P. Equally, a payment by P to A will not discharge P from his liability to X. The position here is stronger, for A is P's agent. However, such a payment may discharge P when X has led him, by words or conduct, to believe that he should pay A, for instance by giving the impression that A has paid X, so that it would be unfair to order P to pay a second time.[5] X is then estopped from denying (eg) that he has settled with A.

1 Below 29.4.0.
2 Blackburn J in *Elbinger AG für Fabrication von Eisenbahn Material v Claye* (1873) LR 8 QB 313 at 317.
3 Diplock LJ in *Teheran-Europe Co Ltd v S T Belton (Tractors) Ltd* [1968] 2 QB 545, [1968] 2 All ER 886, CA.
4 *Teheran—Europe Co Ltd v S T Belton (Traders) Ltd*, supra.
5 *Heald v Kenwrothy* (1855) 10 Exch 739—contra *Armstrong v Stokes* (1872) LR 7 QB 598.

Where the principal is undisclosed

29.3.2   If A contracts with X but does not reveal that he is acting as agent for P, the general rule is modified. X believes throughout that he is dealing with A, and with A alone. He may therefore sue A and, equally, A may sue

X on the contract. If he discovers P's existence X may, alternatively, sue him, although he must choose between A and P. More surprisingly, P may step forward and himself enforce the contract against X. It may seem harsh that X may be held liable in contract to someone of whose interest, and even existence, he was ignorant, and seems to run counter to the notions of consensus and privity of contract. The rule is, however, convenient:

> 'Middlemen, through whom contracts are made, are common and useful in business transactions and in the great mass of contracts it is a matter of indifference to either party whether there is an undisclosed principal or not. If he exists it is, to say the least, extremely convenient that he should be able to sue and be sued as a principal, and he is only allowed to do so upon terms which exclude injustice.'[1]

The rule also prevents circuity of actions, as Diplock LJ has explained;[2] otherwise P could require A to lend his name to an action to enforce the contract against X; and P would be liable to indemnify A against the obligations he incurs towards X.

The rule allowing the undisclosed principal to sue probably has its origin in the 19th century[3] when the increasing pace of commercial life led to an increasing number of bankruptcies, particularly amongst factors. If P has sold property through A to X and before X pays for it, A becomes bankrupt, it would appear unjust to leave P to prove in the bankruptcy while X has the benefit of the property. The rule which allows the undisclosed principal to sue and be sued is in fact merely the inverse of that which allows ratification. Undisclosed agency allows P, who has actually authorised A's actions, to sue and be sued although his existence was not revealed; ratification allows P, for whom A purported to act, to sue and be sued although he had in fact not authorised A's actions. Like ratification, undisclosed agency is subject to a number of limitations, which protect the third party. These are:

(a) A must have P's actual authority at the time when he makes the contract. An undisclosed principal can never ratify.[4]

(b) The undisclosed principal may only enforce the contract if he was in existence and had capacity to make the contract at the time it was made.

(c) The undisclosed principal may not sue on the contract if it expressly prohibits his intervention.

(d) Similarly, he may not sue if the contract impliedly prohibits it. This was held to be the case where an agent entered into a charterparty on behalf of a shipowner but signed the contract in his own name as 'owner'. It was held that by describing himself as the owner of the chartered vessel, A had excluded the possibility of P's intervention.[5] However, the courts have tended to limit this rule; thus when an agent signed a charterparty in his own name as 'charterer' it was held that the undisclosed principal could intervene: 'charterer' was regarded as a neutral description, amounting to no more than 'party to the contract.'[6]

(e) The undisclosed principal may be prevented from intervening if X either had special, personal reasons for contracting only with A or personal reasons for not contracting with P:

(i) X may have special reasons for wishing to contract only with A. This will be the case where, for instance, he makes the contract relying on some special personal characteristics of A, such as his skill or experience, or his solvency. In *Collins v Associated Greyhound Racecourses Ltd*,[7] A, acting on behalf of an undisclosed P, agreed to underwrite an issue of shares. It was held that P could not then come in on the contract because a company has a special interest in the personal characteristics of a person who underwrites its shares. Similarly P will not be able to come in on the contract between X and A if X contracts with A to set off a debt due to him from A against sums due under a contract.[8] P may not come in on a contract which requires personal service from A: thus if A enters a contract of employment, P cannot then claim it was made on his behalf.

(ii) X may have special reasons for not contracting with P. The position here is less clear. In general it seems that P may intervene on a contract made between A and X even though he knew that X would, for personal reasons, have refused to contract with him.[9] However, it seems that P will be prevented from intervening if A positively misrepresents the situation to X, for example if X asks, 'Are you acting for P?' and A dishonestly denies that he is; or, if the contract is such that[10] 'the personal element is strikingly present.' Thus when a theatre critic was banned from a theatre because of unfavourable reviews he had given to past productions, he employed an agent to obtain for him a ticket for a first night. He knew the theatre would not deal with him. When the theatre refused him admission, his claim for breach of contract failed.[11] The case can perhaps be explained by the strong personal element involved in the contract.

The above rules are designed to protect the third party; they prevent the undisclosed principal suing on the contract. There is no authority on the point but it seems that they should not prevent the third party suing the undisclosed principal, if he can be identified.

If the undisclosed principal does sue, the third party may raise against him any defence he could have raised against a claim by the agent. Such defences may include a set off available against a claim by the agent, but only when P's conduct has led X to believe that A is acting on his behalf. The third party who discovers the existence of the undisclosed principal may choose whether to sue him or the agent. Once he has elected to sue one, he may not sue the other. He will be held to have made his election if, knowing of the existence of the undisclosed principal he does some act which shows unequivocally that he is looking only to A or P to meet his claim. Clearly suing one and obtaining judgment against him would amount to an election. However, it has been held that issuing a writ was not enough to amount to an irrevocable election.[12]

If there is an undisclosed agency and X pays any money due under the contract to A, he is discharged from all liability provided that at the time of the payment he was ignorant of P's existence. Clearly, a settlement by P with A will not discharge P from liability to X.

1 Per Lord Lindley in *Keighley, Maxstead & Co v Durant* [1901] AC 240 at 261, HL.
2 In *Freeman & Lockyer (a firm) v Buckhurst Park Properties (Mangal) Ltd* [1964] 2 QB 480, [1964] 1 All ER 630, CA.
3 Explained in Markesinis and Munday, *An Outline of the Law of Agency* (2nd Edn, 1986).
4 *Keighley, Maxstead & Co v Durant* op cit, above 6.1.6.
5 *Humble v Hunter* (1848) 12 QB 310.
6 *Fred Drughorn Ltd v Rederiaktiebolaget Trans-Atlantic* [1919] AC 203, HL.
7 *Collins v Associated Greyhound Racecourses Ltd* [1930] 1 Ch 1.
8 *Greer v Downs Supply Co* [1927] 2 KB 28, CA.
9 *Dyster v Randall & Sons* [1926] Ch 932.
10 *Archer v Stone* (1898) 78 LT 34.

11   *Said v Butt* [1920] 3 KB 497.
12   *Cooke & Sons v Eshelby* (1887) 12 App Cas 271, HL.
13   *Clarkson, Booker Ltd v Andjel* [1964] 2 QB 775, [1964] 3 All ER 260, CA. (X had threatened proceedings against P and A; the threat to sue A was never withdrawn).

Agent and third party

29.4.0   As we have seen, the general rule is that when A acting on behalf of P makes a contract with X, A drops out of the picture and only P and X have rights and liabilities under the contract. However, that rule does not always hold true, as we have already seen. In certain cases A may be liable on the contract, either alone or jointly with P; alternatively he may be liable to X on his own account, either for his own statements or for breach of his warranty of authority.

The agent is liable on the contract

(a)   As we have seen above, when A acts for an undisclosed principal, he is himself liable under and can sue on the contract with X. He will be released from liability if P performs the contract in full or if X, having a right to sue, elects to pursue P and not A. If A discloses the agency but does not name his principal he is not personally liable on the contract under this rule.

(b)   Where an agent personally executes a contract made under seal, he is personally liable on and may enforce the contract to the exclusion of his principal. However, this technical rule does not apply when the agent executes a deed acting under a power of attorney.[1]

(c)   The agent may be held personally liable under a contract if there is a recognised usage to that effect in the particular trade.[2]

(d)   We have already mentioned that there used to be a general rule that where A acted on behalf of a foreign principal, only A could sue and be sued on the contract. However, that is no longer a general rule and the fact that P is a foreigner is only a factor, and generally one of little weight, in deciding whether or not A may sue or be sued.[3]

(e)   The agent may be held liable on a written contract if it appears from the contract that that was the intention of the parties. This will clearly be the case if the contract expressly states that the agent is a party. Difficulties may arise, however, where an agent signs a contract in his own name, if the contract does not expressly make the agent liable. Generally, if an agent signs in his own name, without qualification, he will be held to be a party to the contract. In general it will not be enough for the agent to sign, describing himself as 'agent', 'broker' or 'director': such words could be merely descriptive of his business rather than indicating his representative capacity. This will be so even if the agent is known to be acting for a principal. Thus when a chartered civil engineer signed a building contract on behalf of a client in his own name, adding the words 'chartered civil engineer', he was held personally liable,[4] since he had merely stated his professional qualifications. The presumption that the agent is a party to the contract may be rebutted if his representative capacity is made clear in the body of the contract. The court must then examine all the circumstances of the case. If the agent's representative capacity is made clear in the contract and in the way he signs it, he will not normally be personally liable. In order to avoid personal liability a person signing a contract in a representative capacity should always make that clear and sign 'A, agent for X' or 'A, per pro X', or use similar words.[5] If an agent is liable on a contract in these circumstances he may also be able to enforce it, according to its construction.

(f) Special rules apply to negotiable instruments, including cheques. An agent who signs his name to a negotiable instrument will be personally liable on the instrument unless the signature makes clear that he is acting only in a representative capacity.[6] Thus if two company directors sign a company cheque 'A and B, directors' they may both be personally liable on the cheque, for instance if it is dishonoured. They should sign 'A and B, directors for and on behalf of X Ltd.'

(g) A may intend to be a party to the contract: for instance when he contracts on behalf of himself and his principal jointly. The two may then be jointly liable on the contract. Equally, of course, A would have rights under the contract. This is the case when one partner makes a contract on behalf of his firm.[7]

(h) If A makes a contract on behalf of 'P' when in fact P does not exist, A may be personally liable on the contract. If he is not so liable he will be liable for breach of warranty of authority.[8] When the named principal is an as yet unformed company, the agent will be personally liable by virtue of s 36(4) of the Companies Act 1985.[9]

(i) If A purports to contract on behalf of someone else but in fact is contracting on his own behalf, he is clearly liable on the contract. He may be able to enforce it if either he did not name his purported principal, or, if he did name a principal, the identity of the principal was not material to the other party. However, if A does purport to act for a named principal, and the principal's identity was material to X, it would be unfair to allow A to reveal the truth and enforce the contract, and he therefore may not do so.[10]

1 Powers of Attorney Act 1971, s 7.
2 See eg *Barrow & Bros v Dyster, Nalder & Co* (1884) 13 QBD 635.
3 *Teheran-Europe Co Ltd v S T Belton (Tractors) Ltd* [1968] 2 QB 545, [1968] All ER 886, CA; above 29.3.1.
4 *Sika Contracts Ltd v B L Gill & Closeglen Properties Ltd* (1978) 9 BLR 11.
5 *Universal Steam Navigation Co Ltd v James McElvie & Co* [1923] AC 492, HL.
6 Bills of Exchange Act 1882, s 26(1).
7 Above 32.3.0.
8 Below 29.4.2.
9 Below 33.2.0.
10 *Schmaltz v Avery* (1851) 16 QB 655.

Liability for misstatements etc

29.4.1 An agent is normally employed to negotiate and enter into contracts on behalf of his principal. If during those negotiations A makes a statement to X which is discovered to be false, A may be liable to X in the tort of deceit, if he can be shown to have acted fraudulently,[1] or under the principles of Hedley Byrne & Co Ltd v Heller and Partners if he acted negligently.[2] In addition, P is liable for the torts committed by A within the scope of his authority. Thus P will be liable for false statements made by A in the course of his ostensible authority.[3]

P will also be liable when A's misstatement is wholly innocent but P has deliberately instigated it: eg, when P employs A to make a statement which he (P) knows or ought to know to be false, P is then liable for his own fault. However, when A innocently makes a misstatement which P knows to be false, P is not liable if he does not know that the statement has been made.

A misrepresentation made by A to X during negotiations, even if wholly innocent, will give X a right to rescind the contract. In addition, unless the misrepresentation was wholly innocent, X may be able to claim damages under the Misrepresentation Act. However, unless A is a party to the contract[4] X may only claim damages under the Act, against P.

1 Above 7.1.6.
2 Above 7.1.7.
3 See *Lloyd v Grace Smith & Co* [1912] AC 716, HL; *Armagas Ltd v Mundogas SA, The Ocean Frost* [1986] 2 All ER 385, [1986] 2 WLR 1063, HL.
4 *Resolute Maritime Inc v Nippon Kaiji Kyokai, The Skopas* [1983] 2 All ER 1, [1983] 1 WLR 857.

Breach of warranty of authority
29.4.2 If A makes a contract with X, stating that he is acting on behalf of P we have seen that if A does in fact have P's authority, there is a contract between X and P on which each is liable to the other. Even if A does not have authority when he makes the contract, P may ratify his acts afterwards. Moreover, if P has in some way held A out as having authority to act for him, A will have ostensible authority and P will once again be bound to the contract he negotiates. However, ostensible authority requires some act by P: X cannot safely rely on A's assertion of his own authority. This could, of course, cause difficulties for X. If he had no other protection he would always have to seek verification of A's authority from P. That would impose an unnecessary burden on the businesses of P and X, especially in those areas of commerce such as share and commodity markets where speed is essential. X must be able to rely on A's assertion of authority.

If A deliberately claims authority which he knows he does not possess, he commits the tort of deceit; however, fraud is notoriously difficult to prove. If he claims authority negligently, when he should know his statement to be false, he may be liable under the rule in *Hedley Byrne & Co Ltd v Heller & Partners.*[1] However, X would still have to prove negligence in order to succeed on that ground. X is protected from those requirements by the availability of an action against A for breach of his implied 'warranty of authority'. Whenever A contracts with X, and purports to do so on behalf of P, he impliedly warrants to X that he does have P's authority to make that contract; and if that assertion of authority is in fact false, A is liable to X for breach of that warranty, even though he did not and could not know that it was false. It seems that the assertion of authority, acted on by X, creates a collateral contract between A and X, so that A is strictly liable for its breach. The strict nature of the liability is illustrated by *Yonge v Toynbee*[2] where solicitors were instructed by a client to defend an action. Unbeknown to them the client became insane so that their authority to act for him was terminated;[3] in ignorance of his insanity they continued to act. When the truth was discovered they were held liable for breach of their warranty of authority.

Although the rule protects X and may be thought to facilitate commerce, it is harsh on the agent who is held liable even though he genuinely and reasonably believed he had authority. Its harshness is mitigated in a number of ways, however.

(a) If A is unsure of his position he may warn X that he does not or may not have authority: if he does so and X nevertheless contracts with him, X cannot complain if A's doubts prove to be justified.

(b) If A lacks actual authority but has ostensible authority as a result of P's words or conduct, there is technically a breach of the warranty of authority. However, X can enforce the contract against P by virtue of the ostensible authority, and therefore suffers no loss due to the breach of warranty.

(c) Two statutory provisions protect agents who continue to act in ignorance of the termination of their authority:

(i) when A's authority is terminated by P's bankruptcy, A is protected provided he acted in good faith and without notice of the bankruptcy.[4]

(ii) the donee of a power of attorney is protected in respect of acts done after its revocation provided he was ignorant of the revocation.[5]

If X can bring an action for breach of warranty of authority he is entitled to damages to put him in the position he would have been in had the warranty been true, ie, as if A had had authority. Generally this will entitle him to be put in a position as if his contract with P had been performed. However, if (say) P is insolvent, X may only claim from A such sum as he would have been able to recover in P's insolvency. Since the warranty is contractual, damages awarded for breach are subject to the rules of remoteness in *Hadley v Baxendale*.[6]

1 Above 7.1.7.
2 [1910] 1 KB 215, CA.
3 Below 29.6.2.
4 Insolvency Act 1986, s 342.
5 Powers of Attorney Act 1971, s 5(1).
6 Above 17.1.3.

Principal and agent

29.5.0 The relationship between principal and agent depends upon consent; such consent can be given by the principal after the agent has performed his duties, by the principal ratifying the agent's acts. However, when an agent has only ostensible or apparent authority there is no actual agency relationship between principal and agent at all: the principal never gave consent to the agent acting on his behalf.

There may be, but need not be, a contract between principal and agent: an agent may agree to act gratuitously although it is unlikely that a professional agent will do so. The contract may be express or implied; and if express it may be written or oral, or, in the case of a power of attorney, contained in a deed under seal. If there is a contract, the rights and obligations of the parties inter se will, in part, be regulated by that contract. However, the agency relationship is a special one and the parties will, in addition, enjoy certain rights and be subject to obligations by the law merely as a result of the relationship.

Rights of the agent: remuneration

29.5.1 An agent is only entitled to remuneration if he is acting under a contract of agency. Since the majority of agents with whom we are concerned will be acting in the course of a business, this will normally be the case. Even if there is no express right to payment, a court may imply a term into the contract giving the agent a right to reasonable remuneration, and will normally do so when the agent is a professional or is acting in the course of his business.[1] Such implication depends on the normal rules under which a court will imply terms into a contract. Thus no term can be implied if it would conflict with the express terms of the contract. If the agent has an implied right to remuneration he will recover a quantum meruit for his services;[2] this will be the case where the contract is silent as to the amount of his remuneration, but if the contract provides for him to be paid an amount to be fixed at his principal's discretion and the principal does not fix a sum, the court will not do so, for that would involve the court in substituting its own view for the agreed terms.[3]

If there is a right to remuneration the agent is only entitled to be paid if he has accomplished the task for which he was retained, exactly in accordance with the contract. His right to remuneration will thus depend upon the construction of the contract and interpretation of his task. Moreover, the agent is only entitled to claim remuneration if he has been the effective cause of the result he was employed to bring about, unless the contract provides to the contrary. In *Coles v Enoch*,[4] A was retained to find a tenant for P's premises. While he was describing the premises to an interested party X, T overheard the conversation and asked X where the premises were. X gave only a general description of the location, but T found the premises himself and took a lease from P. A's claim for commission failed: he had not been the direct cause of T taking a lease.

In general it seems that A is not entitled to commission even though he is prevented from earning it by P's own act. Thus A has no claim if he is employed for a fixed term but P closes down his business before expiry of the term.[5] The contract may include an express term which will prevent P hindering A in earning commission; in the absence of an express term the courts are reluctant to imply one. The House of Lords refused to imply such a term in *Luxor (Eastbourne) Ltd v Cooper*[6] where agents were retained to sell two cinemas. Commission of £10,000 was payable on completion of a sale and the agents introduced a prospective buyer. However, the owners refused to sell to them and ultimately sold the shares in the company which owned the cinemas. The agents claimed damages, alleging breach of an implied term. The House held that there was no need of such a term to give business efficacy to the contract; the agents were held to have taken the risk that the owners might pull out of any deal. The House was clearly influenced by the scale of remuneration.

> 'A sum of £10,000 (the equivalent of the remuneration of a year's work by the Lord Chancellor) for work done within a period of eight or nine days is no mean reward and is one well worth a risk.'[7]

However, such a term was implied in *Alpha Trading Ltd v Dunnshaw-Patten Ltd*[8] where P deliberately broke a contract arranged by A and paid compensation to T, intending to take advantage of a rising market.

The question of when exactly the agent can be held to have accomplished his task and so be entitled to commission has several times been considered in the context of estate agency contracts. In such cases the agent's entitlement to commission will depend on the wording of the contract. In the absence of express words, no commission is payable until a sale is completed. Such contracts are normally prepared by the estate agent and the courts have therefore tended to construe them strictly against the agent.[9] It seems that if A is appointed 'sole agent' he will be entitled to commission even if another agent effects a sale; and if he has 'sole right to sell' he will earn commission even if P sells his property privately. As we have already noted, the words 'sole agent' are often used to describe distributors who are not agents in the legal sense but who sell in their own name. Such a 'sole agent' may be able to prevent his supplier (whose goods he distributes) from selling to the public in his own right.[10]

1 Eg *Way v Latilla* [1937] 3 All ER 759, HL.
2 But not necessarily the scale fees of his profession, unless they are sufficiently well known to be regarded as customary, *Wilkie v Scottish Aviation Ltd* 1956 SC 198.
3 *Kofi Sunkersette Obu v A Strauss & Co Ltd* [1951] AC 243, PC; *Re Richmond Gate Property Co Ltd (company director)* [1965] 1 WLR 335.
4 [1939] 3 All ER 327, CA.
5 *Rhodes v Forwood* (1876) 1 App Cas 256, HL; but he may not terminate the agency before its term when part of his business continues; *Turner v Goldsmith* [1891] 1 QB 544, CA.
6 [1941] AC 108, [1941] 1 All ER 33, HL.
7 At p 120.
8 [1981] QB 290, [1981] 1 All ER 482, CA.
9 The Estate Agents Act 1979, s 18 requires the agent to provide the client with particulars of the amount of remuneration and circumstances in which it is payable.
10 *W T Lamb & Sons v Goring Brick Co Ltd* [1932] 1 KB 710, CA, above 29.0.0.

Rights of the agent: indemnity
29.5.2 All agents, whether entitled to remuneration or not, are entitled to be indemnified by their principal against all liabilities and expenses reasonably incurred in the course of their duties. The indemnity only extends to liabilities and expenses incurred whilst the agent is acting within the scope of his actual authority: in addition, an unauthorised agent will be entitled to indemnity if his actions are ratified and an agent of necessity may also claim an indemnity. Where there is a contract between principal and agent, its terms may set out, limit or even exclude the right to indemnity. Certain agents customarily have no right to indemnity unless one is expressly conferred by contract: thus estate agents are only entitled to commission and not to reimbursement of advertising costs, unless express provision is made for the latter.

Where the agent is entitled to an indemnity, he is indemnified against all liabilities incurred while acting in the scope of his authority, including both contractual and tortious liabilities. He may also claim reimbursement of payments made when he was under no legal obligation. For instance when a firm of solicitors were appointed London agents by another firm and instructed counsel, they were entitled to be reimbursed when contrary to instructions they paid counsel his fees. A barrister may not sue for his fees, but a failure to pay would be serious professional misconduct.[1] However, an agent is not entitled to indemnity for liabilities and expenses incurred due to his own default, nor in respect of acts which he knew to be unlawful.[2]

1 *Rhodes v Fielder, Jones and Harrison* (1919) 89 LJKB 15.
2 *Re Parker* (1882) 21 Ch D 408, CA; cf *Adamson v Jarvis* (1827) 4 Bing 66.

Rights of the agent: lien
29.5.3 In order to protect his rights to remuneration or indemnity from his principal, an agent may be entitled to a lien on any property of his principal

which he has in his possession. A lien is simply a right to retain possession of property until a debt is paid. The law recognises two types of lien: a general lien allows an agent to retain his principal's property until any sums due to him from the principal are paid. A particular lien only allows the agent to hold property pending payment of sums due in respect of that property. The law is reluctant to allow an agent a general lien: solicitors, bankers, stockbrokers and factors are recognised as having a general lien; generally other agents have only a particular lien.[1]

The agent has a lien only over that property of his principal which is in his possession in his capacity as agent, and which came into his possession by lawful means. Moreover, the continuation of the lien depends on possession so that the right is lost if the agent voluntarily parts with the property (but not, for example, if the principal recovers it by a trick), or if his conduct shows an intention to waive the lien. The right to a lien may be excluded by an express term in the agency contract.

If the agent is entitled to a lien, it is good not only against the principal but also against all persons claiming rights in respect of the property through him. However, the agent is bound by rights created before he acquired his lien.

1   See eg *Woodworth v Conroy* [1976] QB 884, [1976] 1 All ER 107, CA. Accountants entitled only to particular lien.

Duties of the agent

29.5.4   Where the agency relationship is contractual, the agent's duties, and his rights, may be expressly set out in the contract. However, even if not expressly set out, certain terms will be implied into the agency contract by law, so that they will apply unless expressly excluded. Moreover, even a gratuitous agent is subject to certain liabilities arising either in the law of torts or because of the special relationship between principal and agent. A principal must place himself or at least his interests in the hands of his agent; he must be able to rely on the agent. As a result the agent is placed in a special position of trust and the relationship between principal and agent is said to be a fiduciary one.

Duties of the agent: to obey instructions

29.5.5   The agent is under a duty to carry out his principal's instructions. If he is employed under a contract he is under a duty to act, and is liable for breach of contract if he fails to do the job at all.[1] However, it seems that a gratuitous agent incurs no liability if he simply fails to act. Clearly he cannot be liable on any contract; however, he might, perhaps, be held liable in negligence, at least if he fails to notify his principal of his failure to act and the principal suffers loss as a result. This might happen if A agrees with P gratuitously to arrange insurance on P's property but then neither arranges the insurance nor tells P who, relying on A to insure, does nothing himself. If P's property is then destroyed, and A's failure to notify P could be categorised as negligence, he could be held liable. Whilst there is no authority to support this analysis,[2] a prudent agent, even if he is acting gratuitously, should tell his principal if he intends not to perform his agreed task. On the other hand, even an agent for reward is not liable if he fails to perform an act which would be illegal. Nor will he be liable if his instructions are ambiguous and he acts on a bona fide interpretation of them.[3]

An agent, whether acting for reward or gratuitously, will be liable to his principal if he exceeds his actual authority. As we have seen, his principal may then be held bound by any contract the agent makes, on the basis of apparent authority.

1   *Turpin v Bilton* (1843) 5 Man & G 455.
2   This analysis is doubted by Friedman, *The Law of Agency* and Markesinis and Munday *An Outline of the Law of Agency* (2nd edn, 1986) but is supported by *Bowstead on Agency* and accords with recent developments in the law of negligence; above Ch 7.
3   *Ireland v Livingstone* (1872) LR 5 HL 395.

Duties of the agent: to exercise reasonable care

29.5.6   It seems that all agents, whether they act gratuitously or for payment, owe a duty to their principals to exercise reasonable care and skill in the execution of their authority. Such a liability will arise under the general law of negligence, so that it is clear that once a gratuitous agent begins to act he is liable for failure to exercise reasonable care. Where there is a contract of agency, the duty may also arise as an implied term in the contract; the terms of the contract may, of course, modify or exclude this duty, subject to the Unfair Contract Terms Act 1977.[1]

Where the agent is, or holds himself out as being, a member of a profession, or acting in the course of a business, he will be expected to show the standard of care expected of a reasonably competent practitioner of his trade or profession. A gratuitous agent must show such care as is reasonable in all the circumstances.

The scope of this duty will, of course, depend on the facts of each case. However, it is clear that an agent appointed to sell property must take reasonable care to get the best possible price, by passing all relevant information to his principal.[2]

Whilst an agent is bound to obey his principal's instructions, a professional agent may be bound by this duty to warn his principal if he regards those instructions as unwise.

1   Above 18.0.0.
2   *Keppel v Wheeler* [1927] 1 KB 577, CA; *Heath v Parksinson* (1926) 42 TLR 693.

Duties of the agent: personal performance

29.5.7   In addition to the duties enumerated above, the agent owes his principal a number of duties which arise from the fiduciary nature of the principal/agent relationship. These duties may be excluded or modified by the terms of the contract between principal and agent, but will normally be implied into the relationship. The first of these duties is the duty to carry out his task personally and not to delegate performance to another. This rule is based on the fact that the principal personally selects and puts his trust in the agent: 'confidence in the particular person employed is at the root of agency'[1] so that if an agent delegates performance of his duties without authority, he will be liable to his principal; moreover, the principal will not be bound by the acts of the unauthorised sub-agent, unless the agent had apparent authority to delegate.

However, delegation may be authorised, expressly or impliedly. Implied authority to delegate might exist when the circumstances necessitate delegation: for instance, if P appoints A in Rotterdam to sell his ship and, before a sale can be effected, the ship sails to New York where A has no office.[2] A power to delegate may be implied because of a custom in a particular trade or profession. For instance a provincial solicitor generally has authority to appoint London agents to conduct litigation on his behalf in the courts in London.[3] In addition an agent will have no liability for breach of duty if he delegates the performance of purely ministerial acts, such as serving a notice to quit,[4] or if he delegates performance of his duties to his employees.

If an agent does have authority to delegate, it will be necessary to consider the relationship between principal and sub-agent. It may be that A's only duty is to appoint another agent (A2) to act on behalf of P, and to create a fresh agency contract between them. In that case there will be privity of contract between P and A2, in the normal way, and A2 will owe contractual and fiduciary duties to P. A's duties will be limited to the exercise of reasonable care in the selection of A2. However, where A's only authority is to appoint a genuine sub-agent (S) there will be no contract between S and P. S will be the agent of A, and A will continue to be the agent of P. Thus if S fails to perform his duties, A will be strictly liable to P for breach of contract. In addition, P may be able to hold S liable if he can show that S was negligent; and, if he knows of P's existence, S may owe him the fiduciary duties of an agent.

1 Thesiger LJ in *De Bussche v Alt* (1878) 8 Ch D 286 at 310, CA.
2 See *De Bussche v Alt*, above.
3 *Solley v Wood* (1852) 16 Beav 370.
4 *Allam & Co Ltd v Europa Poster Services Ltd* [1968] 1 All ER 826, [1968] 1 WLR 638.

Duties of the agent: no conflict of interest
29.5.8 We have noted that the agency relationship is based on the trust placed in the agent by the principal. He will normally employ an agent because he requires the agent's personal expertise or because he cannot be in two places at once. In either case, principal must depend on agent and because of that dependency the law imposes on the agent a strict duty to show good faith in his dealings with the principal. One aspect of that general duty is the agent's duty to avoid any situation in which his own interests may come into conflict with those of his principal. If such a situation does arise, the agent is in breach of duty and this is so even if the agent can show that he acted throughout in total good faith and in the best interests of his principal.[1] Such a strict rule is justified because of the risk that an agent faced with such a conflict may favour his own interests over those of his principal. The law requires him not to allow himself even to be exposed to such temptation.[2]

Such a conflict may arise, for instance, when the agent buys property from, or sells his own property to his principal.[3] The possibility of conflict is clear for a seller's concern is to get the best price for his goods; a buyer's is to pay the lowest possible price. If the agent does deal with his principal in this way he is in breach of duty even though he may be able to show that he acted in good faith and the price was fair.

A conflict of interest may similarly arise where an agent purports to act for both parties to a transaction. In this case the conflict is between the interests of the two principals. Certain agents are subject to special rules governing such situations. Thus Rules of Professional Conduct prevent a solicitor acting for two parties between whom there is a conflict of interest.

An estate agent who has a personal interest in land may not enter into negotiations to acquire or dispose of any interest in that land without disclosing his personal interest; failure to comply may allow the Director General of Fair Trading to prohibit him from acting as an estate agent.[4] Particular problems have been raised by the reform of the business of the Stock Exchange, known as the 'Big Bang'. Previously firms were only allowed to act either as 'brokers', buying and selling shares for clients, or 'jobbers', with whom brokers dealt and who held shares on their own account. That strict distinction has now been abolished and one firm may now perform both functions. This creates the possibility of a serious conflict of interest and the Financial Services Act seeks to minimise this conflict by requiring firms to erect 'chinese walls' within the firm to prevent the transfer of sensitive information between different departments performing different functions.[5]

Where a conflict of interest does arise between principal and agent, the latter is liable for breach of duty unless he can show that he made full disclosure of all relevant facts to his principal, who consented to the transaction in question. Where the transaction involves the agent buying or selling property from or to his principal, he must also show that the price was a fair market price. If these requirements are not fulfilled, the principal may set aside the relevant transaction, provided only that he does so within a reasonable time of discovering the conflict of interest.[6] In addition he may either claim damages from the agent for breach of duty, or require him to account for any profit he made from the transaction. He may also refuse to pay the agent any commission.

1 As is illustrated in *Boardman v Phipps* [1967] 2 AC 46, [1966] 3 All ER 721, HL; below 39.5.9.
2 *Bentley v Craven* (1853) 18 Beav 75.
3 See *Lucifero v Castel* (1887) 3 TLR 371.
4 Estate Agents Act 1979, s 21.
5 See generally below 38.0.1.
6 Eg *Oliver v Court* (1820) 8 Price 127: conflict discovered after 13 years.

The duties of the agent: not to make a secret profit

29.5.9 This duty is closely linked to that which prohibits a conflict of interest. It prevents the agent using his position to make a profit for himself over and above his commission. Thus he will be liable for breach of duty if he uses any property of his principal to make a profit for himself. For instance, if P gives money to A to buy goods on his behalf and A invests the money so that it earns interest, he may not keep the interest for himself but must account for it to his principal.[1] 'Property' here includes information which the agent acquires in the course of his agency. In *Boardman v Phipps*[2] two representatives of a trust fund were retained to negotiate with a company in which the fund held shares. Relying on information acquired in those negotiations they bought shares in the company themselves and made a substantial profit. It was held that the profit was made by using information which had come to them in their capacity as representatives of the trust and so they could not keep it. The case is all the more striking because, as a result of their efforts, the fund had also made a profit.

The duty not to make a profit by use of the principal's property may continue beyond the termination of the agency, particularly when the property in question is 'confidential information' (such as details of

customers or secret processes) acquired in the course of the agent's duties.[3]
However, the duty only lasts as long as the information remains confidential.

1   Solicitors are subject to special rules which allow them to keep interest earned on their
    clients' money in certain circumstances, depending on the amount and the length of time for
    which it is held.
2   [1967] 2 AC 46, [1966] 3 All ER 721, HL.
3   See eg *Peter Pan Manufacturing Corpn v Corsets Silhouette Ltd* [1963] 3 All ER 402, [1964]
    1 WLR 96; and see below 30.1.2.

Duties of the agent: not to take a bribe

29.5.10   A bribe is a particular type of secret profit. Despite its name, the
payment of a 'bribe' in this context need not connote any element of
corruption. A bribe is a payment made to an agent by the party with whom
he is dealing on his principal's behalf, which payment is kept secret from the
principal. The law takes a particularly strict view of such payments and
allows the principal a number of remedies against both the agent and the
third party making the payment. Obviously, when a third party makes such
a payment he will expect the agent to reward him by favouring his interests,
but the principal is allowed to claim his various remedies without proof that
the bribe has caused him financial loss. In *Industries and General Mortgage
Co Ltd v Lewis,*[1] P asked A to arrange a mortgage; T agreed to provide a
mortgage and promised A a commission for arranging it with them. That
action vitiated the contract and allowed P to claim the amount of the bribe
from T because the court had to assume that the interest charged by T would
be increased to recoup the payment made to A. In addition, of course, a
bribe may lead an agent not to act in his principal's best interests so that the
rule is closely linked to that against conflict of interest. The payment of a
bribe is a breach of duty unless it is disclosed to the principal.

The remedies available to a principal who discovers that his agent has
taken a bribe are:
(a)   to dismiss the agent immediately without notice;
(b)   to refuse to pay him any commission payable and to recover any
      commission paid on the particular transaction;
(c)   to recover the amount of the bribe from either the agent or the third
      party;
(d)   to claim damages from the agent or the third party for any loss he has
      suffered as a result;
(e)   to set aside the contract with the third party.
A difficult question is whether the principal can claim both (c) (payment of
the amount of the bribe) and (d) (damages) or if he may claim only one. In
Salford Corpn v Lever[2] the corporation requested tenders for the supply of
coal. The defendant promised the corporation agent, who had the job of
selecting the successful tender, a payment of 1 shilling per ton on deliveries if
its tender was accepted. When the corporation discovered the facts and sued
the Court of Appeal held that it could claim both the amount of the bribe
and damages. However, in *Mahesan v Malaysia Government Officers'
Co-operative Housing Society Ltd*[3] the Privy Council doubted that decision
and held that the principal must choose either damages or payment of the
bribe. Whilst to allow him to claim both would have the desirable effect of
discouraging corruption, it would allow the principal a windfall by recovering his loss twice. If *Mahesan* is correct, the principal would obviously

claim the bribe when he could not prove he had suffered any loss, but would claim damages if he could prove loss in excess of the amount of the bribe.

Whatever the position with regard to the choice between claiming damages and repayment of the bribe, the principal's other remedies are cumulative. In addition, if it can be shown that the bribe was paid or received with a corrupt motive, the briber or agent may be guilty of a criminal offence.[4]

1 [1949] 2 All ER 573.
2 [1891] 1 QB 168, CA.
3 [1979] AC 374, [1978] 2 All ER 405, PC.
4 Prevention of Corruption Act 1916, s 1.

Duties of the agent: the duty to account

29.5.11 We have noted that an agent may not make a profit for himself by the use of his principal's property. In addition he is required to keep his principal's property strictly separate from his own and, on termination of the agency, to account to his principal for all such property held on his principal's behalf.[1]

If he does mix the two, the principal is entitled to a charge on the whole mixed fund and if, for instance, the agent uses his principal's money to buy property for himself, the principal is entitled to 'trace' his money into the property which represents it and claim the property. In addition the agent should keep full and accurate books of account, which, of course, is only good business sense since they will protect him as well as his principal, and, on termination of the agency, deliver up to his principal all papers given to him by his principal or prepared for use in the course of their relationship, unless he is entitled to a lien over them for sums due to him from the principal.[2]

1 This is so even if the property is claimed by someone else.
2 Above 29.5.3.

Termination of agency

29.6.0 An agent may be appointed to perform some specific task, for instance to sell a particular piece of property, or, for a specified period. In that case the agency is terminated, of course, on completion of the appointed task or on expiry of the period. Being consensual in nature, an agency can also be terminated, as can any contract, by the mutual agreement of the parties. However, the agreement may also be brought to an end by the act of one of the parties, or by the operation of a rule of law.

Upon termination of an agency, it will be necessary to consider the legal position between principal and agent but also between each of them and any third party with whom the agent deals. The relationship between principal and agent will depend on the terms of their agreement and the way in which the agreement ends. In general, however, the agent is entitled to commission and an indemnity in respect of acts done prior to termination, but not in respect of anything he does thereafter. When the agent is appointed to effect a particular transaction, eg, to sell a ship, completion of the transaction will fulfil the terms of his appointment and, if the agreement provides for commission, entitle him to claim commission. However, termination of the agreement may not affect any third party who deals with the agent in ignorance of the termination. Although termination of the agreement puts an end to the agent's actual authority, he may still possess apparent or ostensible authority so that if he continues to act as if he were still authorised, his principal will be bound to any third party who contracts with him in ignorance of termination of the agency.[1] Of course, if the agent does act in that way after termination of his authority, he will be liable to his principal.

1 See *Drew v Nunn* (1879) 4 QBD 661, CA.

Termination by the parties

29.6.1 It is normally possible for either party to put an end to the agency relationship at any time, reflecting its consensual nature. Thus the principal may dismiss the agent even though the latter was appointed to perform a particular task or for a fixed term which has not yet expired. Such dismissal may be either with or without notice; in either case it will be effective to bring the relationship to an end, although a dismissal without notice or before expiry of a fixed term may amount to a breach of contract by the principal. Whether such a dismissal does constitute a breach of contract will depend on all the facts of the case and terms of the particular clause.

(a) If the agent is appointed for a fixed term, for example, 'to sell the principal's products in the UK for six years' a dismissal before the expiry of the term will normally be a breach of contract for which the agent can claim damages. This will depend on the construction of the agency agreement. In *Rhodes v Forwood*[1] A was appointed for seven years to sell any coal from P's colliery which P might send to the Liverpool area. After four years P closed his business and A claimed compensation for his lost chance to earn commission for three years. The claim failed because on the terms of the agreement there was no guarantee the agreement would remain in force or that P would remain in business. By contrast, in *Turner v Goldsmith*[2] A was retained for five years to sell shirts 'manufactured or sold' by P. P terminated the agreement when his factory burned down, and A's claim for breach of contract succeeded. The agreement was not limited to goods manufactured by P. Early dismissal may be justified if the agent is himself guilty of a breach of duty, for instance, by accepting a bribe.[3]

(b) When the agent is appointed for an indeterminate term the position is more complex. If an express term allows termination by the giving of notice of a specified duration, termination without full notice will be a breach of contract. However, even if there is no such express notice requirement, the courts may imply a term allowing the contract to be terminated on reasonable notice. This will be done when the relationship closely resembles that between employer and employee.[4] Thus *Martin-Baker Aircraft Co Ltd v Canadian Flight Equipment Ltd*[5] A agreed to sell P's products in North America, to spend time and money developing P's business and not to market the products of P's competitors. In return he was appointed sole agent for the sale of P's products and paid a commission of 17½ % on orders taken by him. The court implied a term that the relationship could be terminated on twelve months' notice.

(c) Where an agent is retained to perform a particular task, to be rewarded, it seems that the principal may terminate the relationship before completion of the task and incur no liability.[6]

Since the agency relationship is personal, the courts will not order specific performance of the agency contract.[7] Thus, even a dismissal in breach of contract terminates the agency and the agent's only remedy is to claim damages for breach. However, certain grants of authority are irrevocable at law. This is the case where the agent has an authority coupled with an interest. This would happen when, for example, P owes money to A and gives him authority to sell his (P's) property to discharge the debt. This rule only applies where A had the interest at the time of the grant of authority; it will not protect him when his interest arises after he acquired authority.[8] The agent's claim for commission is not sufficient interest for this purpose. The Powers of Attorney Act 1971[9] similarly provides that a power of attorney may not be revoked without the consent of the donee of the power if it is (a) expressed to be irrevocable and (b) given to secure some proprietary interest of or obligation owed to the donee.

We have spoken above of termination by the principal. Similar principles apply to a termination by the agent so that he may be exposed to a claim for damages if he terminates the contract without proper contractual notice.

1 (1876) 1 App Cas 256, HL.
2 [1891] 1 QB 544, CA.
3 Above 29.5.10.
4 Below Ch 30.
5 [1955] 2 QB 556, [1955] 2 All ER 722.
6 *Luxor (Eastbourne) Ltd v Cooper* [1941] AC 108, [1941] 1 All ER 33, HL.
7 Above 17.1.2.
8 *Smart v Sandars* (1848) CB 895.
9 S 4.

Termination by operation of law
29.6.2 Certain events bring the agency relationship to an end automatically, regardless of the wishes of the parties.

(a) Frustration
Like all contracts, agency is subject to the doctrine of frustration.[1] Thus an agency contract would be terminated if either party became an enemy alien as a result of the outbreak of war.

(b) Death
The death of either party will terminate the agency. If the principal dies it seems that the agent will not even have apparent authority so that the principal's estate will not be bound by his actions. The winding up of a company has a similar effect.

(c) Insanity
The insanity of either party will terminate the relationship. Difficulties arise where the principal becomes insane; there are two apparently conflicting authorities. In *Drew v Nunn*,[2] P became insane but A (his wife) continued to act in his name; upon his recovery, P disclaimed liability for A's acts during the period of disability but was held liable on the basis of A having apparent authority. In contrast in *Yonge v Toynbee*[3] solicitors were held liable for breach of warranty of authority when they continued to conduct litigation on behalf of a client who, unknown to them, had become mentally incapacitated. It thus seems that in such a situation a third party may choose to sue either principal or agent.

29.6.2 *Agency*

Under the Enduring Powers of Attorney Act 1985 it is now possible to create an enduring power of attorney which remains effective despite the mental incapacity of the donor.

(d) Bankruptcy

If the principal becomes bankrupt, any agency he has created is automatically terminated, as his estate falls to be administered by his trustee in bankruptcy. The bankruptcy of the agent will also terminate the relationship if it makes him unfit to continue to act.

1   Above 17.0.4.
2   (1879) 4 QBD 661, CA.
3   [1910] 1 KB 215, CA.

Chapter 30

The Business and the Workforce

30.0.0 Amongst the most important of the relationships which any business may forge is that with its workforce, for the business must normally rely on the efforts of its employees, from shop floor to executive management, to earn its profits. The business must also rely on its employees to represent it in many dealings with the outside world; and, of course, a concerted withdrawal of labour by the workforce may bring the business to a halt.

We have referred above to the relationship between the business and its 'workforce' and in practice the most important relationship will be that which exists on a collective level, between a business and any trade union which represents its employees. However, the law has always tended to focus on the relationship between the business and individual employees. Trade unions are not bodies corporate and do not have a legal personality separate from that of their members.[1] In recent years, it is true, the law has increasingly intervened to regulate the activities of trade unions, but such intervention has largely been aimed at controlling industrial action, by granting, or removing legal immunities for torts committed in the course of industrial action, requiring ballots of the membership before strike action and so on.[2] The balance of such legislation depends, of course, on the political colour of whichever government is in power at any given time, and, indeed, how one regards the balance, or imbalance, of such legislation, depends largely on one's own particular beliefs, policies and prejudices. However, governments of both political complexions have tended to shy away from legal interference with the bargaining relationship between employers and trade unions. When the Industrial Relations Act of 1971 attempted to give legal force to collective agreements, employers and unions alike showed their distaste for importing legal sanctions into their negotiations and almost all collective agreements made during the period in which that legislation was in force contained clauses to the effect that the agreement was not legally binding.[3] The law has been much more comfortable dealing with the relationship between employer and individual employees and it is that relationship on which we intend to focus.

As our comments above indicate, the employees of a business may represent it in its dealings with the outside world. When that is the case the employee is acting as an agent and his power to affect the legal positions of the business and those such as customers, clients and suppliers with whom he deals, will depend upon the application of the agency principles discussed above, and in particular on the scope of the usual authority of a particular class of employee, or the apparent authority of an individual. However, special rules govern the relationship between employer and employee so that they may have extra rights and duties in addition to those of principal and agent.

Reflecting the strong individualistic tradition of the common law and the laissez faire philosophy of the 19th century, the common law analysed the employment relationship in terms of contract, focussing on the contract of employment. As a result the law largely deprived itself of the power to intervene in the relationship between employer and employee, for with the idea of contract came the notion of freedom of contract with its non-interventionist implications.[4] The notion of contract as a freely negotiated bargain between two parties was perhaps nowhere less accurate than in the context of the employment contract, which Kahn Freund has described as 'a command under the guise of an agreement.'[5] The common law's inability to recognise and remedy the inequality of bargaining power between employer and employee has led to two counterbalancing developments. First, the combination of employees into trade unions to give themselves greater bargaining power in their dealings with their employers, and, second, an increasing amount of legislation aimed at giving various statutory rights to the employee, dealing with safety at work, discrimination during employment and the termination of the employment relationship.

The result has been that the last quarter century has seen what ACAS has described as 'a considerable increase in the quantity of law affecting managers, trade unions and employees', together with the erection of a structure of organisations and specialist tribunals to supervise its operation and decide disputes relating to those rights. Indeed, the philosophy of the present Conservative Government has been that the sheer quantity of legislation affecting the employment relationship imposes an unnecessary burden on business and tends to discourage development and the creation of new jobs. It has therefore tended to reduce the statutory rights of employees, particularly those working for small businesses, for instance by extending the qualifying periods for which employees must work before claiming particular rights.[6] Whilst one's reaction to this development must depend to some degree on one's own political preferences, it should not be forgotten that for historical reasons the trade unions remain intensely suspicious of the courts and the law, and that—

> 'most workers want nothing more of the law than that it should leave them alone. A secure job is preferable to a claim to a redundancy payment; a grievance settled in the plant or the office is better than going to a court or an industrial tribunal.'[7]

The law, then, in this area as in so many others, is a safety net: a last resort to be called upon when all else has failed.

1   See below 16.1.5.
2   See above, 6.0.4.
3   The so called 'TINALEA' clause ('This is not a legally enforceable agreement'): see above 13.1.0.
4   See generally 12.0.0.
5   Davies & Freedland (eds), *Labour and The Law* (3rd ed, 1984) p 18.
6   See generally below 30.2.4 and 2.5.9.
7   Wedderburn, *The Worker and the Law* (3rd edn) (1986) p 1.

Categorising the relationship

30.0.1 Not all those who work for a business will be its employees. Some tasks may be done by 'workers' who are in fact in business on their own account, or by workers hired from other employers. Thus, for instance, whilst a chauffeur retained full time to drive the company's managing director may be an employee, a taxi driver who takes him to the airport clearly is not. We have already seen the distinction in relation to agents: an employee may well be the agent of his employer for certain purposes, but not all agents are employees and, indeed, many will be in business on their own account. The use of independent contractors in this way has always been known, but has grown in frequency in recent years as the present Conservative Government has attempted to stimulate and encourage the creation of new small businesses. This use of independent sub-contractors has long been a feature of the building trade, so that not only specialist tasks, such as plumbing or electrical installation, may be put out to separate firms of sub-contractors, but even general labouring work may be done by workers who are nominally independent.[1] The use of independent contractors is now spreading due to changes in business structure. Between 1982 and 1985 the number of self-employed increased by about 400,000. In such cases, whilst there may be a contract between the worker and his 'employer', it is not a contract of employment but a commercial contract between two businesses; a contract for services rather than a contract of service. Alternatively, an entrepreneur may operate by way of a franchise system; public services are increasingly put out to tender; businesses hire workers on a temporary or semi-permanent basis from agencies; and 'executive loans', when a senior manager is 'hired out' to run a particular business for a fixed period have become increasingly common. In these cases the individual worker may be an employee of someone, but his employer is, in all probability, not the business which directly benefits from his labours or expertise.

It may be important on occasion, and for a variety of purposes, to categorise a relationship as one between employer and employee, dependent on a contract of employment. Special terms may be implied into a contract of employment at common law;[2] an employee is charged to income tax under Schedule E of the Income and Corporation Taxes Act, so that tax is deducted from his wages at source, whereas a self-employed person pays tax on the more favourable Schedule D basis; different national insurance contributions may be payable; and, as we have seen, an employer is vicariously liable for the torts committed by his employees in the course of their employment,[3] and owes duties to his employees to take care for their safety. However, perhaps the most important consequence is that many of the statutory employment rights are given to 'employees', defined as those who work under a contract of employment.

It is true that other legislation gives rights to workers according to different classifications, for instance the Sex Discrimination Act 1975 and Race Relations Act 1976 prohibit discrimination against anyone employed under a contract of service or of apprenticeship or personally to execute any work or labour', but for most purposes the contract of employment provides the crucial test.

See below 30.0.3.
Below 30.1.1.
Above 9.0.2.

Recognising a contract of employment

> **30.0.2**   'It is often easy to recognise a contract of service when you see it but difficult to say wherein the difference [between it and a contract for services] lies.'[1]

As we have already seen,[2] the courts have developed a series of tests for distinguishing between the two types of contract. However, none of them can be guaranteed to give accurate results in every case. It should perhaps be borne in mind that the answer to the question 'employee or independent contractor?' may well depend on the reason for asking the question. When the question is raised in the context of vicarious liability, the desire to provide the victim of a tort with a worthwhile (and insured) defendant against whom to proceed will often make the court anxious to recognise the contract as one of employment. Different considerations apply when the question is raised to decide the 'employee's' tax or social security status, or when he claims the protection of the statutory rights; and in this last context, the personal characteristics of the claimant may also influence the outcome of the case.

It will be recalled that the earliest test adopted by the courts depended solely on 'control': the contract was one of employment if the employer could control not only what the employee did but also how he did it. However, as employees became increasingly expert, the judges became unhappy with this test and in 1952, Denning LJ proposed an alternative: the court should ask whether the worker in question was fully integrated into the employer's organisation.[3] This 'integration' or 'organisation' test had its uses, for instance, it categorised as an employee a circus trapeze artiste who was paid only if she performed and who provided her own costumes and safety equipment, but who helped move the circus and acted as an usherette for about three hours each night.[4] However, very often the 'test' would appear to do no more than restate the question. This led MacKenna J to propound a further test which involves the court looking at the contract as a whole and weighing up whether or not its terms are consistent with a contract of employment. In *Ready Mixed Concrete (South East) Ltd v Minister of Pensions and National Insurance*[5] the court had to decide whether the company was liable for national insurance contributions in respect of its lorry drivers. The drivers drove lorries which they were buying on hire purchase from the company. They were required to maintain the lorries themselves, paint them in company colours, use them only for company business, and to wear overalls in the company colours. Drivers were paid on a piece work basis, according to the number of deliveries made; there were no provisions as to holidays or hours of work, and the drivers could employ substitutes to act on their behalf. Evaluating all the factors MacKenna J held that the drivers were not employees. He identified three requirements of a contract of employment:

(a) the employee agrees to provide his own personal work or skill in return for a wage or remuneration paid by the employer;

(b) the employee agrees to be subject to some measure of control by the employer; and

(c) the other provisions of the contract, such as the provision of tools and equipment, payment of holiday or sick pay, tax and national insurance are all consistent with a contract of employment.

Later cases have spoken of looking at the 'economic reality': that is to say, who takes the profits of success or bears the risk of business failure? If the financial risk of success or failure falls on the 'employee' the probability is that the contract is not one of employment at all.

In the past the courts have placed some weight on the label attached to their relationships by the parties themselves. The courts have been especially reluctant to allow a worker, particularly at management or similar level, to consciously choose to be treated as self-employed, so as to gain favourable treatment for tax and national insurance purposes, but then to claim to be an employee so as to take advantage of the statutory protection against unfair dismissal or redundancy.[6] However, the Court of Appeal has recently resiled[7] from this position to some degree: the label attached by the parties to their relationship is but one factor, of relatively little weight, for the court to take into account. The court may thus decide that a worker who has been taxed as if he were self-employed is nevertheless, in reality, an employee; in that case the court or tribunal should notify the Inland Revenue to allow it to take the necessary steps to correct the tax position. However, it should be noted that a worker will not be able to rely on an illegal contract to which he is knowingly a party. Thus if an employee agrees to have wages paid 'under the counter' in cash to avoid tax, he may find himself unprotected if he is later dismissed by his employer.[8]

There is little doubt that the 'multiple' test, by looking at the totality of the relationship between the parties, provides a better yardstick than the earlier tests for distinguishing a contract of service from a contract for services. However, any test provides only an approximation and in recent years, as the pattern of the labour market has changed in the face of economic circumstances and government policy, the courts have had to decide new and difficult questions to which the existing legal tests are ill suited. Thus there has been an increase in the number of 'outworkers' working from home. To date such workers have tended to be women working in the garment and similar trades but the increasing use of new information technology has led to predictions that an increasing number of people in many trades will work from home in the future. The status of such people depends on all the aspects of their working arrangements, but, whilst the courts have on occasions recognised them as employees,[9] they are perhaps less likely to be regarded as employees than those who work on their employer's premises.

Similarly there has been an increase in the numbers of casual workers and an application of the existing tests of employment will generally lead to the conclusion that they are not employees.[10] We have already commented on the growing number of workers working through agencies: it seems that they too, will probably not be regarded as employees of the agency,[11] nor of the business which hires their services. The legal status of trainees on government sponsored training schemes also seems to be precarious; whilst an employer may accept a YTS trainee as an employee, it seems that if he does not expressly do so, the courts will not regard the contract as one of employment.[12]

All these cases involve people who would colloquially be regarded as 'workers' and, indeed, the very sort of persons who are most vulnerable and in need of protection. The application of the existing tests of a contract of employment leads to them being excluded from that protection. By contrast, a company director can have a contract of employment with his company, even if he owns and controls it.[13] However, he is unlikely to be regarded as an employee of the company if he is rewarded only by director's fees[14] rather than salary, and details of his contract of employment are not recorded as required by the Companies Act 1985.[15]

1   Per Denning LJ in *Stevenson Jordan & Harrison Ltd v MacDonald and Evans* [1952] 1 TLR 101, CA.
2   Above 9.0.3.
3   In *Stevenson Jordan & Harrison Ltd v MacDonald & Evans*, above.
4   *Whittaker v Ministry of Pensions* [1967] 1 QB 156.
5   [1968] 2 QB 497, [1968] 1 All ER 433.
6   *Massey v Crown Life Insurance Co* [1978] 2 All ER 576, [1978] 1 WLR 676, CA; cf *Ferguson v John Dawson & Partners (Contractors) Ltd* [1976] 3 All ER 817, [1976] 1 WLR 1213, CA.
7   *Young & Woods Ltd v West* [1980] IRLR 201, CA.
8   *Tomlinson v Dick Evans U Drive Ltd* [1978] ICR 639, [1978] IRLR 77, EAT.
9   See *Nethermere (St Neots) Ltd v Gardiner* [1984] ICR 612, [1984] IRLR 240, CA.
10   *O'Kelly v Trusthouse Forte plc* [1983] 3 All ER 456, [1983] 3 WLR 605.
11   *Wickens v Champion Employment* [1984] ICR 365, EAT.
12   See *Daley v Allied Suppliers Ltd* [1983] ICR 90, [1983] IRLR 14.
13   See *Lee v Lee's Air Farming Ltd* [1961] AC 12, [1960] 3 All ER 420, PC.
14   *Parsons v Albert J Parsons & Sons Ltd* [1979] ICR 271, [1979] IRLR 117, CA.
15   CA 1985, s 318.

The consequences of classification

30.0.3   As we have already commented, the classification of a worker as an 'employee' under a contract of service has a number of consequences. It will affect his status for the purposes of payment of tax and national insurance contributions. On the other hand it may make his employer vicariously liable for his torts and allow him to claim the protection of employment protection legislation. It may affect the standard of care his employer is required to show for his safety, and, in the event of his employer's insolvency, will give him the status of a preferential creditor. Nevertheless from the point of view of the employee, the short term financial benefits of self-employed status may seem particularly attractive. The employer may also be keen to encourage self-employed workers for, although they may not identify with 'the firm' in the same way as employees, he will avoid possible claims for unfair dismissal, redundancy and lay-off payments, which may be highly desirable in areas such as the building trade where business may fluctuate unpredictably, and also save on administrative costs since he will not have to deduct tax at source or pay employers' national insurance contributions. The election to be treated as self employed is, of course, open to abuse. The practice has become widespread in the building trade where 'labour only sub-contractors' (known collectively as 'the lump') have become common. The government, concerned at the potential for tax evasion created by a large itinerant self-employed workforce has therefore legislated so as to require the employers of labour only sub-contractors to deduct income tax from their remuneration and account for it to the Inland Revenue, unless the contractor has an appropriate certificate from the Revenue.[1]

1   Finance Act 1971.

The terms of the contract

30.1.0   An employment contract is not required to take any particular form. It may be in writing, and in the case of a senior employee that will normally be the case. Even in the case of less senior employees there may be at least a letter of appointment which will set out certain important terms, including the names of the parties, the job title, the date of commencement and initial wage or salary. Other documents, such as works rules and the like, may also be incorporated into the contract, by express reference or by implication. However, there is no reason why a perfectly valid contract may not be made wholly orally.

Of course, in such a case there may be difficulties in proving exactly what were the terms of the contract. The parties, in the event of a dispute, would have to give oral evidence as to what was said and, indeed, as to how their relationship was conducted in practice. However, ambiguity about the terms of his employment could be a serious handicap to an employee, so the law now requires the employer to provide every employee with a written statute of the main terms of his employment not later than 13 weeks from the commencement of his employment.[1] Any change in the recorded terms should be notified within four weeks. This statement, which should include any terms relating to the job title, hours of work, rates of pay, holidays, sick pay, pension schemes and disciplinary procedures, will of course provide evidence of what terms were agreed, especially where, as is common, the employee is required to sign and return a copy statement or a tear-off slip. However, contrary to the understanding of many employees, it is not the contract, and a court may decide that it does not accurately record the contract's terms.[2] Unfortunately, evidence suggests that many employers do not comply with the requirement to supply a written statement. In that case the employee may complain to an industrial tribunal, but its only sanction is to declare the terms which should have been recorded; there is no financial penalty for the recalcitrant employer.

Of course, many employees will have terms of employment negotiated for them by trade unions. We have already noted that collective agreements themselves are not normally legally enforceable. However, they may become indirectly enforceable if they are incorporated into the contracts of individual employees. Such terms may, of course, be incorporated by express reference, but the courts have also been prepared to recognise the implied incorporation of terms from collective agreements, provided they are suitable for incorporation into individual agreements and not, for example, policy statements or terms regulating the relationship between employer and union. The exact legal basis of such incorporation is unclear; it may be said that the union could be acting as agent for its members, but that argument will not explain the incorporation of collective terms into the contracts of non-unionists, even though it is clear they are also affected by the collective agreement terms.

1   Employment Protection (Consolidation) Act 1978, s 1.
2   See *System Floors (UK) Ltd v Daniel* [1982] ICR 54, [1981] IRLR 475, EAT; *Turriff Construction Ltd v Bryant* [1967] ITR 292.

The employer's duties

30.1.1   If there is a full written contract it can be expected that it will include express terms relating to the payment of wages, hours of work, holidays and holiday pay and so on. However, even in the absence of express terms, certain terms may be implied, either to give business efficacy to the particular contract[1] or because the law recognises certain terms to be the normal incidents of the employment relationship so that they will normally be implied unless expressly excluded. These terms may be important, particularly in the event of a claim for wrongful or unfair dismissal by the employee: a major breach of his duties by the employer may entitle the employee to walk out and claim he is dismissed; a major breach by the employee may justify his instant dismissal.[2]

(a) Payment of wages

The most fundamental of the employer's duties is his duty to pay wages. 'Wages for work' is the bargain at the heart of the employment contract. Such an obligation will therefore be implied even if not expressly spelt out; the implied obligation will be to pay a reasonable sum. Of course, even if nothing else is expressly agreed, there will normally be express agreement on the amount of wages payable. Difficulties may arise in the absence of express terms to deal with holiday and sick pay. Contrary to popular belief there is no entitlement to paid holiday leave, in the absence of express agreement. The court may imply a term entitling the employee to pay during absence through sickness, but such implication will depend upon all the factors of the case and there is no presumption in favour of a right to sick pay.[3] All employees are entitled to be paid statutory sick pay for the first 23 weeks of absence due to sickness, but this is in effect a social security benefit paid through the employer. Contractual sick pay may be payable for longer, or may top up the statutory entitlement, for instance up to full salary. Deductions from wages are now regulated by the Wages Act 1986 which broadly prohibits any such deductions, for example, for defective workmanship, unless authorised by contract or statute; special rules apply to limit deduction from the wages of workers in retail trades. In order to supply the employee with information about his wages/salary, the employer must provide him with an itemised pay statement showing all deductions.[4]

(b) Work

Traditionally there is no duty on the employer to provide work, so long as he is prepared to pay wages 'Provided I pay my cook her wages regularly she cannot complain if I choose to take all my meals out.'[5] Despite attempts by Lord Denning[6] to argue for a general obligation to provide work in modern times, it seems that an employer is still only obliged to provide work for certain special classes of employee who need to work to practise their skills or keep in the public eye: thus there is an implied obligation to provide work to piece workers,[7] apprentices, skilled employees[8] and actors.[9]

At common law an employer will be in breach of contract if he lays off an employee without pay, unless an express term gives him a right so to do. However, the position is now regulated by statute so that even if there is a contractual right to lay off without pay, the employee will be entitled to a statutory guaranteed payment.[10]

(c) Indemnity

The employer must indemnify employees against liabilities and expenses incurred in the performance of their duties.

(d) Care

The employer is under a duty to take care for the safety of his employees, provide a safe system of work and so on. This common law duty is reinforced by various specific statutory duties, for example, under the Health and Safety at Work etc. Act 1974.[11]

(e) Mutual trust and confidence

The law has long recognised implied duties of good faith owed by employee to employer. In recent years, however, these duties have come to be regarded as mutual so that an employer is under a duty to maintain the working relationship. He may be in breach if he deliberately insults or abuses an employee,[12] especially if in the company of colleagues or subordinates, if he unjustly accuses him of misconduct, incompetence or dishonesty,[13] or if he demotes the employee without good reason. There is likely to be a breach if the employer behaves 'in a way which is contrary to good industrial practice to such an extent that the employee cannot be expected to put up with it any longer.'[14]

(f) Statutory obligations

In addition to the above, a number of statutory obligations are now imposed upon employers. Chief amongst these are the Race Relations Act 1976 and Sex Discrimination Act 1975 which make it unlawful for an employer to discriminate against an employee in the way he affords access to opportunities for promotion, transfer or training, or other benefits, facilities or services or by dismissing or subjecting the employee to any detriment, on the grounds of race, colour, nationality or ethnic origin, or sex or marital status respectively. The Acts prohibit both direct and indirect discrimination. The latter occurs when an employer imposes a requirement, not necessary for the job, which can be fulfilled by a considerably smaller proportion of, women (say) than men. The Equal Pay Act implies an 'equality clause' into the contracts of all employees which requires the terms of employment of men and women to be no less favourable than a member of the opposite sex doing like work, or work rated as equivalent by a job evaluation scheme, or work of equal value. Much detailed learning surrounds these pieces of legislation; it is outside the scope of this volume. Much of the legislation is 'policed' by the Equal Opportunities Commission and Commission for Racial Equality. The employer is also required not to impose detrimental treatment on employees to deter them taking part in trade union activities. Other statutory provisions include a requirement for an employer to allow time off work for employees who are trade union officials, or to take part in union activities, perform public duties or to seek new jobs when faced with redundancy or to seek ante-natal care.

1 See above 14.0.5.
2 See below 30.2.3; 30.2.4.
3 *Mears v Safecar Security Ltd* [1981] 1 WLR 1214, [1981] ICR 409, EAT.
4 Employment Protection (Consolidation) Act 1978, s 8.
5 Per Asquith J in *Collier v Sunday Referee Publishing Co* [1940] 2 KB 647, [1940] 4 All ER 234.
6 *Langston v Amalgamated Union of Engineering Workers* [1974] 1 All ER 980, [1974] 1 WLR 185, CA.
7 *Devonald v Rosser & Sons* [1906] 2 KB 728, CA.
8 *Breach v Epsylon Industries Ltd* [1976] ICR 316, [1976] IRLR 180, EAT.
9 *Herbert Clayton and Jack Waller Ltd v Oliver* [1930] AC 209, HL.
10 EP(C)A 1978, s 12.
11 See generally above 9.0.0.
12 *Palmanor Ltd v Cedron* [1978] ICR 1008, [1978] IRLR 303; *Wetherall (Bond St W1) Ltd v Lynn* [1978] 1 WLR 200, [1978] ICR 205.
13 *Robinson v Crompton Parkinson Ltd* [1978] ICR, 401, [1978] IRLR 61, EAT.
14 Phillips J in *British Aircraft Corpn Ltd v Austin* [1978] IRLR 332, EAT.

Employee's duties

30.1.2. Just as the contract may be expected to impose express obligations upon the employer, so a full contract will set out in detail the employee's duties. However, like the employer, the employee too is subject to implied duties under terms which are implied into the contract at common law. Indeed, perhaps unsurprisingly, the law on employee's duties is more fully developed than that on employer's duties.

(a) Personal service

Just as the payment of wages is the employer's most fundamental obligation, so the employee's first obligation is to do the job for which he is employed. A refusal to work will amount to a breach of contract and thus a strike always involves a technical breach of contract by all the employees who take part in it, enabling the employer to dismiss the strikers without notice at common law.[1] The relationship between employer and employee involves a personal contract so that the employee cannot delegate performance: if he sends someone else to do his job for him, he is in breach of contract.

(b) Obedience

The employee is bound to obey all lawful and reasonable orders of his employer. Failure to do so will entitle the employer to dismiss without notice. The employee is entitled to refuse to obey an unreasonable order, for instance one which would expose him to real personal danger[2] or an unlawful or illegal order, for instance, to falsify tax records.[3] Often an employer with more than one establishment may include a 'mobility clause' in his employees' contracts, by which they can be required to work at any of his establishments. If the contract does include such a clause, the employer is entitled to order the employee to move, and disobedience will amount to misconduct which may justify dismissal. This may be important in the context of dismissal claims.[4]

(c) Care

The employee impliedly undertakes that he is reasonably competent, and to exercise reasonable care in the performance of his duties. There is a further implied obligation to indemnify the employer against liability caused by a breach of this duty, although as we have seen, the right to indemnity is not normally enforced.[5]

(d) Good faith/mutual trust and confidence

This is the equivalent of the employer's duty and, indeed, predates the recent development of that duty. Thus an employee will be in breach of contract if he abuses his employer. However, three other aspects of the duty are of particular importance:

(i) Duty to account The employee must account to his employer for all property of his employer which comes into his possession during the employment. Theft of the employer's property will obviously amount to a breach of duty justifying dismissal;[6] moreover, the employee is, like an agent, under a duty not to make a secret profit or accept bribes in the course of his employment.[7]

(ii) Not to allow a conflict of interest during employment The employee breaks his contract if he allows his own interests to come into conflict with those of his employer. Thus during employment he may not use for his own benefit knowledge of trade secrets, processes and the like, nor knowledge of his

employer's business, such as details of customers or suppliers acquired during the course of his employment. He will be in breach of this obligation if, during employment, he sets up his own business in competition with his employer, or if he goes to work for a competitor of the employer.[8] However, subject to that restriction, there is no implied obligation which prevents 'moonlighting', the taking of a second job outside his ordinary working hours, provided the second job does not interfere with his normal working duties. It would do so if, for example, his job at a night club left him tired so that he fell asleep at work the next day.

The employee is also in breach of his duty if, whilst employed, he prepares to set up a competing business and canvasses his employer's customers[9] or clients, or prepares a list of customers or clients to take with him.[10]

Breach of this duty will justify summary dismissal at common law. The employer may also claim damages, or an account of profits from a competing business, and may seek injunctions to restrain not only the competing employee but also anyone for whom he works.

(iii) Not to allow a conflict of interest after employment The implied duty does survive the termination of employment, but its ambit is narrower than that during employment. The employee may still be restrained from using secret information which came to him during employment. Thus, for example, a chemist who learns a secret process from his employer may be prevented from leaving and setting up a competing business which makes use of that formula, at least so long as it remains secret and is not in the public domain. Whether or not information is so secret as to be so protected will depend on the nature of the employment, the nature of the information, the way it is treated by the parties and how widely it is disseminated to other employees.[11] However, there is no implied duty which prevents an employee canvassing his ex-employer's customers or clients as soon as their employment relationship has ended. Thus in *Fowler v Faccenda Chicken Ltd*[12] the employee set up a highly successful sales operation for his employer. Following a dispute he left and set up his own rival operation, making use of his knowledge of the ex-employer's customers and prices to canvass custom and undercut him. The Court of Appeal held that there was nothing to stop him so doing. The customer and price information was not so secret as to amount to a trade secret. The position would have been different if he had made a list, or canvassed customers, before he left, for he would then have committed a breach during employment. There is nothing to prevent an employee making use during or after employment of information which forms part of his general know-how.

The restricted nature of the employee's implied duty not to compete after employment means that it will generally be desirable for the employer to impose an express restraint of trade clause, on at least senior employees. Of course, such an express restraint will only be upheld if it can be shown to protect a legitimate interest of the employer: this may include the protection of secret information, or of the employer's trade connection, when the employee has developed a specially close relationship with and influence over clients or customers. In addition the restraint must be shown to be reasonable in extent and duration, and not contrary to the public interest.[13] Even if there is a valid express restraint included in the contract, the employer will not be able to rely on it if he himself has broken the contract of employment, eg, by dismissing without notice.[14]

(e) Inventions
An invention made by an employee in the course of his employment may be the property of his employer. It will be so when either (a) it is made during the employee's normal duties in circumstances such that an invention might be expected to result, by an employee with a special obligation to further his employer's interests or (b) it was made during the course of duties specially assigned to the employee, from which an invention might be expected to result.[15] Even if the invention does belong to the employer, the employee may obtain a 'fair share' of the benefit to be derived by his employer if he can show the invention is of outstanding benefit to the employer and he deserves some compensation for his efforts.

1   There may be an unfair dismissal: below 30.2.4.
2   *Ottoman Bank v Chakarian* [1930] AC 277, PC.
3   *Morrish v Henlys (Folkestone) Ltd* [1973] 2 All ER 137, [1973] ICR 482, NIRC.
4   Below 30.2.3ff.
5   *Lister v Romford Ice and Cold Storage Ltd* [1957] AC 555, [1957] 1 All ER 125, HL.
6   *Sinclair v Neighbour* [1967] 2 QB 279, [1966] 3 All ER 988, CA.
7   *Boston Deep Sea Fishing and Ice Co v Ansell* (1888) 39 Ch D 339, CA.
8   *Hivac Ltd v Park Royal Scientific Instruments Ltd* [1946] Ch 169, [1946] 1 All ER 350, CA.
9   *Sanders v Parry* [1967] 2 All ER 803, [1967] 1 WLR 753; *Wessex Dairies Ltd v Smith* [1935] 2 KB 80, CA.
10 *Robb v Green* [1895] 2 QB 315, CA.
11 *Fowler v Faccenda Chicken Ltd* [1986] 1 All ER 617, [1986] 3 WLR 288, CA.
12 Note 11, above.
13 Above 16.0.5.
14 *General Bill Posting Ltd v Atkinson* [1909] AC 118, HL.
15 Patents Act 1979, s 39.

Termination of the contract of employment

30.2.0   The contract of employment can be terminated in the same ways as any other contract. Thus it can be terminated by the mutual consent of the parties, although the courts and industrial tribunals will need clear evidence before interpreting a termination as consensual, especially where pressure is put on the employee.[1] Tribunals should not find an agreement to terminate employment unless it is proved that the employee really did agree with full knowledge of all the implications it had for him. Similarly the contract may be frustrated. This could happen, for instance, when the employee falls sick for a long period so that he is unable to do his job. Whether or not a contract is frustrated by sickness will depend on all the factors of the case, including the nature of the employer's business, the nature of the particular employee's job, the likely length of his absence and so on.[2] It is unlikely that the contract will be frustrated by a trivial illness of short duration; or when the contract provides for payment of sick pay and the employee is likely to return to work before his contractual (not statutory) right to sick pay has expired. The contract could similarly be frustrated if the employee is convicted of a crime and imprisoned so that he is unable to do his job.[3]

Alternatively the contract may be brought to an end by performance. This may occur when the contract is for a fixed term, say a chief executive appointed for five years. At the end of the term his contract will simply expire. A similar result would follow if the employee was retained to perform a particular task: his contract of employment would end when the task was completed.

In addition, the contract will automatically be terminated on the death of either party, on the compulsory winding up of a company, appointment of a receiver or on the employer's cessation of business. Thus, at common law, contracts of employment are automatically terminated if an employer transfers his business to another owner. However, it is now provided that in such a case the contracts of the employees are automatically transferred to the transferee of the business.[4]

In addition to the above situations, the contract may come to an end as a result of the actions of one of the parties. Such a termination may involve a breach of contract by one party or the other and may result in one or more legal claims.

1   *McAlwane v Boughton Estates Ltd* [1973] 2 All ER 299, [1973] JCR 470, NIRC and see *Igbo v Johnson Matthey Chemicals Ltd* [1986] ICR 82, [1986] IRLR 215.
2   *Marshall v Harland & Wolff Ltd* [1972] 2 All ER 715, [1972] 1 WLR 899, NIRC; *Egg Stores (Stamford Hill) Ltd v Leibovici* [1977] ICR 260, [1976] IRLR 376, EAT.
3   *Hare v Murphy Bros Ltd* [1974] 3 All ER 940, [1974] ICR 603, CA; *F C Shepperd & Co Ltd v Jerrom* [1986] 3 All ER 589, CA.
4   Transfer of Undertakings (Protection of Employment) Regulations 1981.

Termination by one of the parties
30.2.1   If the contract is terminated by the employee, it is termed a resignation; if the employer brings the contract to an end, there is a dismissal. Such a resignation or dismissal may amount to a breach of contract. However, it will not be a breach if the contract is terminated in accordance with its terms, or if one party terminates it in response to a serious breach by the other party. Thus, for example, if the employee resigns without notice because he is demoted without reason, he is merely accepting a breach of contract by the employer and will not himself be in breach. Similarly, if the employer catches the employee stealing from work, he will be entitled to dismiss the employee without notice. This is merely an application of the general contractual principle. The breach of contract does not itself end the contract but must be accepted by the innocent party who may elect, instead, to keep the contract alive. When the breach consists of an outright dismissal or resignation the position is less clear: there are conflicting authorities. It seems that the general rule applies and the innocent party still has the option to accept the breach or affirm the contract.[1] However, in practice there is no real choice: a dismissed employee cannot insist on going into work and, in order to claim damages for breach of contract, will be forced to take steps to mitigate his loss by seeking another job.

Whether or not a dismissal or resignation amounts to a breach of contract will depend on the terms of the contract. If the employee is engaged for a fixed term, a termination by either party before the expiry of the term will be a breach of contract, unless the termination was a response to a serious breach by the other party. Thus, for example, if E is employed by A for five years, and, after three his contract is terminated, that is a breach by A, unless the dismissal was justified, for instance, because E had been discovered running his own business in competition with A.

When the contract is for an indeterminate period it can normally be terminated by giving the appropriate notice. The length of notice required to terminate the contract may be governed by an express term; if not, the courts will imply a term that reasonable notice should be given, and the length of 'reasonable notice' will depend on the facts of the case, including the length of the employee's service, the nature and security of his job, his age and so on. In the case of a senior manager a reasonable notice could be as long as twelve months.[2] Of course, the court may only imply a term requiring reasonable notice if there is no express provision as to notice. However, the employee is protected by statute which establishes minimum notice periods. Once the employee has completed 4 weeks' employment he is entitled to at least one week's notice. Thereafter he is entitled to one week's notice for each complete year of employment, up to a maximum of twelve weeks. The minimum notice required to be given by an employee is one week.[3] The contract may provide, expressly or impliedly, for longer notice than the statutory minimum; it cannot provide for less.

When the contract is terminable by notice, it can be terminated at any time by giving full notice in accordance with its terms and such a termination does not amount to a breach of contract. Thus if the employee is entitled to three months' notice and his employer gives him three months' notice of dismissal, there is no breach of contract. A dismissal with no notice, or with less than full notice will be a breach of contract, unless it is a response to a serious breach of contract by the other party.

1 See *Gunton v Richmond-upon-Thames London Borough Council* [1981] Ch 448, [1980] 3 All ER 577, CA. *London Transport Executive v Clarke* [1981] ICR 355, [1981] IRLR 166, CA.
2 *See eg Grundy v Sun Printing and Publishing Association* (1916) 33 TLR 77, CA.
3 Employment Protection (Consolidation) Act 1978, s 49(1).

Claims arising on dismissal
30.2.2 A dismissed employee may be entitled to relief on several grounds. He may be able to bring a claim for wrongful dismissal, unfair dismissal or for a redundancy payment, depending on the circumstances of the dismissal. These claims may overlap and in an appropriate case an employee might be able to claim relief on all three bases. However, sums recovered by each claim may be set off, one against the other, to prevent him recovering twice over for the same loss.

Wrongful dismissal
30.2.3 The common law focussed on the contract of employment and therefore gave either party to the contract a remedy in the event of a breach by the other party. The employee's claim for wrongful dismissal is no more than a claim for damages for breach of contract. A claim is most commonly brought where the employee is dismissed before the expiry of a fixed term contract, or without his full contractual (or statutory, if longer) notice entitlement under a contract for an indeterminate term. As we have observed, technically such a dismissal must, like any other repudiatory breach of contract, be accepted by the innocent party, the employee. However, his only legal remedy in respect of the breach is to claim damages, since the court will not order specific performance of a contract of employment. He therefore has no practical choice but to accept the dismissal. A dismissal without full notice, or before expiry of a fixed term, will only be justified when the employee has himself committed a serious breach of contract. The implied terms of the contract may often be important in this context.[1] Thus summary dismissal will be justified if (for instance) the

employee steals his employer's property, sets up a competing business in breach of his duty of good faith, or if he goes on strike. Often, if there is a full written contract, it will include a non-exhaustive list of circumstances which will justify summary dismissal. It should be noted that the employer may justify a summary dismissal at common law by reference to misconduct committed before but only discovered after the dismissal.[2]

The employee may also bring a claim in respect of any other serious breach of contract by the employer. Thus, for instance, if the employer demotes the employee without good reason, the employee may be justified in walking out, thus accepting the employer's repudiation, and claiming damages.

The employee must bring his claim for wrongful dismissal before the ordinary civil courts, not to an industrial tribunal. Statute[3] gives the Secretary of State power to transfer jurisdiction over such claims to the industrial tribunals. This would make it easier for the dismissed employee to claim wrongful and unfair dismissal, without the expense of funding two sets of proceedings. Since it is a claim for breach of contract, his damages will be assessed according to the rule in *Hadley v Baxendale*[4] and must, so far as possible, put him in the position he would have been in had the contract been performed. Thus he will normally be entitled to the wages he would have earned had he been dismissed with full notice in accordance with the contract. In addition he is entitled to be compensated for the loss of any fringe benefits under the contract, such as the use of a company car, pension fund contributions, health insurance and so on, which he would have enjoyed during the notice period. However, the sum awarded will be subject to a deduction representing the tax he would have paid on earnings during the notice period. Moreover, since the claim is for damages, the employee is under a duty to take reasonable steps to mitigate his loss. He must endeavour to find a new job and may have to take a cut in status and salary. He must certainly claim any social security benefits to which he is entitled. His damages will then be reduced by any amount he receives in such benefits, or from wages from a new job, during the notice period.

Any dismissal will be distressing for an employee, a summary dismissal without good cause will be especially so. However, the law clearly refuses to allow the employee to claim damages for distress or disappointment arising from the loss of his job, or the manner of his dismissal. This rule, first established in 1909,[5] had been criticised and doubted in recent years but was reaffirmed by the Court of Appeal in 1985.[6]

For many employees a wrongful dismissal claim will serve little purpose. Where the employee can be dismissed with relatively short notice, the amount awarded will be low; moreover, the employee must claim in the county or High Court, where the costs of litigation may eat substantially into his damages. In any case, the employer can avoid liability for any claim by dismissing with full notice or, as is common, by dismissing summarily with 'wages in lieu of notice.' However, for a senior employee on a fixed term contract, or with a contract entitling him to long notice, and enjoying valuable fringe benefits, the amount to be claimed for wrongful dismissal may be substantial. For those reasons, such claims tend to be brought by senior executives and managers of football clubs.

Although we have spoken above of claims for 'wrongful dismissal' there is no reason why an employer could not bring a similar claim against an employee who wrongfully repudiated his contract, including a claim for 'wrongful resignation'. However, such claims are rare, for the employer must prove loss, and except in the case of senior and irreplaceable employees, that will not generally be possible.

1 Above 30.1.1.
2 *Boston Deep Sea Fishing and Ice Co v Ansell* (1888) 39 Ch D 339, CA. Contrast the position in a claim for unfair dismissal, below 30.2.4.
3 EPCA (1978), s 131.
4 (1854) 9 Exch 341 above 17.1.3.
5 *Addis v Gramophone Co Ltd* [1909] AC 488, HL.
6 *Bliss v South East Thames Regional Health Authority* [1985] IRLR 308, CA.

Unfair dismissal

30.2.4   Provided the employer does not break the contract, the employee has no claim for wrongful dismissal. The employer need not give, nor even have, a reason for the dismissal; he is safe at common law provided he dismisses with full notice. Thus the employee's position at common law was precarious. The Industrial Relations Act of 1971 introduced a new right to give employees improved protection. The right to claim for unfair dismissal, which is now contained in the Employment Protection (Consolidation) Act 1978 (as amended) allows the dismissed employee to complain to an industrial tribunal if his employer had no good reason for the dismissal, or if he did not adopt a reasonable procedure. Thus, it should be stressed, a wrongful dismissal may yet be fair, and a dismissal in accordance with the contract may nevertheless be unfair.

The procedure for bringing a complaint before an industrial tribunal is both quicker and cheaper than that for bringing a claim in the ordinary courts. Cases are decided at first instance by a panel of three members including a legally qualified chairman with detailed knowledge of employment and two lay members, one from each side of industry, each with practical experience of industrial relations. (It is not unknown for the two lay members to disagree with and outvote the legally qualified chairman). Employees tend therefore to favour claims for unfair dismissal over claims for wrongful dismissal. Moreover although legal aid is not available they will often be able to get trade union support and assistance to bring a claim and as a result of these factors a mass of detailed case law has grown up around the subject. What follows is no more than an overview.[1]

In order to bring a claim for unfair dismissal the employee must first prove his eligibility. Above all he must show that he is an employee, that is, he is employed under a contract of employment.[2] Self-employed contractors are not entitled to protection. Second, he must show he has worked for the employer for the required period of continuous employment. This was increased in 1985 from one year to two years for full time employees who commenced work after 1 June 1985,[3] on the grounds that the risk of unfair dismissal claims was a disincentive to the engagement of new labour, particularly in a speculative business expansion. Certain employees are excluded from the right to bring a claim, including those over normal retiring age, policemen, dock workers, share fishermen, domestic servants and employees who ordinarily work outside Great Britain. An industrial tribunal has no jurisdiction to hear a claim for unfair dismissal when at the time of the dismissal the employer was conducting a lock out or the employee was on strike or taking part in industrial action. Otherwise the tribunal would effectively be called upon to adjudicate on the merits of industrial disputes, something which would be unacceptable to either side of industry. However, the tribunal does have jurisdiction where the employer discriminates against some strikers by either not sacking all of the employees concerned, or by sacking all but then reinstating some.

Second, the employee must prove he has been dismissed. He will be unable to claim if the contract has been frustrated or terminated by agreement. However, dismissal bears an extended meaning for statutory purposes. Thus it includes not only outright dismissal by the employer, but also cases of 'constructive dismissal' when the employee resigns in response to a serious breach of contract by the employer.[4] In addition, the expiry and non-renewal of a fixed term contract is treated as a dismissal. Were it not so, the employer could avoid the legislation by employing all workers on a series of fixed term contracts; he would then never need to dismiss but could remove employees by allowing their contracts to expire without renewal. However, to protect employers in cases of genuine fixed term contracts, the parties may contract out of the unfair dismissal provisions when the contract is in writing and for a fixed term of one year or more.[5]

Provided there is a dismissal, the law then focusses on the reason for it, and the reasonableness of dismissing for that reason. The legislation lists a series of categories of reasons for dismissal; some are automatically unfair; most are potentially fair, depending on the reasonableness of the dismissal; in a few cases the dismissal will be automatically fair. However, it must be stressed that it is for the employer to show his reason for dismissing, and that it was at least potentially fair. If he cannot show a reason at all the dismissal is always unfair. Of course, it might be difficult for the employee to challenge the reason put forward by the employer, but the legislation allows him to request a written statement of the reasons for his dismissal. Such statement may be used in evidence and if the employer unreasonably refuses to provide such a statement within fourteen days, the employee may complain to the tribunal which will order the employer to pay the employee two weeks' wages as a penalty.[6] By contrast with the law of wrongful dismissal, the employer can only resist an unfair dismissal claim on the grounds of a reason known to him at the time of dismissal.[7]

(a) Special reasons: automatically unfair
In certain special cases it is provided that a dismissal is automatically unfair. The most important of these are dismissals 'on the grounds of membership or taking part in the duties of a trade union'; dismissals for reasons connected with pregnancy; and certain dismissals on the grounds of redundancy.

(i) Trade union membership and activities[8] Such dismissals are said to be for an inadmissible reason. Thus it is automatically unfair to dismiss an employee for joining, or proposing to join, or for taking part in the activities of, a trade union. It is also unfair to dismiss an employee who refuses to join a union unless the employer and union operate a closed shop, and the closed shop agreement has been approved by the required majority of the workforce. If there is an approved closed shop it will normally be fair to dismiss an employee who refuses to join. However, even in such circumstances the dismissal may be unfair, on certain grounds, including that the employee has genuine conscientious or religious objections to union membership, or when he has been unreasonably excluded from union membership.

(ii) Reasons connected with pregnancy [9]   It is automatically unfair to dismiss a pregnant woman because she is pregnant or for any reason connected with her pregnancy, unless her pregnancy makes her incapable of doing her normal work and there is no other suitable work to offer her.

(iii) Redundancy [10]   Normally a dismissal on the grounds of redundancy is potentially fair. However, it will be unfair if the employee was selected for redundancy for an inadmissible reason or in breach of an agreed or customary selection procedure.

(b) Potentially fair reasons
In most cases the employer will establish a reason which falls into one of the five potentially fair reasons. These are: [11]
(i)   capability or qualification—which would include gross incompetence and incapability due to ill health;
(ii)   conduct—which would include misconduct such as theft or fighting, repeated absence or bad timekeeping, or disobedience to orders.
(iii) continued employment which would involve a breach of some statutory requirement;
(iv)   redundancy; this is dealt with below. [12]
(v)   'some other substantial reason'. This has been given a wide interpretation and has been held to cover (inter alia) cases of dismissal for 'sound business reasons' such as the employee's refusal to accept a change to his terms of employment as a result of a business reorganisation or rationalisation; [13] dismissals of incompatible employees; [14] and even a dismissal in order to make room to bring a relative into the family business. [15]

Provided the employer establishes a reason for the dismissal falling within one of the above five categories, the tribunal must then consider whether in all the circumstances it was reasonable to treat that reason as sufficient to dismiss. This involves consideration of both the substantive reason for dismissal—was the reason sufficiently serious—and also the procedure by which dismissal was effected. A model disciplinary code of conduct has been promulgated by ACAS detailing procedures which ought to be followed; a revised and much expanded code has recently been published. Obviously the procedural requirements of each case will differ according to the reason for dismissal and the particular facts of the case. However, in general, the employer should investigate a case to make sure he is in possession of all relevant facts before deciding to dismiss; he should give the employee a chance to present his case and to appeal against dismissal. [16] The code is only a guide but many employers have adopted disciplinary procedures based on it, requiring, eg, that before a dismissal for misconduct, the employee be given two oral and one written warning, in order that he has a chance to improve, and appeal against dismissal. In cases of gross misconduct immediate dismissal without warnings may be justified. A failure to adopt a fair procedure will not of itself make a dismissal unfair; [17] on the other hand, an employer who adopts and follows a proper procedure in all cases should generally avoid liability for unfair dismissal claims.

1   For detailed treatment see Smith and Wood, *Industrial Law* (3rd edn 1986) Ch 6.
2   Above, 30.0.2.
3   For employees who commenced work before that time the period is one year, except when the employer employs no more than 20 employees, in which case it is two years.

4 EP(C)A 1978, s 55 (2), as explained in *Western Excavating (ECC) Ltd v Sharp* [1978] QB 761, [1978] 1 All ER 713, CA.
5 EP(C)A 1978, s 54.
6 EP(C)A 1978, s 53.
7 *W Devis & Sons Ltd v Atkins* [1976] 2 All ER 822, [1976] 1 WLR 393.
8 EP(C)A 1978, s 58.
9 EP(C)A 1978, s 60.
10 EP(C)A 1978, s 59.
11 EP(C)A 1978, s 57.
12 See below 30.2.5.
13 *Hollister v National Farmers' Union* [1979] ICR 542, [1979] IRLR 238, CA.
14 *Treganowan v Robert Knee & Co Ltd* [1975] ICR 405, [1975] IRLR 247.
15 *Priddle v Dibble* [1978] 1 All ER 1058, [1978] 1 WLR 895.
16 See eg *British Home Stores Ltd v Burchell* [1980] ICR 303n, [1978] IRLR 379—dismissal for misconduct.
17 *British Labour Pump Co Ltd v Byrne* [1979] ICR 347, [1979] IRLR 94.

Remedies for unfair dismissal

30.2.5 The principal remedy for unfair dismissal is, in practice, an award of compensation. However, when the concept of unfair dismissal was introduced as protection for job security, it was intended that the primary remedy should be an order allowing the employee to return to work. Thus the tribunal has power to order reinstatement or re-engagement. Broadly speaking, reinstatement involves giving the employee his old job back on the same terms; re-engagement may involve him being given a different job or a job on changed terms. In deciding whether or not to order reinstatement or re-engagement the tribunal must consider whether or not it is practicable to comply; it will not be impracticable merely because a replacement has been engaged. It must also consider the employee's wishes. In most cases an unfair dismissal will lead to mutual acrimony and destroy any workable relationship. It is no surprise therefore that orders for reinstatement or re-engagement are made in only about 2% of cases.

As an alternative the tribunal may order the employer to compensate the employee. All compensation orders are made up of two awards: a basic award and a compensatory award. A basic award is calculated according to the same rules as a redundancy payment[1] and depends on the age, length of service and wages of the employee. It is effectively compensation for loss of accrued job security. The compensatory award compensates the employee for wages and other benefits lost due to the dismissal; it will normally include compensation both for loss up to the date of the hearing, and for the future, in practice for a limited period. Fringe benefits and the like may be taken into account and the employee is under a duty to mitigate his loss by seeking another job; any wages from his new employment must be brought into account and will reduce his loss. Furthermore the compensatory award is subject to a financial limit, currently £8,500, which is varied from time to time. Both awards can be reduced on the grounds that the employee has caused or contributed to his own dismissal.

In certain circumstances extra compensation may be payable. Thus if the tribunal makes an order for reinstatement or re-engagement, with which the employer fails to comply, an additional award of between 13 and 26 weeks pay will be ordered. Dismissals for inadmissible reasons (ie trade union activities, membership or non-membership)[2] are especially hazardous for the employer. In such a case the employee may claim even though he has been employed for less than the qualifying period of continuous employment.

There is a minimum basic award in such cases of £2,300, regardless of the employee's age, salary or length of service. Moreover, if in such a case the employee requests reinstatement or re-engagement, a special award may be payable. If the tribunal does not order reinstatement or re-engagement the special award will be the greater of £11,500 and 104 weeks wages, subject to a maximum of £23,000; if reinstatement or re-engagement is ordered but the employer fails to comply, the award will be the greater of £17,250 and 152 weeks' pay; there is no overall maximum.[3]

1   Below 30.2.7.
2   Above 30.2.4.
3   The financial limits may be varied from time to time.

Redundancy payments
30.2.6   The right of an employee to claim a redundancy payment was introduced by the Redundancy Payments Act 1965. Broadly speaking, the right arises when the employee's job disappears so that he is dismissed and not replaced. It has been said that the right to a redundancy payment recognises the employee's property right in his job, comprised in his accrued rights and security, and expectations for the future. It was argued that the existence of such payments would promote labour mobility. The availability of a redundancy payment may be viewed as a carrot to encourage labour to accept management economies and improved productivity.[1] The lump sum payment may serve to reduce the hardship of the loss of a job and, possibly act as an incentive to workers to 'go quietly'; but the sums awarded are rarely large, at least when the statutory scheme is relied upon and particularly where, as is common, employees with the shortest period of service are selected first for redundancy; as the labour market has become depressed in recent years an increasing number of employees have seemed reluctant to accept the carrot of a redundancy payment.

In many cases the statutory redundancy scheme provides no more than a foundation. Thus redundancy agreements negotiated between employers and trade unions representing their workforce may provide for more generous payments, or extend the criteria of eligibility. This is particularly true in the public sector. (However, the majority of employees must rely on the statutory scheme and in view of the weakened position of trade unions since 1980 it is unlikely that collective bargaining will achieve such favourable results in the future.)

In order to claim a statutory redundancy payment an employee must first show that he is qualified to claim. The conditions are similar to those for unfair dismissal; the employee must have completed two years' continuous employment; those over 65 (men) and 60 (women) are excluded, as are several other categories including those who ordinarily work outside Great Britain. The right to a redundancy payment can be excluded if the employee so agrees in writing and is employed under a fixed term contract of one year or more. There must also be a dismissal. The concept of 'dismissal' is the same as that used for unfair dismissal so that constructive dismissal and the expiry of a fixed term contract are included.[2]

A dismissed employee is entitled to a redundancy payment if the dismissal was by reason of redundancy. The statutory definition of 'redundancy', particularly as interpreted by the courts, is much narrower than the idea colloquially conveyed by that word. Redundancy occurs where:

(a) the employer ceases business altogether, or ceases business in the place where the employee is employed; or

(b) the requirements of the employer's business for employees to do work of the kind for which the employee was employed have ceased or diminished, or have done so in the place where the employee was employed.

A total cessation of business is easily recognisable; however, the definition raises two problems of definition: what is 'the place where the employee is employed' and what is meant by 'work of the kind for which the employee was employed'? These questions have been considered several times and the courts and tribunals have answered both by reference to the contract of employment. Thus an employee is employed where he can be required to work under his contract. If his employer has several establishments and closes one, the employee is not redundant if he is 'mobile', ie, he can be ordered to move to another establishment (although he will be redundant if there is an overall diminution in the requirements of the employer's business for employees.) A similar test has been applied to 'work of a particular kind' focussing on the work the employee may be required to do under the contract, rather than the job he actually does. This approach to the definition of redundancy can be restrictive. Thus, when a brewery refurbished a public house with a new 'young' image and replaced its middle aged barmaids with young 'bunny girl' type waitresses, the dismissed barmaids were not redundant;[3] nor was the experienced builder of wooden boats who was too meticulous a craftsman to adapt to building fibreglass boats and faster techniques,[4] even though such people might be colloquially regarded as 'redundant'. Moreover, there is no redundancy if the employee is dismissed for refusing to accept a change in his or her working conditions or terms, such as a new shift system.

> 'It is settled that an employer is entitled to reorganise his business so as to improve its efficiency and, in doing so, to propose to his staff a change in the terms and conditions of their employment; and to dispense with their services if they do not agree.'[5]

It should be stressed that a decision that a dismissal is not 'by reason of redundancy' may be contrary to the interests of the employer, who may then have to justify dismissal on other grounds to avoid an unfair dismissal claim (where the compensation awarded is higher). However, the tribunals would probably regard a dismissal for refusal to accept changed working practices as for 'some other substantial reason.'[6] The combined impact of these decisions, then, is to encourage labour flexibility and strengthen managerial discretion in its management of the workforce, the so-called 'right of management to manage'.

An employee who appears to be entitled to a redundancy payment may nevertheless lose his right. This will be the case when he is dismissed for misconduct; which will include a refusal to obey an order. Thus a 'mobile' employee who refuses to obey an order to move to another establishment will be dismissed for misconduct, not redundancy. Misconduct after notice of redundancy has been given may also affect the right to a payment.[7] The statute also seeks to encourage job flexibility and therefore provides that the employee will lose his right to a redundancy payment if he unreasonably refuses an offer of suitable alternative employment. The tribunal may take into account both the nature of the job, its terms and so on, and the employee's personal circumstances, including family circumstances and the like.[8] If he does decide to accept an alternative job which is offered to him, the employee will have a trial period of four weeks to try out the new job; if during that period either party terminates the contract for a reason connected with the new job, a redundancy payment is payable.[9]

As noted above, a redundancy may amount to an unfair dismissal. In order to avoid this the employer should normally give advance notice of redundancies to individual employees and consider alternative employment for them within his organisation.[10] If there is an agreed or customary procedure for selecting employees for redundancy, he should follow it; if not he should adopt a fair procedure. Many employers select employees on the basis of 'last in, first out' although complex assessment schemes are not uncommon. The employer should also consult as soon as possible with any trade union which represents the employees affected. Failure so to do may make the individual dismissals unfair; it may also allow the union to apply for a 'protective award' on behalf of its members, which requires the employer to continue to pay their wages for a stipulated period. The length of notice required to be given to the union to avoid a protective award will depend on the number of redundancies and the period over which they are to be implemented.[11] The duration of any protective award will normally be equal to the length of notice which should have been given to the union. The employer is also required to give advance notice of redundancies to the Secretary of State for Employment. The length of notice will again depend on the number of redundancies.[12] A failure to give notice may result in a prosecution and possible fine.

1 See Grunfeld, *The Law of Redundancy* (2nd edn 1980) p 5.
2 See above 30.2.4.
3 *Vaux and Associated Breweries Ltd v Ward* (1968) 3 ITR 385.
4 *Hindle v Percival Boats Ltd* [1969] 1 All ER 836, [1969] 1 WLR 174, CA.
5 *Johnson v Nottinghamshire Combined Police Authority* [1974] ICR 170 at 176 per Lord Denning MR.
6 See above 30.2.4.
7 EP(C)A 1978, s 82; EP(C)A 1978, s 92.
8 EP(C)A 1978, s 82(3)–(7).
9 EP(C)A 1978, s 84.
10 See *Williams v Compair Maxam Ltd* [1982] ICR 156, [1982] IRLR 83, EAT.
11 EP(C)A 1978, s 99.
12 EP(C)A 1978, ss 104–105.

Calculation of the redundancy payment
30.2.7 The amount of a redundancy payment depends on the employee's age, length of service, and weekly wage at dismissal. It is calculated according to a formula:
1. For each complete year of employment when the employee was aged 41 or more, he receives one and a half week's pay.
2. For each complete year of employment when he was aged 22 or more but not over 41, he receives one week's pay.
3. For each complete year of employment during which he was aged 18 or over but younger than 22, he receives half a week's pay.
No more than 20 years of employment may be counted, and the maximum week's pay upon which a calculation may be based is £158.[1] The maximum

award is therefore 20 × $1\frac{1}{2}$ × £158 = £4,740. As we have noted, redundancy schemes agreed by collective bargaining may improve on the statutory scheme.

In order to lessen the bill for redundancies which would otherwise fall on employers, the government has operated a rebate scheme under which a proportion of any redundancy payment made by the employer could be reclaimed from a government Redundancy Fund, financed by employers' Social Security contributions. In 1982 the Fund showed a deficit of £282 million and although that figure has been reduced, the rebate scheme has been abolished from October 1986 except for employers of fewer than ten employees.

1   The limit is varied from time to time.

Redundancy, insolvency and business transfer

30.2.8   Many redundancies come about as the result of a business failure, or on the transfer of a business. Indeed, the two events are often linked, failure leading to a sale by a receiver. The employee's rights against an insolvent employer would be precarious but are protected by three special rules. First, an employee's claim for arrears of wages[1] and certain other payments[2] ranks as a preferential claim in his employer's insolvency.[2] Second, where an employer is insolvent, the employee is entitled to claim his redundancy payment, and other sums in respect of payment in lieu of notice, arrears of wages and so on, from the government's Redundancy Fund, leaving the fund to prove in the insolvency.[3] Third, on a transfer of a business as a going concern, the Transfer of Undertakings (Protection of Employment) Regulations of 1981 will apply.[4] At common law there would be a dismissal if the employer disposed of his business since the contract of employment, being personal, could not be transferred. That dismissal would be for redundancy if the transferor thereby ceased business altogether or, as a result, required fewer employees. However the 1981 regulations provide that in such a situation the contracts of employment of all employees employed immediately before the transfer are taken over by the transferee, as if he had always been the employer. Any dismissal by transferor or transferee for any reason connected with the transfer will automatically be unfair unless it is shown to be for an organisational or technical reason entailing changes in the workforce.

1   Up to 4 months' arrears subject to a maximum of £800.
2   See below 36.0.14; Insolvency Act 1986, Sch 6.
3   EP(C)A 1978, s 122.
4   The regulations are notoriously complex.

Part VII
The legal framework of business organisations

Chapter 31

Types of Business Organisation

31.0.0 In the UK the law permits a range of different types of business organisation. At one end of the spectrum is the sole trader or one man unincorporated business; at the other, the massive public limited company whose business operations may have a significant impact on the entire economy. The principal types of business organisation in the UK are the sole trader, the partnership and the corporate association.

Sole trader
31.0.1 The sole trader is the simplest and most flexible legal unit within which to carry on business. It consists of one person carrying on business who may engage employees to work for him. The sole trader is responsible for the conduct of the business and thus for the debts incurred.

In general, there is no requirement for registration, disclosure of financial information or any other form of public accountability. In essence therefore the law applicable to the sole trader is the law which applies to any individual in his personal affairs.

Partnership
31.0.2 Partnership under English law grew from the law of contract and principles of agency[1] as developed by the courts. During the latter part of the nineteenth century, along with other areas of commercial law, partnership law was codified by the enactment of the Partnership Act 1890 (PA 1890). This Act represents a comprehensive, though not complete, statutory framework. The definition of partnership in the 1890 Act is: 'the relationship which subsists between persons carrying on a business in common with a view to profit.'[2] Thus a prerequisite for the existence of a partnership is a business intended to be carried on for profit. The partnership can be formed without formality and without the partners agreeing on a contract. Indeed, it is possible for persons to bring into existence a partnership without realising it.[3]

Under English law separate legal personality is not conferred on a partnership. Partners are collectively called a firm[4] but the firm does not enjoy the separate legal status of a company.[5] Under Scots law, a partnership does enjoy a legal personality separate from that of the partners.[6] Thus the firm can enter into contracts in its own name and can sue and be sued in the same manner as a limited company. Ultimately, however, the partners in a

Scottish firm are, in common with those in an English firm, responsible to the full extent of their personal assets for the debts and liabilities of the firm.

Partners are agents of the firm for carrying on the firm's business in the usual way and entitled to share equally in the profit of the business, in the absence of any agreement to the contrary. The only regulatory control on the freedom to associate in partnership is that partnerships of more than twenty must incorporate unless they are solicitors, accountants, stock-brokers or other partnerships exempted by the Secretary of State.[7]

A special form of partnership was introduced by the Limited Partnership Act 1907. This Act permits the creation of a partnership with one or more general partners who assume a personal liability for the business debts and one or more limited partners with liability limited to their capital contribution. Limited partners are not entitled to share in the management of the partnership, indeed if they do intervene, their limited liability status is lost. Registration of limited partnerships is required with the Registrar of Companies[8] but there are no minimum capital requirements, or continuing disclosure obligations.

Limited partnerships have not proved popular as a form of business association largely because of the rule that the limited partner cannot intervene in the business, even where the capital is being dissipated. Corporate status proved more convenient where all the 'partners' obtained the benefit of limited liability.

1 See Part VI.
2 S 1.
3 See 32.0.0.
4 S 4.
5 See 32.1.0.
6 S 4(4).
7 Companies Act 1985, s 716.
8 See 33.2.2.

Corporate status
31.0.3 The formation of a company results in the creation of a legal entity that enjoys a distinct status quite separate from its members. Once Parliament and the courts had clearly recognised the separate status of business corporations and bestowed the privilege of limited liability on its members, it quickly acquired popularity as a form of business association.

Limited liability and the development of company law
31.1.0 In 1854 a Royal Commission[1] led to a House of Commons resolution to the effect that:

> 'The law of partnership which renders every person who . . . shares the profits of a trading concern liable to the whole of its debts, is unsatisfactory and should be amended to permit such persons to contribute to the capital of such concerns on terms of sharing profits, without incurring liability beyond a limited amount.'

It was forcibly argued during this period that greater accessibility of corporate status and limited liability would bring considerable benefits to society. A select committee in 1850 asserted that changes in the legal framework were desirable on social grounds:

'the great change in the social position of multitudes from the growth of large towns and crowded districts, renders it more necessary that corresponding changes in the law should take place both to improve their condition and contentment, and to give additional facilities to investors of capital which their industry and enterprise is constantly creating and augmenting. It is the conviction of your committee that if such measures were carried into effect, a stimulus would be given to the industry of the community, likely to cause additional employment and contentment without injury to any class and added security to the welfare of all.'[2]

Limited liability was first introduced by the Limited Liability Act 1855. In essence it was seen as a means of promoting the wider investment in joint stock companies that was necessary in order to assist the development of large scale projects on the railways, canals and docks. The 1855 Act contained the basic safeguard that at least 75% of the nominal capital must have been subscribed and that the company could not carry on business if more than 75% of its capital had been lost. Such restrictions were however quickly removed by the Joint Stock Companies Act 1856 which was expressed as having the following objectives:

'The principle we should adopt is this, not to throw the slightest obstacle in the way of limited companies being formed . . . and when difficulties arise, to arm the courts of justice with sufficient powers to check extravagance or roguery. That is the only way the legislature should interfere with the single exception of giving the greatest publicity to the affairs of such companies that everyone may know on what grounds he is dealing.'[3]

There followed the consolidating Companies Act 1862 which laid down the basic constitutional and legal framework which survives to this day.

Under the 1862 Act a company could be formed with seven or more people subscribing their name to a memorandum of association either with or without limited liability. Where the liability was to be limited the memorandum was required to contain the name of the company with the word 'Limited' at the end, the address of the registered office, the objectives for which the company was formed, the declaration that the liability of the members was limited, and the amounts of capital which the company proposed to have registered. The Act also required a register of members to be kept and an annual list of members to be forwarded to the Registrar of Joint Stock Companies.

The type of business organisation that emerged after the mid-nineteenth century was therefore incorporation with limited liability by an easy process of registration. Inevitably, in practice it owed much to the earlier form of unincorporated partnership based on contract. Apart from some basic statutory protections against fraud based on a simple system of registration and disclosure of information, there was no demand for more sophisticated state regulation.[4]

Since the 1862 Act there have been four other consolidation measures. The Companies (Consolidation) Act 1908 formally recognised the private company and granted exemptions to such associations from the disclosure provisions. The Companies Acts of 1928 and 1929 imposed wider reporting requirements on public companies in respect of annual accounts, and the Companies Act 1948 extended these requirements to some private companies, as well as requiring greater disclosure in respect of the profit and loss account, consolidation of subsidiaries' accounts, disclosure of director interests and a strengthened status for auditors.

The Companies Act 1985 (CA 1985) drew together the piecemeal reforms of company law in the period 1948–1981. Such reforms derived from three areas of influence. First the continuing trend towards disclosure of financial information, particularly relating to public companies.[5] Second, demands for greater accountability and responsibility in respect of corporate directors and controllers.[6] Third, the UK's membership of the European Economic Community.[7]

Despite all these developments the basic notion of limited liability has remained intact. It could be said that developments in insolvency law[8] have eroded the principle in the case of directors but in general it remains a central feature of company law.

In practice, in the context of small businesses, directors often have to compromise the protection of limited liability. Creditors invariably seek personal guarantees from the directors before they will extend funds to a small business. Thus the director may obtain the protection of limited liability in dealings with trade creditors and consumers but not in respect of long term commitments with banks or other financial institutions.

1   Report of the Royal Commission on Mercantile Laws 854.
2   1850 BPP Vol XIX 172.
3   Robert Lowe, Parl Deb 1856 Vol 140, col 131.
4   See the quote from Chayes at 1.0.0. note 3.
5   See Companies Acts 1967, 1976, 1980 and 1981.
6   See Companies Act 1980.
7   See European Communities Act 1972, Companies Act 1980 and 1981.
8   See Insolvency Act 1986. See 36.0.14.

Legislative and judicial trends in company law
(a) Disclosure
31.2.0   As indicated above, a central theme of British company law is registration and disclosure. Since 1908 legislation has required companies to disclose progressively more financial information in published accounts and returns to the Registrar of Companies. Such disclosure is justified in terms of a vague notion that it represents the price of limited liability and as a basic report to the shareholders on a stewardship function by directors. As Morris observed however:

> 'Unfortunately few attempts have been made in Britain to determine the objectives of disclosure in financial statements.'[1]

Since the early legislation that gave birth to the limited liability company subsequent changes in respect of the disclosure provisions have evolved from three discernible forces. First, major business scandals and failures have prompted legislation under pressure from public opinion. For example the failure of the Royal British Bank in 1856 led to the Joint Stock Banking Companies Act 1858 and the Punishment of Fraud Act 1857; the collapse of the City of Glasgow Bank in 1878 was followed by the Companies Act 1879; the famous Royal Mail case in 1931 exposed the inadequacy of accounting practices and resulted in reforms in the Companies Act 1948 and the revelations in Department of Trade Inspectors' Reports in the 1970s resulted in provisions requiring greater disclosure of director dealings with a company in the Companies Act 1981.

A second force was the greater public interest in company accounts as a result of more widespread ownership of shares, the development of capital markets and the growth of institutional investors.

Third, the increased pressure to disclose information for the general economic and social good as a form of social accountability. An American academic detects in recent years:

> 'a new policy basis for corporate disclosure . . . Its scope is not yet clear and it has not yet received formal recognition in the law; but its significance cannot be underestimated. This is the idea . . . that disclosure has a role in the regulation of corporations as major power centres of our society. Acceptance of this wider role of disclosure to any degree is to say that there is a direct relationship between corporate disclosure under the securities laws and corporate responsibility . . . It would mean that disclosure is not merely investor orientated but society orientated.'[2]

In 1975 the UK Accounting Standards Steering Committee published 'The Corporate Report' which considered that there is a basic responsibility on every economic entity to report publicly where its size rendered it significant, that is, where the entity has at its command human or material resources on such a scale that the results of its business have significant economic implications for society.

In recent years, however, greater discussion has focussed on relieving companies, especially small businesses, of some of the burdens of registration and disclosure.[3] The Companies Act 1981 allowed small and medium sized companies to present modified financial statements to the Registrar.[4]

Such modifications were justified in terms of relieving the burden on small companies and protecting the competitive position of small and medium sized companies against larger companies. However, it was widely recognised that the preparation of modified accounts involved companies in extra work.[5] There was no evidence to support the view that disclosure affected the competitive position of companies; indeed the Bolton Committee on Small Firms in 1971 found little evidence of genuine detriment to small companies.[6]

The main argument in support of maintaining full disclosure of financial statements for all companies is that it helps maintain an efficient system of credit reporting and represents an index of corporate solvency. Such an argument is only sustainable if the reports are lodged on time and there is an efficient system for monitoring compliance.[7]

(b) EEC membership

A further influential factor in company law in recent years has been the European Economic Community (EEC). On the 1 January 1973 the UK became a member of the Community. One of the principal objectives of the EEC's common industrial policy is:

> 'The creation of a unified business environment involving the harmonisation of company law and taxation, and the creation of a community capital market.'[8]

In its efforts to achieve this objective the Commission has embarked on a programme of company law harmonisation designed to implement Article 543(g) of the Treaty of Rome which calls for 'the co-ordination of the safeguards required from companies in the member states to protect the interests both of members and third parties.'

When the UK joined the EEC the First Directive[9] on company law harmonisation had already been agreed upon by the member states and was implemented by s 9 of the European Communities Act.[10] The section provides some relief against the ultra vires[11] doctrine for third parties dealing with a company.

The principal directives agreed and discussed since the UK joined the EEC are as follows.

The Second Directive[12] dealt with minimum requirements in respect of the formation of companies, and the maintenance of capital. It was implemented by the Companies Act 1980.

The Third Directive[13] deals with mergers where shares are exchanged between public limited companies. It does not deal with takeovers which are the more common form of merger in the UK. It will therefore have a limited impact on the UK. Implementation of this directive has been subject to delay.

The Fourth Directive[14] deals with the disclosure of financial information and the contents of company accounts. It was substantially influenced by UK practice and was implemented by the Companies Act 1981.

The draft Fifth Directive[15] is the most controversial Directive, since it provides for worker participation on company boards. It is expected to take several years to reach agreement on it between member states.

The Sixth Directive[16] complements the Third Directive on mergers. It deals with the operation whereby a public limited company transfers to a number of public limited companies, all of its assets and liabilities in exchange for the issue of shares to the shareholders of the divided company. Implementation was expected to take place in 1986.

The Seventh Directive[17] deals with group accounts and must be implemented by the end of 1987.

The Eighth Directive[18] lays down minimum standards for auditors' qualifications. Discussions on implementation in the UK are currently underway.

(c) Judicial trends

In terms of judicial trends the most significant theme is that of protection of creditors by the application of strict rules on the maintenance of capital. Thus the courts developed strict rules prohibiting a company dealing in its own shares, diluting its share capital by entering into transactions at an undervalue and making improper dividend distributions.[19] The courts also sought to protect shareholders and creditors by developing strict rules that a company's contractual capacity was limited by its statutory objects. Thus if a transaction is outside a company's objects clause it will be ultra vires and void.[20] Despite the ingenuity of legal draftsmen that sought to mitigate the limiting effect of the ultra vires rules the courts' insistence on the application of the ultra vires rules to contracts made by companies prevented misuse by directors of corporate powers. In the words of Lord Cairns:

> 'there is a covenant that no change shall be made in the objects for which the company is established. I apprehend that that includes within it the engagement that no object shall be pursued by the company, or attempted to be attained by the company in practice, except an object which is mentioned in the memorandum of association . . . if that is

so—if that is the condition upon which the corporation is established—
it is a mode of incorporation which contains in it both that which is
affirmative and that which is negative. It states affirmatively the ambit
and extent of vitality and power which by law are given to the corporation and it states, if it is necessary so to state, negatively, that nothing
shall be done beyond that ambit, and that no attempt shall be made to
use corporate life for any purpose than that which is so specified.'[21]

The courts were also quick to recognise the separate legal status of a
company and unwilling to depart from the basic principle laid down in
Salomon v A Salomon & Co Ltd.[22]

In terms of corporate government, the courts have shown a marked reluctance to interfere. Majority rule and management's right to manage have
been the cornerstone of judicial policy. Thus:

'it is not the business of the courts to manage the affairs of the
company. That is for the shareholders and directors'.[23]

1 R C Morris *Corporate Reporting Standards and the Fourth Directive* (ICA Occasional
   Paper, 1974).
2 Schoenbaum, 'The Relationship between Corporate Disclosure and Corporate Responsibility' Fordham Law Review Vol 40 1972 578.
3 See Sealy, 'The Disclosure Philosophy and Company Law Reform' 1981 2 Co Law s 1 and
   see 1.5.5.
4 Companies Act 1985, s 248.
5 See Consultative Committee of Accountancy Bodies: *Memorandum on the Companies
   Bill*, 1981 para 12.
6 *Report of the Committee of Inquiry on Small Firms*, Cmnd 4811, paras 19–25.
7 See Committee of Public Accounts, House of Commons, 1983–84. Reliability of Companies Register which pointed out that up to the summer of 1984 only 42% of eligible
   companies had filed accounts and returns. Since then the position has improved and
   Department of Trade stated that by mid-summer 80% of companies should be up to date.
   In effect however that means some 150,000 to 200,000 companies will still be breaking the
   law. See *Financial Times* 29 April 1986.
8 Commission of the European Communities, *Industrial Policy and the Community*
   (November 1972–73).
9 68/151.
10 Companies Act 1985, s 35.
11 See 33.3.2.
12 77/91.
13 78/855.
14 78/660.
15 See Official Journal of the European Communities, 1983, NOC. 240/c.
16 82/891.
17 83/349.
18 84/353.
19 See 34.2.0.
20 See 33.3.0.
21 *Ashbury Railway Carriage and Iron Co Ltd v Riche* (1875) LR 7 HL 653 at 660, HL.
22 See [1897] AC 22; 33.0.0.
23 *Shuttleworth v Cox Bros & Co (Maidenhead) Ltd* [1927] 2 KB 9 at 12, CA.

Chapter 32

Partnership

Definition and formation of a partnership

32.0.0 Partnership is defined widely as the 'relationship which subsists between persons carrying on a business in common with a view to profit.'[1] However, the relationship between members of a company cannot be a partnership within the meaning of the PA 1890.[2] The courts may however impose obligations on the members of a company akin to those that arise in partnership.[3]

The 'persons' may be individuals or corporate bodies such as a limited company[4] or a local authority.[5] The term 'business' encompasses a potentially wide range of activities and includes every trade, occupation or profession.[6] One would perhaps expect that 'carrying on a business' implies some degree of continuity. However, the courts have been prepared to hold that a single transaction may amount to a partnership. Thus an agreement to purchase, repair and resell a house has been held to be a partnership[7] as was a temporary agreement between coal merchants in order to frustrate industrial action by miners.[8]

Chesterman observes:

> 'Thus the rules of partnership law, which inter alia impose fiduciary duties upon the partners inter se and in most instances render them all liable in respect of a single partner's conduct vis à vis the outside world, may become applicable to transitory or "one off" ventures which in other contexts might not merit the description "business".'[9]

The words 'with a view to profit' make it clear that the objective of the association must be financial reward in the form of a net gain for the benefit of the persons carrying on the business.

Because the law of partnership grew out of contract and agency, the basis of formation is consent, and no particular formality is required. Thus a contract may be entered into orally, by writing or may even be implied by the conduct of the parties.

In many cases it is clear that the parties intend to enter into partnership within the meaning of the PA 1890. However, there are situations where persons engage in some form of joint business activity without realising that they have, in law, entered into partnership. In such a situation the courts will assume the creation of a partnership based upon the conduct of the parties and their presumed intentions and the individuals concerned will thereby incur, perhaps, unexpected liabilities and duties.

At one point in time, it was considered that the receipt of part of the

436

profits of a business was conclusive to establish partnership.[10] A Committee in 1854 commented on the expediency:

> 'of enabling capitalists to lend money to traders at a rate of interest and agents and servants to receive remuneration for their services by money payments, varying with the profits of the business, without being exposed to the hazard of being rendered liable as partners to the creditors of the concern.'[11]

Thus in *Cox v Hickman*[12] the House of Lords accepted the proposition that the sharing of profits, on its own, does not create a partnership but represents cogent evidence of one. Lord Cranworth observed that:

> 'a right to participate affords cogent, often conclusive evidence, that the trade in which the profits have been made was carried on in part for or on behalf of the person setting up such a claim. But the real ground of liability is that the trade has been carried on by persons acting on his behalf. It is not correct to say that his right to share in the profits makes him liable to the debts of the trade. The correct mode of stating the proposition is to say . . . that the trade has been carried on on his behalf, ie that he stood in relation to principal towards the persons acting ostensibly as the traders.'[13]

Section 2 lays down basic rules for determining the existence of a partnership. These provide that:

(a) The joint or common ownership of property does not of itself create a partnership.

(b) The sharing of gross returns does not of itself create a partnership.[14] Gross returns represent funds generated by the business before the expenses are deducted and must be distinguished from net profits.

(c) The sharing of net profits is prima facie evidence of partnership, but the receipt of such a share or of a payment contingent on or varying with the profits of a business, does not of itself make a person a partner of a business. In other words, sharing profits creates a rebuttable presumption of partnership. The Act provides that no presumption of partnership will arise in five specific profit sharing situations. These are, first, the receipt by a person of a debt or other liquidated amounts by instalments out of profits;[15] second, an employee or agent receiving remuneration by a share in the profits of a business;[16] third, a widow who receives an annuity out of the profits of the business in which her husband was a partner;[17] fourth, a written loan agreement under which the lender receives a rate of interest varying with the firm's profits;[18] fifth, the sale of the goodwill of a business in return for a share of profits.[19]

In reality the determining factor is the precise terms of the contract and the intention of the parties as may be inferred from such terms and their conduct. The courts will infer a partnership from the reality of the relationship rather than labels used by the parties.

> 'If a partnership in fact exists, a community of interest in the adventure being carried on in fact, no concealment of name, no verbal equivalent for the ordinary phrases of profit or loss, no indirect expedient for enforcing control over the adventure will prevent the substance and reality of the transaction being adjudged to be a partnership; . . . no

437

phrasing of it by dextrous draftsmen . . . will avail to avert the legal consequences of the contract.'[20]

1   PA 1890, s 1(1).
2   S 1(2).
3   See *Ebrahimi v Westbourne Galleries Ltd* [1973] AC 360, [1972] 2 All ER 492, HL.
4   *Newstead (Inspector of Taxes) v Frost* [1980] 1 All ER 363, [1980] 1 WLR 135, HL.
5   *Jones v Secretary of State for Wales* (1974) 28 P & CR 280.
6   S 45.
7   *Winsor v Schroeder* (1834) 15 TC 602.
8   *John Gardner & Bowring, Hardy & Co v IRC* (1930) 15 TC 602.
9   Chesterman, *Small Businesses* (2nd Edn, 1982) 50.
10 See *Waugh v Carver* (1793) 2 Hy B1 235.
11 First Report of Mercantile Law Commission, 1854.
12 (1860) 8 HL Cas 268.
13 p 274.
14 S 2(2).
15 S 2(3)(a).
16 S 2(3)(b).
17 S 2(3)(c).
18 S 2(3)(d).
19 S 2(3)(e).
20 *Adam v Newbigging* (1888) 13 App Cas 308, HL, Lord Halsbury 325.

Partnership by holding out

32.0.1   Even where a person is not a partner, he may be liable as a partner where he has represented himself, or suffered himself to be represented as a partner. This is no more than the application of the general rules of agency by estoppel or holding out.[1] Thus section 14(1) of the PA provides that:

> 'everyone who by words spoken or written or by conduct represents himself, or who knowingly suffers himself to be represented, as a partner in a particular firm, is liable as a partner to anyone who has on the faith of any such representation given credit to the firm, whether the representation has or has not been made or communicated to the person so giving credit by or with the knowledge of the apparent partner making the representation or suffering it to be made.'

The contract is therefore made on the credit of the person concerned and he is therefore liable to the third party as if he were a partner. Such liability however only extends to partnership debts in respect of the person or persons misled. The partner by estoppel does not thereby become a partner and he does not incur any wider liability for the debts of the firm.

1   See 29.2.4.

Partnership identity

32.1.0   The PA 1890 lays down that persons who

> 'have entered into partnership with one another are for the purposes of the Act called collectively a firm, and the name under which their business is carried on is called the firm's name'.[1]

Under English partnership law the firm does not therefore have separate legal recognition. As Farwell LJ remarked in a case in 1910:

> 'In English law a firm as such has no existence; partners carry on business both as principals and agents for each other within the scope

of the partnership business; the firm name is a mere expression, not a legal entity, although for convenience . . . it may be used for the sake of suing and being sued . . . It is not correct to say that a firm carries on a business; the members of a firm carry on business under the name or style of the firm.'[2]

Under Scots law a firm is a legal person distinct from the partners.[3] In essence, a Scots partnership, in terms of status, lies midway between the English firm and a corporate body; it is a 'quasi-corporation possessing many, but not all, the privileges which the law confers upon a duly constituted corporation.'[4]

Such recognition of the legal status of a firm represents a more rational conceptual foundation for partnership law than does the English position, however, in terms of the overall authority and liability of the partners, there are few practical differences between the two systems.[5]

1   S 4(1).
2   *Sadler v Whiteman* [1910] 1 KB 868 at 889, CA.
3   S 4(2).
4   *Forsyth v Hare* (1834) 13 S 42 at 47.
5   See Burgess and Morse, *Partnership Law and Practice in England and Scotland* (1980).

Partnership name
32.1.1   It used to be the case that where a firm's name did not consist of the true surnames of all partners, the firm must be registered under the Registration of Business Names Act 1916. This legislation was however abolished in 1981 as part of a review of the cost and size of the Civil Service.[1]

The current regulations are contained in the Business Names Act 1985 and dispense with the need for registration, merely requiring publicity to be given in respect of the identity of partners, or if the business is a sole trader, the individual's name. The provisions apply where a business is carried on under a name which does not consist of the surnames or corporate name of all the partners, or in the case of a sole trader, his surname.[2] The use of certain business names is prohibited and certain words and expressions require formal approval from the appropriate government department or other specified body.[3]

1   See *Companies Registration and Business Names: Proposal for Reducing the Functions of the Department of Trade* (1980).
2   S 1.
3   S 2 and 3.

Partners' liability
32.2.0   Unlike the shareholders of a company who have the benefit of limited liability, every partner is liable jointly with the other partners for all the debts and obligations of the firm incurred whilst they remain a partner.[1] Thus each partner is liable jointly with the others and not on his own account. It used to be the case that judgment obtained against all the apparent partners which yielded insufficient funds barred fresh proceedings against a subsequently discovered 'sleeping' partner in the firm.[2] This rule was however circumvented by the procedural practice that a person suing the partners can sue them in the firm's name,[3] and thereby discover the identity of all the partners at the appropriate time. However, under the Civil

Liability (Contribution) Act 1978 judgment recorded against any person liable is no bar to an action against anyone who is jointly liable in respect of the same debt or damage.

1   S 9.
2   See *Kendall v Hamilton* (1879) 4 App Cas 504, HL.
3   See Rules of Supreme Court, Ord 81, r 1.

Partner agency

32.3.0   In relation to the business of the partnership all the partners are agents of the firm and one another.[1] Thus section 5 of the PA 1890 declares that every partner is an agent of the firm and his other partners for the purpose of the business of the partnership; and every partner who does any act for carrying on in the usual way of business of the kind carried on by the firm binds the firm and his partners.

Partners cannot be liable on a contract entered into by a partner without authority if the third party either knows the partner has no authority or does not know or believe him to be a partner.[2] Where a partner enters into a contract outside the scope of the business of the firm, his partners cannot be held liable unless he received authorisation to make the contract.[3]

1   See generally Part VI.
2   S 3.
3   S 7.

Implied or usual authority of partners

32.3.1   For a partner to bind the firm under s 5 his act must relate to the business and be the usual way of carrying on that business. As was stated in Bairds case:

> 'as between the partners and the outside world (whatever may be their private relations between themselves) each partner is the unlimited agent of every other in every matter connected with the partnership business, or which he represents as partnership business, and not being in its nature beyond the scope of the partnership.'[1]

Much therefore rests on the nature of the business and custom and practice in relation to that type of business. In general terms, however, the implied powers of a partner extend to the following transactions:
(a)   to buy and sell goods for the purpose of the business;
(b)   to engage employees for the business;
(c)   to receive payments of debts owing to the firm, and give receipts for them.
In the case of a partnership involved in buying and selling goods, the partner's authority extends to:
(a)   borrowing on the credit of the firm;
(b)   pledging goods or securities for the purpose of the business;
(c)   drawing, making, signing, indorsing, accepting, negotiating and discounting negotiable instruments.
Where the partners place limitations or restrictions on the power of individual partners to bind the firm, such provisions will not bind a third party dealing with a partner unless he has notice of the restriction, or, the particular transaction is outside the implied authority of the partner. Thus in

Mercantile Credit Co Ltd v Garrod[2] two persons entered into partnership in the business of letting of garages and undertaking vehicle repairs. They expressly excluded the buying and selling of cars. In breach of their agreement, one of the partners became involved in selling a vehicle to which he had no title; when the buyers discovered this they sought to recover the purchase price from his partner. It was held that the action should succeed, since selling a vehicle was clearly 'an act of a like kind to the business carried on by persons trading as a garage'.[3] The important factor was what was apparent to the outside world, not any exclusion provisions in the deed of partnership.

1 (1870) 5 Ch App 725, 733.
2 [1962] 3 All ER 1103.
3 At 1106.

Liability of partners in retirement and in tort
32.4.0 Unlike the shareholders of a company who have the benefit of limited liability, every partner is liable jointly with the other partners for all the debts and obligations of the firm incurred while he is a partner.[1] Liability in respect of the firm's contractual obligations is therefore joint. Thus each partner is liable jointly with the others and not on his own account. However, under the Civil Liability (Contribution) Act 1978, judgment obtained against one person jointly liable is no bar to action against others liable in respect of the same debt or damage. In practice a creditor would sue the partners as co-defendants.

1 S 9.

Liability of retiring partners
32.4.1 A retiring partner remains liable for the debts of the firm incurred whilst he was a partner. It is common when a partner retires for the other partners to agree to release him from such liability. However, unless the creditors are parties to such an agreement, the retiring partner remains liable to them with rights of indemnity against his former partners.

In general a retiring partner is not liable for debts contracted after his retirement. However, under s 36(1) of the PA 1890 'where a person deals with a firm after a change in its constitution he is entitled to treat all apparent members of the old firm as still being members of the firm unless he has notice of the change.' Thus in order to avoid continuing liability the retiring partner must give actual notice to existing customers. In respect of persons who have not dealt with the firm but who nevertheless know the person to be a partner, a notice in the *London Gazette* would suffice to protect the partner against liability.[1]

No liability can be incurred for debts contracted after retirement in respect of persons who did not know he was a partner.[2]

1 S 36(2).
2 *Tower Cabinet Co Ltd v Ingram* [1949] 2 KB 397, [1949] 1 All ER 1003.

Liability in tort
32.4.2 In accordance with the rules of agency, the wrongful acts or omissions of any partner acting in the course of business of the firm, or with

the authority of his co-partner, which causes loss or injury renders the firm liable to the same extent as the individual partner.[1] By contrast to a partner's contractual liability, liability in tort is joint and several,[2] so that judgment against one partner is no bar to subsequent action against one or more other partners.

Provided therefore that the wrongful act was committed whilst the partner was acting in the ordinary course of business or with his co-partners' authority, the firm will be liable. Liability for wrongful acts or omissions extends to such actions as negligence, fraud and other tortious act or omissions. It is irrelevant that the particular act was not committed for the firm's benefit.[3]

In respect of misapplication of money or property, the firm is liable for the actions of a partner where the funds were received by the partner within the scope of his apparent authority,[4] or where the funds were received by the firm and subsequently misapplied by a partner whilst in the custody of the firm.[5]

1 S 10.
2 S 12.
3 *Lloyd v Grace, Smith & Co* [1912] AC 716, HL.
4 See Ch 29.
5 S 11.

Duties and decisions

32.5.0 In terms of management rights, duties and decisions as between partners it is a matter of either contractual agreement or implication of the terms of the PA 1890. The Act makes it clear that the rights and duties of the partners, whether expressed in an agreement or implied by the PA 1890, may be varied at any time by the unanimous consent of the partners, which may be express or implied by a course of dealings.[1]

Consistent with the definition of a partnership which envisages carrying on a 'business in common', in the absence of a contrary agreement, every partner has the right to take part in the management of the partnership business.[2] In the event that a partner is excluded from management by his co-partners, a court may agree to the dissolution of the firm.[3] In any event, a partner cannot be expelled from the firm unless there is an express agreement to that effect.[4] The fundamental right to participate in management is so ingrained into partnership law that it has been applied by the courts to the affairs of small companies that are operated on the basis of mutual obligations between the founders of the company.[5]

It is commonplace for the agreement between partners to place a positive duty on them to contribute to the management of the business. Consistent with the right of partners to contribute to the management of the firm, they also have a right to access to the partnership books.[6]

1 S 19.
2 S 24(5).
3 S 35.
4 S 25.
5 See *Ebrahimi v Westbourne Galleries Ltd* [1973] AC 360, [1972] 2 All ER 492, HL and 33.2.5.
6 S 24(9).

Fiduciary duties

32.5.1 Bacon V-C in *Helmore v Smith*[1] observed that:

'If fiduciary relationship means anything . . . I cannot conceive a stronger case of fiduciary relations than that which exists between partners. Their mutual confidence is the life blood of the concern. It is because they trust one another that they are partners in the first place; it is because they continue to trust one another that the business goes on.'

Partnership being a fiduciary relationship based on mutual trust and good faith necessarily imposes upon the partners specific duties. These duties are for the most part codified in the PA 1890. Thus s 28 requires full disclosure by the partners of all things affecting the partnership, and s 29 requires every partner to:

'account to the firm for any benefit derived by him without the consent of the other partners from any transaction concerning the partnership, or from any use by him of the partnership property, name or business connection.'

Section 29(1) encompasses such activities as making a secret profit from a sale to or purchase from the firm,[2] as well as taking a benefit or opportunity which would have gone to or was of concern to the firm.[3]

Under s 30(1) a partner must account to the firm for any profit he makes by carrying on a business of the same nature and competing with that of the firm, unless he has the consent of his co-partners. Thus in *Aas v Benham*[4] a partner in a firm of shipbrokers involved in the chartering of ships used information obtained in the business to promote a shipbuilding company. The court held that the particular activity in question was 'wholly without the scope of the firm's business',[5] he was not therefore in competition and was not liable to account for the fees he received.

As fiduciaries, the majority must exercise their power in good faith for the overall benefit of the firm. The majority cannot expel a partner unless there is an express power to do so[6] and even where such a power exists, it must be exercised in accordance with principles of good faith.[7]

1 (1886) 35 Ch D 436 at 444.
2 See *Bentley v Craven* (1853) 18 Beav 75.
3 See *Industrial Development Consultants Ltd v Cooley* [1972] 2 All ER 162, [1972] 1 WLR 443 which concerned the activities of a managing director. See 35.1.6.
4 [1891] 2 Ch 244, CA.
5 At 256.
6 S 29.
7 See *Blisset v Daniel* (1853) 10 Hare 493 where the majority sought to expel a partner merely because they wanted to buy his share at a lower price.

Management decisions and expulsion

32.5.2 Under s 24(7) no person may be introduced as a partner without the consent of all existing partners. This provision reflects the element of mutual agreement and confidence upon which a partnership is based. It may be, however, that the necessary consent to the introduction of a person to succeed a retiring partner may be given in the partnership agreement itself.

In terms of the day to day management of the business, any dispute 'as to ordinary matters connected with the partnership business may be decided by a majority of the partners, but no change may be made in the nature of the partnership business without the consent of all existing partners.'[1] In practice, the agreement may provide that disputes should be referred to arbitration. There are restraints on the exercise by the majority of their power. Thus, the minority have a right to be consulted even though

> 'his opinion might be overruled, and honestly overruled, but he ought to have had the question put to him and discussed.'[2]

As a general rule the courts will not interfere between partners simply because they disagree.

> 'It is no part of the duty of the court to settle all partnership squabbles: it expects from every partner a certain amount of forbearance and good feeling towards his co-partner; and it does not regard mere passing improprieties, arising from infirmities or temper, as sufficient to warrant a decree for dissolution, or an order for an injunction, or a receiver.'[3]

This reluctance to interfere in the internal affairs of a business has been very much reflected in the judiciary's attitude towards disputes in limited companies.[4]

1   S 24(8).
2   *Coust v Harris* [1824] TR 496 at 525 Lord Eldon.
3   *Lindley on Partnership*, (1984) p 592.
4   See 31.2.0.

Partnership finance and property

32.6.0   In the absence of any agreement to the contrary, all the partners are entitled to share equally in the capital and profits of the business, and must contribute equally towards the losses whether of capital or otherwise sustained by the firm.[1] It may be that one partner provides all the capital for the business and the agreement makes it clear that he retains all rights in respect of that property.[2] In that event, the profits and losses of the business would be shared equally since it is clear from the Act that there is no necessary link between capital contributed and profit and loss. The agreement may additionally lay down the rules for the distribution of profits between the partners: losses would normally be shared in the same proportion as profits unless the agreement provides to the contrary. Simply because one partner works harder for the firm will not be grounds for displacing the agreed division of profits.[3]

A partner is entitled to be indemnified by the firm against personal liabilities incurred and payments made by him in the ordinary and proper conduct of the business; or in or about anything necessarily done for the preservation of the business or property of the firm.[4]

Interest is payable at a rate of 5% per annum on any actual payment or advance to the firm made by a partner, beyond agreed capital contribution.[5] A partner is not however entitled, before profits have been ascertained, to interest on a capital contribution.[6] In common with the other basic rules of partnerships, however, it is always open for the partners to agree to interest to be payable on capital brought into the business.

A partner is not entitled as of right to remuneration for conducting the business of the firm, the rewards for such endeavours are a share of the profits.[7] As far as property is concerned the Act makes it clear that all property, rights and interests in property originally brought into the partnership stock or acquired on account of the firm, or for the purposes and in the course of the partnership business, 'are partnership property'. Such property must be held and applied by the partners exclusively for the purpose of the partnership and in accordance with the agreement.[8]

In essence a partner's interest in partnership property is not a title to specific property but a right to his share after realisation of the assets of the business and payment of the debts and liabilities; partners are effectively joint owners of the property.

Sometimes difficult questions arise as to whether property belongs to the firm or to an individual partner. Thus when a partner brings property to the firm it should be made clear that he retains ownership of the property. In the absence of an express agreement, the intention of the parties must be ascertained as to whether particular items belong to the firm or individual partners. Thus in *Miles v Clarke*[9] two individuals 'drifted' into partnership without reaching a formal agreement. One of them contributed the goodwill and the other equipment and fittings. The business was carried on from premises leased to the partner who provided the equipment. In the context of a dispute over what was partnership property, the courts held that no more agreement between the parties should be assumed than was necessary to give business efficacy to their relationship. Thus, since the only agreement they had was in respect of the sharing of profits, partnership property was only that which had actually been consumed during the firm's business activities, that is, consumable stock in trade.

1   S 24(1).
2   S 24(1).
3   *Robinson v Anderson* (1855) 20 Beav 98.
4   S 24(2).
5   S 24(3).
6   S 24(4).
7   S 24(6).
8   S 20(1).
9   [1953] 1 All ER 779, [1953] 1 WLR 537.

Dissolution

32.7.0   In common with the liquidation of companies[1] a partnership may be dissolved with or without the intervention of the courts. In the case of dissolution without the courts, under the terms of the PA 1890 and subject to any contrary agreement, a partnership is dissolved:

(a) if entered into for a fixed term, by the expiration of that time;
(b) if entered into for a single venture or undertaking, by the termination of such venture or undertaking;
(c) by a partner giving notice in a partnership for an undefined time.[2]

Furthermore, a partnership may be dissolved on the happening of any event which renders the business illegal;[3] by the death or bankruptcy of any partner[4] or at the option of the other partners, or if any partner suffers his share to be charged by the court for his debts on an application by his creditors.[5]

In addition to the statutory grounds for dissolving a partnership, dissolution may be affected because of breach of the agreement giving rise to a right to dissolve.[6]

1   See 36.0.8.
2   S 32.
3   S 34.
4   S 33(1).
5   S 33(2).
6   See *Carmichael v Evans* [1904] 1 Ch 486.

Judicial dissolution
32.7.1   Section 35 lays down the grounds on which the court can dissolve a partnership. These are as follows:
(a) when a partner becomes permanently incapable of performing his part of the partnership agreement;
(b) when a partner has been guilty of conduct prejudicial to the firm's business;
(c) when a partner wilfully or persistently breaks the partnership agreement so that it is not reasonably practicable for the other members to continue;
(d) when the business of the partnership can only be carried on at a loss;
(e) when the court considers it just and equitable to order dissolution. This provision gives a wide discretion to the courts and covers such things as deadlock in the management, refusal to meet on matters of business or quarrelling and animosity such as to undermine confidence between the partners.[1]

1   See *Re Yenidje Tobacco Co Ltd* [1916] 2 Ch 426 at 430, CA.

Implications of dissolution
32.7.2   After the dissolution of a partnership the authority of each partner to bind the firm, and the other rights and obligations of the partners, continue so far as may be necessary to wind up the affairs of the firm and complete transactions initiated before the dissolution.[1] In respect of the settlement of accounts between the partners there are basic rules which must be followed in the absence of contrary agreement. First, losses must be paid out of profits, then out of capital and finally, if necessary, by the partners themselves in the proportion in which they agreed to share profits.[2] Second, the assets of the firm must be applied in the following order:[3]
(a) the debts and liabilities of the firm to non-partners;
(b) paying to each partner rateably what is due from the firm to him for advances as distinct from capital;
(c) paying to each partner rateably what is due from the firm to him in respect of capital.
In the event of there being a residue, it is divided among the partners in the proportion in which profits are divided. Similarly if the assets are not sufficient to repay the partners' capital in full, the deficiency must be borne by the partners in the same proportion as the profits would be divided.[4]

1   S 38.
2   S 44(a).
3   S 44(b).
4   See *Garner v Murray* [1904] 1 Ch 57.

Chapter 33
Corporate Status

33.0.0 The most significant attribute of incorporation is the notion that the company is a legal entity quite separate from its shareholders or officers. Unlike a partnership which under English law is simply a collection of individuals, a company has a separate legal personality of its own. A company is thus able to enjoy rights and is subject to obligations that are quite distinct from the members'. Even where the company is dominated by one person with effective ownership and control over the company's business and is, to all intent and purpose, a one-man operation, the doctrine of separate legal identity still operates.

It was not until the decision of the House of Lords in 1897 in *Salomon v A Salomon & Co Ltd*[1] that the consequences of a separate legal status for limited companies were fully articulated. The facts of the case illustrate the process by which a business is converted into a company. Salomon was a successful boot manufacturer and he decided to convert his business into a limited company. He registered the company, Salomon and Co Ltd, under the Companies Act with seven shareholders, himself with 20,001 shares and his wife and five children each with one share. In reality, therefore, the company was to be a 'one man company', with Salomon as the managing director. The next stage was to formally sell the original business to the newly formed company at an agreed price of £39,000, a sum which Lord Macnaghten described as representing:

> 'the sanguine expectations of a fond owner rather than anything that can be called a businesslike or reasonable estimate of value.'[2]

The price was paid to Salomon in the form of £9,000 in cash, £20,000 fully paid shares and secured debentures for £10,000.[3]

The company did not prosper and eventually went into liquidation leaving a number of unsecured creditors. The central feature of the litigation was a challenge to the priority of Salomon's secured debenture. It was argued that the company was merely acting as Salomon's nominee and agent and that Salomon as principal should not have priority but should indemnify the company's creditors. The High Court and the Court of Appeal accepted that argument but the House of Lords held that Salomon was entitled to be paid on his £10,000 secured debenture in priority to the unsecured creditors.

Lord Macnaghten observed that:

> 'The company is at law a different person altogether from the subscribers to the Memorandum and, although it may be that after

447

> incorporation the business is precisely the same as it was before, and the same people are managers and the same hands receive the profits, the company is not in law the agent of the subscribers or trustee for them nor are subscribers as members liable, in any shape or form, except to the extent and in the manner provided by the Act.'[4]

The decision of the House of Lords gave clear judicial recognition to the one man company and illustrated how it is possible not only to limit liability to the extent of the initial investment but also to avoid serious risk to an investment by subscribing for debentures instead of shares.

The impact of *Salomon* was that even where there was no business risk and no need to attract external investment, traders were induced by the law on an increasing scale to conduct their business in the form of a limited liability company. In effect the decision confirms the inherently insecure position of the creditors of a limited liability company. The decision was described by Kahn-Freund as 'calamitous' since it supported 'the rigidities of the "folklore" of corporate entity "against" the legitimate interests of the company's creditors.'[5]

Persons who deal with a company do so at their own risk, thus it is incumbent on creditors to search a company's file at the Companies Registry, although much of the information, even if filed on time, will be some months out of date. As Lord Watson observed in the *Salomon* case:

> 'A creditor who will not take the trouble to use the means which the statute provides for enabling him to protect himself must bear the consequences of his own negligence.'[6]

Both the courts and Parliament have recognised that the concept of separate corporate personality may be ignored where equitable, economic or moral considerations no longer justify its application.

The judiciary have never wholly overcome the formal restraints of *Salomon* and have displayed a marked reluctance to 'pierce the veil of incorporation'. Thus they have been prepared to disregard the separate entity principal only in cases where a company has been used as an alias or agent in order to perpetrate a fraud or other improper conduct.[7]

An area where the courts have disregarded the *Salomon* principle is in the relationship between a parent company and its subsidiary. It is common practice for a company to form subsidiaries in which the parent company owns all or most of the shares or is otherwise able to control the company. Under the *Salomon* principle each subsidiary is, in law, a separate company and even though it may be controlled by the parent, it is not regarded as its agent. However in *Smith, Stone and Knight Ltd v Birmingham Corpn*[8] it was held that in the circumstances of the case a subsidiary was the tool or agent of the parent company. Atkinson J identified the following six factors to be considered when deciding whether a subsidiary was carrying on the business of the parent:

(a) were the profits of the subsidiary those of the parent company?
(b) were the persons conducting the business of the subsidiary appointed by the parent company?
(c) was the parent company the head and brains of the trading venture?
(d) did the parent company govern the adventure?
(e) were the profits made by the subsidiary company made by the skill and direction of the parent?

(f) was the parent company in effective and constant control of the subsidiary?

In recent years the courts have moved away from an agency-based approach to groups in favour of recognising them as one economic unit. Thus in *DHN Food Distributors Ltd v London Borough of Tower Hamlets*[9] the Court of Appeal recognised the economic unit of the group as a single identity in order to enable them to recover compensation.

Templeman LJ has summarised the position under English company law in the following terms:

> 'English company law possesses some curious features, which may generate curious results. A parent company may spawn a number of subsidiary companies all controlled directly or indirectly by the shareholders of the parent company. If one of the subsidiary companies, to change the metaphor, turns out to be the runt of the litter and declines into insolvency to the dismay of the creditors, the parent company and the other subsidiaries may prosper to the joy of the shareholders without any liability for the debts of the insolvent subsidiary. It is not surprising that when a subsidiary collapses, the unsecured creditors wish the finances of the company and its relationship with other members of the Group to be narrowly examined, to ensure that no assets of the subsidiary company have leaked away; that no liabilities of the subsidiary company ought to be laid at the door of other members of the group, and that no indemnity from a right of action against any other company, or against any individual is by some mischance overlooked.'[10]

Indeed it has been argued that a parent company should be held liable for the debts of a wholly owned subsidiary that has become insolvent.[11]

In terms of financial reporting the Companies Act 1985 treats a group as one entity. Under s 299 where a company has subsidiaries and is not itself the wholly-owned subsidiary of another body corporate, it must prepare group accounts for individual companies in the group. Company law recognises that it is quite legitimate for a company to create subsidiaries perhaps in order to separate different activities within a corporate structure or for economic or administrative convenience, but there is a need to protect the public against the presentation of a misleading financial picture by the requirement to present a group balance sheet and profit and loss account.

Legislation also disregards the separate entity principle in that where the number of members falls below the statutory minimum, every member aware of the fact is liable jointly and severally with the company, for the debts of the company.[12] In addition, if it appears in the course of a winding up that any individuals have been knowingly party to any business carried on with intent to defraud creditors or for any fraudulent purpose, they may be personally liable.[13] This now also extends to directors guilty of wrongful trading.

1 [1897] AC 22, HL.
2 [1897] AC 22 at 49, HL.
3 A debenture is a document of indebtedness and the holder of a secured debenture is afforded some priority in respect of repayment in the event of a liquidation. See 34.3.0.
4 At 51.
5 1944 MLR 54.
6 Ibid p 40.

7   See eg *Gilford Motor Co v Horne* [1933] Ch 935, CA; *Jones v Lipman* [1962] 1 All ER 442, [1962] 1 WLR 832.
8   [1939] 4 All ER 116.
9   [1976] 3 All ER 462, [1976] 1 WLR 852, CA.
10   *Re Southard & Co Ltd* [1979] 1 WLR 1198 at 1208, CA.
11   See eg *Insolvency Law and Practice* Cmnd 8558, 1982, Ch 51.
12   S 24.
13   See Insolvency Act 1986, ss 213 and 214. See 36.0.12.

Consequences of the separate entity

33.0.1   The consequences of the *Salomon* principle and hence the formal advantages of incorporation over partnership, are that a company is able to enter into all forms of commercial transaction in its own name. A company may sue and be sued.[1]

A company also has the advantage of perpetual succession. Until it goes into formal liquidation a company continues and survives the departure of its officers and members. As was commented in 1850:

> 'This unbroken personality, this beautiful combination of the legal characters of the finite with essentials of infinity appears to have been the primary object of the invention of incorporation.'[2]

A further consequence is that the company owns its own property and assets. Shareholders have no proprietary claim over corporate property and assets other than a right to a share of the surplus assets after a company has been wound up. Thus:

> 'shareholders are not in the eyes of the law part owners of the undertaking. The undertaking is something different from the totality of the shareholding'.[3]

The consequences of the *Salomon* principle coupled with the benefit of limited liability and the relative ease with which companies, particularly private ones, could be formed has resulted in the steady growth in company registrations. As stated earlier, the *Salomon* decision encouraged businessmen to form companies, sometimes with a small share capital unable to support effective trading. For example, of the 81,639 companies registered with a share capital in 1982, 52,127 were formed with a share capital of £100 or less. Evidence given to the Jenkins Committee in 1962 referred to the 'irresponsible multiplication of companies' and 'the dangers of abuse through the incorporation with limited liability of very small undercapitalised businesses.'[4]

1   Although this is also now the case for partnerships. See 32.4.0.
2   *Grant on Corporation* (1850) p 4.
3   *Short v Treasury Comrs* [1948] KB 116 at 122, CA.
4   Evidence to the Jenkins Committee cited in *A New Form of Incorporation for Small Firms: A Consultative Document* Cmnd 8171, 1981.

Classification

33.1.0   In essence there are two basic legal approaches to the classification of companies. First, by reference to the liability of the members and second, by reference to private and public companies. Companies registered under the Companies Act 1985 (CA 1985) may be limited by shares, limited by guarantee or unlimited. The former are the commonest type of company whereby each member's liability is limited to the amount that remains unpaid on his shares. In the case of a company limited by guarantee the members' liability is limited to the amount which they agree to contribute to the company's assets in the event of an insolvent winding up; they are used for charitable and educational bodies.

Unlimited companies are companies where the members' liability is unlimited in the event of the company becoming insolvent. The company has all the benefits of corporate status except in relation to the members' liability. Since the availability of limited liability few companies opt for this form. However because of the unlimited liability there is less need for formal protection for creditors in respect of capital maintenance and disclosure of accounts and the rules in the Companies Acts are therefore relaxed for such companies.

The distinction between public and private companies dates back to the Companies Act 1907, which formally recognised the private company for the first time. The legislation restricted the membership of such companies to fifty, prohibited invitations to the public to subscribe for shares and required the constitution of the company to place restrictions on the right of a member to transfer his shares. Private companies were exempted from the ever increasing disclosure requirements laid on public companies.

The private company proved so popular that by 1914 the proportion of private companies being registered had increased to nearly four fifths of the total number of registered companies.[1] This trend continues today.[2] The Companies Act 1967 removed many of the privileges afforded to private companies in respect of non-disclosure. However, reforms initiated because of the UK's membership of the EEC and pressure to remove some of the disclosure burdens from smaller businesses has restored the privileged status to small private companies by exempting them from the need to lodge a full set of accounts with the Registrar of Companies. This trend towards a greater differentiation between private and public companies is likely to continue.[3]

Indeed the trend was hastened by the abandonment of the original 1907 basis of classification by the Companies Act 1980 which was passed to implement the Second EEC Directive. The current position is that the legislation defines a public company and a company that does not fall within the definition is a private company.

A public company is defined as a company limited by shares or by guarantee but having a share capital. The memorandum of the company must state that it is a public limited company (plc) and it must comply with the special provisions for registration of plcs. The major innovation introduced in 1980 was that the nominal value of a plc share capital must be not less than £50,000, of which one quarter must have been paid up. Thus if a company has a share capital whereby the nominal value of each share is £1, it must have allotted 50,000 shares and received at least £12,500 in cash or other consideration. Private companies are not required to have such a minimum capital base.

As a safeguard, a plc may not do business or exercise any borrowing powers until it has satisfied the conditions required by the legislation and the Registrar of Companies has issued a certificate certifying such compliance and entitling it to do business.[4]

The major disadvantage of private company status remains that such companies are prohibited from offering their securities to the public either directly or indirectly. In effect this means that they are limited in terms of the methods they may adopt for attracting funds for corporate growth.[5]

There are numerous other differences between public and private companies scattered around the legislation, some of which we shall identify later. Clearly if private companies are prohibited from offering their shares to the public there is less need for substantive and procedural devices designed to safeguard the public.

1 See Cottrell, *Industrial Finance 1830–1914* (1980) p 54.
2 At the end of 1983, 99.4% of registered companies were private.
3 *Burdens on Business: Report of a Scrutiny of Administrative and Legislative Requirements* (1985).
4 S 117(1). This is in addition to the certificate of incorporation which all companies are required to obtain from the Registrar.
5 See now Financial Services Act 1986, ss 170 and 143(3).

Formation
33.2.0 Companies are formed by the registration of certain documents with the Registrar of Companies. Until the promoters of a company have complied with the statutory registration formalities, the company does not exist. Hence any contracts that are made on behalf of a company before incorporation are not binding on it, nor can they be ratified on incorporation. In such circumstances the CA 1985 provides that a contract made by or on behalf of a company at a time when the company has not been formed shall take effect as one entered into by the person purporting to act for the company and he is liable on it unless the agreement provides to the contrary.[1] In practice it is often the case that persons seeking corporate status for their business may acquire a company from an agency 'off the shelf', that is, a company already registered.

1 CA 1985, s 36(4). See *Phonogram Ltd v Lane* [1982] QB 938, [1981] 3 All ER 182, CA.

Documentation
33.2.1 Incorporation by registration involves lodging with the Registrar certain documents. The main ones are the memorandum and articles of association. In general the memorandum deals with a company's external relations and is therefore required to state the name and country in which it is situated, its objects, liability of the members, initial share capital and the number of shares into which it is divided. The name and address of the original shareholders (subscribers) must be stated and the number of shares they take. If the company is a public company its public nature must be stated.

In respect of the name that a company chooses, it must not be the same as one already on the index of names retained by the Registrar.[1] The use of certain words in a company name requires specific approval from the Secretary of State for Trade or another relevant government official and the Secretary of State has the authority to refuse registration of a name that is offensive. The Secretary of State also has the authority to direct that a company change its name.[2]

The articles of association regulate the internal affairs of the company. In particular they deal with the procedure at meetings, share transfers and transmission, class rights and dividends. It is common practice for companies to adopt, with appropriate modifications, the model articles set out in Table A contained in regulations made under the 1985 Act.[3]

1   S 26.
2   S 28.
3   See The Companies (Tables A-F) Regulations 1985, SI 1985/805.

The role of the Registrar

33.2.2   It is the role of the Registrar to ensure that the documents presented are in conformity with the statutory requirements and all the necessary formalities have been completed. The Registrar has no general supervisory or regulatory role in respect of incorporation, his function is purely administrative. Thus if the documentation is correct, the formalities have been complied with and the purpose of the proposed enterprise is lawful, the Registrar must issue the certificate of incorporation. When the certificate of incorporation is issued it means that the members formally constitute a corporate body and is conclusive evidence of the status of the company and of compliance with the requirements of the Act.[1]

1   S 13(7).

Effect of registration and the doctrine of constructive notice

33.2.3   Because certain documents are lodged with the Registrar and available for the public to inspect, they are termed public documents and everyone dealing with the company is deemed to have notice of the contents of such documents. A company's public documents include its memorandum and articles, special resolutions[1] passed at company meetings and particulars of charges registered on its property.

The effect of this doctrine is that persons who deal with a company without consulting its public documents are treated as aware of any limitations on the capacity of the company or authority of the directors. In terms of the law of agency however the worst effects of the doctrine were mitigated by the development of a rule which provided that if a transaction is apparently consistent with the public documents, persons dealing with a company are not prejudiced by internal irregularities.[2]

The rule was largely abolished in s 9(1) of the European Communities Act 1972, now CA 1985 s 35, in the case of a person dealing with a company in good faith in respect of transactions decided upon by the directors.[3]

1   These are normally passed at meetings authorising constitutional changes.
2   The so called rule in *Royal British Bank v Turquand* (1856) 6 E & B 327, Ex Ch.
3   See 33.3.2.

Continuing disclosure requirements

33.2.4   In addition to the documentation that must be registered as a condition of incorporation, the company has a continuing obligation to file certain documents with the Registrar and hence make them available to the public. Thus a company must make an annual return which represents an update of its registered particulars. It must also file a profit and loss account and balance sheet every year unless it qualifies as a small or medium sized private company in which case certain exemptions apply.[1] In addition, certain other documents must be filed as and when the activity concerned takes place. These include details of special and extraordinary resolutions;[2] particulars of registrable charges;[3] particulars of directors and company secretary; appointment of a receiver or liquidator[4] and resignation of auditors.

In certain cases when the Registrar receives information, in addition to filing it in the company's file, he is required to give wider notice of the issue or receipt of certain documents.[5] Such notice is given in the *London Gazette*.[6]

1   S 248.
2   S 123.
3   S 395.
4   Ss 469 and 534.
5   S 711(1).
6   For a discussion of the rationale of disclosure see 31.2.0. See also *The Delivery of Annual Accounts and Returns to the Registrar of Companies. A Consultative Document* (1984).

Corporate capacity

33.3.0   As stated above the memorandum of association regulates the relationship between a company and outsiders. In particular it contains the objects clause which defines the contractual capacity of the company. Unlike an individual or a partnership a company can only pursue objects which are authorised by its objects clause. If it purports to carry out any activity which is not authorised by its stated objects, that activity will be ultra vires and void.

The so-called ultra vires doctrine had not generally applied to trading organisations prior to the 1850s. This was largely due to the fact that such bodies did not have the benefit of limited liability and therefore creditors had no need of protection. With the granting of limited liability and the growth of the great speculative ventures of that era there became a need to confine trading activities within clearly defined limits. Thus in *Ashbury Railway Carriage and Iron Co Ltd v Riche*[1] the House of Lords was called upon to consider whether the construction of a railway was consistent with objects permitting carrying on business as 'mechanical engineers and general contractors'. Their Lordships held that the transaction was ultra vires and that, being ultra vires, it could not be later validated by the members.

The severity of this decision was somewhat mitigated in the latter case of *A-G v Great Eastern Rly Co*[2] where the court recognised the implied powers of a company so that whatever is reasonably incidental to carrying out express objects will be intra vires.

The natural response of incorporators to the development of the ultra vires rule was to extend the length of objects clauses to include all manner of lawful activities in which the company may wish to engage. Thus Lord Wrenbury observed of the practice in *Cotman v Brougham* in 1918:

> 'It has arrived now at a point at which the fact is that the function of the memorandum is taken to be, not to specify, not to disclose, but to bury beneath a mass of words the real object or objects of the company, with the intent that every conceivable form of activity shall be found included somewhere within its terms.'[3]

The courts vainly attempted to attack such lengthy objects clauses by embracing 'the main objects rule' of interpretation. Thus where an objects clause listed a series of objects the courts would identify what they regarded as the dominant object and treat all others as ancillary thereto.[4] The response from the draftsman of objects clauses was simply to insert a clause to the effect that all clauses were to be regarded as independent and entirely separate objects clauses. Despite the reservations of Lord Wrenbury such clauses were held to be effective by the House of Lords in *Cotman v Brougham*.[5]

Some years later in *Re Introductions Ltd*[6] the Court of Appeal placed some restraint on the utility of such clauses by holding that a *Cotman v Brougham* clause could not convert a power to borrow money into an object in itself. The power to borrow money, even if expressly stated in the objects clause, could only be exercised in furtherance of an object.

In more recent cases the courts have asserted that the question as to whether a 'stated object' is really an independent object or a mere power is essentially one of construction. Even the borrowing of money can be an independent object in the case of an ordinary trading company if, as a matter of construction the memorandum permits it.[7]

A further attempt at evading the ultra vires rule has been the use of very broad subjective clauses. Thus in *Bell Houses Ltd v City Wall Properties Ltd*[8] the court was called upon to consider an objects clause which incorporated a power—

'to carry on any trade or business whatsoever which can, in the opinion of the board of directors, be advantageously carried on by the company in connection with or as ancillary to any of the above business or the general business of the company.'

The court considered that the natural meaning of such a clause was that, provided the directors honestly consider that the activity can advantageously be carried on in relation to the main business, it thereby validates the activity. It remains open to debate whether the courts would take the same approach if such a clause was submitted as one of the main objects of the company.

It will be recalled that the doctrine of constructive notice operates in respect of persons dealing with the company. Thus if it is apparent from the objects clause that the activity in question is ultra vires the contracting party will be unable to enforce the contract. Thus in *Re Jon Beauforte (London) Ltd*[9] a coke merchant supplied coke to a company originally formed to manufacture ladies' clothing. At the time of the order for coke the company was, however, manufacturing wooden panels as was known to the coke merchant. In the context of the merchant's claim for the debt in the company's liquidation, it was held that since he had constructive notice of the company's objects clause and actual notice of ultra vires business the transaction was unenforceable.[10]

Where a person lends money to a company which intends to use the funds for an ultra vires purpose, the lender can recover the funds provided he had no knowledge of the ultra vires purpose.[11]

1   (1875) L R 7 HL 653.
2   (1880) 5 App Cas 473, HL.
3   [1918] AC 514 at 523, HL.
4   See *Re German Date Coffee Co* (1882) 20 Ch D 169, CA.
5   They are often described as *Cotman v Brougham* clauses.
6   [1970] Ch 199, [1969] 1 All ER 887, CA.
7   See *Re Horsley & Weight Ltd* [1982] Ch 442, [1982] 3 All ER 1045, CA. *Rolled Steel Products (Holdings) Ltd v British Steel Corpn* [1986] Ch 246, [1985] 3 All ER 52, CA.
8   [1966] 2 QB 656, [1966] 2 All ER 674, CA.
9   [1953] Ch 133, [1953] 1 All ER 634.
10 But see CA 1985, s 35.
11 See *Re David Payne & Co Ltd, Young v David Payne & Co Ltd* [1904] 2 Ch 608, CA.

Corporate gifts
33.3.1 Payments to charities and educational and research bodies are becoming increasingly attractive in terms of the marketing and public relations policy of British companies, in addition to the more tangible benefits derived from sponsoring research. The Conservative party also derives a substantial proportion of its funds from corporate gifts. The only specific provision of company law dealing with such payments is that they must be disclosed in the annual directors' report.[1]

In general if the making of charitable or political payments is expressly authorised by the objects clause then such payments cannot be challenged on grounds of ultra vires. Indeed in *Re Horsley & Weight Ltd*[2] Buckley LJ observed that:

> 'The objects of a company do not need to be commercial; they can be charitable or philanthropic; indeed, they can be whatever the original incorporators wish, provided that they are legal. Nor is there any reason why a company should not part with its funds gratuitously or for non-commercial reasons if to do so is within its declared objects.'[3]

Where gratuitous payments are not within a company's express objects they may nevertheless be intra vires provided that they are reasonably incidental to the company's business. Thus in *Evans v Brunner, Mond and Co*[4] it was held reasonably incidental to the objects of a chemical company to make donations to research institutions, despite the fact that the company's competitors would derive an equal advantage from such expenditure.

Irrespective of whether the gratuitous payment was made under a clause in the objects or implied by the incidental nature of the payment, if the directors exceed their own powers as laid down in the constitution of the company or otherwise act improperly, the transaction may be challenged. However, since such challenge is not founded on ultra vires, the directors' actions in respect of such transactions could be ratified by the general meeting. Where the directors act improperly in a transaction and the third party creditor is aware of the impropriety, the transaction may be challenged and corporate funds recovered.[5]

1 S 235(3).
2 [1982] Ch 442 [1982] 3 All ER 1045, CA.
3 At 105.
4 [1921] 1 Ch 359.
5 See *Rolled Steel Products (Holdings) Ltd v British Steel Corpn* [1986] Ch 246, [1985] 3 All ER 52, CA; see also 35.0.3.

Effect of an ultra vires transaction
33.3.2 As can be seen from the case of *Re Jon Beauforte*[1] the doctrine of constructive notice and the ultra vires rules as developed by the courts far from protect creditors of a company. Indeed the Cohen Committee in 1945 recommended the abolition of the ultra vires rule in respect of third parties. They observed:

> 'In consequence the doctrine of ultra vires is an illusory protection for the shareholders and yet may be a pitfall for third parties dealing with a company . . . as now applied to companies the doctrine serves no useful purpose but is, on the other hand, a cause of unnecessary prolixity and vexation.'[2]

An ultra vires transaction is void and unenforceable. If it is still possible to trace payment or property it may be possible to recover funds or goods.[3] Furthermore, if an ultra vires loan was used to pay an intra vires debt, the lender is able to 'stand in the shoes' of the intra vires creditor in terms of recovery, although he will not be entitled to the benefit of any security.

Section 9(1) of the European Communities Act 1972 introduced a measure of protection for the creditor of a company caught up in an ultra vires transaction. Since the existing members of the community had already agreed and implemented the First EEC Directive on Company Law harmonisation it was necessary to include provisions in the 1972 Act implementing the directive in the UK. The provisions are now contained in s 35 of the CA 1985 and provide that in respect of a person acting in good faith, any transaction decided on by the directors is deemed to be one which it is within the capacity of the company to enter into, and the power of the director to bind the company is deemed to be free of any limitation under the memorandum or articles. Furthermore, a party to a transaction so decided on is not bound to enquire as to the capacity of the company to enter into it or as to any such limitation on the powers of the directors, and is presumed to have acted in good faith unless the contrary is proved.

The provision clearly does not abolish the ultra vires rule; it simply seeks to protect a creditor by allowing him to enforce an ultra vires transaction against the company should a number of conditions exist. Unfortunately the terms of the provision are drafted in ambiguous and wholly unsatisfactory language.

The first condition that a creditor is required to satisfy is that of good faith. The onus is on the company to establish the absence of good faith. This may be satisfied by proving that the creditor had actual knowledge that the transaction was ultra vires or where it can show that the creditor could not in all the circumstances, have been unaware of the ultra vires character of the transaction.

The second condition is that the person must be dealing with the company. The use of the words dealing and transaction in the section suggests that it is intended to confine the scope of the section to contractual obligations. It is debatable therefore whether it extends to gratuitous obligations and gifts.[4]

The third condition is that the transaction must be decided upon by the directors. If it is intended that the protection should only extend to those transactions actually authorised or at least ratified by the board, then the provision is extremely limited since, proportionately, few transactions are decided upon by the board. Such an interpretation would preclude claims arising out of transactions entered into by a single director, such as the managing director, unless the board has conferred general authority on the director. The Directive itself talks in terms of organs of the company which would encompass transactions by the general meeting, possibly individual officers of the company, as well as the board. The implementing section is however worded in much narrower terms than the Directive.

In one of the few judicial pronouncements on the section Lawton J observed that where a company has only one sole effective director to whom all actual authority to act for the company is effectively delegated, dealings by him would be 'decided on by the directors' within the terms of the section.[5]

1   See 33.3.0 at note 8.
2   Cmnd 6659 para 12. See also *Reform of the Ultra Vires Rule. A Consultative Document* (Dept of Trade and Industry, 1986).
3   See *Sinclair v Brougham* [1914] AC 398, HL.
4   Although under Scots law such obligations may be enforceable as contracts.
5   *International Sales and Agencies Ltd v Marcus* [1982] 3 All ER 551, [1982] 2 CMLR 46; See also *TCB v Gray* [1986] Ch 621, [1986] 1 All ER 587.

Alteration of objects

33.3.3   A company may alter its objects[1] if the alteration is made for one or more of a number of specified purposes. Consistent with most changes to a company's constitution of a major nature, the alteration must be approved by special resolution at a general meeting, that is, one requiring a seventy-five per cent majority of those voting. Minority shareholders and debentures holders have a right to object to the alteration but in practice very few cases are heard.[2]

1   CA 1985, s 4.
2   S 5.

Shareholder status

33.4.0   When shares are acquired in a company the holder does not obtain assets in the form of a claim over the property of the company. In the words of Lord Parker:

'In the case of land the owner possesses a tangible asset, whereas a shareholder has no direct share in the assets of the company. He has such rights as the memorandum and articles give him.'[1]

The Permanent Court of International Justice summarised the status of shareholders in the following terms:

'The decisions of the principle or the highest court of most countries continues to hold that neither the shareholders nor their creditors have any right to the corporate assets other than to receive during the existence of the company, a share of the profits, the distribution of which has been decided by a majority of shareholders and after its winding up a proportion of the assets.'[2]

The nature of the relationship between shareholder and company is purely contractual, based on the memorandum and articles of association. Thus s 14 of CA 1985 provides that—

'subject to the provisions of the Act, the memorandum and articles, when registered, bind the company and its members to the same extent as if they had been signed and sealed by each member and contained covenants on the part of each member to observe all the provisions . . .'

Unlike most contracts which can only be altered by mutual agreement, the shareholders' bargain can be altered by the company at any time. Section 14 states that it is subject to the provisions of the Act, and the Act contains a provision[3] giving the company the power to alter the articles, subject to approval by a special resolution. Thus the minority shareholder is in a somewhat exposed position. In addition, the full range of contractual remedies may not be available to shareholders, only injunction and declaration are considered appropriate.

1   *Short v Treasury Comrs* [1948] KB 116 at 122.
2   *Standard Oil Co Tankers Claim* (1927) BYIL at 156.
3   S 9.

Effect of the memorandum and articles

33.4.1   The precise scope of the shareholders' bargain, as stated in s 14, has been the subject of considerable judicial and academic debate.[1] In general the position may be reduced to the following propositions:

(a)   The member is bound to the company on a contract to observe the terms of memorandum and articles.[2]

(b)   The section only creates rights and duties in respect of the shareholder's membership of the company. Thus, if the memo or articles stipulate other rights for outsiders or rights in respect of the shareholders acting in some other capacity, such as director or company secretary, such provisions do not form part of the contract under s 14. They must be the subject of a separate bargain. For example, if the articles stipulate that a particular shareholder should be the company's solicitor, such a stipulation would not be contractually binding on the company.'[3] However, a stipulation in the articles could, expressly or impliedly, form the basis of a separate contract between the company and the individual concerned.[4] Such a contract would of course be concluded on the basis that the terms of the articles and hence the contract could be altered by the company in general meeting.

It has been suggested that a shareholder may seek to enforce outsider provisions in the articles under a general right to require corporate business to be conducted in conformity with the constitution as embodied in the articles.[5] Whilst the argument has considerable merit, the weight of judicial comment supports the view that—

> 'no right merely purporting to be given by an article to a person, whether a member or not, in a capacity other than that of a member, as for instance, a solicitor, promoter, director, can be enforced against the company.[6]

As Gower points out, however, the section is 'so overlaid with judicial interpretation that, on any count, it no longer means what it says. A rephrasing of it is long overdue . . .'[7]

(c)   A further effect of s 14 is that the shareholders are contractually bound to each other by the terms of the memo and articles, in respect of their membership rights and obligations.[8]

1   See *Wedderburn* (1957) CLJ 193; Gower, *Modern Company Law* (4th Edn 1979), p 337; Prentice, *Company Lawyer* (1980) p 179.
2   *Hickman v Kent or Romney Marsh Sheep-breeders' Association* [1915] 1 Ch 881.
3   *Eley v Positive Government Security Life Assurance Co* (1876) 1 Ex D 88, CA.
4   *Re New British Iron Co, ex p Beckwith* [1898] 1 Ch 324.
5   See note 1 and *Quin and Axtens Ltd v Salmon* [1909] AC 442, HL.
6   Astbury J in *Hickman v Kent or Romney Marsh Sheep-breeders' Association* [1915] 1 Ch 881 at 900.
7   (1979) p 320.
8   *Rayfield v Hands* [1960] Ch 1, [1958] 2 All ER 194.

Alteration of the articles

33.4.2   Subject to the provisions of the Act and any conditions in the memorandum, a company has the right to alter its articles by special resolution.[1] In terms of statutory restrictions on such alteration a company cannot alter its articles to require a shareholder to take more shares, or otherwise increase their liability to the company.[2]

The courts have statutory powers to amend or alter the articles of a company in the context of a variety of disputes.[3] They may also resolve that such alterations cannot be further amended or cancelled without their consent but in the absence of such a condition, the company may amend the articles under the general rule.

Any alteration must be consistent with the overall duty of the corporate controllers to act in good faith for the benefit of the company as a whole. Lindley MR in *Allen v Gold Reefs of West Africa Ltd*,[4] when discussing the power to alter the articles, observed that:

> 'the power conferred by it must, like all other powers, be exercised subject to those general principles of law and equity which are applicable to all powers conferred on majorities and enabling them to bind minorities. It must be exercised, not only in the manner required by law, but also bona fide for the benefit of the company as a whole and it must not be exceeded.'

Since this is one aspect of a general requirement to act in good faith it is discussed at 35.1.2.

1   S 9.
2   S 16(1).
3   See eg ss 5(5), 17(3), 54(6), 461(1).
4   [1900] 1 Ch 656, CA. See 35.1.2.

Chapter 34
Corporate Capital

34.0.0 When discussing the capital of a company it is important to recognise the fundamental distinction between its share capital and loan capital. Every company limited by shares must state in its memorandum the number of shares with which the company proposes to be registered and the nominal value of each share into which the share capital is divided.[1] This nominal capital sets the maximum number of shares that the company may issue. In practice the promoters of the company will, however, only issue the number of shares that are necessary to initially provide the business with sufficient working capital. Further shares may be issued at a later date as and when required and if the company finds that it needs to issue further shares in excess of the original nominal capital, the memorandum may be altered to increase its capital. It will be recalled that the nominal value of a plc's issued capital must be at least £50,000; there is no such minimum for a private company. However, whether public or private, a company must have at least two shareholders. Thus a private company could have a nominal capital of 5,000 £1 shares of which only two have been issued. In such circumstances clearly the company would require to be financed from loans perhaps supported by personal guarantees from the directors.

The nominal value of each share is normally fixed at £1 or under. In practice the nominal or face value attached to a share does not in any way reflect its real value. It is simply a means of assessing the liability of a shareholder; once the nominal value of a share has been paid plus any premium,[2] the shareholder's liability is extinguished. The concept of a nominal value for each share is also of use when calculating dividends since they are invariably expressed as a percentage of the nominal value. The articles may also attach different voting rights to shares with a lower nominal value.

Proposals have been made which would allow companies to issue 'no par value' shares which would focus attention on the actual funds which the company receives for its shares at prices which would vary from time to time.[3]

The articles of a company may divide its share capital into various classes, each with distinct rights. It may be, for example, that the original founders of a company want to ensure their control of the company by taking shares which carry more votes than the other classes. Indeed, issuing shares can be a difficult choice for a company as between the benefits of attracting further finance and the disadvantages of upsetting the existing balance of power in the company by issuing further shares each of which carries one or more votes. The CA 1985 does seek to permit existing ordinary shareholders to maintain their proportionate stake in a company by giving them a right to participate in any new issues[4] but the provisions do allow companies to opt out of such statutory pre-emption rights and a great many do so.

The most common division between shares is into ordinary or equity shares and preference shares. Ordinary shares normally carry full voting rights and equal rights to profits by way of dividends and a share of surplus assets after the winding up of the company. Preference shares carry the right to a fixed dividend expressed as a percentage of the nominal value of the shares, preference as to payment of such dividend and repayment of capital in the event of a winding up. Preference shareholders normally have limited voting rights.

A company which has shares of different classes may require to vary the rights attaching to them. In such a case the company must comply with any procedure for variation of class rights laid down in the memorandum or articles.[5] In addition where the class rights have been varied s 127 gives the holders of not less than 15% of the issued shares of the class in question who did not consent to or vote in favour of the variation the right to apply to the court to have the variation cancelled. The court must disallow the variation if it is satisfied that it would unfairly prejudice the holders of the class of shares concerned.

The courts have taken a very narrow view of what amounts to a variation of rights. For example, it is not considered to be a variation of rights to issue more shares of the same class, thus diluting the effective rights of existing class members.[6] The courts have drawn the distinction between an affecting of the rights of shareholders and an affecting of the enjoyment of the rights; issuing preference shares to the ordinary shareholders merely affects the existing preference shareholders' enjoyment of their rights[7] and hence there is no need to use the variation of rights procedure.

1 S 2(5).
2 An amount in excess of the nominal value of the shares which does reflect its marketability.
3 See Gedge Committee 1954, Cmnd 9112; Jenkins Committee 1962, Cmnd 1749.
4 Ss 89–96.
5 S 125.
6 See *White v Bristol Aeroplane Co Ltd* [1953] Ch 65, [1953] 1 All ER 40.
7 See *Re John Smith's Tadcaster Brewery Co Ltd* [1953] Ch 308.

Value of shares
34.0.1 As indicated above the nominal value of shares does not provide any indication of the real market value of shares for the shareholder or investor. At a simple level the real value of shares may be calculated by dividing the net assets of the company after making deductions for the repayment of any outstanding commitments by the total number of shares.

There are however a number of variable factors which must be taken into account. Obviously in the case of a plc there may be a market in the shares which will result in a price for the shares quoted on the stock exchange. However, only about half the plcs in the UK have their shares quoted on the stock exchange and of course the vast majority of companies are private, in which case there is no official public market for their shares.

It is generally accepted that there are four factors which influence the value attached to the shares of a company.[1] These are capital cover, dividend yields, earnings ratio and marketability.

Capital cover relates to the extent to which a company's net assets at any time are sufficient to repay the share capital to the holders. Capital cover is particularly significant for preference shareholders since they only obtain a fixed dividend irrespective of how much the profits of a company increase. In the case of equity shares, insufficient capital cover could be compensated for in increased dividends and hence higher earnings.

Dividend yield represents the proportion which the dividends paid by a company bears to the price which must be paid for the shares. Obviously since the yield is dependent on the dividend paid, if the company retains a high proportion of its profits and hence distributes only a small dividend, the value of its shares may be adversely affected. The yield on shares can also be affected by the company's gearing, that is, the relationship between fixed return capital (preference shares and debenture interest) and capital with a variable return (such as ordinary shares).[2]

The third factor is the company's actual earnings or profits. All things being equal if a company is generating higher profits than its competitors, then the value of its shares will reflect such profitability. Such will be the case even where the company elects not to distribute any additional profits to the shareholders by way of dividends, but returns them to the business for investment in future expansion.[3]

Finally, there is the marketability factor. This includes such things as the personality of the directorate; the corporate image; whether there is one person or group that holds voting control; the chances of reselling the shares should the need arise. This latter factor is particularly important, since potential shareholders do not want to be locked into a company.[4]

1   See Pennington, *Company Law* (5th Edn 1985) pp 158–162.
2   See Pennington, op cit p 160.
3   And hence future profits and much improved yield.
4   See 34.2.2.

Loan capital

34.1.0   By contrast to the share capital of a company there are fewer legal restrictions on the amount which a company can raise by way of loans. There is no equivalent concept of nominal or authorised loan capital, although in practice the articles may contain some limitations on the ability of a company to raise funds by the issue of debentures. A debenture is simply the document acknowledging a debt. Therein lies the basic distinction between share and loan capital. The holder of a share is a member of the company with rights to participate in its affairs, as expressed in the articles of the company. The shareholder has the right to the return of his capital injection in a winding up provided that there are funds available after the creditors have been paid, otherwise the share capital cannot be returned to the holder by the company.[1] A loan represents a debt against the company, it gives precise contractual rights against the company but does not entail membership of the company. It may be returned to the investor at any time or on or after the expiration of a fixed period. In the event of the winding up of a company the holder of a debenture ranks alongside other creditors and is entitled to be repaid in full before capital is returned to the shareholders.

Invariably a person advancing a loan to a company will require some form of security over the assets of the company. In that event the holder ranks as a secured creditor and in the event of a winding up is entitled to take the benefit of the security to the extent of the amount outstanding on the loan. A secured creditor takes priority over an unsecured creditor such as an ordinary trade creditor.

1 See 34.2.2.

Share capital maintenance

34.2.0 Over the years the courts and Parliament have developed rules specifically designed to ensure that the capital subscribed by the shareholders should remain intact as a guarantee fund for the creditors. Indeed the original justification for the ultra vires rule was that the capital of a company should not be applied to objects not authorised by the memorandum.[1] In reality, it is not always possible to maintain the actual value of the capital: in particular the capital injected into a company by the shareholders has to be used to buy plant and machinery, stock in trade and other items necessary for the business. The value of such items may seriously diminish and if the company makes trading losses the actual value of the company's capital may be reduced below the nominal value of its issued shares. In such circumstances provided that the company remains solvent, such a loss of capital would not prohibit the company from trading.[2]

Indeed this much was recognised by the courts when they conceived the capital maintenance concept. Lord Herschell observed in 1889:

> 'The distinction between a company without limit on the liability of its members and a company where the liability is limited is in the latter case to assure those dealing with the company that the whole of the subscribed capital unless diminished by expenditure upon the objects defined in the memorandum shall remain available for the discharge of its liabilities. The capital might be diminished by expenditure upon and reasonably incidental to all the objects specified. A part might be lost in carrying on the business operations authorised. Of this all persons trusting the company are aware and take the risk. But they have a right to rely and were intended by the legislature to have a right to rely on the capital remaining undiminished by any expenditure outside those limits, or by the return of any part of it to the shareholders.'[3]

Where shares are issued at a premium, that is, at a price above their nominal value, the premium is subject to the same rule. Thus a sum equal to the total amount of the premium must be transferred to a share premium account which to all intents and purposes is treated as share capital. It cannot therefore be returned to the shareholders as a dividend but may be returned as bonus shares.[4]

1 See 33.3.0.
2 In the case of a plc it may however have to call a general meeting to discuss the problem. See s 142.
3 *Trevor v Whitworth* (1889) 12 App Cas 409 at 415, HL.
4 See s 130.

Consequences of capital maintenance

34.2.1 As a consequence of the capital maintenance rule the courts and later the legislature developed specific prohibitions on companies buying their own shares, financing the purchase of their own shares and paying dividends out of capital.

Companies buying their own shares

34.2.2 Since the decision of *Trevor v Whitworth* [1] it has been accepted that a company cannot buy its own shares. This rule received statutory confirmation in 1980 and is now contained in CA 1985, s 143. Gower explains the rationale of the rule in the following terms:

'Such acquisitions are dangerous, not only because they might result in the reduction of capital yardstick to the detriment of the creditors, but also because, if the company paid more than the true worth of the shares, it would dilute the value of the remainder while, if it paid too little, it would increase the value of the remainder and might be used by the directors to enhance the value of their own holdings. Moreover, such purchases might be used by the directors to maintain themselves in control.' [2]

Legislation in 1929 did permit the issue of redeemable preference shares. These represent shares which could be bought back at the instance of the company or the shareholders. They were confined to preference shares since such shares do not afford any voting control and do not fluctuate in value to the same extent as equity shares. In 1981 the provisions were extended to permit a company to issue any class of redeemable shares provided that it has some shares which are not redeemable. [3]

The original facility to issue redeemable shares did not, however, compromise the capital maintenance concept since the shares could only be redeemed out of the proceeds of a fresh issue or out of the company's profits available for distribution. [4] In the latter case, the company must transfer an amount representing the extent of the share capital redeemed out of profits to a special fund known as the capital redemption reserve. [5] The reserve fund is treated in the same manner as if it were share capital and cannot therefore be distributed to the shareholders in the form of dividends. In other words when the shares are being redeemed the share capital they represent is either being replaced by the fresh issue of shares or in the case of redemption out of profits, retained for accounting purposes by the transfer to capital redemption reserve.

In the Companies Act 1981 provisions were however introduced which permitted all companies to purchase or redeem their own shares, and in the case of private companies, to do so out of capital. The provisions were inspired by a Green Paper published in 1980, 'The Purchase by a Company of Its Own Shares'. [6] The importance of the change was summarised in the following terms:

'The Government attaches particular importance to the principal economic arguments in favour of a relaxation of the present law. For private companies, a change should make investment and participation in such companies more attractive, by providing shareholders with a further means of disposing of their shares and by permitting the remaining members to maintain control and ownership of the business. Different considerations apply to companies whose shares are dealt in on a market. Public companies with surplus cash resources could find it useful to be able to buy their own shares and thus return surplus resources to shareholders, thereby removing the pressure on such companies to employ those surplus resources in uneconomic ways, and enabling shareholders to deploy the resources to better effect.'[7]

The main advantages claimed for allowing companies to buy their own shares were expressed in the following terms:

(a) It may enable the company to buy out a dissident shareholder.
(b) It facilitates the retention of family control.
(c) It provides a means whereby a shareholder, or the estate of a deceased shareholder, in a company whose shares are not listed can find a buyer.
(d) It is particularly useful in relation to employee share schemes in enabling the shares of employees to be re-purchased on their ceasing to be employed by the company.
(e) It may help with the marketing of shares by enabling the company to give a subscriber an option to re-sell to the company.
(f) It enables companies to purchase their shares for use later in stock option plans or acquisition programmes.
(g) If redeemable shares are quoted at below the redemption price it enables the company to save money by buying up in advance of the redemption date (a practice which our companies can, and do, adopt in the case of debentures but cannot in the case of redeemable preference shares).
(h) It permits the evolution of the open-ended investment company or mutual fund instead of having to operate through the mechanism of a unit trust.
(i) It provides a company with surplus cash with a further means of using it advantageously.
(j) It can be used to support the market for the shares if this is thought to be unduly depressed, thus preserving for the shareholders the value of their shares as marketable securities.
(k) If the company not only buys its shares but trades in the treasury shares thus acquired it may make money thereby.[8]

The result is that all companies can now purchase their own shares subject to certain conditions and procedures.[9] Such shares are then cancelled.

Purchase transactions can be carried out as a private deal between the company and the shareholder (termed an off-market purchase) or as a market purchase by the company on a recognised stock exchange. Obviously a market purchase can only be carried out by a plc whose shares are dealt with on the stock exchange.

The capital maintenance concept is preserved in that a company when purchasing or redeeming its shares must do so only out of the proceeds of a fresh issue or out of profits; and in the latter event the amount representing the share capital purchased or redeemed must be transferred to capital redemption reserve.

In the case of private companies, however, the capital maintenance concept is compromised in that if there are insufficient profits to cover a purchase or redemption, the company may make up the shortfall, in so far as it is not covered by a fresh issue by making a 'permissible capital payment.'[10] Since this represents an overall reduction in the company's share capital, it must be formally approved by the company and the directors are required to declare that they are of the opinion that there are no grounds to suggest that the company was unable to pay its debts following the payment and that the company will be able to carry on its business as a going concern and to pay its debts as they fall due in the year following the payment.

1 (1887) 12 App Cas 409, HL.
2 Gower, *Modern Company Law* (4th Edn, 1979).
3 See now CA 1985, s 159.
4 CA 1985, ss 160, 170.
5 S 170.
6 Cmnd 7944.
7 P 7.
8 Pp 9–10.
9 See CA 1985, ss 158–178.
10 Ss 171–177.

Financial assistance for the purchase of own shares

34.2.3 A frequent abuse of the capital maintenance concept that developed in the period after the 1914–18 war was the provision of financial assistance by companies for the purchase of their own shares. The commonest example was identified by Lord Green in 1942:

> 'persons—call them financiers, speculators, or what you will—finding a company with a substantial cash balance or easily realisable assets . . . bought up the whole, or greater part, of the shares of the company for cash, and so arranged matters that the purchase money which they then became bound to provide was advanced to them by the company whose shares they were acquiring, either out of its cash balance or by realisation of its liquid investments.'[1]

Successive Companies Acts have sought to tackle such abuses over the years with varying degrees of success. In particular the statutory provisions that existed between 1948 and 1981 cast a very wide net and in some respects deterred the participation of financial institutions in schemes which were entirely in good faith and beneficial from a business point of view.

The current provisions therefore lay much greater stress on the real purpose motivating any financial assistance and the overall good faith of the parties concerned. The general rule is that it is unlawful for a company or its subsidiaries to provide, directly or indirectly, financial assistance for the acquisition of any of its shares. The prohibitions relate to assistance given before, at the time of, or after the acquisition.[2]

The legislation then makes a number of exceptions to the general rule. Some of the exceptions relate to specific transactions,[3] such as distributions lawfully made; allotment of bonus shares; formal redemption or purchase of shares; others are of a more general nature. In particular financial assistance is not prohibited if the company's principal purpose in giving the assistance is not to reduce or discharge any liability incurred by a person for the acquisition of its shares or shares in its holding company; or the reduction or discharge of any such liability is but an incidental part of some larger purpose of the company. In addition, the assistance must be given in good faith in the interests of the company.

An example of such a transaction would be where a company buys a machine from someone knowing that they will use the funds received to

467

acquire shares in the company. Provided that the company genuinely want the machine and the share acquisition is not the main purpose of the transaction, and it is otherwise in good faith, there will be no statutory infringement.

It is also permissible for a company to lend money for the acquisition of its shares, if lending is part of the ordinary business of the company; to provide assistance in accordance with an employee's share scheme and to make loans to persons (other than directors) employed by the company to enable them to own shares in the company.[4] plcs utilising these three exceptions must ensure that their net assets are not reduced, or to the extent that they are so reduced, the assistance is provided out of profits.[5]

In the case of private companies there is a further wide exception. A private company may give financial assistance for the acquisition of its shares or shares in its holding company in any circumstances where the company has net assets which are not thereby reduced or, to the extent that they are reduced, the assistance is provided out of profits. Such assistance must however be made within a rigid framework of procedural and financial safeguards.[6]

These provisions have been particularly helpful in facilitating management buyouts, whereby executives of a business finance the purchase of the business in which they are employed by using its assets as security.

1   *Re VGM Holdings Ltd* [1942] Ch 235 at 239, CA.
2   CA 1985, ss 151–158.
3   S 153.
4   S 153(4).
5   S 154(1).
6   Ss 155–158.

Dividends out of capital
34.2.4   A further consequence of the capital maintenance concept was the rule, largely developed by the courts, that prevented a company from depleting its capital base by making payment out of capital disguised as dividends. Thus a company was prohibited from paying dividends out of capital. There was however a marked contrast between the rules developed by the courts and those developed by the accountancy profession based on prudent standard practice. Thus the courts, for example, would permit a company to pay a dividend out of its current trading profits without setting aside an amount for depreciation,[1] or without making good previous revenue losses.[2] The English courts even permitted a surplus arising from the increase in the book value of a company's assets to be treated as distributable profit even though such profit had not been realised by sale;[3] the more prudent Scottish courts would not so allow.[4]

In the CA 1980 the somewhat lax rules developed by the courts were replaced by a statutory framework implementing the Second EEC Directive; these provisions are now contained in ss 263–281 of the CA 1985. The present provisions reflect the prudent policy that dividends may only be paid by looking at a company's overall performance, taking into account accumulated losses and surpluses over a period. The calculations must be based on actual or 'realised' profits and losses, thus a revaluation surplus cannot be taken into account.

In the case of a plc it must not make a distribution if the amount of its net assets is less than the total of its called up share capital and its undistributable reserves, or if the amount of its net assets after the distribution would be less than its called up share capital plus its undistributable reserves.[5] In other words, the company must make provision for any existing unrealised deficits.

The calculations in respect of profits etc must of course be based on the annual accounts drawn up in accordance with the principles and rules in the Act based on the concept of truth and fairness, and standard accounting practices.[6]

1 See *Lee v Neuchatel Asphalte Co* (1889) 41 Ch D 1, CA.
2 *Ammonia Soda Co Ltd v Chamberlain* [1918] 1 Ch 266, CA.
3 *Dimbula Valley (Ceylon) Tea Co Ltd v Laurie* [1961] Ch 353, [1961] 1 All ER 769.
4 *Westburn Sugar Refineries Ltd v IRC* (1960) 39 TC 45, [1960] TR 105.
5 S 264.
6 Ss 270–276 and generally ss 221–262.

Reduction of capital

34.2.5 A major exception to the capital maintenance concept is the facility given to limited companies to reduce their share capital by means of a special resolution confirmed by a court.[1] A company may reduce its capital in any way, but the Act specifies three particular ways:

(a) By extinguishing or reducing the liability on any of its shares in respect of share capital not paid up.

(b) By cancelling any paid-up capital which is lost or unrepresented by assets.

(c) By paying off any paid-up share capital which is in excess of the company's wants.

The first method is relatively uncommon in contemporary business affairs. The second method reflects the situation outlined in 34.2.0 above, that despite the share capital maintenance concept, the actual value of a company's capital may be reduced below the nominal value of its issued shares, perhaps because of depreciation. In such circumstances, the company may choose to correct such an imbalance by formally reducing its capital. Thus a company may have 20,000 fully paid £1 shares but only net assets to the value of £10,000. The company may therefore choose to reduce its share capital to 20,000 fully paid 50 pence shares thus correcting the imbalance and perhaps ultimately making its shares more attractive.[2]

An example of the third situation would be where a company has more share capital than it needs perhaps because it has rationalised its business operations. Thus it might have a share capital of 20,000 fully paid £1 shares represented by net assets of £20,000 which it could reduce to 10,000 fully paid 50 pence shares and return 50 pence in cash to each shareholder.

In considering whether to confirm a reduction the courts must be satisfied that the interests of the company's creditors have been safeguarded. In addition, the reduction must be fair and equitable as between the shareholders of the company. In particular the reduction of capital must be in accordance with the particular rights attached to classes of shares. Thus if the reduction of capital involves returning capital to the shareholders, the preference shareholders should be paid first because they would normally have preference in respect of return of capital in the event of a winding up.

This would be so even though the preference shareholders could be seen to be penalised by the return because of loss of their investment.[3]

By the same token, if the reduction of capital involves cancelling shares because of trading losses, the ordinary shares would normally be cancelled first because that reflects the order of risk in terms of loss of capital in the event of a winding up.

1 S 135.
2 The court must be satisfied that the assets have fallen in value permanently. See *Re Jupiter House Investments (Cambridge) Ltd* [1985] 1 WLR 975.
3 See *Scottish Insurance Corpn Ltd v Wilson and Clyde Coal Co* [1949] AC 462, [1949] 1 All ER 1068, HL.

Loan and creditor security

34.3.0 We have already seen that the essential distinction between share and loan capital is that a shareholder is a member of the company whereas those who provide loan finance are classed as creditors. In practice company law does not treat such creditors any differently from day to day trade creditors.

However, an increasing proportion of corporate working capital is provided by borrowing from banks or other institutions either by way of overdraft facilities payable on demand or fixed term advances. Such financial institutions are by nature prudent and will not therefore advance funds without some form of security over corporate assets or personal guarantee from the directors. The creditor who stipulates for security does so with the object of minimising potential loss or even avoiding it altogether, should the company go into insolvent liquidation. The act of taking a security gives the holder a proprietary interest in the corporate assets so mortgaged, thus, should the debtor company default on the loan, the creditor is free to realise the security without regard to the effect upon other unsecured creditors.

The basic right of a creditor to demand a security, and thus obtain priority over the creditors in the event of a winding up, is a matter of contract. As Lord Macnaghten said in *Salomon v A Salomon & Co Ltd*,[1] 'Every creditor is entitled to get and hold the best security the law allows him to take.' However, Parliament has increasingly regulated the use and abuse of different types of security by, for example, requiring registration of certain charges with the Registrar, or by rendering certain charges invalid if created in the period prior to liquidation. The difficulty for the law, recognised in recent reports[2], is to balance the legitimate rights of creditors to take security and of companies to grant security in order to attract finance, against the rights of unsecured creditors who are not in a position to obtain such security. As Lord Macnaghten observed in respect of a debenture holder's security:

'For such a catastrophe as has occurred in this case some would blame the law that allows the creation of a floating charge. But a floating charge is too convenient a form of security to be lightly abolished. I have long thought, and believe some of your Lordships also think, that the ordinary trade creditors of a trading company ought to have a preferential claim on the assets in liquidation in respect of debts incurred within a certain limited time before winding up. But that is not the law at present. Everybody knows that when there is a winding up debenture-holders generally step in and sweep off everything, and a great scandal it is.'[3]

1   [1897] AC 22 at 52, HL.
2   See *Insolvency Law and Practice. Report of the Review Committee* Cmnd 8558, 1982.
3   *Salomon v A Solomon & Co Ltd* [1897] AC 22 at 53, HL.

Fixed and floating charges

34.3.1   There are two forms of security which companies may grant over their assets: fixed and floating charges. A fixed charge is a charge created over corporate plant or premises and is created either by a formal legal transaction known as a legal charge or by a simple contract to create the charge by, for example, depositing deeds with a financial institution. The effect of a fixed charge is that the chargeholder can insist that the property mortgaged be sold in the event of default and the proceeds used solely for paying off the loan. The holder of a fixed charge obtains absolute priority over all other creditors including those given some statutory preference.

The disadvantage of a fixed charge from the company's viewpoint is that it effectively freezes corporate assets so that the company cannot deal with those assets in the ordinary course of business without reference to the chargeholder. This means that for practical purposes the class of assets over which fixed charges may be created is limited. Fixed charges may be created by companies and partnerships. Floating charges were devised by the English Court of Chancery in the 1860s, and are restricted to companies.[1]

Under English law a floating charge has three basic characteristics:

(a) it is a charge on a class of assets of a company both present and future;
(b) such assets are of a kind which, in the ordinary course of the business of a company, change from time to time;
(c) it is assumed that, until some specific action is taken by the chargeholder or his representative, the company may carry on its business and deal with the assets in the course of business.

As a security instrument the floating charge is much more flexible than the fixed charge. It provides a simple framework whereby a security can be created over the entire undertaking of a company thereby giving considerable security for the lender, whilst permitting the company to freely dispose of the property. For example, it is common to create floating charges over assets such as stock in trade where it would be impracticable to create a fixed charge.

On the other hand in terms of public policy the floating charge has disadvantages. In particular it allows a company with apparently considerable asset backing to obtain credit from suppliers, and continue to borrow, while the appearance of wealth is compromised by the existence of charges which may be enforced at any time.

As was illustrated by the *Salomon* case, the facility of creating a floating charge enables a trader to minimise the risk of loss of capital and obtain priority over unsuspecting trade creditors. In effect, the practice of creating floating charges over the whole undertaking of a company means that in the event of an insolvent liquidation, the whole assets of a company are out of reach of unsecured creditors, except in so far as those creditors are given statutory preference.

One of the characteristics of a floating charge is that it allows the company to deal with the asset until specific action is taken by the chargeholder. In practice this means that where the company is in default and the holder seeks to enforce the charge by the appointment of a receiver, the charge is said to crystallise. Such crystallisation converts the floating charge into a fixed charge on the assets of the class on which the charge was created. It occurs when the company ceases business or when the holder enforces the security under the authority of the charge. It may, for example occur by the holder of the charge simply giving notice to convert the charge into a fixed charge.[2]

For practical purposes floating charges are restricted to companies.[3] In the event of a winding up the holders of a floating charge will generally be postponed to those of fixed charge holders, the costs of the winding up and the statutory preferred creditors.[4]

1   See *Holyroyd v Marshall* (1862) 10 HL Cas 191. Floating charges were not recognised under Scots common law. It was not until legislation in 1961 that companies registered in Scotland could create floating charges. See Companies (Floating Charges) (Scotland) Act 1961. See now CA 1985, ss 410–424.
2   See *Re Brightlife Ltd* [1986] 3 All ER 673.
3   See Bills of Sale Acts 1878–82 and generally Gower, op cit pp 108–109.
4   See 36.0.15.

Registration of charges
34.3.2   In view of the fact that the creation of charges effectively removes a proportion of corporate assets from funds available to settle the claims of unsecured creditors, it is important that persons dealing with a company are at least made aware of the existence and scope of charges over such assets. Hence, there are provisions which require any legal or equitable charge on a company's land, undertaking or debts, to be registered with the Registrar of Companies.[1] Particulars of the charge must be delivered to the Registrar within 21 days after their creation.

The responsibility for registration lays with the company. However, registration may be effected by any person interested in the charge and the fees recovered from the company.[2]

On registration of a charge, the Registrar issues a certificate of registration which is conclusive evidence that the requirements of the legislation have been complied with. The courts will not therefore inquire into any alleged mistakes or irregularities.[3]

The importance of registration lies in the fact that a failure to register renders the security void as against the liquidator and any creditor of the company. The sufferer is the chargeholder, since security is lost in the event of a winding up and the chargeholder is classed as an unsecured creditor. The charge is not however avoided as against the company so long as it remains solvent. Thus the chargeholder can enforce the charge against the company by the normal remedies but it is void as against the liquidator or any other secured creditors claiming against the property over which the charge was created.

To assist the creditor the statutory provision does however make the money secured by the charge become immediately repayable. The creditor could therefore recover the money lent even though the loan has not yet become contractually repayable. An additional protection for creditors is that the courts have a discretion to extend the period of registration or to rectify errors or omissions in respect of a registration.[4]

1   S 395.
2   S 399.
3   See *R v Registrar of Companies, ex p Central Bank of India* [1986] QB 1114, [1986] 1 All ER 105, CA.
4   S 404.

Priority of charges

34.3.3   In general the holders of a floating charge are postponed to the holders of fixed charges, even where the fixed charge was created after the floating charge. A company cannot create a further floating charge on the same assets ranking in priority to or equally with an existing charge.

It is common practice under the terms of a debenture to restrict the company's power to raise further charges which rank in priority to or equally with the charge being created. Such a prohibition is effective as against later floating charges but not later fixed charges unless the holder was aware of the existence of both the charge and the prohibition. It is not a requirement of the registration process under English law that details of restrictive prohibitions be supplied. Thus it is difficult for the holders of floating charges with such restrictions to bring them to the attention of potential chargeholders.[1]

1   It is common practice for financial institutions to endorse such particulars on the registration documentation which may have the effect of giving actual notice of the prohibition to a potential chargeholder. Under the Scots law provisions of the CA 1985 particulars of any restrictions and prohibitions must be given. CA 1985, s 413(2)(e).

Invalid floating charges

34.3.4   Where a floating charge is created over an existing debt in order to afford some priority to that creditor in an imminent insolvency, the floating charge may be invalidated. Thus under s 245 of the Insolvency Act 1986 a floating charge created at a 'relevant time' is invalid except to the extent of consideration[1] received by the company at the same time as, or after the creation of, the charge. The relevant time is, in the case of connected persons,[2] two years from the commencement of a liquidation or the presentation of a petition for an administration order; in the case of any other person it is one year.[3] In the latter event however the charge will only be invalidated if at the time the company was unable to pay its debts or became unable to pay its debts as a result of the transaction under which the charge was created.[4]

1   Consideration includes money paid, goods, services, the discharge of debts and contractual interests. IA 1986, s 245(2).
2   A person is a connected person if he is a director or shadow director of the company or an associate of such a director or shadow director; or he is an associate of the company. IA 1986, ss 249 and 435.
3   IA 1986, s 245(3).
4   IA 1986, s 245(4).

Default on loans

34.3.5   If a company defaults on a loan it is likely that the company will eventually proceed into liquidation. In any case the creditor has a number of options on such event. These are:

34.3.5 *Corporate Capital*

(a) raise an action for recovery of the principal loan and interest;
(b) apply to the court for an order of foreclosure or sale of the property mortgaged;
(c) appoint a receiver under the authority of the debenture or by application to the courts;[1]
(d) petition for the winding up of the company.[2]

1 See 36.0.4.
2 See 36.0.9.

Chapter 35

Distribution of Corporate Power and Authority in Law and Reality

35.0.0 The theoretical model of corporate government envisages the shareholders' ownership as the basis of power and authority. Such power and authority is exercised collectively at periodic general meetings. Obviously since the general meeting is far too cumbersome to run the company effectively, the shareholders delegate their power and authority to the board of directors. Once delegated, the directors may exercise such power and authority relatively freely, provided that they remain within the legal and constitutional framework laid down by legislation and the company's public documents. Indeed, company law does not attempt to regulate the means by which business decisions are taken or the justification for them. Since the directors derive their authority from the shareholders in general meeting they are ultimately accountable to them and can, for example, be dismissed on a simple majority vote notwithstanding anything in the company's articles or any contract the directors may have.[1]

1   CA 1985, s 303.

The shareholders and the general meeting
35.0.1 In terms of the realities of corporate activity, the legal model is somewhat dated. In all but the smallest private companies where the shareholders participate in management, shareholders do not exercise any meaningful ownership control. This was confirmed in an investigation into the voting behaviour of shareholders in the UK in 1975. Companies were questioned on whether any shareholders in the previous ten years had attempted to exercise control by requisitioning any meetings, proposing or amending resolutions, taking any legal proceedings or initiating any enquiry.

> 'A negative response was given in all cases except that one company recorded an unsuccessful attempt to amend a resolution and another the unsuccessful attempts by a ginger group to defeat the re-election of directors and propose the election of their own choice.'[1]

The same survey revealed that only one quarter of 1% of shareholders attend the general meeting.

Such a situation is the inevitable result of the increased scale of corporate activity which has intensified the separation of ownership and control. The

Cohen Committee on Company Law Reform in 1945 identified the problem in the following terms:

> 'The illusory nature of the control theoretically exercised by share-holders over directors has been accentuated by the dispersion of capital among an increasing number of small shareholders who pay little attention to their investments as long as satisfactory dividends are forthcoming, who lack sufficient time, money and experience to make full use of their rights as occasion arises and who are in many cases too numerous and too widely dispersed to be able to organise themselves.'[2]

It was recognised that even where management has no financial interest in a company 'you can control your company very nicely and very tightly by management itself.'[3] The response of the legislature to these developments has been largely to provide for a greater degree of disclosure by the directorate in respect of financial and related matters, and, somewhat vainly, to seek to restore some power to the general meeting by requiring specific periodic approval of certain actions.[4]

In 1948 a provision was added allowing a director to be dismissed on a simple majority vote.[5] This provision was, however, effectively frustrated by two practices. First, the provision safeguarded a director's contractual rights. Thus if a director was awarded a lengthy service contract prior to the general meeting, the decision to dismiss would be expensive. This practice was, at least in part, tackled by the CA 1980 which required directors' service contracts which cannot be terminated by the company by notice, or can only be terminated in specific circumstances, to be approved by a resolution of the general meeting where the contract is for a period of more than five years.[6] Second, the spirit of the provision can be flouted by terms in the articles, loading the voting rights of directors in the event of a resolution to dismiss them.[7]

At a relatively early stage the courts recognised the constitutional independence of the board of directors. Thus most companies adopt the model provision of Table A[8] which currently declares that the business of the company shall be managed by the directors who may exercise all the powers of the company subject to the legislation and the memorandum and articles and to any directions given by special resolution.

It has always been accepted by the court that having delegated the power to manage the company to the board, the general meeting cannot interfere with the exercise of the board's discretion unless the directors breach the legislation or the company's constitution. This applies even in the event of a majority shareholder securing an ordinary resolution requiring the directors to implement a particular transaction.[9] As the wording of Table A para 70 indicates, however, if a special resolution is secured directing the board to implement a particular transaction they must comply with it.

In the event that the board of directors exceeds the authority bestowed upon them under the terms of the articles, the general meeting, from whom they derive authority, may ratify the unauthorised act.[10] The general meeting cannot however ratify the directors' actions if they are acting ultra vires the company.

As a general rule therefore the shareholders in general meeting possess little real power in terms of management. Apart from those sections of the legislation which confer specific powers on the general meeting, the only time that the shareholders may be required to be involved in management decisions is where the board cannot agree and a state of deadlock exists. In such circumstances the general meeting has residual powers to resolve the deadlock.[11]

1 Midgley, *Companies and Their Shareholders: The Uneasy Relationship* (1975).
2 Cmnd 6659 para 7(c).
3 Ibid.
4 For example the directors' authority to issue shares was subjected to a requirement that it be renewed every five years by the general meeting under the Companies Act 1980 see now CA 1985, s 80.
5 See CA 1985, s 303.
6 See now CA 1985, s 319.
7 See *Bushell v Faith* [1970] AC 1099, [1970] 1 All ER 53, HL.
8 See art 70.
9 *Automatic Self-Cleansing Filter Syndicate Co Ltd v Cuninghame* [1906] 2 Ch 34, CA.
10 See 29.2.7.
11 *Barron v Potter* [1914] 1 Ch 895.

The board of directors

35.0.2 As indicated above, the board of directors has a wide measure of authority to manage the affairs of the company. In practice this authority may be delegated to small committees of executive directors, that is, those involved with the company in a continuing capacity, such as the managing director, chairman, and finance and marketing directors etc. Indeed, in the same way that increasing scale has seen a shift of power from shareholders to the board, so it has seen a shift of power from the board to what might be termed management.

The Bullock Committee on *Industrial Democracy* recognised that:

'The extent to which a main board exercises detailed control of policy is inevitably limited. It cannot exercise detailed influence over every aspect of the company's affairs and it is largely reliant on the proposals and policies put forward to it by management.'[1]

The authors of a study published in 1974 observed that the standard expectation of most directors was that the board collectively does not decide or even seriously discuss anything.

'To be sure the final yea or nay at a board meeting be seen as the decision point, and may so appear in corporate histories . . . Boards of directors are, we feel, best conceived as decision taking institutions, that is, as legitimising institutions rather than as decision making ones.'[2]

In recent years there has been a growing concern to increase the effectiveness of the board in terms of its role in monitoring management. Attention has particularly focused on the appointment of non-executive directors to company boards. Hitherto such directors may have been invited to join the board merely to permit their names to adorn corporate notepaper. However, encouraged by financial institutions, the Bank of England and the CBI, more and more companies are appointing non-executive directors for their professional and commercial knowledge and expertise, in order to give the board additional independent advice and assist in the resolution of conflicts of interest.[3]

1 Ch 7, para 23, Cmnd 6706, 1976.
2 Pahl and Winkler, *The Economic Elite in Theory and Practice,* in *Elites and Power in British Society*, (Stansworth and Giddens (eds) 1974) p 110.
3 See 'Bank of England Quarterly Bulletin' June 1985; 'Non-Executive Directors in Perspective' (Corporate Consulting Group) 1986.

Directors and agency

35.0.3 As indicated above, the ultimate authority in a company lies with the general meeting which delegates such authority to the board. Individual directors have no authority to act as agents of the company. However, it is customary for the articles of a company to allow the board to delegate powers to individual directors or other selected agents.[1] Similarly the articles will permit the board to appoint one of the directors as a managing director and powers will be delegated accordingly.

In terms of the law of agency[2] a director will not therefore possess any apparent authority to act on behalf of the company. Thus unless a director possesses delegated power from the board and hence actual authority, or is held out by the board as having delegated powers,[3] he cannot make a contract on behalf of the company.

A managing director has, however, a fairly wide usual authority to enable him to make contracts in respect of the company's business. Thus he can borrow money on the firm's account and grant security in respect of its repayment,[4] sign cheques and guarantee loans.

It will be recalled that the doctrine of constructive notice operates in the context of a company's public documents.[5] Thus if a transaction with a director or managing director is clearly prohibited under the terms of the company's memorandum or articles, the third party dealing with the director will be deemed to have notice of such prohibition. In order to mitigate the impact of the doctrine of constructive notice the courts developed the so called rule in *Royal British Bank v Turquand*.[6] This provides that so long as a transaction is not prohibited by a company's public documents and is apparently consistent with them, a third party is not bound to inquire into internal procedures and is entitled to assume that such procedures have been complied with.

Thus if a managing director can only make contracts in excess of £20,000 by obtaining the consent of a resolution of the board, a third party may assume that such consent has been obtained. Indeed in such circumstances, a third party has no way of checking that such a resolution has been obtained and the rule is therefore based on business convenience.

The third party cannot rely on the rule where they know or ought to have known of the lack of authority. It has been suggested for example that company directors dealing with their own company could not rely on the rule.[7] If a transaction is in some way unusual or the circumstances suspicious, a third party may be put on inquiry,[8] or if the document which forms the basis of the transaction is a forgery,[9] the rule will not apply.

It will be recalled that the CA 1985, s 35 largely abolished the doctrine of constructive notice where a party deals with a company in good faith in the case of a transaction decided upon by the directors. The section does not, however, assist persons dealing with individual directors unless the company only has one effective director.[10]

1 See Table A arts 71, 72.
2 See Part 6.
3 See *Freeman and Lockyer (a firm) v Buckhurst Park Properties (Mangal) Ltd* [1964] 2 QB 480, [1964] 1 All ER 630, CA.
4 *Biggerstaffe v Rowatt's Wharf Ltd* [1896] 2 Ch 93, CA.
5 See 33.2.3.
6 (1855) 5 E & B 248.
7 *Morris v Kansen* [1946] AC 459, [1946] 1 All ER 586, HL.
8 *AL Underwood Ltd v Bank of Liverpool and Martins* [1924] 1 KB 775, CA.
9 *Ruben v Great Fingall Consolidated* [1906] AC 439, HL.
10 See 33.3.2.

The directors are the company

35.0.4 For the purposes of attributing liability in tort or under criminal law, the courts have adopted the policy of holding that acts or omissions of the directorate or senior management are to be regarded as acts or omissions of the company and hence give rise to corporate liability.[1]

1 See *Lennard's Carrying Co Ltd v Asiatic Petroleum Co Ltd* [1915] AC 705, HL.

Directors' responsibilities and duties

35.1.0 Given the flexible nature of the legal model of corporate government and the considerable discretion that the courts have allowed directors within the 'business decision' concept, it is important that the law lays down at least some minimum standards regulating directors' conduct, behaviour and competence. The rules so laid down consist of certain statutory obligations, prohibitions or disclosure requirements, and extensive common law duties derived from the fiduciary nature of the director's office.

The pattern of legislative reform has been one of piecemeal responses to successive widely publicised abuses and corporate scandals. For example, many of the provisions in the CA 1980 dealing with loans and transactions in which directors are involved were inspired by the findings of Department of Trade investigations in the 1970s.[1]

As far as the common law is concerned the duties of directors are classified under two headings. First, the fiduciary duties which require directors to act in good faith for the benefit of the company, exercising their powers properly for the purpose for which they were conferred and avoiding any direct or indirect conflict of interest. Second, a general duty to exercise due care and skill in carrying out their functions as directors.

1 See eg Department of Trade Inspectors Report into the affairs of Court Line (1978); Dowgate and Hartley Baird Co (1973; London Capital Group (1977); Lonrho (1976).

A duty to whom?

35.1.1 Directors owe their common law duties to the company and not to any individual member. Thus if a director makes use of confidential information in order to purchase some shares from a shareholder at a low price, he incurs no liability to account to that shareholder for the profit he makes,[1] unless it can be proved that the director was acting on behalf of the shareholder as an agent.[2] In certain special circumstances such as in the context of a takeover bid or the running of a small private company, the courts might however take the view that the circumstances imposed on the directors a special duty towards shareholders.[3] In any event if a director makes use of confidential information in dealing with a shareholder, he would be in breach of his duty to the company and therefore liable to account for any profit he makes.[4]

1 *Percival v Wright* [1902] 2 Ch 421.
2 See *Allen v Hyatt* (1914) 30 TLR 444, PC.
3 See respectively *Gething v Kilner* [1972] 1 All ER 1166, [1972] 1 WLR 337 and the New Zealand case of *Coleman v Myers* [1977] 2 NZLR 225.
4 See 35.1.6. and 38.0.5.

Fiduciary duties of good faith
35.1.2 Directors are required to act with loyalty and good faith towards the company, acting within the scope of the powers granted by the company's constitution. However, given the tendency of company articles to grant wide general powers to the directors and the reluctance of the courts to involve themselves in considering the merits of business decisions, cases against directors are confined to fairly clear cut abuses. Provided that the directors can establish to the satisfaction of the court that they honestly believed the action to be right, the courts will not hold them liable. As was said in the Australian High Court:

'I believe the directors' opinion of the needs of the company was imprecise, probably intuitive and may be erroneous, yet each of them addressed his mind to the relevant problem and exercised the power bona fide.'[1]

If, however, the directors are perceived to be acting in the interests of some other party, or their own interests, without reference to the interests of the company, irrespective of dishonest intent, they will be in breach:

'The proper test . . . must be whether an intelligent and honest man in the position of a director of the company concerned could . . . have reasonably believed that the transactions were for the benefit of the company.'[2]

The expression 'benefit of the company' has traditionally been interpreted as referring to the interests of groups such as the workforce, consumers or other sectional interests, only in so far as they coincide with the interests of the general body of shareholders.[3] Whilst the company is a going concern, the directorate can normally justify expenditure in the interests of a particular group or expenditure of a gratuitous nature, since it can be rationalised as in the interests of the shareholders to have a contented workforce or a favourable corporate profile with the public.[4]

It has long been recognised that companies, particularly plcs, have wider responsibilities than those recognised formally by company law.[5] A Canadian judge has said:

'In defining the duties of directors the law ought to take into account the fact that the corporation provides the legal framework for the development of resources and the generation of wealth in the private sector . . . A classical theory that once was unchallengeable must yield to the facts of modern life. In fact, of course, it has. If today the directors of a company were to consider the interests of its employees no one would argue that in doing so they were not acting bona fide in the interests of the company itself. Similarly, if the directors were to consider the consequences to the community of any policy that the company intended to pursue and were deflected in their commitment to that policy as a result, it could not be said that they had not considered bona fide the interests of the shareholders.'[6]

Parliament recognised the interests of the workforce in the CA 1980[7] by providing that:

'The matters to which the directors of a company are to have regard in the performance of their functions include the interests of the company's employees in general as well as the interests of its members.'

It must be stressed, however, that the provision only requires the directors to have regard to the employee interests and to that extent it represents a reflection of general practice. It would be very difficult to make a case against the directors for not complying with the statutory requirement if a general minute appeared in the record of a directors' meeting to the effect that 'the directors paid all due regard to the employee interests in closing down the operation in question'. In any event the requirement would be difficult to enforce by the workforce since the section makes it clear that it is a duty, like all other directors' duties, that is owed to the company and is enforceable by the company.[8] Unless an employee was also a shareholder and could raise an action on the basis of one of the exceptions to the rule in *Foss v Harbottle*[9] whereby shareholders are permitted to bring personal actions against the directors, a challenge by the employees against the directors for breach of the provision is unlikely.

In view of the preoccupation of the judiciary with the capital maintenance concept over the years, it is perhaps surprising that creditors are not considered in the context of the interests of the company. In 1980 Lord Diplock observed that:

'The best interests of the company are not exclusively those of the shareholders but may include those of creditors.'[10]

It would clearly be imprudent for the directors not to consider the interests of creditors in terms of overall corporate policy and planning: however, in terms of the orthodox legal view, such interests are not included in considering the interests of the company.

The notion of acting in good faith for the benefit of the company is a vague expression. As Lord Wilberforce has said:

'This formulation bona fide in the interests of the company is one that is relevant in certain contexts of company law . . . on the other hand (it may) become little more than an alibi for a refusal to consider the merits of the case.'[11]

One area that has proved a fruitful source of litigation against directors is in challenging them for using their powers for a collateral purpose. In particular, in the context of the directors' power to allot shares for the purpose of raising capital, the courts' attitude has been relatively inflexible. A number of cases have held that directors have acted improperly where they use their power to allot shares in order to destroy an existing majority and thereby frustrate a takeover bid.[12] In *Howard Smith Ltd v Ampol Petroleum Ltd*[13] the Privy Council rejected the idea that all that is required of directors with regard to the exercise of their powers is that they must act in good faith in the interests of the company.

> 'Having ascertained on a fair view the nature of this power, and having defined as can best be done in the light of modern conditions, or some limits within which it may be exercised, it is then necessary for the court, if a particular exercise of it is challenged, to examine the substantial purpose for which it was exercised and to reach a conclusion whether that purpose was proper or not.'[14]

Decisions overseas reflect a more flexible attitude in that provided the directors' exclusive concern is the best interests of the company, perhaps because they feel that the bidder is unsuitable, they will not invalidate an allotment.[15] Such an approach is certainly consistent with the business judgement notion which is so enthusiastically adopted by UK courts.

In the event that an allotment is held to be improper the courts have taken the view that the directors' impropriety may be ratified by the company in general meeting.[16]

By way of additonal protection against misuse of the power to allot shares, the CA 1985 requires that the power to allot shares cannot be exercised by the directors unless authorised by the general meeting or the articles.[17] Such authority must be reviewed at least every five years.

1 *Harlowe's Nominees Pty Ltd v Woodside (Lakes Entrance) Oil Co NL* (1968) 42 ALJR 123, (1968) 121 CLR 483.
2 *Charterbridge Corpn Ltd v Lloyd's Bank Ltd* [1970] Ch 62 at 74.
3 See *Parke v Daily News* [1962] Ch 927, [1962] 2 All ER 929.
4 Such payments must of course be within the objects of the company. See 33.3.1.
5 *Responsibilities of the British Public Company* (CBI, 1973).
6 Berger J in *Teck Corpn Ltd v Millar* (1972) 33 DLR (3d) 288.
7 See now CA 1985, s 309.
8 CA 1985, s 309(2).
9 (1843) 2 Hare 461 and see 35.2.1.
10 *Lonrho Ltd v Shell Petroleum Co Ltd* [1980] 1 WLR 627 at 634, HL.
11 *Ebrahimi v Westbourne Galleries Ltd* [1973] AC 360 at 381, HL.
12 See *Hogg v Cramphorn Ltd* [1967] Ch 254, [1966] 3 All ER 420; *Bamford v Bamford* [1970] Ch 212, [1969] 1 All ER 969, CA.
13 [1974] AC 821, [1974] 1 All ER 1126, PC.
14 At 835.
15 See *Teck Corpn v Millar* (1972) 33 DLR (3d) 288.
16 See cases cited at note 12 above.
17 S 80(1).

Conflicts of interest

35.1.3   A further facet of the directors' fiduciary duties is that they must not put themselves in a situation where their duties and personal interests are likely to conflict. As Lord Cranworth observed:

> '. . . it is a rule of universal application that no one having such duties to discharge shall be allowed to enter into engagements in which he has or can have a personal interest conflicting or which may possibly conflict with the interests of those whom he is bound to protect.'[1]

The attitude of the courts in such conflict cases has been strict, in that, once it is established that there is even a real and sensible possibility of a conflict, a breach of duty arises. It is entirely irrelevant that the transaction may be beneficial to the company.

If a conflict arises the company may avoid the contract and require the director to account for any profit that he has derived from the transaction. Given that the transaction in which the director is involved is voidable, the company in general meeting can decide to proceed with it and ratify the director's action after full disclosure. In such event there is nothing to prevent the director concerned from using his votes as a shareholder of the company in order to ratify his own action.[2]

1 *Aberdeen Rly Co v Blaikie Bros* 1854 1 Macq 461, 563.
2 *North West Transportation Co Ltd and Beatty v Beatty* (1887) 12 App Cas 589, PC. But see 35.2.2.

Statutory disclosure of interests and waiver

35.1.4 Under Table A art 85 there is a provision which requires directors to disclose to the board any contract or proposed contract in which they are interested. Such a disclosure requirement is also imposed on directors by virtue of CA 1985, s 317. That section requires disclosure to the board by directors of any contract, transaction or arrangement in which they have an interest.[1] Directors can however make a general declaration of interest regarding specific companies or firms.[2] There is also a statutory requirement that any transaction or arrangement in which a director has a material interest must be included in a note to the annual accounts.[3]

A failure to disclose an interest renders the contract concerned voidable at the instance of the company and the director remains liable to account for any profit. However, article 85 purports to waive the general rule and effectively allow a director to contract out of the conflict of interest duty. It provides that subject to the overall disclosure requirement, a director may be a party to a transaction or arrangement with his company but shall not by reason of his office, be accountable to the company for any benefit which he derives. It further provides that no such transaction or arrangement shall be avoided on the ground of the interest or benefit that the director derived.

It could be argued that article 85 is contrary to a general provision in the CA 1985 s 310, which renders void any provision in the articles or a contract that purports to exempt any officer of the company from liability in respect of negligence, default, breach of duty or breach of trust. However, the fact that the article appears in Table A lends authority to the general proposition that the effect of article 85 is not to exempt directors from liability but to prevent the duty arising in the first place. Provided, therefore, that a director makes a proper disclosure, the strict judicial rules give way to a much more flexible framework.

1 Directors are subject to fines for breach of the provision. S 317(7).
2 S 317(3).
3 S 232.

Statutory regulation of loans and transactions involving a director

35.1.5 Because of abuses revealed by Department of Trade Inspectors in the 1970s and an increasing concern to render company directors more accountable, the CA 1980 introduced a number of new disclosure requirements and prohibitions relating to directors and persons connected with directors. The provisions apply generally to directors, 'a person connected with a director' and 'shadow directors'. A person connected with a director includes a director's spouse, children under eighteen, a company with which the director is associated, a trustee of a family trust and a partner.[1] The notion of a shadow director is intended to cover those persons who, although not formally appointed directors, are able to instruct or direct the board by virtue of their controlling interest.[2]

The effect of the provisions is to prohibit a company from making loans or guaranteeing loans to directors.[3] In addition, public companies are prohibited from entering into loans to a person connected with a director and other forms of arrangements and accommodations involving directors and persons connected with them.[4] There are a number of exceptions to the general rule in respect of transactions involving small amounts, some intra-group transactions and money-lending companies.[5] In respect of those loans and related transactions that are permitted, however, they must be disclosed to the board under s 317[6] and appear in a note to the annual accounts.[7]

An obvious potential abuse is where directors are involved in selling assets to, or buying assets from, their company. In order therefore to frustrate such attempts by the directors to strip a company of valuable assets, any arrangement between a company and its directors or persons connected with the directors involving the acquisition of non-cash assets must be approved by the company in general meeting.[8] Such approval is only required in respect of substantial property transactions, assessed according to specific financial criteria.[9]

1   CA 1985, s 346.
2   S 741.
3   S 330.
4   S 346.
5   See ss 331–340.
6   See 35.1.4.
7   S 232.
8   S 320.
9   See note 8 above.

Profits and opportunities derived from office

35.1.6   Another feature of the fiduciary duty of directors is that they must not make a profit or derive a benefit out of their office. If a director does make a profit then he is liable to account to the company. It is irrelevant that the director concerned acted in all good faith. As Lord Russell observed in the leading case of *Regal (Hastings) Ltd v Gulliver*:[1]

'The rules of equity which insists on those, who by use of a fiduciary position, make a profit, being liable to account for that profit, in no way depends on fraud, or absence of bona fides; or upon such questions or considerations as to whether the profit would or should otherwise have gone to the plaintiffs or whether the profiteer was under a duty to obtain the source of the profit for the plaintiff, whether he took a risk or acted as he did for the benefit of the plaintiff, or whether the plaintiff has in fact been damaged or benefited by his action. The liability arises from the mere fact of a profit having, in stated circumstances, been made. The profiteer, however honest and well-intentioned, cannot escape the risk of being called upon to account.'[2]

The basic condition for liability is that the profit has come to a director by virtue of his position as director in the course of his fiduciary relationship. The rules have been rigidly applied, particularly in the context of opportunities acquired by directors which should have gone to the company. Thus where the directors negotiate contracts for the company and then divert them for their own benefit, they will clearly be in breach.[3] Even where there is little chance of the company being awarded the contract in question, a director will be liable to account if he resigns to take the benefit of a contract negotiated privately between himself and a third party.[4] Such liability is based on the misuse of information.

> 'Information which came to him while he was managing director and which was of concern to the plaintiffs and relevant for the plaintiffs to know, was information which it was his duty to pass on to the plaintiffs.'[5]

The Canadian Supreme Court have held that where the board of a company reject an opportunity in good faith, and individual directors subsequently take it up privately, they are not accountable for the benefit so derived.[6] Such an approach is, however, unlikely to find favour in the UK given the rigid approach of British courts, since it ignores the underlying conflict of interest that the directors are faced with and the potential for abuse that may exist.

Given the fact that directors receive financial rewards for acting as fiduciaries, the relatively uncompromising approach of the British courts is perhaps justifiable. There may, however, be a case for codification of directors' fiduciary duties, with perhaps some modification of the strict rules for directors in private companies. Where the directors act in breach of this aspect of their duty, the general meeting[7] may ratify such a breach. However, if the breach involves actually misappropriating assets it can never be ratified.[8]

1 [1967] 2 AC 134n, [1942] 1 All ER 378, HL.
2 At 147.
3 *Cook v Deeks* [1916] 1 AC 554, PC.
4 *Industrial Development Consultants Ltd v Cooley* [1972] 2 All ER 162, [1972] 1 WLR 443.
5 Ibid at 451.
6 *Peso Silver Mines Ltd v Cropper* (1966) 58 DLR (2d) 1.
7 Including the directors voting as shareholders.
8 *Cook v Deeks* [1916] 1 AC 554, PC. See 35.2.2.

Directors' care and competence
35.1.7 By contrast to the onerous duties that the courts and Parliament have thrust upon directors in respect of their fiduciary duties, the expectations of the law in terms of directors' care and skill are minimal. In part this reflects the traditional reluctance of the courts to involve themselves in business judgements. It also reflects the traditional view of non-executive directors in the UK as genial, amateur, bystanders. Lord Boothby was quoted in 1962 in the following terms:

> 'If you have five directorships it is total heaven, like having a permanent hot bath. No effort of any kind is called for. You go to a meeting once a month in a car supplied by the company, you look grave and sage, on two occasions say "I agree" say "I don't think so" once and if all goes well get £500 a year.'[1]

An American judge has said:

> 'Directors are not specialists, like lawyers and doctors. They must have good sense, perhaps they must have acquaintance with affairs; but they

need not—indeed, perhaps they should not—have any technical talent. They are general advisers of the business and if they faithfully give such ability as they have to their charge, it would not be lawful to hold them liable.'[2]

Regrettably therefore the courts have largely opted out of making decisions which seek to judge the competence and skills of directors against any notional objective standards. In the leading case in this area it was stated that:

'A director need not exhibit in the performance of his duties a greater degree of skill than may be expected from a person of his knowledge and experience.'[3]

Thus, the fewer meetings a director attends, the less will be his experience and the lower his duty of care.[4]

Given the approach of the judiciary in this area of company law, it is hardly surprising that the question has been posed: 'Where else in human affairs can be found so admirable a combination of distinction without anxiety, of reward without toil?'[5]

It is perhaps worth noting that there is scarcely any contemporary judicial pronouncement on the modern director's duty of care and skill. Such as there is suggests that the courts might take a less benevolent view of the role of directors. In an unreported case in 1980 concerning the duties of non-executive directors with accountancy experience, it was considered unreasonable for them not to attend board meetings or display some interest in the company.[6] Given the scope of the statutory obligations now placed upon all directors, it is entirely appropriate that the courts should raise their expectations in respect of the level of competence they require.

Executive directors appointed to specific positions for their professional skills are of course subject to the standards of care and skill expected of a reasonably competent member of that profession or trade.

1 Chamberlain, 'Why It's Harder and Harder to Get a Good Board', Fortune, November 1962, p 109.
2 *Barnes v Andrews District Court* NY 298 Fed Rep 614 (1924).
3 *Re City Equitable Fire Insurance Co Ltd* [1925] Ch 407 at 428, CA per Romer J.
4 See *Re Cardiff Savings Bank, Marquis of Bute's Case* [1892] 2 Ch 100.
5 See Dwight, 17 Yale LJ 33 (1907).
6 *Dorchester Finance Co Ltd v Stebbing* (1980) 1 Co Law 38.

Rendering the directors accountable

35.2.0 We have seen that the legal model of directors' accountability rests on the shareholders in general meeting, supported by legislative disclosure requirements, prior approval provisions and prohibitions in respect of certain transactions. It is essential, as in all democratic institutions, that the directorate secure the continued support or at least acquiescence of the majority of shareholders, in order to retain office. The majority may waive or ratify certain breaches of the directors' duties provided that they act strictly in accordance with the constitution of the company. So long as majority support is secured no further justification or explanation is required. The directors may even use their own votes as shareholders to ratify their own misdeeds, and the courts will rarely examine someone's motives for casting a vote. As Jessell MR observed in 1877:

'Where men exercise their rights of property, they exercise their rights from some motive adequate or inadequate and I have always considered the law to be that those who have the rights of property are entitled to exercise them whatever their motives may be . . . A man may be actuated in giving his vote by interests entirely adverse to the interests of the company as a whole. He may think it more for his particular interest that a certain course may be taken which may be in the opinion of others very adverse to the interests of the company as a whole, but he cannot be restrained from giving his vote in what way he pleases because he is influenced by that motive . . . He has a right, if he thinks fit, to give his vote from motives or promptings of what he considers his own individual interests.'[1]

Despite suggestions that the exercise of a vote is 'subject to equitable considerations which may make it unjust . . . to exercise it in a particular way,'[2] Jessell's comments represent the orthodox statement of principle.

When coupled with the fact that 'shareholders as a body are passive and apathetic about their rights and responsibilities',[3] the principle allowing directors to ratify their own misdeeds, represents a serious threat to the legitimacy of corporate activity. What action, therefore, may a minority of shareholders take against delinquent controlling directors?

In a plc the directors may be exposed to adverse comment in the financial press, informal pressure from financial institutions holding sizeable blocks of shares in the company and ultimately the influence of the market place in terms of the impact of their activities on the market value of their company's shares, which may force them to submit to investigation. A failure to take appropriate action may lead to formal action by City institutions and regulatory bodies or a Department of Trade investigation into the affairs of the company.[4] The simplest remedy for the shareholder is to sell his shares on the open market.

By definition, a private company is not subject to the same market pressure, although their affairs may be subjected to Department of Trade investigation. Furthermore, the dissenting shareholder does not have a public market available whereby he can relinquish his investment in the company. Often shareholders in a private company can become locked into the company, the only route out being to persuade the majority, with whom they disagree, to buy them out or permit the company to buy their shares.[5] The only alternative may be costly litigation. Such litigation may be based on enforcing the shareholders' personal rights, or in the case of a group of shareholders, a representative action on behalf of the group to enforce their rights; or a derivative action whereby the shareholder takes action on behalf of the company in respect of rights derived from the company. In the latter case the benefit resulting from the litigation belongs to the company. In addition to litigation enforcing the directors' duties, a shareholder may seek redress by petitioning for the winding up of the company,[6] or applying for an order against the wrongdoers on the grounds that the affairs of the company have been or are being conducted in a manner unfairly prejudicial to some part of the membership.[7]

1 *Pender v Lushington* (1877) 6 Ch D 70 at 76.
2 *Clemens v Clemens Bros Ltd* [1976] 2 All ER 268 at 282.
3 Midgley, *Companies and Their Shareholders: The Uneasy Relationship* (1975) p 54.
4 See CA 1985, ss 431–453.
5 See 34.2.2.
6 Insolvency Act 1986, s 122.
7 S 459.

Who can sue to enforce directors' duties? The rule in Foss v Harbottle

35.2.1 Since directors owe their duties to the company it must be the company in general meeting that decides to sue, not any individual shareholder. In the words of Lord Davey in *Burland v Earle*:[1]

'It is an elementary principle of the law relating to joint stock companies that the court will not interfere with the internal management of companies acting within their powers and in fact has no jurisdiction to do so. Again it is clear law that in order to redress a wrong done to the company, the action should prime facie be brought by the company itself. These cardinal principles are laid down in the well known case of *Foss v Harbottle*.'[2]

Without such a rule it is argued that companies would be 'torn to pieces'[3] by litigation, 'there would be futile actions and a multiplicity of suits.'[4]

The principle of non-interference originated from the early law of partnership[5] where the courts were averse to interfering between partners unless it was for the purpose of dissolving the relationship. The principle that the proper plaintiff in an action should be the company is no more than the application of the *Salomon* principle.[6]

In practical terms the so-called rule in *Foss v Harbottle* reflects the principle of majority rule.

'If the thing complained of is a thing which in substance the majority of the company are entitled to do, or if something has been done irregularly which the majority of the company are entitled to do regularly . . . there can be no use in having litigation about it, the ultimate end of which is only that a meeting has to be called and then ultimately the majority gets its wishes.'[7]

If strictly applied the consequence of the rule is that if a company's directors are in breach of their duty to the company and can control voting at the general meeting, they can operate with impunity. Such a situation would expose minority shareholders to considerable potential prejudice. Thus the courts have over the years formulated four basic exceptions to the general rule prohibiting action by individual shareholders.

1 [1902] AC 83 at 93, HL.
2 (1843) 2 Hare 461.
3 *Compagnie de Mayville v Whitley* [1896] 1 Ch 788 at 807, CA.
4 *Foss v Harbottle* (1843) 2 Hare 461 at 494.
5 See 32.5.2.
6 See 33.0.0.
7 *MacDougall v Gardiner* (1875) 1 Ch D 13 at 25, CA.

Exceptions to the Foss v Harbottle rule

35.2.2 The following are exceptions to the rule in *Foss v Harbottle*.
(a) Where the action complained of is beyond the capacity of the company, it can never be approved by the general meeting and hence a shareholder is permitted to raise an action against those responsible.
(b) If the articles specify that a particular matter can only be carried out by a special majority and the general meeting purports to carry it out on a simple majority, a minority shareholder would be permitted to bring an action restraining the majority.[1]
(c) Similarly, since a company's memorandum and articles represent a

contract between the shareholders and the company, one would expect that shareholders could bring an action to enforce their own personal rights without being confronted with the rule in *Foss v Harbottle*. If taken to its logical conclusion, any breach by the company of the terms of the articles and hence the shareholders' contractual rights would be sufficient to permit litigation by the shareholder. In reality the courts have allowed shareholders to proceed with litigation where the company has sought to interfere with such rights as the right to vote[2] or the right to have a dividend paid in cash where the articles so specify.[3] They have, however, fallen well short of laying down a general right of shareholders to have the articles observed to the letter. Thus a shareholder does not have a right to require directors to retire in accordance with the articles[4] or a right to have a poll taken.[5] Consistent with the principle of majority rule, a key factor has been whether the alleged irregularity can be put right by an ordinary majority in general meeting. If it can be so ratified, action by the shareholders may not be permitted. In certain circumstances the court may even stay proceedings in order to put the issue to a vote.[6]

(d) Where a fraud has been committed against the minority shareholders and the persons alleged to have committed the fraud are in control of the company and are thereby able to frustrate any action being brought, the minority shareholders will be permitted to bring a derivative action on behalf of the company. In order to succeed the shareholders have to satisfy the twin requirements of fraud and control on the part of the wrongdoer. Fraud is taken to mean any abuse or misuse of the directors' powers. It extends to any appropriation of corporate property, interests or advantages by the majority.[7] Once again consistent with the principle of majority rule, the central question is whether the particular action complained of can be ratified by the majority. A fraud can never be ratified by the majority. On the other hand, making a profit out of their position as directors is ratifiable by the majority.[8] A failure on the part of the directors to exercise a reasonable degree of care and skill may also be ratified by the general meeting[9] but not to the extent that the directors benefit considerably to the detriment of the company.[10] The control factor relates to the fact that the wrongdoers, by virtue of their shareholding, are frustrating any attempt by the minority to challenge them. In general, the minority must be in a position to show that their attempts at challenging the majority have come to nothing. They cannot proceed simply on the basis that the alleged wrongdoers have a controlling majority. An interesting question is whether control means an absolute majority or whether it encompasses minority control. It has long been recognised as a matter of practice that it is possible to exert a controlling influence over a company without actually owning a majority of its shares. The key factor would seem to be whether the wrongdoers are in effective control and this, according to the Court of Appeal in *Prudential Assurance Co Ltd v Newman Industries Ltd (No 2)*[11] embraces a broad spectrum extending from an overall absolute majority of votes at one end to a majority of votes at the other end made up of those likely to be cast by the delinquent himself plus those voting with him as a result of influence or apathy.

1 See *Edwards v Halliwell* [1950] 2 All ER 1064, CA.
2 *Pender v Lushington* (1877) 6 Ch D 70.
3 *Wood v Odessa Waterworks Co* (1889) 42 Ch D 636.

4   *Mozley v Alston* (1847) 1 Ph 790.
5   *MacDougall v Gardiner* (1875) 1 Ch D 13, CA.
6   See *Hogg v Cramphorn Ltd* [1967] Ch 254, [1966] 3 All ER 420.
7   *Cook v Deeks* [1916] 1 AC 554, PC.
8   See note 7 above.
9   *Pavlides v Jensen* [1956] Ch 565, [1956] 2 All ER 518.
10 *Daniels v Daniels* [1978] Ch 406, [1978] 2 All ER 89.
11 *No 2* [1982] Ch 204 at 219, CA.

Statutory protection available to a minority

35.2.3   There are two statutory provisions which offer some protection to an aggrieved minority. The first operates in the context of a winding up of the company and the second offers a general remedy in respect of unfairly prejudicial conduct.

By far the commonest form of dispute that is sought to be resolved under these provisions is the so-called deadlock or corporate squeeze out. The issues raised often go beyond an orthodox breach of the directors' duties and extend into such areas as the rights of a sizeable minority shareholder and director to contribute to management, and the flow of information from the controlling directorate to other directors and shareholders. A typical example of disputes that arise under these provisions would be where a dominant 'founding father' of a business refuses to recognise the legitimate expectations of the directors or family shareholders, or seeks to squeeze out a former partner who provided initial expertise for the business. A particular feature of the cases is that the minority are often asserting a right to take part in management rather than a right specifically arising as a shareholder.

By contrast to the general attitude of the courts in refusing to involve themselves in business judgements, they have displayed an increasing willingness and sympathy towards the plight of aggrieved petitioners in 'quasi-partnership'[1] cases.[2]

1   Business associations that are formally limited companies but which in practice are run on the basis of the principles of mutual understanding, equality and good faith associated with partnership.
2   See *Ebrahimi v Westbourne Galleries Ltd* [1973] AC 360, [1972] 2 All ER 492, HL.

Winding up—misfeasance summons

35.2.4   If it appears in the course of a liquidation that a promoter, director, manager or officer of the company or liquidator or administrative receiver or administrator—

> 'has misapplied or retained or become liable or accountable for any money or property of the company, or has been guilty of any misfeasance or the breach of fiduciary duty, or other duty in relation to the company'[1]

an application may be made to the court requiring the wrongdoer to repay funds, restore any property or pay compensation.

An application would normally be made by the liquidator but may be made by a creditor or shareholder. For shareholders, the advantage of a misfeasance summons is that once the company is in the process of liquidation, litigation cannot be frustrated by the rule in *Foss v Harbottle*.

1   Insolvency Act 1986, s 212.

Winding up on the grounds of justice and equity

35.2.5 The most obvious means of dealing with unreasonable or intolerable conduct by corporate controllers is to terminate the existence of the company. Amongst the grounds for the winding up of a company[1] is a general provision entitling the court to wind up a company if it is of the opinion that it is just and equitable that the company be wound up.

A shareholder can apply for a winding up order under this provision provided he can establish that he has a tangible interest in the winding up. In effect this means that he must convince the court that there will be surplus assets available for himself and other shareholders after the creditors' claims have been settled.[2] If the basis of the shareholder's complaint is the lack of information from the controllers, it is likely that he will not be in a position to assess whether there will be surplus assets. In such a case the courts will normally permit the application to proceed.[3]

In order to prevent persons from buying shares in a company with the object of petitioning for a winding up, a shareholder must normally have held his shares for six months during the eighteen months before the commencement of the winding up.[4] Where a petitioner has an alternative remedy the court may still order a winding up provided that the petitioner is not acting unreasonably in failing to pursue the alternative.[5]

Most of the reported cases under these provisions have concerned companies that operate as quasi-partnerships where the management has become deadlocked or the mutual trust between 'partners' has broken down. Petitions have also been granted where directors have failed to hold meetings and submit accounts and the business has been run down in order to force a minority to sell their shares at an undervalue.[6]

The most influential case has been the decision of the House of Lords in *Ebrahimi v Westbourne Galleries Ltd*[7]. The case concerned two individuals, who originally traded in partnership and subsequently decided to form a company to run their business. They each took 500 shares in the company and both became directors. Soon after forming the company one of the founder's sons joined the company as director and each of the founding directors transferred 100 shares to him. The profits in the company were always distributed in the form of directors' remuneration rather than dividends. Eventually, the two families disagreed and the father and son exercised their majority voting power and removed the founding director quite legitimately under the CA 1948, s 184 (now CA 1985, s 303). The effect of this removal from the board was to exclude him from the management of the company and, in view of the no dividend policy, deprive him of an income from the company. The aggrieved shareholder/director petitioned for a winding up order on the grounds of justice and equity.

The House of Lords held that despite the fact that the controllers were doing no more than they were legally entitled to do and there was no question of fraud or similar impropriety, the petitioner should succeed. In particular they considered that when the two founding partners converted their business to a company it was on the basis of an underlying obligation of mutual trust, good faith and joint participation in management. Once that had broken down it was only just and equitable to formally dissolve the relationship. Lord Wilberforce observed that:

'There is room in company law for recognition of the fact that behind it (a legal entity) or amongst it there are individuals with rights,

491

expectations and obligations inter se which are not necessarily submerged in the company structure. The "just and equitable" provision does not . . . entitle one party to disregard the obligation he assumes by entering a company, nor the court to dispense him from it. It does, as equity always does, enable the court to subject the exercise of legal rights to equitable considerations; considerations of a personal character arising between one individual and another, which may make it unjust or inequitable to insist on legal rights, or to exercise them in a particular way.'[8]

A possible stumbling block for the petitioner was that the conduct he was complaining of affected him in his capacity as director rather than member of the company. Indeed, in respect of the alternative remedy[9] the courts have insisted that the petitioner be affected in his capacity as member. However, their Lordships took a broad view, holding that the petitioner is entitled to rely on any circumstance of justice and equity in his relations with the company or other shareholders.

Lord Wilberforce observed that equitable considerations should apply in respect of certain types of company where one or more of the following factors exist:[10]

(a) An association formed or continued on the basis of a personal relationship, involving mutual confidence. Invariably, this will arise when a partnership has been converted into a company.
(b) An agreement or undertaking in respect of participating in management.
(c) Restriction upon the transfer of the member's interest in the company thus rendering it difficult for a shareholder who has lost confidence in the management to sell his shares.

1 See Insolvency Act 1986, s 122.
2 See *Re Othery Construction Ltd* [1966] 1 All ER 145, [1966] 1 WLR 69.
3 *Re Argentum Reduction (UK) Ltd* [1975] 1 All ER 608, [1975] 1 WLR 186.
4 S 124(2).
5 The alternative may well be a petition under s 459; see 35.2.6.
6 *Loch v John Blackwood Ltd* [1924] AC 783, PC.
7 [1973] AC 360, [1972] 2 All ER 492, HL.
8 At 379.
9 See 35.2.6.
10 At 379.

Alternative statutory remedy
35.2.6 The difficulty with petitioning for the winding up of a company is that it represents an extremely drastic step and the petitioner is faced with the prospect of killing the goose that lays the golden egg, in order to obtain redress. In view of this the CA 1948, s 210, introduced a discretionary remedy available for shareholders where the facts otherwise justify a winding up order. The basis of a complaint under s 210 was that the affairs of the company were being conducted in a manner oppressive to some part of the members.

The section did not provide minority shareholders with an effective alternative remedy. In the period 1948 up to its repeal in the CA 1980, there were only two successful reported cases.[1] The problem with s 210 was that the basic condition of relief under it indicated a course of conduct as distinct from an isolated act. The use of the word oppressive was also considered to be too strong a word to be appropriate in all cases, and certainly would not cover mismanagement of the company. Unlike petitions for winding up, the courts considered that the petitioner must be oppressed in his capacity as a member; exclusion from management was not therefore a ground for petitioning.

The CA 1980, s 75 (now CA 1985, s 459) replaced s 210 with a provision modelled largely on recommendations made by the Jenkins Committee in 1962.[2] The remedy now provides that any member of a company may petition the court for an order on the ground that the affairs of the company are being or have been conducted in a manner unfairly prejudicial to the interests of some part of the members, including the petitioner. The section makes it clear that the conduct complained of may relate to any actual or proposed act or omission of the company.

The provision is a clear improvement on s 210 in that there is no require-ment on the petitioner to establish that the facts otherwise justify a winding up; it extends to single acts or omissions and a petition can be presented in anticipation of proposed prejudicial conduct. The major change, however, was that oppression was replaced by conduct 'unfairly prejudicial'.

The Jenkins Committee considered that unfairly prejudicial conduct represents, at the very least:

> 'a visible departure from the standards of fair dealing, and violation of the conditions of fair play on which every shareholder who entrusts his money to a company is entitled to rely.'[3]

There is no doubt that it covers a wider range of misconduct and malad-ministration than the notion of oppression did. For instance, it has been held that:

> 'without prejudice to the generality of the wording of the section which may cover many other situations, a member of a company will be able to bring himself within the section if he can show that the value of his shareholding has been seriously diminished or at least seriously jeopardised by reason of a course of conduct on the part of those persons who had had de facto control of the company, which has been unfair to the member concerned. The test of unfairness must, I think, be an objective, not a subjective one. In other words it is not necessary to show that the persons who have had de facto control of the company have acted as they did in the conscious knowledge that this was unfair to the petitioner or that they were acting in bad faith; the test I think, is whether a reasonable bystander observing the consequences of their conduct would regard it as having unfairly prejudiced the petitioner's interests.'[4]

The early reported cases on the new provision suggest that the courts are persisting with a narrow interpretation. Indeed in the first reported case[5] the court adopted an approach reminiscent of their approach to s 210 in holding that a petitioner must establish that he has been prejudiced in his capacity as a member. If such an approach is taken it means that the petitioner in the *Ebrahimi* case would not succeed under the unfair prejudice provision and is consequently confined to a winding up petition with its inevitable damage to the company.

Although there are signs of a less restrictive attitude to the provision,[6] the indications are that the narrow approach of the courts to s 210 will be continued when interpreting this provision and, when such an approach is coupled with a refusal to become involved in business judgements, the net result is a modest gain for the interests of an aggrieved minority shareholder/director.

In the event that a court is satisfied that the petitioner's claim is well founded it can 'make such order as it thinks fit for giving relief in respect of the matters complained of.'[7] In particular it may make one of the following orders.

(a) An order regulating the conduct of the company's affairs in the future. This might include the appointment or removal of directors, an alteration of the articles or simply calling of a meeting. In *Re H R Harmer Ltd*[8] the court granted an order under s 210 removing the founder of the business, who ran it in an autocratic and improper manner from his office as director and demoting him to the position of an expert adviser at a fixed salary without any specific duties.

(b) An order requiring the company to refrain from doing or continuing an act complained of by the petitioner or to do an act which the petitioner has complained it has omitted to do.

(c) An order authorising civil proceedings to be brought in the name of and on behalf of the company. In effect this provision enables a petitioner to circumvent the rule in *Foss v Harbottle* by persuading the court to initiate litigation enforcing the directors' duties. However as Farrar points out 'few shareholders will be attracted by a provision which simply authorises further litigation.'[9]

(d) An order providing for the purchase of the shares of any members of the company by other members or by the company itself and, in the latter case, a consequent reduction of the company's capital. This is the most likely order since in a great many cases of unfair prejudice the petitioner is seeking relief in the form of an equitable exit from the company. The difficulty however arises when it comes to placing a value on the shares. When the petitioner is a quasi-partner and petitioning as an alternative to winding up, then the value of his shares will be assessed as a proportion of the company's net worth, not necessarily the market value of the shareholding which would have to reflect the minority status of the holding.[10]

1 See *Scottish Co-operative Wholesale Society Ltd v Meyer* [1959] AC 324, [1958] 3 All ER 66, HL; *Re H R Harmer Ltd* [1958] 3 All ER 689, [1959] 1 WLR 62, CA.
2 See Jenkins Committee, Cmnd 1749, 1962, para 199.
3 Para 204 quoting with approval a passage from *Elder v Elder and Watson Ltd* 1952 SC 49 at 55.
4 *Re R A Noble & Sons (Clothing) Ltd* [1983] BCLC 273. Nourse J approving a statement of Slade J in *Re Bovey Hotel Ventures Ltd* (31 July 1981, unreported), Ch D.
5 *Re a company (No 004475 of 1982)* [1983] Ch 178, [1983] 2 All ER 36.
6 See *Re London School of Electronics Ltd* [1986] Ch 211, [1985] 3 WLR 474.
7 S 461(2).
8 [1958] 3 All ER 689, [1959] 1 WLR 62, CA.
9 Farrar *Company Law* (1985) p 383.
10 *Re Bird Precision Bellows* [1984] Ch 419, [1984] 3 All ER 444, CA.

Chapter 36
Corporate Insolvency and Winding up

36.0.0 Traditionally company law has laid down two methods for dealing with the failure of limited companies—a receivership and a winding up or liquidation. A receivership is the process by which a secured creditor seeks to enforce his security. Invariably receivership is followed by the winding up of the business which is the process by which a company is formally dissolved. The common feature of both procedures is that they require the collection and realisation of corporate assets and the payment of debts.

Where an ailing company has no floating chargeholders then the only option available to it, other than a winding up, is some form of accommodation with its creditors to tide the company over. It could be therefore that some potentially viable companies are forced into liquidation for want of a floating charge under which a receiver could be appointed to protect the secured assets and possibly turn the company round.

The Insolvency Act 1985 (IA 1985) therefore introduced a new procedure as an alternative to receivership, whereby a court is empowered to make an administration order in respect of a company in financial difficulties. In addition the IA 1985 has also introduced a simplified procedure whereby a company can reach a compromise agreement or arrangement with its creditors, in order perhaps to avoid insolvency. The provisions of the CA 1985 and IA 1985 relating to corporate insolvency and winding up are now contained in the Insolvency Act 1986 (IA 1986).

Why do companies get into difficulties?
36.0.1 The actual causes of corporate insolvency are complex involving a variety of factors. Such factors may be: general recession and inflation in the domestic and world economy; the impact of industrial action; changes in government policy penalising certain activities or rendering others less profitable; changes in consumer habits and consumer preferences and a failure to diversify sufficiently; a lack of financial control within the corporate organisation or inadequate management information; a management team that has failed to predict the consequences of the above factors or are otherwise inadequate and incompetent.

Surprisingly, very little research has been carried out specifically on the causes of corporate insolvency.[1] Indeed, the Cork Committee which reported in 1982 on the whole area of *Insolvency Law and Practice*[2] was criticised for a failure to undertake any empirical analysis of business failure.[3]

1   See Argenti, *Corporate Collapse* (1976).
2   Cmnd 8558, 1982.
3   See Farrar, 1983 4 Co Law 20.

The role of the law in insolvency

36.0.2   As a general rule the policy basis of insolvency law has been founded on two central objectives. First, the law is used as an instrument in the process of debt recovery. The threat of receivership or liquidation is a powerful weapon in persuading a defaulting company to settle a debt. Second—

> 'insolvency laws, through their investigative process, are the means by which the demands of commercial morality can be met; any disciplinary measures against the debtor which may appear necessary in the light of this investigating process can be imposed either inside the insolvency proceedings themselves or outside, for example, by the machinery of the criminal law or by professional disciplinary bodies.'[1]

In the government's response to the Cork Report they described the role of modern corporate insolvency law as:
(a) to establish effective and straightforward procedures for dealing with and settling the affairs of insolvent companies in the interests of the creditors;
(b) to provide a statutory framework to encourage companies to pay attention to their financial circumstances so they recognise difficulties at an early stage and before the creditors' interests are prejudiced seriously;
(c) to deter and penalise irresponsible behaviour and malpractice on the part of those managing a company's affairs;
(d) to ensure that those acting in insolvency cases are competent to do so and conduct themselves properly;
(e) to facilitate the re-organisation of companies in difficulties, to minimise unnecessary loss to creditors and to the economy when insolvency occurs.[2]

Given these central objectives, it was concluded that the insolvency law should be radically revised, hence the Insolvency Acts 1985 and 1986.

1   Cork Report, Cmnd 8558, 1982, p 62.
2   *A Revised Framework for Insolvency Law* Cmnd 9175, 1984.

Insolvency practitioners

36.0.3   The Cork Committee recognised that there was a need for greater control to be exercised in respect of the activities of people acting as receivers and liquidators. Any person, however inexperienced, could be appointed a liquidator or receiver. The Committee recommended that some minimum professional qualification and control is necessary:

> 'It is essential that measures are introduced to ensure a high standard of competence as well as integrity in the persons who are eligible for appointment as insolvency practitioners. The existing system is too open to abuse to command public confidence.'[1]

The recommendations were accepted by the government and the Insolvency Act 1986 provides that no person may act as an insolvency practitioner unless he is an individual who is a member of a recognised professional body or has been authorised by the 'relevant authority' set up by the Secretary of State.

Practitioners will also have to provide bonding or insurance for all forms of insolvency proceedings as a safeguard for creditors against losses occurring through misappropriation of funds. These requirements will be laid down by delegated legislation.[2] Professional bodies will be granted recognition by the Secretary of State provided that the rules of the body contain appropriate provisions to ensure that members authorised by it to act as insolvency practitioners are suitably qualified.[3] Where a person is not a member of a recognised professional body, he may apply directly for authorisation to act as an insolvency practitioner to the relevant body appointed by the Secretary of State. In general, the applicant must be a fit and proper person to act as an insolvency practitioner and satisfy prescribed educational and practical training and experience requirements.[4]

Where authorisation has been refused or withdrawn an appeal may be made to an Insolvency Practitioners Tribunal.[5] It will be an offence to act as an insolvency practitioner whilst unqualified.[6]

An individual is disqualified from acting as an insolvency practitioner if:
(a) he is an undischarged bankrupt;
(b) he is the subject of a disqualification order under the Company Directors Disqualification Act 1986 in that he has been convicted of an indictable offence in connection with the promotion, formation, management or insolvency of a company, or he has been persistently in default filing documents with the Registrar, or in the course of a winding up, it appears that he has been guilty of fraud or breach of duty;
(c) he is a patient within the meaning of Part VII of the Mental Health Act 1983.

1 Cmnd 8558, 1982, p 180.
2 IA 1986, s 390(3).
3 S 391.
4 S 393.
5 S 396.
6 S 389.

Receivership
36.0.4 Receivership is concerned with the realisation of the assets of a company which are subject to a floating charge, and payment of the proceeds to the holder of the charge. Secured creditors are entitled to resort to their security quite independently of a winding up and without regard to the unsecured creditors or, necessarily, what is best for the company.

If a company defaults under a secured debenture one of the options available to the creditor is the appointment of a receiver and manager.[1] A receiver may be appointed by the court, in which case he will be an officer of the court. In practice, however, it is most common for a receiver to be appointed directly by the debenture holder under the terms of the debenture. The Insolvency Act 1986 has codified the powers and duties of receivers appointed directly under a debenture[2] secured by a floating charge.

(a) Receiver appointed by the court

In the case of a receiver appointed by the court, since he is an officer of the court, he cannot be an agent for the debenture holders or the company. He is personally liable on contracts that he makes but has a right to be indemnified out of the assets of the company for such liabilities. Once appointed, the receiver assumes the authority of the directors and the powers of the company in respect of those assets covered by the charge.

(b) Administrative receiver

An administrative receiver is a receiver or manager of the whole or substantially the whole of a company's property. He is appointed by the holders of any debentures secured either by a floating charge or by such a charge and one or more other securities.[3] He has a number of statutory powers, including the power:

(a) to carry on the business of the company;
(b) to take possession of the company's property (only in so far as it is covered by the security);
(c) to raise or borrow money and grant security;
(d) to refer issues affecting the company to arbitration and make any arrangements or compromise on behalf of the company. He may also bring and defend any legal action or proceedings;
(e) to appoint a solicitor, accountant, professional adviser or agent;
(f) to present petition for the winding up of the company;
(g) to employ and dismiss employees;
(h) to rank any claim in bankruptcy, insolvency, sequestration or liquidation proceedings against a debtor of the company;
(i) to establish subsidiaries of the company;
(j) to do all other things incidental to the exercise of all the above powers.[4]

The administrative receiver will also have such other powers as are conferred on him by the terms of the debenture under which he was appointed.

Within three months of his appointment the administrative receiver must send a report to the Registrar of Companies, to any trustees for secured creditors and, in so far as he is aware of their addresses, to all creditors.[5] The report must contain details of the events leading up to his appointment; the disposal or proposed disposal of any property of the company and any carrying on of the company's business; the amounts of principal and interest payable to the debenture holders; the amount likely to be available to other creditors; and a summary of the statement of affairs in respect of the company submitted to the administrative receiver by the officers of the company soon after his appointment.[6]

An administrative receiver is deemed to be the company's agent[7] and is personally liable on any contract entered into by him in carrying out his functions.[8]

---

1 The term 'manager' is used because the property subject to the charge may require management.
2 Termed under the Act 'administrative receivers'; s 29(2).
3 IA 1986, s 29.
4 IA 1986 Sch 1.
5 S 48.
6 S 48.
7 S 44.
8 He may, however, contract out of such liability; s 44(1)(b).

Receivers and payment of corporate debts

36.0.5   A receiver is required to pay the company's debts in a particular order. First the costs of selling the property, collecting the debts and enforcing claims against third parties. Second, his own expenses and remuneration. Third, the costs and expenses of the trustees of the debenture. Fourth, the costs of the debenture holder action, if any. Fifth, in the case of debentures secured by a floating charge, the debts of the company which would be preferential debts in a liquidation of the company.[1] Sixth, the debenture holders' debt with interest. This would be followed by any subsequent debenture holder and finally the claims of the ordinary creditors could be settled.

1   See 36.0.15.

The advantages and disadvantages of receivership[1]

36.0.6   As indicated above the appointment of a receiver is essentially a matter for the secured creditor to decide. Such an appointment can, however, have a profound impact on the company. If a business is suffering existing cash flow problems, the expenses of receivership can only serve to add to the problem. Furthermore, the very fact of a receiver being appointed is likely to depress the company's trade since other traders may be reluctant to deal with them except on a cash basis. It is also unlikely that the receiver's staff will have any knowledge of the company's activities and will therefore need to employ management specialists in the area.

On the plus side, however, one could argue that if the assets are not being efficiently deployed and are in jeopardy, they are better realised and employed elsewhere. Receivership does at least enable an ailing business to be subjected to critical monitoring and scrutiny and it may facilitate the sale of viable segments of the company as a going concern.

1   See Farrar, *Company Law* (1985) pp 541–542.

Administration

36.0.7   The Cork Committee[1] recommended that an alternative insolvency mechanism known as an administration be introduced. Such an administrator would be appointed by the court on an application by the company or a creditor of the company. These proposals were accepted in a modified form by the government[2] and are contained in the Insolvency Act 1986, ss 8–27.

The novelty of the provisions is that the remedy, unlike receivership, is not confined to secured creditors. The objective is not therefore geared towards enforcing a security but corporate rehabilitation or at least a more advantageous realisation of the company's assets than would occur in the context of a winding up.

Before making an administration order the court must be satisfied that the company is, or is likely to become, unable to pay its debts and it must consider that the making of an order would be likely to achieve one or more of the following purposes:

(a) the survival of the company, and the whole or any part of its undertaking as a going concern;

(b) the approval at a meeting of the company and its creditors of a composition in satisfaction of the company's debts or a scheme of arrangement of its affairs;

(c) the sanctioning under CA 1985, s 425, of a compromise or arrangement;[3]

(d) a more advantageous realisation of the assets than would be effected in a winding up.[4]

The administrator appointed must be a qualified insolvency practitioner. He will have the same powers and duties as a receiver and manager appointed under a floating charge.[5]

Notice of a petition must be served on any holder of a floating charge and an administrative receiver may still be appointed before the order is made. Where such an appointment has been made the court must dismiss the petition for an order unless the debenture holder consents to the administration order; or any existing security under which a receiver may be appointed would be invalid as against the liquidator.[6]

After an administration order has been made any administrative receiver must vacate office.[7] In general the effect of an administration order is that no steps can be taken to enforce any security over the company property, or to repossess goods under a hire purchase, leasing or retention of title agreement, without consent of the administrator or leave of the court. Also without such consent or leave no other proceedings or legal process may be taken against the company. An administrator will be expected to prepare plans consistent with the purpose behind his appointment. An administrator has powers akin to those of a liquidator; he can for example challenge any transactions entered into by the directors.

As the Cork Committee observed:

'The new procedure is likely to be beneficial only in cases where there is a business of sufficient substance to justify the expense of an administration, and where there is a real prospect of returning to profitability or selling as a going concern.'[8]

1   See Ch 9.
2   White Paper, Cmnd 9175.
3   See 36.0.8.
4   S 8(3).
5   See 36.0.4.
6   S 9.
7   S 11.
8   Para 508.

Arrangements with creditors

36.0.8   If the directors of a company in financial difficulties have entered into an agreement with the creditors for a moratorium on debts, to tide the company over a difficult period, it may be that liquidation could be avoided. A liquidator may also find a compromise agreement with the company's creditors useful in the process of securing a speedy and efficient realisation of the assets of the company, thus avoiding expensive and time consuming disputes and litigation.

If the creditors unanimously agree to a compromise or arrangement, so much the better. The CA 1985, s 425 does, however, provide a procedure for application to the court to sanction an arrangement approved by a majority of the creditors.[1]

The statutory procedure is however rarely used since the level of protection built into the provisions for dissenting creditors has rendered it expensive and time consuming. In general the procedure is unduly formal and complex.[2] With such faults in mind the IA 1986, ss 1–7 has introduced a new procedure to provide an alternative to the formal s 425 procedure. In essence, the objective of the new procedure is to minimise the court's involvement.

The proposed scheme must involve a qualified insolvency practitioner to act as trustee and generally supervise implementation of it.

1   A majority in number representing three quarters in value of the creditors present and voting.
2   See Cork Report, Ch 7.

Winding up

36.0.9   The winding up of a company is the statutory process for bringing the operations of a company to an end, realising its assets and distributing the proceeds amongst its creditors and shareholders in accordance with their rights and interests. Winding up is followed by the dissolution of the company. It is important to emphasise from the outset that a company may be wound up even where it remains solvent.

A company may be wound up in one of two ways:
(a)   compulsorily by order of the courts;
(b)   voluntarily by the members if the company is solvent, or by creditors where the company is insolvent.

Compulsory winding up

36.0.10   Application for a compulsory winding up is made by way of petition presented by the company itself, by shareholders[1], by the creditors and in certain circumstances by the Department of Trade.

The IA 1986 lists seven grounds on which a compulsory winding up may be made.[2] We have already discussed one of the grounds in the context of minority shareholders' rights.[3] Of the other six grounds by far the most important ground is that which is based on the company being insolvent, that is, unable to pay its debts.[4]

In general a company is deemed unable to pay its debts in three situations. First, if a creditor owed more than £750 has served notice on the company demanding payment and has received no satisfaction within 21 days.[5] Second, in the case of a disputed debt, if a court gives judgement against the company on the liability for the debt and the creditor seeks payment by process of the law, and the debt is not satisfied by the company.[6] Third, where it is proved to the satisfaction of the court that the company is unable to pay its debts.[7] In particular, a company is deemed unable to pay its debts if it is proved that the value of its assets is less than the amount of its liabilities, taking into account contingent and prospective liabilities.[8] This method is designed to cover the situation where a creditor due to be paid at some future date feels that given the current and prospective financial position of the company, the debt is unlikely to be satisfied on the due date.

If the court makes a winding up order after hearing the petition, it will appoint a liquidator. In most instances the person appointed will be on the staff of the Department of Trade and Industry, known as an Official Receiver.

1   S 124. The shareholder must have held their shares for six months and prove an interest in the winding up.
2   S 122.
3   See 35.2.5.
4   S 122(f).
5   S 123(1)(a).
6   S 123(1)(b).
7   S 123(1)(e).
8   S 123(IA).

Voluntary winding up

36.0.11   A voluntary winding up is originated by a resolution passed by the company in general meeting.[1] If the directors are willing to make a statement that the company is solvent and able to pay its debts within a period of one year, the winding up will be a members' winding up. Solvency in this context means that the directors have made a full inquiry into the company's affairs and as a result have formed the opinion that it is able to pay its debts within twelve months of the resolution. Should the debts not be paid in full, the directors may be liable to penalties.[2]

The 'advantage' of a members' winding up is that the members can appoint a liquidator of their own choice, who may be someone with a less than rigorous attitude towards the conduct of the directorate. However, the person appointed must at least be a qualified insolvency practitioner.[3]

Where the directors fail to make a declaration of solvency, the winding up is treated as a creditors' voluntary winding up.[4] In that event the company must call a creditors' meeting to be held within fourteen days of the meeting that decided to wind up the company.[5] At each meeting a liquidator must be nominated but in the event of disagreement the creditors' nominee takes preference.[6] In order to protect the interests of creditors, where the members nominate a liquidator most of his statutory powers can only be exercised with the consent of the court up to the date of the creditors' meeting.[7]

1   S 84.
2   S 89.
3   See 36.0.3.
4   S 90.
5   S 98.
6   S 100.
7   S 166.

The liquidator

36.0.12   Since the objective of a winding up is to realise the assets and distribute the proceeds, the liquidator has wide powers and duties with which to achieve such an objective. In some instances his powers can only be exercised with the consent of the court, or if one has been appointed, a committee of creditors.[1] The liquidator is an agent for the company and may therefore bind the company without himself becoming personally liable. The liquidator also has the power to carry on the business of the company in so far as it may be necessary for its beneficial winding up.[2]

1   S 165(2).
2   S 165(3).

Liquidator's right to challenge transactions by the directors prior to winding up

36.0.13 One of the primary objectives of the law, in the context of an insolvent winding up, is to protect creditors by ensuring that the assets are not improperly diverted by the directors in the period prior to the winding up, and that the directors behave responsibly. As the Cork Committee observed a balance must be struck:

> 'No one wishes to discourage the inception and growth of businesses, although both are unavoidably attended by risks to creditors. Equally a climate should exist in which downright irresponsibility is discouraged and in which those who abuse the privilege of limited liability can be made personally liable for the consequences of their conduct.'[1]

The liquidator and in certain cases creditors and shareholders can therefore challenge particular transactions that the directors sanctioned in the period prior to liquidation and thereby increase the funds available for general distribution to the creditors. The principal examples are as follows.

a) Fraudulent trading
The concept of fraudulent trading was developed by Parliament in order to prevent an abuse whereby a controlling director, holding a floating charge and knowing that insolvent liquidation was imminent, 'filled up' his security by causing the company to obtain goods on credit and then appointing a receiver. In such circumstances, the director would obtain the benefit of the goods acquired by virtue of his floating charge and the supplier of the goods be left high and dry.[2]

The IA 1986, s 213 therefore provides that if it appears in the course of a winding up that any business of company has been carried on with intent to defraud creditors, the court may declare that those knowingly a party to such business may be personally responsible for all or any of debts of the company. Breach of the section also involves criminal penalties,[3] and because of the existence of such penalties courts have demanded a strict standard of proof. There must be 'actual dishonesty, involving, according to current notions of fair trading among commercial men, real moral blame.'[4] An application for a declaration under these provisions must be made by the liquidator.[5]

The concept of fraudulent trading as defined by the section and interpreted by the courts has been criticised for its limited scope. Because of the requirement to establish dishonesty, those involved in the administration of insolvent companies have been reluctant to initiate proceedings. An honest director, however reckless, can never be made liable under the section. Even where the director knows the company to be insolvent, but causes it to incur additional liabilities, he will escape liability if he can prove that he honestly believed, however erroneously, that things would take a turn for the better. It was to cover these situations that the concept of wrongful trading was recommended by the Cork Report[6] and subsequently introduced into the law.

b) Wrongful trading
The Cork Committee considered that the concept of wrongful trading should be introduced to cover the situation where an insolvent company incurs liabilities without a reasonable prospect of meeting them. They

considered that liability should be based on an objective test, rather than the subjective test existing under s 213.

The IA 1986, s 214 goes a considerable way towards implementing the Cork proposals. It provides that if in the course of liquidation the liquidator is satisfied that a director is or has been guilty of wrongful trading, he may apply to the court for a declaration that such person is liable to make a contribution to the company's assets. The court must be satisfied that the company has gone into insolvent liquidation and before the winding up the directors knew or ought to have concluded that there was no reasonable prospect that the company would avoid insolvent liquidation.

The test of liability is still however somewhat subjective. A director will be taken to have known that the company could not avoid going into insolvent liquidation if that would have been the conclusion of a reasonably diligent person having the general knowledge, skill and experience actually possessed by that director.[7] A director will not be liable if the court is satisfied that he took every step with a view to minimising the potential loss to the company's creditors he ought to have taken in the circumstances.[8]

One area where the new concept of wrongful trading may be useful is in the case of a heavily undercapitalised company. Since there is no minimum capital requirement for private companies, it is important to encourage directors to satisfy themselves that their companies are adequately capitalised having regard to the scale of operations and level of commitments. If it is established that the company is trading with insufficient share capital and reserves, the directors may be liable for wrongful trading.

c) Preferences and transactions at an undervalue

A primary objective of the law and legal policy in the context of an insolvent liquidation is equality in the treatment of creditors. Thus, if the directors deliberately prefer one creditor over the others such a preference may be challenged as a preference and invalidated.

The provisions on preferences are contained in IA 1986, s 239. A company gives a preference to a person if that person is one of the company's creditors and the company's act has the effect of putting that person in a better position in the event of the company going into insolvent liquidation. The court must be satisfied that the company was influenced by a desire to put the creditor in a better position than he would otherwise have been.[9]

The IA 1986, s 238 also contains a power to challenge transactions at an undervalue. Thus, where a company makes a gift to someone or enters into a transaction with someone for no consideration or a consideration worth significantly less than the value of the benefit given to that person by the company the transaction may be challenged. No order will be made where the company entered into the transaction in good faith and for the purpose of carrying on its business believing at the time on reasonable grounds that the transaction would be of benefit to the company.

To be caught by either of these provisions, either the transactions must have taken place at a time when the company was unable to pay its debts, or the company became unable to pay its debts as a result of the transaction. The transaction must also take place within a specific period before the company goes into liquidation or a petition for an administration order is presented. In the case of a preference the period is six months, extended to two years if the recipient of the preference is a connected person, for example, a director of the company. In the case of a transaction at an under-value, the period is two years.

Applications under the sections must be made by the insolvency practitioner involved with the company and the court has a very wide range of powers including the power to require the return of the property.[10]

d) Avoiding floating charges
This is dealt with in para 34.3.4.

e) Extortionate credit bargains
Where a company has been a party to a transaction in which credit has been provided to the company on terms which are extortionate having regard to the risk accepted by the creditor, the insolvency practitioner concerned with the company may apply to the court for an order to ameliorate the position. The court may investigate transactions within three years of the commencement of the winding up or the administration order.[11]

1 Cmnd 8558, 1982, p 404.
2 See Cork Committee Report, p 29.
3 For the purposes of such liability the company need not be in course of winding up; CA 1985, s 458.
4 Maughan J in *Re Patrick & Lyon Ltd* [1933] Ch 786 at 790.
5 S 213(2).
6 Ch 44.
7 S 214(4).
8 S 214(3).
9 See eg *Re M Kushler Ltd* [1943] Ch 248, [1943] 2 All ER 22, CA.
10 S 241.
11 S 244.

Dealing with delinquent directors
36.0.14 Every officer or employee of the company is under a statutory duty to co-operate with the appropriate insolvency practitioner[1] and provide him with any information he requires.[2] If there is inadequate co-operation an application may be made to the court to order persons to give an account of their dealings or produce appropriate information.[3]

The Cork Committee Report concluded that:

> 'To provide proper safeguards to the general public, the law must also provide that those whose conduct has shown them to be unfitted to manage the affairs of a company with limited liability shall, for a specified period, be prohibited from doing so. It is desirable that restraints of this kind should apply as much to the director of an insolvent company as they apply to the individual who has become insolvent.'[4]

A persistent criticism of company law in recent years has been the ease with which directors involved in an insolvent liquidation could proceed to form a new company, and carry on trading as before, leaving a trail of unpaid creditors. In an attempt to meet such criticisms the Company Directors Disqualification Act 1986 (CDDA 1986) provides for the disqualification of directors in certain circumstances. In particular if it appears to the insolvency practitioner involved with a company which has become insolvent that a director's conduct, either considered in isolation or taken together with his conduct as a director of any other company, makes him unfit to be concerned with the management of a company, he must report the matter to the Secretary of State. If the Secretary of State is satisfied that it is expedient in the public interest that a disqualification order should be made, he may make an application to the court for the director to be disqualified.

In deciding whether a person's conduct is such as to make him unfit to be a director, the court must have regard to factors specified in CDDA 1986. These include general factors such as any misfeasance, breach of duty, misapplication of assets or failure to comply with statutory accounting requirements. They also include specific factors in connection with the insolvency, such as responsibility for the causes of the insolvency or for losses suffered by customers who made advance payments, involvement in any transaction or preference that can be set aside and a failure to comply with statutory requirements relating to the insolvency. The disqualification of a director must be for a minimum period of two years.[5] If a disqualified person involves himself in the management of a company he becomes liable for the debts of the company.[6]

In addition to reporting delinquent directors' conduct to the Secretary of State, the liquidator may initiate proceedings against any officers of the company or any person who acted as liquidator, administrative receiver or administrator of the company, for breach of duty.[7]

1   Termed under IA 1986, s 234(1) 'Office holder'.
2   IA 1986, s 235.
3   IA 1986, s 236.
4   Cmnd 8558, 1982, p 407.
5   CDDA 1986, s 6(4).
6   CDDA 1986, s 13. The Secretary of State maintains a public register of disqualification orders.
7   IA 1986, s 212.

Distribution of assets
36.0.15   When the liquidator arrives at a situation where he can begin to satisfy the claims of the creditors, he is required to make payments in accordance with a rigid classification of creditors. Secured creditors with fixed charges are of course entitled to take the benefit of their security above all other claims. Thereafter the classes and their order of priority are:
(a)   costs, charges and expenses of the winding up;
(b)   the preferential debts (see below);
(c)   the claims of holders of floating charges;
(d)   ordinary unsecured creditors;
(e)   certain deferred debts.
Should there be funds available after satisfying the debts of the company, the shareholders are entitled to the return of their capital and a share in any surplus.

The Cork Committee observed in the context of a discussion on preferential debts that:

'It is a fundamental objective of the law of insolvency to achieve a rateable, that is to say pari passu, distribution of the uncharged assets of the insolvent among the unsecured creditors. In practice, however, this objective is seldom, if ever, attained. In the overwhelming majority of cases it is substantially frustrated by the existence of preferential debts.'[1]

The Committee received a considerable volume of evidence critical of the preferential status afforded to certain classes of debts. As a distinguished Scottish judge observed in 1916:

'Why should individuals be made to suffer for the general good, especially in a case like the present, where the general benefit is infinitesimal but the individual loss substantial?'[2]

Preferential debts include money owed to the Inland Revenue for income tax deducted at source; VAT, car tax, betting and gaming tax; social security and pension scheme contributions; remuneration of employees.[3]

1   Cmnd 8558, 1982, p 317.
2   Lord Anderson in *Admiralty v Blair's Trustee* 1916 1 SLT 19.
3   See IA 1986, s 386 and Sch 6.

Chapter 37

Takeovers and Mergers

37.0.0 One of the principal features of corporate organisation since the industrial revolution has been the increasing concentration of business. Seeking the supposed economic benefits of economies of scale and advantages that sheer size brings to corporate activities, companies have, by a process of takeover and merger, grown larger. Such takeovers and mergers raise two issues for the law and legal policy. First, the need to protect the public interest where a proposed takeover or merger is likely to prejudice the maintenance of competition, the interests of consumers, or generally impede efficiency and innovation or the balanced distribution of industry and employment. This topic is dealt with in Part 1.

The second issue relates to the imposition of some basic standards of fair dealing in the context of takeovers and mergers in order to protect shareholders, creditors and the financial community against self dealing by management or other improper conduct. In general the policy in the UK has been to rely on disclosure and self regulation by City institutions for such protection rather than prescriptive rules of company law.

A takeover is essentially a matter governed by the law of contract, indeed there is no formal statutory framework regulating takeovers. Essentially it involves an offer by one company to the shareholders of the target company to buy their shares for cash or shares in the offeror company or a combination of both. A merger is where the shareholders of two companies agree to combine so that they all become shareholders of one company which owns the assets and business of the two previously separate companies.

Statutory procedures

37.0.1 There are two statutory procedures which may be used to effect an amalgamation or merger between companies or a takeover. First under s 110 of the IA 1986 a company in a voluntary liquidation may resolve to authorise the liquidator to sell the whole or part of its undertaking to another company in return for shares in that other company to be distributed to the shareholders. Alternatively, both companies could be put into liquidation and their business transferred to a third company which then proceeds to issue shares for distribution to the shareholders in the two original companies.

An arrangement under this provision must be sanctioned by a special resolution and thereafter it is binding on all the shareholders. However, a shareholder who did not vote in favour of the resolution may formally dissent to the liquidator and require him either to abstain from carrying out the resolution or purchase his interest.

The creditors' rights must be properly protected and the liquidator will seek to ensure that sufficient assets are retained in order to satisfy their claims. If there is any doubt about the availability of sufficient assets for the creditors then they could frustrate the arrangement by petitioning for the compulsory winding up of the company.

A further procedure is provided by a scheme of arrangement under s 425 of the CA 1985. This procedure can be used for a variety of transactions in addition to takeover or mergers but as we have seen it requires judicial confirmation and is thus formal and time consuming.[1] Its advantage is that once the required majority[2] at meetings of shareholders and creditors has been obtained, and the court has sanctioned the arrangement, it is binding on all the shareholders and creditors.

1   See 36.0.8.
2   75% in number and value of those present and voting in person or by proxy; s 425(2).

The regulation of takeovers

37.0.2   As stated above a takeover is simply a matter of the law of contract; the target company itself does not directly participate in the exercise. As a general rule the offer is expressed as conditional on acceptance by a specific proportion of the shareholders (normally 90%) and conditional on the bid not being referred to the Monopolies and Mergers Commission.[1]

Companies legislation has exercised virtually no control over takeovers. There are provisions which facilitate the acquisition of the remaining shares when 90% acceptances have been received;[2] provisions requiring the disclosure and authorisation of payments to directors for loss of office[3] and general provisions which seek to deter directors from using inside information of a takeover to make a profit or avoid a loss;[4] but there is no statutory code regulating the conduct of takeovers.

In the absence of such a statutory code a working party of the City of London institutions published *Notes on Amalgamation of British Businesses* which in 1968 led to the City Code on takeovers and mergers. The Code represents a self-regulatory codification of good standards of commercial behaviour. The Code has no legal force but is voluntarily observed by financial institutions, stockbrokers and dealers in securities, and merchant banks. It applies to takeovers and mergers in respect of plcs (whether listed on the stock exchange or not) and to private companies whose shares have been dealt in publicly in the preceding ten years.

The introduction to the Code states that:

> 'The Code has not, and does not seek to have, the force of law, but those who wish to take advantage of the facilities of the securities markets in the UK should conduct themselves in matters relating to takeovers according to the Code. Those who do not so conduct themselves cannot expect to enjoy those facilities and may find that they are withheld.'

The Panel on Takeovers and Mergers was established in 1968 to administer the Code and is made up of part-time representatives of financial institutions and a full-time executive. The executive plays a very active supervisory role in giving advice and making swift rulings on matters of interpretation. Given the flexibility of the Code, the executive is as much concerned with ensuring compliance with the spirit of the Code as well as the letter. The Panel is the ultimate arbiter on matters of interpretation.

Given the self-regulatory nature of the Code, the sanctions that can be applied to persons in breach of its provisions are necessarily limited. Ultimately they are restricted to a reprimand, either in private or public, or withdrawing the facilities of the market from the offender. The Panel may refer certain matters to individual organisations such as the Stock Exchange who may take disciplinary action against members.

In general the Panel has—

'become a highly respected self-regulatory body, though still lacking any legally enforceable sanctions. Under its aegis, the Code has been expanded and refined and constitutes a pretty comprehensive set of "Queensbury rules" which, if observed, should ensure that the battle is fought fairly from the viewpoint both of the contestants and of investors.'[5]

Indeed the relative success of the Panel in developing the Code and responding to new tactics employed in the takeover business has to date, been responsible for stemming demands for a formal regulatory Securities Commission.[6]

Although the Panel exercises a supervisory role, it is confined to monitoring subsequent events. It may, however, be consulted in advance on questions of principle but the Panel does not, as a matter of course, see takeover documentation before it goes into circulation. In the case of plcs listed on the Stock Exchange, they are required to comply, in addition to the City Code, with the Stock Exchange's Yellow Book, which does require the prevetting of takeover documentation to prevent misleading information being circulated in the first place.

Despite the fact that the Panel is a self-regulatory body with no legal power its decisions can be scrutinised by the courts under the judicial review procedure.[7] The Court of Appeal has held[8] that since the Panel has immense de facto power and supports public policy in the area of securities regulation and takeover policy, its decisions can be subjected to judicial review. The court would however be reluctant to interfere in the Panel's findings of fact, confining itself to reviewing decisions reached as a result of illegality or irrationality or procedural impropriety. Panel decisions would generally be permitted to take their course and the courts would only intervene 'in retrospect' by making declarations enabling the Panel not to repeat any error and relieving individuals of the disciplinary consequences of any erroneous finding by the Panel in breach of the Code.

---

1 See 2.7.1.
2 Ss 428–432 as amended by s 172, FSA 1986.
3 Ss 313, 314.
4 Company Securities (Insider Dealing) Act 1985. See 38.0.5.
5 *Review of Investor Protection Part 1* Cmnd 9125, 1984, P 135.
6 See 38.0.0.
7 See 2.8.11.
8 *R v Panel on Take-overs and Mergers, ex p Datafin plc (Norton Opax plc intervening)* [1987] 1 All ER 564, [1987] 2 WLR 699, CA.

Conduct of takeovers—the City Code

37.0.3 A takeover offer document is a circular relating to investments within the meaning of s 14 of the Prevention of Fraud (Investments) Act 1958 and it is therefore an offence to distribute documents in relation to takeover unless the distributer is 'authorised', or the permission of the Department of Trade and Industry has been obtained. Amongst the category of authorised persons are licensed dealers, members of the Stock Exchange and exempted dealers which includes merchant banks through which the vast majority of takeovers are conducted. When the Financial Services Act 1986 becomes fully operational its provisions will repeal and replace those contained in the 1958 Act (see 38.0.6).

In respect of licensed dealers, the Licensed Dealers (Conduct of Business) Rules were formulated in 1960 which laid down detailed provisions on the content of takeover documents. However, increasingly the City Code became the key rules to be observed and in 1983 the Licensed Dealers (Conduct of Business) Rules omitted reference to offer documents in favour of the Code. In order to regulate private company takeovers, the Department of Trade issued a General Permission in 1983 which prescribes the information that must be disclosed in respect of takeovers in private companies not caught by the Code.

The Code consists of a number of general principles for the conduct of bids and more detailed rules. The principles emphasise the following:

(a) All shareholders of the same class of an offeree company must be treated similarly by the offeror, and given the same information and advice.

(b) Shareholders must be given sufficient information and advice to enable them to reach a properly informed decision and must have sufficient to do so. No relevant information should be withheld from them.

(c) All documentation and advertisements must be prepared with the highest standards of care and accuracy.

(d) All parties must use every endeavour to prevent the creation of a false market in the securities of the two companies involved.

(e) The directors of the offeree shall not take any action which may frustrate a bona fide bid which has been made or which they know to be imminent[1] unless the general meeting approves such action.

(f) Directors of the companies involved must, in advising their shareholders, act exclusively in the interests of the shareholders, creditors and employees of the company, and must not have regard to their own or their family shareholdings and interests.

Amongst the more important rules are the following:

(a) The information required by Stock Exchange rules must be contained in offer documents and circulars whether the offeror or offeree companies' shares are listed or not.

(b) Secrecy must be absolute before an announcement. All persons privy to confidential information concerning an offer must treat it as secret and may only disclose it if necessary to do so.

(c) Except where the consent of the Panel is obtained where:

(i) any person acquires shares which taken together with shares held or acquired by persons acting in concert with him carry 30% or more of the voting rights, or

(ii) any person, together with persons acting in concert with him, holds not less than 30% but not more than 50% of the voting rights and such person, or any person acting in concert with him, acquires in any twelve months additional shares carrying more than 2% of the voting right, such persons shall extend offers to all shareholders of the class concerned.

This rule is known as the mandatory bid rule and is intended to stop an offeror gaining a controlling interest in a company at a premium price from one or two large shareholders and then, at a later date, buying out the remaining small shareholders at a much cheaper price. The rules prescribe that the mandatory bid must be at the highest price at which the offeror company (or persons acting in concert) has dealt in the offeree company's shares in the twelve months before the holding reached the 30%.

(e) The offeror company must state, and the directors of the offeree comment upon, the offeror's intentions in respect of continuation of the offeree company's business, any major changes to be introduced in the business, including any redeployment of fixed assets and the continued employment of the workforce of the offeree company and its subsidiaries. The offeror must also indicate what it sees as the long term commercial justification for the proposed offer.

In response to criticisms arising out of the £2.5bn takeover bid by Guinness for Distillers, the Panel introduced a number of rule changes in February 1987. These include a rule requiring anyone owning or controlling more than 1% (previously 5%) of the shares of a company involved in a takeover to disclose any dealings made in those companies' shares during the bid.[2] In addition, the owners of such stakes, as well as parties to the takeover and their associates, will not be able to hide behind nominee or 'vehicle' companies. The owner, or controller of the securities, will have to be named. The objective of the changes is to make it more difficult to rig a company's share price through selective buying or selling during a bid.

1   See 35.1.2.
2   See also 37.0.4.

Secret acquisition of shares, concert parties, dawn raids

37.0.4   When a company is considering mounting a full scale takeover, it is common to build up a stake in the company beforehand thus making the ultimate objective of control more likely. So long as the stake does not reach the magic 30% triggering the mandatory bid rule in the City Code, there is nothing to prevent such a practice. However, it is considered contrary to the interests of shareholders and the public to permit someone to acquire surreptitiously blocks of shares[1] in a company through nominees. The CA 1985[2] therefore requires any person who is knowingly interested in 5% of any class of shares of a plc carrying full voting rights to inform the company within five days of any acquisition or disposal. The company must keep the information on a register open to the public.[3] An interest in shares is defined widely and includes any shares held by a person's family or companies which they control.[4]

It is not possible to frustrate the provisions by an agreement with a number of people whereby each will acquire a small proportion of the shares. Such 'concert parties' are treated as a single unit for the purposes of disclosure of interests, thus each of them is deemed to be interested in all the shares in the particular company that the other parties to the agreement are interested in.[5]

A dawn raid is another method whereby a potential bidder attempts to build up a stake in the target company. It involves a well planned and speedy acquisition of shares on the Stock Exchange at a premium price. Such acquisitions offend the central principle of the City Code on equality of treatment for all the shareholders, since only a very small proportion of shareholders are given the opportunity to sell their shares at such premium rates.

In order to ensure such equality, Rules Governing Substantial Acquisitions of Shares are applied by the Council for the Securities Industry. The rules state that a person shall not within any period of seven days acquire 10% or more of the voting rights in a listed company if the acquisition would give them more than 15% of the voting rights in the company, unless a takeover offer is forthcoming or the purchase is from a single shareholder and is their only acquisition of such shares within seven days, or if the purchase is a tender offer. A tender offer involves placing advertisements offering to buy shares in the company thus allowing all shareholders to participate.

1 A practice known as 'warehousing'.
2 S 199.
3 S 211.
4 S 203.
5 Ss 205 and 206.

Chapter 38
Dealings in Securities and Financial Services

38.0.0 The fundamental difference between plc's and private companies is that the shares in a plc may be made available to the public. Most companies begin their existence as private ones but if successful, the need to attract funds may necessitate them 'going public', that is, converting into a plc and eventually having their shares traded on the Stock Exchange (SE). One of the primary reasons for going public is that a company may be in a process of rapid expansion and investment and may not want to depend wholly on borrowing to finance such growth.

The market in securities and the 'Big Bang'

38.0.1 The SE is the recognised market for trading in company shares and securities and government stocks in the UK. It provides a primary market whereby companies can raise finance for growth and a secondary market for the trading of shares between buyers and sellers. Thus without the SE shareholders would have greater difficulty in finding buyers for their shares and companies would be deprived of an efficient means of raising capital by selling shares to the public.

The SE is an unincorporated association of traders in securities which provides a number of important services for its members including a clearing house for settling accounts between traders. On 27 October 1986 the SE was subjected to radical organisation, generally described as the 'Big Bang'. In essence the Big Bang involved deregulation of the SE. Under the old system the SE had two types of member: brokers who accepted orders from investors for shares but who did not hold shares and jobbers who held shares but could only deal with a broker. The broker charged a fixed fee and acted as agent for his client with whichever jobber offered him the best price. The impetus for the change came from the Director General of Fair Trading who considered that competition on the exchange was restricted by the fixed minimum commissions on share dealings. It was also felt by the government that in order to retain its role in the international trading of shares and securities the London market should make membership available to international groups. Thus in July 1983 the government and SE concluded an agreement whereby fixed commissions would be phased out and the challenge to the SE by the Director General of Fair Trading under UK competition law would be withdrawn. Hence the Big Bang which brought about the following changes:

(a) the abandonment of fixed commissions. This will result in greater competition benefitting the financial institutions who are able to negotiate cheaper commissions given the volume of shares which they trade. Charges for small investors are dependant largely on the nature of the service they are seeking from a stockbroker;

(b) abolition of the distinction between jobbers and brokers. In effect jobbers have been replaced by 'market makers' who are wholesalers in shares, holding them at all times and quoting prices in accordance with demand. The result of deregulation was that brokers can now be market makers dealing in securities on their own account as principals as well as acting as agents for their clients' buying and selling through others. Thus brokers may be dual capacity, that is, both market makers and traditional brokers or single capacity (agency brokers) not involved in making markets. Because of the potential conflicts of interest that may arise in dual capacity firms deregulation has been accompanied by extensive changes in the regulation of the market, including the Financial Services Act 1986;

(c) membership of the exchange has been widened to include foreign owned firms.

There are three main markets operated by the SE. These are:

(i) the market in listed shares consisting of the major plc's whose securities are particularly marketable;

(ii) the Unlisted Securities Market (USM) which was launched in 1980 for smaller companies for whom a full listing is inappropriate;

(iii) a third market which commenced trading in early 1987 and is intended to accommodate dealings in the shares of companies too young and small to merit quotation on the USM.

The creation of a third market was largely prompted by the growing over-the-counter market in the shares of unquoted public companies. The market consists of licensed securities dealers making 'mini-markets' in the shares of approximately 160 companies. Invitations to the public to take shares in such companies must be accompanied by the requisite information as prescribed by the CA 1985, Sch 3.[1]

1 Now contained in Financial Services Act 1986. See 38.0.3.

A listing

38:0.2   In order to qualify for a listing a plc must usually have been trading for five years and the market value of the class of shares for which listing is sought must be £700,000.[1] Approximately 2,000 UK companies have securities listed on the SE.

Companies are required to conform to the requirements of the SE's rules on Admission of Securities to Listing[2] (the so called 'yellow book'); in particular their articles of association must contain specific provisions dealing with such things as the procedure at company meetings, directors' powers and share transfers. In addition, a company must comply with the continuing disclosure requirements of the SE. In order to be admitted to listing at least 25% of the shares must be made available to the public (that is persons not associated with the directors or substantial shareholders.)

1 In practice the market capitalisation will not usually be less than £6m.
2 Now given statutory recognition under Part IV of the Financial Services Act 1986.

Statutory controls on public offers—the new framework

38.0.3 Parts IV and V of the Financial Services Act 1986 (FSA), which comes into force in late 1987, are intended to replace the provisions of the CA 1985 dealing with offers of securities to the public, and the Stock Exchange Listing Regulations 1984. Part IV applies to the official listing of securities on the Stock Exchange and Part V to offers of unlisted securities on an approved exchange and in respect of primary and secondary offers of securities.

Under the Part IV provisions no investments can be admitted to the Official List unless an application for listing is made to the 'competent authority' (the Council of the Stock Exchange) and the listing requirements have been complied with. The particulars relating to the securities must be submitted, approved and published and in general must include the following type of information:

(a) details of promoters and profits made by them;
(b) details of the directors;
(c) financial record of the company;
(d) the company's obligations under any material contracts;
(e) details of the share capital and class rights;
(f) details of the capital required by the company.

There is also a new general duty of disclosure in respect of:

> 'all such information as investors and their professional advisers would reasonably require and reasonably expect to find there for the purpose of making an informed assessment—(a) the assets and liabilities, financial position, profits and losses, and prospects of the issuer of the securities; and (b) the rights attaching to those securities.'

The competent authority may, however, exempt specific information from disclosure under the general duty where such disclosure would be contrary to the public interest, seriously detrimental to the issuer, or where the securities are specialised securities.

The Part V provisions seek to control offers of certain non-listed securities by restricting advertisements for such offers unless a prospectus has been registered with the Registrar of Companies. The provisions are aimed at advertisements in respect of admission to dealings on an approved stock exchange such as the Unlisted Securities Market, or in respect of primary or secondary offers. In the case of the former, the prospectus must contain the information specified by the Act unless one of five exceptions apply. These are: if a prospectus in respect of the securities has been delivered within the previous twelve months and the exchange certifies that investors will have sufficient information; if the offer is conditional on the securities being listed under Part IV of the FSA; where the advertisement consists of a registered prospectus or is limited in content; if other securities issued by the same person are already dealt with on the exchange and overseas securities.

Under s 160 no advertisement offering securities which amounts to a primary or secondary offer may be made unless a prospectus containing the prescribed information has been delivered to the Registrar. A primary offer relates to advertisements inviting persons to subscribe for or underwrite securities, or which contain information calculated to lead directly or indirectly to their doing so; secondary offers are offers made by persons other than the issuer, such as may be made by an issuing house that acquires securities with a view to offering them for resale. There are similar exceptions to those that exist in respect of offers on approved exchanges.

1 Defined in s 142.
2 S 142 (6).
3 Listing particulars—formerly known as the prospectus.
4 S 146.
5 S 146.
6 S 158.
7 S 160.
8 S 162 (1).
9 S 159.
10 S 160.

Investors' remedies

38.0.4 An investor who has been misled by the contents of a prospectus has a number of possible remedies against the company or particular individuals concerned. As against the company the usual contractual remedies of rescission and damages for breach of contract are available. If it can be established that a false statement was made knowingly or recklessly with the intention that investors should act upon it and an investor does so act to his detriment, an action may lie against the wrongdoers in the tort of deceit; such actions are rare because of the difficulties of proof.[1]

There are also statutory remedies now contained in the FSA. Sections 150–152 provide a remedy for misrepresentations and omissions in listing particulars; and sections 166–168 provide a similar remedy in relation to unlisted securities. Under s 150(1) any person responsible for listing particulars shall be liable to compensate anyone who has acquired or contracted to acquire an interest in securities and has suffered loss in respect of them as a result of untrue statements, or the omission of anything required to be included under the general duty of disclosure. The persons who may be liable are: the issuer of the securities; the directors of the issuer; anyone who has authorised himself to be named as or having agreed to become a director; and those who have accepted responsibility for the particulars.[2] Defences are available to such persons on the basis of their reasonable belief in the truth of the statements; reasonable belief in the competence of an expert; having taken reasonable steps to correct a defect; reliance on official statements and documents; or knowledge by the person suffering the loss of the falsity of the statement.[3] There are parallel provisions dealing with the liability of those responsible for making offers in respect of unlisted securities.[4]

1 See *Derry v Peek* (1889) 14 App Cas 337, HL.
2 S 150.
3 S 151.
4 Ss 166–168.

Dealings in shares by corporate insiders

38.0.5 One of the most controversial topics of company law in recent years has been the issue of insider dealing. This practice involves the use of confidential information by a person connected with a company in order to trade in the shares of his company either by selling before bad news is made public or buying before good news is made public, thus avoiding a loss or making a profit. In such a situation the person concerned may be in breach of a fiduciary duty and hence be accountable to the company for any profit.[1]

One of the principal arguments against insider dealing is that it offends a basic principle of the market place that all those who deal should do so on a broadly equal basis. The Companies Act 1980 introduced criminal penalties against insider dealing and the provisions are now contained in the Company Securities (Insider Dealings) Act 1985 (CSA 1985). Before these provisions were enacted, the self-regulatory rules of the SE and the Takeover Panel sought to deter insider dealings and the statutory rules now supplement those rules.

The main provisions of the CSA 1985 are as follows:

1. The Act prohibits three categories of transaction. The main prohibition is on dealings in securities of the company by an insider in possession of price sensitive information. Dealings, in this context, refers only to dealings on the SE. The prohibition does not therefore extend to private deals. However, it extends to off-market dealers making a market in advertised securities, that is, the over-the-counter trade.[2] The second prohibition relates to the insider who counsels or procures another to deal, if he knows that that person will deal on the SE. The third prohibition covers communicating information by way of a tip to any other person in order that he may deal or counsel or procure another to deal. In addition to these general prohibitions the Act provides that where an individual has contemplated or is contemplating making a takeover offer for a company in a particular capacity, that individual shall not deal on the SE in securities of that company in another capacity if he knows that the information that the offer is contemplated or is no longer contemplated is unpublished price sensitive information in relation to those securities.

2. Insiders are those who are or who at anytime in the preceding six months have been connected with a company. These include directors, officers, employees or persons who have a professional or business relationship with the company, which may reasonably be expected to give them access to confidential information in relation to the securities of the company. Crown servants and former crown servants who obtain inside information by virtue of their position as crown servants may also be insiders. A person who obtains confidential information, either directly or indirectly, from a person connected with the company or a crown servant may also be classed as an insider (a tippee).

3. For the prosecution to succeed it must be established that the insider was in possession of information which it 'was reasonable to expect an individual not to disclose except for the proper performance of his functions' and he must know that it is unpublished and price sensitive.[3] Price sensitive information is information which relates to specific matters relating to or of concern to a company which are not generally known to shareholders or to anyone else who deals or is likely to deal in the securities of that company, but which if it were generally known to them would be likely to affect materially the price of the securities. Examples of such specific matters would be takeovers, dividend decisions, changes in the directorate, or changes in the capital structure of a company.[4]

4. Consistent with the normal rules of criminal law, a person can only be convicted if he has a guilty mind. Thus he must know that the information is unpublished and price sensitive and know that the relationship by virtue of which he obtained it was that of an insider. In the case of a

tippee, he must know or have reasonable cause to believe that the person from whom he obtained the information obtained it in confidence as a result of a connection with the company, and the tippee must know that it is unpublished and price sensitive.

5. There are a number of defences available to persons who deal in a company's shares in the normal course of business such as market makers, (jobbers), receivers and liquidators. There is also a general defence available to anyone who acts while knowingly in possession of unpublished price sensitive information, 'but otherwise than with a view to the making of a profit or the avoidance of a loss by the use of that information.'[5] For example if a director knows that his company has lost an important government contract and before the news becomes public he sells his shares in order to meet an urgent financial commitment, he may escape penalty if he can establish that the motive for the sale was not avoiding a loss on his shares but meeting a financial commitment.

6. It is worth stressing again that proceedings under the CSA 1985 are criminal proceedings instituted by the Secretary of State for Trade and Industry or by, or with the consent of, the Director of Public Prosecutions.[6] Contravention of the CSA 1985 does not create any remedy in civil law, the transaction in question is not rendered void or voidable.[7]

However, the newly created Securities and Investments Board[8] proposes to issue rules to allow market makers and others who have lost because of insider dealing to sue the wrongdoer for civil damages.

1   See 35.1.6.
2   See 38.0.1.
3   S 1.
4   See eg *Model Code for Securities Transactions by Directors of Listed Companies* (The Stock Exchange).
5   S 3(1)(a).
6   S 8(3).
7   See 35.1.1.
8   See 38.0.6.

Securities regulation—the new framework

38.0.6   Traditionally regulation of the securities market in the UK has been based on self-regulation, underpinned by statutory provisions to deal with certain abuses. A key role is played by institutions such as the SE, the Takeover Panel, the issuing houses and the Council for the Securities Industry. Dealers who operate outside the City's self-regulatory framework are policed by the Department of Trade and Industry and the Bank of England.

In recent years the system of self-regulation has come under increasing criticism.[1] In response to such criticism the Secretary of State appointed Professor Gower in 1981 to review investor protection, the control of dealers in securities, investment consultants and investment managers. After extensive consultation a report was published in 1984.[2] The main recommendation of the report was that there should be a new Investor Protection Act under which the Department of Trade and Industry would play a key role in terms of policy and surveillance. Certain of the regulatory functions should be delegated to self regulatory agencies. The report did not rule out the creation of a statutory Securities Commission along the lines of the Securities and Exchange Commission in the USA.

In 1985 the Department of Trade and Industry published a White Paper entitled *Financial Services in the UK—a New Framework for Investor Protection*.[3] The proposals in the White Paper formed the basis for the provisions of the Financial Services Act 1986 (FSA 1986).

The new framework is centred on a self-regulatory system within a statutory framework. This system was favoured because:

(a) it offers the best possibility of combining adequate investor protection with a competitive and innovative market;
(b) regulation is more likely to be effective if there is significant practitioner involvement in devising and enforcing rules;
(c) a private sector body able to make and enforce rules has greater flexibility in its operations than a statutory body;
(d) practitioners are best equipped to spot breaches of rules and take swift enforcement action;
(e) a private sector body could be established prior to the coming into operation of the 1986 Act and therefore attain a high degree of readiness;
(f) day to day regulatory action is distanced from government.[4]

Under the new framework the Secretary of State for Trade and Industry has regulatory powers in respect of securities and investments. These powers may then be delegated to the Securities and Investment Board (SIB), a private body operating in the form of a company limited by guarantee. The primary function of the SIB is to propagate rules for the conduct of the securities and investment business in the UK in accordance with the principles laid down in the FSA and to grant authorisation to operate in the market. If the SIB is satisfied that a self regulatory organisation (SRO) is able to regulate the admission and conduct of its members, and its rules provide standards equivalent to those operated by the SIB, they may recognise the SRO which will then have power to authorise its own members to operate in the market. The unique feature of the system is that it combines the flexibility of self-regulation with the enforcement advantages of a statutory authority. The SIB will have delegated powers of authorisation, regulation, investigation and prosecution.

Amongst the bodies that are likely to be recognised as SROs are the Stock Exchange, the Investment Management Regulatory Organisation, the Life Assurance and Unit Trust Regulatory Organisation, the Financial Intermediaries Managers and Brokers Regulatory Association and the Association of Futures Brokers and Dealers. The Takeover Panel is not within the new statutory regime.

A particular concern of the SIB and the SROs is the development of strict rules governing conflicts of interest and accountability to clients. We have already noted the potential conflict of interests that may arise in the new dual capacity firms of brokers under the SE deregulation.[5] Thus one firm may have departments each acting as an adviser to numerous different clients who themselves have conflicting aims and requirements. In order to prevent conflicts of interest arising by communication between the different departments of a firm, internal barriers must be erected. Such barriers are termed 'chinese walls' and involve an—

'established arrangement whereby information known to persons involved in one part of a business is not available to those involved in another part of the business and it is accepted that in each of the parts of the business so divided decisions will be taken without reference to any interest which any other such part or any person in any other such part of the business may have in the matter.'[6]

Under the new regime the rules formulated by the SIB and SROs will be strictly monitored by compliance officers looking for evidence of 'cracks' in chinese walls. In addition the insider dealing legislation[7] has been strengthened by giving greater powers to inspectors appointed by the Department of Trade to examine on oath any person whom they consider may have relevant information in respect of insider dealing and to compel witnesses to answer questions under threat of punishment for contempt of court. The inspectors have also been given the power to compel the production of documents. The new powers in respect of insider dealing were brought into force on 15 November 1986, two months in advance of the original implementation date, as a response to revelations of insider dealing by a prominent dealer in securities.

The new framework of investor protection includes recommendations for the creation of ombudsman schemes by SRO's supported by an independent investigation system operated by the SIB. In addition under s 54 of the FSA 1986, compensation may be claimed by an individual investor to reimburse him for money lost due to the financial collapse of a firm either from fraud or mismanagement. Full compensation will be payable for the first £30,000 and 90% of the next £20,000. The scheme will be funded by the SROs.

1 For the advantages and disadvantages of self-regulation see 2.5.1 to 2.5.3.
2 *Review of Investor Protection Report* Cmnd 9125, 1984.
3 Cmnd 9432, 1985.
4 Ibid.
5 See 38.0.1.
6 Licence Dealers Conduct of Business Rules.
7 See 38.0.5.

Index

522